Selected Essays of
ROBERT J. CONNORS

Selected Essays of
ROBERT J. CONNORS

EDITED BY

Lisa Ede
Oregon State University

Andrea A. Lunsford
Stanford University

Published in cooperation with the
National Council of Teachers of English

BEDFORD/ST. MARTIN'S   Boston   •   New York

For Bedford/St. Martin's

Senior Production Editor: Shuli Traub
Production Supervisor: Jennifer Wetzel
Marketing Manager: Brian Wheel
Art Director/Cover Designer: Lucy Krikorian
Text Design: Wanda Kossak
Cover Illustration: Cindy S. Lewis
Composition: Pine Tree Composition, Inc.
Printing and Binding: Haddon Craftsmen, Inc., an R.R. Donnelley & Sons
  Company
President: Joan E. Feinberg
Editorial Director: Denise B. Wydra
Editor in Chief: Nancy Perry
Director of Marketing: Karen R. Melton
Director of Editing, Design, and Production: Marcia Cohen
Managing Editor: Erica T. Appel

NCTE Stock Number: 43113
Published in cooperation with the
National Council of Teachers of English
1111 W. Kenyon Road
Urbana, Illinois 61801-1096
www.ncte.org

Library of Congress Control Number: 2002114958

Manufactured in the United States of America.
8 7 6 5 4
f e d c b

For information, write: Bedford/St. Martin's, 75 Arlington Street, Boston,
MA 02116   (617-399-4000)

ISBN: 0-312-40279-1

ACKNOWLEDGMENTS

"The Rise and Fall of the Modes of Discourse" by Robert J. Connors. From *CCC* 32, December 1981, pp. 444–455. Copyright © 1981 by the National Council of Teachers of English. Reprinted with the permission of NCTE.

Acknowledgments and copyrights are continued at the back of the book on pages 507–508,
which constitute an extension of the copyright page. It is a violation of the law to reproduce
these selections by any means whatsoever without the written permission of the copyright
holder.

A NOTE ON THIS COLLECTION

The essays that follow are ordered chronologically. After considering other options, we chose a chronological organization for two main reasons. First, we did not want to impose our own reading or categorization on Bob Connors's work, as would inevitably be the case had we grouped his essays thematically. More important, perhaps, chronological order allows readers to follow with ease the development of Bob's thinking over the course of his career.

This collection of essays is, of necessity, partial. In making the selections, we aimed for a representative sample of Bob's most influential work throughout his career. To reflect, at least in part, the range of Bob's writerly interests, we have also included several brief nonacademic pieces. And because we cannot think about Bob's writing without thinking about Bob the person, we are grateful to Bob's family and friends for allowing us to include several of our favorite photographs.

Following the essays are several other items we think will be of interest to readers. These include a number of memorial tributes published in professional journals after Bob's death and a full bibliography of his publications compiled by Wayne Robertson. Compiling this bibliography turned out to be quite a difficult process, since all that Bob's colleagues at the University of New Hampshire were able to locate for us were either out-of-date vitas or partial lists of publications. Wayne, however, turned out to be a master sleuth. By combing a number of databases and by physically reviewing the table of contents for each issue of the major professional journals in the field for the last twenty-five years, Wayne has assembled what we believe to be a complete and accurate record of Bob's publications.

When we asked Wayne to undertake this project, we had no idea that the work required would be so substantial, so we want very much to thank Wayne and to acknowledge the importance of his contribution to this collection. There are others whom we also wish to thank. Chuck Christensen, former president of Bedford/St. Martin's, first conceived of this collection as both a memorial tribute to Bob and as a way of keeping his work alive. Joan Feinberg, president, and Nancy Perry, editor in chief, supported this project

from first to last. And Shuli Traub worked her usual wonders as project editor. A number of Bob's colleagues at the University of New Hampshire played key roles in our effort to gather information about Bob's publications. Without the help of Patricia Sullivan, Cinthia Gannett, and Thomas Newkirk, compiling a bibliography of Bob's published works might not have been possible. Colleague and friend Cheryl Glenn read a draft of the introduction and headnotes, providing feedback at a critical time. Others also assisted in this project. At Oregon State University, Julie Baird located and photocopied all of Bob's published articles. Lisa's coworkers at the Center for Writing and Learning—Moira Dempsey, Wayne Robertson, and Saundra Mills—provided much-needed material and emotional support. At Stanford University, Nastassia Lopez and Beatrice Kim assisted in research, and Marvin Diogenes, Alyssa O'Brien, and Christina Huerta provided support and criticism. Finally, we want to thank Colleen Connors for the role she has played in this effort. This book is for Colleen, Aillinn, and Bob.

L. E.
A. A. L.

CONTENTS

INTRODUCTION
Robert J. Connors:
A Life in Writing

Late in the afternoon of June 22, 2000, Bob Connors left the campus of the University of New Hampshire in Durham, where he had just taught the last class of a summer school course, and headed home on his motorcycle. This was a trip that Bob had taken many, many times. This time, however, a sudden and fierce rainstorm—and an inexperienced driver going too fast in a truck with balding tires—brought disaster: the truck crossed the yellow line and collided with Bob's motorcycle. Bob died on the way to the hospital.

In the days and weeks that followed, those who knew Bob, from his family and close friends to a host of professional colleagues, struggled to absorb this loss. Many took solace in acknowledging and honoring Bob's ongoing influence in their professional work and personal lives, and tributes to Bob appeared on a number of listservs and in scholarly journals. The 2001 CCCC program included a session devoted to honoring Bob and his work as well as a memorial gathering sponsored by Bob's longtime publishing partner, Bedford/St. Martin's. The idea for this collection grew out of conversations at these events and represents still another effort to recognize Bob's contributions to the field of rhetoric and composition.

That these contributions were significant is undeniable: during his two decades in the profession, Bob wrote or cowrote ten books and over fifty articles on topics ranging from historiography to nineteenth- and twentieth-century rhetoric to men's studies and the history of citation systems. His scholarly work helped us to better understand composition's history and played an important role in setting the terms of debate for current issues of composition theory and practice. Many readers of this collection, then, already have some sense of the breadth and depth of Bob's work. Newer members of the profession may not know, however, how quickly and strongly Bob made his mark. We therefore begin this introduction by invoking Bob's first years in the profession, first by noting his impact as a scholar and then by situating his accomplishments in the disciplinary and historical context of the period during which he entered the profession.

EARLY CONTRIBUTIONS TO RHETORIC AND COMPOSITION

Bob Connors graduated from the Ohio State University with a Ph.D. in rhetoric and composition in 1980. His dissertation committee included Frank O'Hare (advisor) and Edward P. J. Corbett, and his dissertation topic was "A Study of Rhetorical Theories for College Writing Teachers." Bob's first scholarly publication appeared while he was still a graduate student: in 1979 "The Differences between Speech and Writing: Ethos, Pathos, and Logos" appeared in *College Composition and Communication* (*CCC*). It is now relatively common for students to publish articles while still in graduate school—though publication in the major journal in one's field would still be noteworthy. But in the late 1970s this practice was much less prevalent. Rarer still, both now and then, is the achievement of broad scholarly recognition at the very start of one's academic career. So it seems especially important that in 1982, during his second year of teaching at Louisiana State University, Bob's essay "The Rise and Fall of the Modes of Discourse" won the Conference on College Composition and Communication's Richard Braddock Award for the best article published in *CCC* that year.

As Thomas Newkirk observes in "In Memoriam" (see pages 498 – 500 in this volume), "Bob was part of a talented and productive group of scholars (including James Berlin, Sharon Crowley, John Brereton, Nan Johnson, and others) who helped to map out the history of composition teaching in this country" (498). But Bob did more than help map out this history. For throughout his career, and especially in the period from 1981 to 1990, Bob argued vigorously for the importance of grounding contemporary theories and practices in a richly historicized understanding of the past.

The period from 1981 to 1990 was a critical time in the development of rhetoric and composition as an academic discipline. In the early twentieth century, scholars such as Fred Newton Scott and Gertrude Buck—and later, James Kinneavy, Janet Emig, and Edward P. J. Corbett—had each made many significant contributions to research on rhetoric and on the teaching of writing. But as Kinneavy observed in the introduction to his 1971 *A Theory of Discourse*, despite these and other efforts, composition remained "[. . .] so clearly the stepchild of the English department that it is not a legitimate area of concern in graduate studies, is not even recognized as a subdivision of the discipline of English in a recent manifesto put out by the major professional association (MLA) of college English teachers [. . .], in some universities is not a valid area of scholarship for advancement in rank, and is generally the teaching province of graduate assistants or fringe members of the department" (1).

By the late 1970s and early 1980s, however, the situation was more favorable. Thanks to a number of educational, economic, and political factors, those committed to the scholarly work of composition found an opportunity for change in a new interest in and sense of urgency about the teaching of writing. Thanks to a broad national movement toward greater access to higher education as well as the development and radical expansion of two-year colleges, many students who would not previously have attended col-

lege began to do so. That traditional teaching practices failed to meet the needs of these students became immediately evident, and such efforts as the City University of New York's SEEK (Search for Education, Evaluation, and Knowledge) program were quickly put in place. These developments occurred at a time when the media were proclaiming—as they seem to do regularly, in cycles of about twenty-five years—that the United States was in the midst of a devastating literacy crisis, one that, commentators argued, wreaked educational havoc at all levels. In this context, department chairs, deans, and provosts were, once again, concerned about the teaching of writing on their campuses. Many were willing to fund efforts to develop not only innovative writing programs but new graduate programs in rhetoric and composition as well.

Those who came to the scholarly work of composition in the late 1970s and early 1980s can readily recall the extraordinary sense of possibility that many in the field felt. But that sense of possibility did not necessarily translate into a clear agenda for theory and practice. In hindsight, it might seem that *of course* research on the rhetorical tradition and on North American rhetoric would play a key role in composition's disciplinary development. At the time, however, such an eventuality was anything but certain. Through his scholarly work, Bob Connors helped turn what was at the time simply one of a number of competing possibilities into a reality—and he did so by concretely demonstrating the contributions that such research can make both to theory and to practice.

In the period from 1981 to 1991, Bob Connors published the following works:[1]

- "The Rise and Fall of the Modes of Discourse" (*CCC*, 1981)
- "Current-Traditional Rhetoric: Thirty Years of *Writing with a Purpose*" (*Rhetoric Society Quarterly*, 1981)
- "The Rise of Technical Writing Instruction in America" (*Journal of Technical Writing and Communication*, 1982)
- "Composition Studies and Science" (*College English*, 1983)
- "*Actio:* A Rhetoric of Manuscripts" (*Rhetoric Review*, 1983)
- "Handbooks: History of a Genre" (*Rhetoric Society Quarterly*, 1983)
- "Journals in Composition Studies" (*College English*, 1984)
- "The Rhetoric of Explanation: Explanatory Rhetoric from Aristotle to 1850" (*Written Communication*, 1984)
- "Historical Inquiry in Composition Studies" (*The Writing Instructor*, 1984)
- *Essays on Classical Rhetoric and Modern Discourse* (Southern Illinois UP, 1984)
- "The Rhetoric of Explanation: Explanatory Rhetoric from 1850 to the Present" (*Written Communication*, 1985)

---

[1]This list includes Connors's major scholarly works during this period. For a complete list of his publications, see pages 501–5.

- "Mechanical Correctness as a Focus in Composition Instruction" (*CCC*, 1985)
- "Greek Rhetoric and the Transition from Orality" (*Philosophy and Rhetoric*, 1986)
- "The Rhetoric of Mechanical Correctness" (in *Only Connect: Uniting Reading and Writing*, 1986)
- "Textbooks and the Evolution of the Discipline" (*CCC*, 1986)
- "Grammar in American College Composition: An Historical Overview" (in *The Territory of Language*, 1986)
- "Personal Writing Assignments" (*CCC*, 1987)
- "The Politics of Historiography" (*Rhetoric Review*, 1988)
- "Frequency of Formal Errors in Current College Writing, or Ma and Pa Kettle Do Research" (*CCC*, 1988)
- *Selected Essays of Edward P. J. Corbett* (Southern Methodist UP, 1989)
- *The St. Martin's Handbook* (St. Martin's P, 1989)
- *The St. Martin's Guide to Teaching Writing* (St. Martin's P, 1989)
- "Rhetorical History as a Component of Composition Studies" (*Rhetoric Review*, 1989)
- "Overwork/Underpay: Labor and Status of Composition Teachers since 1880" (*Rhetoric Review*, 1990)

This is an extraordinary record—not only for its productivity but also for the diversity of topics Bob addressed. The subjects of these articles and books range from the modes of discourse to technical writing instruction in America, the history of handbooks as a genre, the rhetoric of explanation, mechanical correctness in composition instruction, the classical rhetorical tradition, personal writing assignments, and more. And yet beneath this diversity we see two recurring themes. First, Bob was convinced that contemporary research on both writing and the teaching of writing needed to be firmly grounded in the rhetorical tradition, and second, he believed that historical studies could play a critical role in establishing and maintaining this connection. In this regard, Bob Connors very much followed in the footsteps of his mentor, Edward P. J. Corbett.

RECURRING METHODS AND THEMES

This is not to say, however, that Bob simply continued a line of research begun by Ed Corbett and others, for Bob demonstrated clear and strong predilections as a scholar. His dissertation study, for example, rests on two principles that inform almost all of Bob's subsequent work: that the teaching of writing is a serious and valuable enterprise calling for careful, rigorous training; and that, as such, the teaching of writing must rest on a strong historical and theoretical basis. Also evident, from his earliest work on the modes of discourse, is what Bob referred to as a realist/empirical stance as a historian, a topic to which we will later return. Above all, however, Bob

maintained an abiding passion for archival scholarship—a passion that helped a generation of historians to recognize that such relics as discarded textbooks from previous teaching eras hold important insights for contemporary researchers.

In fact, thinking of Bob's life in writing calls up no stronger image than of him as a happy bookworm, burrowing away in a library or archive, searching for obscure accounts of teaching practices, dog-eared textbooks, or pieces of student writing from the past. In this sense, Bob's work is insistently materialist. His "Handbooks: History of a Genre," to take a fairly early example (it appeared in *Rhetoric Society Quarterly* in 1983), rests on his examination of the earliest English texts identified as "handbooks" and includes an illustration of a "Theme Card" included in one of them. Like a number of Bob's essays, this one is highly critical of earlier teaching practices, particularly as they are exemplified in handbooks. But this strong criticism is situated in the material conditions associated with the teaching of writing: "The handbook was born," Bob concludes, "out of a 'damage-control' response to teacher overwork. [. . .] Not until we demand that conditions change will we move out from under the shadow of sterile, a-rhetorical correctness that handbooks have come to represent" (23). Here the links among the material artifacts of teaching composition, the material conditions in which such teaching takes place, and the need to situate both in historical and theoretical context are strongly evident. We see the same links at work in many other places in Bob's writing, from "The Rise and Fall of the Modes of Discourse" to *Composition-Rhetoric*.

If Bob's work on the history of writing and writing instruction is basically materialist, it is also almost always narrativized. Like several other key figures in composition studies, Bob was an organizer and taxonomizer. He liked to paint with a broad brush, taking a huge sweep of time and data—some of the latter highly idiosyncratic—and arrange the resulting mass of information into a set of categories that inevitably told a strong story. For example, in the two-part "The Rhetoric of Explanation" (*Written Communication*, 1984 and 1985), Bob's sweeping gaze moves from ancient Greece to the present, recounting the adventures of expository discourse: "The first section of this article followed the rise of a rhetoric of explanation from its roots in the teaching function of homiletic discourse through technical and scientific uses in the seventeenth century to general and written discourse in the eighteenth. The changes in rhetorical instruction that resulted from the novel theories of George Campbell and Hugh Blair gave rise to a new form of pedagogy, seen first on the secondary and then on the college level: a pedagogy of informative discourse" (43). In this essay, Bob categorizes discourse as persuasive or informative and then charts the development of the second category, always in highly readable narrative form. We see similar moves as Bob tells the story of "The Rise of Technical Writing Instruction in America" (*Journal of Technical Writing and Communication*, 1982) or follows the progress of a sometimes heroic subject, *Composition-Rhetoric*.

As committed as Bob was to recovering the past and presenting it from a rationalist, realist perspective, he always kept a weather eye on the usefulness of that past to current concerns in the teaching of writing. In his dissertation, Bob looks carefully at theories of invention, arrangement, and style across a historical span and then uses that analysis to set out a theoretical framework for the teaching of writing in the 1980s and beyond. (Bob's dissertation eventually became the basis for *The St. Martin's Guide to Teaching Writing*, coauthored with Cheryl Glenn and now in its fifth edition.) In a similar way, Bob uses his historical study of calls to abolish the first-year writing requirement to advocate for abolition of that requirement in "The Abolition Debate in Composition: A Short History." In his last published essay, "The Erasure of the Sentence," Bob creates a taxonomy of what he calls "sentence-based pedagogies," traces their history, and then uses his analysis as the basis for arguing that "more has been lost than sentence-combining" (473) in the erasure of these pedagogies in our own time. And in a series of essays on the conditions of writing instruction, Bob drew on his historical knowledge to argue for reform that would value the teaching of writing as well as the teachers and student writers whose work lies at the heart of these endeavors. (See, for example, "Overwork/Underpay: Labor and Status of Composition Teachers since 1880" or "Rhetoric in the Modern University: The Creation of an Underclass.") In these and a number of other essays, Bob resolutely applies his historical investigations to contemporary issues in composition and rhetoric.

Vision of History and Historiography

While Bob can certainly be grouped with other scholars who have helped to write the history of composition and rhetoric, he practiced his own brand of historical exploration. In doing so, he never shied away from unpopular positions on the nature of historical research, arguing for the possibility, not of complete objectivity, to be sure, but rather of realism/empiricism as an appropriate and viable theoretical underpinning for historiography. While Bob acknowledged that the historian's vision was always partial and involved construction of a narrative, he consistently opposed strong social constructionist tendencies within composition as well as what he termed "ideologically based critical historiography." In the introduction to *Composition-Rhetoric*, for example, he insists that he is writing "as history instead of historiography," saying: "If I were to have written this book to conform to one or another of the currently popular theoretical/critical stances [...], I would be afraid that the simple-minded story I hope to tell would get lost in the ideology, would end up serving the theory. I simply have not wit enough to foreground an ideology and also tell the story of what I found and all the complexity I perceive in it. Anyway, the ideologies and theories have plenty of servants already. They don't need my story too" (334). Bob, of course, did indeed have wit enough, and embedded in this statement is the echo of his typically self-deprecating humor as well as of his claim that his "simple-minded story" could somehow stand outside of ideology.

Indeed, Bob's brand of history had more than wit enough to contribute to what might be called canon formation in the field he defined as composition-rhetoric and to tell the story of this field as he saw it. In addition to shaping received understandings of the history of composition-rhetoric, Bob made a series of strategic interventions in the field, almost always aimed at creating a shift in thought or in practice. In "The Rise and Fall of the Modes of Discourse," for instance, he weaves a dramatic narrative whose argument aims at breaking the stranglehold the modes have had on student writers and on teachers of writing: "For years the fact that this schema did not help students learn to write better was not a concern, and even today the modes are accepted by some teachers despite their lack of basis in useful reality. Our discipline has been long in knuckling from its eyes the sleep of the nineteenth and early twentieth centuries, and the real lesson of the modes is that we need always to be on guard against systems that seem convenient to teachers but that ignore the way writing is actually done" (12). As we noted earlier, this essay had a major impact on the field at the time of its publication, and it has been reprinted a number of times since then. Yet twenty years after the essay's publication, it's fair to say that the modes of discourse are alive and well in the teaching of writing, as Bob himself recognizes in *Composition-Rhetoric*: "It remains to be seen whether the taxonomic instinct that maintains the methods of exposition as the current default classification will rest content with the methods or finally depose them—in favor, probably, of another imperfect taxonomy" (256). Strategic interventions, as Bob might say, never guarantee lasting change.

Nevertheless, Bob continued to make strategic interventions in a number of works, from "Composition and Science," in which he offers a corrective to Maxine Hairston's reading (and valorization) of Kuhnian paradigm shifts and questions the faith contemporary composition studies seems to have in science, to his work on Men's Studies, in which he calls on compositionists to take this field more seriously and to attend to the writing of men—and especially male students—with more care and sensitivity. In his two-part essay "The Rhetoric of Citation Systems," Bob seeks to intervene in scholarly paratextual practices, arguing strenuously—and at great length—for the importance of formalist structures in composition but against the "hegemony of some form of the APA name-date citation system" (396) in the humanities. He concludes this particular strategic intervention by urging scholars in the humanities to pay attention to such trends in citation, to recognize the epistemic freight they inevitably carry, and to make decisions about citation practices fully "informed by rhetorical awareness and by a knowledge of the forces that have worked throughout history to affect the ways in which our texts have related to us and to each other" (397).

Composition-Rhetoric: Backgrounds, Theory, and Pedagogy was Bob's penultimate, rather than his final, work. But as a strategic intervention it represents the culmination of his life's work as a scholar. This is not to say that *Composition-Rhetoric* neatly ties up all the strands of Bob's numerous and diverse interests. It does not and could not: such was the richness of his

scholarly work. But the questions and concerns that drive *Composition-Rhetoric* are evident throughout his research. From his earliest interest in nineteenth-century rhetoric in North America to this final study, for instance, Bob was determined to identify and represent rhetorical theories and practices that were suppressed in conventional histories of rhetoric. In *Composition-Rhetoric* this desire was manifested in Bob's insistent challenges to what Richard Young in his 1978 essay "Paradigms and Problems: Needed Research in Rhetorical Invention" terms "current-traditional rhetoric." As Bob says in the introduction to *Composition-Rhetoric,* his archival work led him to believe

> that the almost unquestioned acceptance of Young's term has left the field with a stock phrase that was never completely accurate and has become even more problematical since Young's essay appeared fifteen years ago. What we have reified as a unified "current-traditional rhetoric" is, in reality, not a unified or an unchanging phenomenon. It developed over time [. . .]. It evolved differently in different settings: schools, colleges, universities, Lyceums, literary societies, Chautauquas. The developing tradition of written rhetoric was not monadic, was *never* the rhetorical tradition as a whole; it was always a strand unto itself, reliant upon some elements of the earlier oral rhetoric but also filled with materials that would have been meaningless to oral rhetoricians (320).

Composition-Rhetoric represents Bob Connors's final effort to portray nineteenth-century rhetoric in North America in all its rich complexity and specificity.

As Bob's use of the phrase "in reality" in the preceding quote suggests, *Composition-Rhetoric* also represents Bob's final effort to argue for a particular vision of history and historiography—one that, as we noted earlier, resisted many current trends in the field. In the years preceding his death, we had numerous conversations with Bob about this and other positions, a number of which we resisted and, at times, strongly disagreed with. Yet even as we resisted, and at times argued, we admired the forthrightness with which Bob claimed his positions. And we admired as well the elegance, wit, and self-directed humor with which he did so. Elsewhere in the introduction to *Composition-Rhetoric,* for instance, Bob says, after acknowledging that his project is not "radical" or "subversive" history: "I suppose that means I am (sigh) an epistemologically conservative historian" (332). That sigh is quintessential Bob, and it reminds us of the lively connections between Bob the scholar and Bob the person we had the great good fortune of knowing.

OTHER LIVES

The preceding pages offer one accounting of the life of Bob Connors—his life in writing. But like all of us, Bob lived many other lives. Readers who knew Bob only through his research might be surprised to learn of the range of his passions, including his writerly passions. For somehow in the midst of his

With Edward P. J. Corbett, 1996

The Connors family—Bob, Aillinn, and Colleen, 1998

1999

Selected Essays of
ROBERT J. CONNORS

The Rise and Fall
of the Modes of Discourse

"The Rise and Fall of the Modes of Discourse" was published in *College Composition and Communication* in 1981, when Bob Connors was just two years beyond the Ph.D. Honored with the Braddock Award for the best article published in the *CCC* that year, this essay brought Bob's work to a wide national audience and was, as Bob notes in an afterword that appeared in Lisa Ede's *On Writing Research: The Braddock Essays, 1975–1998* (Boston: Bedford, 1999), "an early signal of the growth of historical consciousness in the rapidly organizing field of composition studies" (121). We would add that this early essay sounds several notes that recur throughout Bob's work: the turn to textbooks from the past as a rich source of historical information about our field; the tendency to organize data into categories or taxonomies; the use of narrative as a guiding structure. Here too we find Bob's characteristically readable and engaging style that brought long-lost or obscure figures from composition's history—Barrett Wendell, John Genung, Adams Sherman Hill—to vivid life. In this, as in many other works, Bob Connors challenged teachers of writing to study the history of writing and of the teaching of writing, not only for their inherent interest but, more importantly, for what the past can teach us about our own practices.

T he classification of discourse into different types has been one of the continuing interests of rhetoricians since the classical period. Some of these classifications have been genuinely useful to teachers of discourse, but others have exemplified Butler's damning couplet, "all a rhetorician's rules / Teach nothing but to name his tools." To explore the question of what makes a discourse classification useful or appealing to teachers, this essay will examine the rise, reign, and fall of the most influential classification scheme of the last hundred years: the "forms" or "modes" of discourse: Narration, Description, Exposition, and Argument. More students have been taught composition using the modes of discourse than any other

From *College Composition and Communication* 32.4 (1981): 444–55.

classification system. The history of the modes is an instructive one; from the time of their popularization in American rhetoric textbooks during the late nineteenth century, through the absolute dominance they had in writing classrooms during the period 1895–1930, and into the 1950's when they were finally superseded by other systems, the modes of discourse both influenced and reflected many of the important changes our discipline has seen in the last century. Looking at the modes and their times may also help us answer the question of what sorts of discourse classifications are most useful for writing classes today.

THE EARLY YEARS: INTRODUCTION, CONFLICT, AND ACCEPTANCE

Most short histories of the modes of discourse (which for brevity's sake will hereafter be called simply "the modes") trace them back to George Campbell's "four ends of speaking" and to Alexander Bain, the Scottish logician and educator whose 1866 textbook *English Composition and Rhetoric* made the modal formula widely known. But, as Albert Kitzhaber points out, the terms we have come to call the modes were floating about in very general use during the period 1825–1870.[1] It is not easy to trace influences among rhetoric texts of this period, since the ideas were presumed to be in currency rather than the specific property of individuals, but the first definitive use of terms similar to our modal terms was in 1827. In that year, they appeared in a small book called *A Practical System of Rhetoric,* by Samuel P. Newman, a professor at Bowdoin College in Maine.

According to the *National Union Catalog,* Newman's text was the most widely-used rhetoric written in America between 1820 and 1860, going through at least sixty "editions" or printings between its first publication and 1856—a huge number for that time. Newman owed much to Hugh Blair's *Lectures on Rhetoric and Belles-Letters* of 1873 and something to George Campbell's 1776 treatise on *The Philosophy of Rhetoric,* but *A Practical System* differed from both books in its penchant for grouping concepts, a fascination with categories which was to become one of the hallmarks of the rigidly formalized rhetoric of the late nineteenth century. Here is Newman's description of the "kinds of composition":

> Writings are distinguished from each other as didactic, persuasive, argumentative, descriptive, and narrative. . . . Didactic writing, as the name implies, is used in conveying instruction. . . . when it is designed to influence the will, the composition becomes the persuasive kind. . . . the various forms of argument, the statement of proofs, the assigning of causes . . . are addressed to the reasoning faculties of the mind. Narrative and descriptive writings relate past occurrences, and place before the mind for its contemplation, various objects and scenes.[2]

Newman uses the term "didactic" in place of the more common "expository" and, as was common in the later nineteenth century, separates persuasion of

the will from argument to the logical faculties, but it seems obvious that his is the prototype of the modal formula.

Newman's terms did not, however, fall on very fertile soil. He had a few imitators between 1827 and 1866, most notably Richard Green Parker, whose 1844 text *Aids to English Composition* added "Pathetic" to Newman's list, and George Quackenbos, who listed Description, Narration, Argument, Exposition, and Speculation in his *Advanced Course of Composition and Rhetoric* of 1854. Few other texts picked up the terms, and the modes hung in suspension, waiting for a powerful voice to solidify and disseminate a formulation.

That voice was found in Bain. Here are "the various kinds of composition" from the first American edition of *English Composition and Rhetoric*.

> Those that have for their object to inform the understanding, fall under three heads—*Description, Narration,* and *Exposition.* The means of influencing the will are given under one head, *Persuasion.* The employing of language to excite pleasurable Feelings is one of the chief characteristics of *Poetry.*[3]

Minus the reference to poetry (which Bain later admitted was extraneous), this was the modal formulation that was to prove such a powerful force in the teaching of writing in American colleges.

Why did Bain's formulation win wide adherence within two decades while Newman's earlier version was not generally accepted? There are two reasons, one having to do with the manner in which Bain used the modes in his text and the other related to the changing temperament of rhetorical education in America during the late nineteenth century.

First, unlike either Newman or Quackenbos, who merely mentioned their modal terms in passing in their texts—Newman spent only two pages on his "kinds of composition"—Bain used the modes as an organizing principle in *English Composition and Rhetoric*. Modal terms inform long sections of his discussion, and one cannot read the text without carrying away a vivid impression of their importance. This is an important key to Bain's success, for the modes were to become generally accepted not merely as a classification of discourse, but as a conceptualizing strategy for teaching composition.

The second reason for the popularity of the Bainian modes was the changing atmosphere of rhetorical education between 1830 and 1900, especially in the United States. At the beginning of this period, American colleges tended to be small and were often religion-based. Curricula were generally classical, and rhetorical study tended to follow the examples set down by the great rhetoricians of the eighteenth century. The work of Hugh Blair was especially influential, and scores of editions of his *Lectures* were printed in the United States between 1790 and 1860. The analyses of belletristic literature that made Blair's work novel had a profound impact on other elements in rhetorical study during the early nineteenth century.

When we consider the popularity of Blair's belletristic approach to rhetoric, it is not strange to find that the leading discourse classification of

the time—the classification the modes were to displace—was based in belles-lettres and classified discourse "according to its literary form—epistle, romance, treatise, dialog, history, etc."[4] This belletristic classification was found in most pre-Civil War rhetorics. Although some texts included journalistic forms such as Reviews and Editorials and some went into minor forms such as Allegories and Parables, the five most common belletristic forms were Letters, Treatises, Essays, Biographies, and Fiction.

Time-proven though this classification was, it lasted only thirty years after the introduction of the modes, largely because rhetorical study in America was transformed after 1860. In tandem with the shift in the structure of higher education from a preponderance of smaller private colleges to a preponderance of larger institutions with more varied and scientific curricula, the study of rhetoric mutated from a traditional (that is, classically-derived) analysis of argument, eloquence, style, and taste into a discipline much more concerned with forms. The culture was calling for a new sort of educated man, and the "Freshman English Course" as we know it today, with its emphasis on error-free writing and the ability to follow directions, was born during this period in response to the call. The shift in classification schemes from belletristic to modal is just a part—though an important part—of this larger change. The teacher of the Gilded Age perceived his students as having needs quite different from the needs of their counterparts of 1830. Treatises, Biographies, Fiction, and such were well and good, but the essentially aristocratic educational tradition they represented was on the way out. What occurred between 1870 and 1895 was a shift from a concrete, form-based model rooted in literary high culture to a more pliable abstract model that seemed to be adaptable to anything which a rising young American might wish to say.

While the belletristic classification was waning, the modes were waxing, but only after a slow beginning. The period 1875–1890 shows no clear victor, though modal texts can be seen advancing, and general acceptance of the modes took two decades after Bain's first publication of them. *English Composition and Rhetoric* itself, after a burst of popularity in 1867, subsided into relative obscurity through the 1870's and early 1880's, and Bain's early followers were not much luckier.

The turning point, the text that really marks the paradigm shift most clearly, did not come until 1885, with the publication of *The Practical Elements of Rhetoric*, by the redoubtable John Genung. As much as Bain himself (whose sales Genung helped boost throughout the late eighties), Genung popularized the modes throughout America. *The Practical Elements* was in print from 1885 through 1904, and only Bain's text, which was in print far longer, A. S. Hill's *Principles of Rhetoric*, which had the cachet of Harvard, and Barrett Wendell's *English Composition* were more popular during the period 1865–1900. Between them, Bain and Genung greatly influenced the theoretical and practical world of rhetoric instruction between 1886 and 1891, and the popularity of their books sounded the death-knell of the belletristic classification in composition courses.

Genung, of course, did not adopt Bain's notion of four modes absolutely, as had Bain's earlier and less successful imitators A. D. Hepburn and David Hill. He distinguished between Argumentation, which he called "Invention dealing with Truths" and Persuasion, which he called "Invention dealing with Practical Issues."[5] These two sorts of arguments were copied and used by derivative textbook authors after Genung until about 1910, when the four standard terms swept all before them. Genung himself adopted the four terms of the standard modes himself in 1893 in his *Outlines of Rhetoric*, the follow-up text to *The Practical Elements*.

THE REIGN OF THE MODES

Of the textbook authors that Kitzhaber calls "The Big Four" of the late nineteenth century—Barrett Wendell, John Genung, Adams Sherman Hill, and Fred Newton Scott (who wrote his texts in collaboration with Joseph V. Denney)—all had implicitly accepted the modes by 1894, and by 1895 all except Wendell were using them as important parts of their texts. Wendell merely mentioned the modes as an accepted convention in his *English Composition*, using instead as an organizing structure his famous trinity of Unity-Mass-Coherence (which he adopted, incidentally, from Bain's discussion of the paragraph). Though he did not use the modes in an important way, Wendell at least advanced no competitive classification, and many later texts adopted both the modes and the trinity as important elements.[6]

A. S. Hill, Boylston Professor of Rhetoric at Harvard, denied the modes throughout the eighties in his text *The Principles of Rhetoric*, which omitted Exposition from its scope. Hill saw the handwriting on the wall in the early nineties, however, when sales of his book dropped off sharply. There was no edition of *The Principles of Rhetoric* in 1894, and when the book reappeared in 1895 in a "New Edition, Revised and Enlarged," the revision recited the modal litany in perfect chorus. So fell into line many of the partially-converted.

Fred N. Scott and Joseph Denney's text, *Paragraph-Writing*, in 1891, dealt as much with paragraphs as with whole essays—using, of course, the paragraph model that Bain had originated 25 years earlier—but the four sorts of essays that Scott and Denney do mention are the familiar quartet. *Paragraph-Writing* was Scott and Denney's most popular text, and aside from its use of the modes it is important for another reason. It is the first truly popular codification of "the means of developing paragraphs" which were to become more and more important in the fifty years following Scott and Denney. Adapted from the classical topics, these "means" included Contrast, Explanation, Definition, Illustration, Detail, and Proofs. Watch these terms, for they will reappear, both as methods of paragraph development and more importantly as the "methods of exposition" that will come to supplant the modes.

This reappearance was not to happen, though, for many years. After 1895, the modes were the controlling classification, having driven the belletristic forms from the field. During the late nineties, non-modal texts almost

completely disappeared; of 28 books dating between 1893 and 1906 surveyed by Kitzhaber, only four made no mention of the modes.[7] There was for a while some disagreement about whether argument and persuasion were truly separate, but by 1910 even these internecine quarrels had died out. That the modes were accepted almost absolutely was evidenced by the growth and spread of texts devoted to treating only one of them, such as George Pierce Baker's influential *The Principles of Argumentation* in 1895, Carroll L. Maxcy's *The Rhetorical Principles of Narration* in 1911, and Gertrude Buck's *Expository Writing* in 1899. As we shall see, these single-mode texts would have an important effect on the future of the modes as a system.

With single-mode and four-mode textbooks controlling the lists, the reign of modal text organization was long and ponderous, lasting from the mid-1890's through the mid-1930's. During this time there were no theoretical advances. Most textbooks were written by followers of Genung and Wendell, and a typical organizing structure of the time was a combination of Wendell's trinity of Unity-Mass-Coherence—later modernized to Unity-Coherence-Emphasis—with "the four traditional forms of discourse." (By 1920 the origin of the modes was lost in the mists of time; they had presumably been carved in stone during the Paleolithic Age.) In terms of new insights, the teaching of composition was frozen in its tracks between 1900 and 1925, and despite a few novel treatments and up-to-date appearances, I cannot find a single text that is not derivative of the authors of the nineties.

Partially this stasis was due to the changing backgrounds of textbook authors, a change which in turn was the result of new directions in the discipline of English. During this period, "philology" was coming more and more to mean the criticism and scholarly study of literature, and rhetoric was being displaced in many schools from English departments. The composition texts of the nineteenth century had generally been written by rhetorical scholars (Barrett Wendell is a notable exception), but in the early years of the new century, the majority of composition texts began to be written by literary scholars who were producing derivative texts in order to put bread on their tables. The pure fire of Bain was kept alive during this period by such literary figures as Percy Boynton, John C. French, and Raymond Pence.

From the middle of the last decade of the nineteenth century, through the Great War, and into the middle of that disillusioned decade following it, the modes controlled the teaching of composition through complete control of textbooks. Nothing threatened, nothing changed. But the world was turning, and the modes were about to be challenged.

THE MODES UNDER ATTACK

It is relatively simple to detail the hegemony of the modes up until the mid-twenties, but at that time, in composition as in the culture at large, great shifts began to occur. Not all of these shifts can be satisfactorily analyzed, but beginning in the late twenties we can note the rise of two trends that would fragment the discipline and result in the gradual diminution of the impor-

tance of the modes. The first—which was, ironically, a by-product of the vast popularity the modes had had—was the rise of single-mode textbooks, especially those dealing with exposition. The second was the appearance of new sort of textbook which I call the "thesis text." Let us examine these trends.

To begin with, single-mode texts had been popular as far back as the nineties, as we have seen, but in the twenties and thirties the texts on argumentation and narration were far outstripped by the ultimate victor: texts concerned with exposition. Books like Maurice Garland Fulton's *Expository Writing,* which was first published in 1912 and which survived until 1953 (making it, by my calculations, the longest-lived text of the century) found new popularity in the thirties, and dozens of new expository-writing texts appeared after 1940. Fulton's text, the grandfather to most which followed it, was organized by what he called "Expository Procedures and Devices." Among them are the following: Definition, Classification and Division, Contrast, Comparison or Analogy, Examples, and Descriptive Exposition. You will notice that these overlap to a large degree with Scott and Denney's 1891 list of "Methods of Paragraph Development." Fulton's Procedures and Devices were to be the first important prototypes for the "methods of exposition" still being retailed (sometimes under different names) in many texts today.

Fulton's list was followed and augmented by many other writers throughout the twenties and thirties. There were disagreements about what the "genuine" methods of exposition were, with different texts offering different choices. By the late thirties, though, the list had largely standardized itself, and the techniques of exposition, as they appeared in a whole series of widely-used texts from the forties through the present time, consisted of selections from this final list: definition, analysis, partition, interpretation, reportage, evaluation by standards, comparison, contrast, classification, process analysis, device analysis, cause-and-effect, induction, deduction, examples, and illustration.[8]

By the 1940's exposition had become so popular that it was more widely taught than the "general" modal freshman composition course. This does not, of course, mean that the other modes had ceased to be taught, but more and more they retreated out of composition classes into specialized niches of their own. Narration and description seceded to become the nuclei of creative writing courses, and argumentation, finding itself more and more an orphan in English departments, took refuge in Speech departments and became largely an oral concern for many years. The very success of the modes—and the fact that exposition was the most "practical" of them in a business-oriented culture—was destroying their power as a general organizational strategy throughout the thirties and forties. The modes were still used in many texts, but by the end of World War II they no longer controlled composition or defined discourse except in a relatively general way.

The second trend that was to result in the passing of the modes was the rise of a new sort of composition textbook, different in its angle of approach from modal texts. Prior to 1930, nearly all composition texts were organized according to a hierarchical view of discourse in which the levels were

discussed impartially—modal organization, the Bain-Wendell trinity of Unity-Coherence-Emphasis, the Bainian paragraph model, traditional three-element sentence theory, and a few other ritual topics. The order of presentation of material in texts was arbitrary, and occasionally the trinity and the modes would change positions in the hierarchy, but the most important classification discussed in the texts was always the modal, and the controlling assumptions about writing underlying these texts were drawn from the theory of modes, as well. Up until the thirties there were few departures from this line.

Then, beginning in 1930 and in larger numbers throughout the forties and fifties, we begin to see this new type of textbook. It is not a text in purely expository writing; it does not use pragmatic classification exclusively; and it certainly does not treat the levels in writing impartially. This new kind of text does, of course, contain a great deal of traditional rhetorical material, but it is marked by an important change in focus: *it announces that one powerful "master idea" about writing should control the way that students learn to write, and it gives precedence to this central thesis, subordinating all other theoretical material to it.* For this reason, I call these new textbooks thesis texts (without at all implying that they focus attention on the need for a thesis in the student's paper). They are *the* modern composition texts, and today they control the textbook world almost completely.

It would not be hard to make a case for Barrett Wendell's *English Composition* in 1891 as the first thesis text. In that book Wendell observed that rhetoric texts in his time consisted

> . . . chiefly of directions as to how one who would write should set about composing. Many of these directions are extremely sensible, many very suggestive. But in every case these directions are appallingly numerous. It took me some years to discern that all which have so far come to my notice could be grouped under one of three simple heads. . . . The first of these principles may conveniently be named the principle of Unity; the second, the principle of Mass; the third, the principle of Coherence.[9]

There in a nutshell is the central doctrine of the thesis text: "All else is essentially subordinate to this." Wendell spent the rest of his book explicating how his three principles could be applied to sentences, paragraphs, and whole themes.

Despite the success of *English Composition* and the flock of slavish imitators it spawned, Wendell did not have a spiritual successor for over forty years; the period following his text, as we have seen, was marked by conventionality and reliance upon modal organization of texts. In 1931, though, a text appeared which was to signal an important departure: Norman Foerster and J. M. Steadman's *Writing and Thinking*. This extremely popular text was in print for over twenty years, and it exerted a profound influence on later authors. Foerster and Steadman's dual thesis was announced on their first page: "Writing and thinking are organically related," and "Writing, in other

words, should be organic, not mechanic."[10] The authors then went on to subordinate the rest of their material—not much of which was genuinely original—to this thesis.

Although *Writing and Thinking* was a popular book, the new trend in texts began slowly; there are only a few books identifiable as being controlled by non-modal theses in the thirties and early forties. The theses that truly established thesis texts, that tipped the balance away from the domination of the modes in the late forties, reflected the two most popular intellectual movements in composition theory at that time: the general education movement with its "language arts/communications" approach, and the General Semantics movement. This essay is not the place for a history of these movements, fascinating as one might be. In brief, the general education/ "communications" movement grew out of the Deweyite interest in "English for Life Skills" during the thirties and emphasized the whole continuum of language activities—reading, writing, speaking, and listening—rather than writing alone. The Conference on College Composition and Communication was formed in 1948 by "communications" enthusiasts. (That's where the "communication" comes from.) General Semantics, of course, was based on the work of Alfred Korzybski as popularized by S. I. Hayakawa in his influential *Words in Action* of 1940, and is most interested in language as a symbol system liable to abuse. Together, communications and General Semantics provided theses for more than half of the new composition texts that appeared between 1948 and 1952.

There were, of course, some thesis texts not based on either communications or on General Semantics. One of the best of them is still going strong: James McCrimmon's *Writing With A Purpose*, the thesis of which is, of course, the importance of the writer's controlling purpose. Most thesis texts not based on communications or General Semantics used theses based on some version of favorite old notions, writing and thinking, writing and reading, the unique demands of American writing. Later the theses in texts would grow out of concepts more complex and interesting: writing and perception, writing and cognition, writing and process. Most expository writing texts also took on characteristics of thesis texts during the fifties, and more and more thesis texts came to use the "methods of exposition."

FALL AND ABANDONMENT OF THE MODES

And where stood the Bainian modes in this avalanche—for an avalanche it became after 1950—of expositionists and thesis texts? As has been suggested, the modes did not completely disappear, but they were certainly changed, truncated, and diminished in power. The new texts that appeared did not subvert the modes because they proved them theoretically erroneous, but rather because their theses or listing of methods took over the role in organizing texts that the modes had earlier played. McCrimmon makes a telling statement in the Preface to the first edition of *Writing With A Purpose* in 1950: "The decision to make purpose the theme of the book made the

conventional fourfold classification of writing unnecessary. Therefore Exposition, Narration, Description, and Argument are not considered as special types of writing."[11] Even when thesis texts mentioned the modes, they were a minor consideration. Essentially, the modes were ignored to death after 1950.

The new thesis texts used a number of original classifications of discourse, and the modes were everywhere being replaced by these novel classifications. After 1955 or so the modes are seen in new texts only when those texts have specifically traditional intent: for instance, Richard Weaver's *Composition* and Hughes and Duhamel's *Rhetoric: Principles and Usage*. Though the theses of the thesis texts would continue to change—from propositions based upon General Semantics or communications in the forties and fifties to propositions developed from transformational grammar, problem solving, and prewriting in the sixties to theses about invention, process, cognition, and syntactic methods in the seventies—all these theses (of which some texts contain several) have one thing in common: they bypass or ignore the modes of discourse. W. Ross Winterowd spoke for authors of thesis texts when he stated in a 1965 textbook that the modal classification, "though interesting, isn't awfully helpful."[12]

In rhetoric texts today, the modes are still expiring. A few texts still mention them as minor elements, but their power in rhetorics is gone. Of the fifteen or so most widely-used freshman rhetoric texts, only one still advances the modal classes as absolute. Though the modes still retain a shadow of their old puissance as an organizing device in certain freshman anthologies of essays, their importance in modern pedagogy is constantly diminishing, and the only teachers still making real classroom use of the modes are those out of touch with current theory. Stripped of their theoretical validity and much of their practical usefulness, the modes cling to a shadowy half-life in the attic of composition legends.

L'ENVOI—THE MODES AS PLAUSIBLE FICTION

Why did the modes of discourse rise to such power, hold it for so long and so abolutely, and then decline so rapidly? At least part of the answer has to do with the relative vitality of the rhetorical tradition during the period 1870–1930, an era when hardly any progressive theoretical work was done in the field. Alexander Bain, Fred N. Scott, and perhaps Barrett Wendell are the greatest figures writing during the period, and (except for Scott, whose influence was limited) they cannot stand beside Campbell in the eighteenth century or Burke in the twentieth. The modes became popular and stayed popular because they fit into the abstract, mechanical nature of writing instruction at the time, and they diminished in importance as other, more vital, ideas about writing appeared in the 1930's and after. Like the "dramatic unities" that ruled the drama of the seventeenth and eighteenth centuries until exploded by Samuel Johnson's common sense, the modes were only powerful so long as they were not examined for evidence of their usefulness.

One of the most damning assessments of the modes' use in the nineteenth century is that of Albert Kitzhaber:

> Such convenient abstractions as . . . the forms of discourse were ideally suited to the purpose of instruction in a subject that had been cut off from all relation with other subjects in the curriculum and, in a sense, from life itself. . . . They represent an unrealistic view of the writing process, a view that assumes writing is done by formula and in a social vacuum. They turn the attention of both teacher and student toward an academic exercise instead of toward a meaningful act of communication in a social context. Like Unity-Coherence-Emphasis—or any other set of static abstractions concerning writing—they substitute mechanical for organic conceptions and therefore distort the real nature of writing.[13]

The weakness of the modes of discourse as a practical tool in the writing class was that they did not really help students to learn to write. When we look closely at the nature of modal distinctions, it is not hard to see why: the modes classify and emphasize the product of writing, having almost nothing to do with the purpose for which the writer sat down, pen in hand. Modal distinctions are divorced from the composition process. As James Kinneavy puts it,

> . . . a stress on modes of discourse rather than aims of discourse is a stress on "what" is being talked about rather than on "why" a thing is talked about. This is actually a substitution of means for ends. Actually, something is narrated for reason. Narration, as such, is not a purpose. Consequently, the "modes" period in history has never lasted very long.[14]

In our time, the modes are little more than an unofficial descriptive myth, replaced in theory by empirically-derived classifications of discourse and in practice by the "methods of exposition" and other non-modal classes. The important theoretical classification schemas of today are those of James Moffett, whose Spectrum of Discourse consists of Recording, Reporting, Generalizing, and Theorizing; of James Kinneavy, who divides discourse into Reference, Scientific, Persuasive, Literary, and Expressive types; and of James Britton, with its triad of Poetic, Expressive, and Transactional discourse. All of these classification schemes have one thing in common: they are based on the writer's purposes, the ends of his or her composing, rather than merely being classifications of written discourse.

In current textbooks, too, the modes are largely displaced by more process-oriented considerations or by heuristic theses that see classification of discourse as unimportant. The most popular discourse classification still found in textbooks is Fulton's "methods of exposition," updated and augmented, of course. Doubtless the most complete system using the methods of exposition is Frank D'Angelo's system of "discourse paradigms." We do not yet know whether the paradigms will become as rigid, abstract, and useless as did their progenitors, the modes.

"Anytime a means is exalted to an end in history of discourse education, a similar pattern can be seen," writes Kinneavy; "the emphasis is short-lived and usually sterile." The modes of discourse controlled a good part of composition teaching during one of rhetoric's least vigorous periods, offering in their seeming completeness and plausibility a schema of discourse that could be easily taught and learned. For years the fact that this schema did not help students learn to write better was not a concern, and even today the modes are accepted by some teachers despite their lack of basis in useful reality. Our discipline has been long in knuckling from its eyes the sleep of the nineteenth and early twentieth centuries, and the real lesson of the modes is that we need always to be on guard against systems that seem convenient to teachers but that ignore the way writing is actually done.

NOTES

1. Albert R. Kitzhaber, *Rhetoric in American Colleges 1850–1900,* Diss. University of Washington, 1953, pp. 191–196.

2. Samuel P. Newman, *A Practical System of Rhetoric* (New York: Mark H. Newman, 1827), pp. 28–29.

3. Alexander Bain, *English Composition and Rhetoric* (New York: D. Appleton and Co., 1866), p. 19.

4. Kitzhaber, p. 191.

5. John F. Genung, *The Practical Elements of Rhetoric* (Boston: Ginn and Co., 1887), Table of Contents.

6. It is interesting to note that Wendell, who mentions the modes only in passing, is the only one of the "Big Four" who admits any indebtedness to Bain. This is especially strange when we consider that Bain's paragraph model was also used in all these texts without direct citation. For more on Bain's paragraph theory—which undoubtedly helped spread the associated doctrine of the modes—see Paul C. Rodgers, Jr., "Alexander Bain and the Rise of the Organic Paragraph," *Quarterly Journal of Speech* 51 (December, 1965), 399–408.

7. Kitzhaber, p. 204.

8. This list is compiled from John S. Naylor, *Informative Writing* (New York: Macmillan, 1942); Joseph M. Bachelor and Harold L. Haley, *The Practice of Exposition* (New York: Appleton-Century, 1947); and Louise F. Rorabacher, *Assignments in Exposition* (New York: Harper and Bros., 1946).

9. Barrett Wendell, *English Composition* (New York: Scribners, 1891), pp. 18–19.

10. Norman Foerster and J. M. Steadman, Jr., *Writing and Thinking* (Boston: Houghton Mifflin, 1931), p. 3.

11. James M. McCrimmon, *Writing With A Purpose* (Boston: Houghton Mifflin, 1950), pp. viii–ix.

12. W. Ross Winterowd, *Writing and Rhetoric* (Boston: Allyn and Bacon, 1965), p. 199.

13. Kitzhaber, pp. 220–221.

14. James L. Kinneavy, *A Theory of Discourse* (Englewood Cliffs, NJ: Prentice-Hall, 1971), pp. 28–29.

Handbooks: History of a Genre

"Handbooks: History of a Genre" appeared in the *Rhetoric Society Quarterly* in 1983. This essay continues Bob's intensive study of textbooks—in this case, handbooks, a genre that, as Bob points out here, appeared in the late nineteenth century and marked an important transition in the teaching of writing. In this essay, Bob's interest in the material conditions of texts—and also of teaching—is clearly evident. In sketching out the history of handbooks from their early development to the present time, Bob considers not only such obvious issues as their nature and organization but also such elements as their physical size. For example, Bob links the shift from "the giantism that began in the 1950's" (22) to the much smaller, pocket-sized handbooks of later years to concrete educational conditions, such as the movement in the early 1960s to challenge a singular emphasis on mechanical correctness in first-year writing. Perhaps even more important, Bob links the development of handbooks to the material situations of teachers of writing. In concluding his essay, Bob points out that "so long as composition instruction is organized so that ill-trained teachers must deal with 100 or 125 student essays every week, handbooks will be the central artifacts of writing courses. Not until we demand that conditions change will we move out from under the shadow of sterile, a-rhetorical correctness that handbooks have come to represent" (24).

T he handbook of composition, a compendium of rules, models, and exercises covering aspects of formal and syntactic convention, is a relatively recent phenomenon in college education. Its appearance in the late nineteenth century marks an important transition in rhetorical instruction, a transition from emphasis on style and communicative effectiveness to primary emphasis on rule-governed mechanical correctness. In this essay I wish to trace the development of the handbook as a form of textbook that mirrored and helped to midwife that transition and eventually came to assert almost total dominance over college-level writing instruction.

From *Rhetoric Society Quarterly* 13.2 (1983): 87–98.

To begin, we must clearly distinguish handbooks in the direct line of instruction-reference from related but dissimilar sorts of books. First to use the title of "handbook" were the "handbooks of conversation" that appeared in the nineteenth century. From the 1840's through the 1890's, handbooks and manuals of usage, politesse, and manners became increasingly popular as the social equalitarianism of the Jefferson-Jackson period receded in America. These handbooks differed from their modern counterparts in a number of ways; most importantly, they were the products of cultural rather than of pedagogical needs. As I discuss elsewhere, changes in the social structure of Victorian America meant that "correctness" and gentility in address had to be given new priority; thus such manuals came to popularity.[1] One of the first of them was Seth Hurd's *Grammatical Corrector* of 1847, which claimed to be "a collection of nearly two thousand barbarisms, cant phrases, colloquialisms, quaint expressions, provincialisms, false pronunciation, perversions . . . and other kindred errors of the English language." (Title Page) Another such proto-handbook was Andrew Peabody's *Handbook of Conversation: Its Faults and Graces* (1855), which put forward the principles which were supposed to govern speaking and writing "among persons of true refinement of mind and character." (p. 7) Such small manuals—later they had titles like *Don't!* and *Discriminate!*—were the fruits of self-improvement fads and a burgeoning system of class distinctions, partially linguistically based, in America. Handbooks of linguistic gentility would not die out until around the turn of the century, when various factors combined to make such social-climb short-cuts unnecessary or ineffective.

We must also distinguish composition handbooks from textbooks of grammar and from prescriptive-usage debates. Vernacular grammar textbooks had been increasingly relied on in American elementary ("grammar") schools since the American Revolution, as Rollo Lyman has shown.[2] Prior to the 1870's, however, such texts were concerned with English grammar as an abstract structure promoting "mental discipline" in its learning. Even after William Swinton's *Language Lessons* of 1873 popularized the combination of grammar with composition in a single course, grammar was still taught as a system to be learned in and for itself. Most grammar texts were written to an obviously elementary level and clearly differ in tone from handbooks; they also ignore questions of style, format, usage, punctuation, and many other handbook necessities. The early methods of teaching grammar—particularly the "false syntax" exercises, which promoted an attitude of constant suspicion, and the rules-based pedagogy—certainly led to the creation of handbooks, but grammar texts are not handbooks themselves.

Similarly, books of prescriptive-usage debate, which became a popular intellectual recreation during the 1860's and '70's, differ from handbooks in that they are oriented toward no rules but those of arbitrary authority. These debates arose in America in 1864, when the Dean of Westminster, Henry Alford, published *A Plea for the Queen's English,* a critique of current usage that singled out Americans for particular opprobrium. Alford was answered and criticized by such now-forgotten champions as George Washington

Moon, Edward S. Gould, Richard Meade Bache and others.[3] The intellectual journals of the period blossomed with their articles, and books appeared with such titles as *The Dean's English; Bad English; Good English, or, Popular Errors in Language; Words: Their Use and Abuse;* and *Vulgarisms and Other Errors of Speech.* Many of these books became prescriptive nit-picking of the worst sort, with their authors descending into lengthy, silly critiques of each others' usage like Milton and Salmasius attacking each other for errors in Latin syntax. Although this prescriptivist debate did work toward creating the intellectual milieu that fostered college handbooks, its works were not handbooks. They dealt only with usage, and they were too arbitrary and chaotic to be of much reference use.

Having determined what were *not* handbooks in the pedagogical sense, we can begin to look at books that *were* handbooks, or at least began to approach handbook status. The first book of prescriptive rules to be used as a handbook in colleges was not originally written for English classes at all; it was Edwin A. Abbott's *How To Write Clearly,* which first appeared in 1874. (It was to be in print for thirty years, which probably surprised even the author.) Abbott, a classics instructor and headmaster of the City of London School, wrote his little manual because his students' translations from the Greek and Latin authors were so poorly done that he felt they needed "help to enable them to write a long English sentence clearly . . . The flat, vague, long-winded Greek-English imposture that is often tolerated . . . diminishes instead of increasing the power that our pupils should possess over their native language." (p. 7) Abbott believed that clear writing (as opposed to stylistically elegant writing) "can be reduced to rules," and his little book consists of 56 mainly stylistic rules under the headings "Clearness and Force" and "Brevity." *How To Write Clearly,* then, was the first college-level text to reduce writing to purely-governed activity.

The book was very successful, especially in America, where it was used less in classics courses than in English composition classes. In 1874, of course, the Freshman English course as we now know it was fairly new, but even that early the evidence was clear: students writing weekly themes for teacher correction made many mechanical errors and produced large amounts of work for the teacher. Some sort of mechanical correction system was needed, and although Abbott's book did not completely fill the bill—it contained no capitalization or punctuation material, used no examples, and assumed pre-existing knowledge of grammar—it was closer than any other book of the time. Teachers ordered it in goodly numbers; between 1875 and 1895 *How To Write Clearly* was required at different times by Harvard, Oberlin, and the Universities of Pennsylvania, Virginia, and Michigan. It far outsold its rivals—such books as Lathem's *Hand-Book of the English Language* and *Outlines of the Art of Expression,* which merely announced upper-level versions of the elementary lessons of grammar without making connections with style and writing. English teachers early realized that it was pragmatic error-based rules and not the rules of abstract grammar that would help them most efficiently, and they chose Abbott's book over all others.

The question most mysterious to anyone investigating the development of the handbook form is why a more recognizable handbook did not appear earlier. Abbott was not really a full handbook, and it was by no means universally used. Certainly all of the factors that made mechanical correction of student papers necessary or attractive to teachers—a weekly-theme policy, heavy overloads, a sociocultural emphasis on "basics" and "correctness"—were in place by 1885. Teachers had need of handbook-type texts, and yet, with one notable exception, no textbooks meant specifically for rule-governed paper correction appeared after Abbott in the nineteenth century. A few textbooks did cover punctuation and capitalization and had since 1870, when John Hart's *Composition and Rhetoric* appeared, but they did not go farther than these areas and were not systematic in their treatments. For the most part, mechanical correction of student papers during the last two decades of the nineteenth century seems to have been done with "Theme Cards" or "Composition Cards," which were printed cards distributed by teachers. Common forms of Theme Cards often printed shortened "rules of correctness" or gave students a list of correction symbols and the terms they were attached to. (See Figure 1.) A few textbooks at the end of the 1880's included such charts, but they covered only one or two pages and seemed stuck in as an afterthought.[4]

The problem with these Theme Cards and Correction Pages was that they simply did not have the room to allow any explanation of the "rule" whose transgression had been indicated. A full-sized book of such rules, symbols, explanations, and illustrations was the obvious next step—and yet it was not taken. The closest thing to it during the *fin de siecle* period was written in 1893 by John F. Genung, whose *Practical Elements of Rhetoric* had been the most popular text of the 1880's. His new book was called *Outlines of Rhetoric*, and it is the first recognizable remedial composition textbook.

Outlines, claimed Genung, was "a new sort of book"; though not truly a handbook of a recognizable sort, it was closer than anything else to the form because it was based on the idea of writing as algorithmic:

> The theoretical part (of *Outlines*), embodying the principles of rhetoric, is given, it will be observed, in the form of rules, which are printed as side-headings, and numbered consecutively from beginning to end of the book. Each rule is accompanied by a brief paragraph of explanation, and by illustrated examples. In this way the attempt is made to bring the core of the rhetorical art into small and manageable compass, the rules being a body of precept to which constant reference is made. (p. iii)

The idea of there being rules to follow in writing was not, of course, new, but the idea that writing could be *entirely compassed* by rules was. Genung's rules numbered 125, and like Abbott he was more interested in stylistic beauty than in syntactic acceptability. Genung did not—indeed, refused to—cover areas such as capitalization, basic punctuation, and sentence structure,

FIGURE 1   A Typical "Correction Card" from the Early Twentieth Century

DEPARTMENT OF ENGLISH

Theme Card.

"The foundation of all right expression is sincerity."

General Directions.

Use the Theme Book provided by the Instructor.

Fill out the card, and paste it in the middle of the cover.

Leave the first two pages for Contents, as in a printed book.

Number the pages following the Contents.

Place the title at the head of the theme.

Indent the paragraphs.

Write only on the left-hand page.

Use black ink, and write with a coarse pen, in a clear, legible hand.

Be careful to space the words properly.

Leave a margin, as in a printed page.

When the book is returned with the Instructor's marks in the margin of the theme, correct on the right-hand page.

Any violation of the above rules for the mechanical form will require the work to be rewritten.

If there is an error (rhetorical) in a sentence, the sentence must be rewritten.

An error in the method of paragraphing will require the theme to be reconstructed.

Particular attention is called to words underscored, and to words or clauses corrected by a line.

Key to the Instructor's marks.

A. Ambiguous.
C. Condense.
Con. Lacks connection.
D. Diction faulty.
E. Expand.
F. Lacks force.
H. Mistake in capital or head letters.
L. Illogical.
M. Figurative language defective.
Ms. Bad manuscript. Theme must be copied.
O. Obscure.
§ Paragraph wanting, or not in the proper place.
P. Punctuation faulty.
R. Repetition.
S. Spelling faulty.
T. Transpose.
U. Lacks unity.
W. Weak. Theme must be rewritten.
? Statement doubtful.
( ) Passage to be omitted.
/ Sentence or clause must be reconstructed.
– Something omitted.
x Some obvious fault.

One of the above marks appearing at the head of the Theme indicates that the fault is a prevailing one.

Works on Rhetoric which are recommended :
Carpenter's "Elements of Rhetoric."
Genung's "Practical Elements of Rhetoric."
Pearson's "Freshman Composition."

Source: From M. Atkinson Williams, *Report on the Teaching of English in the United States* (London: Swan Sonnenschein and Co., 1908), p. 54.

drawing a clear line between what he called "rhetoric" and what he would condemn as "grammar" and refuse to treat of.[5]

Outlines was the only textbook by any of the "Big Four"—Albert Kitzhaber's term for the four influential rhetoricians of the late nineteenth century: Genung, A. S. Hill, Fred N. Scott, and Barrett Wendell—to treat of mechanical correctness. These teachers, the last composition-text authors to be trained in the older rhetorical tradition of Campbell, Blair, Cicero, specifically refused to admit lower-level pedagogies—formal, grammatical, mechanical—into their canons of rhetoric. Genung's *Outlines* is as close as they came, and Genung even admitted, half-ruefully, that the book dealt with elements "which it is not so much an honor to know as a reproach not to know." So long as the texts of the Big Four provided the primary influence on rhetoric—which is to say, from 1878 until the first decade of the new century—mechanical-correctness issues were not featured in textbooks on the college level. The Harvard Reports might fulminate against poor preparation of freshmen, but this last generation of rhetoricians refused to abandon rhetoric to grammar. Thus, by the end of the nineteenth century we see a curious schizophrenia between the central tools of the writing course—the textbooks—and the actual priorities that teachers were enforcing through their paper-marking. In spite of the burgeoning current-traditional rhetorical theory of the time, the vast majority of paper-markings were not rhetorical but mechanical in nature: corrections of surface errors.[6]

The age of rhetoricians was passing, however, and that of composition pedagogues was beginning. The old order changeth, and the first clearly discernible modern handbook of mechanical correctness appeared in 1907: Edwin C. Woolley's *Handbook of Composition: A Compendium of Rules.* Woolley's was the first book to frankly cover every aspect of mechanical correction without apologies; it made no pretension to rhetorical instruction, and was composed of 350 numbered rules which covered many areas never before admitted into college composition texts: spelling, punctuation down to the most basic level, sentence structure, abbreviations. Woolley was a groundbreaker in that he frankly assumed that his readers knew nothing of grammatical or formal conventions. Grammar was no abstract system in this book; Woolley's purpose, he said, was "to make clear the rules in regard to which many people make mistakes." (p. iv)

Woolley's *Handbook* was an immediate success. It spawned several other Woolley books, and after Edwin Woolley's death in 1916 his collaborator, Franklin Scott, began to refer to these varied books as "the Woolley Family." (In addition to the *Handbook,* the Woolley Family included *The Mechanics of Writing* (1909), *The New Handbook of Composition* (1926), *The College Handbook of Composition* (1928), and the *Handbook of Writing and Speaking* (1944).) Despite his early death, Woolley's name remained the one most associated with handbooks as a form until the 1950's; it was not dropped until after the 1958 edition of the *College Handbook.* Edwin Woolley's contribution to composition pedagogy was widely admired and seemed to be what teachers had been waiting for. "This little book deserves the utmost praise," wrote a typical re-

viewer,[7] and the *Handbook* sold very well from the beginning. Other authors lost little time in jumping onto the mechanical-correction bandwagon. There were at first no direct copies of Woolley's rule-controlled format, but by 1910 or 1911 rhetoric texts which incorporated handbook sections *a la* Woolley were becoming common. These dual-identity textbooks, along with the popularity of the Woolley texts, caused a real sea-change in the way that composition ordered its classroom priorities. In 1918, Frank W. Scott complained that handbooks were usurping the place of textbooks of rhetoric:

> For the exposition of vital general principles of rhetoric, too often there has been substituted, among other things, the handbook, which enables the writer ignorant of general laws of composition to remove by external application the more flagrant signs of his deficiencies without touching the underlying ignorance itself.[8]

A few years later, this same Frank Scott would be given the chance to take over the authorship of Woolley's *Handbook* and reshape it as he thought best. As Scott indicates, handbooks and the handbook approach were ubiquitous by the time of WWI.

By the end of that war, Woolley (as the *Handbook* was universally known) was doing so well that other publishers determined to follow in its footsteps, and in 1918 was born Woolley's great imitator and competitor, *The Century Handbook of Writing*, by Garland Greever and Easley S. Jones. With only a few additions and refinements, the handbook as we know it today was to be created by the *Century* and Woolley as they battled it out for control of the handbook market between 1918 and 1935. There were a few other handbooks popular during that period, most notably George Woods' *College Handbook of Writing* and Raymond Pence's *Manual of the Mechanics of Writing*, but it was Woolley and *Century* that forced each other into defining the nature of the modern handbook.

The first Woolley handbook, it must be noted, was meant to be used "for reference at the direction of the instructor, in case of errors in themes." It contained few exercises, and exercises were all in one section; the *Handbook* was clearly not a classroom text. In the 1918 *Century*, however, Greever and Jones made several obvious improvements on Woolley. First, they cannily simplified Woolley's complex 350 rules into a "decimal system" of 100 rules, a chart illustrating which they printed on their end papers. This was a much more accessible and memorable system. Just as important, though, was the novel system of "parallel exercises" offered by the *Century*:

> . . . the book throws upon the student the responsibility of teaching himself. Each article begins with a concise rule which is illustrated by examples; then follows a short "parallel exercise" which the instructor may assign by adding an X to the number he writes in the margin of the theme. While correcting this exercise, the student will give attention to the rule, and will acquire theory and practice at the same time. Moreover, every group of ten articles is followed by mixed exercises; these

may be used for review, or imposed in the margin of a theme as a penalty for flagrant or repeated error. Thus friendly counsel is backed by discipline, and the instructor has the means of compelling the student to make rapid progress toward good English. (p. iii)

Here we strike the true handbook tone.

These exercises were a brilliant stroke; the *Century*'s great emphasis on grammar and usage exercises made it a huge commercial success. Other texts followed Greever and Jones, and soon Woolley's publisher, D.C. Heath, faced a real threat to its hegemony. Edwin Woolley himself was dead by this time, of course, but Heath commissioned an anonymous revision that effectually Greeverized the *Handbook* in 1920, adding more exercises. The market, however, was changing rapidly. In 1922, Walter K. Smart produced his *Handbook of Effective Writing*, which introduced much more rhetorical material into handbook form than any previous book. Smart sold well, and the *Century* replied to it in their 1924 revision: Greever and Jones added larger sections of rhetorical material, effectively turning the *Century* into a handbook-rhetoric. Backs again to the wall, Heath called in Franklin Scott, who had so criticized Woolley in 1918, to do the new revision. Seeing this as his chance to rhetoricize the Woolley he had condemned, Scott dug in and produced the *New Handbook*—an updated Woolley-type book—in 1926, and his own version of a handbook, which owed Woolley nothing but a name, as the *College Handbook of Composition* in 1928. The *College Handbook* took the *Century*'s move toward incorporation of rhetoric even farther; at over 400 pages, it contained nearly all the material in contemporary rhetoric texts *plus* complete handbook coverage. The *College Handbook* was the first of the full-coverage rhetoric-handbooks.

This was, then, the beginning of the next phase: the rhetoric-handbook era. It was the point at which books that had essentially been tools for home reference became complete classroom texts, filled with lessons and exercises as well as with rules and illustrations. Unfortunately, the rhetorical lessons in these 1920's handbooks were the most banal and predictable applications of the degraded current-traditional rhetoric of the time. The *College Handbook* (which was still known to all merely as "Woolley") and the *Century* began a tradition that still continues today (with a few notable exceptions) of the rhetorical lessons in handbooks being the most conservative, reductive, and retrograde rhetoric available.

Throughout the 1930's, the handbook was searching for a final form in a sort of natural-selection process. New handbooks would appear and fail, or appear and prosper, and if they prospered, succeeding authors would copy their features. Through the decade, however, all successful handbooks followed Woolley and the *Century* in their essential contents: they proceeded from Words, through Sentences, Paragraphs, to the Whole Composition, and in addition they covered grammar, punctuation, mechanics, etc., in the form of rules. Other material could be added to this matrix, but authors who chanced unfamiliar organizations courted disaster; textbook firms quickly found that

handbook-using teachers were a *most* conservative audience. These teachers wanted rule-governed composition and yes/no prescriptive usage rules—and they got them. They wanted a symbol system that would allow them to process the overload of themes they were forced to read—and they got it. They wanted exercises that would use up classroom time with a believable show of pedagogical activity—and they got them. Thus, handbooks show little change during the 1930's, in spite of the fact that this was the decade that saw the first widely-based usage studies, the first serious work in error-analysis, and a general re-assessment in language education of the meaning of the concept of "correctness." In the 1930's, the world of the classroom teacher began for the first time to diverge sharply from the findings and pronouncements of pedagogical research. It was a trend that would continue.

Toward the end of the thirties it became obvious to publishers that the handbook had become an absolutely central artifact of composition—that in fact it was the controlling text in most classes. A survey in 1927 had shown that of 27 midwestern colleges, 85% used handbooks in writing classes and 45% used no texts but handbooks;[10] by 1941, James McCrimmon was saying that, "instructors not only consult the handbook they are using, they are likely to con it, get it by heart, and not infrequently, pledge indiscriminate devotion to it."[11] Publishers could not ignore this increasingly central form, and it was around this time that most major houses decided to commission handbooks, often christening them with the house's name. The revised *Century Collegiate,* John Kierzek's *Macmillan Handbook,* and Porter Perrin's *Index to English* appeared in 1939, Albert Marckwardt's *Scribner Handbook* in 1940. These were all good-sized books that mixed current-traditional rhetoric with Woolleyian organization, but none of them was much advanced over the 1928 Woolley *College Handbook.*[12]

Weaknesses were still evident: there remained multifarious systems of competing numbered or lettered rules; there was still overlap between grammatical and "rhetorical" treatments of such elements as the sentence and the paragraph; there were disagreements about whether such forms as letters or such activities as library research should be covered. Woolley was an exemplar, but there was still no complete paradigm.

Then in 1941 there appeared the handbook so successful that it would become that paradigm, the model for all handbooks after it: John C. Hodges' *Harbrace Handbook of English,* the forerunner of today's *Harbrace College Handbook.* Hodges' book was (and remains today) a masterpiece of well-planned minimalism. There was no complex rhetoric-grammer overlap, no hundreds of rule numbers to confuse readers. Hodges had done his homework well; he had researched carefully and come up with the most efficient handbook structure extant:

> The *Harbrace Handbook of English* is a guide to the correction of student themes and also a text for use in class. It presents well-known subject matter in an easily usable form, and thus lightens the instructor's task of grading papers. The book contains only thirty-five major sections. To

> determine the sections actually needed (and consequently the numbers to appear in the correction chart), twenty thousand freshman themes were tabulated according to the corrections by sixteen instructors. (p. i)

This simple expedient of statistically determining what sorts of corrections teachers *really made* on papers was the key to Hodges' success. His thirty-five numbers and lettered subsections proved so durable that they are still unchanged in today's 9th edition. After the *Harbrace* was published, older and more complex systems of organization disappeared quickly; Hodges' plan was simply superior, and by 1950 every handbook used some version of it. In addition, the *Harbrace* introduced the final element which had been missing from pre-1941 handbooks: a chapter on the full research paper, which quickly became *de rigueur* in both handbooks and composition courses.

Handbooks became even more influential during this period. Between 1939 and 1950, they spread down into the high schools in such books as Kibbe et al.'s *Handbook of English for Boys and Girls,* McKee et al.'s *How to Speak and Write: A Junior Handbook,* Woolley, Scott, and Tressler's *Handbook of Speaking and Writing,* and the *Harbrace*'s younger brother, Warriner's *Handbook of English.* Even the deeply rhetorical communications movement of the 1940's was affected by handbook fever and produced specialized "handbooks of communication" like Babcock's *Harper Handbook of Communication Skills.*

During this time, it must be noted, the purely mechanical and grammatical elements in handbooks were softened and as a form handbooks became more rhetorical. Under the aegis of Hodges' ingenious number-letter system, however, the rhetorical material covered was usually organized and treated mechanically itself. Thus we note handbooks through the 1940's tending to treat rhetorical matters as if they were binary correct-incorrect decisions of a grammatical sort. Reductive rhetoric—particularly such doctrines as that of Unity, Coherence, and Emphasis and other static abstractions—was the rule in these handbooks. These lessons took up a good deal of page space, though, and by the early 1950's, most handbooks were as large as typical rhetoric texts. This period also saw the second wave of "house" handbooks: the *Prentice-Hall Handbook* in 1951, the *Harper Handbook* in 1952, the *Modern English Handbook* in 1953, the *Handbook of Current English* in 1955. None of these books was below 500 pages—all were full-sized texts masquerading as handbooks.

Most of the important development of the handbooks form was over by 1960, and since that time there have been only a few novelties in the genre. The giantism that began in the 1950's continued throughout the succeeding decades; through the sixties and seventies, large handbooks and rhetoric texts came to be less and less distinguishable one from another. The name "handbook" now clings to texts such as the *Harper* and the *Modern English* only through historical association. Nearly all full rhetorics incorporate a handbook section discretely, and the difference between these and the large "handbooks" is mainly one of organization and margin appearance.

Not surprisingly, the tendency toward large handbook-rhetorics produced a reaction that has sent one branch of handbook technology toward its

Woolleyian roots. During the 1960's, it was noticed that no extant handbook came anywhere near being able to fit into a hand or pocket, and new, smaller books began to appear to fill the gap. Watkins and Martin's *Practical English Handbook,* Lowry et al.'s *Mechanics of English,* Glorfeld et al.'s *Concise Guide,* Brennan's *Compact Handbook of College Composition* all appeared between 1960 and 1964. These smaller books were a needed corrective to the era of giant-ism in handbooks, for by 1960 the popular conception of a handbook was a *large* text. (A reviewer of the 1960 edition of the *Prentice-Hall Handbook* referred to the 530-page tome as a "basic handbook.")[14]

During the early 1960's, of course, the college composition course itself was being deeply questioned; the high quality of the students of that era caused a re-examination of the traditional mechanical-correctness priorities of freshman English. The rhetoric text, which had almost been displaced by handbooks for a time, made a strong comeback during this decade, and this is probably the reason that the "small-book-of-correctness" concept did not make more headway in the sixties. Only with the beginnings of open-admissions and Basic Writing courses in the early 1970's and the revival of the periodic "literacy crisis" clamor in the mid-seventies did mechanical correctness make a comeback. Handbooks have always been the camp followers of a "back-to-basics" army, and the 1970's were a good decade for them.

As rhetoric once again took a back seat to correctness in many class-rooms, the era of small Woolleyian handbooks came in with a vengeance. Texts such as Corbett's *Little English Handbook,* Herman's *Portable English Handbook,* and Fear and Schiffhorst's *Short English Handbook* began to make strong advances. At present the handbook market seems propitious for such small texts; the era of the very large handbook-rhetoric may be passing. The several new ones which have appeared during the past ten years—most notably Irmscher's *Holt Guide* and Heffernan and Lincoln's *Writing: A College Handbook*—have succeeded more on their names as new-rhetorical texts than as handbooks.

There is no reason to believe that the handbook of composition will not soldier on for many years in the essentially unchanged form it has kept since around 1940. Given the current state of composition teaching—which is to say, 70% of writing courses taught by undertrained and overworked adjuncts—the handbook fills a necessary role as marking-simplifier and touchstone of course priorities. The handbook was born, as I have shown elsewhere, out of a "damage-control" response to teacher overwork, and it remains as evidence of the impulse toward mechanization that appears when work is too onerous to be dealt with by organic attention. Handbooks do not *have* to be used mechanically, but in the hands of teachers without rhetorical training, handbook rules all too easily come to be seen, as James McCrimmon said in 1941, as "the sole criteria of good writing."

The handbook controls many writing courses today for the same reasons it did in 1925: the person who makes herself a correction machine, a grading assistant to the handbook, gets rid of the pain of being a genuine reader. Instructors are not to blame for the spread of handbook-based mechanical

correction; so long as composition instruction is organized so that ill-trained teachers must deal with 100 or 125 student essays every week, handbooks will be the central artifacts of writing courses. Not until we demand that conditions change will we move out from under the shadow of sterile, a-rhetorical correctness that handbooks have come to represent.

NOTES

1. For more information on the cultural and pedagogical background that produced handbooks, see my essay, "Mechanical Correctness in Composition Instruction" (unpublished manuscript). This longer essay is in some senses a counterpart to the present one.

2. Rollo L. Lyman, *English Grammar in American Schools Before 1850* (Washington, D.C.: Government Printing Office, 1922), p. 5.

3. For more information on this debate, see Edward Finegan, *Attitudes Toward English Usage: The History of a War of Words* (New York: Teachers' College Press, 1980), pp. 62–74.

4. See, for instance, William Williams, *Composition and Rhetoric by Practice* (Boston: D.C. Heath, 1890), and Edward R. Shaw, *English Composition by Practice* (New York: Henry Holt & Co., 1892).

5. In his *Working Principles of Rhetoric* of 1900, for instance, Genung took a hard-line attitude toward punctuation instruction that captures the general attitude of the *fin de siecle* text-authors: "Printer's marks are of verious orders. Some, as capitals, apostrophe, and elision marks, diaeresis, hyphen, and quotation-marks, belong to grammar; they are no more a part of rhetoric than is spelling. Others, used for modifying the stress or coloring of a passage, belong to written diction, and are discussed here" (p. 128n).

6. See "Mechanical Correctness in Composition Instruction." See also the examples of student papers and the sorts of teacher comments and markings prevalent in the 1890's found in C. T. Copeland and H. M. Rideout, *Freshman English and Theme-Correcting at Harvard College* (New York: Silver-Burdett, 1901) and in the 1897 *Report of the Overseers of Harvard College.*

7. H. E. Coblentz, review of Woolley's *Handbook of Composition, School Review* 17 (1909), 581.

8. Frank W. Scott, "Composition and the Rest of the Curriculum," *English Journal* 7 (1918), 515.

9. This illustrates the essential principles behind the morbidity of composition pedagogy during most of this century: the reactionary nature of the textbook market—and its tendency to sooner or later co-opt its critics.

10. Ralph L. Henry, "Freshman English in the Middle West," *English Journal* 17 (1928), 302–304.

11. James M. McCrimmon, "The Importance of the Right Handbook," *College English* 3 (1941), 70.

12. The exception, of course, was Perrin's book, which was unique in structure. It did not become "handbooky" until 1942, when the *Writer's Guide* was added, and even then the *Writer's Guide and Index to English* remained the least mechanical book in its genre until after Perrin's death.

13. See my essay "Static Abstractions and Composition" (forthcoming in *Freshman English News*) for more detail on the reductive rhetoric that was based in Unity, Coherence, and Emphasis.

14. W. A. Ferrell, review of Glenn Leggett, C. David Mead, and William Charvat, *Prentice-Hall Handbook for Writers, College Composition and Communication* 12 (1961), 122.

The Rhetoric of Explanation: Explanatory Rhetoric from Aristotle to 1850

In 1984 Steven Witte and John Daly founded a new journal, *Written Communication: A Quarterly Journal of Research, Theory, and Applications*, whose purpose was to treat major, substantive issues in writing from the perspectives of such fields as rhetoric, psychology, linguistics, English, journalism, reading, communications, document design, anthropology, semiotics, and education. Bob's two-part study, "The Rhetoric of Explanation: Explanatory Rhetoric from Aristotle to 1850" and "The Rhetoric of Explanation: Explanatory Rhetoric from 1850 to the Present" appeared in 1984 and 1985 in the first and second volumes of *Written Communication*. In these essays, Bob points out the extent to which most rhetorical history has concerned itself with the theories of argumentation and traces a parallel but less investigated strand of rhetorical history: the theory and practice of explanation. The goal of these "Rhetoric of Explanation" essays is (typically) ambitious: to "provide background to an argument for purposive reintegration of discourse study" (26).

In Part I of "The Rhetoric of Explanation," Bob identifies the roots of explanatory pedagogy from the classical period through the first four decades of the nineteenth century. In Part II, he continues his analysis from Henry Day's *Art of Rhetoric* through contemporary explanatory rhetoric. One of his several provocative insights in Part II is the assertion that "[e]xpository writing is a practice without a past, a method without a proof of its usefulness, a tradition without a theory" (57). In the conclusion to Part II, Bob points out with some prescience that although the study of explanatory rhetoric is only two hundred years old, there are "many signs that the rhetoric of explanation may be the rhetoric of the future. Chief among them are what computer scientists call the 'information revolution,' and the geometrically-increasing importance of explanation in the modern world" (59).

From *Written Communication* 1.2 (1984): 189–210.

Instruction is the proper end of Speech.

— FÉNELON, *Dialogues sur L'eloquence*

T here have been a number of unfortunate conse-
quences of the rise of departmentalization in American colleges during the
period 1875–1910, but few subjects have suffered so severely from the centrifugal stresses of that period as has the study of discourse. Most of us know
the bleak outline of the story: how the novel English departments of the nineteenth century attempted to assimilate rhetoric, oratory, composition, literary
scholarship, and philology; how the rise of literary studies gradually diminished the status of the other fields; how rhetoricians, disgusted with the
neglect they suffered within English departments, broke away in 1914; how
linguists, with the same complaint, broke away in 1924; and how composition, the permanent retarded child of language study, sank into an intellectual oblivion within English, taught principally by untrained part-timers, its
only mission the generation of credit-hours (see Parker, 1967).

It is not my purpose here to bemoan the blindness of our professional ancestors, but rather to provide background to an argument for purposive reintegration of discourse study. The legacy of departmentalization has meant
that for the past century the study of discourse has been unnaturally frag-
mented. On this side of the street we have the speech or communications
scholars who have long been developing sophisticated perspectives on persuasion and oral discourse. On the other side of the street, in English departments, we have a growing discipline of composition studies, reawakened
after a hundred-year sleep, vital and eager to learn all it can about written
discourse. It is, I believe, an accident of history that these two fields, which
share the same intellectual roots and have many similar interests, have been
and continue to be separated.

In order to begin to build bridges between these related disciplines of
rhetoric and composition studies, scholars of written discourse must show
themselves to be as conscious of the historical and theoretical backgrounds of
the discipline they profess as are rhetorical scholars. Let us be honest: Composition studies is playing "catch-up" here, and it cannot pretend to as solid
and continuous an intellectual history as can rhetoric. On the other hand,
there are developments within composition history that rhetoricians may not
be aware of, questions only now beginning to be investigated that are vital to
all discourse scholarship. Of these, perhaps the most important question concerns the classification of discourse into types.

There are many conflicting theories of discourse taxonomy, but for the
purpose of this essay I wish to use the simplest classes possible. Nonbelletris-
tic public discourse consists, I will argue, of explanatory rhetoric and persuasive rhetoric, and all writing or speech must have one of these aims or the
other as primary. Persuasive discourse has been extensively analyzed by

rhetorical scholarship. Explanatory discourse, however, has been given hardly any historical or theoretical attention at all, in spite of the fact that it is and has been for centuries a vital communicative tool. Logic and dialectic, discourse tools that, as Bacon would say, *use* but do not *advance* knowledge, have been minutely examined in their relation to persuasive rhetoric, but simple explanation seems to have been ignored, perhaps because it is so common. In this article, therefore, I wish to examine the concept of explanatory discourse as it developed within the Western rhetorical tradition and investigate the most important components of explanation as it has been discussed in theories and in pedagogy.

Several major points should be mentioned as prolegomena to a historical study of the theory of explanation. First and most important is that explanation is primarily found in written discourse. Its essential purpose is informative, and the cognitive realities underlying efficient informative discourse are different from those governing effective persuasion. The luxuriant redundancy, for instance, that is a hallmark of effective oral persuasion is necessary in that context, in which information must be captured at first hearing or not at all. In explanatory discourse, however, in which pure information and not persuasion is the purpose, we see a different ordering of cognitive priorities, one that favors written transmission over spoken. Hugh Blair, the first great theorist of written discourse, said it best:

> The advantages of writing above speech are, that writing is both the more extensive, and a more permanent method of communication. . . . It likewise affords this advantage to such as read, above such as hear, that, having the written characters before their eyes, they can arrest the sense of the writer. They can pause, and revolve, and compare, at their leisure, one passage with another: whereas, the voice is fugitive and passing; you must catch the words the moment they are uttered, or you lose them forever. (Blair, 1853, pp. 77–78)

Because reading allows this recursion, written information may be given only once with the assurance that it will always then be available. Therefore, a sort of discourse aimed at efficiently transmitting information will naturally tend toward written rather than oral forms.

The second point is a corollary of the first. Since explanation as a discrete form of discourse is so clearly related to literacy on the level of cognitive processing, it is a much "younger" discourse form than is persuasion, at least insofar as enunciated theory and common practice go. Although we can trace "technical writing" of a sort back to Babylon and need come no farther forward than the Roman Republic to find scientific explanation as lucid and sophisticated as any written presently, the conception of a form of discourse pedagogy separate from persuasion is relatively recent. Explanation as an *aim* of discourse is hardly mentioned prior to Bacon, and it is not until the late eighteenth century that "exposition" is seriously spoken of by rhetorical theorists. Clearly the invention of the printing press, the rise of a reading

public, the wider dissemination of books, and the changing ideas of knowledge that were brought about by the scientific revolution of the seventeenth
and eighteenth centuries were the motivating factors behind the conception
of an explanatory form of discourse.

Thus, humanity has been using, practicing widely, and studying the
processes of oral persuasive discourse far longer than it has been paying similar attention to explanation. Scholars of rhetoric, used to a high level of critical development, must therefore be asked to forgive this youngster for its
callowness and the thinness of scholarship surrounding it. Explanation has
yet to find its Aristotle, and if this essay is in some ways an admission of how
little we know about it, I hope it will also be taken as an invitation to delve
into the many issues surrounding explanatory discourse that are as yet
unresolved.

EARLY REFERENCES TO EXPLANATION

We can find mention of essentially informative discourse aims throughout
the corpus of classical rhetorical theory, but in almost every case the purpose
of *teaching* is subservient to the more central purpose of *persuading*. Aristotle
states that a speech has in reality but two parts: "Necessarily, you state your
case, and you prove it" (1414a, trans., 1932). This Aristotelian "statement of
facts," which is also mentioned by Cicero and Quintilian, is explanatory in
nature, but the neutral *narratio* section was always followed immediately by
the argumentative *confirmatio,* which was the center of the speech, building
upon the facts established by the narration. Explanation was not an aim or
purpose by itself in classical rhetoric. It was not held in high enough esteem
by any classical theorist to merit more than a few lines, usually being dismissed with a string of adjectives: Narration was "clear," "concise," "short,"
"lucid," "neutral," and so on. Explanation was not, in essence, considered a
high-level skill.

Thus, the Greek and Roman rhetoricians founded a sort of tradition concerning explanatory discourse: It was a simple skill that could be mastered
by almost anyone; it was not an important aim of discourse; it dealt with
brute facts and not with thought, and therefore was not considered part of dialectic; and it had inherent limitations of length governed by audience
patience. In a culture that was still mainly based in orality, general explanation—as opposed to poetry, storytelling, and persuasive speech—could
have only a small part to play.

After Quintilian there was only one important addition to the tradition
of Western explanatory rhetoric prior to the Renaissance. Augustine in his *On
Christine Doctrine,* the first manual of Christian homiletics, placed stress on
the necessity and importance of teaching rather than of persuading, a shift of
emphasis that affected all preaching:

> to teach is a necessity. For what men know, it is in their own hands either
> to do or not to do. But who would say that it is their duty to do what

they do not know? On the same principle, to persuade is not a necessity, for it is not always called for; as for example, when the hearer yields his assent to one who simply teaches or gives pleasure. (trans. 1952, p. 686)

Augustine lays here the groundwork for the important contribution that homiletics manuals and pulpit oratory would make to the rhetoric of explanation.

Augustine's emphasis on perspicuity and the plain style in Christian teaching had little impact on the classical rhetorical tradition, however. For 1500 years, classical rhetoric remained buried or sterile, with changes appearing only in different conceptions of stylistic beauty. There were certainly no advances in any conception of a theory of informative discourse—indeed, the prose styles popular in the vernacular languages at the close of the sixteenth century would seem to work against the idea of clear explanation, as E. D. Hirsch has shown in his *The Philosophy of Composition* (1977).

The culture of seventeenth-century England was, however, in a very flux of change. Caxton's press had started powerful forces in motion and for the first time books were coming to be within the power of people other than the very rich. Attitudes toward what constituted important knowledge were changing too, and there is no figure more important to that change than Sir Francis Bacon, Baron Verulam. His *The Advancement of Learning* (1605) was the first great call for awareness of the importance of secular knowledge and a survey of the states that diverse fields of learning found themselves in as the seventeenth century opened. It is in Bacon that we find the seeds that will develop into a rhetoric of explanatory discourse.

Extensive attention has been paid by rhetoricians to Bacon's discussion of invention ("It is no Invention, but a Remembrance or Suggestion, with an Application") and of rhetoric ("The duty and office of Rhetoric is to apply Reason to Imagination for the better moving of the will"), but much less is known of Bacon's analysis of what he calls the "Method of Tradition or Delivery." "Tradition" and "delivery" are the Baconian terms for the sort of rational knowledge "which is transitive, concerning the expressing or transferring of our knowledge to others" (1605/1955, p. 299).

Bacon placed his Method of Tradition in the realm of logic rather than that of rhetoric, but tradition is not clearly related to the sort of rigorous, demonstrative dialectic that was even then the common meaning of the term "logic." "The doctrine of Method containeth the rules of judgment upon that which is to be delivered," says Bacon, and he is referring to factual information as well as to reasoning. There are six "diversities of Method" that can be used in the transference of knowledge, according to Bacon: the "Enigmatical and Disclosed," the "delivery of knowledge in Aphorisms or in Methods," "Assertions and their Proofs," "Questions and their Determinations," "according to subject matter which is handled" (abstract/concrete), and "according unto the light and presuppositions of that which is delivered" (old and new information) (pp. 304–307). As we can see, none of these methods of delivery is specifically persuasive or exclusively dialectical; they are in

large part devices for popular and specialized explanation, and when conjoined with Bacon's work on induction, the methods of delivery would result in the first scientific exposition.

Bacon's intellectual legacy, which lay undeveloped during the years of the civil war and the early years of the Commonwealth, was taken up in the mid-1650s by a group of "natural philosophers" meeting in Cambridge and London. The Royal Society of London, as it was to be denominated in its charter of 1662, consisted of scientists and scholars who were drawn together by a dual belief in the importance of "secular knowledge"—knowledge of the workings of the natural world—and in the power of the inductive method of Francis Bacon to solve the riddles that that world proposed to those who studied it. Many of the contributions of the Royal Society have been detailed by scholarship; certainly the Society's contribution to important changes in the English prose style has been shown (Jones, 1930). The neo-Ciceronian tradition of figurative rhetoric that had contributed to the difficulty of reading English prose of the sixteenth century was assailed by the Royal Society; their *Record* stated that in all of the society's writing, "the matter of fact shall be barely stated, without any prefaces, apologies, or rhetorical flourishes" (cited in Howell, 1971, p. 481) and they promised "a constant Resolution, to reject all the amplifications, digressions, and swellings of style . . . bringing all things, as near the Mathematical plainness, as they can" (Sprat, 1667, p. 113).

The great apologist and polemicist of the Royal Society was Thomas Sprat, author of *History of the Royal Society of London* (1667). The *History* does not contain specific references to explanatory discourse as a theory, but the book is filled with references to the methods of the Society's members, and it is clear that their writings were essentially explanatory:

> Their purpose is, in short, to make fruitful Records of all of the Works of Nature or Art, which come within their reach: so that the present Age, and posterity, may be able to put a mark on the Errors, which have been strengthened by long prescription: to restore the Truths, that have lain neglected: to push on those, which are already known: and to make the way more passable, to what remains unreveal'd. This is the compass of their Design. And to accomplish this, they have indeavored, to separate the knowledge of Nature, from the colours of Rhetoric, the devices of Fancy, or the delightful deceit of Fables. . . . They have attempted to free it from the Artifice, and Humors, and Passions, of Sects; to render it an instrument, whereby Mankind may obtain a Dominion over Things, and not only over one anothers Judgements. (1667, pp. 61–62)

It is in this final sentence that we can see clearly the division that Sprat is making between the discourses of his fellow Society members and the essentially artificial devices he imputes to rhetorical discourse. One deals with the realities of nature, while the other merely attempts to sway the fancies of weak men. "Dominion over Things" was to be henceforth one of the primary purposes of explanation.

It is important to realize here that Sprat is opposing scientific discourse to dialectic as well as to rhetoric. The sorts of informational communications he defends here are meant, to use Baconian terms, not merely to *use* knowledge, but to aid in the *progression* of knowledge. Again and again, Sprat draws a contrast between the sterile, self-referential "knowledge" of traditional logic and rhetoric and the fruitfulness of the inductive method. Practitioners of traditional logic and rhetoric have been "wholly employed about the productions of their own minds, and neglecting all the works of Nature that are without them." The experimenter of the Royal Society, on the other hand, "invents not what he does out of himself, but gathers it from the footsteps and progress of Nature." Finally, says Sprat, acceptance of this new sort of discourse can only lead to positive results: "Experimental Philosophy will prevent mens spending the strength of their thoughts about Disputes by turning them to Works." Thus, in the first important defense of the scientific method, we also find the first statement of the purposes and ends of explanatory discourse.

The opinions of Sprat and the Royal Society were extended and made vastly more popular by the work of the man who is arguably the most important intellectual figure in English history: John Locke. Himself a member of the Royal Society, Locke spread its gospel of induction and explanatory discourse far beyond the boundaries of Cambridge and London. As Wilbur S. Howell puts it, Locke gave British learning "a fresh and enduring set of expectations concerning discourse" that "led the intellectual community to see popular and learned exposition as the basic kind of speaking and writing" (1971, p. 501).

Locke himself mentions discourse in relatively few places in his works, but his position upon it is implicit in almost everything he wrote. Most obviously apparent is his active distrust and dislike for the canons of traditional rhetoric. Unlike Bacon, who approved of and even admired rhetoric, and Sprat, who considered it pointless and unnecessary, Locke condemned rhetoric as "that powerful instrument of error and deceit" (1690/1849). In a famous passage, he sets up the desirable ends of discourse against what he considers the false ends promoted by rhetoric: "Wit and fancy" are opposed to "dry truth and real knowledge," "pleasure and delight" to "information and improvement." All the arts of rhetoric, says Locke, "are for nothing else but to insinuate wrong ideas, move the passions, and thereby mislead the judgment"; they "are certainly, in all discourses that pretend to inform or instruct, wholly to be avoided" (1690/1849, p. 328). Up against the "arts of fallacy" of traditional neo-Ciceronian persuasive rhetoric, Locke set out his own desiderata for discourse:

> The ends of language in our discourse with others being chiefly these three: first, to make known one man's thoughts or ideas to another; secondly, to do it with as much ease and quickness as possible; and thirdly, thereby to convey the knowledge of things. (1690/1849, p. 325)

As Howell says, it is obvious that for Locke the basic type of discourse is the explanation, and his basic aim is always communication or instruction.

EIGHTEENTH-CENTURY EXPLANATORY RHETORIC

Up to this point, we have been discussing points of view that are clearly separate from the mainstream of rhetorical theory and instruction, which were until the mid-eighteenth century over-whelmingly neo-Ciceronian, concerned with stylistic and figurative treatments of persuasive discourse. After Locke, however, who instituted a revaluation of all values within English intellectual life, it was inevitable that some accommodation would eventually have to be found between the traditional art of discourse theory and the emerging phenomenon of popular and scientific explanatory discourse. Such an accommodation was not immediately forthcoming, however; rhetoricians stood by their moldering Ciceronianism for more than sixty years while the ever-busier printing presses of the Georgian period piled up mountains of books with which their theories were utterly unable to deal. It was not until the late 1740s, when the polymath Adam Smith, first of the great "new rhetoricians" of the eighteenth century, gave his first course of lectures on rhetoric, that rhetorical theory opened up to explanation.

Although Smith's lecture notes were not published during his lifetime—and he ordered them burned along with other manuscripts as he approached death—his lectures had a keen impact on the other two great Scots rhetoricians of the century, George Campbell and Hugh Blair. When student transcriptions of Smith's rhetoric lectures were discovered in this century, the debt of both Campbell and Blair to Smith's ideas became clear for the first time. Smith was a ground-breaking thinker in a number of ways, but for this discussion we need examine only one element of his theory of rhetoric: his classes of discourse. Smith introduces a rhetorical class that was unheard of by the neo-Ciceronians: the *didactic*:

> Every discourse proposes either barely to relate some fact or to prove some proposition. The first is the kind of discourse called a narrative one; the latter is the foundation of two sorts of discourses, the didactic and the rhetorical. The former proposes to put before us the arguments on both sides of the question in their true light, giving each its proper degree of influence, and has it in view to persuade no further than the arguments themselves appear convincing. The rhetorical, again, endeavours by all means to persuade us, and for this purpose it magnifies all the arguments on the one side, and diminishes or conceals those that might be brought on the other side contrary to that which it is designed that we should favor. Persuasion, which is the primary design in the rhetorical, is but the secondary design in the didactic. It endeavours to persuade us only so far as the strength of the argument is convincing; instruction is the main end. (1963, p. 58)

Later, Smith was to propose that discourse is either historical, poetical, didactic, or oratorical, and to detail the two methods by which didactic writing is accomplished: the analytic and the synthetic.

Smith was the first rhetorical theorist to attempt to make rhetoric a general theory of all types of discourse, not merely the persuasive. His "didactic

discourse" is not general explanation as we now conceive it, since it was based in scientific writing and in the "old logic" of dialectical demonstration, but Smith's thought is important because of the possibilities it opened up for rhetorical theory later in the century—in particular the theory of George Campbell.

If Smith was the first of the new rhetoricians to admit explanation into rhetoric, George Campbell was the greatest. He was a systematic and comprehensive thinker, and he built explanation into his rhetorical system in both abstract and concrete senses. In theoretical terms, *The Philosophy of Rhetoric* (1776) proposed a complete renovation of rhetorical theory, one which broadened the scope of rhetoric to include all discourse, oral and written. On a practical level, Campbell's *Lectures on Systematic Theology and Pulpit Eloquence* brought exposition as a method to the fore in its discussion of homiletic techniques. Both books made important contributions to the rhetoric of explanation and deserve close examination.

The definition of eloquence with which Campbell opens his *Philosophy* is in striking contrast to previous treatments, all of which had involved discussions of persuasion that harked back to Aristotle's definition of rhetoric as "the faculty [power] of discovering in the particular case what are the available means of persuasion" (1355b, trans., 1932). For Campbell, eloquence was a much more general thing: "that art or talent by which the discourse is adapted to its end" (1850, p. 1), and the ends of discourse, for Campbell, were based in faculty psychology and were thus multiple: "All the ends of speaking are reducible to four; every speech being intended to enlighten the understanding, to please the imagination, to move the passions, or to influence the will." Different sorts of discourse were determined by which of these faculties—understanding, imagination, passions, or will—was being addressed.

The most basic of Campbell's faculties was the understanding. Since he considered that the faculties "ascend in a regular progression," every discourse must first address the understanding. Many discourses, however, addressed the understanding exclusively:

> When a speaker addresseth himself to the understanding, he proposes the *instruction* of his hearers, and that, either by explaining some doctrine unknown, or not distinctly comprehended by them, or by proving some position disbelieved or doubted by them—In other words, he proposes either to dispel ignorance or to vanquish error. In the one, his aim is their *information*; in the other, their *conviction*. Accordingly, the predominant quality of the former is *perspicuity*, of the latter *argument*. (Campbell, 1850, pp. 2–3)

Thus the two sorts of discourses addressed to the understanding are the explanatory and the controversial. The other three sorts of discourses, according to Campbell, are imaginative, pathetic, and persuasive, each sort addressed to a corresponding faculty.

Although faculty psychology has long been discredited, we must recognize the importance of Campbell's use of it to widen the horizons of

rhetorical theory. By opening up "nonpoetical oratory" to letters, philosophical dialogues, essays, political writings, historical works, and didactic treatises, *The Philosophy of Rhetoric* paved the way for the more complex rhetorical pedagogy that would be introduced in the nineteenth century.

If Campbell's *Philosophy* was an important theoretical statement on the necessity of widening the definition of rhetoric, his *Lectures on Systematic Theology and Pulpit Eloquence* (1807), given yearly from 1772 through 1795 and published after his death, provided the corresponding practical application. Campbell's lectures have as their unstated theme the fact that pulpit oratory, at the stage of development that the Anglican Church found itself in during the eighteenth century, was essentially explanatory. There is strong evidence that the study of pulpit oratory, of which Campbell's *Lectures* are a popular representative, was the radical principle behind the practical study of methods of explanation in rhetoric.

To understand how the study of pulpit eloquence could act as the parent to explanatory rhetoric, we must remind ourselves that religious eloquence had changed in nature by the eighteenth century. Whereas Augustine in his recommendations to Christian orators could advise a largely conventional Ciceronian persuasive rhetoric to his preachers as they spread throughout the world to make converts, by 1772 most Europeans were Christians and most Englishmen were Anglicans. They did not *need* to be persuaded to join the faith; the element of persuasion was not lost, but it had been undermined by attacks on the Doctrine of Works and increasingly was less important to pulpit orators than was explanation of doctrines. Campbell puts the case well; after introducing his four faculties, he goes on:

> First, then, in order to effect the reformation of men, that is, in order to bring them to a right disposition and practice, there are some things which of necessity they must be made to know. No one will question, that the knowledge of the nature and exent of the duties which they are required to practice, and of the truths and doctrines which serve as motives to practice, is absolutely necessary. The explication of these in the pulpit forms a species of discourses which falls under the first class above mentioned. It is addressed to the understanding, its aim is information, the only obstacle it hath to remove is ignorance. Sermons of this sort we shall henceforth distinguish by the term *explanatory*. (1832, p. 133)

What is particularly striking about the *Lectures* is not that the theory has changed from the *Philosophy,* but rather that Campbell gives so much space to explanatory sermons. Five full chapters are devoted to explanation, and the other sorts of sermons get but one chapter each. It is in the *Lectures,* too, that we meet with the term "exposition" for the first time in a clearly rhetorical context, as Campbell describes the two major sorts of explanatory sermons as *expositions* or *lectures*:

> In discourses of the first class, it is the chief design of the speaker to explain the import of a portion of scripture . . . In the second, it is his great

scope to deduce from a passage . . . useful reflections concerning provi-
dence, the economy of grace, or the conduct of human life . . . the ultimate end of the former is to teach the people to read the scriptures with
understanding, and of the latter to accustom them to read them with reflection. (1832, p. 12)

Campbell's emphasis upon explanatory sermons in the *Lectures* probably did
more to spread the conception of an explanatory rhetoric than the material in
his theoretical treatise; we have long underestimated the effect of the tradition of pulpit oratory on the rhetoric of the late eighteenth and early nineteenth centuries. Although most of Campbell's directions for creating explanatory sermons were technical and rooted in scriptural interpretation, his
stress on explanation and his term "exposition" would appear in the
nineteenth century as parts of a new rhetoric—a rhetoric of writing and
explanation.

Hugh Blair was to be another contributor to this movement. Though not
as original a thinker as Campbell, Blair was a more popular author whose
works found their way far beyond theory and seminary classes. Blair had an
ear more keenly attuned to social changes than Campbell's, and his contribution to the rhetoric of explanation lies mainly in his careful extension of
rhetorical theory to encompass writing as well as speaking. Although Blair's
theory merely parrots Campbell's in many areas—for Blair, eloquence was
"the art of speaking in such a manner as to attain the end for which we
speak"—he goes much more deeply than Campbell into literary and belletristic forms. For that reason, it was Blair and not Campbell who would act
as the intellectual godfather to the college courses in rhetoric and writing that
sprang up as the nineteenth century opened. Blair put great stress on the
practice of *composition,* a term little used in rhetorical theory prior to his
lectures:

The study of composition, important in itself at all times, has acquired
additional importance from the taste and manners of the present age . . .
To all the liberal arts much attention has been paid; and to none more
than to the beauty of language, and the grace and elegance of every kind
of writing. (1853, p. 12)

Seeing in writing an important cultural trend, Blair accordingly devoted
lengthy discussions both to composing and to "discerning and relishing the
beauties of composition."

Although Blair divided prose into generic categories such as historical
writing, philosophical writing, fictitious history, and so on, his literary classification does not add much to any theory of explanation. A more interesting
aspect of Blair's thought is found in his analysis of the different parts of a discourse, especially the part he calls the *"narration"* or *"explication"* section. In
broad terms, the narration section of a speech recommended by Blair corresponds to the *narratio* or statement of facts in classical rhetorical theory: "To

be clear and distinct, to be probable, and to be concise, are the qualities which critics chiefly require in narration." In sermons, however, the narration of a secular speech is replaced by what Blair calls the *"explication"* section, and in his discussion of explication Blair both assumes and extends Campbell's position on explanatory homiletics.[1] The following passage on explication is especially interesting coming from a writer who condemns topical invention:

> To explain the doctrine of the text with propriety; to give a full and perspicuous account of the nature of that virtue or duty which forms the subject of the discourse, is properly the didactic part of preaching. . . . The great art of succeeding in it, is to meditate profoundly on the subject, so as to be able to place it in a clear and strong point of view. Consider what lights other passages of scripture throw upon it; consider whether it be a subject nearly related to some other from which it is proper to distinguish it; consider whether it can be illustrated to advantage by comparing it with, or opposing it to some other thing; by inquiring into causes, or tracing effects; by pointing out examples, or appealing to the feelings of the hearers; that thus, a definite, precise, circumstantial view may be afforded of the doctrine to be inculcated. (Blair, 1853, p. 352)

This passage may well be a "missing link" between the topics of classical invention, which Blair rejected as artificial, and the "methods of exposition," which were to appear during the nineteenth century as specifically informative devices.

RHETORIC AND COMPOSITION

Until the end of the eighteenth century, it is not difficult to follow the rise of explanatory discourse and its incorporation into rhetorical theory. In the early nineteenth century, however, events occurred that would lead to the divorce of rhetoric from composition, oral discourse theory from writing theory, theory itself from practical applications, and, ultimately, explanatory rhetoric from persuasive rhetoric. These separations were all to result from the changing cultural needs of nineteenth-century America. Let us look more closely at how discourse theory fared during that strange century.

Most educational innovations of the nineteenth century were American rather than British, and we must shift our focus to the New World as the century opens in order to understand the development of the rhetoric of "exposition." In 1800, the influence of Blair and Campbell was tremendously strong in America, and Blair's work in particular had made rhetoric a very popular college subject. Courses that had previously used such neo-Ciceronian texts as John Holmes's *The Art of Rhetoric Made Easy* (1755) were switching to Blair's *Lectures* and the early elocutionary textbooks, and students were clamoring to learn elocution and study belles-lettres. New professorships of rhetoric were springing up at both recently founded and estab-

lished colleges, and the rhetoric being taught was more realistic and flexible than it had been for centuries.

Until the appearance of Richard Whately's *Elements of Rhetoric* (1828), curricular matters in rhetorical pedagogy proceeded smoothly enough. Under the aegis of the reforms of Campbell and Blair, rhetoric courses began to deal seriously with written composition and with didactic and explanatory discourse as well as with persuasive oratory. A number of books appeared both in England and in the United States at this time dealing with composition and belles-lettres on the college level, but they were overwhelmingly derivative of Blair's *Lectures* and are thus of little interest. To discover the roots of explanatory rhetoric in America, it is necessary to look at books that appeared during the period 1800–1830 on the secondary and elementary level of instruction. It is in these "grammar and composition" books, and not in college textbooks, that we see explanatory rhetoric develop and also see the beginning of the practical split between expository and persuasive discourse.

It is difficult to know for certain when textbooks first appeared that were meant to teach precollege students composition, as opposed to mere grammar, spelling, and sentence construction. Such books, paper bound and ephemeral, have not survived in large numbers. Those we do have, however, strongly suggest that much of what we have come to know as the pedagogy of explanation developed between 1801 and 1835 in such books as John Walker's *The Teacher's Assistant in English Composition* (1801/1808), John Rippingham's *Rules for English Composition* (1811/1816), Daniel Jaudon's *The Union Grammar* (1811(?)/1828), and William Russell's *A Grammar of Composition* (1798/1823). These secondary-level texts all make the important distinction between writing on explanatory topics and writing on persuasive topics—a distinction that would later become central to discourse education on all levels.

Certainly the seminal book for "composition" as opposed to "rhetoric" must be John Walker's *The Teacher's Assistant,* first published in London in 1801. Walker, an elocutionist, actor, lexicographer, and friend of Samuel Johnson, wrote the book when he was 69, complaining that there was "a scarcity of books on this subject." A scarcity there certainly was, and Walker evolved a set of principles, partly original and partly based in classical rhetoric, that were to become the guiding forces in early composition pedagogy.

Walker's main contribution was the division of compositions into two general sorts, which he called "themes" (this seems to be the first use of this term in vernacular composition rather than translation) and "regular subjects." "Themes" were argumentative—"the proving of some truth"—and were set up using a modified version of classical *dispositio.* Whatever was not argumentative fell into the category of a "regular subject," and regular-subject assignments were usually only a single word: *education, government, peace, war,* and so on. Walker proposed an arrangement for his regular subjects that was novel and easy to teach; regular subjects, he proposed, should

be arranged with the same sort of rigidity as themes, the only difference being that the arrangement form was to be different. Regular subjects had five divisions: *Definition, Cause, Antiquity or Novelty, Universality and Locality,* and *Effects* (1808, pp. 49–50).[2] Walker's "rules for regular subjects" bring us a long step closer to the "methods of exposition." They are a curious amalgam of heuristics for invention and formalized arrangements, and they show the tendency of explanatory techniques to be attached to both *inventio* and *dispositio.* Walker himself says of his "rules":

> There are few subjects that will admit of being treated in so regular a way as to be viewed in all the points set down in the rules. I have been at no small pains to collect so many as I have done (examples of subjects using all five "rules"); and, even in a few of these, I have been obliged to drop some of the points; but as there is not any subject which may not be considered in two or three of these points of view, I flatter myself the method here adopted will be found useful to young people, who must generally be furnished with some hints to be able to say any thing upon any subject. (1808, p. 50)

Walker himself seemed to see his points as partially organizational and partially inventive.

The Teacher's Assistant received at least eleven printings in England between 1801 and 1853, but it had only one American edition, in Boston in 1810. That one edition was enough, however, to make Walker the exemplar for a whole school of composition pedagogy. Walker's most popular follower was Daniel Jaudon, whose *The Union Grammar* of 1811(?) went through at least four printings before 1828. Jaudon used Walker's perspective unchanged (giving no credit): "A Theme is some truth, maxim, or proposition given to be maintained, proved, or illustrated: as '*Delays are dangerous*'; '*Trust not appearances*' . . . etc." This is an exact echo of Walker's treatment, examples and all.

"A Regular Subject," on the other hand, "may be any single word, clause, or member of a sentence, given or assumed, as the ground of an essay: as Time, death, love, beauty, friendship, the advantages of a good education." Jaudon expands on Walker's rules at more length:

1. If your subject require explanation, define or explain it.
2. Show what is the cause of your subject; that is, what is the occasion of it, or what it is derived from.
3. Show whether your subject be ancient or modern; i.e., what it was in ancient times, and what it is at present.
4. Show whether your subject relates to the whole world, or only a particular part of it.
5. Examine whether your subject be good or bad; show wherein that goodness or badness consists and what are the advantages or disadvantages which arise from it. (Jaudon, 1828, p. 201)

Here in Jaudon's version, Walker's "rules" seem to lean more toward invention than organization.

Jaudon made Walker's pedagogy standard, and most secondary texts used it between 1815 and 1840. William Russell, for instance, divided "didactic compositions" into "simple themes" and "complex themes"; simple themes were explanatory and complex themes were argumentative. Thus did the term become generalized, and all student papers have remained "themes" up to the present. Russell's book, *A Grammar of Composition* (1798/1823) is derivative, but it may have contributed toward the college-level acceptance of explanatory rhetoric. Walker's pedagogy, at any rate, soon turned up in college-level texts. A clear example is James Boyd's *Elements of Rhetoric and Literary Criticism* (1844), which divided "the various kinds of original composition" into Narrative, Descriptive, and Miscellaneous Essays. These Miscellaneous Essays were to be written, according to Boyd, using the following method: "The Definition, The Cause, The Antiquity or Novelty, The Universality or Locality, The Effects." By 1844, as can be seen, the heuristic element in Walker's rules had been largely displaced by the organizational element.

Another central influence on explanatory rhetoric—though a negative one—was Richard Whately's *The Elements of Rhetoric* (1828). Whately, of course, denied that rhetoric should be "the Art of Composition, universally"; instead of this Campbellian conception, the *Elements* proposes "to treat of *Argumentative Composition*, generally and exclusively" (1828/1963, p. 6). Though Whately did not limit rhetoric to oral discourse, his influential insistence that rhetoric should be exclusively argumentative did much to undermine the Campbell-Blair reforms of the late eighteenth century. After Whately, a narrow insistence upon argumentative discourse and a growing elocutionary tendency would be the hallmarks of British rhetorical theory for over fifty years.

In America, where the rhetoric of Blair had a powerful hold, Whately was less influential. His book was widely used, but it never approached the almost incredible popularity of Blair's *Lectures*. The hundreds of tiny colleges that sprang up around the country all needed textbooks, and Blair's was the most established text by 1815; as college teachers raised on Blairian rhetoric worked westward, seeding the new colleges and academies with what they had learned in the East, a conception of rhetoric as being concerned with all sorts of discourse took hold in the United States and never really died out.[3] Whately's revisionism caught on late and did not exert any strong influence over the growing and increasingly discrete courses in composition that were being added to the study of elocution and oral rhetoric.

Beginning in the 1820s, we see a new sort of textbook appear in American colleges as a supplement to the Blair or Holmes or Campbell treatises. These new textbooks were usually written by a college teacher as a codification of his course. They were not as theoretical as the older books; they often contained exercises or questions at the end of each chapter. They were meant for use by a class, not as the teacher's lecture notes. They were, of course, the

earliest college-level composition textbooks, and pointing out the first one is not difficult: Samuel P. Newman's *A Practical System of Rhetoric* (1827).

College composition in America began with Newman's book; although largely devoted to belletristic/stylistic concerns of a Blairian sort, *A Practical System* marks the beginning of explanatory pedagogy on an advanced level. Newman was the first clear proponent of a discourse-classification system that would later come to be known as "the modes" or "forms" of discourse, but it is not to that classification ("Writings are distinguished from each other, as didactic, persuasive, argumentative, descriptive, and narrative"), which Newman hardly developed, that we should look for his contribution to explanation. Much more interesting is his discussion of what he called "amplification."

Newman uses the term "amplification" with a meaning completely dissociated from the stylistic meaning of the term given it by Blair and Campbell. Amplification, for Newman, is "the power of enlarging upon the positions and opinions advanced." It is an essentially invention-oriented technique, and Newman's discussion of amplification is the first heuristic treatment of nontopical invention in the literature. The heuristic Newman supplies is simple. Although it is impossible to catalogue all the ways in which writers amplify their propositions, he says, there are a few general principles to be used. For argumentative amplification, Newman recommends Induction, Testimony, and Analogy, all standard Blairian or classical methods. For amplification, the object of which is "the more full exhibition of the meaning of what is asserted," that is, for explanatory amplification, Newman recommends the following methods:

1. By formal definitions of the words, or phrases, used in stating the proposition, or head of discourse;

2. By stating the proposition in different ways, at the same time showing what limitations are designed to apply to it, or wherein there is danger of mistake, which it is necessary to guard against;

3. By stating particular cases, or individual instances, and thus shewing what is meant by a general proposition; and

4. By illustrations, especially by formal comparisons and historical allusions. (1843, p. 23)

These "general principles of amplification" presented by Newman are important not only because they show signs of being early "methods of exposition" but also because they are so clearly inventive in nature. Newman's text was very popular, and his concept of amplification was picked up by a number of other authors.

These, then, were the roots of explanatory pedagogy as it developed during the first four decades of the nineteenth century: (1) the opening up of rhetorical theory implied by Blair and Campbell; (2) the largely explanatory nature of the tradition of pulpit oratory; (3) the growth of courses that treated

writing as a discipline separate from speaking; and (4) the importation from secondary-level text-books of the conception of separate explanatory and argumentative themes and of the methods used to invent and organize explanatory material. During the remainder of the nineteenth century, these factors would coalesce to produce the beginnings of modern explanatory rhetoric.

NOTES

1. We can only guess about the effect that Campbell's lectures may have had on the finally published work of Blair. Indeed, we are not even certain to what degree Blair was influenced by Campbell's *Philosophy of Rhetoric,* published seven years before Blair put his *Lectures* into final form for publication. These lectures, published 24 years after their first delivery, may have gone through many revisions during that time. It would be fascinating to compare student notes from Blair's pre-1776 lectures with his finished book. Whether Campbell's lectures on pulpit eloquence, which were delivered in Aberdeen, might have come in some form to Blair in Edinburgh is a question that eighteenth-century scholars might be able to answer. Presumably both Campbell and Blair were deeply indebted to Smith.

2. Walker wrote a charming poem to illustrate these rules for treating a subject, a poem which I cannot forebear to reproduce here:

If your subject definition do need,
First briefly define it, then proceed:
Thus Education, more at large defined,
Becomes the culture of the human mind.
Next, if you can, find out your subject's cause,
And show from whence its origin it draws:

And thus, if Education's cause be traced,
It will be found in love parental placed.
Ancient or modern, may your subject be;
Pursue it, therefore, to antiquity:
Thus, Education ever will appear,
To have been the ancients' first and greatest care.
Your subject may to distant nations roam,
Or else relate to objects nearer home:
Thus, different modes of Education yield,
To every writer's thoughts, an ample field.
The subject which you treat is good or ill,
Or else a mixture of each principle:
Good Education ranks us with the best,
While bad degrades a man below a beast.
And ere your subject a conclusion know,
The advantage or the disadvantage show.

(A number of textbooks reprinted this poem without credit.)

3. Rudolph (1962, p. 47) estimates that over 700 colleges might have been founded and then collapsed in America during the period 1776–1860. In 1776, there were nine American colleges and in 1860 there were 250, of which 182 still survive.

REFERENCES

Aristotle (1932). *The rhetoric of Aristotle* (L. Cooper, Trans.). Englewood Cliffs, NJ: Prentice-Hall.

Augustine (1952). On Christine Doctrine (J. F. Shaw, Trans.). In R. M. Hutchins (Ed.), *Great books of the Western World* (Vol. 18, pp. 621–698). Chicago: Encyclopaedia Britannica.

Bacon, F. (1955). The Advancement of Learning. In H. G. Dick (Ed.), *Selected works of Sir Francis Bacon* (pp. 157–392). New York: Modern Library. (Original work published 1605)

Blair, H. (1853). *Lectures on rhetoric and belles lettres.* Philadelphia: Troutman and Hayes. (Original work published 1783)

Boyd, J. (1846). *Elements of rhetoric and literary criticism,* 5th ed. New York: Harper and Bros. (Original work published 1844)

Campbell, G. (1832). Lectures on systematic theology and pulpit eloquence. Boston: Lincoln and Edmands.

Campbell, G. (1850). *The philosophy of rhetoric.* London: William Tagg.

Hirsch, E. D., Jr. (1977). *The philosophy of composition.* Chicago: University of Chicago Press.

Holmes, J. (1755). *The art of rhetoric made easy.* London: C. Hitch and L. Hawes.

Howell, W. S. (1971). *Eighteenth century British logic and rhetoric.* Princeton, NJ: Princeton University Press.

Jaudan, D. (1828). *The union grammar,* 4th ed. Philadelphia, PA: Towar and Hogan. (Original work published c. 1811)

Locke, J. (1849). *An essay concerning human understanding.* Philadelphia, PA: Kay and Troutman. (Original work published 1690)

Newman, S. P. (1843). *A practical system of rhetoric.* New York: Mark H. Newman.

Parker, W. R. (1967). Where do English departments come from? *College English, 28,* 339–351.

Rippingham, J. (1816). *Rules for English composition, and particularly for themes.* Poughkeepsie, NY: Paraclete Potter. (Original work published 1811)

Rudolph, F. (1962). *The American college and university: a history.* New York: Alfred A. Knopf.

Russell, W. (1823). *A grammar of composition.* New Haven, CT: A. H. Maltby and Co. (Original work published 1798)

Smith, A. (1963). *Lectures on rhetoric and belles lettres.* J. H. Lothian (Ed.). London: Thames Nelson and Son.

Sprat, T. (1667). *The history of the Royal Society of London.* London: J. Martyn.

Walker, J. (1808). *The teacher's assistant in English composition.* Carlisle: George Kline. (Original work published 1801; first American edition 1810)

Whateley, R. (1963). *The elements of rhetoric.* D. Ehninger (Ed.). Carbondale, IL: Southern Illinois University Press. (Original work published 1828)

The Rhetoric of Explanation: Explanatory Rhetoric from 1850 to the Present

Instruction is the proper end of Speech.

— FÉNELON, *Dialogues sur L'eloquence*

The first section of this article followed the rise of a rhetoric of explanation from its roots in the teaching function of homiletic discourse through technical and scientific uses in the seventeenth century to general and written discourse in the eighteenth. The changes in rhetorical instruction that resulted from the novel theories of George Campbell and Hugh Blair gave rise to a new form of pedagogy, seen first on the secondary and then on the college level: a pedagogy of informative discourse. We have seen how the new multimode rhetoric of Campbell was challenged by Richard Whately's contention that rhetoric is essentially persuasive. This section will begin with an examination of the rhetorical theorist who challenged Whately's views most strongly and established a sophisticated rhetoric of informative discourse in the mid-nineteenth century: Henry Day.

THE EXPLANATORY RHETORIC OF HENRY DAY

In 1850 the rhetoric of explanation made a large step on the road to maturity: Henry Noble Day published his *Elements of the Art of Rhetoric*. Day was the most thoughtful and original rhetorical thinker of the nineteenth century, a polymath who, had he devoted all of his time to rhetoric alone, might have emerged as the dominant voice during the period 1850–1890. Had this occurred, had Day rather than Alexander Bain been the "father of composition," the history of writing pedagogy might have been very different. No one examining Day's works today can escape the feeling that his rhetoric represents a theoretical road not taken—and not taken to our detriment.

Henry Day was born in New Haven and educated at Yale—he was the nephew of reigning President Jeremiah Day—where he studied for the ministry and learned grammar and rhetoric from Chauncey Goodrich. From the Preface to the *Elements,* we know that Day studied homiletics and pulpit eloquence as well as rhetoric. He may have known William Russell and was

From *Written Communication* 2.1 (1985): 49–72.

almost certainly educated in the composition pedagogy of John Walker. The influence of George Campbell and Franz Theremin is powerful in his works. Whatever his training may have been, though—and there is much that we can only guess at—Day's rhetoric, when it appeared, was both a call for a return to Campbellian reforms and a revolutionary tocsin. The *Elements* differs from other rhetorics in three ways that were detailed by Day in his Preface:

1. Day emphasizes invention, not style. Concentration on style, said Day (speaking probably of the texts of Boyd [1844], Newman [1843], and R.G. Parker [1844] that exemplified the sentence-practice pedagogy of the early nineteenth century), has turned composition into "repulsive and profitless drudgeries."

2. He attempts to systematize rhetoric in all of its forms, not merely argumentation.

3. He proposes to treat rhetoric as an art and provide practical instruction, not merely empty theorizing.

Day's initial claim deserves treatment in a comprehensive essay on invention in the nineteenth century,[1] and his final claim treatment in an essay on changing techniques and styles of textbooks. It is his middle claim that affects this inquiry.

Day put his case for discourse-wide rhetorical theory this way:

> Covering the entire field of pure discourse as addressed to another mind, it [rhetoric] is redeemed from the shackles and embarrassments of that view which confines it to mere argumentative composition, or the art of producing Belief. This view of rhetoric, in which Dr. Whately is followed by the writer of the article in the Encyclopedia Britannica, consistently carried out, excludes all Explanatory Discourse. . . . Instruction and conviction are as widely distinguished as perception and belief; and it must appear on a very slight investigation of the subject that "generally speaking the same rules will" *not* "be serviceable for attaining each of these objects." Narration and argumentation have little in common, so far as the conduct of the thought is concerned. There is very little, accordingly, in Dr. Whately's treatise, except under the head of Style, which has any application to Explanatory Discourse (Day, 1850, pp. v–vi).

Thus did Day take on Whately directly, contradicting the most respected "modern" theorist of rhetorical theory.

The rhetoric of Henry Day was organized around what he called the "objects of discourse" that "are but four in number, viz: EXPLANATION, CONVICTION, EXCITATION, and PERSUASION." This was a modified form of Campbellian faculty psychology:

> The process by which a new conception is produced, is by *Explanation*; that by which a new judgment is produced, is by *Conviction*; a change in the sensibilities is effected by the process of *Excitation*; and in the will, by that of *Persuasion* (Day, 1850, p. 42).

This system has some obvious problems of its own, but here we are mainly interested in Day's first discourse process, Explanation.

Within Day's flawed faculty psychology the inner systems were sound. The approach that Day takes is what Kinneavy (1970) would call an "aims of discourse" approach rather than a "models" approach:

> In explanation, the object of discourse is to inform or instruct; in other and more technical words, to lead to a new conception or notion, or to modify one already existing in the mind. . . . The subject or theme of explanatory discourse is some object or truth to be perceived. The state of mind to be produced by explanation, as has been before observed, is a conception. . . . *Conception* is that state of the understanding in which an object or truth is simply perceived, without any affirmation or denial respecting it (Day, 1850, pp. 51–52).

This was the clearest and most modern discussion of the meaning and goals of explanatory discourse that had ever been written. Day's analysis of explanatory processes goes farther, however; in a passage of startling prescience, he goes on to discuss how explanation may be achieved:

> The particular processes by which the explanation of an object or truth may be effected, are five in number, viz: NARRATION, DESCRIPTION, ANALYSIS, EXEMPLIFICATION and COMPARISON or CONTRAST. . . .
>
> 1. Narration, when the object, viewed as a whole, is represented in continuous time or as in succession;
> 2. Description, when the object, viewed as a whole, is represented in space generally;
> 3. Analysis, when the object is regarded as consisting of parts related either to time or to space;
> 4. Exemplification, when the object is regarded as generic, including species or individuals under it, and is represented through one of the class and
> 5. Comparison and Contrast, when the object is regarded as belonging to a class, and is represented through its resemblance or opposition to others of the same class (Day, 1850, pp. 54–55).

Here, in a clearly recognizable form, we have the first version of the present-day "methods of exposition" that have become the central elements of explanatory pedagogy. Day's "processes" differ from Walker's (1808) "parts of a simple theme" in that they are discrete treatments rather than parts of a single theme; they are much less obviously related to the classical topics than are Walker's listings or Newman's types of amplification; and they are clearly meant as invention heuristics, whereas all other lists of this sort had gradually sunk into purely organizational devices.[2] Here is how he illustrates their use:

It is the utter ignorance of what he [the student] is to do when set to the task of writing a composition, as it is called, which makes the task so repulsive. Suppose, for illustration, that "the French Revolution of 1848" be given out as the theme of a composition. No intimation being given in regard to the object in the discussion of the theme, the mind of the pupil is left without an aim, and it cannot work. It will be the merest matter of chance whether he propose to himself any aim at all in the discussion, or whether he do not blindly and confusedly bring together manifold and incongruous aims, and his effort, pursued thus irrationally, give him only disgust from beginning to end. But let him understand that it is as necessary to settle definitely the object as the subject of his composition; to determine that he is to write a narrative of the events of that Revolution, or of its causes or its effects; or a description of its exciting scenes; or argue its necessity or its righteousness or its expediency, or exhibit it as a political movement . . . one or another of these objects and but one, and he is at once prepared to proceed rationally in his work. He knows when to begin, how to proceed, and where to end. The procedure is now all plain, simple, and satisfactory (Day, 1850, pp. vi–vii).

This is one of the most apposite statements on the uses of invention to come out of nineteenth century rhetorical theory.

The Elements of the Art of Rhetoric is by no means a perfect book. It is over-systematized, a common failing during the midcentury period, and it presents several overlapping discourse taxonomies that are never satisfactorily related. But Day's book, for all of its shortcomings, presents a far more fertile and thoughtful rhetorical theory than any since Campbell's. Henry Day went on to write several other rhetorical textbooks promoting his theories: *Rhetorical Praxis* in 1860, a "reconstruction" of *Elements* published as *The Art of Discourse* in 1867, *Grammatical Synthesis* in 1867. He was the most popular American textbook author during the early and mid-1870s, and his work influenced rhetorical pedagogy during that time. But his approach, which emphasized invention and the aims of discourse as well as explanation, did not prosper for long. Day's theories ran counter to another current in nineteenth century rhetoric, a more rigid, mechanical, and stylistic current that was eventually to sweep all other approaches before it. We must now turn to the tradition that Day was up against, a tradition that would hobble the rhetoric of explanation for over 40 years.

ALEXANDER BAIN AND THE SUBMERGENCE OF EXPLANATION

Prior to 1866 there was no serious theory of composition to compete with Day's except the argumentative rhetoric of Whately. Blair's popularity was fading by 1850, as was Newman's. James Boyd's and Richard Green Parker's texts in 1844 and George Quackenbos's in 1854 were all transitional and confused texts, stealing a bit from Blair here, Newman there, Whately there. Quackenbos's *Advanced Course* (1854) did use an early modes of discourse classification that mentioned exposition, but he did not analyze it in any detail as had Day.

These modes of discourse finally found their great champion in the Scots logician and educator Alexander Bain, whose *English Composition and Rhetoric* appeared in 1866. It may be said that the great theoretical battle of the late nineteenth century was between Bain and Henry Day, and that the triumph of Bain's mechanical/modal/stylistic approach over Day's inventive/explanatory approach laid the groundwork for many of the problems that have plagued composition studies even to the present. At the heart of Bain's theory of the "Kinds of Composition"—the modes—was a sort of faculty, psychology that it is surprising to see Bain supporting. It is certainly no more defensible than Day's, and Bain was a trained psychologist. He posits "three departments of the human mind—Understanding, Will, Feelings," and develops his forms of writing around them:

> Those that have for their object to inform the Understanding, fall under three heads—*Description, Narration,* and *Exposition.* The means of influencing the Will are given under one head, *Persuasion.* The employing of language to excite pleasurable Feelings, is one of the chief characteristics of *Poetry.* The Will can be moved only through the Understanding or through the Feelings. Hence there are really but two Rhetorical ends (Bain, 1866, p. 19).

Bain never explains this cryptic passage.

Although Alexander Bain was probably the most influential theorist of rhetoric in the nineteenth century, his contribution to the rhetoric of explanation—or exposition, as it would henceforth be called in the literature—is ultimately negative. There are several reasons for this. First, Bain places Narration and Description outside of Exposition and equal to it. (Day made narration and description processes within explanation, a much more reasonable procedure.) This was to lead to a great deal of confusion and attempted rationalization over the next 80 years and was to rob exposition of several of its most important components. Second, Bain's category of exposition, as he himself handled it, was confined to scientific exposition and not concerned with any sort of popular explanation. As he put it, "exposition is the mode of handling applicable to knowledge or information in the form of what is called the Sciences, as Mathematics, Natural Philosophy, Chemistry, Physiology, Natural History, the Human Mind." This stipulation left out many important explanatory forms and seemed to limit exposition to a very specialized area; as a result of it, the association of exposition with scientific discourse alone did not die out until the 1920s. Finally, Bain's handling of exposition was marred by a crude and confusing schematic representation of various ways of handling it, oversystematized and full of subtle and novel terms (see Bain, 1866, pp. 186–208). The reader's short-term memory is overloaded and his or her patience exhausted by this treatment. By comparison, Bain's analyses of Narration and Description are clear and useful and his discussion of Persuasion is relatively traditional. Only his Exposition section is confusing.

In fine, if Bain had purposefully set out to stymie the growth of explanatory pedagogy, he could not have done a much more effective job. It took the rhetoric of explanation over four decades to recover from Bain's unwitting sabotage and take its place as a central component of modern discourse pedagogy.

In other places I have discussed the rise of the modes of discourse approach to teaching composition (Connors, 1981), and there is no need to recapitulate that information here. An examination of the textbooks of the period 1870–1900 demonstrates what happened to explanatory discourse pedagogy: In the standardization of composition theory, which was the result of changing practices in textbook marketing, explanation became exposition and was assigned to a minor role for over 30 years.[3] Although Henry Day's invention/explanation approach had some followers—A. D. Hepburn (1875), Timothy Whiting Bancroft (1884)—the epitaph for it was engraved in 1878 when Adams Sherman Hill, Boylston Professor of Rhetoric at Harvard, published his *Principles of Rhetoric*. We cannot say that Hill was terribly indebted to Bain as the *Principles* deals mostly with style, sentences, and persuasion, but there are sections on three of Bain's four forms. Conspicuously missing from Hill's book, however, is exposition. There is no treatment of informative discourse in Hill's text at all—and his book had a major influence. Bain's confusing treatment of exposition had caused it to suffer its second major setback.

Beginning in the mid-1870s a number of books began to appear that used a modes of discourse approach, usually with all four modes intact. The discussions of exposition, or didactic writing as it was sometimes called, added nothing new. Most of them did not attempt to follow Bain's complex treatment, opting instead for predictable discussions of tone, style, clearness, simplicity, and the generic literary types associated with exposition (history, travels, the essay, etc.). There is no outstanding text to point to until 1886.

The great popularizer of Bain's theories—because his explanations of them were so much easier to follow than were Bain's—was John F. Genung, whose *Practical Elements of Rhetoric* appeared in 1886, setting down the essential elements of "current-traditional rhetoric" for all who followed. To be fair to Genung, his book owed something to Newman and Day as well as to Bain—but the greater part of his debts was to the Scotsman. In his discussion of exposition Genung did try to remove some of the pure-science stigma that Bain had left on the term. "By exposition," said Genung, "people generally understand *setting forth the meaning of things*; and this we may regard as its fundamental office" (Genung, 1886, p. 383). He mentions criticism and popular exposition as well as scientific exposition, and divides exposition into two "fundamental processes": Intensive Exposition, or Definition, and Extensive Exposition, or Division. Each of these categories takes in certain techniques.

Although not so hopeless as Bain's, Genung's explanation of exposition was still clumsy and oversystematized; the eclipse of this vitally important form of discourse continued. Genung counteracted Hill's dismissal of exposition, but beyond that he did not much advance it, and neither did the next

hugely successful composition textbook, Barrett Wendell's *English Composition* (1891), which generally considered stylistic and structural questions and not discourse taxonomies. It is not until 1893 that explanatory discourse took its next important step.

RENASCENCE OF EXPLANATION

It is not surprising that the rhetoric of explanation should have reached its nadir with Hill, the least interesting of the "Big Four" rhetoricians of the late nineteenth century, and not surprising that it should begin to reappear and be revitalized in the work of the man generally considered the most thoughtful and original of that group: Fred Newton Scott of Michigan. In *Paragraph-Writing* (1893), Scott and his coauthor Joseph Denney made several signal contributions to rhetorical theory as it affects explanation: First, they simplified the complex and confusing expository systems of Bain and Genung and, second, they enunciated a coherent and easily teachable classification system for paragraphs—a system that was to have an important effect on explanation pedagogy.

Scott and Denney followed Genung in that they saw exposition as either scientific or popular, and they presented what they called "Scientific Exposition"—which was largely, in their view, a device for planning an essay, not for organizing one:

> It is evident that the kind of exposition illustrated above is useful mainly for planning and outlining a subject. It is concerned with laying the groundwork for subsequent discussion, description, or narration. It analyzes, defines, divides, and classifies; it plays an important part in planning every essay that is written, whether in description, narration, or argumentation; and for that reason it will be treated under the headings that follow: Analysis by Partition; Analysis by Division; Exposition by Definition; Exposition by Similarity and Contrast—all of these being presented mainly as helps to planning and outlining themes (Scott & Denney, 1893, p. 76).

Again, as in Day's text, we see the purely heuristic nature of these early methods of exposition. Scott and Denney also allowed for Popular Exposition, which was mainly a classification of essays into different types: Didactic Essays, Conversational Essays, Critical Essays.

At the same time that Scott and Denney were recommending these invention-oriented methods of exposition, however, they were offering their theory of the paragraph. The *Paragraph-Writing* theory was built on Bain's, but it bore the same relation to Bain's collection of rigid rules that a sleek 4-6-4 compound locomotive of 1893 bore to a funnel-stacked steam puffer of Civil War vintage. Scott and Denney's paragraph theory, carefully worked out and internally coherent, is the paragraph theory that has lasted with few changes to the present day (in pedagogy if not in theory). What is important about this theory for the present inquiry is that it offers for the first time the

"Means of Developing Paragraphs," which are constants in paragraph theory and powerfully affected explanatory theory.

Scott and Denney's means of development descended in some senses from Newman's conception of amplification, but they were more mechanical in application because of the paragraph's smaller scope:

> If we regard the topic sentence [of a paragraph] as the germ-idea, it is evident that it contains, potentially, all that may be said on the subject in hand. The work of the other sentences is to bring out and develop clearly the thought contained in the topic sentence, or so much of the thought as is necessary for the purpose which the writer has in view. The means by which they do this will of course vary in different cases; and the forms in which the growing idea clothes itself as the paragraph progresses will present many different modifications.

> All of these various forms and means of developing the germ-idea may, however, be grouped, for practical purposes, under the following heads: repeating the theme in other words; defining or limiting the theme; presenting its contrary; explaining or amplifying its meaning by examples, illustrations, or quotations; particularizing by means of specific instances or details; presenting proofs, and applying or enforcing the theme (Scott & Denney, 1893, p. 25).

Here, in its primary form, we have a listing of the means of developing paragraphs that would come to be so generally accepted. We know them, of course, by their short titles: Repetition, Definition, Contrast, Illustration, Details, Proofs, Enforcement.[4]

After *Paragraph-Writing* the rhetoric of explanation once again began to receive attention from teachers and authors, and as the vast popularity of the modes of discourse approach to teaching writing became a stranglehold, nearly all texts fell in line and included a chapter on exposition. (Even A. S. Hill grudgingly included a chapter on exposition in his 1895 revision.) Most of these were still shallow, however; a typical voice is that of Arlo Bates: "Exposition is a statement, an explanation, or a setting forth. . . . Exposition differs from Description in that it deals directly with the meaning or intent of its subject instead of with its appearance" (Bates, 1896, pp. 126–128). And Hill, in his revision, stated: "Exposition may be briefly defined as explanation. . . . [T]he paramount quality in all such writing should be clearness. . . . To secure clearness in exposition a writer should pay special attention to orderly arrangement" (Hill, 1895, pp. 300–314). Dogmatic commonplaces such as these, interlarded with liberal doses of illustrations and examples, provided most of the explanatory pedagogy of the 1890s.

As I have mentioned elsewhere, one by-product of the popularity of the modes of discourse was the appearance, beginning in the 1890s, of books devoted to only one of the four modes. The first single-mode texts were not rhetoric texts but, rather, readers: the "Specimens" series published by Henry Holt & Co., which included George P. Baker's *Specimens of Argumentation*

(1893), closely followed by *Specimens of Exposition* (1894) by Hammond Lamont. (C. S. Baldwin's *Specimens of Prose Description* and W. T. Brewster's *Specimens of Prose Narration* appeared in 1895.) Lamont's book is the one that we must note, despite its derivative nature:

> In brief, then, the term exposition in this volume has been taken broadly to include all writing, the main purpose of which is to explain. Exposition differs from argumentation in that it merely explains, rather than convinces or persuades; from description and narration, in that it deals with a class rather than with an individual. For an adequate exposition the first requisite is clearness, the second, force. To secure these qualities, the most important principles to be observed are unity, logical division and arrangement of material, and illustration of general statements by specific examples (Lamont, 1894, p. xxiv).

Lamont's specimens included examples from science, history, economics, political science, and literary criticism.

In 1895 the division between the rhetorics of argument and explanation was sealed as George P. Baker published his *Principles of Argumentation*, the first post-1870 rhetoric text to treat only persuasive discourse. Baker took up a line that had been little defended since Whately, and his well-written text produced a wave of interest in argumentative discourse. It may indeed be said that Baker, in writing the first modern argumentation text, started in motion forces that would, 19 years later, result in the foundation of the Speech Association of America and the split-off from English departments of devotees of argument and the oral-discourse tradition that seemed to go along with it.

The exceptional success of Baker's book prompted other authors to attempt single-mode rhetoric texts as they had followed him into single-mode readers. The most prolific, although hardly the most successful, of the single-mode authors was Gertrude Buck, who published *A Course in Argumentative Writing*, *A Course in Expository Writing* (both 1899) and *A Course in Narrative Writing* (1906). None of these texts was successful, but *A Course in Expository Writing* must be pointed out as the first explanation textbook as well as the first conscientious attempt to dissect exposition and analyze its relations with other modes. It is unfortunate that Buck, a student of the brilliant Fred Scott at Michigan and an important rhetorical theorist in her own right, should have been such a poor textbook author. *A Course in Expository Writing* was not written to the level of students at all; it was a theoretical investigation of the nature of exposition that attempted to relate organic thought processes to writing as a learned skill. Basing her theory in associationist and early cognitive psychology, Buck leads her reader through description (which to her is cognate with exposition) and definition as the main processes of explaining.[5]

Buck's explanation of exposition is theoretically intriguing, but the book is stylistically turgid, unclear on certain major issues, and written at a level far above that of college students. Rather than revivifying the tradition of explanation as Baker had revived argument, *A Course in Expository Writing*

merely continued the conception of explanation as one mode among others. Buck's book, however, shows that interest in explanation was not dead as it went through three editions despite its problems. The academic climate was changing, and explanation would not stay down for long.

THE WATERSHED: FULTON'S *EXPOSITORY WRITING*

The story of explanatory discourse in the twentieth century is the story of the slow rise of a renewed version of Henry Day's processes of explanation and the gradual incorporation into explanatory discourse of every nonargumentative form of discourse. During this same period courses in general composition gradually came to be called "expository writing" courses and the pragmatic nature of explanation became obvious. In this century the final break took place between "rhetoric"—argument—and "composition"—explanation—as the politics of university departmentalization drove apart the two related disciplines. From this divorce emerged modern English departments and Speech departments, respectively teaching explanation (exposition) and argumentation. Let us examine the way in which this situation arose.

As the new century opened the status of explanation was little better than it had been in 1870. Almost every textbook had a section on exposition and almost every section was the same: "clearness, unity, perspicuity." Some texts offered lists of "types of exposition" that usually mixed the methods of Scott and Denney with generic literary types such as the essay, philosophical dialogues, and so on. Exposition was intellectually moribund; not even the theoretical speculations of a Scott or a Buck seemed able to attract any attention or support. Meanwhile, the burgeoning argumentation industry started by George Baker was attracting interest from serious rhetorical scholars. Men such as C. S. Baldwin gave their real attention to matters rhetorical while churning out derivative writing texts to make money.

It must be admitted that at this time there was no really sound theoretical base for explanation, whereas argumentation could draw on sources from classical antiquity to the present. Most books dealt with exposition by the use of many exemplary passages; outside of the simplest sorts of definitions— "exposition is explanation" and so on—there was no reliable theory. In 1906 a second "Exposition" rhetoric appeared, Mitchill and Carpenter's *Exposition in Class-Room Practice,* but it was a dull and mechanical text that failed quickly. It began to seem during this period that explanatory discourse could not free itself from the shadow of the modal approach, that it had no theory beyond the simplest recitation of commonplaces, that it was indeed a low-level skill. In the absence of a popular approach such as Baker's treatment of argument, the rhetoric of explanation languished.

Then, in 1912 the watershed book appeared: *Expository Writing,* by Maurice Garland Fulton. This was the book that created expository writing as a genre in the minds of most college teachers. *Expository Writing* was not a true rhetoric text: Rather, it was a modified anthology with explanations, containing a long introductory section on the nature of exposition and 43 skill-

fully selected essays illustrating expository writing. Fulton's book did not differ markedly from Lamont's earlier *Specimens of Exposition*—except in the organization of the text, which was to prove paradigmatic for expository writing. *Expository Writing* was the first text—and certainly the first popular and influential text—to organize its selections around what Fulton called the "special processes of expository writing," which included: Definition, Scientific Classification, Division, Statement of a Problem, Description, and Narration. *Expository Writing*, in print from 1912 through 1953, provided the central model for all the exposition texts that followed; and their numbers were legion.

Maurice Fulton himself was hardly an important theoretician. Rather, he was a functionary given to the creation of anthologies who happened to "hit it big" on this one by conjoining two ideas for the first time: the conception of a full-length collection of readings (the logical outgrowth of short collections such as the *Specimens* series), and Scott and Denney's conception of expository types and means of development. He wished, he said, to "centre attention upon exposition since it is the kind of writing that is most directly serviceable in practical life" (Fulton, 1912, p. v), an apologia that would be echoed by many authors in the years to come. To give Fulton his due, he had read and studied every scrap of material on exposition written between 1870 and 1912, and his command of the material allowed him to write an introductory section that remains the best synopsis of early explanatory theory available. Exposition, said Fulton, is "that kind of writing that has as its primary function the essential unfolding of any phenomenon, hypothesis, or generalization to the understanding of the reader" (p. 10). Although nothing in *Expository Writing* was truly original, the book welded together terms and an approach that would henceforth be associated with the term "exposition."

After 1912 the methods of exposition became the accepted means of conceptualizing explanation as a process, and the subsequent history of written rhetoric in this country is essentially a history of the waxing of expository writing. Between 1910 and 1925 there was a tremendous upsurge of interest in exposition that finally matched the post-Baker argumentation boom. The term "Methods of Exposition," which I have been using freely as a standard term, was introduced by John Genung in his revised *Outlines of Composition and Rhetoric* (1915) and soon the methods approach was the unquestioned champion.

TWENTIETH CENTURY EXPOSITION

Explanatory rhetoric, as it developed during this century, was affected by four important elements that determined its nature and position in education. They were as follows: (1) the decay of the modal classification of discourse and the failure of any other taxonomy to supplant it; (2) the concurrent popularity of the Deweyite "English for Life Skills" movement that made the teaching of "practical" exposition seem most logical; (3) the complete acceptance after 1910 of Scott and Denney's means of developing paragraphs, which were

small-scale analogues of the methods of exposition; (4) the tendency for expository genres to split off from general composition once their pedagogy had achieved a sufficiently developed formal character, as has been the case for journalism, technical writing, and business writing. Taken together these elements would come to mean that, following 1950 or so, the teaching of composition and the teaching of exposition would come to be one and the same, and that general composition courses would remain inescapably abstract and unworldly despite the "practical" cachet of exposition.

The decay of the modes of discourse approach to teaching writing I have covered in some detail elsewhere (Connors, 1981). It suffices to say here that the four-modes approach that controlled composition pedagogy (we can no longer say rhetorical pedagogy, for "rhetoric" was a separate area by 1920) from the mid-1890s through World War II began to falter during the 1920s, largely because of inner contradictions. The weakness of narration and description as autonomous classes was early obvious; these forms belonged in fiction writing courses and were increasingly found there. At the same time, rhetoric reclaimed its own and argumentation got its most rigorous treatments from teachers of speech communication. What remained for detailed treatment in composition courses alone was exposition, and writing teachers recognized this fact during the 1920s and 1930s.

At the same time the practical uses of exposition, which in its early days was still heavily identified with science, were becoming clear. Dewey (1916) was recommending that students be given practical skills that would make them productive citizens of a democracy, and the teaching of expository writing fell into the character of a productive skill more clearly than anything else purveyed by English departments. The case was put succinctly in 1920 by Henry Burrowes Lathrop:

> The discarding of systematic treatises on rhetoric was perfectly natural and necessary. The earlier treatises on the art of English composition could be little more than adaptations of Cicero and Quintilian—authors concerned with the art of persuasive oratory.... But Latin and Greek rhetoric was far too narrow as a basis for the theory of modern prose. It had as its aim the production of a type of character essentially unscientific and essentially biased in its whole view of life and letters. The necessity of developing a facile means of communication for the multiform activities of modern life—the need of a discipline in the statement of fact and the explication of ideas for their own sake in fields of science and technology, and of journalism, the complexity of modern business, and the resulting need of a wide-spread command of an accurate and even a fairly refined style as a part of general education, requires the laying of a foundation for writing which does not look to the development of rhetorical ability in the narrow sense as its directing force (Lathrop, 1920, p. viii).

Lathrop went on to apply an interesting form of Lockean associationism to expository methods, tracing all the methods back to comparative conceptualizing.

The same thought expressed by Lathrop was voiced by a number of early (and late) expository pedagogues. Here is Mervin Curl, whose *Expository Writing* (1919) was the first full-scale expository rhetoric text after Fulton:

> "The Anglo-Saxons," Emerson said, "are the hands of the world" — they more than any other people, turn the wheels of the world, do its work, keep things moving. . . . [W]e may safely assert that Expository Writing is the hands of literature. In a world which man even as yet only slightly understands, surrounded as he is by his fellows who constantly baffle his intelligence, and shut up within the riddle of himself, Exposition attempts to explain, to make clear, to tear away the clouds of mystery and ignorance.
>
> Exposition attempts to answer the endless curiosity of man. . . . Obviously, in making the answers the writing will often be garbed in the sack suit of business, will sometimes roll up its sleeves, will pull on the overalls or tie the apron. . . . But it may also appear in the opulence of evening costume, and criticize the ensemble of an orchestra, dismiss the diplomacy of Europe, address us in appreciation of the Arts. . . . In any case, it will be answering the endless curiosity of man (Curl, 1919, pp. 1–2).

With the vocational emphasis obvious in American education as early as 1900, it is not difficult to understand the attractiveness that this most "practical" of the modes had for teachers.

Adding to the attractiveness of exposition was the fact that in the methods of exposition teachers found a neatly packaged and easily taught pedagogical tool, a tool of a sort no other mode offered. The quick standardization of the methods approach was due in large part to its resemblance — down to specific terms — to the extremely popular paragraph pedagogy of Scott and Denney. Over 90% of the textbooks appearing between 1900 and 1930 used the means of developing paragraphs originally introduced in *Paragraph-Writing*: Even the appallingly influential handbooks of grammar and organization that began appearing in the 1900s used Scott and Denney's terms. The lists sometimes differed in specific terms, but there were certain core means that were nearly always found: Definition, Repetition, Details, Specific Instances, Comparison/Contrast, Proof, Cause and Effect. These terms were part of the everyday jargon of the writing teacher by 1920, and more and more they were also found as the informing structures of the "Exposition" chapters of books as well.

Although the means of developing paragraphs helped to spread the terms of the methods, there are important practical differences between the application of such terms on the paragraph level and on the level of the whole discourse. As much as anything, these differences help to explain how the methods of exposition that had begun life in the nineteenth century as invention heuristics came in the twentieth century to be seen as strategies of organization. The crux is this: The paragraph means had always been seen as structural devices within paragraphs, devices almost algorithmic in nature. A paragraph of cause and effect was structured with a topic sentence detailing a cause and four or five following sentences describing the effect; a

paragraph of example consisted of a topic sentence announcing a proposition, followed by four or five sentences of examples of that proposition in action. Although this was a relatively mechanical model, it was plausible at the paragraph level because paragraphs are relatively short units.

When the means and the methods began to run in tandem, however, the methods received a dose of organizational mechanism that ran counter to the invention-oriented methods treatment of Day or Scott and Denney. Along with a conception of the terms of the means of paragraph development, teachers picked up a conception of their generally organizational use, and the methods were transmuted by their association with the means. From being perceived as prewriting tools, they gradually came to be thought of as methods of development—arrangement techniques. The paragraph was often said to be but an essay in miniature, and why, then, could not an essay be a paragraph writ large? As Norman Foerster and J. M. Steadman put the case in 1931: "In principle, a paragraph may be exactly the same as a long theme, a chapter in a book, a work in one volume, a work in many volumes" (Foerster & Steadman, 1931, p. 99). Thus, in keeping company with the seductive but flawed paragraph theory of Scott and Denney, the methods of exposition lost their inventional aspects and were degraded to mere methods of arrangement.

The final element that shaped explanatory pedagogy in this century is what might be called the "secession syndrome." This term is drawn from an obvious tendency within explanatory pedagogy: In this century, whenever general or expository composition produced pedagogic systems that were vocational and relied on concrete rather than abstract methods-based forms, such systems would secede from general composition pedagogy and form the core of a separate and more specialized communications course. The three clear examples of such secession during the last 80 years are journalism, technical writing, and business writing courses. All three of these areas began by teaching exposition, all of them found that the specialized concrete forms that seemed most vital to their interests could not easily fit into a traditionally abstract composition course, and all three left general composition.

The loss of all formal ties to nonacademic writing that is illustrated by journalism, technical writing, and business writing courses moving out on their own has hurt explanatory pedagogy. The rhetoric of explanation has become divorced from such forms as news stories, columnar essays, editorials, letters of all kinds, business and technical proposals, reports of every description—to name just the major forms—and this loss has left the course in general exposition with only audienceless abstractions—the methods of exposition—and an orphan form, the research paper, to teach. From this fact comes much of the continuing sterility of the expository writing course.

THE RHETORIC OF EXPLANATION: MODERN VOICES

The remainder of the historical tale is soon told. Rhetoric in the twentieth century continued, under the auspices of the public speaking movement, to be concerned with persuasion—even though such important voices as I. A.

Richards accused persuasion of "poaching" on other aims of discourse (Richards, 1936, p. 24). In composition, the modal approach to writing instruction waned as the methods of exposition waxed. In texts using the modes, exposition was usually presented as the "first among equals," and nearly every post-1930 educational trend worked to pull down the modes and advance the teaching of exposition. The "American Writing" texts of the 1930s and 1940s, the "communications" and "General Semantics" texts of the 1940s and 1950s, all used some version of the methods of exposition. After 1950 there was hardly any need to continue to identify exposition texts by name, because by that time the revolutionaries had become the government and composition was firmly in the hands of those committed to expository writing. By 1970 the modal system had become a ghostly remnant and no discourse taxonomy put forward had the staying power of the methods of exposition. They became, de facto, the central conceptual structures of most standard composition courses. Advanced by "readers" as well as rhetorics, they stand today as living representatives of a pedagogy with almost no idea of its own genesis.

Expository writing is a practice without a past, a method without a proof of its usefulness, a tradition without a theory. Halloran (1976) has pointed out the difference between a theory and a tradition in rhetorical history, and the story of the rhetoric of explanation bears out his duality. There have been theorists of explanation—and here we can return to the more exact and less pretentious term—but their ideas have never been as important to pedagogy as have the methods. It is sad but true to say that there was no real rhetorical theory attached to explanation. The pedagogy worked itself out in textbooks according to laws of the marketplace and cultural stimuli; nothing new or innovative was propounded. It was not until the early 1960s, when composition studies began to shake off the lethargy that had long been associated with its second-class status within English departments, that we again see a vital scholarly tradition in explanatory rhetoric, a tradition that had been missing since the death of Fred Scott. Out of this renaissance in composition came the two primary modern statements on explanatory rhetoric, James L. Kinneavy's treatise on *A Theory of Discourse* (1970) and Frank J. D'Angelo's *A Conceptual Theory of Rhetoric* (1974).

Kinneavy's seminal book proposes a taxonomy of discourse based on a synthesis of classifications created by theorists as diverse as Roman Jakobson and C. S. Peirce. The classes of discourse derived by Kinneavy are these: Expressive, Referential, Literary, and Persuasive, corresponding to the common terms "personal writing," "explanation," "creative writing," and "argument or persuasion" (Kinneavy, 1970, p. 61). These four classes are based on the aims of discourse (as were Henry Day's classes) rather than on an after-the-fact judgment about what a piece of discourse has accomplished (as were Bain's modal classes).

Kinneavy's reference discourse, which is essentially cognate with what I have been calling here explanation or exposition (a term upon which Kinneavy frowns, for various plausible reasons), puts its "emphasis on the

reality to which reference is made," hence the name. It is a sort of discourse meant to give us, in Sprat's words, "a Dominion over Things, and not only over one another's Judgements." Reference discourse is further subdivided into three sorts: exploratory, informative, and scientific. "Exploratory discourse fundamentally asks a question," says Kinneavy. "Informative discourse answers it. Scientific discourse proves it" (Kinneavy, 1970, p. 89). *A Theory of Discourse* goes into great detail on the syntax, semantics, and pragmatics of each of these subdivisions. The depth and breadth of Kinneavy's scholarship has produced an impressive range of support for his theoretical proposals.

Much more speculative than *A Theory of Discourse* is Frank D'Angelo's *A Conceptual Theory of Rhetoric*. D'Angelo's thesis in this short book is that both thought and discourse are structural, that both are controlled by certain inherent conceptual patterns, and, therefore, that thinking relates invention, arrangement, and style in ways that have as yet been little understood. The same mental processes are used in each canon. "We call these processes 'topics' when they serve a heuristic function," says D'Angelo, "we call them patterns of arrangement when they are used to organize discourse; we call them stylistic when they inform sentences. All, in fact, are symbolic manifestations of the same underlying thought processes" (D'Angelo, 1974, pp. 28–29). Having made this statement, D'Angelo goes on to give instances of it in action.

The most obvious and popular application of D'Angelo's conceptual theory has been his use of the "conceptual patterns of arrangement," or "paradigms," as he calls them. The paradigms, says D'Angelo, are "dynamic organizational processes, not merely static conventional patterns." They are "universal patterns of discourse containing structural features which underlie all languages." When D'Angelo finally comes to list the paradigms in his textbook *Process and Thought in Composition,* we are not surprised to see that they are familiar: Analysis, Description, Classification, Exemplification, Definition, Comparison, Analogy, Narration, Process, Cause and Effect. There is a sense of deja vu about this list; although D'Angelo works hard to reify these paradigms as conceptual structures, they are presented in his text as straight mechanical methods of development. D'Angelo may be right in his contention that the paradigms are avatars of basic conceptual patterns but, despite his plausible theoretical rationale, the paradigms seem not to have advanced beyond the old methods of exposition in any practical sense.[6]

CONCLUSION: THE FUTURE OF EXPLANATORY RHETORIC

This overview of the development of the rhetoric of explanation leads unavoidably to a comparison of the rhetorics of argumentation and explanation. For any reflective person such a comparison can reveal only one truth: At the present our rhetorical knowledge of explanation is much less developed than our knowledge of persuasion. As we have seen, there are good reasons for the immaturity of explanatory rhetoric: the study of explanation is only 200 years old; spurious modal distinctions obscured the importance of explana-

tion for years; general explanatory theory was deserted by the most important of its concrete forms during this century; explanation seemed for too long the responsibility of "the comma-splice brigade," as one of my colleagues in Speech refers to freshman-English instructors. The rhetoric of explanation has suffered some serious setbacks and we cannot wonder that it is less developed than traditional persuasive rhetoric.

There are, however, many signs that the rhetoric of explanation may be the rhetoric of the future. Chief among them are what computer scientists call the "information revolution," and the geometrically-increasing importance of explanation in the modern world. Student realization of the importance of explanation is shown in the skyrocketing enrollments in specialized business and technical writing courses, not to mention the ever-more-common practice of industries hiring special consultants in communications. Explanation is becoming as important as persuasion in our increasingly complex and intermediated world.

Our knowledge about how explanation may best be accomplished is growing as well, although much work currently being done is speculative. Modern discourse theory and text linguistics will obviously have important ramifications for explanation and information transfer: Particularly promising is what is called "new/old information theory," which analyzes communication in terms of previous knowledge and level of information need (see, for example, Vande Koppel, 1982). It is hoped that this will be an area in which explanatory theory can be highly developed, because comprehension of information is much easier to order to scientific measure than is level of adherence or assent to a proposition.

Important work is also being done on questions of audience for explanation, particularly in the field of technical communication. Even the field of explanatory stylistics is awakening from its slumber, and the traditional calls for clearness and perspicuity in explanatory style are being supplemented by sophisticated discussions of other stylistic options available to writers and speakers (Bradford & Halloran, 1984). The very structures by which usable information is delivered are being investigated in novel and rigorous fashion by a new sort of linguistic analysis, analysis of cohesion (Halliday & Hason, 1976). As even this short list shows, the rhetoric of explanation is tending away from its traditional home in English and toward interdisciplinary approaches, with important contributions coming from psychology, linguistics, and information theory.

The rhetoric of explanation is at an important point in its development, a crossroads from which it could take a number of paths. One path leads to further disciplinary fragmentation, with practitioners in English, communications, linguistics, and psychology continuing to work independently of one another. Another path leads toward synthesis, with all practitioners sharing information and learning from one another without departmental boundaries interfering, developing explanation into, if not a science, at least a coherent body of knowledge. My vote is for the latter path. The history of the rhetoric of explanation shows the results of following the path of fragmen-

tation. If all of us can learn from our mistakes, perhaps the future will give evidence of how clearly superior is the path of cooperation.

NOTES

1. The question of invention in nineteenth-century America is discussed by James A. Berlin (1981). But Berlin is less concerned with practice or textbooks than with theory. He does not mention Newman, and his reference to Day seems to discount the fact that Day's approach to invention was quite popular.

2. My thanks to Nan Johnson for pointing out to me the importance of Day's thought to the rhetoric of explanation.

3. It is about this time that a new element enters the picture that we have of the development of composition theories: the idea of the marketplace. By the early 1880s textbook publishing companies were established, many of which—Harper, Houghton Mifflin, Scribner—still exist. Rhetorical theories had to begin to "sell themselves" in this ever-more-competitive marketplace by selling textbooks. The marketplace idea in text publishing meant, in practice, that instead of several separate theoretical approaches co-existing (as the neo-Ciceronian and Blairian views had in the eighteenth century or the Blairian and Whatelian views in the early nineteenth), the economic squeeze was on to push out whatever methods sold fewer texts. This Darwinian selection process would lead, by the end of the 1880s, to the demise of a vital rhetoric of explanation, and by the end of the century to a unified and unchallengeable model of composition pedagogy that would last, little changed, into our own time.

4. For more information on the history of the paragraph form, see Rodgers (1965).

5. For more information on Buck, see Burke (1979).

6. See Lunsford (1980) for a critique of D'Angelo's theory.

REFERENCES

Bain, A. (1886). *English composition and rhetoric.* New York: D. Appleton.

Baker, G. P. (1893). *Specimens of argumentation.* New York: Holt, Rinehart & Winston.

Baker, G. P. (1895). *The principles of argumentation.* Boston: Ginn.

Baldwin, C. S. (1895). *Specimens of prose description.* New York: Holt, Rinehart & Winston.

Bancroft, T. W. (1884). *A method of English composition.* Boston: Ginn.

Bates, A. (1896). *Talks on writing English.* Boston: Houghton Mifflin.

Berlin, J. A. (1981). The transformation of invention in nineteenth century American rhetoric. *Southern Speech Communication Journal, 46,* 292–304.

Boyd, J. R. (1844). *Elements of rhetoric and literary criticism.* New York: Harper & Row.

Bradford, A., & Halloran, S. M. (1984). Figures of speech in the language of science and technology. In R. Connors, L. Ede, & A. Lunsford (Eds.), *Classical rhetoric and modern discourse* (pp. 179–192). Carbondale: Southern Illinois University Press.

Brewster, W. T. (1895). *Specimens of narration.* New York: Holt, Rinehart & Winston.

Buck, G. (1899). *A course in argumentative writing.* New York: Holt, Rinehart & Winston.

Buck, G., & Woodbridge, E. (1899). *A course in expository writing.* New York: Holt, Rinehart & Winston.

Buck, G., & Morris, E. W. (1906). *A course in narrative writing.* New York: Holt, Rinehart & Winston.

Burke, R. J. (1979). *Gertrude Buck's rhetorical theory.* Manhattan: Kansas State University.

Connors, R. J. (1981). The rise and fall of the modes of discourse. *College Composition and Communication, 32,* 444–455.

Curl, M. J. (1919). *Expository writing.* Boston: Houghton Mifflin.

D'Angelo, F. J. (1974). *A conceptual theory of rhetoric.* Cambridge, MA: Winthrop.

Day, H. N. (1850). *Elements of the art of rhetoric.* Hudson: Skinner.

Day, H. N. (1860). *Rhetorical praxis.* New York: American Book Co.

Day, H. N. (1867). *The art of discourse.* New York: Scribner.

Day, H. N. (1867). *Grammatical synthesis: The art of English composition.* New York: Scribner.

Dewey, J. (1916). *Democracy and education: An introduction to the philosophy of education.* New York: Macmillan.

Foerster, N., & Steadman, J. M. (1931). *Writing and thinking.* Boston: Houghton Mifflin.

Fulton, M. G. (1912). *Expository writing* (rev. ed.). New York: Macmillan.

Genung, J. F. (1886). *The practical elements of rhetoric.* Boston: Ginn.

Genung, J. F., & Hanson, C. L. (1915). *Outlines of composition and rhetoric.* Boston: Ginn.

Halliday, M.A.K., & Hasan, R. (1976). *Cohesion in English.* London: Longmans.

Halloran, S. M. (1976). Tradition and theory in rhetoric. *Quarterly Journal of Speech, 62,* 234–241.

Hepburn, A. D. (1875). *Manual of English rhetoric.* Cincinnati: Wilson, Hinkle.

Hill, A. S. (1878). *The principles of rhetoric and their application.* New York: Harper & Row.

Hill, A. S. (1895). *The principles of rhetoric* (rev. ed.). New York: American Book Co.

Kinneavy, J. L. (1970). *A theory of discourse.* Englewood Cliffs, NJ: Prentice-Hall.

Lamont, H. (1894). *Specimens of exposition.* New York: Holt, Rinehart & Winston.

Lathrop, H. B. (1920). *Freshman composition.* New York: Century Co.

Lunsford, A. A. (1980). *On D'Angelo's conceptual theory of rhetoric.* Paper presented at the Conference on College Composition and Communications, Washington, D.C.

Mitchill, T. C., & Carpenter, G. R. (1906). *Exposition in class-room practice.* New York: Macmillan.

Newman, S. P. (1843). *A practical system of rhetoric.* New York: Mark H. Newman. (Original work published 1827)

Parker, R. G. (1844). *Aids to English composition.* Boston: R. S. Davis.

Quackenbos, G. P. (1854). *Advanced course of composition and rhetoric.* New York: Appleton.

Richards, I. A. (1936). *The philosophy of rhetoric.* New York: Oxford University Press.

Rodgers, P. C. Jr. (1965). Alexander Bain and the rise of the organic paragraph. *Quarterly Journal of Speech, 51,* 399–408.

Russell, W. (1823). *A grammar of composition.* New Haven, CT: A. H. Maltby.

Scott, F. N., & Denney, J. (1893). *Paragraph-writing, with appendices on newspaper style and proof-reading.* Boston Allyn and Bacon.

Vande Koppel, W. (1982). Functional sentence perspective. *College Composition and Communication, 33,* 50–63.

Walker, J. (1808). *Teacher's assistant in English composition.* Carlisle: George Kline.

Wendell, B. (1891). *English composition.* New York: Scribner.

Whately, R. (1963). *Elements of rhetoric.* Carbondale: Southern Illinois University Press. (Original work published 1828)

The Genius

When we first read "The Genius," a short story that Bob published in *Road & Track* in 1985, we could see immediately why Bob might want to write a narrative about model cars. Even after he became an established scholar—and a husband and father—Bob talked nostalgically of his days as a truck driver. And he loved motor vehicles of all sorts. Bob was also a skilled craftsman who would spend endless hours working in stained glass, so we could readily imagine his becoming absorbed in the world of model car construction. What surprised us, however, were the Ambrose Bierce–like details of this story. What was it that so compelled Bob about this idea—the notion of someone stealing cars and then somehow magically (or diabolically) shrinking them to model size—that he interrupted his teaching and writing at the University of New Hampshire to write this story? We invite readers to consider this question as they read this short story—the last of three pieces of fiction Bob published.

N o, that one's not for sale. Both of them are mine. Yes, they're Warren Johnson models. He was the greatest modeling genius the world ever saw, I allow. Know him? You bet I knew him. Better than anyone else around here. He was a strange one, all right, but I liked him. I sometimes wonder where he is now.

I expect it must have been around April of last year when I saw him for the first time. He was kind of mooching around in front of the store with a big cardboard box under his arm. He'd walk on by, looking in the window like a dog in front of a butcher's, disappear, then come back. I was setting up a Tyco raceway in the back, so I don't know how long he was out there.

Finally the door chime rang, and he came in, kind of gliding in cheap sneakers. A big fat guy, the sort who always looks shiny even in the winter. Ban-Lon shirt and greasy jeans: he looked like the fat kid in "Gasoline Alley," except older and gone baggy. About 40, pink cheeks, curly yellow hair. And with this big cardboard box he carried real carefully.

From *Road & Track*, August 1985, 58–60, 64.

The store was quiet just then. He put the box down on the counter and stood moving from one foot to another, like he had to go or something. And I asked him if I could help him.

"You, uh . . ." he said, his voice sounding scared, "you buy models as well as sell them, huh? My friend said you bought them."

I went over. "Yes, we buy models. But only antiques or very special models. Not your old Revells."

"This isn't an old Revell. Do you want to see?"

"Okay, sure. What have you got?"

He took the top off and began to pull out cotton wool from the box. I looked, saw a flash of chrome, and then he reached down very carefully and slowly drew out a model car, a green 1967 Chevy, and put it on the counter in front of me.

It was not a commercial model. It was about 18 in. long, every line correct. Reaching out, I touched the fender with my forefinger, and the car rocked on tiny springs. Tiny coil springs. The model was all metal.

"Nice, huh?" He sounded proud. "All the details work, too. You have to use these tweezers and this needle." Fumbling the tools from a shirt pocket, he unlatched and opened the Chevy's door (it gave a high squeak). The seats were of worn vinyl, the driver's covered with a miniature cool-seat. Reaching in with the long needle, he pressed the horn ring, and a thin blatting came from under the hood. He poked open the minuscule vent window.

"Pretty good model, huh?"

I was trying to keep my voice steady. "Not bad, not bad. Let me look more carefully." I went and got my 20× magnifier while he stood there shifting from foot to foot.

Now, I think I know model cars as well as anyone around this city. They can be pretty damned nice. The Pochers are beautiful, the Solidos are fine models. I've seen those hand-cast and bolted Bugattis from Switzerland—lovely! I've seen photos of little Mercers a man builds that actually run. I know the market. But never in my life had I ever seen *anything* to approach the detail of this little Chevy. The tires were pressurized. The radio antenna went up and down. The doors all opened, the windows all raised and lowered (well, the driver's side didn't; broken, he said). All the tiny things were right: the little chrome Impalas were there. The wipers worked, the lights went on and off, it even had tiny rust holes and a bitty ding in the bumper. I mean, it was *perfect*. It had little *casting holes* in the back of the steering wheel, for crying out loud.

I tried to be blasé. This fella was the greatest modeler in the world and didn't seem to know it. "Not bad," I said jokingly, "a little rusty, though." He looked pained. "That's for realism," he said stoutly. "You could repaint it anyhow, couldn't you? It runs good, real good."

Staring, I said, "Runs? The motor?"

"Sure. Look." Reaching carefully in with the tweezers, he turned the microscopic key in the dashboard. A high-pitched, whirring sound, then a sharp growl from under the car. "Needs a new muffler," he explained. "Is it a V-8?" I asked sarcastically. "No, just a six. Watch it go."

He gingerly set it on the floor, where it was regarded with amazement by a couple of kids who had come in. Reaching in clumsily with an index finger, he moved the automatic transmission lever over; the growl changed. Holding the car back by the edges of the roof, he straightened the steering, then let it go. It crept, about 6 in./sec, down the aisle of the store. The kids were bug-eyed.

Warren (that was the name he told me, Warren Johnson) ran and stopped the car, turned it off, then looked up at me. "Well, are you interested?"

I nodded. "Come on into the office. Bring the car."

Well, the long and short of it was that I ended up paying him $375 for the Chevy. I told him I had never seen a Chevy so fine and that any time he had any more models like that to come and see me. He was pleased, I was pleased, we shook hands and he twitched out the keys and gave them to me. I asked him how long it had taken to put the Chevy together. He looked confused for a second, then said just a couple months. He had some others under construction now and would show them to me when they were ready. He left then, walking fast.

I looked the car over. God, it was something. A little battery the size of your fingernail, an automatic transmission 3 in. long. Every nut and bolt perfect. There was even a flat spare and a miniature bag of rock salt in the trunk. I put the car in the window with a sign reading "World's Most Detailed Model," and three days later a man from Cleveland bought it for $1100. When I took it from the window there was a little pool of oil under where the engine had been.

I didn't see Warren for a few weeks after that, and thought it would take him months more to complete another model—I mean, it should have taken *years* to put a model like that together. He was a genius, that's all. That's what I told myself. Then about three weeks later he came in with two more models.

His clothes were new. He had on a cheap green polyester leisure suit that made him look like a watermelon, and the cardboard box was heavier.

"Hi, boss. I see you sold the Chevy." His manner was different now; he was confident. I don't know why he called me boss.

"Right. Got any more?"

"You bet. Can we go in the office?"

He had a Volkswagen Beetle model and a really nifty little old fastback Mustang. The details, everything, were just as perfect and amazing as those on the Chevy had been. He had somehow even duplicated the spare-pressure windshield-washer on the Bug.

"I, uh, have to tell you," he said, casting his eyes down, "the VW has a blown engine. Doesn't run. For realism, y'know?"

"Realism. God, Warren, any more realism and I'll expect you to produce a little human being out of your pocket and have him drive the cars away." I was fascinated, tinkering with the 4-speed of the Mustang. "How do you get that weathered-paint look?"

He spoke quickly. "Oh, sanding, and a special paint I mix up myself. Do you want these?" He never seemed to like to talk about his techniques.

"Do you have any more?"

"I have some almost finished and some in the works. How much do you think these are worth? Do you want them?"

I couldn't help it. I had to ask. "How in the world can you part with them for money after all the work you put in? I would want to keep them forever."

"These?" He almost laughed. "Just a VW and an old Mustang? They're nothing. I've got others in the works. But I need the money for these."

Yes, I know. Strange. But not for me to wonder why like the man says. I made a deal with Warren: I would be his exclusive distributor and he would sell all of his works of art (Who could call them just models? They're worth tens of thousands today) through me. I gave him a grand on spec for the two he had brought and he promised to return within the month.

So we started our business relationship, Warren and me. I sold the VW for $1500 and the Mustang for $2300 to a Ford nut. The week afterward I got a call from a man who had seen the Chevrolet and wondered if I had any more Johnson models. I took his number.

Two days later Warren mooched in with a yellow Pinto and a pretty Datsun B210 model. The polyester outfit was gone: now he was wearing a wool sportcoat. His nails were clean. "Hot stuff, huh, boss?" he said happily. Hot stuff it was: both models were gone in a week. His cars were getting known around the state and collectors often called me. At one point I just had to tell people I'd put them on a list.

It went like that. He would show up at odd times, and he'd have the damnedest models. Over the next few months he brought in a VW 412, a Sunbeam Alpine, two Plymouth Dusters, and a 1965 Valiant. That sort of car.

Most modelmakers do the classic cars, the Model Ts and the 1955 Chevys, the Cords and Bugattis. That's what most people want models of. But this fella—the greatest modeler who ever lived, I expect—did only cheap, everyday cars. "I like those cars best," he said when I asked him about it. "Those are the cars I grew up with." And he kept on with the Mavericks and Toyota Corollas.

I know: I should have suspected something. In six months he came up with 16 complete model cars, and each one sold for more than $3000. I put an ad in *Model World* and selling them was no problem. I kept a third and he got two-thirds. My share came to more than $21,000. That's a lot of money.

Throughout all this Warren kept completely to himself. He never told me where he lived, never gave me a phone number. "You take care of the business end, boss," he said. "Everything." He would come into the store at odd intervals with a model or two, talk a little while about prices, pick up his money and leave. He always asked for cashier's checks. His clothes were much more expensive, I noticed, and one day when he left I saw him drive past a minute later in a gray XJ-S.

As I say, this went on for about half a year. The models sold well, but they were not, never would be, the classic cars that collectors would kill for. I finally figured that I needed to talk with Warren about it. One day after he

had brought in a beautifully detailed but sort of ratty 1967 Ford pickup truck model. I sat him down in the office.

"Listen, Warren," I said, "how long do you want to go on with this penny-ante modeling? You can keep making these Checkers and Dodges at three grand a throw forever . . ."

"Yeah, the money's pretty good!" he interrupted enthusiastically.

I went on. "Or, you can start to make some real money."

He looked confused. "Real money?"

It was time to give him my big gun. "I got a phone call yesterday from the president of the regional MG club. They're willing to pay $9500 for one of your models. But it has to be an MG TC. Not another Malibu or Falcon."

He swallowed. "Almost ten grand? For one car?"

"Yes. And that's peanuts compared to some. We could get more for others. There've been several people who wanted to order models, and I've had to tell them you were an eccentric genius who only did models of damnfool cars."

"Ten thousand dollars," he said wonderingly, and walked out the door in some sort of daze. Three days later he came back with his box: a perfect darkblue 1949 MG TC. You can't put together a Pocher kit in three days, and this TC was 50 times more detailed.

I should have known then that something wasn't right. But I expect that the dollar signs were in my eyes too. When the president of the TC Society came to pick up the model, he was flabbergasted. He looked at it for a moment, nudging the fabric of the top with a finger, sliding the side curtains back and forth.

"Unbelievable. Unbelievable."

As he was making out his check I put the TC into one of the glass display cases I had had made up for Warren's cars. "Where you going to put this model, Mr. Gallant?" I asked.

"Right in the lobby of my building," he answered, tearing off the check.

"I'm going to lock this handbrake so it doesn't roll around during the tr—hmmm. I guess not." The handbrake lever had no tension; cable broken maybe.

"It broke?" Gallant came over. "Hmmm, no tension," I said, moving the lever up and down to show him.

"Well, don't worry about it. Just pack it in shavings or something . . ." He stopped, looked closely at the car again. "You know, the handbrake on Jack Castine's car was always loose like that. Same color, too. Last I heard he was selling that car. Maybe your man used it as a model."

"Might be, might be. Thank you, sir."

All right, all right. But in all honesty, there was nothing illegal about what I did. The models were all sold legally. I have all the tax records. They were all bought and paid for. I run a clean shop; I sell no airplane glue to kids.

The operation changed for a while after that. Warren Johnson models had gotten so well known that I could name the prices; from middle-income and regional collectors our customers became top-level national and even in-

ternational people. The days of Gremlins and Galaxies were over; after that MG. Warren let me know he'd accept orders.

"It might take me a little longer, boss," he said as I made out his bank check for $8000 (I worked on percentage by then; he got smarter). And he did take longer—he would sometimes be gone for a month before he showed up with what the collector had ordered.

I tell you, those were the glory days. We got orders from all over; for a Z-car, a Jag E-Type, a Lotus Elan, and Warren kept the models rolling in. God, they were lovely. No more misplaced "realism," no more rust and dings. The models were gems, just gems. The 240Z sold for $13,500, and I heard it just changed hands for $37,000 last week.

But Warren would only take certain orders, nothing too old, nothing too rare. "I always have to get more for the model than the car itself," he told me once, "it's a point of pride. If one man built a Pinto, it'd be expensive too." So I had to turn away the Cord and Duesenberg people, the serious individual collectors. And the number of people with big money who want modern car models is limited.

The day came finally. Warren walked in with a really heart-breaking model of a Mazda RX-7 (the little Wankel engine made a high whining sound) and wanted to know what was next. I had to tell him there were no more orders.

"No more orders? For *my* cars?" he repeated dumbly, eyes round. "Sure, I've got orders." I replied, "orders for a Bugatti Type 35, a Duesenberg SJ, a boat-tail Auburn, a . . ."

"All right, all right," he growled, "you know what I told you about those cars. Too hard to blueprint, too hard to do . . ." He sounded unconvincing.

"Hard to do?" I made my voice sarcastic. "Look at your detail work on this Mazda. Look at that wheel. Look at those headlights. Hard to do!"

There was a long silence. Then he said slowly. "Do you have any pictures of the Bugatti?"

So we started the third and last phase of our partnership. Two months after that night he brought in the Bug. When the man came to get it, he stood for a second and peered at the little blue car on the counter. Walked closer, looked carefully. Then his back convulsed, and two huge tears trickled from behind his Coke-bottle lenses. "It's . . . it's . . . the most beautiful thing . . ." he said brokenly. I said $25,000.

When Warren brought in the Doozie, I seriously considered stealing it for myself. It was a 1932, chocolate-brown and black, with a long 2-seat Murphy body, gray upholstery, that purring straight-8 engine with the miniature super-charger . . . I can see it now, twinkling on the counter. That counter there. They tell me that car's gone now, stolen. I'm not surprised. It went to a private collector, then was resold, then stolen. No, I'm not surprised. That model was like the Hope diamond: I wouldn't be surprised if someone killed for it.

What came next? Oh yes, the Model A. Beautiful little rumble-seat coupe, bright yellow, black fenders. That one was cheap then, only $12,000. I guess Warren figured he could loaf a little; the Duesenberg had gone for $38,000. We were both well off.

We had a long-standing order for an Auburn, and I think he was in the middle of doing it when Mr Gottschalk came in for the first time. I looked up from a Lionel tank car I was trying to repair and there was this figure in black, all black. His skin looked white and puffy, sort of . . . in my mind I called him the Pillsbury Doughboy, although he must have been at least 60.

"Are you the agent for Johnson models?" His voice was cold and twangy, real precise.

"Yes, I handle business for Warren Johnson."

"Then I have a commission for you." He talked that way, never looking straight at you, speaking as if he'd just eaten sour persimmons.

"I am Sidney Gottschalk. You may have heard of me. Gottschalk Refining, Pretoria, Bern and Rochester."

I allowed as how I had.

"I wish a model of a vehicle I own. A 1938 Delahaye with coachwork by Figoni et Falaschi. Can your man build such a model?"

I allowed as how he could. For a large sum of money.

"I am prepared to pay $40,000 if the model is of the quality of the others I have seen."

I allowed as how it would be. We signed paper.

"I will expect to hear from you within three months."

"You will. I'll need good quality 8 × 10s of the car from the side, front, rear, top, bottom."

"My chauffeur will bring them. Good day, sir."

When Warren showed up with the Auburn, I was appalled. It was beautiful, of course, but then I opened the hood—and the engine was a Chevy V-8. Inside the cockpit—the car was an automatic!

"Some—something wrong?" Warren quavered. "It's perfect, isn't it?" I closed my eyes, put my head down on the desk. "What's wrong?"

"Warren," I finally moaned, "why in the name of God have you built a model of a modern replicar—a fiberglass Auburn body on a Chevrolet chassis?"

"Re—replicar?" he stammered. "It isn't a real . . . ?"

"Oh, cripes," was all I could say. He didn't seem to know anything about classic cars at all, and instead of a $30,000 model we had a useless piece of miniature junk. Well, not completely. I salvaged something by selling the model to the Indianapolis company that makes the replicar bodies. But it was a big loss.

"Get it right next time, you lunk-head!" I told him. He was plenty sheepish, and promised not to screw up on the Delahaye.

"Jeez, boss, I've never seen a car like this around anywhere. Who wants it?" I wished he wouldn't call me boss.

"Never mind. There are only eight cars like it in the world. Can you do it?"

He hesitated. "I guess so . . . it may take time—couple, three months."

It was a couple of days later when I was packing up the fake Auburn for shipment and my eye fell on something. I was crumpling up newspapers,

and the word "Duesenberg" on a page made me stop and read. It was the Detroit *Free Press* for about three months before; I don't know where it had come from. The story was only a column on page 8: VINTAGE AUTO DIS-APPEARS.

"Police continued today to investigate the mysterious theft of an antique 1932 Duesenberg roadster from the locked garage of industrialist Fred T. Prianowski early this morning. The brown convertible, more than 16 ft long, disappeared without the heavily electronically alarmed garage door being opened. 'The locks weren't tampered with,' said Sgt Thomas Cochrane. 'A small window was broken, but hardly even big enough to get the bumper out. It just seemed to disappear into thin air.' The car was valued at more than $100,000."

No. Really, I don't know anything. There's nothing that can be proven. I just sell hobby supplies. I don't know anything about auto thefts. I threw out the paper and forgot all about it. Just forgot it. Forgot the whole thing.

When Warren finally brought in the Delahaye I didn't talk much to him. But when I called up Gottschalk to tell him his model was in, he was not excited. His cold voice sounded carved from ice now.

"Three days ago someone forced the door of my storage facility and made off with three cars from my collection, including my Delahaye. Yes, I am aware that we have a contract. My chauffeur will be in to pick up the model."

He did, the next day. "Mr. Gottschalk is really down in the dumps," he said, looking over the shiny curves of the body work. "He loved this car better'n any of 'em. His big Daimler and the gray Caddy got ripped too, but this Delahaye was the only car he drove himself. He's hell to live with these days. Well, nice model, here's the check. See you later." And he went out the door.

Seemed like the chime had hardly stopped ringing when Gottschalk himself was back in, his pasty face now a fiery red. "What have you done with my car?" he shouted, waving a small piece of black rag in front of my face. The model Delahaye was clutched in his other hand; his grip was so tight that the sheet metal of the top was crumpling. "My car!" I couldn't quiet him down.

"You see this?" He waved the black scrap of cloth. "I drive car last weekend, it's hot, I take off my coat, put it in the boot. Now in boot of this car, this toy car, my coat! Toy coat! And again I ask where is my Delahaye??" He was dancing with fury; his eyes were bugging out.

I'll tell you, that was an afternoon. I got him out finally with the help of the chauffeur, who was an okay guy really, but how do you convince a man that you haven't magically reduced his most prized possession to a toy?

Warren came back in a couple of days later. I hadn't had any orders when he last came in with the Delahaye, but he had a big box with him.

"Hey there, boss. No orders yet, huh? Got a couple of new ones here any-how . . ." But I decided: No more.

"Hold it, Warren. Don't take the cover off. I think I know what you've got." He looked at me.

"You've got two cars. One is English and one is gray." He turned that color himself. "I thought so," I said, as he sagged against the counter.

"Now listen, Warren, I want you to go away. Today. Now. I don't know what it is you're doing or how you're doing it, but it's starting to catch up with you. No, don't say anything. My advice is to get out of town, out of the state, as fast as you can. I never want to hear from you again. If they ask me what I know I'll say nothing, and it'll be the truth. I don't want to know anything."

His face looked like a melting candle, and his hand was leaving a big sweaty print on the counter. "So go on," I said. "Beat it quick. I don't think you've hurt anybody really bad yet. Keep it that way." And he gulped, and he stammered, and finally said, "Th-thanks," and he left, running, without the box. And I never saw Warren again.

It was about three weeks later when the four Army guys from Ft. Belvoir came and showed me a photo of a younger, thinner Warren in a corporal's uniform and said that Johnson wasn't his real name and wanted to know if I ever saw him with a big suitcase or a backpack or if he ever bought any dry-cell batteries from me. And I told them all I've told you. Mostly. And they mumbled about National Security and Good Citizenship and The Research Race, but I didn't know where Warren was then and finally they went away.

So, no, those aren't for sale and never will be. I have some nice Tamiyas and Pochers over here. This Alfa's a honey. But the Daimler and the Cadillac are mine. Warren Johnson models are real collector's classics now, and those are the last two. No, as far as I know they never caught him.

The Rhetoric of Mechanical Correctness

"The Rhetoric of Mechanical Correctness" was published in 1986 in
Only Connect: Uniting Reading and Writing, a collection of essays
edited by Thomas Newkirk; a shorter version of this essay appeared in *College Composition and Communication* during the previous year. In this essay, Bob turns his attention to the historical
conditions that led to "the single-minded enforcement of standards
of mechanical and grammatical correctness in writing" (72), and he
does so by looking at the history, nature, and status of the required
course in English composition in the United States. As he typically
does in his research, Bob attends with particular care to material
conditions, especially the working conditions of teachers of writing
after 1870. Bob estimates, for instance, that Barrett Wendell, who in
1884 pioneered the daily theme at Harvard, read "855 themes
weekly, or 22,230 for the year" (83). In response to demands such
as these, Bob argues, teachers developed strategies, including
simpler assignments and an emphasis on reading for mechanical
correctness, "to protect themselves from insanity and to get on
with their work" (84). Bob concludes this essay with a statement of
optimism that we think especially reflects the sensibility of many
in the field in the mid-1980s: "At last the reductive traditions of the
first half of the century are being questioned and challenged.
Teachers are better trained every year. Newer textbooks are providing even traditionally-oriented teachers with more defensible
course content than the 'shall-will' rules. [. . .] We have made
strides, and more will be made" (95). Like many who came to the
work of composition in the late 1970s and early 1980s, however,
Bob later found it hard to maintain this sense of optimism and of
disciplinary progress.

From *Only Connect: Uniting Reading and Writing,* ed. Thomas Newkirk (Upper Montclair, NJ: Boynton/Cook, 1986), 27–58.

He that despiseth little things shall perish little by little.

– APOCRYPHA

T
hroughout most of its history as a college subject, English composition has meant one thing to most people: the single-minded enforcement of standards of mechanical and grammatical correctness in writing. The image of a grim-faced Miss Grundy, besprinkling the essays of her luckless students with scarlet handbook hieroglyphs, is still a common stereotype; it is only in the last twenty-five years that composition instructors have seriously begun to question the priority given to simple correctness in college-level instruction. Most scholars of rhetorical history have wondered at some time about the forces which turned "rhetoric" into "composition," transformed instruction in wide-ranging techniques of persuasion and analysis into a narrow concern for convention on the most basic levels, transmogrified the noble discipline of Aristotle, Cicero, Campbell, into a stultifying error hunt. In this essay I'd like to examine some of those forces, both cultural and pedagogical, which shaped nineteenth-century rhetorical history and resulted in the obsession with mechanical correctness which for so many years defined the college course in written rhetoric.

The required course in English composition is a uniquely American institution. Less than any other college subject has it been informed by a genuine body of knowledge crying out to be disseminated; more than any other subject has it been shaped by perceived social and cultural needs. College writing courses began in the nineteenth century as rhetoric lectures in the traditional British mold, studying mental faculties, taste, style, and *belles-lettres*. The general spirit of the age, however, was one of radical equalitarianism, and culturally there was little pressure for formal correctness in writing. Only with the beginnings of a structured system of social classes in America—a system based both on wealth and on education—did an ethic of gentility and "correctness" arise in Americans' attitudes toward speaking and writing. Around the same time, new pedagogical techniques in the teaching of vernacular grammar ingrained the habit of scrutinizing sentences for errors. With the growth of a native literary-intellectual culture—in specific, an identifiable college and university culture—linguistic insecurity arose, and it was exacerbated by post–Civil War evidence that the writing abilities of new college freshmen were indeed atrocious. The result: the first "back-to-basics" movement, the first stab at remedial college English. Teachers were swamped with "themes" to "correct," and their overwork created a booming business in supportive educational technology—handbooks, workbooks, etc.—meant to aid them in their drudgery. These tools came all too quickly to control their masters, however, and the subsequent history of composition instruction until recently is a history of poorly trained instructors pressed by overwork and circumstance to enforce the most easily-perceived

standards of writing—mechanical standards—while ignoring or short-changing more difficult and rhetorical elements.

Things are better now, but this is a sad enough story—a story of well-meaning teachers and administrators swept by ignorance and shortsightedness through an eighty-year pedagogical bad dream. To understand how it all began, we must go back to the first third of the nineteenth century and examine the attitudes toward language, culture, and education held at that time.

ATTITUDES TOWARD LANGUAGE IN THE EARLY NINETEENTH CENTURY

During the first fifty years of the nineteenth century, the new nation of the United States was striving to define itself as a culture. Jeffersonian and then Jacksonian democracy had produced an ethic of equalitarianism that extended into all areas of national life, including education and language. During the earlier part of the century, Americans tended to be almost contentious in their rejection of imposed hierarchies of value; it was a unique cultural situation, and was due partially to the American educational structure. In 1831, when Alexis de Tocqueville made his tour of the United States, he saw thousands of public elementary schools but relatively few colleges.[1] As Tocqueville put it, "there is no other country in the world where, proportionally to population, there are so few ignorant and so few learned individuals as in America. Primary education is within reach of all; higher education is hardly available to anybody."[2]

The equality of prospect which Tocqueville marked as the most obvious feature of American democracy was to have several effects upon the national attitude toward language use. Most people were taught reading and writing in elementary school and emerged at the age of twelve or so with all the schooling they were to see; thus grew up a common denominator of expression. For a time, it seemed that linguistic class distinctions would disappear:

> ... when men are no longer held to a fixed social position, when they continually see one another and talk together, when castes are destroyed and classes change and merge, all of the words of a language get mixed up too. Those which cannot please the majority die; the rest form a common stock from which each man chooses at random ... Not only does everyone use the same words, but they get into the habit of using them without discrimination. The rules of style are destroyed. Hardly any expressions seem, by their nature, vulgar, and hardly any seem refined.[3]

Tocqueville visited a nation in which elementary schools were emphasizing grammar instruction as an abstract "mental discipline" and where only a very few men could aspire to college training—training which led nearly inevitably to the closed circles of pulpit and bar. Such college-educated men were too few and too specialized to provide a real linguistic aristocracy, and thus for a time the common denominator prevailed in language.

Nineteenth-century America, however, was a culture in transition, and the linguistic leveling that Tocqueville reported was beginning to melt away even as he published his first volume of *Democracy in America*. The period 1830–1870 saw the rise of forces that would gradually overcome the equalitarianism of the earlier part of the century. At some point after 1840, the common denominator stopped falling and began to rise as Americans became aware of and concerned about their speaking and writing habits.

The reasons for this awakening interest in correctness of usage and the niceties of grammatical construction are both cultural and pedagogical. Culturally, the period 1820 through 1860 was the "American Renaissance," an era that saw the rise of a secular literary-intellectual culture in America. For the first time, the New World produced writers and poets who could stand with the best of the Old—and who also wished to stand separate from the old. Tocqueville's comment that "American authors may fairly be said to live more in England than in America," might have seemed accurate in 1831, but by 1840 it was rapidly becoming outdated by such writers as Irving, Hawthorne, Poe, Emerson, and many others. The "frontier" was being pushed westward, and Eastern cities were developing cosmopolitan attributes, generating indigenous intellectual elites and atmospheres far removed from the rough-and-tumble equalitarianism of the earlier part of the century. Classes, based both upon wealth and upon education, were beginning to form—and where there is class distinction, linguistic distinctions are not far behind.[4]

In addition, the character of school instruction in language was also changing. As Rollo Lyman has shown, grammar instruction in the United States became an important aspect of primary education:

> English grammar gained momentum as the hold of Latin Grammar weakened (during the post–Revolutionary War period), and by the end of the first quarter of the nineteenth century it became so generally taught that the common term grammar school, formerly applied to the secondary school of the Latin-grammar type, was now by common consent used to designate an intermediate school with English grammar as its central study. After 1825 the prominence of English grammar became gradually more marked, until it reached its height about 1850–1875.[5]

Lyman calls the period around 1860 "the heyday of grammar," and it is no accident that it coincides with the first great period of American linguistic insecurity.

This rise of interest in vernacular grammar had led by the 1840s to a new awareness on Americans' parts of the concepts of "correctness" and "grammaticality." In large part, this new awareness resulted from new instructional methods in grammar classes. Lindley Murray, whose immensely popular *English Grammar* was the best-selling grammar text in America prior to 1825, utilized a "correct-incorrect" duality borrowed from the pedagogy used to enforce the learning of Latin grammar, and his approach emphasized a

binary, good-or-bad attitude toward each sentence studied. Samuel Kirkham, whose 1829 *English Grammar in Familiar Lectures* took up the market as Murray began to falter, made heavy use of "false-syntax" exercises—lists of sentences larded with errors in grammar and usage which students were supposed to identify and correct. These exercises fostered an attitude of suspicion toward everything written, and as Edward Finegan suggests, Murray and Kirkham have to be held at least partly responsible for later negativistic and absolutist attitudes toward language.[6]

The age of Victorian gentility was beginning, and in the 1840s we begin to see a new movement in the United States, a movement whose desiderata were proper usage and grammatical correctness in speech and writing. This new interest seems to have sprung from two distinct proximate causes: the Eastern reaction against the "roughness" and "crudeness" of frontier America, an attitude which wished to set standards of propriety in language as in all other aspects of life; and the desire for self-improvement and "getting ahead," which was an important part of the American mythos during the nineteenth century. These two elements were found mixed into most of the early works on "good language." The first can be seen clearly during the late 1840s in an address given to the Newburyport Girls' High School by Andrew Peabody, chaplain at Harvard College. Peabody spoke to the girls on "Conversation," and the point of his remarks was that his audience should strive to establish a proper and correct linguistic ambience about them, should "raise the tone" where they were:

> Young ladies do more than any other class in the community towards establishing the general tone and standard of social intercourse . . . you are fast approaching an age when you will take prominent places in general society; will be the objects of peculiar regard; and will, in a great measure, determine whether the social converse in your respective circles shall be vulgar or refined . . . [7]

Peabody goes on to warn against faulty pronunciation, "ungrammatical vulgarisms," and other "untasteful practices" in conversation. His *Handbook of Conversation: Mistakes of Speaking and Writing Corrected* included this address as well as several other short pieces of linguistic prescription, and it remained in print from 1855 through 1882. Peabody's *Handbook* shows how early the cultural lines between "refined" and "vulgar" language were being drawn. His use of "vulgar" is especially noteworthy; it's not a term previously heard very often in America outside of lectures on rhetoric. It's an essentially elitist term foreign to the ethos of Jeffersonian and Jacksonian democracy, but through the forties, fifties, and sixties we will hear it used more and more.

In 1847, the year that Peabody first gave his Newburyport address, there appeared a book less popular but more important as a harbinger of things to come. This was Seth T. Hurd's self-improvement manual, *A Grammatical Corrector*. Between 1826 and 1834, Hurd had spent his winters as a "public

lecturer" on English Grammar, probably at the Lyceums then coming to popularity. In his capacity as a traveling lecturer—a sort of early Chautauqua figure—he visited "almost every section of the United States." Hurd explained his method thus: "The common errors and peculiarities of speech, which were found to prevail in different communities, were carefully noted down and preserved, not only as a source of amusement (to myself), but for the purpose of correction and comment in the Lecture-room."[8] Given this *modus operandi*, it is no wonder that Hurd kept moving on. The epigraph on his title page describes the contents of the *Grammatical Corrector* better than anything else:

> Being a collection of nearly two thousand barbarisms, cant phrases, colloquialisms, quaint expressions, provincialisms, false pronunciation, perversions, misapplications of terms and other kindred errors of the English language peculiar to the different States of the Union. The whole explained, corrected, and conveniently arranged for the use of schools and private individuals.

Painful though it might have been for them, Hurd's audiences in the 1830s were interested in having their "barbarisms" corrected, in being told that *"done up brown"* was *"a very low phrase."* The general audiences at such Lyceum lectures obviously had wider agendas than mere politeness or gentility; theirs was an interest in self-improvement that must have been as much concerned with getting ahead as it was with "raising the tone." Hurd was more than an early Victorian John Simon, shaking his readers down while he attacked their language habits as "uneducated," "impolite," "inelegant," and "vulgar"; there are elements of Dale Carnegie's commercial approach to influencing businessmen in his book as well.

Usage, Correctness, and Social Position

These beginnings of linguistic status-anxiety in the 1840s and fifties grew stronger in the 1860s, when much of the American intellectual community was influenced by a small book written by an Englishman. *A Plea for the Queen's English*, by Henry Alford, who was Dean of Westminster and a noted British intellectual, appeared in 1864; it would see eleven British and American printings and remain in print until 1893. In it, "the Dean," as he was called by his opponents and fellow controversialists, attacked much current usage, both literary and popular, striking out at poor pronunciation, wrong words, improper sentence construction, and other "objectionable" misuses of English. The Dean's book raised a number of hackles in England, but to Americans it was a particularly stinging rebuke, for Alford was bitterly anti-American in addition to being a linguistic purist:[9]

> . . . the language of a people is no trifle. The national mind is reflected in the national speech . . . Every important feature in a people's language is reflected in its character and history.

Look, to take one familiar example, at the process of deterioration which our Queen's English has undergone at the hands of the Americans. Look at those phrases which so amuse us in their speech and books; at their reckless imagination, and contempt for congruity; and then compare the character and history of the nation—its blunted sense of moral obligation and duty to man; its disregard for conventional right where aggrandizement is to be obtained . . . Such examples as this . . . may serve to show that language is no trifle.[10]

These was fightin' words in 1864, and America was not long in producing champions to field against the Dean. The great prescriptive-usage war of the Victorian era was on.

Best known of the Dean's antagonists in these debates were George Washington Moon, an expatriate American living in England, and Edward S. Gould, a New York journeyman intellectual. Moon slashingly attacked Alford's own grammar and usage in his *The Dean's English* of 1865 and *Bad English* of 1867. Gould's contribution was published in 1867 as *Good English: or Popular Errors in Language*, and it shows how conscious the American reading public was becoming of language:

The present age is pre-eminently an age of progress; and, unfortunately, the progress is not limited to "things of good report." Error follows fast upon the footsteps of truth, and sometimes truth is left behind in the race.

For example, the English language, within the last quarter of a century, through the agency of good writers, critics, and lexicographers, has in many respects been greatly improved; but, through the heedlessness of those who should be its conservators, and the recklessness of those who have been, and are, its corruptors, it has deteriorated in other respects in a greater proportion.[11]

Dean Alford was wrong about where the deterioration lay, argued Gould and Moon, but neither argued that it did not exist. In fact, the deterioration of English at the hands of uneducated frontiersmen was what these Easterners excoriated most violently. A linguistic base for class distinctions seems to be the hidden agenda of this debate. Richard Meade Bache put the case most clearly in the preface to his 1869 *Vulgarisms and Other Errors of Speech:*

Many persons, although they have not enjoyed advantages early in life, have, through merit combined with the unrivalled opportunities which this country presents, risen to station in society. Few of them, it must be thought, even if unaware of the extent of their deficiency in knowledge of their language, are so obtuse as not to perceive their deficiency at all, and not to know that it often presents them in an unfavorable light in their association with the more favoured children of fortune. Few, it must be believed, would not from one motive or the other, from desire for knowledge, or from dread of ridicule, gladly avail themselves of opportunities for instruction.[12]

More than any of the other early prescriptive philologists, Bache realized that the changing nature of American society itself was behind the interest in correct speech and writing that sold so many of the nit-picking books of Alford, Moon, and Gould.

The Alford controversy had powerful consequences in an increasingly self-conscious America. As a result of it, William Mathews wrote in 1876, "hundred of persons who before felt a profound indifference to this subject . . . have suddenly found themselves . . . deeply interested in questions of grammar, and now, with their appetites whetted, will continue the study . . ."[13] The 1870s and 1880s saw a spate of non-academic little "manuals of correctness" covering both conversation and writing.[14] The general ethos of these manuals can be summed up by the quote from Swift that Alfred Ayres (Thomas E. Osmun) chose as the epigraph to his *The Verbalist: A Manual*: "As a man is known by his company, so a man's company may be known by his manner of expressing himself." Though we tend today to think of the Gilded Age as a time when wealth, status, and vulgarity combined in an unprecedented way, it was also a time when the concept of "proper society" exerted a powerful conservative influence. Wealth might make vulgarity tolerated, but it could never make *arrivistes* truly acceptable; thus the children of horny-handed "captains of industry" were carefully tutored by hired intellectuals and shipped to Harvard, Yale, and Princeton to be finished off. Propriety—most obviously reflected in a person's way of speaking—was the desire of even the crassest "new money," and true propriety could not be purchased; it had to be learned.

Colleges had always assumed part of that burden of socialization, and during the 1870s they began to react directly to these changing cultural attitudes. This was, of course, a period when American college education was undergoing a number of profound shifts in emphasis. For the first time, the professional aspects of a college education were beginning to rival the social aspects. New sorts of schools were opening, and the older college ideal of classical study and mental discipline was fast retreating as colleges, striving to attract students and meet changing cultural needs, instituted sweeping curricular changes. Their potential clientele, they were discovering, no longer consisted of aspiring lawyers, ministers, and gentlemen; the growth of vocational specialties and of the concept of college as training in social acceptability meant that the purposes behind enrollment were much broader. Students wanted something new after the Civil War, and the colleges scrambled to try to give it to them.[15]

CHANGES IN THE COLLEGE RHETORIC COURSE

It was impossible that the college course in rhetoric and writing should be unaffected by these shifts, and beginning in the 1870s we see the focus of writing instruction in America undergo a radical change. The forty years 1865–1905 were years of wrenching necessity and desperate invention for rhetoric. Like the rest of the traditional college curriculum, rhetorical instruc-

tion was forced to move away from the abstract educational ideal of "mental discipline" and toward more immediate instructional goals.[16] The immediate goals, in this case, came to involve, not more effective written communication, but rather, simple mechanical correctness. Let us examine how this occurred.

First of all, it must be understood that the idea of teaching grammatical or mechanical correctness on the college level does not go farther back than 1870. From the classical period up through 1860 or so, the teaching of rhetoric concentrated on theoretical concerns and contained no mechanical material at all. Usage and style were, of course, major areas of rhetorical consideration, but traditional prescriptive advice in these areas assumed a student able to handle grammatical construction and to produce an acceptable manuscript with complete facility. These were, after all, supposed to be the subjects of students' earlier course, the grammar course taught by the *grammaticus*, or usher, or master in the boys' school. Such elementary skills as handwriting, punctuation, capitalization, and spelling might be critiqued by the professor of rhetoric, but officially they had no place in rhetoric throughout most of history. They were thought to be the domain of pedagogues and pedants; rhetoric was a higher mystery, the domain of dons and professors, and it didn't degrade itself to the level of mere correctness.

In a sense, the history of the college composition course in America is a history of this heretofore "elementary" instruction taking over a commanding place in most teachers' ideas of what rhetoric was. Between 1865 and 1895, such base-level elements of mechanical correctness as grammar, punctuation, spelling, and capitalization, which would never have been found in pre-1850 textbooks, came to usurp much of the time devoted in class to rhetorical instruction and most of the marking of student writing. What came more and more to be taught and enforced was correctness, but as Albert Kitzhaber points out, "the sort of correctness desired was superficial and mechanical."[17] (The very use of the word "correct" changed between 1870 and 1910 from a meaning of "socially acceptable" to one of "formally acceptable.")

We have already examined some of the general causes of this interest in correctness, but for its direct introduction into the rhetoric course we can also identify a proximate cause: in 1874, Harvard University introduced an entrance examination featuring, for the first time, a writing requirement. The reasons for the introduction of this writing requirement were several: a growing awareness of the importance of linguistic class distinctions in the United States; poor showings in written assignments by Harvard undergraduates; a desire to demonstrate that Harvard had the highest standards and deserved its leadership position in American education; a declaration that henceforward writing would be an important element in the college rhetoric course; perhaps a challenge to the academies that supplied the Cambridge institution with raw material.[18] The examination was introduced and given for the first time during the summer of 1874, and, when the English faculty at Harvard received this first test of candidates' writing ability, they were deeply

shocked. The scrawled pages revealed that the graduates of the best academies and preparatory schools in America were writing essays filled with formal and mechanical errors of all sorts. Punctuation, capitalization, spelling, syntax—at every level, error abounded. More than half the students taking these early examinations failed to pass. As Adams S. Hill, who took over the administration of the exam in 1876, put it, "the examination makes a poor showing for the schools that furnish the materials whereof the university which professes to set up the highest standard in America, has to make educated men."[19]

Harvard and other colleges strove mightily to pin the blame for poor freshman writing on the preparatory and secondary schools—where, indeed, much of it did lie—but at the same time, colleges found themselves forced to deal somehow with the results of the poor training they were decrying. The errors students made on their exams were beginning to get a good deal of publicity and were even becoming something of a national scandal.[20] This could not be borne, and the seventies and eighties saw a good deal of pedagogical innovation as teachers engaged in the first great wave of college-level remedial English.

It was quickly obvious to writing teachers that the old abstract rhetoric of Blair, Whately, and Day wouldn't solve the problems uncovered by the Harvard examinations. What good, they asked, did knowledge of tropes or amplification do a student who couldn't spell or punctuate? Beginning in the 1870s, college-level teaching tools of a simpler sort began to appear. New texts were published which contained simple right-wrong sentence exercises as well as theoretical advice, and during the late seventies college texts began for the first time to include sections on such simple formal elements of writing as capitalization and punctuation.[21] All sorts of treatments of materials were tried out by teachers, but the most popular was what came to be known to teachers as "grammar." Uncased from its elementary school framework and its general association with abstract mental discipline, grammar began to be introduced to college students in the 1870s in the hope that somehow a theoretical knowledge of the structure of English would act as a prophylaxis against errors in writing.

Thus was born the soulful trust in the powers of "grammar" that still rules the methods of some instructors today. Teaching abstract grammar didn't work in the 1870s as it doesn't work now; college teachers turned to it out of the idea that somehow students' elementary grammar instruction hadn't "taken," and that it needed to be repeated until it did somehow take hold. This was an *essentially* incorrect idea. As A. S. Hill realized, students wrote poorly because they had never been given any practice in composition during their secondary school careers; vernacular composition wasn't taught in most American high schools until the 1880s. Students failed on the Harvard exams because they had never been asked to do much writing, not because they had failed to grasp their elementary grammar lessons. But once the grammar-based college pedagogy became enshrined in textbooks there was no escaping it, as we shall see.

The Harvard exams seemed to pinpoint mechanical problems as the important troubles of freshmen writers, and it was natural that such exams would tend to make "error-free" writing the central definition of "good" writing in many teachers' minds. This conception quickly gained great power, and after 1885 or so, the very nature of the freshman writing course came to be defined by error avoidance rather than by any sort of genuine communicative success. As Kitzhaber points out, this meant in practice that composition had to be taught as a series of explicable rules, and that the writing desired from students was writing that violated none of these rules.[22] The rhetorical theory developed between 1865 and 1895 above the sentence level—most importantly, the modes, the paragraph structure, static abstractions, and the methods of development—was all an attempt to rule-govern the written product. The heart of the rules orientation, however, always remained in grammatical and mechanical rule-application at the sentence level.

After the mid-eighties, this rule-and-form orientation constituted a sort of "hidden agenda" in college writing courses. Unlike the rhetorical theory of the period, which was all developed in textbooks, we find relatively little textbook evidence of the mechanical-correctness aspects of the composition courses of the eighties and nineties. The correctness emphasis was there—as we know from non-textbook sources—but texts hardly mention it, concerning themselves with paragraphs, modes, abstractions, etc. The fact that college composition was fast becoming error-obsessed was like a shameful secret during this period, mentioned only obliquely. Of the four great rhetorical voices of the *fin de siècle* period, only one—John Genung—ever wrote a college-level textbook dealing with rule-governed formal correctness; what sketchy treatments there were are found in texts by lesser authors. Albert Kitzhaber infers that this lack of textbook treatment of lower-level mechanical questions is a result of the "paragraph boom" of the nineties and of the low opinion of grammar study developing in the elementary education level.[23] He is undoubtedly correct, but there is, I believe, a further reason: college teachers were ashamed to be found professing grammar, punctuation, and lower-level skills (as many were in 1971 during the second great remedial period, and as many still are).

Thus, in spite of growing evidence of the poor writing of college freshmen—especially the evidence presented to the sound of trumpets by the Harvard Reports of the nineties—the most notable college teachers of rhetoric refused to admit publicly that they should deal with the problem, or that they were dealing with it every day. Instead, they constantly cried out for deliverance by some sort of secondary-school *deus ex pedagogia*. E. L. Godkin, one of the Harvard Report authors, was the most outraged spokesman for this Old Guard attitude; throughout the nineties he urged that college teachers be "delivered, in large part at least, from the necessity of teaching the rudiments of the language."[24] Barrett Wendell, that enthusiastic man, dealt not at all with mechanics in his famous textbook *English Composition*, nor did A. S. Hill in his college texts (though he had no aversion to including mechanics in his lower-level texts and in his college-level "adjunct mate-

rials"). John Genung, in spite of having authored the rules-oriented *Outlines of Rhetoric* in 1893, drew the line at teaching sentence mechanics, sneering in 1900 that basic-level punctuation elements "belong to grammar; they are no more a part of rhetoric than is spelling."[25] And Fred N. Scott, the last of Kitzhaber's "Big Four" rhetoricians (and the most perspicacious), rejected mechanical emphases for somewhat higher reasons: "These matters, after all," he wrote, "are subsidiary . . . They are means to an end. To treat them as an end in and for themselves is to turn education in this subject upside down."[26] As a result of these attitudes, we see very little mechanical material in the most popular rhetoric texts of the late nineteenth century.

In this case, however, these major texts are somewhat misleading. The later 1880s and the 1890s were times of extreme changes in the way that writing was taught—changes half-obscured, but no less real for that. The college rhetoric course was being deformed by novel stresses and was quickly generating new tools to try to solve the problems that were arising. We need now to look more closely at some of these problems and at the solutions they engendered.

OVERWORK

First of all, we must understand the most pervasive reality of the rhetoric teachers at nearly all colleges after 1870: gross overwork. We may still have a way to go today before teachers are given realistic teaching loads in composition, but the composition instructors of the nineteenth century faced situations far grimmer. It is difficult for us today to imagine, but the standard practice during the period 1880–1910 was for teachers to be assigned writing courses that were lecture-sized. Most teachers were responsible for teaching between 140 and 200 students. Barrett Wendell at Harvard in 1892 said that he had in his writing class "within one or two of 170 men."[27] This may have been a large class, for Wendell was a popular teacher, but it was by no means extraordinary. (By 1900, Harvard had adopted the policy of hiring non-professorial help to take charge of the freshman course, and there, at least, the average class size dropped to between 60 and 70.)[28] At Yale's Sheffield Scientific School, one professor and one instructor were responsible for 250 students (as well as for three non-freshman courses totaling 306 students).[29] At the University of Iowa, the average class size for freshman and sophomore courses was 80, and again, over 250 students were the responsibility of one professor and one instructor.[30] At Chicago, which prided itself on its small classes, the courses in "required theme writing" averaged over 65 students per class.[31]

These very large lecture-sized sections were the result of some of the rapid changes taking place in American universities. As Lawrence Veysey says, after 1870 three basic types of instruction came to prominence: the laboratory, the lecture, and the seminar.[32] The laboratory, of course, was conceived as a specialized scientific instructional form, and the labor-intensive seminar (or seminary, as it was referred to) was usually reserved for upper-

class and graduate students. This left the lecture-sized section as the form of choice for most freshman and sophomore courses. The large lecture, of course, is a perfectly defensible technique for courses with testable subject-content that might be fashioned into fruitful lecture material. In composition courses, though, its use, though widespread, always presented problems.

Leaving aside the question of the worth of abstract lecture material to the struggling writer, the large class sizes of lecture-organized sections meant two things: first, that the teacher could give little individual attention to students, even if a large course was split into smaller classes; and second, that the number of papers each teacher was expected to read and grade was staggering.

There are few statements extant today recording the effect of having to grade hundreds of papers each week on nineteenth-century teachers, but it must have been exhausting. Most teachers tried to present a "stiff upper lip" about their struggles. Here is Barrett Wendell, who in 1884 pioneered the "daily theme," which spread from trend-setting Harvard to many other schools, on his workload during the 1892–3 school year:

> The daily theme, as it exists at Harvard College, started in one of my courses perhaps eight or nine years ago . . . I introduced in my elective course the practice of requiring from every student a daily theme, which consists of a single page of probably fifty to a hundred words . . . I have at this moment in my class at Harvard College within one or two of 170 men, and they write these themes every day, and it happens this year to be my duty to read those every day and to make some sort of note on them . . . of course, I must do it rather hastily. It is a matter of two or three hours a day.[33]

A little math indicates the extent of Wendell's reading. Assuming a 26-week school year, he read 855 themes weekly, or 22,230 for the year. This was, of course, in addition to Harvard's required fortnightly themes, which were longer and had to be critiqued in more depth. 170 of these every two weeks adds 2,210 additional papers for the year. Even the effervescent Wendell must have been daunted.

The grading load was terribly heavy even at schools that didn't use the daily theme. Fred Newton Scott of the University of Michigan, the greatest rhetorical theorist of the period 1875–1925, was also the most honest and outspoken about the overwork teachers endured:

> . . . I have read and re-read this year something over 3,000 essays, most of them written by a class of 216 students . . . That the instructor should somehow lay hold of the student as an individual is, for successful composition work, simply indispensable . . . But . . . in the larger universities the day of small and cosey classes is long past. Now the hungry generations tread us down. We hardly learn the names and faces of our hundreds of students before they break ranks and go their ways, and then we must resume our Sisyphean labors.[34]

Scott paints a dark picture, but it must be accepted as a true one. The reasons for such conditions are not difficult to infer. Then, as now, teachers of composition were ill-organized and suffered from a code of "professionalism" that frowned upon public complaint about conditions. Many were low in status, unsure about how their courses should be run, unwilling to demand changes in conditions. College administrators, for their part, probably didn't realize that the introductory English course was qualitatively different from the introductory History course; thus both were organized as large lectures. The result, as we have seen, was the destructive overloading of writing teachers. As George R. Carpenter *et al.* put it in 1903, "It is not uncommon for teachers of English . . . who are conducting twenty hours of recitation a week . . . to sit up until twelve o'clock night after night in order to correct the compositions of their pupils."[35] We will never know the degree to which this glut of theme-correcting destroyed rhetoric as a scholarly discipline by driving sensitive scholars into other fields—particularly literature—but it must have been considerable.[36] This situation persisted from around 1880 through the middle part of the 'teens, when conditions slowly began to improve.[37]

REACTIONS TO OVERWORK: ASSIGNMENTS, READING STYLES, AND ADJUNCT TECHNOLOGY

Faced with this gross overwork and with growing social and professional pressure to enforce "the basics," teachers were forced to evolve strategies to protect themselves from insanity and to get on with their work. We are still seeing versions today of the strategies, several in nature, evolved by the writing teachers of the late nineteenth century to cope with those conditions.

First of all, teachers moved quickly to scrap the older abstract paper topics that had been popular between 1800 and 1870, substituting instead simpler assignments that could be scanned quickly for obvious flaws. As Kitzhaber shows, the trend was away from assignments requiring special knowledge, complex conceptualizations, or detailed explanations, and toward essays based on personal experience and observation. In terms of the modal division of discourse then popular, it was a switch from an emphasis on exposition (which was more complex in the nineteenth century than it became in the twentieth) and argument to an emphasis on narration and description. Topics such as "Curiosity" or "The Evanescence of Pleasure" were replaced by "Our Newsboy" and "An Early Morning's Fishing" (and eventually by the notorious "How I Spent My Summer Vacation").[38]

Kitzhaber's contention that this personalization and simplification of theme topics was the result of dissatisfaction with the older abstract topics is certainly true, but he doesn't go into much depth on the reasons for that dissatisfaction. That such topics as "Selfishness" produced bad writing from college freshmen is easy to understand. More important for the current discussion, however, is that such abstract topics produce writing that is *cognitively more demanding and therefore slower to read and grade.* I believe that this is the central reason behind the adoption of narrative and descriptive topics; as

every teacher knows, personal-experience writing is the easiest reading we see. Criteria for judging narratives and simple descriptions are easy to set, paper content often suggests itself, and the organization of such essays is usually simple chronology or spatial reference. Personal-experience papers can be read and evaluated much more quickly and with far fewer difficult judgment calls than the older sort of abstract-analysis papers, and in short, the newer topics took over because grading them was easier work for teachers snowed under by too many themes.

With questions of content and organization radically simplified, the reading and grading of students' papers entered a whole new era. At some point between 1870 and 1900, the act of a teacher reading and commenting on the general communicative success of a piece of student writing—form and content—was succeeded by a simplified concept: the teacher as spotter and corrector of formal errors. Student essays ceased to be "literary efforts" and became instead exhibits of rule-worship, to be examined "with a lawyer's eyes," as Mina Shaughnessy tellingly puts it. Skill in writing, which had traditionally meant the ability to manipulate a complex hierarchy of content-based, organizational, and stylistic goals, came to mean but one thing: error avoidance.

This new emphasis upon mechanical correctness grew out of the "illiteracy" furor we have discussed, but more importantly out of the understandable need of teachers to somehow deal with their huge stacks of student themes. As every writing teacher knows, truly reading a paper—any paper—is mentally demanding and time-consuming. It requires complete attention to all levels of style, form, meaning, full presence of mind. Full editorial reading is tiring and cannot be done efficiently for long stretches of time.

On the other hand, merely scanning a paper for formal and syntactic correctness is a rather mechanical act; with practice it can be done with almost as little concentration as riding a bicycle. Far more students' papers can be passed through such a mechanism in a given period of time than can be passed through a full reading. The writing teachers of the 1880s and 1890s, faced with a reading task that was essentially impossible, were forced to cut their losses as best they could; substituting rapid scanning-for-errors in place of full readings, they came to see this simple correcting procedure as what they were expected to do. Yes, they "read" the 170 themes a day or the 216 themes a week—after a fashion. They "corrected" and graded them, and rationalized this sort of reading by claiming that they were giving students what students really needed most. The work was demanding; it took time; it was onerous—but it was not impossible, as genuine reading would have been. Faced with killing work levels, teachers had to give something up; what went, unfortunately, was rhetoric. Real teacher responses to student papers went the same way as complex and challenging assignments.

With primary teacher attention and nearly all paper correction being devoted to the formal aspects of student writing, it was inevitable that the nature of the college composition course should change. During the eighties and nineties we can see the changes slowly taking place, not so much in textbooks as in adjunct technologies. The mechanical grading and evaluation

that teachers were being forced into invited mechanical support systems, usually in the form of systems of rules to which students could be referred. These systems of mechanical rules were found in two primary sources: as "composition cards" containing abbreviated rules and correction marks, and later, in specialized textbooks. Let us examine both of these developments.

"Correction Cards," or "Theme Cards," printed on heavy stock and given out to students, were first used in high schools in the 1870s, but their use quickly spread to the college level. The most common sort contained short directions on manuscript preparation and a key to the system of correction marks used by the instructor. Many of these systems of marks were based on the one recommended in E. W. Huffcut's 1887 *English in the Preparatory Schools*, but they varied a good deal from school to school. Some sort of card system of this sort was the rule at most colleges by 1890. Adams S. Hill assembled one for sale at Harvard, and many other colleges followed suit. The rules of "grammar" might not be good enough for a place in rhetoric textbooks, but no teacher could do without some means of referring to them. These cards were highly ephemeral and few have survived; the one reprinted here is a high-school card from 1908.[39] (See Figure 1.)

Use of these cards, while better than nothing, presented several problems. First of all, their correction systems were varied and could be confusing to students. More seriously, they couldn't provide enough space for satisfactory explanations of the key correction marks. Teachers clearly felt a need for some sort of bridge between the rhetoric texts—which overwhelmingly rejected syntax, grammar, and form as "baby-work"—and composition cards. Such bridges were slow in appearing. A few rhetorics appeared which contained a page or two of composition-card material, but they were the exception rather than the rule.[40]

THE GENESIS OF THE HANDBOOK

The obvious answer to the problem was a new sort of textbook, one that would explain and exemplify the sorts of rules that teachers were increasingly asking their students to learn and practice, and through the last quarter of the nineteenth century several attempts to find the form for such a book were made, none of them completely successful. The first and most obvious answer to the problem of teaching students "grammar" (which by 1885 was a sort of catch-all term used by English teachers to mean formal correctness of all kinds) was merely to update the grammar rules taught by elementary schools. This was done by Alonzo Reed and Brainerd Kellogg in their 1877 high school text, *Higher Lessons in English*, and on the college level by Joseph Gilmore in his 1875 text *Outlines of the Art of Expression*, which used a sort of Baltimore Catechism question-and-answer method to inculcate grammatical rules. The book grew, said Gilmore, "in the author's class-room, out of an attempt to supplement the defective early training of his pupils." Gilmore used an expansive definition of grammar: "Grammar," he said, "may be defined as the art of correctly expressing our thoughts. It lays the foundation for

FIGURE 1   A Typical "Correction Card" from the Early Twentieth Century

Only Connect

"AIM AT UNITY OF THOUGHT AND VARIETY
OF STATEMENT." —Dr. F. N. Scott

. . . .	I. Manuscript	a Legible	1 Letters 2 Spacing 3 i's and t's
. . . .		b Capitals c Hyphens	
. . . .		d Italics e Quotation marks	
. . . .		f Punctuation	1 Comma 2 Semicolon 3 Colon
. . . .			4 Period
. . . .			5 Question mark
. . . .	II. Words	a Formation b Good use	1 Verb 2 Possessive
. . . .			3 Spelling
. . . .		c Precision d Simplicity	
. . . .		e Brevity f Variety	
. . . .	III. Sentences	a Correctness	1 Complete 2 Subject and verb 3 Participle and noun 4 Pronoun and antecedent
. . . .			5 Case 6 Shall, Should 7 Infinitive
. . . .		b Unity	
. . . .		c Mass	1 Beginning 2 End
. . . .		d Coherence	1 Order of words 2 Parallel construction 3 Precise conjunction
. . . .		e Variety	1 Periodic and loose 2 Long and short
. . . .	IV. Paragraphs	a Unity	1 Topic Sentence 2 Length moderate
. . . .		b Mass	1 Beginning 2 End 3 Proportion
. . . .		c Coherence	1 Order of sentences 2 Parallel construction 3 Precise conjunction
. . . .			4 Tenses
. . . .	V. Theme	a Unity	Summary in one paragraph
. . . .		b Mass	1 Beginning 2 End 3 Proportion
. . . .		c Coherence	Order of paragraphs

Based on Barrett Wendell's ENGLISH COMPOSITION

rhetoric, which superinduces, upon mere *correctness* of expression, Clearness, Energy, and Elegance . . ."[41] Gilmore went on to deal in such questions as "Define a simple sentence and an act of thought," and "Give the exceptions to the general rules for forming the plurals of English nouns."

Gilmore's book had some initial popularity, but this question-answer format was by necessity abstract and hard to use as a reference. Much more popular than Gilmore's approach was the "rules" approach taken by Edwin A. Abbott in his 1874 manual *How To Write Clearly: Rules and Exercises*. This book, which went through 25 printings between 1874 and 1914, is the earliest recognizable prototype for all the "handbooks of composition" that came after it. "Almost every English boy can be taught to write clearly," said Abbott, "so far at least as clearness depends upon the arrangement of words . . . Clear writing can be reduced to rules."[42] *How To Write Clearly* contains 56 rules, most of them dealing with sentence construction and style, many of them similar to certain of today's handbook prescriptions. Unlike Gilmore's question-answers, Abbott expressed his rules in positive commandments followed by exemplifications: "32. In a long conditional sentence put the 'if-clause' antecedent, or protasis, first," and "41. Antithesis adds force, and often clearness." Abbott covered few questions of usage, no spelling or punctuation, very little basic syntax or grammar; and yet it was in print for over 40 years. Harvard required students to purchase the book through the 1880s, and it also seems to have been required at different times by Oberlin and the Universities of Pennsylvania, Virginia, Michigan, and Colorado.[43] As early as 1880, teachers were casting about for convenient systems of enforceable reference rules.

What is most surprising about Abbott is not that it was fairly popular, but that it wasn't more widely copied. A few texts appeared during the eighties that treated of mechanics—punctuation, usage, etc.—but no American authors seemed willing to write an Abbott-style rulebook treating all of the questions of mechanics. In 1893, John Genung published his *Outlines of Rhetoric*, which was organized according to rules but which is more accurately seen as the first college-level Basic Writing text than as a book in the reference mode. Genung's attitude toward basic-level instruction in the elements of correctness was paradoxical; he was the only one of the "Big Four" to write anything like a remedial-English college text, yet he didn't seem proud of his chosen task: "(Rhetoric) has as its lower and elementary stages, comprising the procedures that lie at the foundation of all composition, things which it is not so much an honor to know as a reproach not to know; these are what the present treatise is mainly concerned with . . ."[44] Genung proposed that these basic areas could be reduced to 73 rules, based on Usage, Phraseology, and Style, which he numbered consecutively and printed as side-headings throughout the text; a digest of them was printed at the end of the book "to facilitate the correction of the student's written work." "By simply writing the number of the rule in the margin of the student's paper," wrote Genung, "the teacher can call his attention to the error involved."

Outlines was another popular success for Genung, who was one of the first English authors to make textbooks financially rewarding, and it remained in use until at least 1915. As mentioned earlier, however, it started no trends, and the influential textbooks of the time remained set against treatments of basic mechanical material. The authors of the eighties and nineties were the last composition teachers trained in the remnants of the great tradition of rhetoric, and they would not recant their beliefs that rhetoric involved higher mysteries than grammatical correctness.

The day of the rhetoricians, however, was passing, and the day of the composition pedagogues was dawning. The spirit of questing experimentation that had fueled composition in the nineties failed after 1900, and as the torch of rhetorical theory guttered, the practical problems of classroom pedagogy came to the fore. By 1905, Hill, Genung, and Endell had all but retired from teaching and writing about composition, and the few rhetorical theorists still active at that time—mainly F. N. Scott and his disciples—were increasingly voices crying in the wilderness. Textbooks at this time became predictable and derivative, unwilling to experiment with new treatments. Materials on mechanical correctness bloomed, and in 1907 there appeared a new sort of text-book, the logical culmination of the move toward rule-governed composition that had been going on since 1875: the modern handbook of composition.[45]

The first handbook was Edwin C. Woolley's *Handbook of Composition: A Compendium of Rules.* Woolley provided in a primitive form nearly all of the elements that make up today's handbooks: it dealt with punctuation, spelling, legibility, sentence structure. The *Handbook* saw no element of writing as beneath its scope; it had no rhetorical pretensions. Woolley himself argued the case for his handbook most succinctly in his 1909 *Mechanics of Writing:*

> The chief benefit derived from theme-writing lies probably in the instructor's indication of errors in the themes and his showing how these errors are to be corrected . . . But . . . how shall the instructor, as he indicates these eight hundred errors (in the fifty themes he must hand back the next day), furnish the information called for by each one? Obviously he must use some kind of shorthand. Suppose, then, that he writes opposite the incorrect "whom" above quoted the expression "Gr." or "b.E." or "case." Do these expressions furnish the student with the information he needs regarding that "whom"? It seems to me that they do not . . .
>
> Yet shorthand must be used in correcting themes. Is there no system of shorthand which conveys to the student the information he should have regarding each error marked in this themes? There is such a system; it consists of references to a book . . . The *Handbook* was designed, and the present book has been designed, to be used in this way.[46]

This was Woolley's credo. And how did teachers react to this new sort of text? With overwhelming approbation. In a representative review in 1909, H. E. Coblentz spoke for most of the college teachers of the day: "This little

book deserves the utmost praise ... Every teacher of English will find this the handiest book of its kind."[47] At last the cat was out of the bag, and teachers of writing no longer tried to hide the primarily mechanical nature of their readings.

With the *Handbook*, Woolley began what would later be referred to as "the Woolley family" of handbooks, a family still represented by the collateral descendant of the 1907 *Handbook*, today's *Heath Handbook*, 10th edition. He also began the handbook era, initiating a new sort of writing text that would quickly come to be at the heart of most college writing courses. Since the first Woolley *Handbook*, composition pedagogy has been transformed. Needs had shaped the texts, and now the texts shaped the writing courses; this was especially true of handbooks, which were always the favorite texts of untrained writing teachers and thus exerted a great, although often hidden, influence.

The twenty years following the Woolley *Handbook* might be called the Great Handbook Boom. Between 1907 and 1927 at least fifteen different handbooks were published.[48] As important as the numbers of handbooks, however, were the changes the handbook form was causing in the rhetoric texts of the period and the broadening of the purposes of the handbooks themselves. Beginning around 1910 we see the rapid crumbling of rhetoric texts' authors' unwillingness to include mechanical-correctness materials in their books. Clippinger's *Illustrated Lessons*, Foerster and Steadman's *Sentences and Thinking*, Young and Young's *Freshman English* all reflected a novel handbook-oriented emphasis on lower-level elements of mechanical correctness: punctuation, spelling, grammar. Clippinger in 1912 actually included a separate handbook section in his rhetoric—probably the first such conjunction. During this period the last vestiges of the old abstract-theory tradition in composition died out, and with it died any sense of professional history. By 1925 most of the great nineteenth-century rhetorical theorists had been forgotten, and their doctrines were assumed to have always existed. In the hands of overworked part-timers and graduate students, Freshman English entered its Dark Ages: unenlightened toil, a benighted processing of students through the obstacle course of mechanical correctness.

In "Handbooks: History of a Genre" I have discussed how Woolley's home-reference handbook grew first into a book of rules and exercises and then into a full-scale textbook meant for use both at home and in class: the rhetoric-handbook. Woolley and Scott's *College Handbook of Composition* in 1928 marked the beginning of this phase of textbook development, a phase which effactually meant that the mechanical organization and algorithmic rule-governed approach of the handbook extended themselves into all aspects of rhetoric. The predictable result was that the derivative rhetorical theory of the period became even more debased, even more removed from the actual process of communication. Handbook rhetoric was always the most reductive form of current-traditional dogma, and by the 1920s there was little rhetorical theory not influenced by handbook approaches. Fewer and fewer rhetoric texts were found that didn't incorporate a handbook or rules-type section, and after 1925

or so it seemed a tacit assumption that the average composition course was an essentially remedial endeavor. As John French said in his book *Writing* in 1924: "This book attempts to supply in one volume material adequate for such a course in English Composition as includes the review of elementary principles and the *anticipation* of mature studies in English and other subjects. Consequently it gives much space to rules for correctness."[49] For the freshman of 1924, mature writing was something only anticipated.

Bereft of a theoretical discipline and a professional tradition, teachers during this period had nothing to turn to for information about their subject—except their textbooks. It is during the first two decades of this century that we first see the pattern of writing teachers as the only college-level instructors who know no more of their discipline than is contained in the texts they assign their students—a sad pattern that still, alas, continues today at too many schools. And when we examine the books these teachers of the 1920s depended upon, it is not difficult to see why I. A. Richards called rhetoric "the dreariest part of the waste the unfortunate travel through" during their first year of college. Quite literally, after 1925, handbooks and handbook-rhetorics were in control of composition classes. A survey taken in 1927 showed that of 27 representative colleges in the Midwest, 85% used handbooks in their writing courses—and more importantly, 41% used no texts *but* handbooks.[50] Rhetoric had truly been transmogrified into the dread discipline of "Freshman English."

REMEDIAL TECHNOLOGY

If the period 1875–1900 nurtured the elements leading to an obsession with mechanical correctness and the period 1900–1925 turned composition from a subject (distantly) concerned with communication into an error hunt, the period following 1925 was what might be called the remedial-technology era. It was a time when composition teachers, at their nadir in terms of experience and interest, were lured farther and farther into mechanism by ever-more-sophisticated "classroom aids" put out by textbook firms. Handbooks became the central reference point for teachers who had never studied any rhetorical theory (and no teacher English-trained could have been taught rhetoric between 1915 and 1950); even those whose training in critical reading made them sensitive readers of student writing were too overworked to bring useful criticism to bear on the papers they graded, and these teachers did what they could: they enforced correctness and made it the heart of their demands.

We cannot overestimate the effect of textbooks on the teaching and paper-grading done during this period; it was everything. Especially influential were the handbooks, which after 1930 assumed a larger and larger place in the pedagogical scene and eventually became the single most important element of stability in the entire composition course. Writing in 1941, James McCrimmon identified the reasons behind the growth of popularity of handbooks: their role in transmitting values. "Instructors," said McCrimmon, "not only consult the handbook they are using, they are likely to con it, get it by heart, pledge indiscriminate devotion to it. Herein lies its power . . . for the

English handbook is often the teacher's teacher." Since most composition teachers were untrained graduate students without experience, McCrimmon stated, they have no idea what besides the handbook to teach:

> Little wonder that in such a sea of confusion he (the teacher) clings to his handbook as a shipwrecked sailor clings to his raft, and by an interesting human weakness, soon comes to believe that these rules, which only yesterday were unknown to him, are the sole criteria of good writing.[51]

Forty-three years later, the phenomenon remarked by McCrimmon is still with us.

Handbooks arrived and proliferated because they were tools for the task of enforcing correctness. Their main purpose, in theory at least, was as support systems for instruction that was still supposed to be rhetorical: student essays read by the teacher. Following closely behind handbooks, however, were their dark siblings: drillbooks and workbooks, which introduced completely a-rhetorical practice in error recognition and sentence construction into the college writing course. Beginning in the mid-twenties and becoming a thriving industry by 1935, the "remedial racket," as Porter Perrin called it, introduced high school–level exercises in grammar, punctuation, and usage into college classrooms. Such books as Howard Grose's *Exercises in Everyday Writing*, Dana Jensen's *Corrective English Exercises*, and Easley Jones's *Practical English Drillbook* were selling well by the mid-thirties, and college composition was close to its most mechanistic point. Perrin's voice was one of the few raised in protest against the workbook approach:

> These exercises obviously violate the lone principle that present teachers of composition have salvaged from the 2500 years of the discipline of rhetoric, that one learns to speak and write by speaking and writing. . . . Why do we adopt them? Well, they're easy to handle: like every popular "advance" in pedagogical method, they are ultimately easier for the teacher. . . . We find a comforting certainty in grading exercises in the most elementary conventions of the language that is a great relief in a field where so little is certain, where the real work is eliciting variables in a growth. We may realize that these absolutely certain elements are few and are the least, or at any rate the lowest, factors in style. But we cannot help breathing more freely as we pass from the sand of better-or-worse to the pavement of supposed right-or-wrong.[52]

Perrin could certainly understand the weakness that made teachers turn to drillbooks, but he could not condone it. His was the first voice in a rising chorus of criticism of the status quo in college composition that began in the 1930s.

The Loyal Opposition

It was during this decade that we see the beginnings of the curious schizophrenia that has afflicted college composition since: the split between the scholars and theoreticians of the discipline and the great mass of classroom

teachers. The descent into mechanism that occurred in the thirties was a result of the beliefs and activities of the latter group, but we must note that it took place against a background of serious and capable research and even protest from the former. Scholars of language began during this decade to bring together some of the research that had been ongoing since the teens; studies of errors in writing, of remedial techniques, of the efficacy of grammar drill were all scrutinized, and all of them pointed to the conclusion that the popular sorts of classroom grammar drills were essentially futile as attempts to improve student writing.[53] Sterling Leonard's pioneering study, *Current English Usage*, appeared in 1932, striking a powerful blow against the prescriptive-usage doctrines that were part of the mechanical-correctness tradition. The NCTE, which had existed since 1911, truly found its voice during the 1930s and began to declaim a Deweyite gospel of education for social goals, "tying up literature and composition with the business of living."[54] These pragmatic goals usually meant that the organization worked against sterile drills and mechanistic pedagogies. In sum, a motley crowd of linguists, educationists, and rhetoricians began to coalesce during the thirties and to struggle against the overwhelmingly mechanical classroom methods of the time.

It looked at first to be a futile battle. The forces of overwork and professionally-countenanced ignorance were very great. Handbooks, workbooks, drillbooks appeared in larger numbers each year, continuing the feedback loop of mechanical criteria as the only valid criteria of good writing. But the seeds of dissent had been planted, and through the forties and fifties the anti-mechanical reaction to the standard composition course began to grow strong in the profession of English. Rhetoric, which had been dormant within composition since the 1890s, began to make a reappearance after 1944, when the first communications courses were taught at the University of Iowa. Communications courses quickly spread to other schools, bringing together scholars from English and Speech departments for the first time since the tragic split between the disciplines that occurred in 1914, teaching all four of the "communications skills"—reading, writing, speaking, and listening. Rhetoric, which had been in the keeping of Speech departments during the twentieth century, was a vital part of these courses, and many English teachers learned for the first time what some of the alternatives to mechanical correctness might be.

This reintroduction of rhetoric into composition was to prove extremely vivifying. The idea of successful communication and not mere grammatical correctness as the central aim of writing was novel and exciting to English scholars, who once again began to investigate the great traditions of rhetoric; the newly-formed Conference on College Composition and Communication became the professional vehicle for this movement away from composition-as-grammar. It was inevitable that large parts of this emergency scholarship would involve intense self-criticism by English teachers, and indeed, beginning around the late forties, we do hear voices raised in plaintive criticism of the methods of brother teachers both past and present. Porter Perrin, who

had been a soldier in the rhetorical trenches for over twenty years, spoke in 1951 of the years 1900–1935 as "a conspicuously narrow era of instruction" which showed "a general surrender of the broad aims that have made the study (of rhetoric) great to a concentration on minutiae of usage (actually a triumph of grammar over rhetoric)."[55]

By this time, however, Perrin's voice was not the only one being raised in criticism of the mechanical-correctness emphasis in writing instruction. Others were coming to the realization that student disgust for the writing course was no irrational response. Ruth Davies in 1950 wrote that "many teachers of freshman English waste much of their energy trying to enforce rules and standards universally ignored . . . While we are engrossed with the scrawny skin and brittle bones of composition, the flesh and blood and heart of the matter are almost forgotten."[56] Jacques Barzun struck out at the hypocrisy of educational systems that claimed to be "progressive" and eschew narrow insistence on formal correctness—but continue to enforce it:

> I know very well that correctness was supposedly given up long ago. The modern teacher does not mention it. But if the teacher marks spelling and grammatical errors and speaks of little else, what is a child to think? . . . Meanwhile the things that are teachable, the ways of translating the flashes of thought into consecutive sentences, are neglected.[57]

And Barriss Mills, in his seminal "Writing as Process" of 1953, strongly condemned the "police-force concept of usage" that still prevailed in most classrooms. 'Nothing is more blighting," wrote Mills, "to natural and functional written communication than an excessive zeal for purity of usage in mechanics."[58]

All of this criticism of the traditional mechanical priorities appeared during the late forties and early fifties in what can only be called a spontaneous reaction to a notably deficient pedagogical paradigm, a revolt against the current-traditional methods of teaching and thinking about composition that took its impetus from the rediscovery of rhetorical issues as they applied to writing. From its beginning in the late 1940s, this revolt gathered strength during the fifties and suddenly burst into full flower during the early sixties. Suddenly theorists and teachers everywhere were actively—and sometimes heatedly—discussing the purposes and methods of teaching composition, and the reign of mechanical correctness, which had largely depended on continued teacher ignorance, was being threatened.

I need not, I think, rehearse here the disputes of the last two decades over such issues as formal marking, theme correction, the nature of revision, the teaching of grammar. These debates can all be viewed as the mechanical correctness tradition defending itself against attacks made in the name of rhetorical priority. On the one hand are the theorists, the rhetoricians, the proponents of writing as discovery or communication; on the other are the traditionalists, the front-line teachers, the proponents of writing as vocational skill. Both sides make valid points, and if the rhetoricians often get the best of the abstract arguments, the traditionalists can still point to savage overwork

as an occupational reality for many writing teachers—a reality that makes real rhetorical instruction difficult or impossible. A teacher with 100 papers to grade in a weekend, say the traditionalists, cannot possibly respond effectively to each one as communication—and they are right.

There is no doubt that the composition-as-mechanical-correctness tradition has suffered serious setbacks during the last thirty years, but it is not a tradition that can be overcome so long as administrative priorities overwork undertrained teachers. There are still too many "four and four" teaching assignments, and such cynical exploitation of the victims of the depressed academic marketplace only creates grist for the mills of mechanism. Of the making of handbooks there is no end—and too many teachers are still given no training beyond their Harbrace charts. Overwork and ignorance have ever been the parents of destructive overemphasis on mechanical correctness, and these are not conditions we can get rid of easily.

We can, however, rejoice in the gains we have made. At last the reductive traditions of the first half of the century are being questioned and challenged. Teachers are better trained every year. Newer textbooks are providing even traditionally-oriented teachers with more defensible course content than the "shall-will" rules. Administrators have gradually been made to understand that 40 students are too many for one class, and most now accept 30 as too many. We may eventually be able to convince them that 25 are too many as well, and that four writing courses per term is too heavy a load for any teacher. We have made strides, and more will be made.

The enforcement of standards of mechanical correctness is not a tradition that can—or should—die out of composition instruction. Mechanical errors, as Mina Shaughnessy says, are "unprofitable intrusions upon the consciousness of the reader" which "demand energy without giving any return in meaning," and helping students overcome their own unintentional sabotage of the process of communicating their thoughts is certainly an important part of our work. But it is not all of our work. Striking a balance between formal and rhetorical considerations is the problem we now face, and it is a delicate one. We cannot escape the fact that in a written text any question of mechanics is also a rhetorical question, and as a discipline we are still trying to understand the meaning of that conjunction. We may spend the rest of our professional lives investigating how the balance between rhetoric and mechanics can best be struck—a difficult question, but one heartening to see asked, for the fact that we are confronting such questions shows that composition studies is once again a genuine discipline and no longer a purblind drifting on the current of unexamined tradition.

NOTES

1. Tewksbury lists 54 American colleges extant in 1831; this was just prior to the great Protestant college-building boom of the period 1830–1850. See Donald G. Tewksbury, *The Founding of American Colleges and Universities Before the Civil War* (New York: Teachers' College, Columbia University, 1932), pp. 32–54.

2. Alexis de Tocqueville, *Democracy in America*, trans. George Lawrence (Garden City, NY: Doubleday, 1969), p. 55.

3. Tocqueville, *Democracy in America*, p. 480.

4. It is no accident that around this time we also see the beginnings of dialect humor in the Sam Slick books, the writings of Artemus Ward, etc.

5. Rollo LaVerne Lyman, *English Grammar in American Schools Before 1850* (Washington, D.C.: Government Printing Office, 1922), p. 5. As Lyman shows, the period 1820–1850 saw the largest number of new grammar texts appear. Numbers are: 1811–1820—41 texts; 1821–1830—84; 1831–1840—63; 1841–1850—66. (Lyman, p. 80)

6. Edward Finegan, *Attitudes Toward English Usage: The History of a War of Words* (New York; Teachers' College Press, 1980), pp. 47–54. Another well-written source on certain nineteenth-century language phenomena is Dennis E. Baron, *Grammar and Good Taste: Reforming the American Language* (New Haven: Yale University Press, 1982). Baron concentrates more on linguistic protest and reform movements, Finegan more on the history of usage debates. Both perspectives are useful to anyone studying the development of composition in America.

7. Andrew Peabody, *Conversation, Its Faults and Its Graces* (Boston: Shepard and Lee, 1867), pp. 10–11.

8. Seth T. Hurd, *A Grammatical Corrector* (Philadelphia: E. H. Butler and Co., 1847), p. v.

9. Alford was actually anti-Union (he was an open Confederate sympathizer like many Britons), but he extended his critique to all Americans.

10. Henry Alford, *A Plea for the Queen's English* (London: Alexander Strahan, 1864), pp. 5–6.

11. Edward S. Gould, *Good English: or Popular Errors in Language* (New York: W. J. Widdleton, 1867), p. 1.

12. Richard Meade Bache, *Vulgarisms and Other Errors of Speech* (Philadelphia: Claxton, Remsen, and Haffelfinger, 1869), Preface.

13. William Mathews, *Words: Their Use and Abuse* (Chicago: S. C. Griggs, 1876), p. 5.

14. See, for instance, Alfred Ayres (Thomas E. Osmun), *The Verbalist: A Manual* (New York: D. Appleton, 1881), and the Sheperd and Lee series of social-language handbooks, including Samuel Fallows' *Discriminate!* of 1885 and Harlan H. Ballard's *Handbook of Blunders* of the same year. Probably the longest-lived of these handbooks of linguistic *arrivisme* was Oliver Bell Bunce's classic *Don't* (New York: D. Appleton), which appeared in 1883 and was last reprinted in 1921.

15. A good overview of this period is found in Frederick Rudolph, *The American College and University: A History* (New York: Knopf, 1962).

16. For information on this movement, see Lawrence R. Veysey, *The Emergence of the American University* (Chicago: University of Chicago Press, 1965), pp. 1–20, 57–118.

17. Albert R. Kitzhaber, *Rhetoric in American Colleges 1850–1900* (Dissertation, University of Washington, 1953), p. 312.

18. The only dependable information we have on the introduction of this examination seems to be in A. S. Hill's essay "An Answer to the Cry for More English," and Hill was not even on the Harvard faculty when the exam was first introduced in 1874. (He took it over two years later.) The essay is found in *Twenty Years of School and College English* (Cambridge: Harvard University Press, 1896).

19. A. S. Hill, "An Answer to the Cry for More English," p. 11.

20. They were even provoking scornful laughter from the general public. See Caroline B. Le Row, *English As She Is Taught: Genuine Answers to Examination Questions in our Public Schools* (New York: Cassell, 1887), which prints funny examples of student writing. Example: a definition of "mertia" as "the negative quality of passiveness

either in recoverable latency or incipient latescence." The beginning of a long tradition of rather cruel humor.

21. See, for instance, Henry Jameson, *Rhetorical Method* (St. Louis: G. I. Jones & Co., 1879), and Henry Coppens, *A Practical Introduction to English Rhetoric: Precepts and Exercises* (New York: Catholic School Book Co., 1880).

22. Kitzhaber, *Rhetoric in American Colleges,* p. 319.

23. Kitzhaber, p. 306.

24. E. L. Godkin, "The Illiteracy of American Boys," *Educational Review* 8 (1897), 7.

25. John F. Genung, *The Working Principles of Rhetoric* (Boston: Ginn and Co., 1900), p. 128n.

26. Fred Newton Scott, "What the West Wants in Preparatory English," *School Review* 17 (1909), 19.

27. Barrett Wendell, "English Work in the Secondary Schools," *School Review* 1 (1893), 659–660.

28. C. T. Copeland and H. M. Rideout, *Freshman English and Theme-Correcting in Harvard College* (New York: Silver, Burdett, 1901), p. 1.

29. William Morton Payne, ed., *English in American Universities* (Boston: D. C. Heath, 1895), p. 30.

30. Payne, *English in American Universities,* p. 83.

31. Payne, p. 86.

32. Veysey, *The Emergence of the American University,* p. 153.

33. Wendell, "English Work in the Secondary Schools," pp. 659–660.

34. Fred Newton Scott, in Payne, *English in American Universities,* pp. 121–122.

35. George R. Carpenter, Franklin T. Baker, and Fred N. Scott, *The Teaching of English in the Elementary and Secondary School* (New York: Longmans, Green, 1903), p. 329.

36. This is illustrated by "a private letter by a teacher in an Eastern University" quoted in Carpenter *et al.* in which the anonymous author says, "I have never done any rhetorical work at_____ except in connection with my courses in literature, and I thank God I have been delivered from the bondage of theme-work into the glorious liberty of literature" (p. 329n).

37. It was early obvious that the lecture-sized class was the wrong sort of setting for composition, but nineteenth-century administrators, as many today still do, turned their backs on the obvious evidence of overwork and meditated instead on the bottom line. Seminar-type writing courses seem never to have been considered, but some schools were wealthy enough or had prestigious enough faculty members so that their writing courses were taught as "laboratory" courses. John Genung at Amherst led this movement most obviously. These first lab-type courses were not much different from regular classes except in their numbers—Henry Frink, the freshman teacher at Amherst, had five assistants for a class of 110 students—but numbers were so important that a movement in favor of composition as "laboratory work" became very vocal and had by 1900 gained some power. If composition is truly laboratory work, said Fred Scott in 1895, "why should it not be placed on the same footing as other laboratory work as regards manning and equipment?"

Such support, despite outcries from teachers, was not rapidly forthcoming. In 1911, the NEA and NCTE organized a committee to investigate the labor involved in composition teaching. Edwin M. Hopkins, chair of this committee, said in his first report that "composition teaching has been described as a 'laboratory subject' for a fairly long time," but that adequate conditions had never been provided for such teaching and only existed, when they did, as "the result of a fortunate chance." The Hopkins Committee Report, issued in 1912, put their findings bluntly:

> Under present average conditions, English teachers are assigned more than twice as much work as they can do. Some of them try to do it by working more than

twice as much as other teachers do. This is wrong, because it disables them. Others do only what they reasonably can and let the rest go. This is wrong in another way, because it is an injustice to the pupil and a waste of his time . . . Under present average conditions of teaching English expression, workmen must choose between overwork and bad work; between spoiling their material or killing themselves. . . . (Edwin M. Hopkins, "The Labor and Cost of Composition Teaching: The Present Conditions," *Proceedings of the NEA* 50 [1912], 750.)

This report was the first shot in an NCTE campaign to lower class size in writing courses, a campaign that has lasted into our time. Conditions did improve during the twenties and thirties; by that time, however, teachers had been set in pedagogies shaped by the bad old days.

38. See Kitzhaber's discussion of this change in *Rhetoric in American Colleges*, pp. 169–177.

39. This correction card is reprinted from M. Atkinson Williams, *Report on the Teaching of English in the United States* (London: Swan Sonnenschein and Co., 1908). Williams, a young Englishwoman touring the schools and colleges of the U.S. in order to report on their methods to her fellow Britons, says about the use of these cards, "I wish I could be sure that the pupils made as much use of them as the teachers" (p. 52)

40. See, for instance, William Williams, *Composition and Rhetoric by Practice* (Boston: D. C. Heath & Co., 1890) and Edward R. Shaw, *English Composition by Practice* (New York: Henry Holt & Co., 1892).

41. Joseph H. Gilmore, *Outlines of the Art of Expression* (Boston: Ginn Bros., 1876), p. 5.

42. Edwin A. Abbott, *How To Write Clearly: Rules and Exercises on English Composition* (Boston: Roberts Bros., 1874), p. 5.

43. This is an extrapolation from data in the *National Union Catalog*.

44. John F. Genung, *Outlines of Rhetoric* (Boston: Ginn & Co., 1893), pp. 3–4.

45. See my essay-bibliography "Handbooks: History of a Genre" (forthcoming, I hope) for more detailed information on this extremely important textbook form.

46. Edwin C. Woolley, *The Mechanics of Writing* (Boston: D. C. Heath, 1909), pp. vi–viii.

47. H. E. Coblentz, review of Edwin C. Woolley, *Handbook of Composition, School Review* 17 (1909), 581.

48. See the bibliography at the end of "Handbooks" for the authors, titles, and dates of these handbooks.

49. John C. French, *Writing: A Textbook of Structure, Style, and Usage* (New York: Harcourt, Brace & Co., 1924), p. v. Italics are mine.

50. Ralph L. Henry, "Freshman English in the Middle West," *English Journal* 17 (1928), 302–304.

51. James M. McCrimmon, "The Importance of the Right Handbook," *College English* 3 (1941), 70–71.

52. Porter G. Perrin, "The Remedial Racket," *English Journal* 22 (1933), 384–388.

53. See, for instance, Roy Ivan Johnson, "Persistency of Error in English Composition," *School Review* 25 (1917), 555–580, and William Asker, "Does Knowledge of Formal Grammar Function?" *School and Society* 17 (1923), 109–111.

54. Stella C. Center, "The Liberalism of the NCTE," *Education* 53 (1932), 164.

55. Porter G. Perrin, "A Professional Attitude for Teachers of Communication," *Education* 72 (1951), 488.

56. Ruth Davies, "A Defense of Freshmen," *College English* 12 (1950), 442.

57. Jacques Barzun, "English As She's Not Taught," *Atlantic Monthly* (December, 1953), pp. 28–29.

58. Barriss Mills, "Writing as Process," *College English* 15 (1953), 21.

Textbooks and the Evolution of the Discipline

In "Textbooks and the Evolution of the Discipline," published in *College Composition and Communication* in 1986, Bob looks at what he—with typical wit and elegance—terms "the intricate quadrille that textbooks have danced with the teaching of writing in America" (100). After identifying the factors that fueled the development of composition textbooks in the nineteenth century—"a paucity of new rhetorical material [. . .] the weakness and ignorance of undertrained teachers [. . . . and] the increasing power of a newly technologized publishing industry" (105)—Bob traces the development of textbooks until the present day. He concludes by noting the extent to which the textbook industry and professional associations have offered competing visions of, and suggested practices for, the teaching of writing. As is often the case in Bob's writing, his narrative relies strongly on dualisms. Bob characterizes "[t]he history of research on writing and composition teaching from the 1940's through the present," for instance, as a "history of epistemological warfare, of progressive theoretical and empirical research struggling with entrenched traditional pedagogy" (112). But even as he does so, he persistently reminds readers that material conditions—particularly "the changing qualifications of the teachers in the composition classrooms" (113)—are at the heart of developments in the field.

The way out does not lie in tools but in sheer teaching.
—PORTER PERRIN, 1933

T he last twenty-five years have seen an unprecedented surge in the scholarship surrounding writing and the teaching of writing. We are in the midst of an information boom, and for those of us

---

From *College Composition and Communication* 37.2 (1986): 178–94.

whose professional views have been developed and shaped by reading scholarly journals it is difficult to imagine things any other way. But today's discipline of composition studies is really a very new one. Before 1930, the teaching of rhetoric and writing in American colleges went forward with no important influence from journals at all. During the eighteenth, nineteenth, and early twentieth centuries, composition theory and pedagogy were overwhelmingly shaped by one great force: textbooks. The course we have inherited today owes much to the forms and genres of textbooks that rhetoric spun off as it devolved after 1860 from a theoretical to a practical pedagogy. In this essay I want to examine the intricate quadrille that textbooks have danced with the teaching of writing in America. Such an examination will show that composition textbooks as they developed between 1820 and the present have always responded to the preferences of the teachers cast up by the culture, meeting their perceived needs and recreating these and other needs in later teachers shaped by the texts.

What, first of all, *is* a composition textbook? We cannot, I think, define it as any book used in any way in a rhetoric or composition course, because books of countless unrelated sorts have been dragged into writing classes over the years, as Albert Kitzhaber has shown.[1] Even books that are specifically rhetorical are not always texts, since not every rhetorical book was written to structure a pedagogy in writing. Rhetoric books before 1800 were treatises, not textbooks. American composition grew from rhetoric, and although composition theory is not rhetorical theory, many of the formal elements of composition texts are essentially those of the rhetorics that preceded them.

The tradition of books about rhetorical techniques from Aristotle through Campbell, Blair, and Whately was an *ex post facto* descriptive tradition;[2] that is, most manuals of rhetoric made it their business to describe what works in persuasive discourse and to analyze why it works. They did this by creating abstract categories, generalizations, taxonomies, rules. Indeed, rhetoric as it exists in books has always been primarily a theoretical and only secondarily a pedagogical discipline. Writing is a technology for extending and storing thought, and printed books are nonpareil at one thing: containing complex information that cannot be easily committed to memory. Thus, the reader of a rhetoric treatise or book of lectures has one central task: mastering the information. The book is the teacher, and no other teacher is really needed. Such books were reference sources rather than directly pedagogical materials for most courses.

This pattern of the rhetoric as reference book is followed up through the end of the eighteenth century and into the early nineteenth. Thus we see the popularity of the works of Campbell, Blair, Whately, Priestly, Witherspoon, and Lawson, all of which are either lectures or analytical treatises. During the early and mid-nineteenth century, however, the patterns of influence in rhetoric slowly began to change; fewer and fewer theoretical writers were turning to the synthesis of classical authors—John Quincy Adams was perhaps the last important lecturer in the neo-Ciceronian vein—and more and more were rely-

ing on Hugh Blair's belletristic approach. We need to examine this period, 1800–1850, very closely, because here begin the great changes in the rhetoric course that would eventuate in the founding of American college composition.

THE EXAMPLE OF HUGH BLAIR'S *LECTURES*

Rhetoric entered the nineteenth century as a discipline based around the pedagogy of large lectures and accepting the idea of "mental discipline"—the enforced learning of large numbers of abstract concepts—as central to education. It covered a broad range of theoretical topics based on the tradition of oral discourse and belletristic analysis, contained no component of affective writing, and was ruled by a lecturer who depended on books for content and not for pedagogy. Rhetoric exited the nineteenth century as the new discipline of "composition," based around large lecture-sized discussion classes, accepting the idea of constant writing practice as central to education. Instead of the broad synthesis of the old rhetorical tradition, composition covered a narrow range of textbook topics based generally on the authors' intuitive theorizing about writing. The new discipline contained a large component of writing— the enforced composing of short assigned "themes"—and was run most commonly by a low-level teacher who depended utterly on his textbook for both course content and pedagogy. During that century, in other words, rhetoric was degraded, textbooks went from servants to masters, and teachers were correspondingly demoted until finally they were little more than grading assistants to the textbook author they chose as *seigneur*. Let us look more closely at how this happened.

American college culture and teaching differed from British in certain crucial ways, perhaps the chief difference being the much heavier American reliance on books and "book learning." The trained ushers and masters supplied in good numbers by the English school system were much rarer in America. Great Britain traded many goods to her colonies, but scholars were never a notable export, and thus Americans, always culturally subordinate, got used to knowledge arriving on these shores in the form of English books, not Englishmen.[3] The instruction in rhetoric that a London or Edinburgh student could have by sauntering down to the College weekly could be had in Philadelphia only between leather covers, and thus American college teachers came to rely much more on books, especially student-owned books, than did their European counterparts.

By 1800, of course, America was producing a small number of genuine scholars of its own, but old habits die hard, and Britain continued to dominate American language instruction long after she had ceased to dominate America politically. The teaching of English grammar in America was shaped by Lindley Murray's *English Grammar* of 1795, and American rhetoric was for more than fifty years completely in thrall to Hugh Blair's *Lectures*. The case of Blair is important and paradigmatic enough to warrant special attention, because not only did Blairian rhetoric predominate theoretically, it also introduced a new pedagogy that redirected American rhetorical instruction.

Lectures on Rhetoric and Belles-Lettres was published in London in 1783, and during the next 80 years it saw 18 British (English and Scottish) editions, the last in 1863, and eight abridgments, the last in 1822.[4] Clearly Blair's rhetoric was popular in England and Scotland, but just as clearly his book was not central to British education. Turning to American imprints we find a much different story, a tale of rhetoric triumphant, turned into a veritable centerpiece of education both in secondary schools and in colleges. Following its first Philadelphia printing in 1784, Blair saw *at least* 66 full-length editions in the United States before 1874. Even more important for this argument, 74 abridged versions of the *Lectures* were also published between 1803 and 1911 in America. Examining these editions and abridgments, we can begin to see the development of a new rhetoric pedagogy around Blair's theories, one that would seriously change students' relations with rhetoric books by introducing simplistic questions that made the text rather than the teacher the centerpiece of the course.

We don't see this happen immediately; the first twenty-five years of Blair in America are not particularly noteworthy. A number of editions were published, but all merely copied the corrections and additions of the most recent London or Edinburgh editions. Abridged versions of the *Lectures* began to appear in 1803, probably for the use of the many academies that were springing up throughout the East, but these shortened versions added nothing pedagogically new. In 1818, however, the first abridgment appeared that added *questions* to the end of each abridged lecture, specifically announcing that it was "for the use of schools and academies." The year 1820 saw a Hartford edition of Blair "reduced to Question and Answer by John Marsh."

Clearly a trend was shaping here, and in 1829 it culminated with an edition of the *Lectures* "to which are added copious questions and an analysis of each lecture by Abraham Mills, Teacher of Rhetoric." This was to become the "cheap stereotype edition" published by Carvill in New York and the Kay Brothers and T. Elwood Zell in Philadelphia—the inexpensive edition that flooded onto the market by the thousands of copies after new mechanical processes made hand-setting of type unnecessary.[5] The Mills editions, which became the college standard, contained questions that were absolutely catechetical, demanding nothing more than rote memorization of the exact lines of Blair. Following the chapter on style, for instance, Mills asks, "Of what kinds of style did our author treat in the last lecture? With relation to what, was style considered?" etc.[6] Mills, an educational drone, was rendered wealthy beyond the dreams of avarice by this farrago.

What do these editions of Blair with questions added signify? Simply, that the way rhetoric was taught was undergoing significant change. First in academies and then in colleges, teachers were coming to depend less and less on straight lecturing and more and more on the use of recitation and perhaps even discussion. With these interactive forms of pedagogy came a need for new support systems for the use of teachers. As it always would, the young textbook industry scrambled to meet the perceived needs of teachers. I will argue that these editions of Blair with questions are the first specifically pedagogical rhetoric books—the first textbooks.

REASONS BEHIND THE NEW PEDAGOGY

The reasons for the switch from lecture-based to question-answer classes in rhetoric are complex, and they begin on the secondary rather than the college level.[7] During the early nineteenth century, we see in many disciplines a new importance given to question-answer methods. Textbooks in geography, history, mathematics are suddenly all full of questions; rhetoric merely went with the trend. Almost certainly this flood of questions was due to the sudden popularity of the monitorial classroom system proposed by Joseph Lancaster in his influential 1803 book *Improvements in Education*.[8] Lancastrian teaching, which had its heyday between 1810 and 1835, took sole responsibility for classroom activity off the teacher and put much of it on classroom "monitors," students who drilled other students on the lessons. These monitors were usually older students, but they were untrained in pedagogy and often had little more knowledge of the subject than the students they were drilling. They needed textbooks of a new and very directive sort, and in every subject such textbooks rapidly appeared. Usually the new texts contained catechetical questions that untrained monitors could easily use, and thus in rhetoric we see the growth of question-and-answer abridgments of Blair.

Teachers were not undivided in their opinions of this change in classroom methods. Even some of those authors who included questions in their texts feared the mechanism inherent in slavish use of them. The Rev. J. L. Blake warned in his abridgment of 1822 that:

> It is also suggested to teachers that their pupils would find great advantage in fixing their minds more upon ideas and less upon the words than is usual—to answer as much as possible in their own language, instead of committing to memory and repeating *verbatim* from the book. . . . This remark applies in all its force to the method of teaching by "Question and Answer," as it is termed—one of the most erroneous principles of education ever adopted unless it be for small children not become capable of much reflection.[9]

Questions were considered a great advance by others, however; two years later, Nathaniel Greene prefaced his abridgment of Blair by noting that "the mode of communicating the ideas of Blair, by practicing in Question and Answer, has been found of great utility. This Edition carries that system into very complete operation."[10]

That a textbook-based question-and-answer system might take hold of rhetoric at the secondary level is easy to understand, arguable though its utility might have been. On the college level, however, where tutorials and lectures had always emphasized thought rather than rote memorization, the growth of such a system is harder to explain. Many schoolbooks before 1870, of course, were written to be used on either the secondary or the college level,[11] but we cannot ignore the use of recitation methods in college-level books. The great numbers of question-ridden editions of Blair caused Samuel

Newman, author of the first American college-level text, to plead in 1827 for more thought-oriented pedagogy in American colleges: "Above all things, let not the mockery of set questions and set answers be practiced, in teaching what pertains to the philosophy of rhetoric."[12] Newman's book, *A Practical System of Rhetoric*, followed this precept, being mostly composed of treatise material, but his plea went largely unheeded as question-laden books proliferated.

This degradation of college rhetoric from a lecture-tutorial system to a catechetical recitation-based discipline is largely due to the development of American colleges between 1820 and 1850, the period during which what Frederick Rudolph calls "the college movement" was at its most powerful. Almost incredible numbers of small colleges were founded throughout America during these years, especially in the frontier states. As Rudolph states,

> College-founding in the nineteenth century was undertaken in the same spirit as canal-building, cotton-ginning, farming, and gold-mining. In none of these activities did completely rational procedures prevail. All were touched by the American faith in tomorrow, in the unquestionable capacity of Americans to achieve a better world.[13]

According to Donald G. Tewksbury, as many as 700 colleges were founded before the Civil War, of which fewer than 200 were still extant in 1932.[14] Throughout the 1820's, 30's, and 40's, then, this great wave of small colleges, usually religiously-affiliated, spread throughout the land. Many of them did later fail (Ohio had 37 colleges in 1880, only 17 in 1930), but during the boom period prior to 1850 the educational resources of the country were seriously strained. Only nine American colleges predated the Revolution; only 25 existed in 1800. When the college movement began around 1815, there was a sudden serious shortage of trained college-level teachers and no corresponding mechanism for producing them.

This shortage created a pedagogical problem. The traditional college tutorial methods of Socratic questioning require from teachers considerable knowledge of the field and considerable ability to deploy that knowledge flexibly. These qualities became harder and harder for the many new colleges to find in their teachers. There were simply not enough men trained by the established colleges—only a few hundred a year, and most of these went to bar or pulpit. Harvard, of course, could always find a reputable scholar for the Boylston Chair, and Yale had scores of scholars on which to draw. But for the overseers of Wabash Presbyterian College in the frontier town of Rockland, a trained rhetoric teacher was a rarity.

The problem: a shortage of trained, effective college rhetoric teachers. The solution: many of the newer and less established colleges were forced to turn to less skilled and less highly trained teachers. The pedagogy: highly inflexible recitation techniques like those many of the new teachers were used to using on the secondary level. The tools: question-answer textbooks like

Greene's abridgment of Blair and the mass-produced stereotyped editions of Blair that featured the mindless catechetical questions of Abraham Mills.

Thus were rhetoric textbooks born: out of a paucity of new rhetorical material, out of the weakness and ignorance of undertrained teachers, and out of the increasing power of a newly technologized publishing industry that was quickly gaining the ability to control the content of textbooks by the exertion of market pressure. For more than a century afterwards, these three conditions would continue to be key elements affecting composition textbooks.

THE NEW COMPOSITION TEXTS: DRILLS AND EXERCISES

To this point I have been speaking generally of rhetoric, the ancient discipline of persuasive discourse, but now we need to follow rhetoric as it was transmuted from a discipline of oral to one of written discourse—as it became composition. Composition texts, unlike rhetoric texts, could not make do merely with the questions and answers of a discipline that still paid lip service to "mental discipline." Composition was ineluctably practical; students were expected to *write*. Teachers could, of course, have asked students merely to do a great deal of writing and have examined and discussed it with them, but that would seem to scant the rhetorical theory that composition carried over from the older discipline; in addition, such a pedagogy would have been unimaginably arduous given the huge lecture-sized writing classes of the nineteenth century.[15] Class time could not be all lectures or recitation—it had to be made to include writing, *but not the sort of writing the teacher needed to look at*. The obvious answer was "composition practice," in the form of sentences, paragraphs, short exercises, and drills.

Teachers could, of course, create their own assignments, exercises, topics, check-drills, but to do so was a demanding task. Furthermore, few teachers had very clear ideas about what such exercises and assignments should look like. Should they be more complex versions of grammar-school composition exercises, based primarily on Murray's *English Grammar* and Walker's *Teacher's Assistant in English Composition*, or should college exercises be something essentially different? These were questions that were answered only gradually between 1820 and 1860.

The answers required a reshaping of the pedagogy of "mental discipline" implicit in lecture-treatise and recitation methods. Up to this point, it had been taken for granted that the teacher's job was to produce and disseminate raw information in certain standard forms—the treatise, the lecture series, the rhetorical lesson—and that students' jobs were to capture this information in notes, learn it, and be able to feed it back in synthesized form. This instructional strategy of requiring absorption and regurgitation had lain behind the entire pedagogy of abstract rhetorical theory (as opposed to the older practice-oriented pedagogy of rhetoric as a form of verbal action) that had been growing up since the sixteenth century. It was a pedagogy based around learning abstract concepts, but even when confronted with a

concrete, skills-oriented subject like composition, *it would not let go*. Thus writing, a practice-based skill, became tangled with the insistence on abstract "mental discipline" of the early nineteenth century, and the conception grew that one learns to write by consciously learning ideas about writing and then practicing the application of those ideas. The story of the growth of composition textbooks is the story of the abstract and theoretical rhetoric that was the legacy of the treatise forcing itself into realms of skill development not easily conformable to it.

The change from abstract treatises to abstract textbooks was accomplished by adding exercises, drills, questions, and assignments to the rhetorical lessons that were the heart of each treatise-chapter. These exercises, like the chapters themselves, were atomistic, breaking down writing into many discrete subskills and observance of conventions of writing into hundreds of unrelated small elements. Newman's *Practical System* of 1827 used some assignments, but they were a minor part of the back of the book. It is to one of Newman's competitors in the freewheeling textbook market of the early nineteenth century that we must turn for the first full-scale "activities" textbook.

Richard Green Parker was a professional textbook author. He had popular texts in geography and history, but his primary works were in the field of rhetoric, or, as it would increasingly be known after 1840, composition. Parker's *Progressive Exercises in English Composition* was published in 1832 and sold very well in the burgeoning education marketplace of the time. Heartened by its success, Parker investigated the subject at the college level and realized quickly that there was no book applying to the higher study of writing the popular exercise-based pedagogy that had made *Progressive Exercises* such a hit on the elementary level. He lost no time in lashing together a college version of this method, and in 1844 it appeared as *Aids to English Composition*, subtitled "Specimens and examples of school and college exercises." This was a *locus classicus* of the textbook meant for use by exceedingly uninformed teachers—"those," as Parker admits openly in his Preface, "who have neither the leisure nor the inclination to seek in the wide fields of literature for other and deeper sources of information."[16]

Aids was a college text unlike any before it, proceeding inductively and atomistically through series of short lessons based on the lessons in elementary texts. The book begins with simple grammatical and logical materials— Events, Objects, Names, Words, Phrases, Clauses—and works up to questions of style, revision, and various literary genres. Each short chapter includes a "lesson" which is explained in abstract terms, an example of the lesson as illustration, and exercises that ask the student to practice the lesson using given materials. This was by no means a novel pedagogy, even in writing,[17] but never before had this simple pedagogy been offered on the college level.

And it prospered. *Aids* was very popular, remaining in print for more than 30 years and seeing at least 21 printings. Other similar books appeared, like James R. Boyd's *Elements of Rhetoric and Literary Criticism* (1844) and

George Quackenbos' *Advanced Course of Rhetoric and English Composition* (1855), which also used a lesson-illustration-exercises approach. The college boom of the period had created a sort of pedagogical vacuum, and professional textbook authors like Parker and Quackenbos filled it with their new and simpler texts.

I don't wish to suggest that these exercise-oriented texts ever completely dominated the scene. "Rhetoric," as opposed to "composition," was still taught from treatises and books of lectures (although increasingly the older theoretical rhetorics were being supplanted by newer elocutionary texts). Some college teachers, especially in the East, *were* well enough educated and confident enough to do without a textbook's pedagogical support, and such professors continued to use Campbell, or Blair *sans* questions, or Richard Whately's *Elements of Rhetoric*, or Henry Day's *Art of Rhetoric*. Prior to the Civil War, textbooks and treatises shared the rhetoric/composition market.

THE THEORETICAL INTERREGNUM IN POSTWAR RHETORIC

After the Civil War, composition texts underwent another great mutation. The 1860s, of course, mark a great change in rhetorical history—in educational history, for that matter—in the United States. As I have discussed elsewhere, the Morrill Act of 1862, which provided for the establishment of land-grant agricultural and mechanical colleges, was instrumental in creating a new sort of populist education in America. At the same time, the postwar culture, with its growing emphasis on applied technologies and its increasing social stratification, was demanding even of the older colleges a new sort of education. From being essentially based in orality, rhetoric—increasingly called "composition"—was becoming a writing-based discipline, and between 1860 and 1900 composition gave birth to that set of practical and theoretical doctrines that we now usually refer to as "current-traditional rhetoric."[18]

This period of rhetorical history is commonly conceived, following Albert Kitzhaber, as a long continuous breakdown of the old abstract rhetorical theories as newer exercise-based and mechanically-oriented pedagogies gained popularity. Indeed, that perspective is a defensible one. But looking at the textbooks and only the textbooks of the period, we might form a different idea. Post-1860 texts, in stark contrast to Boyd's, Quackenbos', and especially Parker's exercise-oriented texts of the 1840's and 1850's, look much more like treatises and much less like drillbooks. Though a number of postwar texts did contain exercises, the exercises were few in number and often located near the simpler grammar-based sentence material usually found at the beginning of many books. Through the sixties, seventies, and eighties we see a surprising swing away from basic mechanical texts and back toward more abstract and theoretical books.

What are the reasons for this seeming turnabout? Most importantly, the size, nature, and number of colleges in America. In comparison to the 1820–1850 period of almost frenzied college establishment, the years 1860–1890

were a time of consolidation, when college space was created by the growth of universities rather than by the foundation of new colleges.[19] Rather than seeking to find teachers and professors as best they could, the better-supported schools that had survived the shakeout of the fifties and sixties could concentrate on quality of education and on the establishment of curricula. Institutions were aided in this search for professionalized and competent faculty by the growing influence of the German model of higher education: after 1860, more and more faculty members possessed and were expected to possess advanced degrees in the subjects they professed.

The day of the amateur professor was coming to an end, and with the growing experience and expertise of the American professoriat came a corresponding rejection of simplistic or elementary methods. Thus we can understand the seemingly curious fall of the first wave of exercise-based composition texts. As Alexander Bain noted in the Preface to his influential *English Composition and Rhetoric* of 1866, dicta and not practice or exercises were the proper substance of a book:

> All the principles and rules of composition that seem to me capable of affording aid or direction in the art I have attempted to bring together. . . . The fulfillment of this design has ended in a work more closely allied to Campbell's Philosophy of Rhetoric, Blair's Lectures, or Whately's Rhetoric, than to the majority of recent works on English Composition.[20]

Bain did include a few exercises in his book, but in the main it consists of abstract lessons and observations.

There follows Bain a curious sort of interregnum between two overtly exercise-based and mechanics-oriented periods in textbook style. Between 1870 and 1895, the exercises of the earlier part of the century were relegated to secondary school texts, while college texts became treatises. Certainly the three most important texts of the period are classic rhetoric treatises in the mold of Whately and Newman rather than Parkerian exercise-books. A. S. Hill's *Principles of Rhetoric* of 1878, John Genung's *Practical Elements* of 1886, and Barrett Wendell's *English Composition* of 1891 all eschewed basic practice materials and concentrated on deductive lessons based on their authors' observations. These books dealt little with grammatical and mechanical considerations, seeming to consider rhetoric an essentially conscious application of carefully-learned abstract principles.

These three textbooks are crucially important to the development of composition in America for several reasons. First was their sheer popularity. Hill was in print from 1878 through 1923, Genung from 1886 through 1914, Wendell from 1891 through 1918. These books went through printing after printing, and these were not the small printings of 2000 copies which had characterized the imprints of earlier in the century, but great steam-driven mass productions of 10,000 and 20,000 copies. The large houses which still control much text publishing today were being formed and were establishing extensive sales and distribution networks; after 1870 their most popular texts

defined the content of disciplines in a way that had been rare before the advent of cheap stereotyping. Hill, Genung, and Wendell were among their most popular authors, and, along with Bain, these three created the rhetorical theory that would shape American composition through the 1960s.

Second, these authors were the first genuine rhetoricians to deal completely with the theoretical problems posed by the shift from oral to written discourse. Rhetoricians since Blair had attempted it, but most of their theories had bogged down in belletristic analysis, poorly adapted oral rhetoric, or cumbersome taxonomic systems. Bain had begun to adapt, but his books were arid and hard to read. In Hill, Genung, and Wendell we have the first attempts at a modern written rhetoric, the first rhetoric of the century to really go beyond the orally-based theories of earlier rhetoric. Much of this composition theory had to be sheerly *invented* out of the whole cloth of personal observation, supposition, and selective plagiarism, and thus were born the modes of discourse, Unity, Coherence, and Emphasis, the patterns of exposition, Clearness, Force, and Energy, the organic paragraph, and other classic elements of current-traditional rhetoric. Whatever we may think of this theory, it remained the heart of composition textbooks for over sixty years.[21]

Finally, these books are important because they carry on the central *formal* characteristic of oral rhetorical theory: they are atomistic in perspective, dividing and subdividing the subject into many, many discrete classes, levels, figures, skills, behaviors, and rules. In spite of the fact that much of the theoretical *content* of these three books was recent, the *form* of these treatises was very traditional. Rhetoric was perceived as a collection of observations about the properties of successful written products, and the composition student was expected to bring the conscious insights of the book's author to bear on his own writing. Genung, in his Preface to the *Practical Elements*, admits that such an approach does not supply answers to all needs, but claims that a textbook cannot do more:

> Some elements of rhetoric, though very real and valuable, are not practical, because the ability to employ them cannot be imparted by teaching. They have to exist in the writer himself. . . . Literature is, of course, infinitely more than mechanism, but in proportion as it becomes more a text-book of rhetoric has less business with it. It is as mechanism that it must be taught; the rest must be left to the student himself.[22]

And Barrett Wendell's "Note for Teachers" at the beginning of *English Composition* makes it clear that for him, too, composition is a mechanical skill to be built up piece by piece, from the smallest pieces to the largest.[23]

THE AGE OF IRON

By Wendell's day, however, the theoretical interregnum was almost over. The great changes that occurred after the 1890s were not so much theoretical as formal: treatises gave way to textbooks filled with exercises and assignments

as well as lessons. Between 1890 and 1930, the textbook as we see it today was developed by placing the invented theory of the nineteenth century into a lessons/exercises format perfected on the secondary level, and then feeding the resulting product into an increasingly centralized mass textbook market.

In other essays I have traced the rise of criteria of mechanical correctness, the growth of grammar and skills drills, the inception of handbooks and workbooks, and other elements of the history of teaching composition that reflect the influence of textbooks,[24] and for now I will merely summarize. The "literacy crisis" of the 1880's and '90's created a felt need for new sorts of composition teaching, and the cry then as in the 1970s was "Back to the Basics!" In the late eighties textbooks began to appear with the term "by practice" somewhere in their titles. Taking advantage of the general move toward giving students strenuous doses of writing practice, these books incorporated mechanical and formal exercises that had been unheard of in colleges for several decades. Such books prospered in the crisis atmosphere gripping the nation, and soon other authors were penning texts that proposed to use "written exercises, both critical and constructive, designed to cultivate in progressive and systematic order the students' sense of the leading requisites of composition," as John Genung put it in *his* exercise book, *Outlines of Rhetoric*, in 1893.[25]

By 1900 the trend had caught on most seriously, and with a few exceptions the textbooks that were being produced were, in formal respects, modern: filled with lessons, illustrations, and practice exercises. During the early part of this century, almost every text covered obligatory elements like the levels of composition—word, sentence, paragraph, whole composition—and modes of discourse—narration, description, exposition, argument—as well as a number of minor fields that shifted with the book's emphasis—grammar, spelling, punctuation, figures of speech, outlining, proofreading, letter-writing, etc.

Over the next forty years, very little was added that was novel, although some changes took place in texts. Most obviously, textbooks became very specialized; instead of the one central book of 1900 the field gradually evolved complex squadrons of rhetorics, exposition texts, handbooks, drillbooks, readers, sentence books, and all varieties of combinations and permutations. This movement began in the 1890's, with the first composition readers, Holt's "Specimens" series, which covered the four modes with a different anthology for each. Edwin Woolley produced the first handbook of composition in 1907, the perfect symbol of the mechanism of the period: composition crystallized into 500 mechanical rules. In 1912 the first "Patterns of Exposition" text appeared. In the late twenties, "exercise pads" appeared, large loose-bound books of exercises with perforated pages that would later be called workbooks; soon such books were staples of college teaching.[26] And always there were the rhetorics, with their endlessly derivative treatments. As time went on a few new electives were added—the business letter, the research paper, the literary essay—but most rhetorics remained depressingly similar.

This static situation, which lasted until after 1940, was the result of further development of phenomena we have already discussed: an unrealistic and atomized theory based on observation of finished products and on solipsistic intuition, and a centralized and highly competitive textbook marketplace that squeezed out approaches that didn't immediately sell. The most important cause of the morbidity that has caused some historians to label 1900–1930 the "Dark Ages" of composition was, however, the appallingly ignorant and reactionary nature of the audience for textbooks after 1900: the writing teachers. Interesting theory was not forthcoming because it did not sell as well as it had in the 1890's. And why not?

Composition was moribund during this time for the same reason that had caused the popularity of simplistic textbooks a century before: the qualifications of the teachers in the classrooms. In 1830 the young usher-professor, having had little rhetorical training and no pedagogical training, had *needed* a copy of Blair-cum-Mills in order to run his rhetoric class at Missouri Methodist College. The system in 1830 was not producing enough trained teachers, and such textbooks had helped take up the time. In 1930 the young literary graduate student needed *his* copy of Rankin, Thorpe, and Solve's *College Composition* and his *Century Collegiate Handbook* to run his class at Penn State, having had no rhetorical training and little pedagogical training. The system, considering composition intellectually valueless, had not taught him anything about teaching writing, and for the teacher of 1930 as for the teacher of 1830, textbooks taught the only way he knew. "Little wonder," as James McCrimmon put it, "that in such a sea of confusion he clings to his handbook as a shipwrecked sailor clings to his raft, and by an interesting human weakness, soon comes to believe that these rules, which yesterday were unknown to him, are the sole criteria of good writing."[27]

Textbooks thus came to have a unique place in the profession of composition. In most developed intellectual disciplines, the function of texts has always been essentially conservative: textbooks, which change with glacial slowness, provide stability amid the shifting winds of theoretical argument. They serve as sources for the proven truths needed for students' basic training while advanced scholarship extends the theoretical envelope, usually in journal articles. This is a model of information testing and dissemination accepted by disciplines from history to biology. The great difference between composition and other college-level disciplines is that for all intents and purposes, composition studies *had* no scholarly professionals between 1900 and 1930. English departments during that period saw composition as degrading hackwork, apprenticeship to higher literary studies, and did not encourage theoretical speculation. There was only one journal in the field, and as late as 1930 the *English Journal* had only 1,000 subscribers.

As a result, the usual disciplinary balance between journals and textbooks was destroyed; the conservative influence of textbooks became pervasive. There was nothing to move textbooks forward in correspondence with new discoveries in the field. There *were* no new discoveries. There was hardly any field. What debate was carried on in *English Journal* was usually rather

low-level and was read by few; a popular textbook, on the other hand, was the commonest artifact in a teacher's world. A textbook was placed in her hands as a graduate student, and most teachers assumed that the wisdom of the text was the wisdom of the world. They read their texts, they studied their handbooks, they taught their tools. Composition was the only college-level course consistently carried on by people whose only real training came from the rules and tenets found in the textbooks they asked their students to buy.

KNOWLEDGE, POWER, AND MARKETS

Slowly, however, glacially, changes began to take place in the structure of the discipline—changes that would strongly affect textbooks. The National Council of Teachers of English, founded in 1911, had made little headway during its first two decades, remaining a shrunken in-group of mostly midwestern teachers until 1930 or so. Around that time, however, the expansion of *English Journal* into a high school and a college version began to attract more university teachers, and the growing influence of John Dewey in colleges of education led to greater membership in the Deweyite NCTE. In 1938 the college membership of the NCTE had become so numerous that *EJ* underwent mitosis and a separate journal, *College English*, was spun off. Eleven years later the Conference on College Composition and Communication was formed, and its members, feeling that they needed their own journal, founded *College Composition and Communication*. Suddenly, within only about twenty years, there was a *literature* on the problems of college writing, a growing body of knowledge being developed by a growing group of practitioners. For the first time, writing teachers could turn to something other than their textbooks for information about how best to do their work.

As a result, the last four decades' worth of textbooks have been a remarkably experimental group when contrasted to pre-1940 texts. The effects of the new journals and of the burgeoning educational culture of post–World War II America led to a real questioning of the older sorts of textbooks, and we have seen General Semantics texts, Communications texts, structural linguistics texts, and different sorts of thesis texts[28] come and go in a seemingly endless parade of novelties. We have seen many educational fads, but after the "abstraction ladders" had fallen down, the "four communications skills" had melted back into expository writing, the "structural linguistics" heirophants had been Chomskyized, the day-glo covers had faded beneath the harsh light of back-to-basics, the textbook of 1980 was mostly material that would be familiar to a teacher of 1950.[29] Not even the rhetorical revolution of the 1960's had a powerful effect on textbooks, at least not until recently.

The history of research on writing and composition teaching from the 1940's through the present is a history of epistemological warfare, of progressive theoretical and empirical research struggling with entrenched traditional pedagogy. We who read the journals have tended to characterize the struggle as a war between good and evil, discovery and reaction.[30] In the most pragmatic sense, however, things are considerably simpler: it is a struggle for

epistemological primacy between journals and textbooks, and textbooks are changing because they have begun, for the first time, to lose the battle.

It is a curious war, this, with both sides dependent to some degree on each other, and with a constant movement of troops—that is, teachers and "composition theorists"—back and forth from one camp to another. Textbook publishers and journal authors, who often promulgate vastly different visions of what composition teaching should be, are yet symbiotic.[31] Fascinating as this coëvolutionary socioculture is, however, it is tangential to our central inquiry here. What we need to note here is that once again textbooks are changing, and this time it is a genuine shift, slow but powerful, and not the scattered ad hoc experimentalism that passed for textbook change from 1965 to 1980. A shift has occurred, and fairly recently: for the first time in this century, more textbook adoption decisions are being made by rhetorically-trained persons than by rhetorically ignorant persons. And that means that finally the dream of Fred Newton Scott in 1909 and of Porter Perrin in 1933 and of Albert Kitzhaber in 1960 has a chance of realization, and the intellectual discipline of composition can finally start to take control of its tools once again.

This shift is not due to any new liberality on the parts of text publishers. It is occurring for the same reasons that have motivated the other great textbook shifts we have examined in this essay: the changing qualifications of the teachers in the composition classrooms. We are seeing today, I believe, a sort of repeat of the post–Civil War situation. The average teacher of composition today is much more likely to be knowledgeable about the field than she was even ten years ago. The average composition program is much more likely to be directed by a trained specialist than ten years ago. Practicums, colloquia, wider journal coverage, more professional respect, and a drastically changing job market have all come together to change the preparation and thus the needs of the average writing teacher, and when the average teacher changes, textbook publishers react. Fewer and fewer young, trained writing teachers are willing to surrender their teacherly autonomy to the master-teacher behind the textbook, to exercises and canned discussions and mechanical paper marking. Text publishers are realizing that stasis is no longer safe, not even for current-traditional warhorses like McCrimmon's *Writing with a Purpose*.

The battle for better teaching continues always, of course, and it remains to be seen whether the evolutionary change in teachers and writing programs that I have been describing will prevail. But textbooks *are* beginning to appear that concentrate on having students learn the processes of writing rather than abstract concepts *about* writing, that liberate the teacher to listen to her students rather than enslaving them to an author's theories. More and more involved, trained teachers are gravitating to these texts. The shift is relatively new, and the movement toward better textbooks has far to go; the forces of tradition and dependency are very strong. But if we will keep training teachers to stand by themselves, we can continue to re-invent textbooks in the image of their best nature—as our tools, not crutches we depend upon for all support. Texts can be powerful servants, but only our own pride in

and knowledge of our subject will keep them from turning on us and becoming, as they have in the past, oppressive masters.

NOTES

1. Albert R. Kitzhaber, *Themes, Theories, and Therapy: The Teching of Writing in College* (New York: McGraw-Hill, 1963), pp. 8–26.

2. It could, I think, be argued that Quintilian's *Institutio Oratoria* is an exception, an essentially pedagogical rather than an analytical work; even Quintilian, however, is filled with descriptive and analytical detail.

3. The letters of the Founding Fathers, especially those of Franklin and Jefferson, are filled with references to sending and receiving books from Europe and to the excitement of such imported learning.

4. According to the *Catalogue of the British Museum*.

5. The stereotyping process, which was invented by the French printer Didot in the 1790's, allowed printers to cast solid page-sized plates from *papier-mache* molds rather than setting individual pieces of type. These plates could then be used again and again, allowing reprints of books to be made far more cheaply. The Mills edition of Blair, cast in 1829, remained available through 1873, brought out by a number of different publishers. (Carvill and Zell apparently sold stereotype plates to whoever could afford them.) During those 44 years the pagination, questions, and "analysis" remained completely unchanged.

6. Hugh Blair, *Lectures on Rhetoric and Belles-Lettres, To Which Are Added, Copious Questions: And an Analysis of Each Lecture By Abraham Mills, Teacher of Rhetoric and Belles-Lettres* (Philadelphia: Porter and Coates, 1873), p. 215n. This was the last year that the 1829 Mills "University, College, and School Edition" was published in Philadelphia.

7. The introduction of Blairian rhetoric in secondary schools was itself a novel development. Prior to 1800 students might have read a few orations prior to college, but systematic rhetorical study had not been often taught in lower grades. Blair's rhetorical approach, however, which allowed the combination of rhetoric with the ever-increasing study of vernacular literature, was incredibly popular, and its popularity encompassed younger students than had ever been taught rhetoric before. In one sense, then, textbooks did not ascend to rhetoric; rhetoric descended to educational levels where question-answer apparatus had existed for years.

8. Joseph Lancaster, *Improvements in Education* (London: Darton and Harvey, 1803).

9. Rev. J. L. Blake, *Abridgment of Lectures on Rhetoric by Hugh Blair* (Concord: Hill and Moore, 1822), p. iii.

10. Nathaniel Greene, *Abridgment of Lectures on Rhetoric by Hugh Blair* (Boston: True and Greene, 1824), p. iii.

11. As William G. Carr says, "The history of the textbook since 1860 is primarily a history of increased differentiation and grading. The early books were written 'for schools, academies, colleges, and teachers' institutes.' It was apparently assumed that children of all ages were equal in ability, had the same interests, and could be benefited by identical subject matter and methods of instruction" (William G. Carr, "The Evolution of the Junior High School Textbook in English," *English Journal*, 16 [February 1927], 120).

12. Samuel P. Newman, *A Practical System of Rhetoric* (New York: Mark H. Newman, 1843), p. 14.

13. Frederick Rudolph, *The American College and University: A History* (New York: Alfred A. Knopf, 1962), pp. 48–49.

14. Donald G. Tewksbury, *The Founding of American Colleges and Universities before the Civil War* (New York: Teachers College, Columbia University, 1932), pp. 15, 28. My reading of Tewksbury's somewhat confusing statistics is more conservative than that of Rudolph, who extrapolates over 700 colleges founded *and defunct* before 1865. (Rudolph, p. 47n.)

15. For more on this problem, see my essay "Mechanical Correctness as a Focus in Composition Instruction," *College Composition and Communication*, 36 (February, 1985), 61–72.

16. Richard Green Parker, *Aids to English Composition* (Boston: R. S. Davis, 1844), p. i.

17. Such a method had previously been used in books like Daniel Jaudon's *Union Grammar*, John Rippingham's *Rules for English Composition*, George Quackenbos' *First Lessons in English Composition*, and Parker's own *Progressive Exercises*.

18. C. H. Knoblauch, in his talk, "Neither Current, Nor Traditional, nor a Paradigm" (Modern Language Association Conference, Washington, DC, December 1984), delivered a usefully astringent corrective to the casual adaptation of Daniel Fogarty's term "current-traditional rhetoric," to mean the congeries of intuitions and assumptions from the nineteenth century that have informed most twentieth-century composition teaching. The term seems, however, to have developed a sinister life of its own, and I heave a sigh as I realize that inventing a new term would be harder and more confusing than continuing to (mis)use the old one.

19. It is true that the Morrill Act established some new colleges, but its importance lies primarily in the ways in which it changed the nature of established schools and gave them certain kinds of financial support. According to Arthur Comey, there were 38.1 college students per 100,000 Americans in 1850 and 41.3 per 100,000 in 1880. During this period the U.S. population itself more than doubled. Since we know that relatively few new private colleges were founded during this period, the natural assumption is that most of these new students were the result of the founding of the A&M colleges after 1862 and the subsequent enlargement of many older colleges into prototypical universities. (Arthur M. Comey, "Growth of Colleges of the United States," *Educational Review*, 3 [February, 1892], 124–127.)

20. Alexander Bain, *English Composition and Rhetoric: A Manual* (New York: American Book Co., 1866), p. 4. Bain was not American, but his implied sneer at Parkerian books reflected contemporary American professorial attitudes.

21. We now tend to think of these theories and constructs as relics of a barbarous era, epistemologically questionable and pedagogically useless, but we must remember that the rhetors behind this theory were attempting to chart an almost completely unknown territory. That their maps were not accurate is hardly to be wondered at; we sigh today not because of the maps' inaccuracy, but because so many have for so long unquestioningly followed their directions into the desert.

22. John F. Genung, *The Practical Elements of Rhetoric* (Boston: Ginn, 1886), pp. xi–xii.

23. Wendell had his students read his book, chapter by chapter, beginning with the "Words" chapter and working up to the "Force" and "Elegance" chapters. They would after these readings analyze their fortnightly essays looking for elements specifically relating to the chapters read. "Repeated use of this scheme," says Wendell, "certainly fixes the book in their minds to a rather surprising degree." Doubtless true. See Wendell, *English Composition* (New York: Scribners, 1903), pp. [1–4]. This Note is dated May 1894, and does not appear in editions predating that year.

24. See "Mechanical Correctness"; "Grammar in American College Composition," in Donald M. McQuade, ed., *The Territory of Language: Linguistics, Stylistics, and the Teaching of Composition*, rev. ed. (Carbondale, IL: Southern Illinois University Press, forthcoming); and "Handbooks: History of a Genre" in *Rhetoric Society Quarterly*, 13 (Spring, 1983), 87–98.

25. John F. Genung, *Outlines of Rhetoric, Embodied in Rules, Illustrative Examples, and a Progressive Course of Prose Composition* (Boston: Ginn & Co., 1893), p. iii.

26. See Porter Perrin's diatribe against the use of drillbooks in his classic article "The Remedial Racket," *English Journal*, 22 (May, 1933), 384–388.

27. James M. McCrimmon, "The Importance of the Right Handbook," *College English*, 3 (October, 1941), 71.

28. Thesis texts are the quintessential modern composition texts; I call them thesis texts because each one purveys a central idea about writing or learning to write. This central idea controls the presentation of the pedagogy. For a fuller discussion of thesis texts, see "The Rise and Fall of the Modes of Discourse," pp. 451–452.

29. For an illustration of this *plus ca change* phenomenon as illustrated by a popular text, see my article "Current-Traditional Rhetoric: Thirty Years of *Writing with a Purpose*," *Rhetoric Society Quarterly*, 11 (Fall, 1981), 208–221.

30. Two of the most thoughtful of these critiques are Donald C. Stewart, "Composition Textbooks and the Assault on Tradition," *CCC*, 29 (May, 1978), 171–175, and Mike Rose, "Sophisticated, Ineffective Books: The Dismantling of Process in Composition Texts," *CCC*, 32 (February, 1981), 65–74.

31. See, for instance, David Tedlock's rather rueful "Confessions of a Textbook Writer," *College English*, 42 (October, 1980), 167–170, and Arnold and Charlene Tibbetts' darkly negative "Can Composition Textbooks Use Composition Research?" *CE*, 44 (December, 1982), 855–56.

Grammar in American College Composition: An Historical Overview

A powerful premise undergirds "Grammar in American College Composition: An Historical Overview," an essay published in Donald McQuade's 1986 edited collection *The Territory of Language: Linguistics, Stylistics, and the Teaching of Composition*. It is that despite contemporary scholars' instinctive desire to turn away from the restrictive and often idiosyncratic practices associated with traditional grammar instruction, we need to acknowledge that "the old days may be gone theoretically but remain with us on the level of practical pedagogy." As a consequence, Bob argues, "[w]e ought [. . .] to learn more about them" (118). In this essay, Bob fulfills his own dictum by tracing grammar instruction in America from the eighteenth century to the present. The essay is less polemical than some of Bob's scholarly work, but as his essays often do, it concludes with an elegantly written vision of ongoing struggle within composition: "A great deal of the history of composition in America seems to be a clumsy shuffle-dance of grammar with rhetoric, with first one and then another leading. It will not end soon, for the wish for certainty and algorithmic closure represented by the one struggles always with the desire for originality and creativity represented by the other. So long as language is part science, part art, and part magic, the grammarians and the rhetoricians will be struggling with each other to lead the dance" (136).

T he relationship between the teaching of writing and the various bodies of knowledge and prejudice called "grammar" has always been problematical. In a volume such as this, which investigates, among other issues, the relation of writing to the most modern linguistic phenomena, it might at first seem unwarranted to cover the "bad old days," when pinch-faced champions of "literacy" forced gobs of questionable prescription down adolescent throats. A look, however, into the handbooks and the workbooks that still pour from the presses for use in both remedial and freshman

From *The Territory of Language: Linguistics, Stylistics, and the Teaching of Composition*, ed. Donald McQuade (Carbondale: Southern Illinois UP, 1986), 3–22.

English will show that the old days may be gone theoretically but remain with us on the level of practical pedagogy. We ought, I think, to learn more about them.

English Grammar: Background

In order to understand how grammar has affected the teaching of writing, it will first be necessary to look briefly at the ways in which traditional grammar was taught in America prior to the rise of modern linguistics. The study of formal English grammar became a popular subject in the common schools of America around the time of the American Revolution. Rollo L. Lyman has set 1775 as the date for the beginning of a fifty-year rise of vernacular grammar in elementary and secondary schools.[1] English grammar replaced the study of Latin grammar among the earlier school grades as Latin and Greek ceased to be the absolute core of every curriculum. Soon grammar was so much at the center of elementary study that elementary schools became known as "grammar schools," an appellation that exists even today. Study of English grammar reached its peak influence around 1850, at a time when grammar was the main subject of a pupil's first six grades.

Early grammar instruction—before 1850 or so—had nothing to do with composing essays or even with constructing sentences. It was an absolutely formal discipline that demanded a great deal of rote memorization of terms, complex analyses of given sentences, and suspicious patrols through other sentences searching for "errors." As Charles C. Fries says, the basis of this early formal grammar study was very different from modern linguistic science and had as its end not "*description* for the sake of *prediction*" but "*analysis* for the sake of *classification*."[2] Grammar was not, in any sense, a creative field of study; rather, it was meant as a "mental discipline," training the mind for rigorous thought.

Before 1850, traditional grammar methods were threefold, and none of the three traditional pedagogies was concerned with the development of writing skill. First, pupils were made to memorize the parts of speech, all the "rules" of declension, conjugation, gender, number, case, degree, tense, mood, person, and countless others. Second, they were forced to apply and demonstrate these rules in oral exercises called "parsing," which asked pupils to give definitions and applicable rules for every word in a sentence provided by the teacher. Here is an example of a sentence partially parsed, from what was the paradigmatic grammar text for nineteenth-century America, Lindley Murray's best-selling *English Grammar* of 1795:

"We should be kind to them, who are unkind to us."

We is a personal pronoun, of the first person, the plural number, and in the nominative case. (*Decline it.*) *Should be* is an irregular verb neuter, in the potential mood, the imperfect tense, and the first person plural. (*Repeat the present tense, etc.*) *Kind* is an adjective, in the positive state. (*Repeat the degrees of comparison.*) *To* is a preposition. *Them* is a per-

sonal pronoun, of the third person, the plural number, and in the objective case. (*Decline it.*) *Who* is a relative pronoun, and in the nominative case. (*Decline it*). . . .[3]

The example goes on, but the point is made. The third sort of grammar exercise was introduced by Robert Lowth in his *Short Introduction* of 1758, and was used by every major grammar textbook through 1850. It consisted of the teacher's providing examples of ungrammatical sentences, either orally or in written form, and asking pupils to correct the ungrammaticality and then state the rules and definitions by which the repair was made. These "false syntax" exercises fostered a spirit of anxiety and suspicion about grammar that was not long in pervading the entire linguistic culture of the new nation.[4]

Around 1850 the methods of teaching grammar began to change as inductive forms of pedagogy were imported from Europe. Creative and compositional elements were gradually added to the memorization and dissection exercises already used. Most important to this movement toward incorporating writing and grammar were the many editions of Samuel S. Greene's *Analysis* of 1847. Greene was the first important grammarian to include the writing of original sentences as part of each of his grammar lessons, usually ending a series of models and parsing exercises with instructions. For instance, "Write fifteen sentences of your own, limiting the subjects of the first five by a compound adjective element, the predicates of the next five by a compound objective element, and the predicates of the last five by a compound adverbial element."[5] In spite of Greene's popularity, however, the field of grammar continued to be overwhelmingly formalistic and abstract, having little to do with communications skills as they really existed. Grammarians contrived to accept Lindley Murray's definition of grammar as "the art of speaking and writing the English language with propriety," and school grammar was still an attempt to instill, through rigid taxonomic practice, this knowledge of correctness.

Teaching of formal grammar in American elementary and high schools reached its high point around 1850 and then began to lose popularity. More and more teachers and school board officials began to see the "mental discipline" claims of grammar instructions as will-o'-the-wisps and the claims that knowledge of grammatical categories fostered literate skills as demonstrably false. William H. Wells, one of the earliest professors of the system of inductive grammar (his textbook appeared in 1846), had lost faith in grammatical study by 1865, when he wrote that a student "may have the whole grammar book by heart, and yet not be able to make a respectable speech. . . . The great object to be attained, is not the mastery of a text-book in grammar, but the acquisition of language."[6] Indeed, some began to question whether English *had* a grammar, so poorly did the language seem to fit into the accepted inflected structure of Latin grammar. In *Words and Their Uses* in 1870 Richard Grant White claimed that English was a "grammarless" language, and many believed the claim.

The traditional teaching of formal grammar was in deep trouble by the 1880s. The state of Connecticut dropped all grammar teaching during this

period, claiming it was "hateful" to students and did not help them to speak or write better.[7] On the level of theory, more and more philologists were coming to agree with pioneer linguist George P. Marsh:

> So far as respects English or any other uninflected speech, a knowledge of grammar is rather a matter of convenience as a nomenclature, a medium of thought and discussion *about* language than a guide to the actual use of it, and it is as impossible to acquire the complete command of our own tongue by the study of grammatical precept, as to learn to walk or swim by attending a course of lectures on anatomy.[8]

Marsh believed that in English "grammar has little use except to systematize," and more and more people were questioning why such an abstract system should be at the core of American school education.

Yet grammar, though its early methods were being seriously questioned, was far from defunct. Educators, a conservative group in the nineteenth century, were shoring up fragments against the ruin of their central subject, and between 1850 and 1880 a new pedagogy for grammar was born, one based not on abstract learning of formal grammar but rather on using grammar in sentences. This method, based on Greene's *Analysis*, came to be called "sentence building" or "language lessons," after William Swinton's extremely popular textbook *Language Lessons*, which appeared in 1873.[9] This pedagogy focused on writing and then examining the student's own sentences rather than on rote memorization and parsing. It was given a great boost in 1877, when Alonzo Reed and Brainerd Kellogg first published their *Higher Lessons in English*.

Reed and Kellogg admitted that grammar "is very insecure. Children are not enthusiastic in praise of grammar, most parents recall without pleasure their own trials with it, and many men of culture and of wisdom openly advise its banishment from the school-room."[10] Reed and Kellogg believed that grammar is necessary, but warned that "it must bear on its branches more obvious and more *serviceable* fruit, or the tree will be hewn down and cast out of the way" (p. 3). The answer in *Higher Lessons* was to "make the Science of the Language, of which all the essentials are thoroughly presented, tributary to the Art of Expression" (p. 3). The book was filled with practices, exercises, and drills, but these were not so different from Swinton's drills. What really set Reed and Kellogg apart was their invention of the sentence diagram, the familiar straight-line diagram that was still used in the 1970s to demonstrate sentence structure.

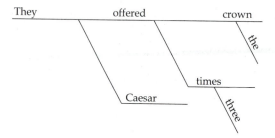

Reed and Kellogg provided a new defense for sentence-based grammar pedagogy, one that soon became extremely popular. It can be said, in fact, that the diagram-based analysis of sentences that *Higher Lessons* originated was *the* essential grammar pedagogy from 1880 through 1970. It was critiqued around the beginning of the century by several theorists, most notably Gertrude Buck,[11] for its mechanical and linear nature; other critics of diagram-based texts called attention to the extremely confusing variation of names and terms in different grammar texts.[12] Despite the criticism leveled at it, however, no system was put forward to supplant the Reed and Kellogg–based "sentence study" method. This became the background method for most of the discussions of "grammar" conducted on the college level prior to 1925 or so, and this traditional grammatical system is the system that came under heavy attack almost as soon as modern descriptive linguistics was established as a discipline.

GRAMMAR AND RHETORIC

When assessing grammar's effect on the teaching of writing, we need to remember that the conflation of grammar and rhetoric is an exclusively modern phenomenon, unknown before 1870 or so. The Greek or Roman rhetorician would have been scandalized by the suggestion that he profess the structure of the language on any level. That job, dirty but necessary, was the responsibility of the *grammaticus*, the lower-grade teacher who made certain that pupils could speak with *correctness*. Only when this knowledge of pure and correct language was assured would the rhetorician take over and teach the pupil to discourse with *eloquence*. This essential split between grammar and rhetoric existed unchanged through the eighteenth century. As the brilliant George Campbell, hardly a purveyor of unexamined tradition, put it in 1776,

> Now, the grammatical art hath its completion in syntax; the oratorical, as far as the body of expression is concerned, in style. Syntax regards only the composition of many words into one sentence; style, at the same time that it attends to this, regards further the composition of many sentences into one discourse. Nor is this the only difference; the grammarian . . . requires only purity. . . . The orator requires also beauty and strength. The highest aim of the former is the lowest aim of the latter; where grammar ends eloquence begins. Thus the grammarian's department bears much the same relation to the orator's which the art of the mason bears to that of the architect.[13]

Campbell is not sneering here at grammar—he discusses grammatical purity at some length when covering good usage—but he does wish to differentiate it clearly from the rhetorical theory that absorbed his interest.

Campbell's attitude toward grammar was not, however, shared by Hugh Blair, whose 1783 *Lectures on Rhetoric and Belles-Lettres* became the most

influential of the eighteenth-century rhetorics. Instruction in formal English grammar had begun in both England and America around 1750, and Blair saw, as Campbell did not, that an English rhetoric would have to come to terms with English grammar. Grammar, wrote Blair in one of his two chapters covering it,

> is apt to be slighted by superficial thinkers as belonging to those rudi-
> ments of knowledge, which were inculcated upon us in our earliest
> youth. But what was then inculcated before we could comprehend its
> principles, would abundantly repay our study in maturer years; and to
> the ignorance of it, must be attributed many of those fundamental de-
> fects which appear in writing.[14]

Blair gave grammar a place in two of his forty-six lectures, covering all the parts of speech and something of the origins of English. This discussion, thought Blair, was necessary, for without a knowledge of grammar as a formal system good writing was impossible. Good style demanded grammatical purity and propriety, and "If any imagine they can catch it merely by the ear, or acquire it by a slight perusal of some of our good authors, they will find them- selves much disappointed."[15] This statement became an article of faith for sev- eral generations of teachers of vernacular composition, who came to see a complete knowledge of English grammar as a panacea for all ills in writing.

The gradual absorption of grammar by rhetoric began slowly, however. There were early textbooks with titles like *A Grammar of Composition*, but most of the texts of the pre-1850 period are either based upon Blair's *Lectures* and contain much rhetorical theory and a passing mention of grammar, or upon Lindley Murray's *English Grammar* and are overwhelmingly grammatical with perhaps a few pages on "purity, propriety, precision, and perspicuity" in writ- ing. Rhetoricians were generally able to assume preexisting understanding of the "rules" and terms of grammar on the parts of their readers. At the very least, students of rhetoric were supposed to have mastered the necessities of "Correctness," which, as Samuel Newman put it in his *Practical System* of 1827, "is to be learned from the rules and principles of syntax."[16]

Rhetoric, however, was still mostly thought a higher mystery, one con- cerned with more than the grammarian's correctness. The rhetoric of the period before 1850 was overwhelmingly abstract and theoretical, concerned with systems of rules and principles rather than with creative methods. There was very little actual practice in composition in rhetoric courses before 1875 or so; such courses consisted of lectures on or textbook study of a system. For such a rhetorical tradition, chock full of its own theoretical content, there was little need for the "rules" and definitions of grammar, a separate system.

BEGINNINGS OF COMPOSITION

But rhetoric in America was changing. As Albert Kitzhaber has shown, the period 1850–1900 was a time when systematic theoretical rhetoric was re- placed by an intensely practical course in correct writing, and a large part of

this change came about as a result of the mixture of the "practical" sentence-based grammar of Greene and Reed and Kellogg with the newly practical subject of English composition. During the 1850s and 1860s, instruction in actual writing was in its infancy in American colleges, but it became quickly apparent to teachers who demanded writing from students that the older theoretical rhetoric of Blair, like the formal grammar of Murray and his imitators, had no effect on students' abilities to write. Only one early text, G. P. Quackenbos' *Advanced Course of Composition and Rhetoric*, tried mixing the new "sentence-building" grammar with rhetorical lessons.

During the 1860s, however, several phenomena converged to create a new situation for grammar. First, formal grammar, as we have seen, came under attack as sterile and impractical. Second, the teaching of rhetoric came to be more and more concerned with writing, and thus with *correctness* as well as eloquence. Third, the United States culture as a whole began to become more aware of correct speaking and writing as indices of status and professional worth. In 1865 Henry Alford, dean of Westminster, published his *Plea for the Queen's English*, an attack on the poor grammar and bad usage he saw all around him—and noted especially in America. Several American writers answered and debated him, and the prescriptive-usage debate that raged throughout the 1860s and '70s drew the attention of the American intellectual community to linguistic issues as never before.[17] After the Civil War, with the Union saved and the beginnings of the drastic social stratification of the Gilded Age, proper language came to have new importance.

A few theorists saw that rhetoric and grammar would be melded in the developing discipline of composition and strove to create an intellectually defensible systhesis of the two. Some, like grammarian William Wells, saw a new discipline in which practice in writing would be the central pedagogical technique, "where analysis and parsing will find their appropriate place as collateral aids in connection with the daily living exercises in the use of the English tongue."[18] Rhetorician Henry Day, always a theoretical pioneer, published his *Grammatical Synthesis: The Art of English Composition* in 1867. This book, which meant to unite grammar, rhetoric, and logic in one study because all were "grounded in the basis of Thought," never attained great popularity; like most of Day's work it was too original for its own good. *Grammatical Synthesis* showed, however, that by the late 1860s at least some colleges were beginning to mix grammar with composition.

In the 1870s grammatical elements advanced even more rapidly into the teaching of writing, largely because of the influence of Harvard College. Harvard teachers of English had been noticing for some years that their students had trouble with the written language, and as the older academic system of lectures and exams gave way to the newer classroom discussion and essay-writing methods, this problem became even more obvious. In addition, the growing importance of linguistically influenced class structures and Harvard's desire to demonstrate that it had the highest standards and deserved its leadership position led to the introduction in 1874 of a written examination that determined admission to the college.[19] When the Harvard faculty

read these first exams they were shocked by the poor writing and the number of egregious grammatical errors produced by the graduates of America's best academies. More than half of the students taking these early tests failed.

This began an "illiteracy" uproar in academia that lasted for more than two decades and resulted in the internment of most of the old traditions of rhetoric and the creation of a new course and subject that soon became *de rigueur* in American colleges: freshman composition courses patterned after "English A," the course Harvard instituted to grapple with its literacy problems. Much anxiety was apparent in the public prints after the mid-seventies bemoaning the "illiteracy of American boys" and suggesting various solutions to the problem. The most popular remedy prescribed for the cure of "illiteracy" was the collection of form-based mechanical lessons that came to be known as "grammar." College students could not write, the reasoning went, because their early grammar lessons had not "taken." Thus the lessons needed to be repeated until the knowledge of parts of speech and rules would transform into the ability to write. We now see this as an *essentially* incorrect idea, and identify students' poor writing in 1874 as a result of their lack of composition practice in the academies and schools. Yet the power of grammar as a panacea for writing ills was still strong in the 1870s and '80s.

Several books appeared in the mid-seventies which reflect the rather sudden introduction of grammar to the composition course. Joseph H. Gilmore's textbook *Outlines of the Art of Expression* set out, quite clearly, to make grammar a college-level subject. Gilmore, a professor at the University of Rochester, stated in his preface:

> This little book has grown, in the author's class-room, out of an attempt to supplement the defective early training of his pupils.
>
> Those pupils had, when they entered college, some practical acquaintance with English composition. . . . *English* Grammar, many of them had never studied at all—few if any, of them, as the author conceives it should be studied.[20]

For Gilmore, grammar was "the art of correctly expressing our thoughts," and his 112-page book mixed formal grammar and prescriptive advice with some low-level stylistic rhetoric. *Outlines* was neither a grammar book nor a true rhetoric, but its combination of sentence-level advice and grammatical rules made it popular until nearly the turn of the century.

Much more popular and important was a book that originated in England, Edwin A. Abbott's *How to Write Clearly* (1875). Abbott had originally written his book to help his students translate Greek and Latin into acceptable English, since "the flat, vague, long-winded Greek-English and Latin-English imposture that is often tolerated in our examinations . . . diminishes instead of increasing the power that our pupils should possess over their native language."[21] Abbott's answer, unlike Gilmore's, was to try to discern the main grammatical principles most commonly violated and to create a new sort of prescriptive rule that would warn against that specific violation. This

was often a grammar-based rule but was by no means always a grammatical rule. For instance, where Gilmore covers adverbs according to their traditional definitions and classes, Abbott assumes this knowledge and proffers three specific prescriptions: "Adverbs should be placed next to the words they are intended to affect"; " 'Only' requires careful use"; and "When 'not only' precedes 'but also,' see that each is followed by the same part of speech." In short, *How to Write Clearly* is the first identifiable handbook of composition. Amazingly popular in the U.S., it remained in print from 1875 until 1914 and was required by colleges in all parts of the country.

THE TRIUMPH OF GRAMMAR IN COMPOSITION

Gilmore and Abbott together illustrate how pervasively grammar had infiltrated composition by 1880. Curiously, however, we find little evidence of the advance of grammar in most rhetoric texts of the day. Alexander Bain, A. S. Hill, Barrett Wendell, and Fred Newton Scott all wrote extremely popular rhetoric texts that had no important grammatical components at all. Of all the major rhetoricians of the last two decades of the century, only John Genung in his *Practical Elements of Rhetoric* (1886) and *Outlines of Rhetoric* (1893) touched on grammar in any important way.[22] Genung's willingness to deal with grammatical elements (he called them "Fundamental Processes") in his books was part of the reason for his tremendous success: between 1887 and 1894 or so, *Practical Elements* was the most popular composition textbook. Genung realized that rhetoric was going to have to make peace with grammar one way or another and figured that it might as well be done with dignity. "But even in employing grammatical processes as working-tools," Genung wrote, "rhetoric imparts to them a new quality distinctively rhetorical, the quality by which they become methods in an art, means to an end."[23] His *Outlines of Rhetoric* of 1893 was even more open in its acceptance of grammatical theory and syntactic exercises. *Outlines* is a collection of 125 illustrated rules not unlike an expanded version of Abbott's *How to Write Clearly*. Of these, thirty-one were overtly grammatical rules. *Outlines* was the first major text to be so practice-oriented and prescriptively organized.

Genung may have been the only rhetorician of the "Big Four" to include grammatical elements in his rhetoric, but beginning in the late eighties other text authors made the jump from "rhetoric" to "composition." The words "composition" and "by practice" in a book title were often the code terms for books that included lower-level formal sections and sections on grammar. William Williams' *Composition and Rhetoric by Practice* (1888) devoted its first sixty pages to grammar and to sentence practice and remained extremely popular into the 1920s. Williams was immediately copied by Edward Shaw, whose 1892 *English Composition by Practice* was even less concerned with traditional nongrammatical rhetoric than was Williams' book.

The period of the nineties was a time of warfare between the old-fashioned rhetoricians and teachers who believed that grammar and rhetoric should remain separate and the newer teachers and authors who had no

such qualms. The old guard, many of whom had been educated in Blair's systematic tradition, looked down on the new field of composition as it burgeoned. They decried the illiteracy of students but insisted that secondary schools take the responsibility for education in grammar and formal correctness. E. L. Godkin, one of the authors of the famous Harvard Report of 1892, pleaded that college teachers be "delivered, in large part at least, from the necessity of teaching the rudiments of the language."[24] It was increasingly clear, however, that they would not soon be so delivered, and younger members of the authorial community increasingly produced textbooks that took advantage of the trend toward grammar.

Though more and more traditional grammar was included in college rhetorics after 1895, those who wrote about English pedagogy seemed at that time curiously reticent about admitting that the "practicalization" of the course in rhetoric, so much lauded, really meant the supplanting of abstract lectures by low-level formal exercises. The very word "grammar" seldom appeared in many books except as part of a short discussion about its relation to rhetoric. Hardly mentioned was the fact that basic grammatical correctness was coming to be regarded as the prime desideratum for composition. One must look at some of the student papers of the period and the comments teachers made upon them to realize how essentially formal the criteria for good writing were. At the same time that article-writers in *Educational Review* were discussing "philological training" and "the science of language," however, teachers were making their students buy Abbott's *How to Write Clearly*, A. S. Hill's pamphlet on grammatical correctness, or one of the newer texts that carefully straddled the line between high school and college composition.

Teaching grammatical correctness in college accelerated after 1900, and it soon became obvious that new tools would be needed to make college grammar more effective. In 1907, Edwin Woolley's *Handbook of Composition* reduced the system of English grammar to a series of prescriptive error-based rules. Woolley was much more complete than Abbott, covering 350 rules to Abbott's 56. Woolley's *Handbook* was not a grammar treatise of the old sort; as he said in his preface, "The aim of the book is not scientific, but practical. The purpose is to make clear the rules in regard to which many people make mistakes. No material has been put into the book for the sake of formal completeness."[25] A far cry from the aims of traditional grammarians from Lowth onward, but Woolley defined here the sort of "grammar" that would henceforward be most people's definition: a set of rules about words and sentences that define mistakes as perceived by an English teacher.

The development and use of handbooks after Woolley is another story, one told elsewhere.[26] For the purposes of this essay, it is enough to say that insofar as grammar was part of composition after 1910, it was found in the increasingly popular—eventually almost ubiquitous—handbooks. As the handbook moved closer and closer to centrality in the teaching practices and especially in the paper-grading and marking practices of teachers, the field of grammar became more and more important. For secondary-school students,

grammar meant the "sentence-building" book or the "language" book; for college students, grammar meant the handbook.

Rhetoric waned during the period 1910–1930. Frank Scott wrote in 1918 that "for ten years or so there has been a steady diminution of the amount of rhetorical theory offered in [college textbooks]; that which has been retained has been made more and more elementary."[27] Meanwhile, the sort of grammar being taught in college courses reflected the most old-fashioned, rigid, and puristic prejudices of the nineteenth century.

EARLY LINGUISTIC THEORY

If a gap had developed between rhetoric as it perceived itself and the grammar oriented composition course as it was taught, a gap just as large began to open between the grammar that English teachers taught and the growing insights of the scientific philologists and linguists active in English studies during the late nineteenth and early twentieth centuries. Such important early linguistic scholars as Thomas Lounsbury, Brander Matthews, and George P. Krapp began, in the years after 1900, to suggest that a new way of viewing grammar, one based on a descriptive and flexible objectivity rather than on the prescriptive purism of the older grammar, might be the linguistics of the future.

Support for a universal grammar and a rigid purism in usage declined rapidly among genuine philosophers of language after 1900, but, sadly, little was carried over from the descriptive language studies such as those of Krapp, Otto Jespersen, Henry Sweet, or George Curme. As early as the 1880s a few philologists had criticized teachers' total acceptance of traditional rigid grammar,[28] but before 1900 there was no organized critique of this purblind dependence on an increasingly discredited system.

With the work of Lounsbury, Matthews, and Krapp a new scientific and descriptive spirit appeared in philology. Arguing against a fixed standard of grammatical propriety in *The Standard of Usage in English*, Lounsbury grittily proclaimed that "in order to have a language become fixed, it is first necessary that those who speak it should become dead. . . ."[29] George Krapp, in his *Modern English* of 1909, made an important differentiation between *standard* English as taught by the rigid prescriptive grammarians of the schools and *good* English, language that treads the boundary between *convention* and *invention*. "Language is valuable only as it effects the purposes one wishes to attain," wrote Krapp,[30] unconsciously echoing George Campbell's definition of rhetoric in 1776 as "that art or talent by which the discourse is adapted to its end."

By World War I a whole generation of philologically trained teachers had made themselves conversant with both the history of the English language and with its similarities to and differences from other language systems. This generation of scholars—no more than a few hundred in number, in comparison to the thousands of literary specialists and composition teachers—founded the Linguistic Society of America in 1924. Linguistics thus officially

declared itself independent of English, classics, anthropology, and psychology, complaining that "the standing of our science in the academic community leaves much to be desired."[31] In an almost anguished *apologia* for the LSA, published in the first volume of *Language*, Leonard Bloomfield charged that

> Our schools are conducted by persons who, from professors of education down to teachers in the classroom, know nothing of the results of linguistic science, not even the relation of writing to speech or of standard language to dialect. In short, they do not know what language is, and yet must teach it. . . . [32]

Bloomfield's charge was all too sadly true. As I have noted, S. E. Lang, Gertrude Buck, and others had launched various disorganized attacks upon prescriptive grammar before 1910, but no organized group of critics had been forthcoming. By 1925, however, there was already the beginning of a movement to try to set composition on a sounder linguistic basis.

THE ANTITRADITIONALISTS

The National Council of Teachers of English had been formed in 1911, but only slowly did it come to be a prime mover behind attacks on purism and prescriptivism in grammar. Most early NCTE members, it appears, were satisfied with Woolley's prescriptive-handbook approach, but a few of the most active and influential members were aware of the trends in linguistics and began in the late teens to fire off salvoes against prescriptive grammar and usage. Fred N. Scott, as reliably ahead of his time on this issue as on others, attacked inflexible prescriptive standards in the 1917 *English Journal*. In the following year, he was seconded by G. P. Krapp, who was still exploring the question of acceptability of usages, and the youthful Sterling A. Leonard, whose "Old Purist Junk" still remains a classic of witty denigration. It begins, "The purist is surely one of the strangest of God's creatures," and includes the plaint, modern-sounding even in the eighties, that

> in our weary preoccupation with a hundred mere insignificant conventions of wording and idiom we have left almost untouched more fruitful topics. . . . Our nice conscientiousness has been sadly misled by dictatorial and wise-sounding but often densely ignorant pronouncements, into a teaching, not only of fiddle-faddle niceties, but of positive untruth about present usage. I suggest that for a very considerable part of the actual difficulties and regrettable ill successes of our English teaching—I know at least that it is true of my own—the blind leading of purists is responsible.[33]

Leonard was one of the most important figures in establishing the empirical reality of the doctrine of usage with his posthumously published *Current English Usage* of 1932. (Leonard drowned while boating in Wisconsin with

I. A. Richards in 1931; his tragically early death robbed English studies of a natural leader who might have brought about needed reforms much earlier.) But as early as 1917 he had already spoken out strongly in favor of the liberal and reformist ideas he had learned as Scott's student at Michigan.

The decade of the teens also brought forth the first series of attempts to measure empirically the worth of grammar to literacy skills. Most of these early experiments involved elementary and secondary schools and affected college grammar only indirectly. Yet the fact that they were done at all indicates a new professionalism in education, an unwillingness to accept the received wisdom that grammar was indispensable. Studies such as those of Hoyt in 1906, Briggs in 1913, Charters in 1915, and Johnson in 1917 cast increasing doubt on the idea that grammar instruction carried over into composition.[34] William Asker in 1923 correlated the grammatical knowledge of high school seniors with their freshman composition grades in college and found that "knowledge of formal grammar influences ability to judge the grammatical correctness of a sentence and ability in English composition only to a negligible degree."[35]

By the 1920s, the antiprescriptivists had begun to assemble an impressive array of theorists and studies unified by the belief that traditional grammar was not useful. Krapp, Leonard, and Scott insisted that the insights of Bloomfield, Sapir, Jespersen, and other scientific linguists could be ignored only at peril. Around the mid-twenties Charles C. Fries added his voice to this chorus of criticism. Throughout his long and active career in the LSA, the MLA, and NCTE, Fries constantly strove to make English teachers aware of linguistic insights. In Fries's first important book, *The Teaching of the English Language* (1927), he wrote:

> Even after more than a hundred years of linguistic study based upon the historical method, the fundamental principles upon which the modern scientific view of language rests and the results of scholarly investigations in the English language have not reached the schools. On the whole the schools still perpetuate with very little change the eighteenth century point of view. . . . This book is an effort to interpret the modern scientific view of language in a practical way for teachers.[36]

Fries discusses at length the folly of rule-worship, the doctrine of the standard of usage, where the concept of acceptable grammar originated, and other elements of informed language teaching. For the next forty years, which included presidencies of the LSA and NCTE, Fries would continue to press the fight against destructive prescription in grammar.

By the mid-twenties the defenders of formal grammar, while ascendant in the classroom, were on the defensive in scholarly journals. Leon Mones was one of the few who made any attempt to defend the teaching of formal grammar against the flood of attacks. Grammar was under such an attack, complained Mones, that "an argument in its favor must ring like either grumpy reaction or hysteric reform. Well, grumpy some of us are, and

hysteric too. We have seen the 'No Formal Grammar' army march on to victory and leave chaos behind it."[37] Mones' nostalgia for an ordered past was not the usual position found in journals after 1920, however. The greater number of post-1920 journal articles on grammar either report the findings of ill-designed studies about whether grammar helps students read and write, or attack the idea of prescriptive usage, or report on minor teaching techniques involving grammar without taking sides, or make technical descriptive points within traditional grammar. Meanwhile, in the classrooms, handbooks and their sinister new siblings, "drillbooks" and "workbooks," held almost unchallenged sway.

During this period, the public attitude toward grammar instruction was mixed; most people had hated their school grammar, but large numbers felt it had done them good and many thought traditional grammar needed to be continued.[38] The public had little idea of the formidable forces building a case against grammar instruction within academe until Sterling Leonard's *Current English Usage* in 1932 and Marckwardt and Walcott's *Facts about Current English Usage* in 1938. These books were widely perceived as a surrender on the part of English teachers to an "anything goes" ethic in usage, and various funerals were held in popular magazines for "grammar." When the NCTE in 1935 published its *Experience Curriculum in English*, a document which more or less summed up the pedagogical opinions of the Deweyite wing that composed the group's vocal minority, few were surprised to see a general comdemnation of grammar teaching:

> Because scientific investigators haved failed to show the effectiveness of grammar in the elimination of usage errors, it is not here organized for that purpose. There is no scientific evidence of the value of grammar which warrants its appearance as a prominent or even distinct feature of the course of study.[39]

LINGUISTICS AND ENGLISH: CROSS-PURPOSES

After 1935 a number of factors came together to make the relations between linguistics and composition complex and polemical. Edward Sapir and Leonard Bloomfield had published their *magni opi*, both entitled *Language*, in 1921 and 1933, and in the thirties their students moved more and more rapidly toward a genuinely scientific linguistics. In practice, this meant that after 1930 linguistics and composition moved further and further apart in terms of their ultimate goals. Linguistics was becoming exclusively interested in comparative and structural description that had nothing at all to do with teaching or specifying good or bad usage. Such labels, dear to English teachers, were becoming genuinely embarrassing to linguists.

Except for a few teachers like Fries, who had deep roots in both English and linguistics, there were not many who could carry the message of this essential disjunction over to English. Since Bloomfield's *Language* in 1933, linguistics had hardly concerned its investigations with writing at all, assuming

that writing was secondary to oral speech, but few teachers were even aware of that. Most had never had specific training in linguistics, although the NCTE had been calling for such training for English teachers since 1928.[40] English teachers knew *something* was happening in linguistics, and they had heard it was scientific and impressive; when, they tended to ask, would this new grammar give them something they could use in classrooms to replace the oft-critiqued old grammar?

Such applications were not forthcoming. Linguists after 1940 hardly bothered to criticize the sort of grammar taught in English. They merely rolled their eyes and sighed. The linguistic frontiers were far away from the handbook and the classroom. As many large universities formed departments of linguistics, linguists literally moved away from English and away from the turmoil that continued in English over the use of "grammar" to teach writing.

For the period after 1940 we must carefully distinguish the controversies within the field of linguistics from those in English whose ostensible subject was linguistics. Linguists increasingly disputed analytical techniques, categories, philosophical and psychological perspectives, and purposive paradigms. English teachers disputed two questions: what should "grammar" be and how can it help students read and write better? While this is not the place for a history of linguistics in America (those interested can turn to a number of books on that subject[41]), it must be noted that the knowledge and attitudes of most English teachers were increasingly outdated. Fries' *American English Grammar* of 1940, financed by the NCTE, was meant to inform teachers about contemporary grammatical knowledge and thus reduce the "futile and even harmful practices which have resulted from ignorance."[42] The book seems not to have had much impact, however, despite its practical intentions and readability.

During the forties and early fifties grammar teaching in college was damped down by the growth of two trendy movements: General Semantics and the Communications movement. The General Semantics movement, popularized by S. I. Hayakawa's *Thought and Language* of 1940, concerned itself with words and their representational functions. The "communications" movement in general education wished to concentrate on all four communications skills—reading, writing, speaking, and listening—and thus had a great deal of nongrammatical material to cover. Meanwhile, handbooks of grammar grew from small home-reference manuals into fairly large books that attempted to rule-govern the entire process of composition. It is unfortunate but true that of the dozens of handbooks published between 1930 and 1960 only a handful even attempted to utilize the insights of linguistics, and only one of these had any influence—Porter Perrin's *An Index to English* (1939), which, like all of Perrin's work, was rigorous in its scholarship and not satisfied to mouth the contemporary pieties.

In 1952, the indefatigable Charles Fries published *The Structure of American English*, a textbook which attempted to apply the insights of linguists since Bloomfield to constructing English sentences. Fries's basically

descriptive, nonnormative approach would gradually come to be called "structural grammar" and would be one of the key issues in grammatical arguments that would rage a few years later.[43] In 1952, however, *The Structure of English* caused barely a ripple. Many teachers examined it, but few taught it. Most English teachers continued to slumber through a long summer of lethargic acceptance of linguistic ignorance, leading W. Nelson Francis to cry in 1953 that

> in no reputable academic discipline is the gap between the pioneers of research and the pedagogical rank and file more shockingly great. . . . Our situation is as anomalous as if our scientific colleagues were to teach geocentric astronomy, pre-Darwinian biology, and chemistry based on the four elements.[44]

The combination of ignorance and willful refusal to abandon traditional grammar and the "standards" that many people thought it represented continued throughout most of the 1950s. Many teachers shared the common public attitude that "standards" had been sliding in English for many years, and especially since Sterling Leonard and Charles Fries and their band of radical hotheads had begun cutting the ground out from under traditional grammar. By the mid-fifties, however, this position was little defended except in *sotto voce* staffroom complaints. Most of the publishing members of the profession were increasingly coming to see a pro–traditional grammar attitude as a hallmark of ignorance and solipsism.

THE GREAT STRUCTURALISM DEBATE

With the mid-fifties we enter a fascinating era, one that really deserves an essay all its own. I cannot do full justice to the complexity of the positions held or the arguments advanced; such huge theoretical shifts rocked both linguistics and composition between 1956 and 1965 that the picture is often less than clear. Before 1956 or so there was relatively little interest in or activity concerning grammar as a intellectual concept or a pedagogical challenge, and after 1965 we emerge into the recognizable modern landscape well described by W. Ross Winterowd.[45] Between those two dates, however, a veritable ferment of interest in linguistics came to English, leaving the discipline shaken and changed forever.

This new era probably began with Fries' 1952 *Structure* as much as with anything else. Though not a popular textbook, it motivated several other authors to write textbooks using "structural grammar" as their essential model. Paul Roberts' *Patterns of English*, Donald Lloyd and Harry Warfel's *American English in Its Cultural Setting* and Harold Whitehall's *Structural Essentials of English* all appeared in 1956. Suddenly, like it or not, English teachers were faced with having to choose between books that tacitly supported the old dispensation and those that trumpeted the new. As happens so often in composition, the knowledge that journal authors had been trying to promote for years was actually delivered by textbooks.

Not, I hasten to add, that the "structural" textbooks took over the field; in fact, they did rather poorly, considering how much had been said about the "new grammar." Some teachers tried the structural approach, hopeful, perhaps that this "new" grammar could rekindle the flame of belief that seemed to be guttering for the old grammar. But Roberts, Fries, and Lloyd-Warfel never became the touchstones they sought to be. Their problems were well diagnosed by Charlton Laird in 1957:

> If we are to attempt teaching English in the near future by extensive use of structural linguistics, we are presented with at least the following staggering facts: (1) structural linguistics is a difficult concept and an exacting practice, when compared, for instance, with an engaging amusement like general semantics; (2) the linguists themselves do not as yet agree entirely, either in the analysis of English or in a method of teaching it; (3) no large-scale test of the approach using unselected teachers has yet been attempted, and (4) there is no immediate prospect of producing a considerable body of teachers versed in structural linguistics.[46]

Laird went on to question the entire structuralist enterprise, but he was aware even as he critiqued descriptivism that the old grammar was no more defensible. His essay provoked several responses.

By 1959, the question of structural linguistics and its relation to English was getting ready to explode. In late 1958 the venerable Wilbur Hatfield had come out in favor of teaching structural grammar in English,[47] and the fuse was lit in 1959 by Harry Warfel's argument in the February *College English*. In his typically winsome and delicate fashion, Warfel began:

> The science of structural linguistics has put new tools into our hands. Just as nucleonics has penetrated into the minute operations of the atom, so structural linguistics has unlocked the secrets of language. The established conclusions and the emerging theories seem likely to force other disciplines to reshape current procedures wherever they are dependent upon or impinge upon language. . . . The teaching of composition must undergo a revolutionary change.[48]

From this humble beginning, Warfel went on to lecture his audience on the "vast array of facts" amassed by structural linguists from which come "principles, rules, and laws that have relevance to general composition. Warfel argued that the function-based grammar then accepted by most linguists was a better basis for composition learning than anything else. He inveighed against the "outmoded gadgetry" of traditional handbooks, workbooks, and grammars, but he also condemned the (sometimes extreme) "thought" and "general education" methods of the period. "The study of semantics has been a will-o-the-wisp. . . . Most books of reading selections have been productive of little good. The preoccupation with ideas as opposed to the student's mastery of the language system has been self-defeating" (p. 212). This hectoring tone continued throughout the article.

Warfel's structuralist boosterism seems vaguely sad and ironic to us today— "Look upon my works, ye mighty, and despair"—but in 1959 it was little less than a call to arms. He was replied to quickly, and soon the journals were filled with essays for and against structural linguistics in English. The denigration of linguistics in the popular prints was continuing, with Jacques Barzun leading the charge against the "new grammarians," and from 1960 through 1963, linguistics and its impact on composition were fighting issues. *College English* devoted the better parts of four issues to the linguistic controversy between 1960 and 1965, and the battles raged. Structuralists explained patiently again and again why their discipline better explained the facts of language than did the traditional grammar,[49] while at the same time numerous English teachers wrote essays complaining about the nonjudgmental aspects of descriptive linguistics. Polemicists had a field day; W. Nelson Francis criticized Barzun and Mario Pei, John Sherwood criticized Charles Fries, A. M. Tibbetts criticized W. Nelson Francis, platoons criticized Harry Warfel . . . The entire discipline seemed to feel that a great question impended; as Allain Renoir put it, "The necessity to make a considered choice between traditional grammar and structural linguistics is one which teachers of freshman composition can no longer avoid. . . ."[50]

In the midst of this controversy a number of rational points of view also appeared. Among those who took this rational middle ground were Renoir, who admitted that the structuralists' "extreme accuracy in linguistic description is certainly desirable but by no means necessary to the teaching of composition. The main job of the teacher of composition is *not* to describe language, but rather to teach his students how to *compose*." And Charles Fries himself, in several magisterial statements in 1960 and 1961, defended linguistics but tried to disassociate himself from its thoughtless popularizers. "Linguistic science, like all science, is concerned with knowing and understanding, not with doing," wrote Fries. If applications were to be made, he was certain that they could not be the result of forcing English teachers to take one or two linguistics courses to master techniques. Nor did Fries believe in the simple-minded adaptations that some of the "linguistic science-fiction" writers like Warfel had proposed. Fries was utterly certain that such adaptations were futile, and his statement is worth noting today:

> In my view, it is not the tools and the techniques of linguistic science that should be brought into the classroom; but in some way, the substance of the knowledge and understanding won by linguistic science must be thoroughly assimilated and then used to shed new light upon the problems that arise wherever language is concerned.[51]

The structuralist controversy seemed to many teachers and English based linguists to be a battle for the very soul of composition teaching itself. Some asked: would the discipline stagnate, a purveyor of outworn and discredited conventions, or would it take the high road of science and accept the future? Others asked: would English surrender to the "anything goes" radical wing or proudly continue its traditional role as safeguarder of standards?

Only a few early saw the futility of the battle, the foredoomed fate of both structuralists and traditionalists. While the usual suspects—Warfel, Fries, Francis, Barzun, Allen, Roberts, and many others—worried the question of structuralism from 1959 through 1963, a young student of Zellig Harris's named Noam Chomsky readied the linguistic revolution that would, at least in America, relegate the entire structuralist enterprise to the history books. As early as 1961 James Sledd saw it coming in a thoughtful article called "A Plea for Pluralism." As usual, Sledd minced no words:

> For American teachers of English, the year's principal developments in language-study have been two. First, Chomsky, Halle, Lees, and their disciples have sustained their attacks on structural linguistics with increasing vigor and success. Second, with increasing success and vigor the evangels of the Anglists have sustained their effort to convert the high schools and colleges to structural linguistics. Yesterday's Left has thus become today's Right, a new Left has emerged which is in some ways closer to yesterday's Right than to today's, and today's Right, internally divided and calling itself the Center, works at ignoring the new Left as it evangelizes the old Right. The result may well be that men who have argued creditably against traditional dogmas will now saddle the country's schools with the opposite dogmas of American structuralism at the precise moment when many of those dogmas are being discredited.[52]

That is what happened for a little while, but not for long. After 1965, linguistics in America was clearly in the hands of the MIT axis, and the structuralist debate was effectively over. The old Right, handbook traditionalists, remained in English, but even the tenuous bridges between linguistics and handbook grammar that the structuralists had built were impossible to maintain after the ascent of transformational-generative grammar. If Friesian function categories and juncture theory were hard for English teachers to follow, phrase-structure rules and obligatory transformations were completely impossible for most of them. After 1965, linguistics as an ongoing exploration had less and less to do with teaching English. As genuine linguistics became less accessible, "grammar" in English became the strange amalgam of buzzwords, legends, handbook nostrums, half-understood transformational concepts, and decayed eighteenth-century prescription that most of us know today.[53] Traditional grammar did not flourish openly, especially after the famous and seemingly final verdict of *Research in Written Composition* in 1963 that "the teaching of formal grammar has a negligible or, because it usually displaces some instruction and practice in actual composition, even a harmful effect on the improvement of writing,"[54] but it continued its malevolent half-life in its accustomed lair: handbooks and workbooks.

In 1963, the concerted leap forward in rhetorical theory that we now think of as the "rhetorical revolution" was just beginning, and some nonmainstream linguistic theories such as tagmemics were instrumental parts of it. A few enthusiasts believed that transformational-generative theory could

be made the keystone of the new rhetoric, but results were inconclusive, and the full story of TG applications takes me beyond 1965, where I arbitrarily mean to end this history.

The tale of grammar is by no means over; even today sentence diagramming has voluble champions, and traditional grammar, against all odds, is attempting a comeback. A great deal of the history of composition in America seems to be a clumsy shuffle-dance of grammar with rhetoric, with first one and then another leading. It will not end soon, for the wish for certainty and algorithmic closure represented by the one struggles always with the desire for originality and creativity represented by the other. So long as language is part science, part art, and part magic, the grammarians and the rhetoricians will be struggling with each other to lead the dance.

NOTES

1. Rollo L. Lyman, *English Grammar in American Schools before 1850* (Washington, D.C.: Govt. Printing Office, 1922), p. 5.

2. Charles C. Fries, "Linguistic Science and the Teaching of English," in *Perspectives in English*, ed. Robert C. Pooley (New York: Appleton-Century-Crofts, 1960), p. 152.

3. Lindley Murray, *An English Grammar*, 7th ed. (New York: Thomas Wilson, 1842), p. 333.

4. For an informative discussion of this phenomenon, see Edward Finegan, *Attitudes toward English Usage: The History of a War of Words* (New York: Teachers' College Press, 1980), pp. 30–60.

5. Samuel S. Greene, *Greene's Analysis* (Philadelphia: Thomas, Cowperthwaite, 1847), p. 79.

6. William H. Wells, "Methods of Teaching English Grammar," *Barnard's American Journal of Education*, 5 (1865), 148–49.

7. F. A. Barbour, "History of English Grammar Teaching," *Educational Review*, 12 (1896), 487–507.

8. George P. Marsh, *Lectures on the English Language* (New York: Scribner's, 1860), pp. 87–88.

9. C. Homer Bean, "How English Grammar has Been Taught in America," *Education*, 34 (1913–14), 311.

10. Alonzo Reed and Brainerd Kellogg, *Higher Lessons in English* (New York: Clark and Maynard, 1877), p. 3.

11. See especially Buck's "Make-Believe Grammar," *School Review*, 17 (1909), 21–33.

12. See, for instance, C. R. Rounds, "The Varying Systems of Nomenclature in Use in Our Texts in English Grammar," *Educational Review*, 40 (1910), 82–88.

13. George Campbell, *The Philosophy of Rhetoric* (London: William Tegg, 1850), p. 35.

14. Hugh Blair, *Lectures on Rhetoric and Belles-Lettres* (Philadelphia: Troutman and Hayes, 1853), p. 78.

15. Blair, *Lectures*, p. 101.

16. Samuel P. Newman, *A Practical System of Rhetoric* (New York: Mark H. Newman, 1843), p. 136.

17. For more information on this debate, see my essay "Mechanical Correctness in Composition Instruction," forthcoming in *College Composition and Communication*, and Finegan, *Attitudes toward English Usage*, pp. 62–75.

18. Wells, "Methods of Teaching English Grammar," p. 149.

19. For more on this examination, see A. S. Hill, "An Answer to the Cry for More English," in *Twenty Years of School and College English* (Cambridge: Harvard Univ. Pr., 1896), pp. 6–16.

20. Joseph H. Gilmore, *Outlines of the Art of Expression* (Boston: Ginn, 1876), p. 3.

21. Edwin A. Abbott, *How to Write Clearly* (Boston: Roberts Bros., 1875), p. 7.

22. Some texts did incorporate grammar, but they were rare. C. W. Bardeen's *A System of Rhetoric* of 1884, for instance, included 139 pages of straight grammar—numbered with Roman numerals and called an "Introduction"—but it also utilized a more pragmatic organizational system than most popular texts and did not sell well.

23. John F. Genung, *The Practical Elements of Rhetoric* (Boston: Ginn, 1886), p. 109.

24. E. L. Godkin, "The Illiteracy of American Boys," *Educational Review*, 13 (1897), 7.

25. Edwin C. Woolley, *Handbook of Composition: A Compendium of Rules* (Boston: D. C. Heath, 1907), p. iv.

26. See my essay, "Handbooks: History of a Genre," *Rhetoric Society Quarterly*, 13 (1983), 87–98.

27. Frank W. Scott, "Composition and the Rest of the Curriculum," *English Journal*, 7 (1918), 515.

28. For instance, Edward A. Allen in 1887: "But our grammarians, refusing to study their language in its marvelous process of development for the last thousand years, have been content either to create rules for the use of it . . . or to borrow the rules of those languages which have a differently developed system of grammar. . . . No student should be deluded into the belief that he can become a grammarian by the study of the grammar alone" ("English Grammar Viewed from All Sides," *Education*, 7 [1887], 466–69).

29. Thomas Lounsbury, *The Standard of Usage in English* (New York: Harper, 1908), p. 71.

30. George Krapp, *Modern English: Its Growth and Present Use* (New York: Scribner's, 1909), p. 330.

31. "The Call for the Organization Meeting," *Language*, 1 (1925), 6.

32. Leonard Bloomfield, "Why a Linguistic Society?" *Language*, 1 (1925), 5.

33. Sterling A. Leonard, " 'Old Purist Junk,' " *English Journal*, 7 (1918), 296. See also his *Current English Usage* (Chicago: Inland Press, 1932).

34. These studies are mentioned and evaluated by James F. Hosic in "The Essentials of Composition and Grammar," *School and Society*, 1 (1915), 581–587.

35. William Asker, "Does Knowledge of Formal Grammar Function?" *School and Society*, 17 (1923), 109–11.

36. Charles C. Fries, "Preface," *The Teaching of the English Language* (New York: Thomas Nelson, 1927).

37. Leon Mones, "A Word on Formal Grammar," *Education*, 44 (1923–24), 234.

38. See, for instance, C. R. Rounds, "Is Grammar Useful?" *Education*, 46 (1925–26), 551–559.

39. Wilbur Hatfield et al., *An Experience Curriculum in English* (New York: Appleton-Century, 1935), p. 228.

40. See Harold B. Allen, "From Prairies to Mountains: Linguistics and Composition," *College English*, 26 (1965), 266.

41. Two good historical sources are John P. Hughes, *The Science of Language: An Introduction to Linguistics* (New York: Random House, 1962), and John Lyons, *Introduction to Theoretical Linguistics* (Cambridge: Cambridge Univ. Pr., 1968).

42. Charles C. Fries, *American English Grammar* (New York: Appleton-Century, 1940), p. vii.

43. Fries was not, of course, the only or even the most important contributor to the terms "structural grammar" or "structural linguistics." The terms had existed

since the thirties, and in linguistics such books as Zellig Harris' *Methods in Structural Linguistics* (1951) and George Trager and Lee Smith's *Outline of English Structures* (1951) were much better known than Fries'. Fries, however, brought the terms to popular use in English and was almost certainly responsible for such later titles as A. A. Hill's *Introduction to Linguistic Structure* (1958) and W. Nelson Francis' *Structure of American English* (1958).

44. W. Nelson Francis, "Our Responsibility to the English Language," *College English*, 14 (1953), 329.

45. W. Ross Winterowd, "Linguistics and Composition," in *Teaching Composition: Ten Bibliographical Essays*, ed. Gary Tate (Fort Worth: Texas Christian Univ. Pr., 1976), pp. 197–221.

46. Charlton Laird, "The Parts, or Vestigial Remnants, of Speech," *College English*, 18 (1957), 337.

47. Wilbur W. Hatfield, "Will Structural Grammar Help?" *English Journal*, 47 (1958), 570–72.

48. Harry R. Warfel, "Structural Linguistics and Composition," *College English*, 20 (1959), 205.

49. Samuel R. Levin, "Comparing Traditional and Structural Grammar," *College English*, 21 (1960), 260–65.

50. Allain Renoir, "Traditional Grammar or Structural Linguistics," *College English*, 22 (1961), 484.

51. Charles C. Fries, "Advances in Linguistics," *College English*, 23 (1961), 37. See also his essay, "Linguistic Science and the Teaching of English."

52. James Sledd, "A Plea for Pluralism," *College English*, 23 (1961), 16.

53. Again, James Sledd has an apposite comment on structural linguistics: "That version of modernity is now quite rejected and forgotten, having been succeeded by several other abiding truths; but despite the confusion of the shifting doctrines, a clear result has certainly been attained—namely, a state of utter confusion among school teachers and blank ignorance among their pupils. We have taught the teachers to despise our one established grammatical tradition; we have given them nothing stable to put in its place; and consequently the average student in our colleges and universities today knows nothing of any grammatical system whatsoever and is totally at a loss when in any of his classes strange vocables like *noun* and *verb* are uttered." ("What Are We Going to Do About It Now That We're Number One?" *American Speech*, 53 [1978], 184.)

54. Richard Braddock, Richard Lloyd-Jones, and Lowell Schoer, *Research in Written Composition* (Champaign, IL: NCTE, 1963), pp. 37–38.

Personal Writing Assignments

The question of what Bob chose *not* to discuss in "Personal Writing Assignments," published in *College Composition and Communication* in 1987, is almost as interesting as the question of what he chose to discuss. For by 1987, debates over what James Berlin and others termed "expressivism" in composition were certainly a central feature of the scholarly landscape. And since most critics identify a focus on personal writing as a feature of expressivist teaching, Bob might well have situated his essay in the context of this debate. Although Bob does gesture toward this debate in the conclusion of the essay, he focuses primarily on providing a systematic history of writing assignments from the classical period to the present. And the story that Bob tells is one of the ascendancy of personal writing assignments in America, with the result that "[f]rom the 1890's through today, personal writing assignments have remained central to the teaching of composition" (150). In the concluding section of his essay, Bob examines some contemporary backlashes against personal writing and identifies "a curious discomfort in English teachers' attitudes toward students writing from personal experience," a discomfort that arises from conflicts between "different ideas about what students should know and control in their writing" (151). Bob concludes his essay by calling for teachers to take what he characterizes as a "middle position" on this issue (154).

The question can be asked this way: what are students of discourse supposed to know, supposed to be able to speak and write about? This is a question that faces us whenever we organize courses and make writing assignments. Should we emphasize "honest, personal" writing, stress "academic," "argumentative," or "practical" subjects, or try somehow to create a balance among these discourse aims? This inescapable question is one that teachers have argued about for the last hundred years and more. I want to examine here a small element of rhetorical history — the sorts of subjects that teachers have assigned students, and their change from objective,

---

From *College Composition and Communication* 38.2 (1987): 166–83.

centripetal writing tasks to subjective, centrifugal tasks. This topic has important ramifications for teachers and opens out, as I will show, on an entire shift of emphasis within western culture, a shift that we still are in the midst of and are striving to understand today.

THE IMPERSONALITY OF CLASSICAL RHETORIC

Throughout most of the history of rhetoric, the answer to the question above was clear enough: the student of discourse was supposed to be able to speak and write on any objective subject given. Indeed, this concept of rhetoric having no specific province of its own, being able to cover any area of knowledge, is older than Plato and Aristotle. As Richard Leo Enos has shown, rhetorical theorists from the first sophists forward trained young students from their earliest lessons to master fully-formed objective speech tasks of many sorts. There were those in antiquity who felt quite sincerely that this meant the true rhetor must know everything—as Cicero puts it in *De Oratore*: "In my opinion, no one can be an absolutely perfect orator unless he has acquired a knowledge of all important subjects and arts" (I, 4, 20). Quintilian, the greatest rhetorical educator of the ancient world, does not go this far, but does recommend a complete literary and philosophical education as preparatory to the learning of rhetoric, "for there is nothing which may not crop up in a cause or appear as a question for discussion" (II, 21, 22).

The technics of classical invention all militated in favor of outward-directed investigation. The Aristotelian topics, which were the point of entry to classical invention, were all based in logos—the nature of the subject—and much less in questions of ethos, the nature of the speaker. When a subject was assigned to a student of rhetoric—the superiority of trade over agriculture, for instance—the pupil was expected to complete a full topical analysis of all the arguments that could be made. All of Aristotle's four common topics and 28 special topics could be brought into play, and students were expected to master the use of all of them. The lines of argument produced by topical invention are overwhelmingly *impersonal*. They take into consideration historical forces, contemporary feelings, testimony of authorities, class expectations. Everything is useful to the speaker, but until a speaker had established his own ethos, usually through community service or previous rhetorical success, his own experiences and opinions were not important to his discourse. The one line of argument that no one expected or would accept would be the argument that trade was preferable to agriculture because the speaker was familiar with it and liked it better.

Rhetorical exercises mirrored the classical belief that the world—the brute facts of it, the doings of the persons in it, the nature of their feelings, judgments, beliefs—was the grist for the mill of rhetoric. From the earliest age, students were to be trained to see the world, to know what had been thought and said about it, and to hammer that knowledge into discourse that could change it. To learn to do this, pupils were given exercises called progymnasmata, which led them through various sorts of writing practice in a

sequence designed to give them continuing challenges and ever-increasing engagement with real issues.[1] Such sequences were the essential tools used with beginning writers. Quintilian recommends that, in addition to being initially taught literature, boys should begin writing by practice in historical narratives, then moving to refutation and confirmation of narratives, then to speeches of praise and denunciation, then to theses concerned with comparisons between things ("which is preferable, town or country life?"), and finally to the praise and denunciation of laws (II, 4, 1–40).

What I wish to stress here is that ancient rhetoric was a public discipline, devoted to examining and arguing questions that could be shared by all members of the polity. Even children were expected to read and argue from myth, history, and contemporary questions. Proofs of arguments were impersonal, and the students were taught from the nursery up that to obtrude merely personal opinions was both hubristic and stupid, proceeding "from a passion for display that would do credit to a common mountebank" (II, 4, 15).

In addition to the progymnasmata, the central pedagogical technique used by rhetorical teachers of classical times was *imitation*—exercises in the deliberate surrendering of the students' writerly autonomy to the authority of a "master." Such imitation exercises as learning by heart, translations from one language to another, paraphrase, and emulation were all parts of basic education in Greece and Rome. Here was complete submergence of the personality of the student in the works of another, all for the purpose of eventual mastery. Through imitation, wrote Quintilian, students

> will form an intimate acquaintance with the best writings, will carry their models with them . . . they will have a plentiful and choice vocabulary and a command of artistic structure and a supply of figures which will not have to be hunted for, but will offer themselves spontaneously, from the treasure-house, if I may so call it, in which they are stored. In addition they will be in the agreeable position of being able to quote the happy sayings of the various authors, a power which they will find most useful. . . . (II, 7, 3–4)

Imitation, in other words, was meant to be the foundation for creative mastery rather than mere "servile copying."

In addition to impersonal *topoi*, sequenced assignment of public rhetorical tasks, and the use of imitation exercises, the classical educational tradition had as its essential quality the concept of synthesis—of looking to the world, gathering what is good there, and using it according to a slowly-developing wisdom. For this purpose there was no better practice than the keeping of a commonplace book.[2] By the creation and use of commonplace books, the student was expected to have access to the *copia* of material that was the mark of an educated man. Even accomplished scholars kept commonplace books, and such books, either personally kept or printed and bought, underlay the attitude toward discourse of the classical tradition.

Such attitudes informed classical rhetoric and controlled the teaching of discourse from 400 B.C. up until A.D. 1800 or so. They form a necessary

backdrop to any examination of the teaching of speech and writing in America, and what I want to emphasize about them is this: The classical tradition in *rhetoric*—as opposed to literature, which was a less demanding part of education and taught much earlier in a student's career—was essentially unconcerned with personal expression of personal experience. There was no branch of ancient learning that meant to teach students how to "express themselves" in any personal way; the very idea of teaching such a thing was alien to the ancients. For classical educators, the likes and dislikes of the student, his own style, the entire expression of his private personality, were of very little account. Through the Roman Empire, the Middle Ages, and the early Renaissance this tradition held sway. The individual was held in small regard, was continuingly subservient to the King, the Court, the Lord, the State, and especially the Church. Rhetoric served these ends.

EPISTEMOLOGICAL SHIFTS TOWARD INDIVIDUALISM

As the seventeenth century opened, this impersonal tradition continued as part of both the neo-Ciceronian and Ramean traditions in discourse education. But changes were occurring, slow shifts in the epistemological fabric of western culture. What we begin to see during the seventeenth century is the rise of the individual—personal tastes, feelings, perceptions, experiences—as a worthy and important part of public life, and especially of the life of words. In large part, of course, this was due to the burgeoning of vernacular literature itself, which had, as opposed to Latin and Greek post-classical writing, celebrated the individual, the self, the personal. The very genre of narrative, most commonly occupied in history and rhetoric with heroes, archetypes, great non-personal forces, became in the narratives of the vernacular stories of increasingly realistic individual persons: Beowulf giving way to the Wife of Bath; Everyman giving way to Shylock. By 1700, all the literary groundwork had been laid for the rise of novels, books of personal essays, travel books, realistic narrative and overtly personal poems—indeed, for all of the forms of literary discourse that burgeoned in the eighteenth century.

All of this mirrors, of course, the rise of the middle classes and the increasing threats they presented to the traditional hierarchies. These changes stirred European culture to its bones. We must realize, however, that throughout the first half of the eighteenth century, rhetoric was almost completely divorced from the growing importance and literary celebration of the individual. Not until Adam Smith's rhetoric lectures of 1749 did rhetoric begin to free itself from the dead hand of neoclassicism, try to determine what the common people might find effective and persuasive, and begin to consider the nature and meaning inherent in vernacular literature. By 1783, though, the incorporation of literature and rhetoric was speeded by the most popular rhetoric of its time, Hugh Blair's *Lectures*, which made literary criticism and taste important and complementary parts of education for the next seventy years. For the first time, a primary definition of education came to be the ability to make personal, reasoned and appreciative judgments about

the literary effusions of others. Taste and criticism as components of rhetoric reflect the increased appreciation for sentiment and personality as elements of life.

The nineteenth century was to see a profound shift in rhetoric resulting from the proto-romanticism of the eighteenth century. Rhetoric, though enhanced theoretically between 1749 and 1783, had remained essentially classical in outlook—that is, the subjects of the rhetorician (as opposed to the critic) were still held to be public events and opinions, to be investigated, amplified, arranged, and presented. The nineteenth century saw this classical approach change, in a relatively few years, into a rhetorical praxis far more personal, private, intimate—in short, a praxis informed by Romanticism rather than by Classicism.

The Romantic Movement, important though it is to literary studies and, indeed, to any understanding of the development of European and American culture, has until recently been given little consideration as a force in nineteenth-century rhetoric.[3] There is no doubt, however, that rhetoric and composition were powerfully influenced by Romantic thought. Nineteenth-century rhetoric shows many of the classic signs of the Romantic shift, changes in the ways that writers viewed themselves and in the way that rhetoric viewed writing. Language recommended to students gradually changes from the Ciceronian "high style" to something closer to the Wordsworthian "language really used by men." The world of external nature comes more and more into rhetorical consideration (though never as powerfully as it had into poetry) as description became one end of rhetoric. The emphasis comes to be on discourse as more organic than mechanical, needing to be nurtured, growing out of the writer's purpose. And most importantly, the personal feelings, experiences, thoughts, and appreciations of the writer come to have a centrality and power in rhetorical education after 1875 that would have shocked rhetoricians of even fifty years before. Let us examine these changes in detail.

THE DECLINE OF INVENTION

Giving students specific subjects on which they were to write goes back to the ancient world, as we have seen, but composition subjects do not begin to appear in textbooks until the early nineteenth century. Up through the Civil War, English composition was devoted, as rhetoric had been, to teaching the received ways of handling public topics by deploying gleaned knowledge mixed with commonly-held beliefs. At the academies and high schools, writing, when taught at all, was taught using rhetorical precepts and assignments. So for more than fifty years, students were expected to learn to write by discoursing on "Time," or "Temperance," or "Gaming," or "Luxury," and were given later assignments on such subjects as "Familiarity Breeds Contempt," "The Necessity of Exercises," and "The Baneful Effects of Indulgence."[4] Early textbooks merely picked up and expanded these old topics. John Walker's *Teacher's Assistant in English Composition* of 1801, for instance,

began the trend by dividing composition up into "Regular Subjects" and "Themes," which roughly correspond to explanation and argument—the two "senior members" of what would later be called the modes of discourse.[5] Walker provided examples of the topics that could be assigned for both subjects and themes, and, not surprisingly, these topics are all non-personal: topics for regular subjects included "Education," "Government," "Peace," "War," and those for themes were the proof of maxims like "Trust not appearances."

Walker's pedagogy was more or less *ab ovo*, and so, efficacious or not, it was picked up and used by other authors, especially in the United States, where the common schools were teaching composition to an ever-larger percentage of children. Newer composition texts also offered lists and lists of potential subject assignments, all of which were completely, utterly, relentlessly impersonal. R. G. Parker's *Progressive Exercises* of 1832, for instance, presented an alphabetized list of 302 topics, beginning with "On Attention," "On Adversity," "On Affectation," "On Affection, Parental," "On Ardour of Mind," etc., and proceeding to such complexities as "Female Virtues" and "The Progress of Error."

And what were students supposed to do with these creaking abstractions? Exactly what rhetoric students had always done with their assignments: search through their reading, their memories, their commonplace books for something to say. With the disappearance of classical study from the vernacular grammar schools, however, student knowledge of non-personal topics declined markedly, and here Walker was again influential. He had developed a kind of corrupted topical invention system for handling his abstract subjects, asking students to handle his abstract "subject" topics by concentrating on "Definition," "Cause," "Antiquity or Novelty," "Universality and Locality," and "Effects." (His argumentative "theme" topics were handled by a version of the classical six-part oration.) This system, mechanistic though it was, appeared in many textbooks between 1810 and 1850. Adopting Walker's turgid five-element invention heuristic, students could come up with at least *some* things that needed to be found out before the topic could be attempted, and if the results were mechanical they at least reflected a minimal knowledge of the facts of the outside world. Although the wide-ranging reading that was a legacy of the classical education was seen less and less, mechanical heuristics like Walker's allowed students to at least come up with *some* sort of material. Thus impersonal topics could be made to seem workable.

In the transitional composition-rhetoricians of the period 1800–1850 we see the last hurrah of formalized invention systems meant for use in the old way of rhetoric—as keys meant to explore the writer's resources, which were assumed to consist of a considerable store of cultural knowledge. The ability to write at all on such subjects, it becomes clear, was intimately bound up with some method of invention, usually a mechanical form based loosely on some of the classical topics. Walker's five-part form for subjects and six-part form for themes were popular, but other writers evolved their own

mechanistic invention systems. George P. Quackenbos' *Advanced Course* of 1854 stressed invention and in specific stressed the necessity for using heuristics to deal with abstract subjects:

> It is [invention] that furnishes the material of composition, and on which, in a great measure, its value depends. Here moreover, lies most of the difficulty which the young experience in writing. Let them have definite thoughts and they will generally find it easy to express themselves. But how are they to deal with intangible things . . . ? (325)

Quackenbos spends two complete chapters on explaining the method of his topically-based system, and follows up his explanation with 506 suggested topics that can be run through it. None of them, predictably, are personal or experiential; they do not need to be, since using Quackenbos' system would allow students to write—not necessarily well, but to write—on any abstract subject.

Henry Day's impassioned defense in 1850 of invention against Richard Whately's seeming dismissal of it is in the same vein: "The mind, having thought to express, and being animated by a perceived object in expressing it, when furnished with the guiding principles in such expression, acts intelligently, easily, and with satisfaction to itself" (iii–iv). Day realized that most students could not write on "The Rise of Popery" or "The Corrupting Effects of Slavery" without the assistance of some system.

These authors—Parker, Quackenbos, and Day—represent the end of the line for invention because of the deep changes going on in the culture after 1825 or so. A number of historians have commented on the demotion of invention to a subsidiary role in the rhetorical theory of the later nineteenth century (Crowley, 1985, Young, 1980); what has not been emphasized, however, is that the retreat from invention was actually a conscious move away from the complex or mechanical invention systems that were a necessary part of trying to use the old abstract rhetorical assignments in a changed world.

THE MODES OF DISCOURSE AND THE REPUDIATION OF IMPERSONAL SUBJECTS

And the world of teaching was changing. It was expanding rapidly, encompassing more and more people, mutating to try to meet their needs. Increasingly, students were arriving at schools and colleges possessing only the broad, unspecialized education of the common schools and frontier academies. These were not the classically-prepared students of the earlier, more elitist educational tradition. They did not have their Caesar, their Aristotle, their Demosthenes—not even their Ramus. They had a little readin', a little writin', a little 'rithmetic, and they needed a different sort of training. As a result, after 1860, composition teachers began to reject abstract, impersonal topics. The movement began with the realization—probably quite early—that the essays students were turning out in response to topics like "Joy" and

"Herbal Delights" were very poor writing. As early as 1850, Henry Day (whose own book is filled with objective, impersonal assignments) was complaining that

> whenever a familiar and, at the same time, a broad and comprehensive theme is selected . . . only general, familiar views can be taken, and there is no life of invention. It is a cold, inanimate work of the memory recalling dead thought. There is no inspiration, no satisfaction. There must be some new view taken, something original, or the work of invention must necessarily be laborious and heavy. (40)

The revolt against abstract subjects did not, however, really begin until after the Civil War, when we see a sort of concerted disgust with these general topics begin to appear. For instance, Simon Kerl's *Elements of Composition and Rhetoric* of 1869, though still based on expository and argumentative subjects—"The Planetary System," "Instincts of Animals," "Lying"—was one of the first texts to offer students a few obviously personal topics as well—"My Grandmother," "Songs I Remember" (364–65).

The modes of discourse—narration, description, exposition, and argument—which were formalized in 1866 by Alexander Bain, had a powerful effect on writing topics in the U.S. During the 1870's and 80's the modal system had been growing more popular, and with its gradual triumph in the 90's, due mostly to the books of Alexander Bain and John Genung, the two personal modes—narration and description—became the first elements of composition taught in most classes. Commonly there were whole chapters devoted to these modes, and narration and description were the gates through which personal writing entered composition instruction. In early books, we sometimes see narration and description treated impersonally, but never do we see personal writing assignments unrelated to these personal modes.

It was John M. Hart's very popular *Manual of Composition and Rhetoric* of 1870, however, that really opened the floodgates to personal writing in composition courses. Hart was the first text author to take real advantage of the personal-experience writing potential of narration and description. Although his book is not modally organized, Hart saw that narrative and descriptive writing could go far beyond the retelling of history and the simple travelogues that they had theretofore been. Hart proposed that students tackle a series of subjects ranging from simple to complex: compositions on objects ("Paper," "Dogs," "Penknives"), transactions ("Going to School," "Cultivating Flowers"), abstract subjects ("Fear," "The Danger of Bad Company"), imaginary subjects ("The Man in the Moon," "A Tour on the Flying Dutchman"), personal narratives ("How I Spent My Vacation," "Ascent of Mt. Washington") and descriptions ("A Visit to a Picture-Gallery," "A Description of a Rolling-Mill"). Here, in a short compass, we have the old and the new: the abstract subjects of the old sort—"fear," "memory"—and the first textbook statements of new personal-experience topics, including the classics, "Going to School," and "How I Spent My Vacation" (341).

Hart is clearly transitional; although he condemns book-learned assignments as "least conducive to the development of the power of invention," begetting in the student "the habit of copying," he still includes assignments clearly meant to be researched or written from books. But throughout the seventies the dam was preparing to burst. Student writing was being scrutinized and increasingly pronounced unreadable. Authors still believed in abstract subjects, but more and more they sought ways to make them personal, to get students to avoid the bland padding that older topics-based invention systems increasingly created. Personal experience writing showed the way. During this decade we can see invention methods snap inside out, from primary emphasis on recall and synthesis of sources to a new emphasis on choosing and analyzing aspects of personal knowledge. Before the Civil War, invention methods had meant to find and discover things to say, ways to approach a given subject. Invention was primarily accretive; it meant to pile up impersonal material. After personal experience topics began to attain popularity, however, invention shifted purposes; from the vast raft of their personal experiences students had to choose something, narrow it to a workable theme topic, and develop it in some way. Invention became primarily selective — devoted to narrowing and channeling experience — rather than accretive. Information, to be made meaningful, had to be personalized. Depth replaced breadth as central desideratum.

We see this begin in Brainerd Kellogg's books in the late 70's and 80's. Kellogg was one of the first authors to outright reject abstract subjects. "Choose your subject long before you are to write," said Kellogg and Alonzo Reed in 1877's *Higher Lessons in English*: "avoid a full, round term like *Patriotism* or *Duty*; take a fragment of it; as *How Can a Boy be Patriotic?* or *Duties Which We Schoolmates Owe Each Other*" (302–03). Kellogg's higher-level *Textbook on Rhetoric* stuck more with the objective assignments, but still proposed narrowing general subjects to specific branches as the most important phase of invention.

The romanticism that had been an important element in literature since 1798 begins to appear in composition in earnest after 1870, and we see a new emphasis on writing as a first-hand rather than second-hand responsibility. Textbooks had sometimes mentioned before 1865 that writers should write from personal observations, but without the modal system, without narrative and descriptive tasks, the possibilities of observation were limited. By the 1870's, however, personal observation is often included in lists from which materials for writing are to be accumulated. "Knowledge obtained by one's self is always more clear, fresh, and interesting than if obtained at second hand," wrote David J. Hill in his *Elements* of 1878. "Do not go to Homer for a sunrise when you can see one every morning" (13). By the time of John Genung's very popular *Practical Elements of Rhetoric* of 1886, observation was listed first under "Mental Habits that Promote Invention." Observation, said Genung, is "the most potent stimulus and aid to original production . . . In a sense, all the activities of authorship are reducible to this" (227).

Despite the unwillingness of some teachers to give up on the idea that their writing students would be well-read, it was becoming clear to all by the 1880's that the old abstract subjects were not being explored by students as once they had (or were thought to have) been. When Charles Bardeen recommends beginning with narration and description, it is because students can do little else when beginning. "Abstract general topics are meaningless to them . . . Many pupils put together a composition as they would a banquet, seeking in memory or in books for elegant phrases to arrange, and as little understanding to originate an idea as to construct a moss-rose" (310). Exactly what teachers were up against is illustrated by a theme quoted by Bardeen on the assigned subject of "Virtue":

> "Virtue is a good thing to get a holt of. Whenever a feller gets a holt of virtue, he better keep a holt." (310)

Here is the problem well illustrated. This student, confronted with the necessity of saying something about "virtue," looked to his resources as students always had. Through Classical, Medieval, and Renaissance times, even up to the eighteenth century, the student would probably have read widely in Classical literature, imitating and translating it. Very probably he would have been keeping a commonplace book, perhaps indexed. He would be used to examining philosophical concepts through the words of great authors, would have a ready store of illustrations, examples, maxims. He would have been able to write a theme on virtue—a theme servile, unoriginal, and larded with commonplaces, but a theme that made a point, developed it, and concluded. The unfortunate whose theme is quoted above did not even have that option. Having been trained only in the vernacular language, classical illustrations and examples were denied him. Commonplace books had faded away, replaced by the ubiquitous vernacular "readers" that proliferated after 1820. The "gems of literature" in these readers were not imitated or translated, and thus a student could only make use of them in a theme by copying directly from them, as Bardeen suggests happened. Without commonplace books, students *had* no immediate personal access to impersonal knowledge; committing it to subconscious memory was no longer part of education. If a student had no books handy to copy from, he floundered. Thus this completely bankrupt "virtue" theme.

By the nineties, teachers were beginning to be unanimous in their realization that the old subjects did not work any more. With what seems surprising suddenness and vigor, the old ways were outright rejected. Alphonso Newcomer wrote in 1893:

> In selecting subjects for compositions avoid in general those which are too broad and comprehensive for precise treatment; those which are difficult and abstruse, requiring the knowledge and accuracy of one long trained in methods of scientific investigation, or the authority of a matured and logical thinker; those which have been worn out by the use

and abuse of successive generations of essay-writers; those which can have no living interest for your readers and hearers; those which draw upon no personal experience, or appeal to no knowledge or taste of your own. Thus, avoid abstract subjects, such as Patience, Perseverance, Idleness, Duty, Character, True Manhood and Womanhood and the old triad, Faith, Hope, and Charity. You can scarcely expect to say anything old in a new way; all the changes have been rung upon them long ago. Life and the world offer too much that is new and attractive, for us to be wasting our time on these outworn themes. (2)

Newcomer's book was filled with personal experience assignments—incidents from school life, autobiographies, character descriptions of friends, all the essentially "modern" personal subjects we see today. During the nineties the rejection speeded up tremendously, and by the first years of the new century, the reaction was so complete that Howry Espenshade could marvel in 1904 that "a treatise on composition printed only a quarter of a century ago suggests the following as suitable subjects for students' themes: "War," "Mountains," "Disease," . . . The teacher who assigns to his pupils such theme-subjects . . . cannot reasonably complain if they conceive a hearty dislike for theme-writing" (24).

THE ELEMENTS OF PERSONALISM

If the old abstract subjects were no longer viable, what could replace them? Textbooks relied increasingly on two concepts that marked a good subject: *narrowness* and *novelty*. Narrowing the large subject, as we have seen, goes back to the texts of the 1870's, with advice like Reed and Kellogg's to narrow "Patriotism" into "How Can a Boy be Patriotic." By the late 80's, the influential John Genung was warning against such general "subjects" as "too comprehensive, too general, for treatment. They contain no hint of one kind of treatment more than another, no indication of fitness to place, public, or form of discourse; no suggestion of limits or direction. It is clear that they are not as yet in shape to guide the writer as his working idea" (249). Genung proposed that such subjects be narrowed to themes, "concentrated, by means of directive limitations, upon a single issue." The way in which this concentration worked depended for Genung upon the nature of the subject and the mode of discourse, but for later (and more simplistic) authors, this process of concentration was simple "narrowing" of subject to theme, the gist of which must be statable as a *proposition*—later called the *thesis*. "Mountains" becomes "A Tramp to the Mountains," "Disease," becomes "The Anthrax Plague in our Village."

Strongly related to this advice on narrowing the subject is advice on the necessity of *novelty*, of escaping the dead hand of past writers by "making it new." The idea began to circulate in composition classes that a writer's job was to please a reader. It seems strange to us, but the concept of writing interestingly for an audience was *not* brought out strongly by composition texts

until after 1885. Only then do we begin to hear authors saying that "to write interestingly, [the writer] must have something new or striking to tell" (Mead 128). Newcomer asks,

> What then is interesting to the reader? That which is *new* to him. It may almost be said that we spend our lives in the search after novelty—new truth, new power, new beauty. . . . When you were tramping through the woods last Saturday you found growing wild in an out-of-the-way spot a great bed of white violets. What a discovery. . . . Why, you can write a delightful account of this and your schoolmates will be far more interested in it than they would in any essay on plants carefully written up out of botanies and encyclopedias, or in any sentimental rhapsodizing over flowers in general. (7)

By 1900, personal writing assignments, their "narrow/select/develop" invention pedagogy, their corollary concepts of the need to write "interestingly" out of "actual experience," had gained all but complete acceptance. New textbooks proliferated after 1910 that bore down hard on the observation/ experience side of writing: texts based on personal narration ("Write a reminiscence based on some incident in your experience"), texts with observation exercises ("Observe the main street of your town"), and texts including pictures and photographs to which students were to respond. "He who would write a theme must . . . become alive to the perceptions of his five senses," wrote Arthur Nason in 1917; "He must deal with things that are actual and material, not with abstract ideas" (10). Students were encouraged to write about these material, actual things. Theme assignments included: "How I Caught the Woodchuck," "The Largest Fire I Have Seen," "An Hour in the Study Hall," "The Loneliness of Freshmen," and "Why I Came to School." We have come a long way from "Joy," "Parental Affection," and "Instincts of Animals" (320).

From the 1890's through today, personal writing assignments have remained central to the teaching of composition. Almost every writing course includes personal writing, most start with it, and many concentrate on it. Personal writing is not only widely assigned, but is widely accepted by students. A study in 1930 of the topics for written composition in high school showed that out of all of the topics possible under the aegis of the four modes, these were the ten rated highest and done most often by students:

> 1. Narration of personal incident, 2. Narration of program heard over the radio, 3. Criticism of school procedure, 4. Criticism of a motion picture, 5. Narration of story of a game, 6. Criticism of school marks, 7. Reaction to a school subject, 8. Comment on books, school activities, current events, people, etc., in diary form, 9. Directions for making something, 10. Descriptions of a hobby. (Symonds 774)

Things have probably not changed all that radically in today's high schools.

BACKLASH AGAINST PERSONAL WRITING

I don't wish to suggest that personal experience assignments ever completely took over or dominated the teaching of writing. They did not, have never done so. Although after 1900 personal writing was (and has remained) a large part of composition, it was prevented from overwhelming other kinds of writing by the same mechanism that made personal writing possible: the modes of discourse. Modal distinctions made teaching narration and description possible, thus creating formats for personal experience, but dealing with all four modes meant that teachers also had to move on to exposition and argumentation—the "impersonal" modes. And it is interesting to note that the impersonal modes took on a separate and new life of their own very quickly after the triumph of personal writing in the general composition course. George P. Baker's *Principles of Argumentation* of 1895 slammed the door closed on personal writing in favor of old-style objective, researched argument—and it was very popular. Courses in argument followed Baker, diverging for a while into Speech departments before returning to English. Exposition, the other "impersonal mode," had its own specific textbook as early as 1899 in Buck and Woodbridge's *A Course in Expository Writing*, and went on to develop its own complex laws and pedagogy. Exposition, as we now know, would after 1930 become the most important of the four modes in the eyes of writing teachers.[6]

The rise of the "impersonal modes" so quickly after the "personal modes" had been accepted signifies, I think, a curious discomfort in English teachers' attitudes toward students writing from personal experience. This discomfort led to some obvious strains and disagreements in pedagogy during the twentieth century as different ideas about what students should know and control in their writing clashed. The old-style general topics had been routed by the romantic attack of the eighties and nineties, but impersonal topics had not, and after 1910 a "return of the repressed" can be seen in various ways. The privileging of exposition (and to a lesser degree, argument) is one obvious way that teachers could move away from "merely" personal writing. By teaching all of the various "methods of exposition," teachers after 1920 could make certain that their students wrote modern versions of the old-time objective papers. The topic was "How to Raise Lettuce," or "The Advantages of Owning a Home in a Recently Developed Section of (Your Town)," rather than "The Progress of Error," but the idea of forcing students to handle a world beyond immediate experience was the same. What exposition-text authors sought was a subordination of personality to information for practical purposes, a demonstration that exposition was, as one author put it, "the hands of literature."

The rise of the "research paper" as a genre in freshman composition is another way that teachers tried to transcend the personal writing that occupied the early stages of any course.[7] Library research, often unconnected to any writing purpose beyond amassing brute facts for regurgitation into a "research paper," became very popular around 1920 and has remained a staple

in writing courses since. The rationale for such work is that it is good practice for other college writing. "Since a good deal of college work is acquiring and becoming able to discuss the information and ideas of others, a standard method of discovering material, making notes of it, and presenting it has been developed," as Porter Perrin put it in 1942. "Preparing a research paper gives practice in using this method" (320). The whole idea of a specific "research" paper would have been without meaning in 1880, of course, because prior to the reign of personal writing, teachers naturally assumed that students had no choice but to write something transmitted and synthesized from their reading.

The final and most controversial way of transcending personal experience writing was the use of literature in composition courses. Some writing courses, of course, had always relied on literature, but at Harvard and the many schools that followed its example, courses in "pure" literature and composition courses were at first kept rigorously separate. Only gradually did the use of belletristic literature make its way into many freshman classes, usually in the latter portions of the class, after the "personal modes" had been worked through. Thus in the later 'teens we begin to see textbooks which feature both assignments like "How Snow is Removed in Your Town" and "The Character of Macbeth." For many teachers, literature and literary analysis provided a way out of the world of personal writing that made them uncomfortable. In addition, of course, the teacher of a literature-oriented writing course is able to focus on teaching material she is familiar with in a fashion congenial to most English-trained persons. The question still rages today about the amount of belletristic literature that should be "allowed" in a composition course, although the issues that began the use of literary works in composition have been almost completely forgotten.

"Write what you know," has been perhaps the most common advice given to writers, and the movement toward personal writing assignments has been the inevitable result of taking that dictum seriously within a culture whose educational institutions give most of their clients only a shallow knowledge across a broad range of fields. The natural subject to turn to—the *only* subject about which most students know more than a few threadbare (or misremembered) facts—is personal experience. The alternatives I have been discussing—expository writing, research papers, literary analyses—were all thrown into the breach during the first part of this century by teachers who felt, usually in an inchoate fashion, that something had gone radically wrong with education if it was producing students whose only coherent subject matter was themselves and their experiences.

Teachers seldom discussed this discomfort, but it was there nonetheless. It pops up amidst the blithe encomia for personal writing that have filled many textbooks and articles for the past 70 years. Sometimes it took the form of a sort of sub-channel despairing of student mentality, as in C. H. Ward's malignant *What is English* of 1917: "What should students write about? Always about familiar matters in which they have a real interest. . . . If you ever feel sure that their minds really contain some elementary criticism, try that;

but the experiment is of doubtful utility" (204). Sometimes this discomfort took the form of a kind of resignation about how students asked to write on political or social or educational problems lose themselves in "the intense inane of the general, the intangible, and the vague." As Samuel Green put it in 1939, the student "feels the force of the mighty new ideas [in the anthology]; he supports, he refutes, he advances solutions of his own—panaceas for social ills, programs for the peace of the world; he aims to please; and it is all as sounding brass and tinkling cymbals" (693). And sometimes it took the form of encouragement to go beyond personal writing into something else, as in a paragraph Porter Perrin added to his *Writer's Guide* in 1942: "Often the choice of subjects in college should grow out of your desire to *extend* your experience, *to know more than you do* about something in history, literature, economics, biology . . . wherever your interest has been aroused" (293, my italics).

Clearly, then, there were and are conflicts in teachers' attitudes toward personal writing. Despite all of the supplements to and withdrawals from the use of personal experience writing in freshmen courses, however, such subjective assignments have remained the central core of many of the essays students are asked to do, and the original impulse—to make writing meaningful to student writers—has never disappeared. Our recent history has seen what might be called a revival of romanticism, a conscious shift on some influential theorists' parts *away* from exposition, abstraction, "school writing." In the wake of the progressive education movement of the early 1960's, such writers as Ken Macrorie, Peter Elbow, Janet Emig, and James Britton formalized the critique, only implicit in the nineteenth century, of non-personal writing assignments as useless and meaningless. One can almost hear an echo of Newcomer in Macrorie's contention that good student writing should be students "speaking in their own voices about things that counted for them" (21). This crusade against "Engfish" seemed to peak around 1975, when its essential romanticism was met by a neoclassical countermovement insisting on traditional skills-and-social-usefulness teaching: the "back-to-basics" movement.

Since that time there has been no clear ascendant; romantics and classicists coexist—usually amiably—in almost every English department. The question persists as to what place telling personal stories and citing personal observations should have in the process of teaching students to write. Many advocates of the writing process movement seem to opt, at least tacitly, for personal writing as the only honest and revealing sort of discourse. At the other end of the spectrum, the advocates of "cultural literacy" have formalized many of the vague disquiets I discussed above, claiming that student writing is threadbare because students simply don't know enough about their culture to say anything beyond their own experience.

The question of personal writing is uncomfortable for many teachers because it presents such a clear mirror of one's individual philosophy of education. It is easy to feel that one's teaching is not striking the balance well between making writing meaningful to the student and making the student

meaningful to the community. Debates over the last two decades between advocates of "honest, personal writing" and those of "writing that gets the world's work done" will probably continue, because the seductions of an emotional "knockout punch" are no less real for teachers than the seductions of a well-planned and carefully done research paper. The continuing debate, tacit and sub-channel though it may be, indicates that we as a profession have not yet come to agreement about the larger purposes of writing in this culture. The question of personal writing assignments forces us to take an implicit stand about what we think is important, for students and for society—and making important decisions is always uncomfortable.

On the level of practical teaching, most of us take, I think, a sort of middle position. For us, the world of written discourse is a continuing conversation, to which all are welcome who can contribute. Learning that one has a right to speak, that one's voice and personality have validity, is an important step—an essential step. Personal writing, leaning on one's own experience, is necessary for this step, especially when one is being encouraged to enter the conversation at age eighteen. Extrapersonal writing is difficult at an age before most people have completed the shaping and motivating decisions that constitute adulthood, have chosen the path of interest that will give them voices to speak confidently on extrapersonal subjects. But as teachers, we always have to encourage, even demand attempts at the next step—to go beyond *merely* personal accounts, either outside into encompassing the world in discourse, or inside into shaping our personal observations into the touching, deeply empathetic and finally metapersonal stuff of which the greatest writing is made.

WORKS CONSULTED AND CITED

Baker, George Pierce. *Principles of Argumentation*. Boston: Ginn & Co., 1895.

Bardeen, C. W. *A System of Rhetoric*. New York: A. S. Barnes, 1884.

Berlin, James A. *Writing Instruction in Nineteenth-Century American Colleges*. Carbondale: Southern Illinois UP, 1985.

Britton, James, *et al. The Development of Writing Abilities (11–18)*. London: Macmillan Education, 1975.

Buck, Gertrude, and Elisabeth Woodbridge. *A Course in Expository Writing*. New York: Henry Holt, 1899.

Canby, Henry S. and John B. Opdycke. *Elements of Composition for Secondary Schools*. New York: Macmillan, 1913.

Cicero. *De Oratore*. Trans. E. W. Sutton and H. Rackham. Cambridge: Harvard UP, 1942.

Clark, Donald Leman. *Rhetoric in Greco-Roman Education*. New York: Columbia UP, 1957.

Connors, Robert J. "The Rhetoric of Explanation: Explanatory Rhetoric from Aristotle to 1850." *Written Communication* 1 (1984): 189–210.

———. "The Rhetoric of Explanation: Explanatory Rhetoric from 1850 to the Present." *Written Communication* 2 (1985): 49–72.

Crane, William G. *Wit and Rhetoric in the Renaissance*. New York: Columbia UP, 1937.

Crowley, Sharon. "Invention in Nineteenth Century Rhetoric." *College Composition and Communication* 36 (1985): 51–60.

Curl, Mervin J. *Expository Writing*. Boston: Houghton Mifflin, 1919.

Day, Henry N. *Elements of the Art of Discourse*. Hudson: Skinner, 1850.

Espenshade, A. Howry. *The Essentials of Composition and Rhetoric*. Boston: D. C. Heath & Company, 1913.

Genung, John F. *Outlines of Rhetoric*. Boston: Ginn and Co., 1893.

————. *Practical Elements of Rhetoric*. Boston: Ginn and Co., 1886.

Green, Andrew J. "Significant Theme Content." *College English* 1 (1939): 691–99.

Hart, John M. *A Manual of Composition and Rhetoric*. Philadelphia: Eldredge & Brother, 1870.

Hill, David J. *Elements of Rhetoric and Composition*. New York: Sheldon & Company, 1878.

Howes, Raymond F. "Freshman Assignments." *English Journal* 17 (1928): 154–57.

Kellogg, Brainerd. *A Text-Book on Rhetoric*. New York: Clark & Maynard, 1880.

Kerl, Simon. *Elements of Composition & Rhetoric*. New York: Ivison, Phinney, Blakeman, 1869.

Kitzhaber, Albert R. *Rhetoric in American Colleges 1850–1900*. Diss., U of Washington, 1953.

Lomer, Gerhard R., and Margaret Ashmun. *The Study and Practice of Writing English*. Boston: Houghton Mifflin Co., 1914.

Macrorie, Ken. *Uptaught*. Rochelle Park, NJ: Hayden Book Co., 1970.

Mead, William E. *Elementary Composition and Rhetoric*. Boston: Leach, Shwell & Sanborn, 1894.

Nason, Arthur Huntington. *Efficient Composition: A College Rhetoric*. New York: New York UP, 1917.

Newcomer, Alphonso G. *A Practical Course in English Composition*. Boston: Ginn, 1893.

Parker, Richard Green. *Aids to English Composition*. New York: Harper & Brothers, 1845.

————. *Progressive Exercises in English Composition*. Boston: Robert S. Davis, 1832.

Perrin, Porter G. *An Index to English*. Chicago: Scott, Foresman & Company, 1939.

Quackenbos, George P. *Advanced Course of Composition and Rhetoric*. New York: D. Appleton, 1854.

Quintilian. *Institutio Oratoria*. Trans. H. E. Butler. Cambridge: Harvard UP, 1920.

Reed, Alonzo, and Brainerd Kellogg. *Higher Lessons in English*. New York: Clark & Maynard, 1877.

Scott, H. P. "Making Themes Mean Something." *English Journal* 12 (1923): 93–97.

Symonds, Percival M. "Real Topics for Writing and Speaking," *School Review* 38 (1930): 765–75.

Walker, John. *The Teacher's Assistant in English Composition*. Carlisle: Kline, 1808.

Ward, C. H. *What is English?* Chicago: Scott, Foresman, 1917.

Young, Richard. "Arts, Crafts, Gifts and Knacks: Some Disharmonies in the New Rhetoric." *Reinventing the Rhetorical Tradition*. Ed. Aviva Freedman and Ian Pringle. Conway, AR: University of Central Arkansas, 1980, 53–60.

NOTES

1. The progymnasmata which have survived are those of Aphthonius, which propose the following sequence: fable, tale, chreia (enlargement on a thesis), proverb, refutation and confirmation, common place, encomium, comparison, impersonation, description, thesis, and finally legislation. (Clark 179–206)

2. Although it is certain that such books were kept by many in antiquity, it is not until after the advent of printing that advice on the keeping of commonplace books became widely distributed. If a student or rhetorician wished to base his learning on

his own selection and compilation of authors, a personal commonplace book was the way. As Ludwig Vives wrote in his *An Introduction to Wisdom* of 1540:

> and if thou perceyve any thing taken of the wise sort, or to be spoken quyckely, gravely, learnedlye, wyttilye, comely, beare in minde, that thou mayst, when thou shalte have occasion; use the same. Thou shalt have always at hand a paper boke, wherein thou shalt write such notable thynges, as thou redest thyself, or herest of other men worthy to be noted, be it other feate sentence, or word, mete for famil-iar speche, that thou maist have in a redynes, what time requireth. (From *An In-troduction to Wisdome*, made by Ludovicus Vives and translated into Englishe by Richarde Morysine, Aiii recto. Quoted from Crane, p. 32.)

3. James Berlin has done much to spur investigation of romantic influences on rhetoric, most obviously in his *Writing Instruction in Nineteenth-Century American Colleges* (1985).

4. Many early composition texts were written by ministers, and this method of providing a phrase—usually an old cliche or maxim—for analysis and argument par-allels the similar practice in Protestant homiletics as it had developed since the early eighteenth century. In a sermon the minister would choose a scriptural passage as the "Doctrine," and after explicating it would proceed to the "Application" of the text.

5. For more information on Walker's book and its importance for composition teaching, see Connors 1984, 204–206.

6. For more on the rise of expository writing in composition courses, see Connors 1985.

7. No texts except exposition and argument texts were able after 1910 to avoid be-ginning with narration and description, but some authors gradually moved more to-ward impersonal materials. Note, for instance, the 1917 revision of Lomer and Ashmun's *Study and Practice of Writing* (1914), which repeats the personal-writing as-signments of the first edition but adds a chapter on library research—something the book's users had obviously recommended.

Frequency of Formal Errors in Current College Writing, or Ma and Pa Kettle Do Research

We admit to a special fondness for "Frequency of Formal Errors in Current College Writing, or Ma and Pa Kettle Do Research"—and we do so not just because one of us (Andrea) collaborated with Bob on this essay, which was published in *College Composition and Communication* in December 1988. Our fondness arises from the fact that, in this more than in any other of his published works, Bob's wacky sense of humor and propensity toward self-deprecation are most clearly visible. Who would have imagined that an essay reporting on an empirical study of the patterns of errors in more than 21,500 papers from 300 teachers all across America would have subheadings that manage to mix classical organizational schemes with titles that have a strong "down-home" flavor, as in the following example: "*Confutatio*: Ma and Pa Suck Eggs" (161). There is definitely a serious side to this essay, however, for it represents an effort to get, if not a definitive report on students' current writing practices, then at least a window into these practices—and into the error-marking practices of their teachers.

PROEM: IN WHICH THE CHARACTERS ARE INTRODUCED

The labyrinthine project of which this research is a part represents an ongoing activity for us, something we engage in because we like to work together, have a long friendship, and share many interests. As we worked on this error research together, however, we started somewhere along the line to feel less and less like the white-coated Researchers of our dreams and more and more like characters we called Ma and Pa Kettle— good-hearted bumblers striving to understand a world whose complexity was more than a little daunting. Being fans of classical rhetoric, *prosopopoeia*, *letteraturizzazione*, and the like, as well as enthusiasts for intertextuality, *plaisir de texte*, *differance*, etc., we offer this account of our travails—with apologies to Marjorie Main and Percy Kilbride.

From *College Composition and Communication* 39.4 (1988): 395–409. This article was coauthored by Andrea A. Lunford.

EXORDIUM: THE KETTLES SMELL A PROBLEM

Marking and judging formal and mechanical errors in student papers is one area in which composition studies seems to have a multiple-personality disorder. On the one hand, our mellow, student-centered, process-based selves tend to condemn marking formal errors at all. Doing it represents the Bad Old Days. Ms. Fidditch and Mr. Flutesnoot with sharpened red pencils, spilling innocent blood across the page. Useless detail work. Inhumane, perfectionist standards, making our students feel stupid, wrong, trivial, misunderstood. Joseph Williams has pointed out how arbitrary and context-bound our judgments of formal error are. And certainly our noting of errors on student papers gives no one any great joy; as Peter Elbow says, English is most often associated *either* with grammar or with high literature—"two things designed to make folks feel most out of it."

Nevertheless, very few of us can deny that an outright comma splice, its/it's error, or misspelled common word distracts us. So our more traditional pedagogical selves feel a touch guilty when we ignore student error patterns altogether, even in the sacrosanct drafting stage of composing. Not even the most liberal of process-oriented teachers completely ignores the problem of mechanical and formal errors. As Mina Shaughnessy put it, errors are "unintentional and unprofitable intrusions upon the consciousness of the reader. . . . They demand energy without giving back any return in meaning" (12). Errors are not merely mechanical, therefore, but rhetorical as well. The world judges a writer by her mastery of conventions, and we all know it. Students, parents, university colleagues, and administrators expect us to deal somehow with those unmet rhetorical expectations, and, like it or not, pointing out errors seems to most of us part of what we do.

Of course, every teacher has his or her ideas of what errors are common and important, but testing those intuitive ideas is something else again. We became interested in error-frequency research as a result of our historical studies, when we realized that no major nationwide analysis of actual college essays had been conducted, to our knowledge, since the late 1930s. As part of the background for a text we were writing and because the research seemed fascinating, we determined to collect a large number of college student essays from the 1980s, analyze them, and determine what the major patterns of formal and mechanical error in current student writing might be.

NARRATIO: MA AND PA VISIT THE LIBRARY

Coming to this research as historians rather than as trained experimenters has given us a humility based on several different sources. Since we are not formally trained in research design, we have constantly relied on help from more expert friends and colleagues. Creating a sense of our limitations even more keenly, however, have been our historical studies. No one looking into the history of research on composition errors in this country can emerge

very confident about definitions, terms, and preconceptions. In almost no other pedagogical area we have studied do the investigators and writers seem so time-bound, so shackled by their ideas of what errors *are*, so blinkered by the definitions and demarcations that are part of their historical scene. And, ineluctably, we must see ourselves and our study as history-bound as well. Thus we write not as the torchbearers of some new truth, but as two more in the long line of people applying their contemporary perspectives to a numbering and ordering system and hoping for something of use from it.

The tradition of research into error patterns is as old as composition teaching, of course, but before the growth of the social-science model in education it was carried on informally. Teachers had "the list" of serious and common errors in their heads, and their lists were probably substantially similar (although "serious" and "common" were not necessarily overlapping categories).[1] Beginning around 1910, however, teachers and educational researchers began trying to taxonomize errors and chart their frequency. The great heyday of error-frequency seems to have occurred between 1915 and 1935. During those two decades, no fewer than thirty studies of error frequency were conducted.[2] Unfortunately, most of these studies were flawed in some way: too small a data sample, too regional a data sample, different definitions of errors, faulty methodologies (Harap 440). Most early error research is hard to understand today because the researchers used terms widely understood at the time but now incomprehensible or at best strange. Some of the studies were very seriously conducted, however, and deserve further discussion later in this paper.

After the middle 1930s, error-frequency research waned as the progressive-education movement gained strength and the "experience curriculum" in English replaced older correctness-based methods. Our historical research indicates that the last large-scale research into student patterns of formal error was conducted in 1938–39 by John C. Hodges, author of the *Harbrace College Handbook*. Hodges collected 20,000 student papers that had been marked by 16 different teachers, mainly from the University of Tennessee at Knoxville. He analyzed these papers and created a taxonomy of errors, using his findings to inform the 34-part organization of his *Harbrace Handbook*, a text which quickly became and remains today the most popular college handbook of writing.

However Hodges may have constructed his study, his results fifty years later seem problematic at best. Small-scale studies of changes in student writing over the past thirty years have shown that formal error patterns have shifted radically even since the 1950s. The kinds and quantities of formal errors revealed in Mina Shaughnessy's work with basic writers in the 1970s were new and shocking to many teachers of writing. We sensed that the time had come for a study that would attempt to answer two questions: (1) what are the most common patterns of student writing errors being made in the 1980s in the United States?, and (2) which of these patterns are marked most consistently by American teachers?

CONFIRMATIO I: THE KETTLES GET CRACKING

The first task we faced was gathering data. We needed teacher-marked papers from American college freshmen and sophomores in a representative range of different kinds of schools and a representative range of geographic areas. We did not want to try to gather the isolated sample of timed examination-style writing that is often studied, although such a sample would probably have been easier to obtain than the actual marked papers we sought. We wanted "themes in the raw," the actual commerce of writing courses all across America. We wanted papers that had been personally marked or graded, filled with every uncontrolled and uncontrollable sign of both student and teacher personalities.

Gathering these papers presented a number of obstacles. In terms of ideal methodology, the data-gathering would be untouched by self-selection among teachers, and we could randomly choose our sources. After worrying about this problem, we finally could conceive of no way to gather upwards of 20,000 papers (the number of papers Hodges had looked at) without appealing to teachers who had marked them. We could think of no way to go directly to students, and, though some departments stockpile student themes, we did not wish to weight our study toward any one school or department. We had to ask composition teachers for help.

And help us they did. In response to a direct mail appeal to more than 1,500 teachers who had used or expressed interest in handbooks, we had received by September 1985 more than 21,500 papers from 300 teachers all across America.[3]

To say that the variety in the papers we were sent was striking is a serious understatement. They ranged in length from a partial page to over 20 pages. About 30% were typed, the rest handwritten. Some were annotated marginally until they looked like the Book of Kells, while others merely sported a few scrawled words and a grade. Some were pathologically neat, and others look dashed off on the jog between classes. Some were formally perfect, while others approximated Mina Shaughnessy's more extreme examples of basic writing. Altogether, the 21,500+ papers, each one carefully stamped by paper number and batch number, filled approximately 30 feet of hastily-installed shelving. It was an imposing mass.

We had originally been enthusiastic (and naive) enough to believe that with help we might somehow look over and analyze 20,000 papers. Wrong. Examining an average paper even for mechanical lapses, we soon realized, took at the very least ten busy minutes; to examine all of them would require over 3,000 Ma-and-Pa-hours. We simply could not do it. But we could analyze a carefully stratified sample of 3,000 randomly chosen papers. Such an analysis would give us data that were very reliable. Relieved that we would not have to try to look at 20,000 papers, we went to work on the stratification.[4] After stratifying our batches of papers by region, size of school, and type of school, we used the table of random numbers and the numbers that had been stamped on each paper as it came in to pull 3,000 papers from our tonnage of papers. Thus we had our randomized, stratified sample, ready for analysis.

Confutatio: Ma and Pa Suck Eggs

But—analyzed using what? From very early on in the research, we realized that trying to introduce strict "scientific" definitions into an area so essentially values-driven as formal error marking would be a foolhardy mistake. We accepted Joe Williams' contention that it is "necessary to shift our attention from error treated strictly as an isolated item on a page, to error perceived as a flawed verbal transaction between a writer and a reader" (153). Williams' thoughtful article on "The Phenomenology of Error" had, in fact, persuaded us that some sort of reader-response treatment of errors would be far more useful than an attempt to standardize error patterns in a pseudo-scientific fashion based on Hodges' or any other handbook.

We were made even more distrustful of any absolutist claims by our further examination of previous error-frequency research. Looking into the history of this kind of research showed us clearly how teachers' ideas about error definition and classification have always been absolute products of their times and cultures. What seem to us the most common and permanent of terms and definitions are likely to be newer and far more transient than we know. Errors like "stringy sentences" and "use of *would* for simple past tense forms" seemed obvious and serious to teachers in 1925 or 1917 but obscure to us today.[5]

While phenomena and adaptable definitions do continue from decade to decade, we knew that any system we might adopt, however defensible or linguistically sound it might seem to us, would someday represent one more historical curiosity. "Comma splice?" some researcher in the future will murmur, "What a strange term for Connors and Lunsford to use. Where could it have come from?"[6] Teachers have always marked different phenomena as errors, called them different things, given them different weights. Error-pattern study is essentially the examination of an ever-shifting pattern of skills judged by an ever-shifting pattern of prejudices. We wanted to try looking at this situation as it existed in the 1980s, but clearly the instrument we needed could not be algorithmic and would not be historically stable.

We settled, finally, on several general understandings. First, examining what teachers had marked on these papers was as important as trying to ascertain what was "really there" in terms of formal error patterns. Second, we could only analyze for a limited number of error patterns—perhaps twenty in all. And finally, we had no taxonomy of errors we felt we could trust. We would have to generate our own, then, using our own culture- and time-bound definitions and perceptions as best we could.

Confirmatio II: Ma and Pa Hit the Road

Producing that taxonomy meant looking closely at the papers. Using the random number tables again, we pulled 300 papers from the remaining piles. Each of us took 150, and we set out inductively to note every formal error pattern we could discover in the two piles of papers. During this incredibly boring and nauseating part of the study, we tried to ignore any elements of

paper content or organization except as they were necessary to identify errors. Every error marked by teachers was included in our listing, of course, but we found many that had not been marked at all, and some that were not even easily definable. What follows is the list of errors and the numbers of errors we discovered in that first careful scrutiny of 300 papers:

Error or Error Pattern	# in 300 Papers
Spelling	450
No comma after introductory element	138
Comma splice	124
Wrong word	102
Lack of possessive apostrophe	99
Vague pronoun reference	90
No comma in compound sentence	87
Pronoun agreement	83
Sentence fragment	82
No comma in non-restrictive phrase	75
Subject-verb agreement	59
Unnecessary comma with restrictive phrase	50
Unnecessary words/style rewrite	49
Wrong tense	46
Dangling or misplaced modifier	42
Run-on sentence	39
Wrong or missing preposition	38
Lack of comma in series	35
Its/it's error	34
Tense shift	31
Pronoun shift/point of view shift	31
Wrong/missing inflected endings	31
Comma with quotation marks error	28
Missing words	27
Capitalization	24
"Which/that" for "who/whom"	21
Unidiomatic word use	17
Comma between subject and verb	14
Unnecessary apostrophe after "s"	11
Unnecessary comma in complex sentence	11
Hyphenation errors	9
Comma before direct object	6
Unidiomatic sentence pattern	6
Title underlining	6
Garbled sentence	4
Adjectival for adverbial form—"ly"	4

In addition, the following errors appeared fewer than 4 times in 300 papers:

Wrong pronoun

Wrong use of dashes

Confusion of a/an

Missing articles (the)

Missing question mark

Wrong verb form

Lack of transition

Missing/incorrect quotation marks

Incorrect comma use with parentheses

Use of comma instead of "that"

Missing comma before "etc."

Incorrect semicolon use

Repetition of words

Unclear gerund modifier

Double negative

Missing apostrophe in contraction

Colon misuse

Lack of parallelism

As expected, many old favorites appear on these lists. To our surprise, however, some errors we were used to thinking of as very common and serious proved to be at least not so common as we had thought. Others, which were not thought of as serious (or even, in some cases, as actual errors), seemed very common.

Our next step was to calibrate our readings, making certain we were both counting apples as apples, and to determine the cutoff point in this list, the errors we would actually count in the 3,000 papers. Since spelling errors predominated by a factor of 300% (which in itself was a surprising margin), we chose not to deal further with spelling in this analysis, but to develop a separate line of research on spelling. Below spelling, we decided to go arbitrarily with the top twenty error patterns, cutting off below "wrong inflected ending." These were the twenty error patterns we would train our analysts to tote up.

Now we had a sample and we had an instrument, however rough. Next we needed to gather a group of representative teachers who could do the actual analysis. Fifty teaching assistants, instructors, and professors from the Ohio State University English Department volunteered to help us with the analysis. The usual question of inter-rater reliability did not seem pressing to us, because what we were looking for seemed so essentially charged with social conditioning and personal predilection. Since we did not think that we could always "scientifically" determine what was real error and what was style or usage variation, our best idea was to rationalize the arbitrariness inherent in the project by spreading out the analytical decisions.

On a Friday afternoon in January 1986 we worked with the fifty raters, going over the definitions and examples we had come up with for the "top twenty," as we were by then calling them. It was a grueling Friday and Saturday. We trained raters to recognize error patterns all Friday afternoon in the dusty, stuffy old English Library at OSU—the air of which Thurber must have breathed, and probably the very same air, considering how hard the windows were to open. On returning to our hotel that night, we found it occupied by the Ohio chapter of the Pentecostal Youth, who had been given permission to run around the hotel giggling and shouting until 3:30 a.m. In despair, we turned our TV volumes all the way up on white-noise stations that had gone off the air. They sounded like the Reichenbach Falls and almost drowned out the hoo-raw in the hallway. After 3:30 it did indeed quiet down some, and we fell into troublous sleep. The next day the Pentecostal Youth had vanished, and Ma & Pa had research to do.

AMPLIFICATIO: MA AND PA HUNKER DOWN

The following day, rating began at 9:00 a.m. and, with a short lunch break, we had completed the last paper by 5:00 p.m. We paused occasionally to calibrate our ratings, to redefine some term, or to share some irresistible piece of student prose. (Top prize went to the notorious "One Night," one student's response to an assignment asking for "analysis." This essay's abstract announced it as "an analysis of the realm of different feelings experienced in one night by a man and wife in love."[7]) The rating sheets and papers were reordered and bundled up, and we all went out for dinner.[8]

The results of this exercise became real for us when we totaled up the numbers on all of the raters' sheets. Here was the information we had been seeking, what all our efforts had been directed toward. It was exciting to finally see in black and white what we had been wondering about. What we found appears in Table 1.

PERORATIO: THE KETTLES SAY, "AW, SHUCKS"

The results of this research by no means represent a final word on any question involving formal errors or teacher marking patterns. We can, however, draw several intriguing, if tentative, generalizations.

First, teachers' ideas about what constitutes a serious, markable error vary widely. As most of us may have expected, some teachers pounce on every "very unique" as a pet peeve, some rail at "Every student . . . their . . ." The most prevalent "error," failure to place a comma after an introductory word or phrase, was a *bête noire* for some teachers but was ignored by many more. Papers marked by the same teacher might at different times evince different patterns of formal marking. Teachers' reasons for marking specific errors and patterns of error in their students' papers are complex, and in many cases they are no doubt guided by the perceived needs of the student writing the paper and by the stage of the composing process the paper has achieved.

TABLE 1

Error or Error Pattern	# Found in 3000 Papers	% of Total Errors	# Found Marked by Teacher	% Marked by Teacher	Rank by # of Errors Marked by Teacher
1. No comma after introductory element	3,299	11.5%	995	30%	2
2. Vague pronoun reference	2,809	9.8%	892	32%	4
3. No comma in compound sentence	2,446	8.6%	719	29%	7
4. Wrong word	2,217	7.8%	1,114	50%	1
5. No comma in non-restrictive element	1,864	6.5%	580	31%	10
6. Wrong/missing inflected endings	1,679	5.9%	857	51%	5
7. Wrong or missing preposition	1,580	5.5%	679	43%	8
8. Comma splice	1,565	5.5%	850	54%	6
9. Possessive apostrophe error	1,458	5.1%	906	62%	3
10. Tense shift	1,453	5.1%	484	33%	12
11. Unnecessary shift in person	1,347	4.7%	410	30%	14
12. Sentence fragment	1,217	4.2%	671	55%	9
13. Wrong tense or verb form	952	3.3%	465	49%	13
14. Subject-verb agreement	909	3.2%	534	58%	11
15. Lack of comma in series	781	2.7%	184	24%	19
16. Pronoun agreement error	752	2.6%	365	48%	15
17. Unnecessary comma with restrictive element	693	2.4%	239	34%	17
18. Run-on or fused sentence	681	2.4%	308	45%	16
19. Dangling or misplaced modifier	577	2.0%	167	29%	20
20. Its/it's error	292	1.0%	188	64%	18

Second, teachers do not seem to mark as many errors as we often think they do. On average, college English teachers mark only 43% of the most serious errors in the papers they evaluate. In contrast to the popular picture of English teachers mad to mark up every error, our results show that even the most-often marked errors are only marked two-thirds of the time. The less-marked patterns (and remember, these are the Top Twenty error patterns overall) are marked only once for every four times they appear. The number of errors found compared to the number of errors marked suggests a fascinating possibility for future research: detailed observation of teacher marking, accompanied by talk-aloud protocols. Such research seems to us a natural follow-up to the findings presented here.[9]

Third, the reasons teachers mark any given error seem to result from a complex formula that takes into account at least two factors: how serious or annoying the error is perceived to be at a given time for both teacher and student, and how difficult it is to mark or explain. As Table 1 shows, the errors marked by the original teachers on our papers produce a different (although not completely dissimilar) ranking of errors than the formal count we asked our raters to do. Some of the lesser-marked errors we studied are clearly felt to be more stylistic than substantive. Certain of the comma errors seem simply not to bother teachers very much. Others, like wrong words or missing inflections, are much more frequently marked, and might be said to have a high "response quotient" for teachers. In addition, we sensed that in many cases errors went unmarked not because the teacher failed to see them, but because they were not germane to the lessons at hand. A teacher working very hard to help a student master subject-verb agreement with third-person singular nouns, for instance, might well ignore most other errors in a given paper.

Teachers' perceptions of the seriousness of a given error pattern seem, however, to be only part of the reason for marking an error. The sheer difficulty of explanation presented by some error patterns is another factor. Jotting "WW" in the margin to tip a student off to a diction problem is one thing; explaining a subtle shift in point of view in that same marginal space is quite another. Sentence fragments, comma splices, and wrong tenses, to name three classic "serious" errors, are all marked less often than possessive apostrophes. This is, we think, not due to teachers' perception that apostrophe errors are worse than sentence-boundary or tense problems, but to their quickness and ease of indication. The its/it's error and the possessive apostrophe, the two highest-marked patterns, are also two of the easiest errors to mark. This is, of course, not laziness; many composition teachers are so chronically overworked that we should not wonder that the errors most marked are those most quickly indicated.

Fourth, error patterns in student writing are shifting in certain ways, at least partially as a result of changing media trends within the culture. Conclusions must be especially tentative here, because the time-bound nature of studies of error makes comparisons difficult and definitions of errors

counted in earlier research are hard to correlate. Our research turned up several earlier lists of serious errors in freshman composition, however, whose order is rather different from the order we discovered.

Roy Ivan Johnson, writing in 1917, reported on 198 papers written by 66 freshmen, and his list of the top ten error patterns in his study is as follows (wherever possible, we have translated his terms into ours):

1. Spelling
2. Capitalization
3. Punctuation (mostly comma errors)
4. Careless omission or repetition
5. Apostrophe errors
6. Pronoun agreement
7. Verb tense errors and agreement
8. Ungrammatical sentence structure (fragments and run-ons)
9. Mistakes in the use of adjectives and adverbs
10. Mistakes in the use of prepositions and conjunctions

In 1930, Paul Witty and Roberta Green analyzed 170 papers written in a timed situation by freshmen. Here is their top ten list, translated into our terms where possible:

1. Faulty connectives
2. Vague pronoun reference
3. Use of "would" for simple past tense forms
4. Confusion of forms from similarity of sound or meaning
5. Misplaced modifiers
6. Pronoun agreement
7. Fragments
8. Unclassified errors
9. Dangling modifiers
10. Wrong tense

As we mentioned earlier, the largest-scale analysis of errors was done by John C. Hodges in the late 1930s. Unfortunately, we know very little about Hodges' research. He never published any results in contemporary journals, and thus it is difficult to know his methods or even very much about his findings, because we can see them only as they are reflected in the *Harbrace Handbook*, which today still uses the exact arrangement that Hodges gave it in its first edition in 1941. In the "To the Instructor" preface of his first edition, Hodges says that his 20,000 themes "have been tabulated according to the corrections marked by sixteen instructors," which suggests that his raters

looked only for teacher-marked errors (Hodges iii). In a footnote on the same page, Hodges gives the only version of his top-ten list ever published:

1. Comma
2. Spelling
3. Exactness
4. Agreement
5. Superfluous commas
6. Reference of pronouns
7. Apostrophe
8. Omission of words
9. Wordiness
10. Good use

That is all we know of Hodges' findings, but it does not seem unreasonable to assume that he reports them in order of frequency.

In terms of how patterns of error have changed, our findings are, of course, extremely tentative. Assuming that Hodges' *Harbrace* list constitutes some version of the error patterns he found in 1939, however, we note some distinct changes. In general, our list shows a proliferation of error patterns that seem to suggest declining familiarity with the visual look of a written page. Most strikingly, spelling errors have gone from second on the list to first by a factor of three. Spelling is the most obvious example of this lack of visual memory of printed pages seen, but the growth of other error patterns supports it as well.[10]

Some of the error patterns that seem to suggest this visual-memory problem were not found or listed in earlier studies but have come to light in ours. The many wrong word errors, the missing inflected endings, the wrong prepositions, even the its/it's errors—all suggest that students today may be less familiar with the visible aspects of written forms. These findings confirm the contrastive analysis between 2,000 papers from the 1950s and 2,000 papers from the 1970s that was carried out by Gary Sloan in 1979. Sloan determined that many elements of formal writing convention broke down severely between the fifties and seventies, including spelling, homophones, sentence structure elements, inflected endings, and others (157–59). Sloan notes that the effects of an oral—and we would stress, an *electronic*—culture on literacy skills are subversive. Students who do not read the "texts" of our culture will continue to come to school without the tacit visual knowledge of written conventions that "text-wise" writers carry with them effortlessly. Such changes in literate behavior have and will continue to affect us in multiple ways, including the ways we perceive, categorize, and judge "errors."

Finally, we feel we can report some good news. One very telling fact emerging from our research is our realization that college students are *not* making more formal errors in writing than they used to. The numbers of er-

rors made by students in earlier studies and the numbers we found in the 1980s agree remarkably. Our findings chart out as follows:[11]

Study	Year	Average Paper Length	Errors per Paper	Errors per 100 Words
Johnson	1917	162 words	3.42	2.11
Witty & Green	1930	231 words	5.18	2.24
Ma & Pa	1986	422 words	9.52	2.26

The consistency of these numbers seems to us extraordinary. It suggests that although the length of the average paper demanded in freshman composition has been steadily rising, the formal skills of students have not declined precipitously.

In the light of the "Johnny Can't Write" furor of the 1970s and the sometimes hysterical claims of educational decline oft heard today, these results are striking—and heartening. They suggest that in some ways we *are* doing a better job than we might have known. The number of errors has not gone down, but neither has it risen in the past five decades. In spite of open admissions, in spite of radical shifts in the demographics of college students, in spite of the huge escalation in the population percentage as well as in sheer numbers of people attending American colleges, freshmen are still committing approximately the same number of formal errors per 100 words they were before World War One. In this case, not losing means that we are winning.

Epilogos

Our foray into the highways of research and the byways of the Pentecostal Youth are over for a time, and we are back on the farm. From our vantage point here on the porch, we can see that this labor has raised more questions than it has answered. Where, for instance, *do* our specific notions of error come from? Can we identify more precisely the relationship among error patterns in written student discourse and other forms of discourse, especially the mass media? Could we identify regional or other variations in error patterns? How might certain error patterns correlate with other patterns—say age, gender, habits of reading, etc.? How might they correlate with measures of writing apprehension, or the "ethos," the ideology of a specific curriculum? Most provocatively, could we derive a contemporary theory of error which would account for the written behaviors of all our students as well as the marking behavior of teachers? These are a few of the problems we'd like to fret over if and when we decide to take to the research road again.

NOTES

1. As an example of shifting perceptions of student error patterns, it is worth noting that Charles T. Copeland and Henry M. Rideout, writing in 1901, identified the most serious and common grammatical error in Harvard freshman papers as a confusion of the rules for use of "shall" and "will" to express futurity (71n).

2. For a list of most of these studies, see Harap 444–46.

3. We wish here to express our gratitude to the College Division of St. Martin's Press, which graciously offered respondents a choice from the St. Martin's trade book list in exchange for 30 or more teacher-marked student papers or xeroxes of student papers. We are especially grateful to Nancy Perry, Marilyn Moller, and Susan Manning, without whose help this research could never have been accomplished. From assistance with mailings to the considerable tasks of paper stacking, stamping, sorting, and filing, they made the task possible. Their support, both institutional and personal, is deeply appreciated.

The demographics of the papers we were sent were interesting, as we found when examining them for our stratified sample. After pulling all the papers that were illegible, or were not undergraduate papers, were too short to be useful, or were clearly papers from ESL courses, we were left with 19,615 papers. We divided up the U.S. into seven fairly standard geographical regions:

1. Northeast
2. Southeast
3. Midwest
4. Mid-South
5. Plains States
6. Southwest (including Hawaii)
7. Northwest (including Alaska)

Here are the raw numbers of how the papers were distributed as they came in to us:

Region	1	2	3	4	5	6	7	Total
Total number of papers	3,652	3,478	3,099	4,974	1,229	2,292	891	19,615
Total number of teachers	61	51	54	55	18	47	14	300
Total number of 4-year schools	47	35	40	39	14	24	7	206
Total number of 2-year schools	14	16	14	16	4	23	7	94
Total number of state schools	44	49	48	48	18	44	13	264
Total number of private schools	17	2	6	7	0	3	1	36
Number of schools with total enrollment under 1,000	2	2	0	1	1	1	1	8
Enrollment 1–3,000	9	13	7	11	3	5	4	52
Enrollment 3–5,000	13	5	5	14	2	7	2	48
Enrollment 5–10,000	19	9	16	10	6	7	4	71
Enrollment 10–20,000	14	9	13	13	1	15	2	67
Enrollment over 20,000	4	13	13	6	5	12	1	54

4. We wanted to find out whether the sample of papers we had received mirrored the demographic realities of American higher education. If it did not, we would have to adjust it to represent the student and teacher populations that were really out there.

When we looked at *The Digest of Education Statistics*, we found that some of our numbers approximated educational statistics closely enough not to need adjustment. The breakdown between 4-year colleges and 2-year colleges, for instance, is 71%/29% in the statistical tables and 69%/31% in our sample. The state schools/private schools ratio is statistically 79%/21%, while our sample ratio was 88%/12%, but the over-representation of state schools did not seem serious enough to worry about for our purposes. In terms of enrollment, we found middle-sized schools slightly over-represented and very small and very large schools slightly under-represented, but in no case was the deviation more than 7% either way:

	% of Students Nationally	% in Sample
Number of schools with total enrollment under 1,000	4	2
Enrollment 1–3,000	11	17
Enrollment 3–5,000	13	16
Enrollment 5–10,000	21	24
Enrollment 10–20,000	25	22
Enrollment over 20,000	25	18

We found the most serious discrepancies in the regional stratification, with some regions over- and others under-represented.

Region	1	2	3	4	5	6	7
% of students nationally	23	12	23	15	4	19	4
% of students in sample	19	18	15	25	6	12	5

On the basis of the regional discrepancy we found, we decided to stratify the sample papers regionally but not in any other way.

For help with the methodological problems we faced, and for advice on establishing a random stratified sample of 3,000 papers, many thanks to Charles Cooper. When the going gets tough, the tough go ask Charles for advice.

5. These two examples of old-time error patterns are cited in Pressey and in Johnson.

6. The term "comma fault" was by far the most popular term to describe this error pattern until the ubiquitous *Harbrace* seeded the clouds with its terms in 1941, advancing "comma splice," previously a term of tertiary choice, into a primary position by 1960. See Lunsford, Glenn, and Connors, "Changing Pedagogical Nomenclature," forthcoming when we can all stop panting.

7. This paper, five lovingly-written pages of classic Victorian pornography, was extremely popular with the raters. Example passage: "Tammy's own arousal came with suddenness. Bill's urgent caresses kindled a delicious warmth in her flesh and then a melting trembling heat." We would quote more, but we're prudes, and this is a family magazine. For an original xerox copy of this extremely interesting piece of pedagogical history, send $25.00 and a plain brown self-addressed envelope to the Ma and Pa Kettle Go To Waikiki Fund, c/o this magazine.

The teacher's comment on this paper, incidently, was curt. "This is narration," wrote the teacher, "Sorry you didn't use analysis to explain. Remember the definition of explanatory prose?" Another kick in the teeth for Art.

8. In addition to the error-rating sheets, on which the raters kept track of errors found and errors marked, we asked them to write down on a separate list every misspelled word in every paper they saw. This spelling research is only partially tabulated and will be presented in another study.

9. We were also intrigued to find that of the 3,000 papers examined, only 276 had been marked using the letter-number system of any handbook. Handbooks may be widely used, but fewer than 10% of our papers relied on their systems. The rest had been marked using the common symbols and interlinear notes.

10. With our spelling research partially tabulated at this point, we are struck by the prevalence of homophone errors in the list of the most commonly misspelled words. The growth of *too/to* and *their/there/they're* error patterns strongly suggests the sort of problem with visual familiarity suggested by our list of non-spelling errors.

11. These comparisons are not absolutely exact, of course. Johnson counted spelling errors, while Witty and Green and we did not. The numbers in the chart for Johnson's research were derived by subtracting all spelling errors from his final error total.

WORKS CITED

Copeland, Charles T., and Henry M. Rideout. *Freshman English and Theme-Correcting at Harvard College*. Boston: Silver, Burdett, 1901.

Elbow, Peter. Unpublished document. English Coalition Conference. July 1987.

Harap, Henry. "The Most Common Grammatical Errors." *English Journal* 19 (June 1930): 440–46.

Hodges, John C. *Harbrace Handbook of English*. New York: Harcourt, Brace & Co., 1941.

Johnson, Roy Ivan. "The Persistency of Error in English Composition." *School Review* 25 (Oct. 1917): 555–80.

Pressey, S. L. "A Statistical Study of Children's Errors in Sentence-Structures." *English Journal* 14 (Sept. 1925): 528–35.

Shaughnessy, Mina P. *Errors and Expectations*. New York: Oxford UP, 1977.

Sloan, Gary. "The Subversive Effects of an Oral Culture on Student Writing." *College Composition and Communication* 30 (May 1979): 156–60.

Snyder, Thomas D. *Digest of Education Statistics 1987*. Washington: Center for Education Statistics, 1987.

Williams, Joseph. "The Phenomenology of Error." *College Composition and Communication* 32 (May 1981): 152–68.

Witty, Paul A., and Roberta La Brant Green. "Composition Errors of College Students." *English Journal* 19 (May 1930): 388–93.

Introduction to
Selected Essays of
Edward P. J. Corbett

The "Introduction" to the *Selected Essays of Edward P. J. Corbett*, published in 1989 by Southern Methodist University Press, was a labor of love for Bob, who took several classes with Corbett while completing his Ph.D. at the Ohio State University. In 1984, we collaborated with Bob on a collection of essays on *Classical Rhetoric and Modern Discourse* in Ed's honor. But in *Selected Essays of Edward P. J. Corbett*, Bob wanted to present Ed's own scholarly writing. Bob wanted to do so, he notes in the introduction, not only because Ed's scholarly work contributed so much to the development of rhetoric and composition in America but also because Ed himself was so strong a presence in the words on the page. The same, we believe, is true of Bob in this introduction, and in all of Bob's writing. In his introduction Bob says of Ed Corbett: "No mere writings can give us the full man" (180). We agree—but we are grateful for this introduction, which tells us much not only about Ed Corbett but about Bob as well.

T his book brings together a selection of essays and addresses written and delivered by Edward P. J. Corbett between 1958 and 1986. These were years in which rhetoric became increasingly important in the discipline that would come to be called composition studies—an increasing importance for which Edward P. J. Corbett's influence was largely responsible. As a compendium of his work, this book represents not only the evolving thought of one of the field's major voices, but also a sort of history of the birth and evolution of many of the important ideas informing composition studies. Edward P. J. Corbett has taught at the University of Chicago, Creighton University, and, since 1966, at Ohio State University. He has held almost every office in the Conference on College Composition and Communication. He edited the journal *College Composition and Communication* from 1973 to 1979. His contributions to the field have been so numerous and varied that it is difficult to imagine it without him, but in order to understand the importance of those contributions, we must first look briefly into the history of composition in American colleges.

From *Selected Essays of Edward P. J. Corbett* (Dallas: Southern Methodist UP, 1989), xi–xxii.

Between 1960 and 1975 the discipline of composition studies was born in American colleges and universities. Before 1960 there had been, of course, a great deal of composition *teaching*, but we cannot point to a clear intellectual discipline behind most of that teaching. Composition pedagogy, as it had evolved in American colleges since 1800, was a practice without a coherently evolved theory, a constantly reinvented set of ad hoc experiments stretched over a cumbersome matrix of taxonomic and mechanical abstractions.

College teaching of written rhetoric had always been problematical. When courses in practical composition, as opposed to lecture-based courses using Hugh Blair's *Lectures on Rhetoric and Belles Lettres*, began in the 1830s, their teachers realized quickly that the rhetorical tradition as it existed in classical and even modern sources would not serve them well. Student writers did not need extended discourses on The Beauties of Johnson; they needed *some* kind of information about what made prose clear, readable, and mechanically correct. Textbook authors immediately strove to concoct books that would provide this information. Some of the theory purveyed by these texts was adapted fragments of classical rhetorical theory; some of it was snippets of George Campbell, Hugh Blair, Richard Whately. But the largest amount of the material we now call "current-traditional rhetoric" was derived from text authors' attempts at inductive understanding of the structural rules they supposed must govern the production of good writing. As David J. Hill put it in his 1877 book *The Science of Rhetoric*, "Rhetoric cannot make laws for composition, but it can discover them." The nineteenth century "discovered" a number of conflicting "laws" for composition, and much of the material that governed the teaching of writing after 1830 was simply made up out of this whole cloth of inductive assertion.

The college freshman composition course founded on this material perpetuated the errors in these current-traditional theories. The required freshman writing course had been invented by the staff of Harvard in the 1880s as a response to the perceived "illiteracy of American boys" purportedly uncovered by the Harvard entrance examinations. Harvard placed the blame for the large percentage of failures of this exam squarely on the academies and preparatory schools, but the college could not wait for secondary schools to solve the problem. The college was determined to solve the problem of "illiteracy" that existed in its own ranks. Thus, in 1885, was born "English A," Adams Sherman Hill's simplified written-rhetoric-cum-grammar class. All freshmen had to take this course, and soon many colleges were aping Harvard's ways. Freshman composition bloomed all over America, soon outdrawing the sophomore- and junior-level rhetoric courses that had preceded it.

The problem with freshman composition was social. From the beginning it had been a "remedial" course, specifically divorced from "genuine" college English courses (which after 1890 were largely literary in scope). As a remedial course it did not attract the interest or work of scholars or critics, who were overwhelmingly attracted to upper-level courses. As a result, freshman composition was nearly always detailed after 1890 or so to graduate students, lower-level instructors, new assistant professors, faculty spouses, and other

English department fringe people. In addition, the endemic overworking of composition teachers—whose load was presumed no heavier than that of literature teachers, in spite of the fact that composition usually entailed three times as much paper marking as literature—drove many from the field.

This overwork and lack of status meant that the number of scholars and theorists attracted to composition questions dropped radically after 1895. The senior professors, who had been trained while the older discipline of rhetoric was still coherent and respected, either retired or switched allegiance to literary or dramatic subjects. They were not replaced, and the newer junior teachers of composition had neither the time nor the inclination to become scholars in the field that occupied most of their teaching energy. Those teachers interested in rhetoric felt more and more ignored and marginalized in English departments, and after 1914 they seceded into the newly created Speech and Communications departments.

During the period 1900–1940, nearly all "theory" in composition was carried on by textbooks, whose contents were seldom questioned. English composition teaching went on without respect and without access to any deeper tradition of ideas about discourse. As a result, there was no continuing core of theorists and investigators to create a "discipline" of composition studies. Thus, through most of this century, composition teaching proceeded in an overwhelmingly atheoretical way. The few journals that existed to serve writing teachers were well intentioned but intensely repetitive and pragmatic in outlook. The few books that appeared concerning the teaching of composition between 1900 and 1960 were curricular and "Monday-morning" practical works. Cut off from vital roots in the millennia-old traditions of discourse theory and education, freshman composition went on its way, the "dreariest part of the waste that the unfortunate travel through" in freshman English, as I. A. Richards lamented in 1936. Debilitated since the 1890s, composition awaited a revitalization.

It would be dramatically satisfying to be able to point to a single date or person responsible for the revitalization that occurred, but what Edward P. J. Corbett calls "the recovery of the rhetorical tradition" in composition did not take place in a single burst in the early 1960s. The roots for it extend back to the late 1940s, when three unrelated phenomena in the discipline of English prepared the discipline for the shifts that would come later.

One of these was the post-war "Communications" movement in general education, which brought together Speech and English scholars for the first time since Speech had become a separate discipline in the early part of the century. Communications courses sought to bring together oral and literate skills, teaching reading, writing, speaking, and listening in a cooperative fashion. English and Speech teachers worked side by side for the first time in forty years, and both learned from the experience. Although the Communications movement was short-lived, having essentially run its course by 1958, it made English teachers aware that there *was* a rhetorical tradition, one that had been kept alive in Speech since 1914. English teachers began to explore the possibilities that the traditions of rhetoric might offer their students.

Another professional shift was the general move within literary scholarship to a New Critical methodology. New Criticism was an essentially populist movement within the field of English, a method whose "practical" close-reading approach made it appealing and practicable for almost any reader, even one without extensive philological or scholarly background. New Criticism, with its emphasis on explication and the search for predetermined qualities like irony or ambiguity, was a species of rhetorical criticism. One of its central questions had to do with the qualities that *defined* literature as opposed to nonliterary language, and its approach to literary texts made many scholars conscious—often, as Corbett tells it, painfully so—of the different ways of reading they applied to "literary" and "student" texts.

Finally, the socioculture of English studies was changed radically by the aftermath of World War II. Students poured into the colleges on the GI Bill, more of them than colleges had ever dreamed of. Graduate schools grew rapidly and by the early 1950s were turning out hundreds of new Ph.D.'s a year instead of the scores that they had produced before the war. Higher education was becoming a big business—but more importantly, it was also becoming more populist. The nature of the American professoriat was no longer as rarefied and elitist as it had been during the period 1890–1940; the "new men" (and women) were often from lower-middle-class backgrounds and had been thrown into intellectual channels by the great convulsion of the war. Unlike the small elite group of earlier college English teachers, for whom any literary study after the eighteenth century had been a questionable enterprise, they were willing to accept the teaching of modern fiction, modern poetry, American literature, folklore—and the teaching of composition.

Slowly, but with increasing force through the late forties and early fifties, this new group of teachers made itself felt. Communications pedagogy and New Critical theory were discussed everywhere, and composition teaching, the essential assignment for all new instructors, was suddenly being reexamined with an intensity not seen for half a century. The Conference on College Composition and Communication (CCCC), founded in 1949, had at first fewer than 200 members. By 1954 its membership had climbed only to 351. But in the next nine years, the organization's numbers took an amazing leap, to 1656 in 1957 and to 2888 by 1962. Along with this almost tenfold increase in numbers, the CCCC began to act as an important national clearinghouse for ideas on composition teaching. The journal *College Composition and Communication* (*CCC*), which had at first done little more than reprint talks given at the annual conference, started to publish articles by respected scholars and serious debates about the uses and purposes of the composition course.

With all of this growing activity in composition, however, there was a clearly felt lack of a center. The journal articles of the period 1955–1960 are filled with proposals that link composition with grammar, logic, language, speaking, research, teacher training—but they are also filled with a sense that, as Albert Kitzhaber put it, "freshman English courses as they exist now are not something we can be content with, much less be proud of." This dis-

satisfaction with the received wisdom that had so long informed the freshman composition course was not absolutely new in the profession, but never before had there been such widespread and vocal discussion of it. More importantly, never before had so many bright and committed young scholars stepped forward to try to do something about it. Between 1960 and 1965 the efforts of these new theorists changed the face of the field forever. Looking through back issues of *CCC*, one is struck by the fact that the 1960 journal, with its endless debates on logic, usage, and structural grammar, seems the product of another historical period, while the 1965 journal, filled with Richard Braddock, Robert Gorrell, Francis Christensen, Richard E. Hughes, Edward White, Edward P. J. Corbett, seems essentially modern both in tone and content. A sea-change has taken place. Issues are being defined and agreed on; histories are being discovered; solid research and testing of assertions are being demanded; philosophical assumptions are being argued out; and most importantly, a whole generation of practitioners has voluntarily dedicated itself to the exploration of a previously disdained field. Composition studies is born.

This is not the place for a full history of that rebirth of composition during the period 1960–1970 or for an adequate recognition of the many persons who were instrumental in giving composition studies its identity as a respectable field. There is, however, no doubt that one primary concept lay behind most of the theory and practice that we now think of as defining the early period of composition studies. The concept was rhetoric.

The suddenness with which rhetoric swept over composition studies is striking. Virginia Burke, who was intimate with the work done at that time, reported that there were no rhetorically oriented workshops at CCCC before 1958. There was almost no mention of the term "rhetoric" before 1960, when *CCC* ran a list of projected workshops for the 1961 conference. One of them was titled "Rhetoric—the Neglected Art in the C/C Course?" This workshop, co-chaired by Carl Dallinger of Iowa State and Edward P. J. Corbett of Creighton University, took place at the CCCC in March of 1961. It was the first CCCC workshop to bring rhetorical principles to the fore as a programmatic move. In 1962 there was a workshop panel on "History and Philosophy of Rhetoric and Composition." The theme of that 1962 conference was "What is English?" and the 1963 CCCC, chaired by Robert Gorrell, was to be an answer to that question called "The Content of the English Course."

The CCCC met in Los Angeles that March of 1963. Rhetoric was not overly represented in the program in any obvious sense, but many who were there recall the 1963 conference as qualitatively changed from earlier conferences. Over 1500 attended, more than had ever before come to a CCCC meeting, and panels and workshops were all packed. Something new seemed to be in the wind. Wayne Booth gave a presentation on "The Rhetorical Stance," Francis Christensen gave "A Generative Rhetoric of the Sentence," Gene Montague gave "Rhetoric in Literary Criticism," Robert Lambert gave "Assignment in the Rhetoric of Involvement," and Edward P. J. Corbett gave "The Usefulness of Classical Rhetoric." The "Rhetoric in Freshman English"

workshop was no longer No. 12 or No. 19: it was Workshop No. 1. The workshop passed two resolutions: "Resolved, that rhetoric, generally conceived as effective adaptation of writing skills to particular ends and/or audiences, be accepted as an integral part of the freshman course," and "Rhetorical principles should be the organizational principle of the freshman English course and the evaluating criteria for grading student papers."

The tendency toward sudden attention to rhetorical issues was so emphatic that Ken Macrorie, the new editor of *CCC*, trumpeted across the cover of the October issue the phrase that would come to delineate the movement: "Toward a New Rhetoric." In November the executive committee voted to sponsor a Scholars' Seminar in 1964 devoted to the subject of rhetoric. Participants were Wayne Booth, Virginia Burke, Francis Christensen, Edward P. J. Corbett, Robert Gorrell, Albert Kitzhaber, Richard Ohmann, James Squire, Richard Young, and Karl Wallace. This gathering began to change current thinking about composition teaching in some fundamental ways; suddenly writing teachers had a whole new body of knowledge to draw from and explore. "Rhetoric is the word, or is becoming the word," reported Gorrell in his article about that seminar.

Indeed rhetoric was the word, throughout the rest of the 1960s and into the mid-1970s. Rhetorically oriented scholarship of all sorts, from rediscoveries of older rhetorics to "new rhetorics" of Christensen and Burke, led composition studies out of the backwater area where it had been glumly encamped for so long. In 1968 a group of rhetorical scholars founded the Rhetoric Society of America, "for the advancement of the study of rhetoric," and the Rhetoric Society meetings quickly became known to the CCCC *cognoscenti* as the salons of choice for news about the most interesting work being done in the field of composition. Hundreds of articles appeared with the word "rhetoric" in their titles. Scores of composition texts appeared claiming allegiance to rhetoric.

The great efflorescence could not last indefinitely, of course, and limits to growth were eventually reached. By the middle 1970s, rhetoric had lost some of its trendiness, and certain scholars were quick to see the rhetorical revolution as a passing fad within composition. Was not rhetoric, they argued, merely the current version of "oral English," "general semantics," "communications," "structural linguistics," and the other members of yesterday's Hit Parade of pedagogical fads? Would it not fade away into the oblivion that awaits each trumpeted pedagogical movement when it has run its course?

The answer was no. Rhetoric did not disappear. Its ascendence leveled off, yes, but throughout the seventies and eighties rhetoric has continued to be a powerful force within composition teaching. The reason for the continuing relevance of rhetoric lay in its sheer expansiveness and flexibility. The rhetorical tradition, as it was recovered and expanded by the written-discourse theorists of the New Rhetorical period, could simply cover more ground, entertain more questions, and explain more phenomena than other potential approaches within the field. The traditional canons of rhetoric, which became and remain the bases for the indispensable current bibliography of the field, Gary Tate's

Teaching Composition, have been able to subsume most of the major areas of investigation within composition studies. More importantly, the relation of philosophical and rhetorical thought, begun in the 1960s, has continued to provide a discourse-based theory of knowledge and learning which embraces almost every aspect of discourse and pedagogy.

As a discipline we have searched hard, but there seems to be no disciplinary rubric as adaptable, spacious, and comprehensive as rhetoric. Grammar and linguistics, which had looked for a time in the 1950s and 1960s as if they might become the bases for a new approach to teaching writing, were gradually perceived as too algorithmic, too concerned with demonstrable right/wrong dualities, to be widely applicable beyond the sentence level. The research strand in composition studies, beginning with Richard Braddock, Richard Lloyd-Jones, and Lowell Schoer's call for better research in *Research in Written Composition* (Urbana: NCTE, 1963), became and remains a vital element in the study of teaching and discourse. Important as it is, however, composition research cannot provide for axiological ordering of the facts it discovers; research questions are framed by rhetorical categories, and interpretation of research results must always be dialogic. Research must rely on rhetoric to embed its findings in social contexts or pedagogical methods, and thus research can be only a part of the larger picture. The writing-process movement, which proposes that one learns to write simply by writing and practicing revision under the guidance of a sympathetic editor, has developed some of the most helpful and humane teaching methods yet seen in composition, and it is an integral part of the newly revived discipline. Process-based teaching is, of course, profoundly rhetorical, but the majority of its practitioners remain essentially atheoretical, uninterested in deeper explanations of the results they achieve.

So rhetoric has remained vital primarily because it is the most embracing study of discourse production and teaching. It can encompass discourse theory and linguistic explorations beyond the sentence. Experimental and naturalistic research studies give meaning to what they discover by explaining it within general rhetorical frameworks. Process-oriented teachers can look to rhetorical theories for help with specific questions and problems that come in their interactions with texts and with students. The recent interest in the social and ideological construction of reality through discourse communities has an intrinsically rhetorical basis. Rhetorical approaches, once recovered for composition, could not die out because finally, rhetoric must be at the heart of all discourse study. As the oldest and newest of the humane disciplines, it is able to embrace psychological, social, cultural, methodological, philosophical, and practical questions in a way that no mere "approach" can. That Terry Eagleton and other contemporary literary theorists are today calling for a unified discourse study under the aegis of rhetoric is not surprising; what is more surprising is that literary theory did not rediscover the utility of rhetoric sooner.

To try to point to one single individual who "revived rhetoric" within composition studies would be hubristic and foolish. It took the continuing

dialectical efforts of many people to shove the recalcitrant and atheoretical proto-discipline in the direction of supportable work that was not directly pedagogical. In the primary group of scholar-teachers whose efforts revived rhetoric, however, Edward P. J. Corbett must be given an honored place. His significant discovery of Hugh Blair and subsequent self-immersion in the originals of classical rhetoric eventuated in a long series of essays and books that reshaped composition teaching. He made accessible to writing teachers a long but buried tradition of theory and practice that they could use as a touchstone and criterion. He made the serious study of style feasible for thousands of students who would otherwise have been unable to do more than make impressionistic claims. He brought out the contributions of historically under-appreciated rhetorical thinkers like Locke and Newman and has made us reevaluate other rhetoricians like Isocrates. Beginning more than thirty years ago, Edward P. J. Corbett made rhetoric available to us, and his work has kept it central. The selected essays in this book, as readable and compelling today as they were when they were first written, have taught us much about who we are as teachers and theorists—and they still have much to teach.

The essays within these covers are the outward and visible signs—or at least the generally sharable signs—of a professional effort that still continues today. As those who know and love Edward P. J. Corbett are aware, his writings can tell only a part of the story of his contribution to the maturation of his chosen field. These pages cannot speak of the thousands of undergraduate students Mr. Corbett has touched, of the scores of graduate students for whom his careful training has been a key to the doors of their lives, of the hundreds of colleagues who have been moved by and have learned from him. They cannot convey the forty years of hard work, the workdays beginning at 6:00 A.M., the hundreds of courses, the dozens of workshops, committees, task forces, offices, responsibilities. No mere writings can give us the full man, can provide us with the "leaping spark" that Plato claimed was the only true tradition of learning. These are only his compositions.

And yet . . . listen to the voice here. Perhaps the man is not so far away. From the very first essay we can hear the clarity, the concern for the reader that has always characterized Edward P. J. Corbett's writing. Even more apparent is the broad, deep synthesis of knowledge lying behind each of the deceptively simple sentences. The bootstrap, self-motivated scholarship that supports those beautifully readable early articles is never advertised or paraded; we simply accept that this writer *knows*, and will give us what he knows.

These two qualities, modesty and generosity, surpassing rare in the academic world, are continuing touchstones in all of Edward P. J. Corbett's writing. They shine forth from the man himself in that clear, wise, humorous, self-deprecating voice that helped so much to give us all professional voices, disciplinary selves. Today Edward P. J. Corbett is still explaining things to us, still teaching us that the best of scholarship is a delight in discovery and sharing. You will meet him in these essays.

Overwork/Underpay: Labor and Status of Composition Teachers since 1880

The story that Bob tells in "Overwork/Underpay: Labor and Status of Composition Teachers since 1880," published in *Rhetoric Review* in 1990, is a familiar one. By that time, Bob and other scholars had narrated the tale of how "[r]hetoric as a college-level discipline entered the nineteenth century as one of the most respected fields in higher education" but over the course of a hundred years changed "from an academic desideratum to a grim apprenticeship, to be escaped as soon as practicable" (181). But there is an edge to this essay that reveals that it was written in the aftermath of the optimism—and, later, the deep pessimism—generated by efforts surrounding the Wyoming Resolution. (For more information, see Linda R. Robertson, Sharon Crowley, and Frank Lentricchia, "The Wyoming Conference Resolution Opposing Unfair Salaries and Working Conditions for Post-Secondary Teachers of Writing," *College English*, March 1987 [49]: 274–80.) The essay also paints a particularly rich and detailed portrait of the work of writing teachers from 1880 to the present and of the ways in which graduate education influenced their view of teaching writing. Bob closes "Overwork/Underpay" with a strong and forceful argument: "Unless and until teaching and studying writing can be made work the entire English faculty wants to share in, irresistible social forces will maintain the underclass and all of the unhappiness and poisonous inequality that have always followed in its train" (195).

Rhetoric as a college-level discipline entered the nineteenth century as one of the most respected fields in higher education. The teacher of rhetoric at that time was an honored and respected figure, often occupying a chaired position like Edinburgh's Regius Professorship or Harvard's Boylston Chair. When, however, we look at the teacher of rhetoric a mere century later, what a sad change we find. Rhetoric has changed in a hundred years from an academic desideratum to a grim apprenticeship, to be escaped as soon as practicable. Instead of being an esteemed intellectual

From *Rhetoric Review* 9.1 (1990): 108–25.

figure in community and campus, the rhetoric teacher of 1900 is increasingly marginalized, overworked, and ill-paid. Instead of being a senior professor, he, or she, is an instructor or a graduate student. Instead of being sought by students, rhetoric courses are despised and sneered at, and their teachers have fallen from the empyrean of named chairs to the status of permanent underclass "composition teachers": oppressed, badly paid, ill-used, and secretly despised. In this essay I want to examine some of the issues of labor and status that have surrounded the composition underclass, which is with us today in forms that would be all too familiar to the writing teachers of 1900.

The creation of the composition underclass cannot be understood without examining an essential change that took place in America during the nineteenth and early twentieth centuries. This was the shift from oral to written discourse within rhetorical training, with its result an incredible rise in the amount of individual academic work that each teacher of rhetoric must do. This overwork, along with the increasing bureaucratization of the universities, allowed the formation of permanent low-status jobs in composition which were *not* filled by upwardly mobile scholars, who increasingly gravitated to literary work, which was easier, offered a lighter load, and was given more respect.

Teaching Conditions in Composition Courses

Composition teaching, which grew with literary study out of the decline of the older oral rhetorical tradition, came to be despised in part because it could not boast the Germanically based scholarly cachet of philology or literary history. It was not that there was no rhetorical scholarship; some rhetoricians, after all, separated from English departments and built their own scholarly discipline of Speech. But within the emerging English departments of the period 1880–1900, there was little interest in making composition into a scholarly field. It was within English departments that the teaching underclass was formed and it is at these emerging departments that we must look. Why did rhetoric come to rest in English as required composition?

In the 1860s, linguistic correctness came to be a cultural preoccupation in America with the onset of the great transatlantic usage debates between Henry Alford, G. W. Moon, Richard Gould, and others (Finegan 62–74). The educated classes in America were suddenly swept up in a wave of anxiety about the propriety of their speech and writing, and educational institutions responded to this anxiety. Harvard College instituted its first entrance examinations in written English in 1874, and to the horror of professors, parents, and the intellectual culture as a whole, more than half the students taking the exam failed it. Clearly something had to be done.

The Harvard exam and the continuing problems students had with it (and with the host of similar writing tests quickly set up by the many colleges that took Harvard for a model) created the first American college literacy crisis and the first experiments in required basic writing instruction on

the college level. Adams S. Hill argued incessantly for a required freshman English course at Harvard: "Could the study [of writing] be taken up at the threshold of college life, the schools would be made to feel that their labors in this direction were going to tell upon a pupil's standing in college . . ." (12). In 1885 such a basic freshman course was offered. Very quickly, other colleges followed Harvard's lead, and mandatory freshman composition was the rule at most schools by the late 1880s. This highly symbolic response to a perception of threatening cultural conditions fit in neatly with the increasing demand for literate functionaries in business and industry. In addition, coeducation, which was spreading rapidly, helped promote the idea that rhetoric was mainly written and private rather than oral and public. Essay writing rather than traditional oral agonistic rhetoric fit the psychological demands of coeducation more easily, since many men were uncomfortable competing or debating orally with women in any educational or public forum.[1]

For all these reasons, rhetoric became more and more oriented toward writing. We need now to examine more closely what went on in these new rhetoric courses after 1875. It was through these courses that composition came to be despised and the underclass came to exist. Its genesis there had to do with the nature of the composition work itself, and the conditions under which teachers were expected to do it. It was an initial failure to understand these classes, to realize what composition pedagogy demands of a teacher, that made a composition underclass inevitable.

American college classes from the Revolutionary period through the Civil War had typically been rather small, in part at least because the colleges themselves were small. At Bowdoin, a representative small American college, the graduating class averaged nine students per year 1810–1815, 25 students 1825–1830, and 50 students 1845–1850. Yale was always the largest of the pre–Civil War colleges, and in 1855 Yale had only 472 students. Allowing for limited electives in sciences and modern languages, which became possible after 1800 at many colleges, the average size of the college course before 1860 was seldom larger than 40 or 50 students. Though we may today think that 40 students is a large class, there is no evidence that professors of that period felt overwhelmed by their work. They had no publication demands and very simple service requirements, so they could devote most of their time to their students.

Rhetorical instruction before 1880 was often in both oral and written discourse, and we need to look more closely at these pedagogies. Oral discourse teaching relied on the same rhetorical principles that had been used for centuries in colleges: lecture for the theory, and forensics, orations, and debates for the practice. Note that these teaching techniques are not in any important way dependent on the numbers of students in a course. A lecture can be to 20 or 200 students; oral practice can be organized in groups or teams, and a teacher's comments on an oration may be heard and digested by all in a class. As the American colleges gradually enlarged, oral discourse teaching changed little in its presentation, and the demands it made on the teacher remained stable.

Writing instruction, however, did change radically. "As the meaning of the word *rhetoric* changes gradually in practical application," wrote C. S. Baldwin in 1894, "a corresponding change is taking place in the relation of the instructor to the individual student" (290). It was a change toward encouragement of student self-expression and toward much more individualized contact between teacher and student. "Instead of memorized literary criticism the courses in rhetoric deal largely in practice in self-expression," wrote Frances Lewis in 1902, "and the class-room work, once entirely recitation from a text-book, is now often on the laboratory plan . . ." (15). The rise of "laboratory work" in composition, while pedagogically productive, meant that a completely different set of demands were being placed on teachers. Writing, in comparison to oral rhetorical instruction, was seen to demand by its nature an essentially individualized pedagogy. Writing is an interior activity, and although techniques can be used to share writing among students, a primary transaction in any serious composition course came to be seen as between the student and the teacher. Each student came to be seen as deserving a measurable individual chunk of the teacher's time and energy. It might be much or it may be little, but it had to be there. This inescapable demand, which came from the best-known teachers and schools in America—and the related inability of teachers and administrators to grasp its meaning in a changing college environment—led to the nightmare of overwork that composition courses became.

At first the problem developed very slowly. During much of the first half of the nineteenth century, college rhetoric classes were often devoted to both writing and speaking. In addition, with small classes, professors were able to give each student individual time without real hardship. Nathaniel Hawthorne told of conferences he had over his themes at Bowdoin College with the respected Samuel Newman, and Edward S. Hale reports that during Edward T. Channing's long tenure as Boylston Professor of Rhetoric at Harvard, "we had to write a theme for his examination once a fortnight."

> The stuff which most of us wrote in those first themes was enough to make even optimistic angels weep. . . . But such as it was, we carried it in at three o'clock on alternate Friday afternoons. . . . You sat down in the recitation-room, and were called man by man, or boy by boy, in the order in which you came into the room; you therefore heard his criticism on each of your predecessors. . . . Everything was said with perfect kindness . . . and if you had said a decent thing, or thought anything that was in the least above the mud, he was so sympathetic. Poor dear man! to read those acres of trash must have been dispiriting. (361)

Hale's comment in 1893 about the efforts of Edward Channing in 1840 is instructive. Channing was much beloved by his students and taught written rhetoric at Harvard from 1819 to 1851; he worked hard, but there is no evidence that he was oppressed, or miserable with overwork. By 1851, when he retired, Channing's largest course, the sophomore rhetoric course, was prob-

ably no more than 60 students, up from approximately 35 in 1819, when he was appointed. These were numbers that could allow a fortnightly theme conference without hardship. And yet by 1893, Channing is pitied by Hale, who continues his narrative thus: "Half a century afterwards, when I was an overseer, the president of the time [Eliot] said to me, 'You cannot get people to read themes for many years together.' I said, 'I thank God every day of my life that Ned Channing was willing to read themes for thirty-two years.'" (361). We can see the change that has obtained between 1840 and 1890: From an honored professoriate, the Boylston Chair has descended—even in the mind of the Harvard president—to the status of an academic sweatshop, which wears out its people like ball bearings, which then have to be replaced.

The reason for this change is simple: numbers of students.[2] Composition courses of the latter nineteenth century became hells of overwork which drove away all those teachers who were mobile and ground down those who were not. To understand how this happened, we must look more closely at the structures of courses as they evolved at colleges, especially in the 1880s and 1890s.

NUMBERS OF STUDENTS IN COMPOSITION COURSES

American college courses under the classical curriculum were all required up until the 1820s. The Latin professor, for instance, would teach his Latin course to the entire sophomore class, however large it was. Only with the beginnings of elective courses in the 1830s do we see the concept of splitting a class into several subgroups for specialized training. With the rise of the scientific schools, however, and the growing popularity of electives like the modern languages, such class-splitting became more and more common. By the post–Civil War era, when the Germanic specialties began to be popular, many of the courses at most colleges were split courses.

The rise of the elective principle in colleges is usually closely associated with Charles W. Eliot, President of Harvard from 1869 to 1909. During Eliot's reign, Harvard became the uncontested collegiate and university model. It also completely revamped its curricular requirements, abandoning subject requirements for seniors in 1872, juniors in 1879, sophomores in 1884. By 1894 the only required courses for freshmen were rhetoric and a modern language (Rudolph 294). And by 1897 the only required course at Harvard for any student was English A Freshman Composition.

While the elective system did not take hold at *all* American colleges and universities, it was increasingly adopted throughout the country. Students might be expected to fulfill certain requirements for major departments, but after 1885 the old required curriculum was on the wane. Instead of a few professors teaching a very limited range of courses to entire college classes, American schools increasingly offered a larger number of highly trained and specialized professors teaching smaller courses open to a range of classes.

Except, of course, for rhetoric teachers.

Just as rhetoric as a discipline seemed to many Americans to hark back to the trivial tradition of the old English-based college, so the structure of the

rhetoric course—and the freshman composition course based in rhetoric—seemed to hark back to the older whole-class based college curriculum. The traditional sophomore rhetoric course, and more absolutely the required freshman course were typically taught to an entire class, just as they always had been.

These were not, however, the classes of twenty or forty or sixty students that had been common before the Civil War. The average size of the freshman class at Harvard was over 200 students by 1870, and by 1903 it had grown to more than 600. Even in smaller institutions growth was the rule, and by 1900 the enrollment of all of the most important state universities and nearly all of the influential Ivies was above 1,000 students.[3]

With these ever-larger numbers of students to serve and no class-splitting or elective system to help ease their burden, rhetoric teachers were in a serious situation. The average freshman class was two hundred or more students in many institutions, and these teachers were attempting to teach a course that required a certain amount of personal attention to each student. The expectation around the turn of the century was that each teacher would provide 6–8 hours of personal conferences to students for each two hours of class time (Hart 370). These teachers could not use mass recitations or simple tests. They had to read the writing of more students than was possible without real hardship.

What happened? They did it—or at least they tried hard. And the resulting overwork drove away any possibility that rhetoric as a field could attract the talented scholars who might have been able to forge it into a modern scholarly discipline despite its lack of Teutonic breeding.

We need only look at a few numbers to see what the rhetoric teachers of the late nineteenth century faced. At Harvard in 1892, Barrett Wendell read daily and fortnightly themes from 170 students—over 24,000 papers each year.[4] At Yale, one professor and one instructor were responsible for 250 composition students; the same was true at Iowa. At Wellesley one professor and three assistants taught 600 students. At Minnesota one professor and three assistants taught 800 students in the Department of Rhetoric.[5] Fred Newton Scott of Michigan, writing in 1895, reported that

> I have read and re-read this year something over 3,000 essays, most of them written by a class of 216 students. . . . That the instructor should somehow lay hold of the student as an individual is, for composition work, simply indispensable. . . . But it must be borne in mind that in the larger universities the day of small and cosey classes is long past. Now the hungry generations tread us down. We hardly learn the names and faces of our hundreds of students before they break ranks and go their ways, and then we must resume our Sisyphyaean labors. (Payne 121–22)

However much we may today complain about our composition loads, these early teachers had a far worse situation to deal with. What is most amazing today, however, is the relative lack of direct complaint we hear from

them. Barrett Wendell's tone in reporting his work with 170 students is cool and neutral: "it happens this year to be my duty to read [the daily themes] every day and to make some sort of note on them . . . of course, I must do it rather hastily. It is a matter of two or three hours a day." (Wendell 660) These daily themes added immensely to the work of composition teachers at Harvard, but even the more standard weekly themes presented teachers with appalling overloads.[6]

We have no complete or detailed information on teaching loads outside of such anecdotal references until the early part of the twentieth century. In 1909, however, the Central Division of the MLA (which was F. N. Scott's home base) voted to establish a committee to investigate the labor and cost of composition teaching at American colleges. Edwin M. Hopkins of the University of Kansas was appointed the chair of this committee, which began its labors in 1910 but did not complete them until 1913.

The Hopkins Report, as it was known, is a shocking indictment of the conditions and labor involved in teaching college composition. It is the more powerful for being written in a carefully understated tone. The Hopkins Committee based its report on nationwide surveys conducted between 1909 and 1913; these surveys were completed by over 600 teachers and represented around 20 percent of all American colleges. The Hopkins Report surveys were carefully tabulated and designed to err on the side of litotes, but the picture they paint is grim indeed. They found, for instance, that students were required to produce around 650 words each week on the average, that teachers could read around 2200 words per hour, and that teachers could read themes for only two hours a day (ten hours a week) without strain.

Given these numbers, the Hopkins Report made simple calculations about upper limits of students teachers could effectively teach. Even with the most optimistic view of paper-reading skills, the calculations indicated that 61 writing students per teacher was the upper limit. Unfortunately, the surveys reported that the average number of composition students assigned to a teacher was 105, and that to read all of their students' work, writing teachers would need to spend thirty hours each week only on theme-reading (20). In fact, the teachers reported spending only 21 hours per week on theme-grading—two-thirds of what they were "expected" to do, but twice what they could do well (26).

The results of the surveys were summarized by the committee in two pages; from that summary we may note the following as primary elements:

> . . . the average necessary duty of an English instructor according to the class and hour standards in effect was almost double (approximately 175 per cent) that of an instructor in any of the other departments concerned. (20n)

> . . . the theme reading labor expected of a college freshman composition instructor is more than double (250 per cent) that which can be carried on without undue physical strain. (20)

> The results of the work are unsatisfactory and are the subject of general academic and public complaint. (21)

> Conscientious and efficient teachers are brought to actual physical collapse and driven from the profession. (21)

The Hopkins Report begins to give us some idea of why teachers—beginning as early as the 1890s—suddenly began to see rhetoric as drudgery and to desert it in large numbers. While teachers in other fields were dealing successfully with the larger numbers in their classes by evolving techniques of discussion and lecture, composition teachers were tied to the reading of thousands of themes. As Hopkins reports, "Even some of the best of the colleges testify that it is more difficult to retain instructors in English composition than in any other subject. Other reports certify to wearing out, suffering from indigestion and nervous exhaustion, loss of efficiency, impaired eyesight, shattered nerves, and in certain instances, a complete nervous collapse . . ." (25). This is why Charles Eliot lamented his administrative difficulty in keeping composition instructors. This is why a former writing teacher notes in a letter, after having transferred to a different department, ". . . I thank God I have been delivered from the bondage of theme-work into the glorious liberty of literature" (Carpenter et al. 329n). Thus could Hopkins quote the following pathetic lines from writing teachers queried about their status: "I have a better place in view"; "I refuse to overwork, slighting my classes when necessary"; "I have been trained for this work and can do nothing else, hence am helpless to change"; "We hope for better things" (28). And this is why even Barrett Wendell's students could feel his lot was hard, writing, "How pitiful it must be for a man to peruse about 200 odd sermons every day, week after week, and, worst of all, like the shades in Hades, not be permitted to die" (C. H. Burdette, quoted from Newkirk, notes).

COMPOSITION TEACHING AS ORDEAL AND APPRENTICESHIP

The terrible overwork to which rhetoric teachers were subjected was, for many of them, rendered supportable only by the hope that it would someday end, to be replaced by "the glorious liberty of literature." The conception of composition as an apprenticeship to the "real" work of literature had begun as early as the 1890s, when the use of graduate students as TAs first became widespread in universities. With these TAs at the bottom of the pole, the modern hierarchy of English departments was in place: TAs, instructors, assistant, associate, and full professors. And more and more, the teaching of rhetoric in college was detailed to the low ends of the scale, the hapless bottom-feeders: TAs and instructors.

The appearance of this division of labor in the 1890s was coterminous with the gradual entrenchment of the freshman composition course in its modern form. As Edwin Hopkins put it in 1915, "The genesis of the present situation in English may be found in the change from memory training to

laboratory training that was made perhaps thirty-five or forty years ago. When that change occurred, no attempt seems to have been made to ascertain the physical conditions necessary in the application of new methods, as is always done in business and scientific training" (*Proc. NEA* 115).

In order to understand the composition underclass as it developed in the 90s, we must understand the psychology of the instructors who made it up. The PhD degree was less rigidly defined at that time than it is presently; a typical doctorate took only three years beyond bachelor's work to achieve, and the final year of doctoral study often coincided with the first year of an instructor's position. Teaching assistantships existed, but not in the numbers they now do, and the rank of instructor was typically where a young man started.[7] Since the PhD was an investigative or research degree which contained no rhetorical or pedagogical training, the young instructor emerged blinking from his isolate study into a world that was filled with alien work and dreadful drudgery.[8] "To the college instructor," said Franklin Snyder, "a section of English A has been, if not an actual symbol of academic serfdom like the iron collars of Gurth and Wamba, at least a badge of apprenticeship—something to be accepted as initially inevitable, but from which relief would come with the passing of time" (200).

It was early seen that the disparity between the work a young PhD was trained for and that he actually had to do was a serious problem. James Cox said in 1913 that "the PhD as at present conceived is not a teacher's degree but an investigator's degree. . . . Very few can hope to make investigation a lifework and practically all are constrained to teach" (207) and the teaching work was nearly all composition. A questionnaire sent to English departments in 1915 showed that 39 schools required their new people to teach some form of freshman composition, while only eight allowed them to teach noncomposition "junior-college literature" ("Report" 25). New instructors were regularly assigned three, four, or five sections of composition—sometimes while they were still attempting to finish their dissertations.

The result, predictably, of this situation was that young instructors quickly came to hate rhetoric and composition with a passion that almost matched the feelings of their unfortunate charges. Lyle Spencer put the case tellingly in 1913 in a discussion worth quoting at length:

> During the years of his training for teaching the instructor-to-be has not only been taught composition, but he has been led to regard the work as dull, uninteresting. He has been taught, if not by precept, certainly by example, that composition teaching is menial work, drudgery, a pursuit to be avoided. He has been taught to look forward to research work. The vision held before him has been that of scholarship. In his dreams he has seen himself the discoverer of the ur-*Hamlet*, of the lost version of *Love's Labour's Won*, or the other six books of the *Faerie Queen*—and the world rising up to call him blessed. Consequently he has looked forward to teaching anything but composition.

But when his last college day has closed and he is rudely awakened from his dreams, the only position open to him is composition, into which he is compelled to go for the bare necessity of a living. There he finds himself unprepared for the work, with no interest in it, and with the courses looming before him as so much drudgery. . . .

It is the calamity of our present-day composition teaching that our instructors are—the majority of them—not only without special training in their subject, but using the work merely as a stepping-stone for advancement. They do not expect to teach composition always; their interest is in other lines of work; and they either are only filling in, waiting for a man higher up—in Shakespeare or eighteenth-century literature or Middle English—to die, or else are teaching the subject only until they can get an assistant who will take what is regarded by them as the menial work. (In discussion following Greenough, 118–19)

The composition work was thus perceived as mean in addition to being gross overwork, and this attitude in many young instructors poisoned their relationship with teaching in general and with rhetoric in specific.

Thus, very early in the creation of the modern university system was born the tradition—still, sadly, with us today—of graduate students and young faculty members "voting with their feet" against teaching composition and in favor of teaching literature. As J. M. Thomas (one of F. N. Scott's PhDs) said in 1916, the whole training of graduate students "has been such as to give them a notion that courses in composition are little more than a necessary evil" (453).

This separation [between composition and literature] is made more pronounced by the feeling on the part of certain men that such utilitarian work is unworthy of their own high gifts, and that the training they have received, if it has not made them unfit for it, has at least fitted them for higher things. . . . In our colleges, at least, I feel that [the problem] springs in part from the fact that the older men confine their work to courses in literature, and that the courses in composition are generally taught by young men with no experience, or with very limited experience. Furthermore, they are put in charge of classes, and, without any sort of oversight or direction, or even competent advice, are left to work out their own destinies. In no other business in the world would such a waste of energy be tolerated. They are asked to learn to teach in the same way that boys used to learn to swim. They are thrown into deep water and are left to sink or to save themselves. There are a few who swim, there are a few more that manage to struggle out, they know not how, and forever after look with horror on composition. Many sink; a few are rescued by sympathetic friends, and never afterward venture out of the shallow but safer waters of courses in "literary appreciation." (456–57)

It is not hard to see why literary courses were so sought after, and so completely safeguarded as their own by the senior professors. Then, as now,

literary courses were easier to teach, drew more obviously on traditional graduate training, offered a lighter load, and could be shaped to the taste of the individual teacher.[9]

There is also a great deal of evidence that the young aesthetically oriented, highly specialized students of literature being turned out by graduate schools and philology were exceedingly poor composition teachers. They were "inexperienced, unfitted by nature for the work, ill-trained, and sometimes, in addition, reluctant and disaffected," as an NCTE committee reported in 1918 ("Preliminary Report" 593). In his controversial "English and the Ph.D." of 1925, Harry T. Baker excoriated the influence of the degree in scathing terms:

> The missing characteristics of the fledgling Doctor of Philosophy are best shown by his often pathetic attempts to wrestle with the problem of teaching Freshman composition. Frequently he has to teach this for several years before being promoted to the delights of misrepresenting literature to undergraduates. Since his doctorate training and his natural temperament have not been largely concerned with the matter of good English he finds his work dull, and his pupils find it duller. The Freshman course in writing is the standing joke of American universities. The middle-aged doctors are not required to teach it, and the young ones teach it badly. (148)

Teaching, claimed Baker, was primarily a human problem, and PhDs were trained to investigate subjects, not teach students. Howard Savage in 1921 called the required composition course a "salvage dump for young doctors of philosophy, and especially for men and women of uncertain or negative qualifications" (439).

It was early realized that PhD training, though it was increasingly a necessary prerequisite for college teaching, often worked actively against effective teaching by inculcating arrogant and elitist attitudes in the young doctors being produced. Composition students would always be "impervious to learning of any kind . . . young yokels that rush to the universities without thought of culture beyond that thin veneer necessary to get along with their fellow Babbitts . . ." (486), as W. B. Gates sneered in 1929. His attitude can also be seen in a graduate student's comment on a freshman theme, quoted by V. T. Thayer in 1926: "'You should develop a grace of style and depth of comprehension. You need, too, to understand the esthetic and spiritual values of the great masterpieces of the world's art, literary and pictorial.'" (773). Here, clearly, is a gulf between teacher and student that boggles the mind.

The final indignity heaped on the rhetoric teacher after 1900 was the extremely poor pay given for teaching writing. The Hopkins Report found that "The average teaching cost of college English, including all English subjects, is below that of any other department compared, the next in cost exceeding English by 17 per cent. . . . College freshman English composition with the same unit of comparison costs about one-third less than the average for all

English subjects, and 43 per cent less than the average cost for the next lowest department after English" (21). Hopkins found that the average total English departmental budget for his reporting institutions was almost $18,000, out of which only $3,000 was budgeted for composition. Departments budgeted only 56 percent as much per student for composition students as for literary students. The average cost per instructor in literary courses was $2,600 and in composition courses was $1,000 (31). In other words, English was the least expensive college subject to teach, and composition was by far the cheapest sort of English to teach.

Graduate teaching assistants during the first decades of the twentieth century did more composition work than any other sort, and their average salaries lay in a range between $350 and $850 yearly, with the average around $650. By 1929, 34 percent of all colleges were using TAs to teach composition, and 47 percent of larger institutions relied on TAs regularly (Taylor 22). Instructors, who typically taught full time, did little better, averaging around $950 annually. Contrast these salaries with the annual salary of a full professor in 1907, which was over $2,300 (and was over $3,500 at many of the more prestigious universities) (Carnegie Report 10–11, 42–45). By 1920 the average professor made $3,616, the average instructor $1,653. By 1929 the differential was $4,407 and $1,995. In a study of teachers' salaries in 1932, Viva Boothe found that instructors were the only college-teaching rank to consistently run at a financial deficit; their combined expenditures ran to 103.4 percent of their meager salaries (122).[10]

We can note a rough correlation between professorial and instructor salaries. If Associate Professors were earning $9,500 in 1961, instructors were usually earning around $3,500–4,000, and graduate students were earning $1,800–2,000. In general it remained true from 1900 through the 1940s that the instructor corps, which typically taught the same number of hours as the professoriate, earned between 40 and 45 percent of what the professors earned (Boothe 12–13). At my own institution, this ratio was a little worse throughout the 1950s; Donald Murray reports that on his BA graduation in 1948 he was offered an instructor's position at $900 per year, at a time when assistant professors were earning around $3,000.[11] Such examples abound, but no one in an English department needs to be told about these ratios; they are the guilty secrets lurking in nearly all of our liberal humanistic closets.

THE COMPOSITION OF THE UNDERCLASS

And yet, young PhDs, though underpaid and disaffected, took entry-level composition jobs through this century in great numbers. They had little other choice; if they were to work at all, the entry-level jobs were the only ones available. To enter into business with the PhD was the only other alternative, and at least the composition teaching "kept the hand in" and kept the young teacher on a campus. But the "treadmill of freshman English," as Savage called it, was bitter drudgery for all who worked it. Out of this dreary grind the young PhD might eventually be promoted into "the glorious liberty of lit-

erature," but the composition grind would forever mark each English teacher. Rhetoric would always be, to each sufferer under a four-and-four teaching load, a wasteland of "small pay, smaller encouragement, and opportunities for adding to the sum of human knowledge smaller still" (440). They would escape if they could, and would despise and turn away from those who could not.

Those instructors who remained teaching writing knew they could look forward to little better treatment—as long as they remained instructors, as long as they remained composition teachers. Though some members of this underclass were merely passing through, others chose, or were forced by circumstance, to remain. Who were these permanent members of the freshman composition staff and why were they willing to remain in the overworked underclass?

The answer to that question is complex and can only be provisionally sketched here. A part of the answer can be found in gender studies; it seems inescapably true that a disproportionate percentage of the instructor corps in composition has been women. After 1900 more and more women attended graduate school, and the statistics on their attendance versus that of men are very telling. The following table tells the story:

Year	# of Male Grad Students	# of Female Grad Students	# of Male PhDs Granted	# of Female PhDs Granted	# of Male Grad Stu. per PhD	# of Female Grad Stu. per PhD
1900	4,112	1,179	322	20	13	59
1910	6,504	2,866	365	44	18	65
1920	9,837	5,775	439	93	22	62
1930	29,070	18,185	1,692	332	17	54

(John 13–19)

What we see here is simple; there existed a very significant gap between the percentage of male graduate students who attained the PhD degree and the percentage of female graduate students. During the first three decades of the twentieth century, the differential was approximately three to one; where between 7 and 16 percent of men in graduate school would achieve a PhD within a decade, that figure never rose from between 3 and 5 percent for women.

What these figures meant, of course, was that, despite the rise in absolute numbers of women in graduate school and the absolute number of female PhDs, there were vastly larger percentages of uncompleted female than male PhDs. Women often ceased study after the masters degree or even before its attainment. Since after 1900 the PhD was almost absolutely necessary for promotion out of instructor rank (Stewart 250), most of these women, if they chose to remain in college teaching, were forced to settle into the rank of permanent instructor. And, indeed, Taylor's study in 1929 showed that of all composition instruction nation-wide, 38 percent was being conducted by female instructors (22). This is certainly the highest percentage of female

instruction found anywhere in colleges, with the exception of the home economics departments.

That women were a disproportionate percentage of the composition staff was noted by Stith Thompson in 1930, discussing the Taylor Report. Thompson, by 1930, has become so inured to the existence of the underclass that he even asks whether it is not a good thing. "The pertinent question is raised as to whether a certain nucleus of rather permanent freshman composition teachers may be valuable, and this brings up the subject of women instructors—who do often seem to be willing to settle down to a life of efficient freshman teaching without any idea of going further in their academic career" (555).

Why were women willing to accept these conditions, and this pay? The answer is complex and can only be surmised. The academic culture as it existed from 1880 through the growth of the women's movement in our own time certainly did not encourage women PhDs, though it allowed them. Although most women took their degrees in humanities fields—many in English—even in the humanities they had a hard time competing with men for the jobs given out by very real Old Boy networks. Many women chose to marry, and raising children was seen as the woman's job; full-time scholarly competition was difficult for active mothers of young children. Many women chose part-time work for the freedom it gave them in child-raising. And in addition, the close-contact work of freshman composition, time-consuming though it is, seems to have been appealing to women in a way it was not to male PhDs.

For whatever reasons, the nurturing of younger college students through their required composition courses, while it never became an absolutely feminine activity, was work done on a permanent basis by many women, from the First World War up through modern times. In 1962 we find Warner Rice echoing Stith Thompson's claim thirty-two years earlier, "We find, however, some students—especially young women—who are excellent teachers of lower-division English and who lack some of the interests or qualifications required for the PhD as it is traditionally given" (473). Even today, freshman staffs contain more female instructors than any other instructor corps on campuses.

The other permanent members of the underclass are the part-timers, who trade job status for the hours they desire, and the surplus PhDs, those unfortunates who make the long march only to find their achievement turned to dross by job market conditions. As early as the 1920s their fates had been clear; indeed, except for an anomalous period during the 1960s, there seem always to have been more English doctorates than satisfactory tenure-line jobs, and this unhappy fact has stocked the composition underclass throughout the century. Oscar J. Campbell commented tellingly on it in 1939:

> The truth is that one of the most distressing products of the Freshman English machine is the academic proletariat that is has created. In the nature of the case, for the vast majority of those who begin their careers as

section hands in Freshman English there is no future in the profession. They cannot hope for even moderate academic promotion. But, for all that, crowds of young men and women have been lured into the teaching of English by the great numbers of positions annually open at the bottom of the heap, and there they stick, contaminating one another with their discouragement and rebellion. I know of large departments of English in which no one has been promoted from an instructorship to an assistant professorship for over ten years. Instead, men from other institutions have been brought in over the heads of the wretched section hands. This process is natural—yes, inevitable—because the work of a Freshman English instructor does not fit him for the teaching of literature. So at the bottom of almost every large English department lies a kind of morass of unhappy, disillusioned men and women which poisons all its fairer regions. (Campbell 181–82)

Although I do not share Campbell's tendency to blame the victims of institutional shortsightedness for damage to its "fairer regions," it is in the spirit of his pungent and still-true observations that I will close this essay. The composition underclass we have always with us, and many of the reasons for its inception still control its use and development today.

Although the 200-student composition overloads of the past are mostly gone now, the overwork of composition teachers remains a key defining term in the problem of the underclass. It will remain a key problem unless distinctly addressed by rhetoricians, because composition teaching and literary teaching are not comparable in their demands on a teacher. This is hard to talk about, given the way our departments function. We must, however, come to terms with it somehow.

The fact is, as everyone knows who has taught both, that composition is harder and more energy-consuming than literature to teach well. Literature teachers do not delegate composition instruction to instructors only because literature has more cachet; literature is less work to teach. Because it is not required, attracts upperclass students, and has infinitely variable content, it is often more enjoyable to teach. And until English departments begin to address this reality—probably by creating some system of extra teaching credit for faculty who agree to teach writing courses—most tenure-line faculty members (in literature *and* in rhetoric) will continue to use the century-old variety of stratagems and arguments developed to avoid teaching writing as much as they can, and the work will continue to fall to a structurally necessary underclass. Unless and until teaching and studying writing can be made work the entire English faculty wants to share in, irresistible social forces will maintain the underclass and all of the unhappiness and poisonous inequality that have always followed in its train.

NOTES

1. I have been developing this thesis about coeducation and rhetorical instruction in a long essay called "The Feminization of Rhetoric," of which as yet only one section is ready to be published. "The Exclusion of Women from Classical Rhetoric" will

appear in *A Rhetoric of Doing*, ed. Neil Nakadate, Stephen Witte, and Roger Cherry, forthcoming in 1990.

2. We must tread carefully through the minefield that is late nineteenth-century educational statistics. There is no period for which statistics are as confusing and potentially misleading. Our two major sources, the Reports of the US Commissioner of Education and those of the US Office of Education, disagree sharply on many important numbers. It is not strange that numbers may turn untrustworthy when we consider the difficulty of defining such terms as *faculty, student,* and *degree* during the period 1870–1900, when American universities were inventing and defining themselves.

What the statistics clearly do *not* show is a radical increase in the student/faculty ratio between 1870 and 1900. Here are some relevant numbers:

	1869–70	79–80	89–90	99–00
Faculty #	5,553	11,522	15,809	23,868
Student #	52,286	115,817	156,756	237,592
Ratio	(9.4)	(10.1)	(9.9)	(9.9)

(Source: Harris, 932. Harris' book contains a completely different set of statistics for these same realities on p. 924, gleaned from disparate sources and confusingly presented. I prefer these numbers, all drawn from the Digest of Educational Statistics, because they are more consistent with degree totals. "Lies, damned lies . . .")

The story told by these numbers is simple: the overall college student/faculty ratio remained almost exactly constant, at around ten students per faculty member, throughout this extremely important period. So we cannot claim that all college teachers were suddenly subject to dreadful overloads of students. Composition teachers, however, clearly were.

3. According to figures derived from Harris, pp. 936–39, the "average" undergraduate enrollment for the 30 most influential schools in the United States was 1,204 students by 1903.

4. For a fuller discussion of this issue, see Connors, 39–41.

5. In the Department of Language and Literature, the same number of students were taught by three professors and three assistants. (See Payne for details.)

6. At Stanford, the professors voted to cancel the freshman composition course because they were "worn out with the drudgery of correcting freshman themes." "Had this salutary innovation not been accomplished, all the literary courses would have been swept away by the rapidly growing inundation of Freshman themes, and all of our strength and courage would have been dissipated . . ." reported Melville B. Anderson in 1894. The composition course was turned over to two "approved teachers and to the various secondary schools," but Anderson reports that the department will hire more composition instructors because "it would be bad policy to allow any instructor to devote the whole of his attention to the work in English composition; for, however great a man's enthusiasm for such work may be, it is incident to human nature that no man can read themes efficiently for more than three hours at a stretch" (Payne 52).

7. This remained true until the 1960s. Earning the doctorate did not until the late sixties automatically guarantee promotion to the professional ranks, which might come considerably later. See Archer 446–48.

8. There were a few practicum-style courses for new teachers at schools with "advanced" ideas. In 1912 Harvard began to offer English 67, a practicum-style course for new TAs, and by the mid-1920s, Donald L. Clark of Columbia was offering a course in composition pedagogy on the graduate level there. These were, however, rare cases. Most new TAs were given a textbook and some lore and shoved into the classroom to sink or swim. See Wyckoff 217.

9. We can hear the scorn in Thomas' voice as he describes the situation in 1916: "It is my personal opinion that the comparative ease of the task of teaching literature, of arousing enthusiasm in regard to works that have a perennial charm, accounts as much as anything for the great attraction this field has for all young men entering upon the teaching of college English. There is on the contrary no field which so quickly searches out a man's weakness, which puts his ingenuity and resourcefulness to as keen a test, which really proves his ability as a teacher so quickly, as English composition" (456).

10. A sadly representative set of figures is found in Clifford Griffin's history of the University of Kansas. During severe budget cutbacks in 1933, all professors were forced to take salary reductions, and Griffin mentions several individuals' salary cuts. A chemistry professor was cut from $4,800 to $3,620. A history professor was cut from $4,500 to $3,425. And Edwin M. Hopkins of English, who was then in his forty-third year of composition teaching at KU, had his salary cut from $3,800 to $2,960. Thus thy wages, good and faithful servant.

11. Murray spurned this offer, taking instead a position that offered him $300 more per year as an office boy at a magazine. When he did return to UNH in 1963, as a Pulitzer-prize winning journalism teacher, he was offered the princely sum of $9,000 per year.

WORKS CITED

Alden, Raymond M. "Preparation for College English Teaching." *English Journal* 2 (1913): 344–56.

Archer, Jerome W. "Professional Career of the College English Teacher." *College English* 23 (1962): 445–69.

Baker, Harry T. "English and the PhD." *Educational Review* 69 (1925): 147–49.

Baldwin, C. S. "The Value of the Office-Hour in the Teaching of Rhetoric." *Educational Review* 8 (1894): 290–93.

Boothe, Viva. *Salaries and the Cost of Living in Twenty-Seven State Colleges and Universities, 1913–1932.* Columbus: Ohio State UP, 1932.

Brown, Rollo W. *Harvard Yard in the Golden Age.* New York: Current Books, 1948.

Campbell, Oscar James. "The Failure of Freshman English." *English Journal* 28 (1939): 177–85.

Carpenter, George R., Franklin T. Baker, and Fred N. Scott. *The Teaching of English in the Elementary and Secondary School.* New York: Longmans, 1903.

Connors, Robert J. "The Rhetoric of Mechanical Correctness." *Only Connect*, ed. Thomas Newkirk. Montclair, NJ: Boynton/Cook, 1986, 27–58.

Corbett, Edward P. J. "The Cornell School of Rhetoric," *Rhetoric Review* 4 (1985): 4–15.

Cox, John H. "What is the Best Preparation for the College Teacher of English?" *English Journal* 2 (1913): 207–14.

The Financial Status of the Professor in America and in Germany. New York: Carnegie Foundation, 1907.

Finegan, Edward. *Attitudes Toward English Usage: The History of a War of Words.* New York: Teachers College P, 1980.

Gates, W. B. "In Defense of the PhD in English." *English Journal* 18 (1929): 482–87.

Graff, Gerald. *Professing Literature.* Chicago: U of Chicago P, 1987.

Greenough, Chester Noyes. "An Experiment in the Training of Teachers of Composition for Work with College Freshmen." *English Journal* 2 (1913): 109–21.

Griffin, Clifford S. *The University of Kansas: A History.* Lawrence: U of Kansas P, 1974.

Harris, Seymour E. *A Statistical Portrait of Higher Education.* New York: McGraw-Hill, 1972.

Hart, Sophie Chantal. "English in the College." *School Review* 10 (1902): 364–73.

Hill, Adams S. "An Answer to the Cry for More English." *Twenty Years of School and College English.* Cambridge: Harvard UP, 1896.

Hopkins, Edwin M. "The Labor and Cost of Composition Teaching: The Present Conditions." *Proceedings of the NEA.* 1912. 747–51.

———. "The Cost and Labor of English Teaching." *Proceedings of the NEA.* 1915. 114–19.

———. *The Labor and Cost of the Teaching of English in Colleges and Secondary Schools with Especial Reference to English Composition.* Chicago: NCTE, 1923.

John, Walton C. *Graduate Study in Universities and Colleges in the United States.* Washington, D. C.: U. S. Government Printing Office, 1935.

Lewis, Frances W. "The Qualifications of the English Teacher." *Education* (Sept. 1902): 15–26.

Newkirk, Thomas. Personal research notes from Harvard archives. 1989.

Payne, William Morton, ed. *English in American Universities.* Boston: Heath, 1895.

"Preliminary Report of the Special Committee on Freshman English." *English Journal* 7 (1918): 592–99.

"Report of the Committee on the Preparation of College Teachers of English." *English Journal* 5 (1916): 20–32.

Rice, Warner G. "Teachers of College English: Preparation, Supply, and Demand." *College English* 23 (1962): 470–83.

Rutland, J. R. "Tendencies in the Administration of Freshman English." *English Journal* 12 (1923): 1–9.

Savage, Howard J. "Personnel for College Composition." *English Journal* 10 (1921): 439–49.

Snyder, Franklyn B. "Twenty-Five Years of Trying to 'Teach' English." *English Journal* 24 (1935): 196–208.

Stewart, Charles A. "Appointment and Promotion of College Instructors." *Educational Review* 44 (1912): 249–66.

Taylor, Warner. *A National Survey of Conditions in Freshman English.* Madison: U of Wisconsin Research Bulletin No. 11, 1929.

Thayer, V. T. "The University as a Training School for College and University Teachers." *School and Society* 24 (1926): 773–79.

Thomas, J. M. "Training for Teaching Composition in Colleges." *English Journal* 5 (1916): 447–57.

Thompson, Stith. "A National Survey of Freshman English." *English Journal* 19 (1930): 553–57.

Veysey, Lawrence R. *The Emergence of the American University.* Chicago: U of Chicago P, 1965.

Wendell, Barrett. "English Work in the Secondary Schools." *School Review* (1893): 638–67.

Wykoff, George S. "On the Revision of PhD Requirements in English." *English Journal* 17 (1928): 213–20.

How in the World Do You Get a Skunk out of a Bottle?

"How in the World Do You Get a Skunk out of a Bottle?" was published in the regional magazine *Yankee* in 1991. This was actually the second of Bob's essays to appear in that magazine. The first, "Ode to the Age of the Beetle," was published there in 1981. "How in the World Do You Get a Skunk out of a Bottle?" recounts an experience that is aptly foretold by the essay's title—but the narrative is about much more than the title suggests. (Readers will be interested, we think, to know that when Bob listed this publication on his vita, he followed it with the statement "Not my title!") This essay provides insight into both Bob the stylist and, with its concluding words "joy, joy, joy," Bob the man.

T he sandy dirt of Canterbury Road is just right as I pant my way past Johnson's hayfield. The air cool enough for delight but not cold enough for long johns and stocking cap, the early sun slanting low. No sound but my labored breathing and the chunking noise of sneakers on dirt. Just another morning. Or so I think.

Then I see him, off to my right. Twenty-five feet or so from the road in a cut-over hayfield. A skunk. One of the kind that are mostly white, with the black mainly on their sides. From the corner of my eye I watch him turn, move. I detour to the other side of the road.

But something seems wrong, in the way that he moves or the way that he looks. Some glint of strangeness. I slow my pace, looking over my right shoulder. The skunk moves through the stubble toward the road. I stop and shade my eyes against the low sunlight. The skunk comes closer. And then I see it.

A glass jar. About 4½ inches long, about three inches in diameter, with a pinched-in neck—a large baby-food jar, perhaps. It is jammed over the skunk's head, completely covering it past the ears. Unable to hear or smell, the skunk raises his head in a clumsy, unnatural way. His dim eyes catch sight of my bright purple warm-up jacket. He begins, slowly but unmistakably, to come toward me.

From *Yankee*, June 1991, 68–71.

As you probably know, this is not what skunks or any wild animals typically do. But as I stand on the bright, hard-packed road, this skunk is clearly coming toward me. More, I can't help but feel that he is coming *to* me.

I begin to talk to him. Only later does it occur to me that he is probably unable to hear anything with the jar on his head, but the talk is more for my sake anyway.

"Oh, boy," I say, as the skunk trundles closer, "if you aren't a textbook case in conservation ethics, I've never seen one." I back away a step. What if he's rabid? He lifts his head, feebly, to the right, to the left. I can see the long white silky hairs of his back, the fogged translucence of the glass jar.

I have a sudden desire to turn, go, keep running, get home.

By this time the skunk has reached the high grass at the edge of the road. And there he stops. His sides heave; the tight neck of the jar can hardly admit any air, and each breath is a struggle of seven or eight seconds' duration. The skunk is shivering as well, slight tremors running through his whole body as he crouches, watching me. Clearly, the skunk is going to die and not of starvation. He is suffocating as I watch.

"What do you want me to do?" I say. "You've got to come to me. I can't come to you. Who knows what mental state you're in?" The skunk looks at me. "Look, I'd love to help you. But the covered end of you isn't the end I'm worried about." The skunk wags his head slightly, tries to breathe. "What were you looking for in there anyway, you dumb-head? That jar's been out here empty for years."

By now I realize that this skunk is my responsibility. The police would probably kill him in order to save him. Getting someone from Fish and Game would take hours. I am the one here, now.

Maybe I can throw a big rock and break the jar. Not get close enough to be sprayed, but break the glass. Let the skunk breathe.

No. Any rock heavy enough to break the glass from a distance couldn't be thrown accurately. It might hit the skunk and injure him. Even if the glass broke, the edges might slash the skunk's face or get into his eyes. And with that kind of jar, the neck might not break with the bottle part, leaving the skunk with a jagged necklace of razor-edged glass that would sooner or later kill him. No, the rock idea is out.

Perhaps I can find something to throw over him—a coat or a blanket so he can't spray me—and grab the jar. But all I have is this warm-up jacket— too small to cover him and too light to keep him from turning.

"I don't know, old skunkoid," I say, moving slightly closer to where he sits, motionless except for the shivering. "There's no way that I'm just going to go over to you and pull that jar off." One step closer. I have no idea what I *am* going to do. Hunkering down, I keep on talking. "You understand my position. I have to go teach college today. If you spray me, you will seriously undercut my efficiency." He is still not moving. Stand up, move one step closer. Squat down again.

"I'm not going to hurt you. I present no threat. I'm scared to death of you, and you probably are of me." Stand up, one step closer, squat down.

I can see the bloody scratches along the skunk's neck where he tried with claws to free himself from the jar. I keep on talking, just to make noise, piling nonsense on nonsense.

Stand, step, squat, and I am three feet from the skunk. He regards me. Deep breath. Then, very slowly, I reach out with my right hand. "Don't worry now, bubba. I'm not here to hurt you. This jar is the problem." Slowly, slowly, reaching, the skunk still quiet, then *got it!* My hand clamps down on the warm rigidity of the jar.

Suddenly the skunk, until now motionless, is galvanized. He pulls back in panic, his paws scrabbling at the grass, at my hand. I pull hard on the jar. Now it will come off and he will run away. One way or another, this is it.

But this is not it. Pulling hard, I find I am dragging the skunk, who pushes frantically backward, onto the dirt road. His head is *impacted* into the jar. It will not come out.

"Oh, boy, come *on*." The skunk is now completely in the road, struggling furiously to get away, twisting and turning as I hold the jar-tight. The one good thing at this point is that he is so completely wedged that he can't turn and fire, although there is little doubt that he regrets this keenly. As long as I have his head, I'm safe. I pull again and am only able to drag the skunk farther. "Oh, *great*. Now I get to take you home." He grunts audibly, pulls again, scrabbling up packed dirt.

There's nothing for it. I have to grab him with one hand and try to pull the jar off with the other. With my left hand, I grasp him around the shoulder blades. His hair is soft. He would be nice to stroke. "Come on come on come on. . . ." I twist the jar hard to the left, and his head inside assumes a crazy angle, but he stops struggling. I pull hard on the jar. It does not move. "Come on, you. . . ." The jar is *really* socked onto his neck, which has swollen in some way. Grabbing hard at his shoulder blades, I twist and pull harder.

I am exerting all my strength now. And I see the threads of the jar turn, slowly, then more quickly. "OK, something moving, heads up," then more movement, an upward sliding, and then with an audible *pop* the jar is off.

Without any thought except *escape*, I jump up, whirl, run. Unscathed. Unsprayed. At a safe distance, I stop and look back. The skunk stands in the middle of the road. He breathes deeply, several times, shakes himself from stem to stern, takes a few tottering steps across the road.

On the other side, he halts, then turns to look at me. I look back. For perhaps 30 seconds, we regard each other with great benignity. Then I hold up my index finger in a tutorial fashion.

"Next time you see me," I say, "don't spray me." He watches me gravely a moment more, then turns and plods off into a cemetery across the road.

There is something in my hand. An empty jar. Starting to run up the long hill to Main Street, I pitch it as hard as I can, sidearm, way out into a swamp. I hear it splash as I run on up the hill into a sunny morning whose colors are joy, joy, joy.

Writing the History
of Our Discipline

In "Writing the History of Our Discipline," published in 1991 in Gary Tate's and Erika Lindemann's *An Introduction to Composition Studies*, Bob describes the origins of the subfield of composition history, distinguishing it from rhetorical history and emphasizing the prominent role that Albert Kitzhaber's 1953 dissertation, "Rhetoric in American Colleges 1850–1900," played in enabling subsequent historical studies. After acknowledging the contributions of later historians, including James Berlin, Donald Stewart, Sharon Crowley, and others, Bob discusses a number of issues relevant to those undertaking historical scholarship in composition, such as the nature and availability of sources. He closes by considering recent methodological and epistemological debates that have engendered much discussion among historians of rhetoric. As we reread this section of Bob's essay, we were struck both by Bob's fairness in characterizing positions with which he disagreed and by his wit, which is displayed in comments such as the following: "Though we may wax nostalgic for the simple days when the Decline and Fall narrative provided continuity, when textbooks clumsily mated and bred without sociocultural influence, and when neat taxonomies made everything understandable, that is not how we think about things anymore" (217–18).

Near the end of his essay Bob observes that "The writing of the history of composition is still at a very early stage. Much remains to be done" (217). We agree—and we wish very much that Bob was still at his desk working away.

Composition studies is both the oldest and the newest of the humanities, and our gradual realization of this dual nature is probably the reason for the growing importance of historical study in composition. Traditionally melioristic and oriented toward a beckoning future, composition scholars are realizing that the future can most fruitfully be studied with a knowledge of more than a century's experience in teaching and studying

From *An Introduction to Composition Studies*, ed. Gary Tate and Erika C. Lindemann (New York: Oxford UP, 1991), 49–71.

writing. We may not always be able to claim that we see far because we stand on the shoulders of giants; we do, however, stand on the shoulders of thousands of good-willed teachers and writers surprisingly like us, who faced in 1870 or 1930 problems amazingly similar to those we confront each time we enter the classroom. Listening carefully, those of us who have begun to try to hear their voices have found much there we can learn from. Impatient dismissal of the past was a hallmark of our field's early years, and as we mature as a discipline, we will need to draw more and more deeply on the experience of the teachers who came before us. Only in such a context can we discern useful from harmful paths. This essay will be about our development and current state as historians of composition teaching and composition studies.

RHETORICAL HISTORY AND COMPOSITION HISTORY

We need at the beginning to understand that "history of composition" is not a *sui generis* subfield of composition studies. Like composition studies itself, history of composition is a branch of the larger field of rhetorical studies, which has existed for over 2000 years. Though composition emerged from rhetoric, there is no sense in which we can really say that "rhetoric" ended and "composition" began on any certain date. As James J. Murphy's recent collection *A Short History of Writing Instruction* has shown, instruction in the composition of discourse has always been a part of rhetorical pedagogy. The special field of written rhetoric, which came to be called "composition," grew during the nineteenth century out of the older and more accepted practice and teaching of oral rhetoric, which we can trace in considerable detail all the way back to 500 B.C. The history of composition in rhetorical scholarship has, however, been problematical until recently.

Rhetorical history as a scholarly field has existed for nearly as long as rhetoric itself; rhetoricians have always seemed to feel it important to honor or argue with their forebears. All rhetorical writings contain elements of history, and rhetorical history has thus been remarkably well preserved and documented. Even so, to someone reading the standard modern histories of rhetoric or anthologies of important works, there is a sense of inexplicable hiatus after the eighteenth century. A standard rhetorical history text like Golden, Berquist, and Coleman's *The Rhetoric of Western Thought* gives a good example. In that book, the history of oral discourse begins with Corax and Gorgias in ancient Greece, proceeds through Hellenic and Roman rhetoric and into patristic and medieval works. With the Renaissance we read of a great burst of neoclassical and Ramist activity, all well documented, and then the seventeenth and eighteenth centuries see a tremendous empiricist revolution in rhetoric, culminating between 1776 and 1828 in the ground-breaking works of George Campbell, Hugh Blair, and Richard Whately.

And then, after Whately in 1828, rhetoric as described in these books falls off the edge of the earth. The traditional rhetorical histories end abruptly with Whately, and the rest of the nineteenth century is an echoing tomb. The

story picks up again in the 1920s, with I. A. Richards and Kenneth Burke, and from there we hum along merrily through modern to contemporary oral rhetoric, now usually called speech communications. What we see in these books is an intentional excision of a hundred years of rhetorical history, a wiping out of most of the nineteenth century as if it had never existed.

This historical void, which for most of the twentieth century left written rhetoric without a history, is the unfortunate result of the rise of departmentalization in American universities. In early American colleges, oral rhetoric and writing were usually taught by the same generalist professor. There were no academic departments. After the Civil War, however, when scholars began traveling to Germany and bringing back the ideas that would create modern American higher education, the organization of the university into departments of scholars studying similar phenomena seemed natural. Modern English departments appeared quickly, teaching philology, literature, and composition. The older field of oral rhetoric, however, having no Germanic scholarly pedigree, never found a comfortable home in English.[1] In 1914, rhetoric teachers, discouraged by their inferior status in English, left the National Council of Teachers of English to form the National Association of Academic Teachers of Public Speaking, which became the Speech Communication Association—and to form their own separate Departments of Speech. It was in these Speech departments that most of the serious scholarship in rhetorical history has been done in this century.

Speech department scholars defined themselves (naturally, and often polemically) by their interest in oral discourse, and thus we shouldn't be surprised to see a clouding or submergence of the history of written rhetoric in their work. Speech department historians begat histories of an oral rhetoric that seemed to close down or disappear as soon as rhetorical work shifted primarily to written composition in the early nineteenth century. They begin coverage again with the rise of Speech departments as scholarly institutions, creating a new college-based discipline and theory of speech communication. Like literature, composition was seen as an "English concern," and was thus no part of rhetorical history. So high and frowning were departmental walls that it seemed not to matter that most nineteenth-century composition textbooks had "rhetoric" in their titles somewhere, or that their authors clearly saw themselves within the rhetorical tradition. For Speech scholars, rhetoric was oral discourse or it did not exist.

But what of English departments? With composition being taught to great numbers in English, with so many renowned scholars in English from Francis James Child onward, why was no history of composition-rhetoric written? The answer is, sadly, obvious to anyone conversant with the history of English departments.[2] English departments have always been two-tier departments, with the teaching and theorizing about literature given more status and better conditions than the teaching of composition. There was little interest in theorizing about composition or analyzing its history among the burgeoning group of literary scholars, philologists, and critics that controlled English departments after 1895. As the MLA was coalescing and

scholars were working to create the organization and bibliographical tools that would result in the modern field of literature, composition teaching increasingly went on in a sort of twilit underground, taught by unwilling graduate student conscripts and badly paid non-tenured instructors. In short, there simply never evolved a discipline of composition studies comparable to literary studies in English. Composition teaching was done, but no degree specialties in composition existed, and no real scholarship surrounded it except for a few articles in education journals and in *College English*. From 1885 until after World War II, composition existed as a practice without a coherent theory or a developed history.

The status of composition did not change until after 1950. The modern field of composition studies grows out of a great change wrought in the American professoriat, especially in English, after World War II. Before that time, college had tended to be for an elite social class and the professors there had been an elect group. After the war, however, the GI Bill made educational loans easy for servicemen to get, and a great rush of veterans into colleges and universities resulted. Colleges groaned at the seams; many grew precipitously to serve all their new students. And from this mass of GI Bill students came a generation of graduate students and young faculty members who changed the face of English. These younger men, who were from all American social classes, brought fresh ideas with them, many of which democratized the staid old English field. In literature they championed American literature and the New Criticism; their teaching changed textual analyses from something only a trained philologist could do to something any earnest student was capable of. In composition their populist influence was even more powerful. Young professors had always been forced to teach composition, and most of them had gritted their teeth, served their time, and escaped to literature as soon as possible. A notable group within this post–World War II generation, however, determined to study composition, analyze it, and try to do it as best it could be done.

At the same time that this GI Bill generation of teachers was beginning to emerge from graduate schools, the general education movement was sweeping America. Based on the idea that too narrow a subject specialization was not useful in life, the General Education movement sought to bring separated disciplines together. In the language arts this General Education movement was called the "communications" movement. The subjects it meant to conflate were reading, writing, speaking, and listening, and the departments that it got talking to one another, after thirty-five years of frigid silence, were Speech and English.

It is here, in the late 1940s and early 1950s, that we can see the emergence of the new field of composition studies, as opposed to composition teaching. The post–World War II generation of active young teachers in English, brought together for the first time with colleagues from the older tradition represented by speech, began to forge during these years a new scholarly field. Its nature was represented by the name they gave the organization they founded in 1949: The Conference on College Composition and

Communication. Immediately they established a journal: *College Composition and Communication*. At the beginning of the CCCC's existence, the writing appearing in the journal was nearly always concerned with actual issues in the contemporary teaching of writing. But by the late 1950s, writers on composition issues were beginning to reach out toward collateral fields, looking at the theory behind the practice, beginning to investigate rhetoric and linguistics in a serious way. Composition studies was coming into its own as a discipline. And it was here, in this rapidly changing decade, that the first great research into the history of composition teaching was done: Albert Kitzhaber's 1953 dissertation, *Rhetoric in American Colleges, 1850–1900*.

THE GREAT EXEMPLAR: ALBERT R. KITZHABER

Albert Raymond Kitzhaber was born in 1915 and took his MA in 1941. He served in the European Theatre in World War II, returning to work toward his Ph.D. at the University of Washington, and between 1950 and 1953 he researched and wrote his dissertation. *Rhetoric in American Colleges 1850–1900* was written under the direction of Porter G. Perrin, who had himself written a dissertation in 1936 on eighteenth-century American rhetoric. (Perrin, who is now almost forgotten, was one of the great figures of composition teaching in America between 1925 and 1960.) Under Perrin's careful scholarly guidance, Kitzhaber assembled an imposing mass of research materials in nineteenth-century rhetoric and composition, read through and mastered all of it, and then in his writing analyzed and discussed those lost, pivotal fifty years, 1850 to 1900, in a style marked by understated elegance and brilliant synthesis.

Kitzhaber's tone was never one of disinterested scholarship; he looked about him at the serious problems besetting the teaching of writing and sought to trace them to their sources in the theory and practice of post–Civil War rhetoric teachers. "The years from 1850 to 1900 cannot in any sense be called a great period in the history of rhetoric," wrote Kitzhaber. "Composition teaching became, in a very real sense, drudgery of the worst sort, unenlivened by any genuine belief in its value, shackled by an unrealistic theory of writing, and so debased in esteem that men of ability were unwilling to identify themselves with it permanently" (351). He saw his task as providing the necessary information to change the conditions he saw around him: "If a teacher is to have any perspective on his subject, he must know the tradition that lies behind it, know the place of himself and his times in the tradition, and, through this knowledge, be able to put a proper value on new developments in his subject as they appear" (352).

Rhetoric in American Colleges can be coruscating; it is often bitterly critical. With Kitzhaber comes the tendency, seen in much of the later historical work that used his dissertation as a basis, to create heroes and villains out of figures in the history of composition. Kitzhaber's heroes—Fred Newton Scott, Gertrude Buck, John Genung—became the heroes of such second-generation historians as Donald Stewart and James Berlin; his villains—primarily Adams S. Hill and the "Harvard crowd"—became our villains. And for all

later historians of composition, Kitzhaber became "the lion in the road": we could not go around him without dealing with his work. That work—its amazing assembly of sources without any previous bibliographic help, its informed analysis of destructive ideas and methods in composition teaching, its attractive division of our forebears into competing camps, and its narrative of the tragic victory of the mechanistic, form-obsessed "bad guys" who created our own troubled period—influenced in ways great and small everything that followed it in composition history.

It's not hyperbolic to state that with Kitzhaber's dissertation the history of composition studies gained its first really respectable work—and then ended for a quarter-century. *Rhetoric in American Colleges 1850–1900* was never published.[3] It remained an underground classic available only from University Microfilms, passed around in *samizdat* Xerox copies by the small group of people interested in composition history. Kitzhaber went on to a distinguished career at Dartmouth and the University of Oregon, where he continued to work in composition studies and to fight for defensible teaching methods that eschewed both useless traditions and the trendy pedagogical fads of the 1950s and 1960s. And the history of composition in American colleges remained a field little examined. There were, of course, educational histories that touched on composition in college, and a few biographies of figures like Harvard's Barrett Wendell who had also made literary contributions. By and large, however, Kitzhaber's ground-breaking dissertation was not followed up—even by him—during the 1950s and 1960s.

During these years, of course, the general field of composition studies was building itself. Like Whitman's spider, it threw out thread after thread to other disciplines, hoping that some would catch. The primary work during these years was recuperation of the rhetorical tradition, from classical rhetoric onward, and what Janice Lauer calls "analogical-theoretical research," which makes claims for composition studies on the basis of its similarities to other more developed fields, of which the favorites were linguistics and psychology. The technologies of empirical research in composition were re-examined and tuned up, and an improved experimental tradition began. But as the field was creating itself, historical research was a very minor part of it.

THE SECOND GENERATION OF HISTORICAL SCHOLARS

Not until composition studies had evolved to the point where it was granting its own specialized doctoral degrees, in the 1970s, do we see the real beginnings of a scholarly tradition in composition history. Before that point, though certain related historical studies had been done in education departments[4] and in speech departments,[5] only Kitzhaber had explored college-level composition history in any detail. Slowly, however, the flowering scholarship turned toward historical issues.

Like much feminist historical work, early composition history was polemical history. Wallace Douglas bitingly reinterpreted Harvard's place in

the teaching of writing in his "Rhetoric for the Meritocracy" essay of 1976.[6] Again like feminist scholarship, composition history began to search for marginalized forebears, and the greatest of these, Fred Newton Scott of Michigan, was re-introduced to composition studies by Donald Stewart in a series of articles beginning in 1978. In 1980 James Berlin weighed in with articles in *Freshman English News* and *College English* that helped define the forces that had opposed Fred Scott. Borrowing a term from Richard Young (who had borrowed it from Daniel Fogarty's *Roots for a New Rhetoric*), Berlin called the congeries of teaching methods and theories that had evolved through the nineteenth and early twentieth centuries "current-traditional rhetoric." It was a term of opprobrium, and it stuck.

Beginning with Stewart and Berlin, the scholarly study of the history of composition took off. Slowly at first, then with more speed, scholars began to examine the nineteenth and early twentieth centuries for materials useful to current analytical needs. In 1981 Andrea Lunsford published an essay on rhetoric in nineteenth-century Scots universities, Leo Rockas published an essay on John Genung of Amherst College, and Robert Connors published a piece on the modes of discourse, which won the CCCC's Richard Braddock Award the following year. This organizational imprimatur for historical scholarship seemed to give impetus to a whole new generation of scholars, and from 1983 through the present, historical scholarship in composition has been increasingly accepted as an essential branch of the field.

Most contemporary scholars writing on composition history were trained at the doctoral level in both literature and rhetoric, so a historical perspective and access to historiographic methods are not strange to them. Lunsford, Connors, Katherine Adams, Sharon Crowley, William F. Woods, John Brereton, David Russell, Nan Johnson, David Jolliffe, Anne Ruggles Gere, and others have all applied traditional historical methodologies to the primary and, increasingly, to the secondary sources they use and generate. Like all historians, members of this group bring varied perspectives and intentions to the scholarship they do. Some historical scholars specialize in delineating large movements and trends in composition history, while others tend toward smaller-scale works or straight biography of important figures they have researched. Some prefer an attempt at neutral presentation of their findings, while others are openly polemical, operating from a declared Marxist or vitalist or social-constructionist point of view. In a fairly short period of time, composition history has come to be a microcosm of the larger field of historical scholarship.

Most of the work done thus far in composition history has been in the form of journal articles and book chapters. We seem as yet not to have completed the base-level scholarship necessary to producing in-depth studies of book length. As Donald Stewart put it in 1983, "My best guess is that a truly definitive work on this period cannot be written before 1990."[7] The only longer works done since Kitzhaber have both been by James Berlin: his two monographs *Writing Instruction in Nineteenth-Century American Colleges* in 1984 and *Rhetoric and Reality* in 1987. These books remain the most widely

read introductions to composition history used today, and scholars seeking more specific secondary works have to look without much bibliographic assistance through almost every journal in composition studies today; articles on history have appeared in *College English, College Composition and Communication, Freshman English News, Rhetoric Society Quarterly, Rhetoric Review, English Journal, Written Communication, Pre/Text,* and *Rhetorica.* The work done over the past fifteen years has deepened and extended the original territory mapped out by Kitzhaber in 1953, but composition history is still in a very early stage of development. We have a few exemplars, but no masterworks as yet. Small pieces have been admirably accounted for, but the entire picture still remains to be pieced together.

THE QUESTION OF SOURCES

Like historians in any field, historians of composition studies face certain practical and methodological problems. Primary among them are problems of sources. Like conscientious practitioners in many historical fields, composition historians at best seek always to work from primary sources. (Though there is a body of secondary sources building up, it is not yet so large or canonical as to be necessary except for background consultation.) And it is in the search for primary sources that the historian most often finds frustration.

Most of our problems with sources are traceable to the marginalized status of composition up until a decade or so ago. When any field of activity is primarily staffed by part-timers and non-tenured teachers with a high turnover rate, we cannot expect many depositories of professional papers to exist. When the primary pedagogical tools and means for training new teachers are "non-scholarly" textbooks, library holdings of them will almost certainly be incomplete. When no Ph.D.s are being granted in a field, we cannot be surprised that the journals for that field are not being stocked by the college library. And when a field is tacitly felt by those controlling the department in which it resides to be either unworthy or actually nonexistent as scholarly activity, we cannot expect that many people will take care to gather together and preserve the physical evidences of it.

Unlike much of previous rhetorical history, written rhetoric is defined by the paper trail it left. But that trail can sometimes be very cold. Certain sources, like the very popular textbooks of the 1890s, are relatively easy to find, while others, such as pedagogical materials and student papers, are quite rare. It is hard, in fact, to imagine any recent historical artifacts more ephemeral than the pedagogical documents that have actually shaped the teaching of writing at specific schools. Syllabi, teachers' notes, correction cards, course descriptions, class exercises, and handouts from the writing courses of the last 100 years do exist, but in minute quantities and only at a few schools. They were simply not saved at most places. Before the advent of easy duplicating technology in the 1940s, copies of typed documents could be made only in limited numbers using the painful and messy carbon paper method, and before typewriting became common in offices around 1900,

there was no way of duplicating documents except to set them in type and print them. Thus we have almost no nineteenth-century pedagogical materials that were not printed in some form.

Another important source of information on composition history is, of course, students' papers. Unfortunately, our problem in finding pedagogical ephemera is matched by the problem we have in locating students' papers. Especially in the freshman composition course, it seems, neither students nor their teachers were as likely to keep and save papers as they might be in other, later courses. Except at Harvard, which has extensive archives in both ephemera and papers, no large collection of nineteenth-century composition essays is known currently to exist. There are some isolated papers in college archives here and there, but thus far we have no comprehensive record of what exists and where. So outside of Harvard's courses (which were important models, of course, but not necessarily representative), we have only an impressionistic idea of exactly what student essays were like.

Most of the primary sources accessible to the average historical researcher in composition studies are, then, printed sources of different kinds. Of these, the most often used sources have been textbooks and journals. Since Kitzhaber, who derived the great majority of his information from and based his analyses of rhetorical trends on textbooks, their use as effective reflections of pedagogical reality has been heavy. In an essay in 1982, Susan Miller was the first to critique historians' sometime overuse of texts as sources.[8] Since that time historians have striven to search out as many other kinds of sources as they can. Textbooks remain, however, a major source of information on rhetoric and composition in the nineteenth century and a *sine qua non* for a serious historical investigation. Our histories would be poorer by far without them.

Textbooks are important to any rhetorical historian, but they are of special interest to the composition historian because of their incredible proliferation and variety during the nineteenth century and because, unlike rhetorical treatises of earlier days, textbooks were written and sold with specifically pedagogical intentions.[9] Rhetorical treatises were meant to be read (or heard in lecture form, possibly). Rhetorical textbooks, on the other hand, were meant to be taught in classrooms. We can thus learn a great deal about the rapidly shifting rhetorical theory of the nineteenth century from them (much of that theory never appeared anywhere else) and we can also learn much about how authors thought that theory could be applied and learned through exercises, assignments, authors' introductions, and prefaces. In addition, some of the most fascinating information to be found in old textbooks is no part of the author's intention; student notes, inscriptions, doodles, and *sotto voce* complaints on pages and flyleaves also testify feelingly about how the book was used and its claims received.[10] From Lindley Murray and John Walker in the 1790s through the latest process-oriented rhetoric, textbooks can help the historian get a feel for what rhetorical *ars* and *praxis* both were at any point in American history.

Journals having to do with teaching writing, both those originating in education and those from the field of English, can be very useful to the historian as well. Specialized magazines about education go back surprisingly far

into the past (*Barnard's American Journal of Education* started publication in 1856; *New England Journal of Education* started in 1875; *PMLA* began in 1886; *Educational Review* began in 1887; *School Review* started in 1893; and the *English Journal* started in 1912). The great surprise in examining journals and articles even a century old is in noting how "modern" they often sound. Nearly every historian who has looked into these journals, especially the *EJ*, has been astonished by how progressive many of the articles in them seem. But that astonishment should also sound a warning about the unquestioning acceptance of claims made by journal articles. Unlike textbooks, which reflect for better or worse what students were actually supposed to be doing and learning in courses, journal articles often reflect mainly what authors *wished* or *hoped* students were doing or learning.

Indeed, some of the most profound insights that composition historians have come to are based on the disparity between the world of pedagogy set forth in many of the journal articles of the period 1910 to 1940 and what the textbooks show was actually being done in classrooms. Those reading the journals might get a picture of the freshman course across America in the hands of thoughtful, forward-looking teachers who welded experience with humanism and a willingness to seek out and use new methods; even the "discipline in crisis" articles (a century-old genre) give the impression that intelligence and good will shall prevail over the problems. Oral English, or a new grading scale, or using newspapers, or structural grammar, or small-group meetings will make the course pay off. We must examine these articles carefully, however. A few classrooms might have been using small-group meetings and practicing revision as the journals suggested, but thousands of others were sweating through textbook punctuation exercises, or trying to apply Unity, Mass, and Coherence, or attempting to write Three Examples of the Paragraph of Classification. It is only by comparing, year after year, the journals' claims and statements, which were read by a few thousand teachers at most, with the content of textbooks, which were read and used by hundreds of thousands of students, that we begin to get an accurate picture of what composition theory and practice really were like.

Historians must be aware of other sources as well. Professional books about the teaching of writing go back to the 1890s, when the first media-driven "literacy crisis" had produced the freshman composition course as one of its answers. That course created its own methodological problems for curriculum planners, and specialized books for teachers have existed since then. Useful as these books are, they must be examined with the same reservations as journal articles are; they present the world of teaching only as the author sees it, and sometimes as the author hopes it is. Biographies and memoirs of various figures can be very helpful, although few full-scale biographies of central figures in composition history have yet been done and memoirs are about as rare. And only recently has the collection of oral histories from older or retired members of the field begun to be explored.[11] The gathering of these oral histories and recollections is clearly an important task for composition historians, and one we cannot put off.

Locating and evaluating these sources of data have been traditional problems for composition historians. As mentioned, few schools have saved old pedagogical materials or student papers, but I have found library holdings even in the printed sources to be very unpredictable at different universities. Unlike literary historians, composition historians cannot automatically assume that their libraries will have any holdings in their field at all. Old textbooks and even the older professional books have been "de-accessioned" by policy at many libraries. Holdings in the older education journals such as *Barnard's* and the important *Educational Review* are very spotty, and even older volumes of the indispensable *EJ* can be hard to find. Most college libraries get the NCTE journals *College English* and *College Composition and Communication*, but other important journals for historical work—*Freshman English News, Rhetoric Review, Pre/Text, Written Communication, Rhetoric Society Quarterly*—may not be on the shelves. We also face the growing tendency to put older journals on microfilm, which makes the sort of browse-reading so important to historical background tedious and unpleasant.

In addition to confronting problems with primary sources, historians must also cope with inadequate scholarly tools. There are almost none. The field of literary studies has the wonderful MLA Bibliographies as well as a host of more specialized bibliographic tools for both primary and secondary sources. Composition studies, however, has not yet even seriously begun the task of choosing and editing primary sources. Right now, in fact, we do not even have a complete list of such sources; the closest things we have to useful bibliographies of primary texts are the bibliographies at the end of Kitzhaber's and Berlin's books. These lists, while admirable, are far from complete. And scholarly editions of primary sources promise to be long in coming. When it appears in 1991, Andrea Lunsford's edition of Alexander Bain's *English Composition and Rhetoric* of 1866 will be the first scholarly edition of a textbook clearly associated with composition (which is to say, previously ignored by scholarly editors from Speech). For journal articles from the nineteenth and early twentieth centuries, there is no source approaching completeness. General bibliographic sources outside of Donald Stewart's essays for Winifred Horner's two collections, *Historical Rhetoric* in 1980 and *The Present State of Scholarship* in 1983, simply don't exist; each historian has to examine all the primary sources for him- or herself. For secondary work since 1975, of course, the ERIC system is helpful, but it does not cover several important historical journals such as *RSQ* and *Rhetorica*. The *Longman Bibliography* (now the *CCCC Bibliography*), which is issued yearly, bids fair to be our best source on secondary historical work, but it begins only in 1984, and everything before that date must be catch as catch can.

METHODOLOGICAL AND EPISTEMOLOGICAL ISSUES

For a part of the field that has only been active for a decade or so, composition history has already generated a considerable list of controversies and disputed issues. The disputes tend to fall into methodological and epistemological areas, although most refuse to fit neatly into one class or another.

An example of a dispute that spans categories is the issue of whether composition historians should write histories of theory or histories of practice. One strong tacit tradition in rhetorical history has been to write theoretical histories, narratives that show how one set of ideas was propounded, criticized, adopted, revised. "Influence studies" is the term often given this sort of scholarship in literature. Some of the most impressive works in rhetorical history have been written to trace and categorize these theoretical influences, most notably Wilbur Samuel Howell's two magisterial volumes on English logic and rhetoric from 1500 through 1800, which cover every rhetorical treatise written during those years but make little attempt to situate rhetoric culturally.[12] The other strong tradition has been to describe rhetorical *praxis* and education in the context of their times and cultures, paying more attention to the meaning and uses of the discipline than to the content of its theory. George Kennedy's books on classical rhetoric in Greece and Rome and Brian Vickers' recent *Defense of Rhetoric* exemplify this tradition.

The immense influence of Albert Kitzhaber moved composition history in both directions, but ultimately his work tended to head more toward theoretical than toward cultural histories of composition. Coverage and theoretical analysis of early composition textbooks were Kitzhaber's great strength; like Porter Perrin and Glenn Hess before him, Kitzhaber worked primarily from the artifacts he had gathered and mastered, which were textbooks, and, to a lesser degree, journal articles. Since textbooks remain the largest mine of evidence concerning nineteenth-century composition theory and teaching, and since they remain more easily (although randomly) available to researchers than most other data, and since Kitzhaber had made their use respectable, the early members of the "second generation" of composition historians—primarily Stewart, Berlin, Connors, and Johnson—relied on textbooks to a great extent. As a result, the early work in composition history tends, with the exception of Wallace Douglas' Marxist readings of Harvard records, to be about the theories found in early composition texts and about how those theories evolved.

Even at their most theoretical, however, composition historians have never approached the almost complete lack of interest in culture and practice seen in some theoretical histories of rhetoric. They have remained *involved*. The main reason for this practical and cultural focus in composition history has been the fact that most composition historians are also writing teachers. They are immediately implicated in their subject. Speech historian W. S. Howell could afford a certain distance toward his discovery that Adam Smith in 1749 approached rhetoric with more acumen than John Holmes did in 1755. The fact may have been interesting, but the work of neither of them affected Howell and his daily world of professional reality very much. From Kitzhaber on, however, composition historians have never had the luxury of scholarly distance. They exist, as composition specialists have for a century, in a world of complex social and institutional problems whose solution is writing teachers' charge, and thus even the theoretical and "textbook" histories of the field have always been implicitly polemical. We followed Kitzhaber not only to his sources, but also to the sometimes savage indignation about current conditions that often characterized his work.

So Kitzhaber's methodological legacy has been two-pronged; early composition history had a tendency to look at the past in terms of its theory and textbooks, and it had a distinct tendency to view the past through the sometimes narrow lens of how it seemed to affect the troubled present. We found the works of our heroes—Fred Newton Scott, Gertrude Buck, Joseph Denney, Franz Theremin, Henry Day, C. S. Baldwin, Sterling Leonard, Porter Perrin—and celebrated them. We traced the elements in composition teaching that we thought were questionable back to their lairs in the works of our pantheon of villains and dupes—Samuel Newman, Richard Whately, Alexander Bain, Adams S. Hill, Barrett Wendell, John Genung, Edwin Woolley, John Warriner, John Hodges. This early work was clearly *sided* history.

The perspective on American composition taken in most of these analyses is easy to understand in retrospect: historians writing in a troubled present constructed a narrative of its genesis based on sources at hand. Thus the metanarrative of most work before 1984 or so might have the subtitle "Decline and Fall." It was a tragic tale of bad theory driving out good, of the loss of the liberal tradition in rhetoric, of calculating, hegemonic Harvard taking over the rhetorical world, of a noble Fred Newton Scott fighting a hopeless rear-guard action against encroaching barbarisms like "grammar" and "workbooks." It ended with the ugly triumph of Bain's formalism over Emerson's and Theremin's idealism and with the onset of our current Iron Age, where until recently the lamp of rhetorical humanism guttered low.

This was a rattling good story, and in certain ways it is even an accurate one. But it was not the complete story, and work in composition history since 1985 has been struggling to add some depth to the all-too-simple tale of Decline and Fall. The essential problems with the old narrative are, first, that it ignores or discounts too much information we now have, and, second, that it does not look deeply enough into the social, cultural, and ideological contexts of rhetoric and composition as they developed in their own eras. For instance, it was a natural and necessary step to trace paragraph theory back to Alexander Bain in 1866 and then to show how his theory is not accurate or useful according to our current knowledge. The harder task confronting historians now is to draw the analysis out in deeper and stronger ways. What led Bain to this theory? How does it relate to changing ideas of English prose style? Why were teachers attracted to it? What do formal theories suggest about pedagogic attitudes?

Perhaps we see the most important sign of maturation in historical research in the crumbling of the simple heroes-and-villains narrative. While no one would deny Fred Scott his eminence, we no longer see his work as the touchstone of all that is True and Good. And after more than thirty years as everyone's *bête noire*, Harvard's A. S. Hill is being seen as the much more complex thinker and actor that he was.[13] We are looking at a broader range of sources and learning that our metanarrative has been too simple. While I would hope that composition history never completely loses touch with the dissatisfaction that fueled its earliest works with fervor and gave meaning and passion to its narratives, our work is richer now. Historians' growing

awareness of the causal complexities and sociocultural motivations that are as important as any theoretical history to the development of our field can only make sharper our awareness of current conditions and make more realistic our hopes for solving contemporary problems through understanding them.

Another set of current issues in the writing of composition history has to do with the development of research and with the presentation of data after they've been found. It's our version of the old Platonic/Aristotelian debate about deduction and induction. Some historians tend to see, to research, and to present their findings within overt and carefully created frameworks of meaning, and others eschew this approach. Of contemporary historians, James Berlin is probably the best-known "framework" researcher. In each of his books, Berlin creates a taxonomic structure and follows its implications by fitting various figures and works into it; in *Writing Instruction in Nineteenth-Century American Colleges* his taxonomy breaks nineteenth-century rhetoric into classical, psychological-epistemological, and romantic types, while in *Rhetoric and Reality* he classifies twentieth-century movements into objective, subjective, and transactional classes. Wallace Douglas' Marxist analyses, which use an existing class-structure perspective, are also examples of "framework" research.

Other historians opt for a more inductively derived historical narration, one that takes up a problem at the "beginning"—the first place their research can discover it—and follows it through to contemporary times, or that traces the work and influence of one figure. Paul Rodgers on the Bainian organic paragraph, or David Russell on writing across the curriculum, or my work on the development of handbooks are all examples of problem- or figure-based history.

Both the overt framework histories and the problem- or figure-based works are, of course, subject to the criticism that they present narratives based on *a priori* viewpoints that control and constrain the research beneath them. Berlin chooses his classes, then seeks evidence that reifies them; I start with an *a priori* definition of handbooks and only look at books that fulfill that definition. I cannot think of any work of composition history that cannot to some degree be accused of this sort of *a priori* subjectivism; historians disagree mainly on how much of it exists. In a review of *Writing Instruction in Nineteenth-Century American Colleges*, I once critiqued James Berlin for filtering his research effort through powerful terministic screens and for failing to take important alternate perspectives into consideration. Berlin's reply was that such screens are inevitable in any research project, and that since objectivity is impossible, any historical research project is automatically interpretive and thus radically subjective; all a historian can do is try to be aware of the terministic screens that exist for him or her.

This whole issue of how and when a researcher reaches closure—of where the data she is discovering begin to assemble themselves in her mind into a structure that will form a thesis claim and will then inevitably guide and constrain subsequent research—leads to the great historiographic

question of facts versus interpretations. Some of the field's major historians met in an "octolog" at the 1987 CCCC to discuss these complex issues, and in spite of some real methodological disagreements there was surprising agreement from most of the participants. Of the eight panelists discussing "The Politics of Historiography," seven were working historians, and one, Victor Vitanza, was a historiographic theorist. When the dust settled, it was clear that: (1) No one on the panel believed that any "objective" or definitive history was possible or even desirable; all believed that multiple histories are possible and desirable; (2) The seven working historians all believed, tacitly or explicitly, that "evidence" or "data" or "sources" or "historical materials" were essential stuff of their day-to-day researches. Of the eight panelists, only Vitanza valorized language and its infinitely regressive possibilities as the central component of history. ("Is there any evidence for evidence?" he asks.)

That there was so much tacit agreement in a panel specifically convened to air disagreements is less surprising when we consider that the participants were rhetoricians as well as historians. They all expressed an essential rhetorical position: that assent could be based both on inartistic proofs—evidence—and on artistic proofs—the perspective, the method of presentation, the language. The working historians all accepted the concept that evidence must be searched for and weighed, that prejudices must be taken into consideration, and that induction and deduction were both necessary parts of historical research and writing.

The entire question of historiographic theory animating this 1987 octolog has been brought to the fore in the last five years largely through the efforts of Victor Vitanza, who has used his journal *Pre/Text* to advance various radical critiques of current historical works and practices. Vitanza has attracted a brilliant group of younger scholars to the journal, and one of their primary interests has been in historiographic issues. Such scholars as Susan Jarratt, John Schilb, Jan Swearingen, and James Berlin have weighed in with historiographic articles in *Pre/Text*. Although only Schilb (and, to a lesser extent, Jarratt) might be said to hold many ideas in common with Vitanza, the general effect of Vitanza's efforts has been to valorize historiographic questions. Since 1986, the theoretical and epistemological issues surrounding the writing of history have been much discussed.

The proponents of "revisionist historiography," as it has come to be called, fall roughly into two camps: those who seek to promote a specific program or perspective, and those who point out the incompleteness, potential for totalization, or naivete of any specific program or perspective. Into the former camp might fall Sharon Crowley and Jan Swearingen, who have both been engaged in recovering heretofore marginalized figures in rhetorical history: the sophists and women. Here, too, we find James Berlin and Wallace Douglas, who take the perspective of neo-Marxists and argue for dialectical history and class-based historical analyses. The implicit program of this group is action-based; they make the claim that traditional histories are biased, or incomplete, or controlled by sexist or racist or class purposes.

The other group of revisionist historiographers are the epistemological radicals, primarily Victor Vitanza, John Schilb, and Susan Jarratt. (It is interesting to note that with the exception of Jarratt, who is the least radical and most obviously "political" of the group, the epistemological radicals have themselves primarily written critiques of historical writing rather than history itself.) The critiques coming from this end of the table mainly descend from the interpretive issues popularly argued over in literary criticism during the past fifteen years: the undecidability of meaning in texts; the aporias that riddle every text and source; the interplay of social conditioning and understanding or ordering of meaning; the hegemony of linearity and "clearness" as criteria for worth in historical writing; the utter lack of support for any concept of objectivity. In radically undercutting meaning systems, Vitanza is probably the most extreme; like his eidolons Deleuze and Guattari, his own prose style is deliberately playful and hallucinatory, and his suspicion of all proffered meaning-systems as totalizing and potentially fascistic makes him the great epistemological anarchist in the field.

Thus far the working historians have tended to react to the Vitanza position with a mixture of humor, discomfort, and distracted annoyance.[14] We cannot supply proofs for proof, in Vitanza's terms, but thus far no historian has been willing to allow the theoretical uncertainty underlying his or her making of meaning to close down the enterprise. We may argue about the relative power of facts versus interpretations, but finally the community of working historians feels constrained by and dependent on both. All we can do is continue to be aware of the necessary balance between induction and deduction in any research enterprise, trying to avoid totalizing perspectives that force us to closure too early in the research process. No historian sets out deliberately to twist the truth, but Vitanza's critique remains a salutary reminder that our natural prejudices constantly create terministic screens that control what we see—and can control what we look for as researchers.

The writing of the history of composition is still at a very early stage. Much remains to be done. We need to continue looking closely at the connections between rhetoric and writing instruction—indeed, at *all* the issues surrounding the relation of orality and literacy. We need much more work on the period 1790 to 1850, which still remains the subject of only a few articles and dissertations. We still know very little about the teaching and learning of writing outside the United States and Canada; the other English-speaking countries are only beginning to be examined. We need to articulate our knowledge, to connect college issues with the increasingly detailed historical work being done on elementary and secondary schooling. We also must put our research ever more strongly in context by making ourselves aware of the larger issues of class, gender, race, and franchise that have always been the "silent" realities behind college education. The larger issues of literacy and power, which have begun to appear in historical works of the last few years, will be inescapable for historians in the future. Though we may wax nostalgic for the simple days when the Decline and Fall narrative provided

continuity, when textbooks clumsily mated and bred without sociocultural influence, and when neat taxonomies made everything understandable, that is not how we think about things anymore.

Historians of composition in the future will need to be both peripatetic and widely read. The primary sources are out there, and finding them—especially the ephemeral pedagogical materials and the almost-as-ephemeral student papers—will be a challenge. We will need to evolve serious collections and depositories of composition materials.[15] In addition to being scholar-gypsies, composition historians of the future will need to immerse themselves in collateral reading about their subjects and periods, as good rhetorical scholars always have. We cannot understand the teaching of writing in 1870 without understanding the causes of the Civil War; we cannot understand the "American English" movement of the 1940s without understanding the McCarthy era. We are ineluctably tied to the movements of our cultures, and as rhetoricians we have to watch the signals. Only then will we write histories truly informed by all the good evidence needed to gain a hearing from an increasingly skeptical discourse community.

Composition history, like rhetorical history, is only one channel of the knowledge we in composition studies must seek. Yet without it, we are cut off from information of vast usefulness. We are not here alone; others have come before us, and from their situations, struggles, victories, and defeats we can build the context that will give our work as teachers and theorists background, substance, and originality. Only by understanding where we came from can we ascertain where we want to go.

NOTES

1. For more information on how this lack of scholarly credentials led to the decline of rhetoric, see my essay "The Creation of an Underclass," forthcoming in *The Politics of Writing Instruction*.

2. The classic essay on this question is William Riley Parker's "Where Do English Departments Come From?" *College English* 28 (1967): 339–51.

3. *Rhetoric in American Colleges*, with a new introduction by John Gage, has recently been reprinted (Dallas: Southern Methodist UP, 1991).

4. Glenn Hess' dissertation *An Analysis of Early American Rhetoric and Composition Textbooks from 1784 to 1870* (U of Pittsburgh, 1949), Janet Emig's Qualifying Paper *The Relation of Thought and Language Implicit in Some Early American Rhetoric and Composition Texts* (Harvard, 1963), Gene Piche's *Revision and Reform in the Secondary School English Curriculum 1870–1900* (U of Minnesota, 1967) and Stephen Judy's *The Teaching of English Composition in American Secondary Schools 1850–1893* (Northwestern, 1967) are some of the important examples of work from Education.

5. Warren Guthrie's dissertation *The Development of Rhetorical Theory in America 1635–1850* (Northwestern, 1940) is the only example I know of a historical dissertation from Speech that was not overwhelmingly concerned with oral-discourse issues.

6. This essay is found in Richard Ohmann's *English in America* (New York: Oxford UP, 1976), 97–132.

7. Donald Stewart, "The Nineteenth Century," in *The Present State of Scholarship in Historical and Contemporary Rhetoric* (Columbia: U of Missouri P, 1983), p. 158. From the

perspective of 1990, when this was being written, Stewart's assessment looks optimistic.

8. Miller made her charges in her essay "Is There a Text in This Class?" in *Freshman English News* 11 (1982): 22–33.

9. For more information, see my essay "Textbooks and the Evolution of the Discipline," *College Composition and Communication* 37 (May 1986): 178–94.

10. I have before me two books that illustrate this kind of information. In an 1893 copy of Genung's *Rhetorical Analysis*, Nettie Lawson of Bradford Academy has painstakingly written out on the flyleaf four paragraph rules, which she no doubt was asked to consult again and again. Every chapter in the book has pencilled notes from the teacher's lectures. On the other hand, in a 1901 copy of Lockwood and Emerson's *Composition and Rhetoric for Higher Schools*, "Marion, Lily, and Laurena, Members of the Spectator Club" have written "Sing me a song of the south, a song of the sunny south," "On A Beautiful Night With A Beautiful Girl," and the complete lyrics to "When I Get You Alone Tonight." In their own ways, these inscriptions tell the story of an English class, too.

11. There are as yet few examples of these sorts of retrospective interviews. Dixie Goswami and Maureen Butler interviewed Janet Emig in 1983, and parts of those interviews are used in Emig's collection *The Web of Meaning*. Lisa Ede and Andrea Lunsford interviewed Edward P. J. Corbett in 1987, and portions of that interview are used in the *Selected Essays of Edward P. J. Corbett*. R. Gerald Nelms of Ohio State is currently completing a dissertation based on oral histories, but thus far few scholars have ventured out into the field with tape recorder in hand. It must be done, and soon.

12. Wilbur Samuel Howell, *Logic and Rhetoric in England, 1500–1700* (Princeton: Princeton UP, 1956) and *Eighteenth-Century British Logic and Rhetoric* (Princeton: Princeton UP, 1971).

13. See, for instance, David Jolliffe's essay "The Moral Subject in College Composition: A Conceptual Framework and the Case of Harvard, 1865–1900," in *College English* 51 (1989): 163–73. Thomas Newkirk is also doing fascinating research in the Harvard Archives that is showing Harvard's early pedagogy to be strikingly similar to modern "process" and "whole language" pedagogies. Newkirk began to report on this material at CCCC in 1990 with his talk "Barrett Wendell and the Birth of Freshman Composition."

14. The reaction of working historians to the Vitanza position, in fact, is reminiscent of the reactions of Anglo-American literary critics to the early sallies of deconstruction, circa 1975–1982, a mixture of "Very interesting . . ." with "Oh, come *on!*" This position of "glum common sense," as it has been called, will probably have to be maintained until professional necessity rises and twitches its mantle blue, declaring the Vitanza position to be, as it has declared deconstruction to be, not wrong but merely passé.

15. As of this writing, only one such public collection exists: the Richard S. Beal Collection at the University of New Hampshire.

SUGGESTED READINGS

Berlin, James. *Rhetoric and Reality: Writing Instruction in American Colleges, 1900–1985.* Carbondale: Southern Illinois UP, 1987.

———. *Writing Instruction in Nineteenth-Century American Colleges.* Carbondale: Southern Illinois UP, 1984.

Brereton, John, ed. *Traditions of Inquiry.* New York: Oxford UP, 1985.

"Historiography and the Histories of Rhetorics: Revisionary Histories." *Pre/Text* 8 (Spring/Summer 1987).

Horner, Winifred, ed. *Historical Rhetoric: An Annotated Bibliography of Selected Sources in English*. Boston: G. K. Hall, 1980.

————. *The Present State of Scholarship in Historical and Contemporary Rhetoric*. Rev. ed. Columbia: U of Missouri P, 1990.

Kitzhaber, Albert R. *Rhetoric in American Colleges 1850–1900*. Dallas: Southern Methodist UP, 1990.

Murphy, James J., ed. *The Rhetorical Tradition and Modern Writing*. New York: MLA, 1982.

————. *A Short History of Writing Instruction from Ancient Greece to Twentieth-Century America*. Davis, CA: Hermagoras, 1990.

"Octalog: The Politics of Historiography." *Rhetoric Review* 7 (Fall 1988): 5 – 57.

Dreams and Play: Historical Method and Methodology

In "Dreams and Play: Historical Method and Methodology," Bob continues a disciplinary conversation that was well under way by the time this essay appeared in 1992 in *Methods and Methodology in Composition Research*, edited by Gesa Kirsch and Patricia A. Sullivan. Addressing five major questions—What constitutes data in historical studies? How are data used in producing knowledge, generating theories, and building models? What kinds of questions can and can't be answered by historical research? What problems emerge in the process of inquiry? and What issues are raised by historical methodologies?—Bob provides general answers, illustrating them with stories from his own experience as a historical researcher. Bob defines historical data as comprising "present awareness, archival retrieval, and realization of prejudice" (222). In discussing the prejudices of historians, Bob acknowledges that "[a]ll of historical work [. . .] is provisional, partial—fragments we shore against our ruin. [. . .] It is always a construction. It is always tottering" (226). But this seeming nod to a social constructionist view of history is in tension with many other statements in this essay. In fact, he concludes this meditation on a historian's intriguing search through the Archive ("where storage meets dreams, and the result is history" [223]) by talking about the great importance of recovering the history of composition that "had been lost for 150 years" (234). Though that history may sometimes be murky, Bob sees it as real and recoverable. To that end, he devoted a great deal of his scholarly career.

Historical research, until a decade ago only a minor part of the ongoing activity in composition studies, has recently been evolving into one of the recognized strands in our burgeoning field. Unlike certain other research strands, however, historical research uses methods more closely related to traditional humanities inquiry than to scientific or social-scientific paradigms. What, exactly, does writing composition history presuppose and entail?

From *Methods and Methodology in Composition Research*, ed. Gesa Kirsch and Patricia A. Sullivan (Carbondale: Southern Illinois UP, 1992), 15–36.

WHAT CONSTITUTES DATA IN HISTORICAL STUDIES?

It has been common until recently to think of data in historical research as composed of historical "facts." These facts would be uncovered by assiduous gleaning of sources, pieced together like a jigsaw puzzle (which has, of course, only one possible correct solution), and presented to readers as "the historical truth." Historians and careful students of history, however, have always known that such an idealized view of their work with data was false. In reality, data in historical studies are made up of at least these three elements: the historian's perceptions of the present, her assemblage of claims based on study of materials from the past, and an ongoing internal dialogue about cultural preconceptions and prejudices and the historian's own. These three elements—present awareness, archival retrieval, and realization of prejudice—are the pieces of information that the historian brings to the attempted solution of the historical problem facing her. Let's look at these elements in more detail.

It may sound strange to say that among the most important data for the historical researcher in composition studies are perceptions of the present day, but every narrator knows it. Until we have some knowledge of the situation a posteriori, our ability to understand the prior situation is hopelessly lacking. Partially, of course, knowledge about the present is central data for the historian because causes can be clearly understood only in the light of their effects; each generation of economic historians since the New Deal has understood and analyzed Roosevelt's policies differently as more and more cause-effect data have come in. But I am also calling perceptions of the present central data because they stimulate questioning, excitement, and curiosity, without which history of any sort is a dead compiling of facts without affect. Without intellectual curiosity, without the wish to discover and explain something about life, history *is* a dust bin.

Knowledge of the present is important data for any historian, but it is particularly fundamental to the history of composition studies, because that history is relatively short. Historians of classical rhetoric, for instance, use their knowledge of the present day primarily in a general way; they examine claims and written sources from ancient Greece with their own perceptions of rhetorical action and their own knowledge of human and institutional behavior in mind. The knowledge of the present they bring to the task is of general human nature and of the slow evolution of large institutions. This is how historians of the remote past must operate, since the "causes" seen at a remove of two millennia must have relatively broad and general effects today. But the historian of composition studies, an essentially modern discipline, sees all around her the direct and specific effects of the activities whose genesis she studies. There, in that classroom next door, is the new edition of the *Heath Handbook*; not even D. C. Heath knows it's really the fourteenth, not the twelfth edition—but the historian knows it was the first handbook, born in 1907. Here, in this curriculum meeting, someone is arguing for the "old four modes from classical rhetoric," and the historian knows that the modes were

made up by Alexander Bain in 1866. A news magazine rends the welkin with warnings about "the new illiteracy," and the historian knows this is the fourth great American literacy crisis. All around us are the data of the present, and they constantly press on us the immediate question, "What shall we do?" The historian tries to help answer this by looking into less immediate but essential questions, "What have people done in the past?" and "How did things come to be this way?"

From these observational data we begin. All around the composition historian are phenomena that need to be explained. Why is freshman English the only course required for every student? Where does the paragraph come from? Why do students at many colleges fold their papers in half lengthwise before passing them in, without being instructed to do so? Why are there instructors? Why do many literature specialists despise composition? When did the grading system begin? Is student writing worse now than it was in 1900? In my own case, the vital question often used to be, "How did things get this bad?" History nearly always begins as simple curiosity about how we got here.

The next kind of data must be uncovered by painstaking research. We take our questions and our perceptional data, as all historians must, into the Archive, the storehouse of data about the past. The Archive must be explored, analyzed, cross-checked, deconstructed, reconstructed, made meaning of, be stripped, checked, and polished. Here, for the composition historian, is the world of the written word, the printed word, the picture, the table, the diagram, the voice on the tape. The Archive is where storage meets dreams, and the result is history.

The overwhelming bulk of data from the past that the historian of composition studies must deal with is in written and printed form, and what I am calling the Archive actually consists of two discrete kinds of sources, library and archival. Libraries are repositories for printed and published materials generally, while institutional archives deal in more specific primary sources, many of which exist nowhere else and were never meant to be published. A great deal of the material for composition history is available in good research libraries, since most records having to do with teaching writing in general—as opposed to composition teaching at a specific school—were printed and distributed in either books or journals and magazines. From the 1820s on, rhetoric and writing instruction were important issues in American education, and there is a great deal of information to be sifted through in library sources.

When doing library research, the historian must initially determine whether secondary sources exist, how complete they are, and whether they must be consulted. Only a decade ago, this was much less of an issue, but recently the list of creditable secondary sources in composition history has grown markedly. We now have five or six good short books on composition history, and fifty or sixty respectable journal articles. About even the best of these works, most historians have mixed feelings. On the one hand, it is important to know who has been doing work in the area and what they have

found out. No one wants to reinvent the cotton gin. Sharing sources and methods is not just collegial; it is good sense. On the other hand, as the field has grown, so too has a healthy tendency grown to disregard secondary sources, to go directly to the primary sources. Some historians refuse to read secondary sources, especially the better-known works by such authors as Kitzhaber and Berlin, because they want to approach the primary works without preconceptions they could have avoided. Too much reliance on secondary sources may result in historians' efforts being relegated to "normal science," cleaning up small-scale problems within the larger paradigm of the existing source's conception. Perhaps the best answer is to read many secondary sources voraciously, seeking for methods, style, coherence, looking for models to pattern your own history on—in any specific area but your own. Then, go to the primary sources. See what *they* say to you.

And what are those primary sources? Composition textbooks since the beginning of composition history have been obvious sources, able to tell us much about both the theory and the practice of writing pedagogy. From John Walker's *Teacher's Assistant in English Composition* of 1795 onward, they were used as the theoretical matrices of courses. Soon after 1810, questions to be asked in classes became part of textbook apparatus, thus providing classroom organization. Beginning in the 1830s, rhetorics also came to include written exercises, devices which organized homework activities for students. These "do-everything" books could be used by less-experienced teachers as the pedagogical organizing tools for entire courses, and with them the "modern" form of the rhetoric text was set. We can learn about theory, questions, exercises, advice, and assignments from these books. Historians argue about the degree to which we should assume that textbook organization really informed classroom practice, but no one claims that older textbooks do not constitute important data.

Specialized journals and even general magazines also represent important primary sources. From the 1840s onward, education journals like *Barnard's* dealt with pedagogical and even more specialized language and rhetoric issues. With the *Educational Review, PMLA, School Review*, and *Journal of Education* in the late nineteenth century, a recognizably modern literature on educational issues was created, and the researcher can find in them many articles on composition teaching. Finally, in 1912 comes *English Journal*, the first English-pedagogy journal, and throughout the rest of the century this journal and its eventual spinoffs, *College English* and *College Composition and Communication*, constitute the central fora for professional discussion. In addition, there have been periods—especially the late nineteenth and early twentieth centuries—when composition issues have been seen as so important that general-interest magazines such as *Harper's* and *Atlantic Monthly* would discuss them, and so traditional bibliographic tools like the *Poole's Index* of nineteenth-century magazines can be called into play.

The final primary source likely to be found in libraries is the "professional book" written for teachers or practitioners. Professional books about the teaching of writing go back to the 1890s, when the first media-driven

literacy crisis had produced the freshman composition course as one of its answers. That course created its own methodological problems for curriculum planners, and specialized books for teachers have existed since then. There are descriptions of programs, tips for teachers, various forms of braggadocio and apologia among these books. Biographies and memoirs of various figures can be helpful, although few full-scale biographies of central figures in composition history have yet been done, and memoirs are about as rare.

With textbooks, journal and magazine articles, and professional books, the primary sources available at general scholarly libraries have probably been covered. Archives are specialized kinds of libraries that usually contain materials specific to one institution or activity. The archival record contains those rarest and most valuable of data, actual student writings, teacher records, unprinted notes and pedagogical materials, and ephemera that writing courses have always generated but rarely kept. Unlike printed sources, by nature meant for distribution and multiple copies, these notes, papers, and ephemera existed in only a single copy (or sometimes carbon-copy form). As a result, such important data are much more difficult for historians to get hold of than are printed sources. Unlike books and journals, which are cataloged by circulation in libraries and can thus be accessed through bibliographic search and interlibrary loan, archival papers and notes tend to be cataloged separately. Usually researchers have no way to know what college archives contain without hands-on examination, and that can be expensive and difficult for many scholars. There is to this point no central clearinghouse or depository for this sort of archival material; Harvard University's collection is the largest and most detailed, but it refers only to one school's work. The Richard S. Beal Collection at the University of New Hampshire was begun in 1989 as a central depository for composition archives, and over the next decade it should develop into a diverse collection in composition studies.

These are, then, what I call the Archive, those written and printed materials that most people think of as the only real historical sources. But finally, along with the historian's current perceptions and the inert archival material that can be worked with or discarded, there is one more source of data that the conscientious historian must keep in mind: his or her own prejudices. No person exists without prejudice. Our entire life experience functions to predispose us favorably toward some ideas or practices and less favorably toward others. Constitutional affinities and ideological positions form what Kenneth Burke calls *terministic screens* through which we view both current reality and archival materials. The question we face is how we work with our prejudices. No historian is free from prejudiced ideas, but no historian wishes to try for anything less than fair presentation of her findings. So the only way of dealing with our always already being prejudiced is to study the prejudices *as data*. Why do we admire Fred N. Scott and despise Adams S. Hill? Why do we dismiss the terms *clearness, force,* and *elegance* while we accept *unity, coherence,* and *emphasis*? Why do we find a sneer in our voices when we say the word "workbook"? We may not always be able to see all of our own terministic screens, certainly, but then again we cannot claim to

know all of current reality or to have found all the possible archival sources. We work with what we can find of all three kinds of data.

All of historical work, then, is provisional, partial—fragments we shore against our ruin. We are trying to make sense of things. It is always a construction. It is always tottering.

How Are Data Used in Producing Knowledge, Generating Theories, and Building Models?

We always start with a hypothesis or a question. In some historical research, this question may be abstract, or prompted by other historians' assertions, or based on newly discovered archival material. In composition history, however, it is much more common for the motivating question to arise out of simple curiosity about one or both of two general situations: (1) Why are things around me as they are? or (2) Why do I see and judge things around me as I do?

Why, for instance, does every teacher know the four "modes of discourse" when they are so little treated in modern textbooks? That was the vague curiosity that began the research that ended in my essay "The Rise and Fall of the Modes of Discourse." In another case, the question arose in my mind, "Why do many teachers mark only the mechanical errors in papers?" That was a reasonable perception-data question. If that had been the only question I had considered, the result might have been a straight historical narrative that took no strong position on the phenomenon of journal marking. I had to admit, however, that I found superadded a more complex and interesting corollary question based on my own prejudices: "Why do I condemn formal-criterion grading when I consider it?" With this question, you see, we plunge into the complex world of the historian's own training, context, personality, ideology, and experience. And only from there do we go to the Archive for confirmation or denial.

So how do data first interact in historical research? Most historical writers, if they are honest, will admit that perceptions and prejudices always must come first in shaping a research question. Seldom does anyone plunge cold into the Archive without something to look for, something they're hoping to find, hoping to see proof of. To try to approach the Archive without even a general hypothesis would go against the human instinct to make sense of things. We gravitate toward organizing ideas. Old composition materials are seldom fascinating or enjoyable to read as art-prose, and we enter that jungle because we think something is there for us to track.

So theory generation is never really *ab ovo*. We start from theory, at least from a theory about building challenging, supportable hypotheses, and historians seldom work through serious archival research unless they have a hypothesis that they tacitly think is supportable. My hypothesis about formal-criteria marking went, at the beginning, something like this: "Paper-marking for mechanical correctives began sometime in the middle of the nineteenth century, probably as a result of handbook use, and it's a bad, a-rhetorical way to mark papers, used then, as now, by lazy, untrained teachers." Now I'm not claiming

this is a good hypothesis. It's shot through, as early historical hypotheses often are, with vague assumptions, unsupported assertions, huge gaps in knowledge. It is, in fact, largely false. But it was a place to start. From that questionable but real starting place, built on perception and prejudice, I could go to the Archive with the initial distinctions I needed to begin work there.

What do historians do in the Archive, when they confront that inert, dusty mass of past records? Though it would be neat to be able to say that they sift through everything with hypothesis in hand, "keeping up a running fire of exclamations, groans, whistles, and little cries," drawing scientific deductions Holmes-like, t'aint true. What historians really do in the Archive—and really need to do—is play. Search is play.

How can I describe the work of historians in the Archive? It is not, cannot be, a forced march from hypothesis to support to further support to thesis, since more than half of all sources examined with hypothesis in mind turn out to have little or nothing to do with the question at hand. I might leaf through three or four volumes of early *English Journal*, as I did for a recent essay on the status and salaries of composition teachers, without seeing a single article on the topic. But neither is my examination of archival data ever a random stroll, turning pages without purpose. Historians seldom conduct basic research of that sort. Archival reading is, instead, a kind of directed ramble, something like an August mushroom hunt. There are various concurrent intentions in it: I am looking for information on my specific question; I am looking to increase my own general knowledge of various periods and persons; I am seeking to be better acquainted with the sources themselves; I am looking for fascinating anomalies; I am hoping for unexpected treasures; and of course I am seeking those conjunctions of historical evidence with sudden perception or understanding that occasionally light up the skies for the lucky historian and reveal a whole world whose genesis and current realities have been subtly reshaped—the "Ah!" of realization that is always the historian's true payoff.

To shift down a step, what we do is browse with directed intention. There is a track, constraint exercised by the developing hypothesis, but we may and must dart off the track to follow a likely scent, a fascinating claim, a mysterious author, a curious fact. I wander about the library with a stack of five-by-eight notecards and a legal pad—the cards for bibliography and citations, and the legal pad for the slowly accumulating "brainstorming" insights that accrue from gradual mental conjunction of the materials examined. The path is always circuitous. Following up one lead may take all afternoon, forcing me to chase through an early *College English* volume, then to the *National Union Catalog*, then to the library circulation computer and the Online Catalog for the Library of Congress computers, then over to my own office to check my database program, then back to the stacks, and finally— oh, frustration!—to the interlibrary loan office, which means a two-week wait before the chase can be taken up again.

As Nan Johnson once put it at a historians' "octolog," or symposium, we often seem unwilling to admit that our research can be exciting, can satisfy

curiosity, can be . . . fun. But it can. Historical research at its best is detective work, with all the intellectual rewards of problem and puzzle solving. Of course, for every moment when "the game is afoot," there will always be hours of careful slogging through quotidian facts, deadly educational statistics, dreadfully written accounts of how writing is taught. But we must come out and say it—much archival research is fascinating, and much of the challenge of history is the challenge of puzzle solving.

What, specifically, do historians do as they read, browse, sift, write notes and cards? There are three primary parts to traditional historical analysis: external criticism, internal criticism, and synthesis of materials. These are not "stages" that must take place only in linear order; they are recursive steps that can take place in various orders. Let me, however, go through them one at a time.

External criticism has primarily to do with the choice of sources the historian will read. Given a hypothesis, she must first establish what sources are available that might support (or disprove) it, and then determine whether those available sources are indeed appropriate to the task or able to handle it effectively. It is here, at this primary stage, that researchers really need to know their Archives. What books, journals, paper, ephemera do they have access to? Which are the most likely to serve the needs of the project? For my recent essay, "The Creation of an Underclass," dealing with the status and labor of writing teachers, I was forced to a whole new level of external criticism, one not demanded by earlier projects. For previous work on textbooks, for instance, I had become familiar and comfortable with the University of New Hampshire Library holdings in old textbooks. But a complex sociocultural inquiry about the conditions surrounding composition teaching required very different sources. I had to acquaint myself with economic studies of college teaching, with educational reports and statistics, with histories of individual colleges and universities, with the few reports English professors ever wrote concerning their own status. I had to go to new journals; I had to explore new sections of the library stacks; I had to examine novel secondary sources; and I had to make extensive use of interlibrary loan. Poring over all this new material was quite a departure from the simpler history-of-ideas research that informed much of my early work, and possible sources seemed to ramify in countless directions. But I had to get as many sources as possible into my hands, and after a search of some months, I was confident that I had at least the rudiments of the map, if not a complete vision of the territory.

At the same time that she searches for and judges sources, the historian must also engage in the next stage of analysis—internal criticism. Internal criticism examines the sources found with the intent of making sure they are judged correctly. Historians check the language and usage of their sources, examine them for obvious or subtle biases, try to eliminate glosses or corruptions. Most importantly, internal criticism implies a search for corroborative support of claims made by sources. If thoughtful, defensible history has a methodological nexus, it must be in this search for corroboration. All records we have are written by human, all-too-human, agents. They are necessarily

filled with self-justification, optimistic delusion, pessimistic distortion, partisan argument. Not a one can stand as the complete and trusty truth—not even the statistics. And so a process of comparison and corroboration is central work for the historian.

This internal criticism is especially important when studying the history of composition, because for the last century and a half, teaching writing has been an arena echoing with claims and counterclaims—a genuine rhetorical situation. As I have argued elsewhere, freshman composition is the only college-level course that was instituted to solve a perceived social problem rather than to investigate a branch of knowledge, so claims about its methods, necessity, and usefulness have always been as argumentative as they were expository. Composition historians must dig through this mass of claims and rejoinders. If we cannot always make judgments about whose arguments were right, we can at least try to determine certain factual realities. Barrett Wendell, for example, claims to have invented the "daily theme" at Harvard in the 1880s. Did he? This was the question that my colleague Tom Newkirk faced recently. Was this a claim that Tom, as a historian, wished to endorse? Through a process of internal criticism, he had to test this claim. What did Wendell's students say? What do the Harvard records and memoirs say? What did Wendell's colleagues think? What, if Tom could find evidence in the Harvard archives, do Wendell's teaching notes or student essays show? Only after a thorough cross-check of all these sources could the historian really support the claim.

As you can see, it is never possible to separate internal criticism from external criticism completely, because one often sends a historian out into a round of the other. To understand and accept any claim internal to a document, it must be compared to claims in other documents. When I was searching for information on instructors' salaries in 1920, I could not be certain about the figures I found until I had a second source that gave me approximately the same figures—a second source I had to get from interlibrary loan. Barbara Tuchman, in *Practicing History*, says that she never accepts a single primary source as effective evidence, but always contrasts at least two different accounts. This is not always possible in composition history, but enough different kinds of evidence exist to give a careful historian a sense of whether the archival fact will support a developing hypothesis.

The depth of corroboration needed for a historical claim has a direct relationship to the novelty and current acceptance of that claim. (This is why we cannot completely dispense with reading secondary sources.) What is the researcher's discourse community likely to know already, likely to accept as given? If I claim, for instance, that composition teaching burgeoned after the Civil War because of the growth of universities and the needs of a capitalist economy, I will hardly have to do more than cite one or two secondary sources. No one disagrees with those claims, and they need little corroboration today. But if I claim, as I have been doing lately, that composition burgeoned in America because of the demand of women to be taught rhetoric, the corresponding responses of men, and the general educational changes

forced on colleges by coeducation after 1840, I will need to provide considerable evidence and extensive corroboration for that claim. It is a novel claim,
and one that must be strenuously supported if it is to be accepted. My internal criticism of sources, given the intensely polemical nature of most of the
nineteenth-century debates on coeducation and rhetorical training for
women, will need to be deep. That is why I am currently four years into this
project and have thus far published little about it.

When external and internal criticism have been brought forcibly to an
end—and it is nearly always necessary to bring the research period to an end
forcibly, since by its nature research is never "done," and investigation always seems more comfortable than conclusions—the final stage of analysis
is synthesis of materials. This step corresponds in some ways to *dispositio* in
classical rhetoric. The historian structures the scattered and disparate sources
she has located and compared, bringing into play ideas of cause and effect,
inductive generalizations, patterns of influence, taxonomic groupings, and
all of the other various systems of connection by which we make sense of the
world. Of course, since the research has itself been guided by a hypothesis,
the synthesis of materials has in a sense been going on since the inception of
the project. But even as the index cards mount up, even as the legal pad fills
with hastily scrawled connections and insights, the shape of the final thesis-
and-support often cannot be seen until the organizing and actual composing
begin.

The way this usually happens for me is that the archival sources build up
and interinanimate until they produce a subhypothesis that then generates
further search. In the case of my "Creation of an Underclass" piece, which
had as its general hypothesis the low pay and status of composition teachers,
this subhypothesis developed as I struggled to understand why rhetoric
came to be so despised at nineteenth-century American universities when it
had been so respected at American colleges. What differentiated universities
from colleges? Lawrence Veysey's *Emergence of the American University* told
me that the answer was specialized schools. What were the most obvious
kind? Graduate schools. What did graduate schools produce? Ph.D.'s. So that
was one line of evidence.

Then I turned to biographies of English professors and teachers active
from 1880–1900—Adams Hill, Fred Newton Scott, Barrett Wendell, John
Genung, Henry Frink. What I found there—what I had always vaguely known
but had never really brought together in my mind—was that there *were* no
Ph.D.'s in rhetoric. Where Ph.D.'s existed, they were in philology or literature.
Except at Michigan between 1896 and 1927, no American university had ever
granted rhetoric Ph.D.'s until speech departments took rhetoric over and separated it from written discourse. Why had this been the case? For the answer to
that I had to go to the history of international graduate study, especially to the
country after whose higher learning nineteenth-century Americans patterned
their own: Germany. And there I found my answer, in sources on the German
university system that I had never seen before: there was no German intellectual tradition of rhetoric after 1810, and no German rhetoric Ph.D.'s. So by

synthesizing my study of American universities and colleges, the development of English departments and their associated literary and compositional luminaries, and the German intellectual condemnation of rhetoric, I was able to come up with a working subhypothesis: that composition teachers were marginalized because they had no Ph.D. licensure and no way to advance in the university hierarchy that licensure had created.

This subhypothesis existed through much of my research, of course, and when time came actually to draft the essay, the synthesis of materials was done on a much smaller scale. The questions involved in *writing* history are stylistic, presentational, small-scale. What order should the stack of note cards take? Which of these juicy quotes must be discarded as redundant? Of the two major modes of presentation available, thematic and chronological, which should be chosen where? How much general explanation does the background of the intended audience require? These are synthetic questions that have more to do with presentation than with research, yet that does not make them unimportant; many times a perceived need for better support during composing has sent me back (grudgingly, and sometimes frantically) to external and internal criticism.

So that is how developing data build theories in historical research. Occasionally a beautiful hypothesis is supported for a while only to be killed by a cruel counterfact, but more often hypotheses start as vague suppositions that are sharpened and directed by accumulating archival evidence.

WHAT KINDS OF QUESTIONS CAN AND CAN'T BE ANSWERED BY HISTORICAL RESEARCH?

Obviously historical research can give fairly solid answers to discrete factual questions about the past. I can tell you what the first composition workbook was, and who invented the methods of exposition. David Russell can run down for you the first programs to use writing across the curriculum. Donald Stewart can name all of Fred Newton Scott's publications. And if we don't have the facts at our fingertips, we know where to get them, or at least whether they are likely to be had.

But these discrete historical facts hang in a vacuum, useless, without the interpretations that order them in all historical writing. And so the two questions that are continually argued about in historical writing are these: (1) Does this interpretation of the historical data seem coherent, reliable, interesting, useful? and (2) What can this interpretation of the past show us about the present and the future?

For the first question, there are criteria that can be applied to allow us at least provisional answers. We can make informed judgments about any historian's basic knowledge, depth of research, imaginative facility, ideological predispositions, and writing ability, to determine who writes history we will call "good." How original is the thesis? How broad is the explanatory power? How many primary sources were consulted? Were any important sources missed or scanted? Are there careless generalizations? Are the

assertions backed up with enough proof? Is there any attempt at explaining alternative interpretations, or is it a presentation of only one single strong side? Is the narrative written in a way that draws the reader along? Are the issues explored important or involving to the readership? These and other questions can clarify for us the "quality" of the history being presented.

For the second question, however, the one that historians are always being asked, the answer is much less clear. *Can* we learn about the present or the future from the past? On some levels, obviously, we can be advised by the lessons of the past. But can we learn enough, in enough systematic ways, to make any historian's view of the past an accurate guide to the present and future? The answer to this question must be, sadly, no.

Historical research cannot tell us what we should and should not do in any given set of circumstances. It cannot even give us the plausible "certainties" provided by statistical analysis. History is always written from probabilistic, and therefore rhetorical, points of view. All it can do is tell us stories, stories that may move us to actions but that in themselves cannot guide our actions according to any system. If history were, or could be, systematic, things might be different. But history is not, and never has been, systematic or scientific. Any attempt to make history predictive would have to assume that there are dependable recurring circumstances, which is simply not the case. In fact, history is narrative, and every attempt to create a system to give that narrative a predictive meaning is fraught with peril.

This is not to say that we cannot learn *anything* from history. If history does not allow us to predict or anticipate what is coming on the basis of what has been, it certainly does paint pictures of the past for us from which we can draw lessons. For example, the great literacy crisis of 1885 was followed by fifteen years of frantic attempts to solve it, and these attempts were then followed by thirty years of dogmatic torpor. I would appear foolish if I were to say that the great literacy crisis of 1976 would have to be followed by exactly the same scenario. History has too many cunning passages for that to be simply the case.

But what can I say, with any confidence, on the basis of knowing about the literacy crisis of 1885? Surely I can compare the social and cultural conditions of the time. Surely the economic reasons for and the pedagogic results of the 1885 crisis might tell me something about our own era. Surely the student papers of the time could give me insight into today's basic writing students and their papers. The point is that although what we face as teachers and scholars every day is always new, it is never completely new. Others have been here before, facing similar problems and choices. The story of their hopes, ideas, struggles, disappointments, and triumphs can tell us about our own stories. We may not learn how ours will end from how theirs ended, but we can gain valuable insight into people and their conditions, their motives, and their responses to problems.

So we cannot learn what to do from history. All we can learn is what others have done, perhaps a little about what not to do, and, perhaps, a little about who we are.

WHAT PROBLEMS EMERGE IN THE PROCESS OF INQUIRY, AND WHAT ISSUES ARE RAISED BY HISTORICAL METHODOLOGY?

The most obvious problem we face as historical researchers and writers is how to make our narratives reliable and persuasive. Practically, this issue comes down to the way in which induction balances deduction during the research process itself. How much do our preexisting ideas about what we will look for in the Archive create the data paths we then actually follow, rendering our narratives self-creating? The Chicago formalist critics used to castigate New Criticism as "a priori" criticism because New Critics would often choose some literary element a priori—an element like irony or ambiguity—and simply chase it down through a text or texts, ignoring other important formal elements at work there. Historians can always be pronounced guilty of this same offense, of course, because we hardly ever step into the archival forest without an existing hypothesis. We are always looking for something. The sticky point remains how the hypothesis we are using may constrain our search and make us less sensitive to other important elements in the historical equation. If an a priori hypothesis is too strong, too neat, it may take over the entire work of seeking archival data. The historian may end up searching through the stacks with blinders on, seeking only confirmation of the hypothesis. Similarly, if a historian depends too much on secondary sources and received wisdom, her hypotheses are apt to be constrained by those sources, and her research is apt to present no threat to standard ideas. That way lies orthodoxy, and bad history.

Again, the case of Barrett Wendell can illustrate this danger. The grandfather of composition history, Albert R. Kitzhaber, pronounced the verdict in his seminal 1953 dissertation, *Rhetoric in American Colleges, 1850–1900*: Barrett Wendell was an interesting eccentric but a dogmatic, retrograde rhetorician whose Harvard department put composition teaching on the road to ruin in the 1890s. Since Kitzhaber's 1953 pronunciamento, nearly all other historians have taken his damnation of Wendell and Harvard as accurate. Donald Stewart and James Berlin in particular, in works they wrote extolling Fred N. Scott and contrasting Scott's University of Michigan department with Harvard, continued Kitzhaber's dismissal of Wendell. The hypotheses historians evolved about Wendell grew out of the Kitzhaber legacy of received wisdom, and the research line followed the hypotheses, which—surprise!—were supported by the research.

Not until 1987, when newer historians such as David Jolliffe and Thomas Newkirk began to investigate the Harvard archives, were a new Barrett Wendell and a new *fin de siècle* Harvard writing program revealed. When historians looked carefully at the heretofore despised Harvard program, they found that under Wendell the Harvard writing courses had been taught almost like contemporary "process writing" courses, with student topic choice, revision, and individual conferences. The myth of the error-obsessed, mechanistic Harvard course that became the freshman composition prototype was exploded.

What's the lesson here? Not, certainly, that all received wisdom is wrong, but that all received wisdom is partial, incomplete. It must be examined again and again, not merely accepted. That, finally, is why there are, and why we need, multiple histories. There can never be any history so magisterial that it precludes the need for other histories. The scholar who claims, as does a classicist I know, that his intention is to write *the* book on Protagoras—one that would render any other book on Protagoras forever unnecessary—is living in an epistemological time warp. We should, of course, always strive to write the most reliable, valid, thorough, coherent, and fair-minded narratives we can, but no one narrative can ever, or should ever, shut down the narrative enterprise. There are too many interesting perspectives for that to be desirable.

This necessity for multiple histories can, of course, be taken on a theoretical level all the way to a claim about the validity of any history—to epistemological atheism, as it were. Victor Vitanza, that loving gadfly of rhetorical historians, is fond of asking "What's the proof for proof? What's the evidence for evidence?" Against so thoroughgoing a critique of any belief system as Victor mounts, historians can only continue to proffer their hard-won narratives and say to readers with A. E. Housman's Terence, "I will friend you, if I may." Simply, we hope to do some good. If we cannot really controvert the deconstruction of all epistemic certainties, we can at least keep the voices going, keep talking to one another, keep telling the stories that finally are all that can ever body us forth one to another.

Because that is what history is: the telling of stories about the tribe that make the tribe real. That is why the recovery of composition history after it had been lost for 150 years is so important. Finally, we are telling the stories of our fathers and our mothers, and we are legitimating ourselves through legitimating them. Yes, the story is sometimes discouraging; yes, many false paths and useless methods were tried; yes, there were long periods of dogma and desuetude. But we in composition studies have a history. It's murky in places so far, and much of it has not been well explored. But it exists. We are part of a discipline that is twenty-five hundred years old, and our continuity from Aristotle and the earliest rhetoricians cannot now be doubted by anyone. Our history is its own justification, and if our methods can grow more solid and sophisticated our motives should not. The methods are not new, nor can they be; the effort there is to wield them with more control, more self-awareness. But our motives for writing our history are what such motives have always been: we write histories to define ourselves on the stage of time.

WORKS CITED

Bain, Alexander. *English Composition and Rhetoric: A Manual*. New York: D. Appleton, 1866.

Berlin, James. *Rhetoric and Reality: Writing Instruction in American Colleges 1900–1985*. Carbondale: Southern Illinois UP, 1987.

———. *Writing Instruction in Nineteenth-Century American Colleges*. Carbondale: Southern Illinois UP, 1984.

Connors, Robert J. "Rhetoric in the Modern University: The Creation of An Underclass." *The Politics of Writing Instruction: Postsecondary*. Ed. Richard Bullock and John Trimbur. Portsmouth, NH: Boynton/Cook, 1991, 55–84.

———. "The Rhetoric of Mechanical Correctness." *Only Connect: Uniting Reading and Writing*. Ed. Thomas Newkirk. Upper Montclair, NJ: Boynton/Cook, 1986, 27–58.

———. "The Rise and Fall of the Modes of Discourse." *College Composition and Communication* 32 (1981): 444–55.

Horner, Winifred, ed. *Historical Rhetoric: An Annotated Bibliography of Selected Sources in English*. Boston: G. K. Hall, 1980.

———, ed. *The Present State of Scholarship in Historical and Contemporary Rhetoric*. Columbia: U of Missouri P, 1983.

Jolliffe, David. "The Moral Subject in College Composition: A Conceptual Framework and the Case of Harvard, 1865–1900." *College English* 51 (1989): 163–73.

Kitzhaber, Albert R. *Rhetoric in American Colleges 1850–1900*. Dallas: Southern Methodist UP, 1990.

Newkirk, Thomas. "Barrett Wendell and the Birth of Freshman Composition." Paper read at CCCC, Chicago, IL, March 1990.

———. "Octolog: The Politics of Historiography." *Rhetoric Review* 7 (1988): 5–57.

Tuchman, Barbara. *Practicing History: Selected Essays*. New York: Knopf, 1981.

Veysey, Lawrence R. *The Emergence of the American University*. Chicago: U of Chicago P, 1965.

Vitanza, Victor J. "'Notes' Towards Historiographies of Rhetorics." *PRE/TEXT* 8 (1987): 63–125.

Wendell, Barrett. *English Composition*. New York: Scribner's, 1891.

Teachers' Rhetorical Comments on Student Papers

In the course of his archival research, Bob became increasingly interested in the comments that instructors wrote on student texts, and he took great pleasure in describing some of the more unusual comments he had found in the cache of papers stored at Harvard, purportedly attesting to the illiteracy of American boys. When Bob's research (with Andrea in preparation for the first edition of *The St. Martin's Handbook*) resulted in gathering together over 21,000 contemporary student essays that had been marked by instructors of first-year writing, he dove in, almost gleefully, to record and categorize all the instructor comments on a stratified, randomized sample of 3,000 papers. The resulting essay, "Teachers' Rhetorical Comments on Student Papers," published in *College Composition and Communication* in 1993, typically sets this study in historical context, reminding readers of the development and proliferation of grading scales and correcting sheets, and linking these to a particular vision of the teacher's role as judge and rater rather than rhetorical responder. After tracing a shift to rhetorical response to the communications movement of the 1950s and noting that few of the subsequent scholarly essays on teacher response were grounded in "numerical depth" (241), the authors turn to their own numerical analysis and findings. Perhaps most notable, in retrospect, was the overwhelming use of comments to justify grades and the concomitant negative messages sent to students. We haven't been able to let our own comments on student papers go unexamined since this essay was published—a fact we think would please Bob very much.

As far back as we can trace student papers, we can see the attempts of teachers to squeeze their reactions into a few pithy phrases, to roll all their strength and all their sweetness up into one ball for student delectation. Every teacher of composition has shared in this struggle to address students, and writing helpful comments is one of the skills most teach-

From *College Composition and Communication* 44.2 (1993): 200–23. This essay was coauthored by Andrea A. Lunsford.

ers wish to develop toward that end. Given that writing evaluative commentary is one of the great tasks we share, one might think it would have been one of the central areas of examination in composition studies.

Indeed, a number of thoughtful examinations of written teacher commentaries exist, most of them measuring empirically the comments of a relatively small teacher and student population. No studies we could find, however, have ever looked at large numbers of papers commented on by large numbers of teachers. We do not have, in other words, any large-scale knowledge of the ways that North American teachers and students tend to interact through written assessments. There are clear logistical reasons for this lack of large-scale studies; the gathering and analysis of a large data base are daunting tasks, and evaluating rhetorical (as opposed to formal) commentary is a challenge. But we had the data base gathered from previous research, and in the great tradition of fools rushing in where wise number-crunchers fear to tread, we thought we'd take a look at this question of teacher commentary.

As inveterate historical kibbitzers, we naturally started research by asking what sorts of comments teachers had made on student papers in the past. Have teacher comments become more or less prescriptive, longer or shorter, more positive or more negative? We headed for the stacks to try to find out. Rather to our amazement, we discovered that what we were proposing to look at—teachers' rhetorical comments on student papers—was a relatively recent phenomenon in general composition teaching.

THE HISTORICAL TRAIL

Evidence of widespread acceptance of teachers acting as rhetorical audiences for their first-year students simply does not exist much farther back than the early 1950s.[1] Before that time, the most widely accepted idea was that teachers' jobs were to correct, perhaps edit, and then grade student papers. Now and then someone attacked this approach, but it seems to have held wide sway through the first half of this century. As Walter Barnes put it in 1912, writing students live

> in an absolute monarchy, in which they are the subjects, the teacher the king (more often, the queen), and the red-ink pen the royal scepter.... Theme correction is an unintelligent process.... In our efforts to train our children, we turn martinets and discipline the recruits into a company of stupid, stolid soldierkins—prompt to obey orders, it may be, but utterly devoid of initiative. (158–59)

The teacher who "pounces on the verbal mistake, who ferrets out the buried grammatical blunder, who scents from afar a colloquialism or a bit of slang" (159) seemed to Barnes a weak writing teacher, but by far the most common kind.

The idea that the teacher's most important job was to rate rather than to respond rhetorically to themes seems to have been well-nigh universal from

the 1880s onward, perhaps as a result of the much-cried-up "illiteracy crisis" of the 1880s and 1890s. Those who have examined older college themes preserved in archives at Harvard and Baylor have noted that teacher "comments" overwhelmingly comprised formal and mechanical corrections (for example, see Copeland and Rideout). College programs, in fact, very early came up with "correction cards," editing sheets, and symbol systems that were meant to allow teachers numerically to assess students' adherence to conventional rules, and it seemed reasonable to extrapolate that approach to issues of content, organization, and style. Thus were born during the first decade of this century, the various "rating scales" that represented the first systematic attempt we know of to deal with the issue of rhetorical effectiveness in student writing.

This is not the place for a complete history of the rise of rating scales, the various purposes they covered, the arguments they engendered, or the epistemological assumptions that fostered their development. Suffice it to say that between 1900 and 1925 a number of scales were proposed for rating composition. It's probably fair to say that these scales evolved from the rising status of scientific method and statistics and from writing teachers' uncomfortable awareness of exactly how "subjective" their grading of papers was (James). Teachers wished for a defensible rating instrument, and, beginning with the Hillegas Scale in 1912, educational theorists proposed to give them one. Many developments and variations of Hillegas's scale followed: the Thorndike Extension, the Trabue Scale, the Hudelson Scale, the Harvard-Newton Scale, the Breed-Frostic and Willing Scales, and others (Hudelson 164–67).

We don't want to suggest that these composition scales were entirely devoted to formal and mechanical ratings; their interest for us, in fact, lies primarily in their attempts to evolve an early holistic-style set of standards by which the more qualitative elements of composition could be "reliably" judged. This pedagogically interesting attempt found a supporter in no less than Sterling Leonard, much of whose early work in composition involved his attempt to build more rhetorical awareness into rating scales he felt were too much weighted toward formal aspects (Leonard 760–61). Interest in the perfect rating scale, however, eventually waned, doubtless because rating rhetorical elements was simply too complex and multi-layered a task for any scale. As two scale-using researchers admitted in 1917, after having been through a complex study using a variant of the Harvard-Newton Scale, "This study raises more questions than it answers. In fact, it cannot be said to have settled any question satisfactorily" (Brown and Hagerty 527).

The fact that rating scales usually served as instruments for administrative judgment rather than for student improvement also led to their gradual abandonment by many teachers. Fred Newton Scott, with his customary sagacity, identified this problem early on, noting in 1913 that "whenever a piece of scientific machinery is allowed to take the place of teaching—which is in essence but an attempt to reveal to the pupil the unifying principle of life—the result will be to artificialize the course of instruction" (4). Scott drew a strong distinction between a system which grades a composition for administrative pur-

poses and that which evaluates it as a stage in the pupil's progress. Hillegas's Scale clearly served the former purpose, and thus Scott ended his discussion of it with this Parthian shot:

> I leave this problem with you, then, with the seemingly paradoxical conclusion that we ought in every way to encourage Professor Thorndike and Dr. Hillegas in their attempts to provide us with a scale for the measurement of English compositions, but that when the scale is ready, we had better refrain from using it. If this sounds like the famous recipe for a salad which closes with the words "throw the entire mixture out the window," you will not, I am sure, if you have followed me thus far, be under any misapprehension as to my meaning. (5)

The liberal wing of the profession (including most of Scott's PhD students) followed this line, and the controversy over rating scales lasted for better than a dozen years.

By the mid-1920s, the excitement over rating scales died down as teachers began discussing the most effective ways of "criticizing a theme" outside of the question of grading it. Various kinds of advice were advanced: raise the standards as the course advances; don't be too severe; always include a bit of praise; don't point out every error.[2] All good advice, but the attitude of these authors toward the job of the teacher was almost universally in support of critical/judgmental rather than editorial/interventionist relations with students. "Correction" of papers was always uppermost, even to "liberal" teachers and writers. James Bowman, whose "The Marking of English Themes" of 1920 provides a sensible discussion of teacher marking, devotes only one short paragraph to the whole issue of teacher comments: "The comments are of far greater importance than the mark which is given the theme. These should be stern and yet kindly. While they should overlook no error, they should, in addition, be constructive and optimistic. It is necessary, above all, for the teacher to enter intimately and sympathetically into the problems of the student" (242–43). No one would argue with these ideas, but, even if well-intentioned, they are immensely general. Against that one paragraph, the rest of the article discussed correction of errors and assignment of grades.

This ratio held sway in most quarters. Oh, there were the forward-looking articles that always surprise first-time readers of old volumes of the *English Journal*—like Allan Gilbert's "What Shall We Do with Freshman Themes?" which proposes a socially-constructed and process-oriented regimen of peer review and group conferencing.[3] But for every Gilbert or Leonard or Scott or Gertrude Buck there were ten Hilda Jane Holleys, for whom "Interest and originality" was but one of ten areas rated (and third from the bottom of her chart, too, way after "Grammar" and "Vocabulary") and Louise Griswolds, proposing to reread each graded theme and change the grade to F if every formal error had not been corrected.

Such formal-error correction characterized teacher response through the twenties, thirties, and early forties, and the centrality of the correction

approach was not widely questioned until the advent of the communications movement during the late forties. Then, the concept of teachers best serving students by "correcting" their papers, like many other accepted traditions in writing pedagogy, began to come under sustained fire from a new generation of writing teachers.[4] Jeffrey Fleece in 1951 made what seemed to many a novel suggestion: that teachers actually consider themselves as students' real audiences and respond to their essays accordingly. Since "purpose" was the watchword of the communications movement, said Fleece, why not stop pretending that the teacher was not the only final and actual audience for students, and make use of that audience relationship? On papers with a real purpose, said Fleece, "the teacher should react to the content in some way, to guarantee the student's continued confidence in his interest" (273).

Fleece's view hardly seems radical today, but at the time it was received as a startling suggestion about the relations that students and teachers in writing might have. Even students were unused to having what they *said* in papers taken seriously. In an essay called "Conversing in the Margins," Harold Collins reported in 1954 that:

> When I return the themes, hands go up over pained faces, and injured innocence makes itself heard.
>
> "Aren't you supposed to stick to the grammar and punctuation and that sort of thing and not bother about what we say, the—er—content of our themes?"
>
> "I had only one error in spelling and three in punctuation. What do you mark on?" (He means, "Why didn't I get an A or a B?")
>
> "Do we have to agree with you? That doesn't seem. . . ."
>
> I must justify my extensive commentary, explain why I have seen fit to stray from such textbook concerns as diction, spelling, punctuation, sentence structure, and organization. With some warmth, I protest that I am not a theme-reading machine, a new marvel of electronics grading for grammar. Though it may be hard to credit, I am a real human being, and so I am naturally interested in what my students say in their themes. . . . (465)

Between 1900 and 1940, the concept that most students could have anything to "say" in their writing that would *really* interest the teacher was hardly imagined except by a few rare teachers.[5]

By the middle fifties, however, educators were more and more expected to try to address their students' essays as "real" audiences and to write long personal comments. "It requires extra time and care on the teacher's part," admitted Delmer Rodabaugh. "Perhaps it is not strictly his job to go to so much trouble, but trouble turns to pleasure when he begins to get results" (37). Rodabaugh admitted that what he proposed was not new, but was "a deliberate and persistent attempt to extend what we all do." This new effort, based on the idea that students should get full-scale rhetorical comments both in margins and at the end of papers, was very much in place by the end

of the 1950s, and new teachers after that time who gave no rhetorical advice along with their formal corrections did their work with certain guilt.

But what, exactly, did that work really come to? The attitudes that first appeared during the heyday of the communications movement still control much of what is presumed today about written teacher responses to student writing. Since the 1950s the field of composition studies has waxed, and its attitude toward teacher response to student writing has remained marked by the essential assumption that the teacher must and should engage the student in rhetorical dialogue. Around this assumption lies a large literature, which began to burgeon in the middle 1960s, hit a peak in the early 1980s, and has recently come up for discussion again in an excellent collection of essays edited by Chris Anson.[6]

We won't review this literature here, since so many people in the Anson collection have already done that better than we could. But we did notice, as we looked through the many thoughtful essays about teacher response, how few of them have studied the subject in numerical depth. Many discussions about response are inspiring, but most are either prescriptive, idealistic, or theoretical. Now and then a discouraging word has been heard—Albert Kitzhaber's flinty assessment of how few Dartmouth teachers actually wrote any comments on papers in the early 1960s, Cy Knoblauch and Lil Brannon's glum assertion in 1981 that no kind of written comment from teachers did much good or harm or had much attention paid to it, or Nancy Sommers's study of 35 teachers responding at Oklahoma and NYU, which concluded that "the news from the classroom is not good," that teachers were not responding to students in ways that would help them engage with issues, purposes, or goals (154). But most of the rest of the college-level literature is largely exploratory. No really large-scale study of the sorts of comments teachers were actually making on student papers existed, at least none that we knew of. We thought we'd give it a try.

THE SAMPLE AND THE METHODOLOGY

In 1986, we had collected 21,000 teacher-marked student essays for a national study of patterns of formal error. After identifying a randomized, stratified sample of 3,000 papers, we asked 50 analyzers to find examples of the top twenty error patterns in the writing of contemporary college students. The results of that study were published in 1988 as "Frequency of Formal Errors in Current College Writing."[7] As we sat through the long day of analysis and talked afterwards about what we'd seen that was interesting, everyone agreed that the whole issue of the ways in which the teachers responded to the student writing was something we ought to study. Not, of course, the ways in which teachers marked up the formal and mechanical errors, which nearly always tended to be done using either handbook numbers or the standard set of mysterious phatic grunts: "awk," "ww," "comma," etc. No, what we wanted to try to look at was a sometimes vague entity that we called

"global comments" by the teachers. What were teachers saying in response to the *content* of the paper, or to the specifically *rhetorical* aspects of its organization, sentence structure, etc.? What kinds of teacher-student relationships did the comments reflect?

We had a data base that we could use. Back in 1985, when we had been soliciting papers from teachers nationally, we had specifically asked that we be sent only papers that had been marked by teachers; some of the papers had very minimal markings, but each one had been evaluated in some way, had passed under the eye and been judged by the pen of a teacher. Our original request letter asked only for student papers "to which teachers have responded with interlinear, marginal, or terminal comments." The Methodology Police would probably bust us for the way the sample was gathered; the 300 teachers who sent us papers were a self-selected group who responded to an initial mailing (offering books from the St. Martin's Press trade list in exchange for commented papers) that went to over 8,000 teachers. We can't be sure why these folks were the ones who came forward, but even though the paper sample itself is randomized and nationally stratified by region, size and type of college, and so on, the teachers themselves were self-selected. Though it would be more satisfying to be able to say we had papers from 3,000 teachers who were chosen randomly from some giant national bingo drum, getting such a sample is simply beyond us. As it stands, we have a larger sample, and a better national distribution, than any previous study. Nothing, as one of our students once wrote, is extremely perfect.[8]

Okay, the data base was in hand. Now, as before, we faced the question of what instrument we would use to try to understand what we might find in the 3,000-paper sample.

We figured that we might as well work as inductively as we could, so we again selected 300 random papers, 150 for Andrea and 150 for Bob. We then looked carefully at these 300 papers, trying to note any important patterns we could see of teacher response to global rhetorical issues. Each of us came up with a list, and then we compared lists. We found that we had both noted some responses based on individual comments and some that were based in the *forms* and *genres* of teacher comments. We melded our lists and came up with a checklist form that we hoped would capture a substantial number of the different kinds of global comments our readers might see.

With lots of help from Eric Walborn, Heather Graves, and Carrie Leverenz in the Ohio State graduate program, one Saturday morning in May 1991 we assembled a group of 26 experienced writing teachers and eager readers. Lured by the prospect of a promised twelve feet of high-quality submarine sandwiches, these champions of the proletariat plunged into a learning curve and then into large stacks of papers, looking only at the teacher comments on each paper, and searching for a number of specific elements to record.[9]

We were specifically interested in what we called "global comments" by teachers, general evaluative comments found at the end or the beginning of papers. Such comments may be quite long or as short as a single word, or

they may take the form of marginal or interlinear comments in the body of the paper which are rhetorically oriented and not related to formal or mechanical problems. Global comments by teachers are meant to address global issues in students' writing: issues of rhetoric, structure, general success, longitudinal writing development, mastery of conventional generic knowledge, and other large-scale issues.

In other words, we asked our readers to ignore any comments on the level of formal error, grammar, punctuation, spelling, syntax, etc., unless those comments were couched in a specifically rhetorical way, i.e., "Your audience will think harshly of you if they see lots of comma splices." What we wanted to try to get at were the ways in which teachers judge the rhetorical effectiveness of their students' writing, and the sorts of teacher-student relationships reflected in the comments that teachers give. The following table summarizes what we found.

GRADES AND PATTERNS OF COMMENTARY

We looked at 3,000 papers. Of that number, 2,297 (77%) contained global comments. We had asked in our letter only for teacher-marked student papers, not for specifically "global" comments, so this percentage seems heartening. In fact, the 77% of teachers who took the time and effort to write even minimal global comments on student papers seem to us rather to diminish the claim sometimes heard that teachers do nothing with student papers except bleed upon errors. Of our sample, more than three-quarters dealt in some way with larger issues of rhetorical effectiveness.

The number of papers bearing some sort of grade was 2,241, or 75% of the total. These grades did not, we hasten to say, always appear on papers with global comments; in fact, our readers noted with some amazement how many of the graded papers contained no other form of commentary on them. The overwhelming impression our readers were left with was that grades were implicitly—or often explicitly—overwhelming impediments both for teachers and for students. If papers had no other markings, they had grades or evaluative symbols.[10]

The grades themselves took an extraordinary variety of forms, ranging from standard letter grades, with pluses and minuses; to standard 100-point number grades; to cryptic systems of numbers, fractions, decimals; and finally to symbolic systems of different kinds, including varieties of stars, moons, checks, check-pluses and -minuses. We had meant to attempt an average of these grades, but the different systems they used and the different contexts out of which they came made such an attempt seem silly; we had no idea how to average notations such as ***, 94/130, 3.1, +, F+, and ☺. So we desisted.

Of the 3,000 papers, 1,934 (64%) had identifiable terminal or initial comments on them. Such comments, appearing at the end or the beginning of a paper, serve as the teacher's most general and usually final comment on the work of the paper as a whole, and so we paid very close attention to them. Of

Numerical Results: Global Commentary Research

Total Number of Papers Examined: 3,000	# of 3,000	Percentage
Number of papers with global or rhetorical comments	2,297	77% of all Ps
Papers without global or rhetorical comments	703	23%
Number of papers graded	2,241	75%
Number of papers with initial or terminal comments	1,934	64%
Number of initial comments	318	16% of Ps with I or T comments
Number of terminal comments	1,616	84% of Ps with I or T comments
Purpose of comments:		
To give feedback on draft in process	242	11% of Ps with I or T comments
To justify grades	1,355	59%
Global comments in general:		
Comments that are all essentially positive	172	9% of Ps with I or T comments
Comments that are all essentially negative	451	23%
Comments that begin positively and then go to negative	808	42%
Comments that begin negatively and then go to positive	217	11%
Comments that lead with rhetorical issues	692	36%
Comments that lead with mechanical issues	357	18%
Very short comments—fewer than 10 words	460	24%
Very long comments—more than 100 words	101	5%
Comments focused exclusively on rhetorical issues	472	24%
Comments focused exclusively on formal/mechanical issues	435	22%
Comments that argue with content points made in paper	478	24%
Comments that indicate use of mechanical criteria as gate criteria ("The comma splices force me to give this an F despite. . . .")	150	8%
Comments that give general reader response ("like/dislike")	322	17%
Comments evaluating specific rhetorical elements:		
Supporting evidence, examples, details	1,296	56% of all Ps with comments
Organization	643	28%

Numerical Results: Global Commentary Research (*Continued*)

Total Number of Papers Examined: 3,000	*# of 3,000*	*Percentage*
Purpose	240	11%
Response to assignment	246	11%
Audience	137	6%
Overall progress, beyond commentary on paper	176	8%
Comments that deal with specific formal elements:		
Sentence structure	767	33% of all Ps with comments
Paragraph structure	417	18%
Documentation	154	7%
Quotations	142	6%
Source materials	133	6%
Paper format	372	16%

the two styles, the terminal comments were by far the most common. We found that only 318 papers (16% of all the papers with overview-style comments) placed that general overview at the beginning of the paper; the other 84% of teachers using these comments placed them at the end of the paper, usually along with the grade. There are probably simple reasons for this phenomenon. Terminal comments, especially those with grades to justify, are written on the last page of the essay, seeming to result from the reading process more naturally. They flow when the teacher's memory is freshest, at the point when she has just stopped reading. Their being buried in a later page allows them to be more private and even secret, unlike initial comments, which announce the teacher's judgment to the world in public fashion. But some teachers seem to prefer initial overall comments, perhaps because they hope to engage the student in thinking about central issues *before* looking at the rest of the commentary.

As we looked over the patterns of general commentary our readers found, we were reminded of how much rhetorical *forms* can tell us about the purposes and attitudes of those using them. Every intellectual field might be said to have its announced public values and its secret soul. Most composition teachers know what the field *says* is important—our public "tropes," so to speak. We talk and write often of purpose, of audience, of organization, of proof, of process and invention and revision and so on. These words fill our journals, our professional books, our conferences, and especially our textbooks. But do we really follow through? Do comments on papers show us acting on these public tropes, giving them more than lip service? Or do we have more genuine and less overt agendas? That was one of our major questions as we looked at these longer comments. As we examined the longer comments, we began to find patterns, and we came more and more to see our findings as a sort of exploration of the tropics of teacher commentary. Teachers, we found, tend to return to well-understood topoi as well as to familiar terms, phrases, and locu-

tions as they make their judgments on student writing. These topoi and tropes of commentary have several origins: they are public and private, conscious and habitual, social and individualistic. They are powerful tacit genres, and we were particularly interested in how these patterns of commentary reflected the beliefs of the field of composition studies.

Initial and terminal comments in particular have, we discovered, certain patterns and genres that they tend to fall into. The rarest of these tropes is the comment consisting of nothing except praise and positive evaluation. Of the papers with global comments, only 9% exhibited this pattern of totally positive commentary. These figures correlate with Daiker's Miami of Ohio study and illustrate how American teachers tend to be trained in finding and isolating problems in writing (104). Rarely can teachers keep themselves to completely positive commentary. As our readers noted, these positive comments tended to be the shortest of all the global comments found, as well as the friendliest. They were nearly all found next to A-level grades, and the teachers seem commonly to have felt that such good grades needed little explanation or commentary. Interestingly, our readers mentioned that completely positive global comments were the most personal comments, and were even commonly signed with the teacher's initials—a phenomenon not noted in mixed or negative global comments. "Very well done," "Your usual careful job," and "Superb!" were all examples of this pattern, which by its rarity and the sometimes surprising intensity of the praises rendered probably indicates how starved teachers feel for work they can wholeheartedly praise.

The next most common pattern we found consisted of comments that began by critiquing some aspect of the student's writing—very often a formal or mechanical aspect—and then moved into a positive commentary on the effective aspects of the papers. We called this *admonitio*, and it was still rather rare, with only 11% of the comments falling into the class.

More than twice as common was the comment consisting of nothing except negative judgments. Of our commented papers, 23% fell into this category, and they usually accompanied the worst grades. These completely critical comments ranged from savagely indignant to sadly resigned, but all gave the message that the teacher was seriously disappointed with this effort and was not equal to the task of finding anything about the paper to like. On a paper about the writer's feelings after being called to an accident scene where a sixteen-year-old girl had died, the comment was, "Learn to use subordination. You might have given us more on the drunken driver and your subsequent thoughts about him. You are still making comma splices! You must eliminate this error once and for all. Is it because you aren't able to recognize an independent clause?" George Hillocks, reviewing studies relating to teacher comments in his *Research on Written Composition*, found that although negative comments did not have any definitive effect on the quality of students' writing, they did strongly affect students' attitudes toward writing (160–68).

The most common trope in global comments proved to be the comment that began positively, with some praise of some element of a paper, and then turned negative toward the end. "Jodie—You describe much of Rodriguez's

dilemma well. I'd like to see some of your own ideas expanded—they deserve more attention! And be careful of those apostrophes!" A full 42% of all terminal and initial comments—almost half—fell into this category. The reasons for its popularity probably derive from the by-now traditional wisdom about always trying to find something to praise in each student's work. Seeing that many teachers do conscientiously try to find at least one good point to comment on in a paper was heartening.[11]

In terms of the order of presentation of materials in the terminal and initial comments, the most common order was *global/local*, leading with rhetorical comments, followed up by comments on mechanical or formal issues. Twice as many comments—36%—began with rhetorical comments as with formal comments, and this order ties in with the positive-negative duality; the single most common kind of comment we found consisted of a positive rhetorical comment followed by complaints and suggestions of different sorts, often concerning mechanical elements in the paper. "Paul, you've organized the paragraphs here well to support your thesis, but your sentences are all still short and simple, and you really need to check the comma rules."

The lengths of terminal and initial comments ranged widely. The longest comment we found was over 250 words long, but long comments were far less common than short. The average comment length throughout the run of papers was around 31 words, but this is not a very meaningful figure. Very short comments—fewer than ten words—were much more common than longer comments. A full 24% of all global comments had ten words or fewer; of these, many were a very few words, or one word—"Organization" or "No thesis" or "Handwriting—learn to type!" or "Tense!" Conversely, only 5% of comments exceeded 100 words. The portrait of teacher-student interchange painted by these numbers is one in which overworked teachers dash down a few words which very often tell students little about how or why their papers succeed or fail. The rarity of longer comments seemed to our readers to indicate not so much that teachers had nothing to say as that they had little time or energy to say it and little faith that what they had to say would be heard.

We found that only 22% of the longer comments were concerned exclusively with formal issues, indicating that 78% of all the longer global comments made by teachers took cognizance of rhetorical issues in the paper. (This number corresponds to the very small number of papers whose comments indicated that formal or mechanical criteria had been used as "gate criteria," without success in which a passing grade was impossible. Only 8% of the comments indicated uses of such gates as "The comma splices force me to give this paper an F despite. . . .") Some comments (24%) were focused exclusively on rhetorical issues and never went into any detail about mechanics, but the most common tropes of teacher comment took *both* rhetorical and mechanical elements of the paper into consideration. In general, teachers seem determined to respond to what their students are saying as well as how they say it, which is interesting news to those critics of contemporary teaching who claim that writing teachers are obsessed only with errors (and which substantiates what we found in our previous study of formal errors).

TROPES WITHIN COMMENTARY

One section of our tally sheets was devoted to recording numbers for how often teachers commented on some of the more common rhetorical elements that are a staple of freshman textbooks and teaching. What we found was instructive, and somewhat surprising. From the comments counted by our readers—and here we counted all global comments, not just terminal and initial comments—teachers comment in large numbers only on two general areas: supporting details and overall paper organization. A full 56% of *all* papers with global comments contained comments on the effectiveness—or more commonly, the lack—of supporting details, evidence, or examples. The next most commonly discussed rhetorical element, at 28%, was overall paper organization, especially issues of introductory sections and issues of conclusion and ending, and thematic coherence.

Since most textbooks, and many teachers, put considerable stress on the two large issues of purpose and audience, we might expect that teacher comments would similarly emphasize these issues. We were surprised, then, to find that very few teacher comments discussed them. Only 11% of the papers we examined had comments that could, even with liberal interpretation, be considered to be about purpose in the essay. Even rarer were comments about the writer's approach toward audience, with only 6% of papers mentioning anything about audience considerations such as tone or voice. According to our readers, the impression left by reading most teacher comments was that the audience for the writing was clearly the teacher, only the teacher, and nothing but the teacher, and thus most comments on audience outside of those parameters seemed redundant.

We also found that 11% of the papers contained comments concerned with how successfully the paper responded to the assignment. Many of these papers were clearly written either to formal assignments ("comparison/ contrast paper," "narrative essay," "research paper," etc.) or to full content-based assignments ("Give a synopsis of the Orwell essay followed by your own examples of doublespeak," etc.). Many of these papers did not contain comments specifically directed toward the assignment in spite of their clear nature as assignment-driven, but very often when the writer chose an incorrect genre or failed to take some specific instruction into proper consideration, the teacher would call it out as a serious failure. "This really is not a process analysis at all," complains one teacher about an essay called "What Are Friends For?" "You haven't given instructions to follow in performing or achieving something." The paper, which seemed acceptable to our readers except for failing to meet these generic expectations, received a D+.

Finally, we asked our readers to look at comments that went beyond the paper at hand to relate this piece of work to other work the teacher had seen the student accomplish. "Jennifer, I've enjoyed having you in class, and we've really seen some improvement. Good luck! I hope that next quarter you find more people that you fit in with." Here, again, we found that such commentary was thin on the ground; only 8% of the papers displayed any

comments that dealt with the writer's work as a developing system. The other 92% dealt only with the individual work at hand, making no comments on progress or development. Various reasons may account for this lack of longitudinal commentary. Our most immediate hypothesis is that teachers simply have too many students and too many papers to have time to look for the "big picture" of any one student's development.

While this research was meant to deal with global or rhetorical comments rather than mechanical elements in student writing, we couldn't separate those two factors absolutely. The formal and the mechanical are always rhetorical as well, and we wanted to try to look at the ways in which teachers commented on the rhetorical effectiveness of formal decisions student writers had made. Here we found that the most widely noted formal feature was sentence structure, with 33% of the commented papers mentioning it. (These were not merely syntactic or grammatical complaints or corrections, but longer comments on the effectiveness of sentences.) Paragraph structure was also mentioned in 18% of the commented papers, which was a bit of a surprise, since textbooks bear down so hard on paragraphs as organic units. General paper format—margins, spacing, neatness, cover sheets, etc.— elicited response on 16% of the commented papers.[12]

Finally, we examined the terminal and initial comments for their purpose. It was not always possible to divide comments into clear categories, of course, but we wanted to see what we could tell about the writing processes encouraged in the classrooms of the teachers whose comments we had. We found that the majority of the comments at the beginning or end of the papers served one purpose: to justify and explain final grades. Over 59% of the initial and terminal comments were grade justifications, "autopsies" representing a full stop rather than any medial stage in the writing process. In contrast, only 11% of the papers with such comments exhibited commentary clearly meant to advise the student about the paper as an ongoing project. It's probable that our process of paper-gathering specifically solicited papers at the final stage of the writing process, papers which had already been revised and which had been submitted for final grading. Nevertheless, this study suggests that consistent and wide-spread use of multiple drafts and revisions may hold more in theory than it does in practice.

READER IMPRESSIONS

We worked on recording numerical information for about five hours, at which point we broke to munch subs and talk about what we'd seen in the teacher comments on the papers and about our impressions. These impressionistic responses are, of course, just that—and therefore are not generalizable. We nevertheless found them fascinating, because they emerged immediately from the people who read through all those 3,000 papers. Because numbers tell only one story, we want to include our readers' voices here.

The primary emotion that they felt as they read through these teacher comments, our readers told us, was a sort of chagrin: these papers and

comments revealed to them a world of teaching writing that was harder and sadder than they wanted it to be—a world very different from the theoretical world of composition studies most readers hoped to inhabit. It was a world, many said, whose most obvious nature was seen in the exhaustion on the parts of the teachers marking these papers. Many of the more disturbing aspects of the teacher-student interaction revealed by these comments could be traced to overwork. A teacher with too many students, too many papers to grade, can pay only small attention to each one, and small attention indeed is what many of these papers got. A quarter of them had no personal comments at all, a third of them had no real rhetorical responses, and only 5% of them had lengthy, engaged comments of more than 100 words.

Just as students invent the university every time they write, teachers invent not only a student writer but a responder every time they comment. One characteristic of the responder that many teachers construct, our readers said, was its nature as a general and objective judge. Many of the comments seemed to speak to the student from empyrean heights, delivering judgments in an apparently disinterested way. Very few teachers, for instance, allowed themselves the subjective stance implicit in telling students simply whether they liked or disliked a piece of writing. This kind of reader-response stance was found in 17% of the global comments; the other 83% of comments pronounced on the paper in a distanced tone, like reified pesonifications of Perelman's Universal Audience. "You've structured the paper well in the block format," "You have a suitable opening paragraph with thesis statement," or "There are some lapses in style that need attention" were much more common than comments like "Don't get discouraged. Good writing takes years."

Similarly, teachers seemed unwilling to engage powerfully with content-based student assertions or to pass anything except "professional" judgments on the student writing they were examining. Only 24% of the comments made any move toward arguing or refuting any content points made in the paper, and many of these "refutations" were actually formal comments on weak argumentative strategies. In some way, then, teachers seem conditioned *not* to engage with student writing in personal or polemical ways. What we found, in short, was that most teachers in this sample give evidence of reading student papers in ways antithetical to the reading strategies currently being explored by many critical theorists.[13] (It's our guess that even the most devoted reader-response critics, by the way, tend to produce similar disinterested commentary on student papers.) For whatever reasons, our readers found evidence to support the contention of Robert Schwegler that "professional practices and assumptions have encouraged composition instructors to suppress value-laden responses to student writing and ignore the political dimensions of their reading and teaching practices" (205). Schwegler's conclusion that "the language of marginal and summative commentary . . . is predominantly formalist and implicitly authoritarian" is one our study clearly supports (222).

The authoritarian attitude came through most clearly in the insensitivity our readers felt some of the teacher comments evinced. They sensed, they

said, not only exhaustion but a kind of disappointment on the parts of many teachers, and, as a result, patience was often in short supply. "Do over, and pick one subject for development. This is just silly." "Throw away!" "You apparently do not understand thing one about what a research paper is." At times the harshness, which might be justified in particular contexts, even segued into a downright punitive state of mind; one teacher wrote at the end of a paper, "Brian, this is much too short, as I'm sure you know. You've not fulfilled the requirements of the course. Besides receiving an F for the paper, I'm lowering another grade 20 points. You should have consulted with me." Another teacher wrote:

> I refuse to read this research paper. You have not done adequate research, you have not narrowed the topic as directed, you have not followed the format described, *and you have not been directed by my comments during the research assignment.* (emphasis added)

Here is disappointment brimming over into accusation and acrimony.

Some teachers were disturbed when students seemed not to have a grasp of materials that teachers expected them to have mastered. This disappointment, our readers said, seemed to stem from a disjunction between what teachers thought they taught and what they then evaluated. "Ken, you know better than to create comma splices at this point in the semester!" wrote a teacher in rueful disappointment, but Ken obviously did not. In assuming that Ken purposefully had "created" some comma splices after no doubt being taught that such creations were to be avoided, the teacher showed a dissociation between *her* knowledge as she assumed it was disseminated into the class and *Ken's* grasp of some fairly complex and experience-based conventions.

Our readers also told us that the large number of short, careless, exhausted, or insensitive comments really made them notice and appreciate comments that reflected commitment to students and to learning. They noted lengthy comments from teachers who seemed really to care, not only about students' writing, but also about the students themselves:

> Elly—this is not a good essay, but you'd have to be superhuman to write a good essay on this topic, given how important and immediate it is for you. I *feel* for your situation—I know what it is like to feel like a different person in a different place, and however much people tell you it is possible to change anywhere, it surely is MUCH harder in some places than others. (Run away to NYC!) Unfortunately, my job is not to encourage you to run away, but to write a good essay. Let's make it a short but specific one: tell me *one* incident that will show how you used to put yourself down, and *one* incident during your visit to NYC that shows how you didn't put yourself down or were even proud of yourself.

Some might complain that this teacher is being too directive, telling the student exactly how to revise, but after looking at many papers with no

evidence that a revision option had ever existed and no evidence that the teacher cared much for the student or her situation, this kind of comment really captured our readers' attention.

Another trait our readers admired was the skill of careful marginal comments. Teachers who use marginal comments and a revision option were praised by our readers for their thoroughness and the care they took in calling all sorts of rhetorical elements—not just very large-scale ones—to students' attention. One teacher particularly won raves from the readers; his marginal questions were dense—questions like "When did she do this?" and "You didn't know how to steer?" were interspersed with shorter notes like "Paragraph?"—and the whole was followed up with a half-page typed response to the paper, giving comments and suggestions for the next draft. At the same time we admired this teacher's work and care, however, we also wondered, as one reader put it, "When does this guy ever sleep?"

It was also good to discover teachers experimenting with different systems to help students revise. Although, as we suggested, many teachers seemed to see revision as merely the editing out of formal errors, other teachers clearly encouraged revision for content issues. One teacher had even invented a "contract" form for revision, which was a sort of written proposal of the changes the student would make in a draft, and a promise from the teacher—signed and dated—of what grade would be given the paper if the changes were successfully carried out.

Many of the teachers commenting in our study did seem to use the concept of teaching the writing process in their responses to students, but all too often the process reflected a rigid stage model. Some students were asked to attach their outlines or invention materials to the draft handed in, leading to comments like "This is terrible prewriting!" Our readers saw few attempts to discuss any recursive model of writing, and although prewriting was sometimes mentioned, revision had very little place in the comments we read. With only 11% of the papers showing any evidence of a revision policy (and we deliberately asked our readers to use the most liberal definition of "draft in process" possible, even to the extent of defining a graded paper as a draft if it gave evidence of being the final draft of a previous series), and many of the "revisions" suggested being the editing and correction of errors, the practices mirrored by these comments are still governed by the older form of "one-shot writing."

Although we had not meant to look at formal or mechanical comments, our readers told us that it had been impossible for them to ignore the editing and corrections they saw. There was, they said, a pervasive tendency to isolate problems and errors individually and "correct" them, without any corresponding attempt to analyze error patterns in any larger way, as is recommended by Mina Shaughnessy and the entire tradition that follows her. The "job" that teachers felt they were supposed to do was, it seemed, overwhelmingly a job of looking at papers rather than students; our readers found very little readerly response and very little response to content. Most teachers, if our sample is representative, continue to feel that a major task is to "correct" and

edit papers, primarily for formal errors but also for deviation from algorithmic and often rigid "rhetorical" rules as well. The editing was often heavy-handed and primarily apodictic, concerned more with ridding the paper of problems than with helping the student learn how to avoid them in the future.

In spite of what we know about how grading works against our goals, our readers saw evidence everywhere that much teacher commentary was grade-driven. A large number of teachers used some form of dittoed or xeroxed "grading sheet" clipped or stapled to the student's essay. These sheets, which varied in format, were sometimes obviously departmental in origin, but a number of them were individual. They were great boons to grading, because teachers could circle a few words or phrases, rate several different elements in the paper independently and easily, and go on to the next paper with hardly any personal commentary on the paper. These rating sheets also allowed teachers to pass hierarchical judgments on rhetorical matters; one teacher used an editing sheet that gave checks and points for the quality of the prewriting. Our readers discerned a relationship between use of these grading sheets and lower grades on papers, which they ascribed to the atomistic division of the paper such sheets encourage and the teacher's resulting difficulty in seeing the piece of writing holistically or with much affect. Some teachers had a set of "penalty points" criteria which produced an automatic F if a certain number of types of error was found. "I stopped here," wrote one teacher in the middle of a research paper. "You've already messed this up to the point of failure."

One notable subset of these rating sheets were the "correction sheets," sometimes found in labeled "correction folders." Correction sheets were not merely reactive, but prophylactic as well. Some contained written instructions demanding that students examine their teacher-marked paper, then list the error symbol, the error name, the rule that the error had broken, and the rewritten sentence in which the error originally had appeared. This technique, which appeared in a number of papers, did not always use a separate sheet; very often, students were asked to rewrite elements with formal errors as part of the *post-grading* work on the paper. In one case, in fact, we found a teacher who, after each error marking, placed a row of numbers—1, 2, 3, 4, 5—on succeeding lines in the margin. The student's task, as far as we can reconstruct it, was to identify the error and then write the correct word or phrase out five times in the margin so as to really "get it through her head."

But even those teachers not using grading sheets often gave few reasons why they approved of or condemned some aspect of a paper. The judgments expressed in writing by teachers often seemed to come out of some privately held set of ideals about what good writing should look like, norms that students may have been taught but were certainly expected to know. One of our readers called this tacit assumption the problem of "writer-based teacher response," and it was as pervasive among our teachers as writer-based prose is among students.

The reactions of our readers made us realize anew how difficult the situations of many teachers remain today. Behind the abstractions we push about

as counters in our scholarly game, there exist real persons facing real and sometimes grim circumstances. We have a long road ahead of us if we are to make real and useful so much of what we confidently discuss in our journals and our conference talks. So the news we bring back from the Tropics of Commentary is both good and bad. The good news is that teachers are genuinely involved in trying to help their students with rhetorical issues in their writing. Counter to the popular image of the writing teacher as error-obsessed and concerned only with mechanical issues, the teachers whose work we looked at clearly cared about how their students were planning and ordering writing. The classical canons invoked in more than three-quarters of the papers we examined were invention and arrangement, not merely style. Similarly, more comments were made on the traditional rhetorical issues of supporting details/examples and general organization than were made on smaller-scale issues. Very few comments were entirely negative, and very few showed use of formal and mechanical standards as completely dominating standards of content. Grading standards have softened up a little in the last 70 years, but not as much as many people may have thought.

The bad news is that many teachers seem still to be facing classroom situations, loads, and levels of training that keep them from communicating their rhetorical evaluations effectively. Even given the nature of our sample, there was not much reflection in these papers of revision options, or of contemporary views of the composing process. The teachers whose comments we studied seem often to have been trained to judge student writing by rhetorical formulae that are almost as restricting as mechanical formulae. The emphasis still seems to be on finding and pointing out problems and deficits in the individual paper, not on envisioning patterns in student writing habits or prompts that could go beyond such analysis. As D. Gordon Rohman put it as long ago as 1965, merely pointing out errors or praising good rhetorical choices is based on a fundamental misconception, the idea that:

> if we train students how to recognize an example of good prose ("the rhetoric of the finished word"), we have given them a basis on which to build their own writing abilities. All we have done, in fact, is to give them standards to judge the goodness or badness of their finished effort. *We haven't really taught them how to make that effort.* (106)

For reasons of overwork, or incomplete training, or curricular demand, many of the teachers whose comments we looked at are still not going beyond giving students standards by which to judge finished writing.

It may be, in addition, that to some degree teachers perceive that their comments *don't count*—that students ignore them, that the discursive system at work in institutional grading won't allow for any communication *not* algorithmic and grade-based. As our readers, with their admirable idealism, told us, many of the comments they saw seemed to be part of a web of institutional constraints that made teacherly "voice" in commentary a rare thing. If we're accurate in this perception, it is the entire industry and institution of

rank ordering, hyper-competition, and grading that is culpable, and teachers are as much victims of it as students.

Janet Auten's recent claim that we need a rhetorical context for every disruption we make in a student text is certainly compelling, and her suggestions that teachers become aware of their separate roles as readers, coaches, and editors are helpful (11–12). What we would like to see are future studies that would build such awareness by describing *in detail* the topography we have only sketched in here, perhaps in "thick descriptions" of teacher-responders at work, in their full context. Ethnographies of response would certainly provide a starting point for analyses of instructional constraints, for the ideologies of teacher response, and for the ethos of this particular teacher-student interaction. But in addition to knowing more about the complex act of response, we have to work at seeing that what we know *now* is enacted in writing programs. We need to start putting into programmatic practice what we've learned about effective teacher commentary from scholars like Nancy Sommers, Lil Brannon, and Chris Anson. Doing so might best begin, for each of us, at home—by cataloguing and studying our own tropics of commentary. By determining those genres and tropes of response we tend to privilege, perhaps we can begin to learn how our students "read" these teacherly tropes, which seem so obvious and helpful to us but may not be so easily deciphered by those still striving to enter the community we take for granted.

NOTES

1. During the nineteenth century, of course, when most writing courses were taught at the sophomore level and above, teachers at the better colleges often engaged with their students' essays at some length in commentary. This practice of serious and lengthy engagement died out quickly, however, after the first freshman writing courses began to evolve with their drastic overwork and underprepared students. By 1900 the practice of engagement with the content of student essays was the rare exception to the rule.

2. Those who thought this piece of advice was relatively new will be surprised to learn that it can be dated with certainty back to 1921, and we have no doubt that, traced truly, it predates Quintilian. Each generation seems to feel that truly humanistic pedagogy began only a decade or two ago. See Bowman, 249–53, Hewitt, 85–87, and Daiker, 105.

3. Gilbert, writing in 1922, is a startlingly "modern" voice who often sounds a lot like David Bartholomae or Ann Berthoff. Listen:

> The course in freshman rhetoric—without plenty of reading—is an attempt to make bricks of straw only. . . . The teacher of Freshman English must deserve his right to stand on the same level as any other teacher of Freshmen, and must deal with big things, ideas, and books that hit the intelligence of the students. This does more to improve slovenly sentences, than does constant worrying of details. The mint, anise, and cumin must be tithed, but the teacher of Freshmen who gives himself to trivial things and neglects the weightier matters of good literature does not make his course a power for literacy. (400)

Gilbert goes on to recommend literature as a springboard for students' own choices of what to write, then suggests that students read their papers before the class because to do so "gives the writer an audience," after which comes group criticism, then personal

conferences with the teacher, then group conferences. Sadly, Gilbert was a rather lonely voice in his time.

4. For more information on the importance of this generation to composition pedagogy, see the "Introduction" to *Selected Essays of Edward P. J. Corbett*.

5. Fred Newton Scott had been encouraging teachers to read their students' essays rhetorically, of course, but although we admire Scott today, his influence (and that of his students) was not enough to change composition pedagogy in general.

6. For an overview of the work done during the seventies and early eighties, see Griffin. For good discussions of contemporary ideas and attitudes, see the essays in Anson, several of which have very complete bibliographies.

7. Those who want to know the details about how the 3,000 randomized and stratified papers were selected for this study are referred to the long footnotes in our 1988 study. These papers are not the same ones, but they were pulled from the pile of 21,000 using exactly the same methodology.

8. One of our *CCC* referees made the irrefutable point that the self-selected nature of our sample meant that this study could make no claim of reflecting all of the possible kinds of student-teacher interaction:

> For instance, if I had received the request to send in a set of papers, and the set I had currently at hand were papers I mark in preparation for personal conferences, to discuss how the paper should be revised for a further draft, then indeed I would become one of the 7,700 who declined, simply because my commenting on that type of draft is extremely minimal. . . . I wouldn't send the set in because I am sure the researchers would be able to make little out of it, and yet the very kind of conferencing and push toward revision and treatment of writing as an act in progress and not as a completed copy is the kind of teacher commentary that the authors complain they found little of in the "database."

This observation is very accurate, and it is a prime reason why we make no attempt to claim that our sample represents all teachers, or to derive percentages about teachers using revision, etc. What we wanted to try to analyze here was specifically *written* commentary, the rhetorical interaction that goes between teachers and students via the traditional marginal and terminal commentary. We make no claims at all about the various other sorts of student-teacher interaction possible; indeed, there is no way we can know any more than what is suggested by the papers we studied. Nonetheless, we can't agree with Lil Brannon's assessment, given at a panel on this research at the 1992 CCCC, that "we do not learn very much from this kind of study." For many teachers and students, written commentary remains the primary interchange they have, and understanding it better cannot be unimportant.

9. The ratings of our 26 readers were not checked for traditional kinds of inter-rater reliability either by us or by repeated ratings. Because of the "slippery" nature of rhetorical possibility, such tight controls were simply not realistic. We counted on the number of readers and their level of expertise to give our study the only kind of reliability we thought practical. We have little doubt that 26 other readers looking at 3,000 other papers would come up with slightly different numbers, but we would be surprised if those numbers led to substantially different inferences.

10. As our readers looked at these papers, they had the impression that the grading curve on them was lower than their own, and while we could not, as we said, complete a serious statistical analysis of the grades because we had no context for many of them, a very rough analysis of the first 350 pure-letter grades on our sheets turned up the following, which, for the sake of interest, we contrast with similar information gleaned from Bowman (248) on grades at the University of Missouri in 1920:

	1915–1920	*1980–1985*
A-range grades	4%	9%
B-range grades	21%	39%
C-range grades	52%	37%
D-range grades	16%	12%
F grades	7%	3%

Sue Carter Simmons's research with Barrett Wendell's gradebook provides an interesting corroboration of those early figures. His English A grades at Harvard between 1887 and 1890 were in these ranges: A—4%, B—16%, C—46%, D—30%, and F—4% (178–79). Our findings are very speculative, and concentrating only on the pure letter grades clearly skews the results in this rough comparison, but certainly we see some grade inflation, especially at the B-range level. At many schools today, grade inflation has turned the old "gentleman's C" into the "partier's B," thus putting a crack in the classic bell curve, but these numbers do not seem to us to be completely out of line with grading expectations from our own teaching.

11. Of course, these sorts of comments can easily become mechanically formulaic, as was early recognized. For a funny (and early) view of these and other rhetorical commentary formulae, see Eble.

12. In this same section of the study we also asked our readers to look for comments aimed at uses of quotations, use of source materials, and use of documentation and citation forms; all three of these elements elicited comments from between 6% and 7% of all commented papers. The conclusion we draw from these numbers is simply that between 6% and 7% of the papers examined were generic "research papers," and could thus be expected to contain quotations, sources, and cites, all of which are likely to be commented on by teachers. Quotations were seldom found outside of research papers and literary analyses; students, it seems, rarely use sources or citations unless pushed to do so by specific assignments.

13. This whole question of how teachers engage as readers of student writing has tantalizing implications about men's and women's ways of knowing and about gendered response and teacher-student interaction. In this study, we did not build in any systematic ways of identifying the gender of either teachers or students. Given our data base, it could have been done, but it would have made what we did do immensely more complex. That piece of research remains in the future, but we do hope to take it up.

WORKS CITED

Anson, Chris M., ed. *Writing and Response: Theory, Practice, and Research.* Urbana: NCTE, 1989.

Auten, Janet Gebhart. "A Rhetoric of Teacher Commentary: The Complexity of Response to Student Writing." *Focuses* 4 (1991): 3–18.

Barnes, Walter. "The Reign of Red Ink." *English Journal* 2 (Mar. 1913): 158–65.

Bowman, James C. "The Marking of English Themes." *English Journal* 9 (May 1920): 245–54.

Brannon, Lil. "Response." Conference on College Composition and Communication. Cincinnati, 20 Mar. 1992.

Brown, Marion D., and M. E. Hagerty. "The Measurement of Improvement in English Composition." *English Journal* 6 (Oct. 1917): 515–27.

Collins, Harold R. "Conversing in the Margins." *College English* 15 (May 1954): 465–66.

Connors, Robert J., and Andrea A. Lunsford. "Frequency of Formal Errors in Current College Writing, or, Ma and Pa Kettle Do Research." *College Composition and Communication* 39 (Dec. 1988): 395–409.

Copeland, Charles T., and H. M. Rideout. *Freshman English and Theme Correcting at Harvard College.* New York: Silver-Burdett, 1901.

Corbett, Edward P. J. *Selected Essays of Edward P. J. Corbett.* Ed. Robert J. Connors. Dallas: Southern Methodist UP, 1989.

Daiker, Donald A. "Learning to Praise." Anson 103–13.

Eble, Kenneth E. "Everyman's Handbook of Final Comments on Freshman Themes." *College English* 19 (Dec. 1957): 126–27.

Fleece, Jeffrey. "Teacher as Audience." *College English* 13 (Feb. 1952): 272–75.

Gilbert, Allan H. "What Shall We Do with Freshman Themes?" *English Journal* 11 (Sep. 1922): 392–403.

Griffin, C. W. "Theory of Responding to Student Writing: The State of the Art." *College Composition and Communication* 33 (Oct. 1982): 296–301.

Griswold, Louise. "Getting Results from Theme-Correction." *English Journal* 18 (Mar. 1929): 245–47.

Hewitt, Charles C. "Criticism—Getting It Over." *English Journal* 10 (Feb. 1921): 85–88.

Hillocks, George Jr. *Research on Written Composition: New Directions for Teaching.* Urbana: NCRE, 1986.

Holley, Hilda. "Correcting and Grading Themes." *English Journal* 13 (Jan. 1924): 29–34.

Hudelson, Earl. "The Development and Comparative Values of Composition Scales." *English Journal* 12 (Mar. 1923): 163–68.

James, H. W. "A National Survey of the Grading of College Freshman Composition." *English Journal* 12 (Oct. 1926): 579–87.

Kitzhaber, Albert R. *Themes, Theories, and Therapy: The Teaching of Writing in College.* New York: McGraw-Hill, 1963.

Knoblauch, C. H., and Lil Brannon. "Teacher Commentary on Student Writing: The State of the Art." *Freshman English News* 10 (Fall 1981): 1–4.

Leonard, Sterling A. "Building a Scale of Purely Composition Quality." *English Journal* 14 (Dec. 1925): 760–75.

Phelps, Louise W. "Images of Student Writing: The Deep Structure of Teacher Response." Anson 37–67.

Rodabaugh, Delmer. "Assigning and Commenting on Themes." *College English* 16 (Oct. 1954): 33–37.

Rohman, D. Gordon. "Pre-Writing: The Stage of Discovery in the Writing Process." *College Composition and Communication* 16 (May 1965): 106–12.

Schwegler, Robert. "The Politics of Reading Student Papers." *The Politics of Writing Instruction: Postsecondary.* Ed. Richard Bullock and John Trimbur. Portsmouth: Boynton/Cook, 1991, 203–26.

Simmons, Sue Carter. "A Critique of the Stereotypes of Current-Traditional Rhetoric: Invention and Writing Instruction at Harvard, 1875–1900." Diss. U of Texas at Austin, 1991.

Sommers, Nancy I. "Responding to Student Writing." *College Composition and Communication* 33 (May 1982): 148–56.

Scott, Fred Newton. "Our Problems." *English Journal* 2 (Jan. 1913): 1–10.

Women's Reclamation of Rhetoric in Nineteenth-Century America

In "The Exclusion of Women from Classical Rhetoric" (published in a 1992 festschrift for James Kinneavy, *A Rhetoric of Doing*), Bob began addressing gender issues. Three years later, in "Women's Reclamation of Rhetoric in Nineteenth-Century America," Bob reiterates this focus on exclusion, identifying the rhetorical tradition as "quintessentially agonistic" and "absolutely male." Bob sees this tradition as most seriously challenged during the nineteenth century, as women began to achieve access to formal higher education and, along with it, rhetorical training and culture. "Rhetoric entered the nineteenth century," he says, "as a central argumentative discipline. [. . .] Rhetoric exited the nineteenth century as 'composition'" (262). What accounted for such a monumental change? In a word, women, whose incursion into the academy brought about a change in teacher-student relationship ("from challenging and judgmental to nurturing and personalized"); in medium of communication ("from oral rhetoric to writing"); in genre (from argument to "a multimodal approach that privileged explanation"); and in topics for writing (from "abstract, distanced subjects" to "more personal assignments") (263). As he explores and defends these claims, Bob presents a wealth of archival data along with fascinating and sometimes quirky details, such as a description of the Davidson College faculty suppressing rebellious math students in 1855. The essay that follows is one of Bob's most controversial works, and the heated conversation it helped begin is still in progress.

Throughout most of Western history, rhetoric was the property of men. The continuing discipline of rhetoric was shaped by male rituals, male contests, male ideals, and masculine agendas. Women were definitively excluded from all that rhetoric implied. Beginning in the nineteenth century, however, with the opening of higher education to women, the theretofore closed field of rhetoric began to shift and change. The shift from a

From *Feminine Principles and Women's Experience in American Composition and Rhetoric*, ed. Louise Wetherbee Phelps and Janet Emig (Pittsburgh: U of Pittsburgh P, 1995), 67–90.

male-dominated rhetoric to one that can encompass other purposes is still taking place, powerfully shaping and changing the discipline over the past two decades and—even more important—shaping us as individuals and teachers. This chapter tells the story of how some of those changes began in the nineteenth century and how they have affected women and men and the ways we think about, use, and teach discourse processes.

The term *rhetoric* is used in this chapter as it would have been used by its practitioners through 1850—that is, as the 2,500-year-old discipline of persuasive public discourse. From its inception in the probate courts of early Syracuse, the techniques of rhetoric were evolved for a single purpose: to create persuasive arguments, to develop and win cases, to put forward opinions in legislative forums, to stake out turf and verbally hold it against opponents in public contest. To use a term popularized by Walter Ong, rhetoric was a quintessentially *agonistic* discipline—concerned with contest. It was ritualized contest, yes, but contest, nonetheless. Argument and debate are verbal agonistic displays, and as Ong has argued, ritual contests of all sorts have been central to Western culture for as long as we have recorded history. In his book *Fighting for Life*, Ong traces the strands of agonistic ritual contest between males that exist in nature and in the convoluted, codified forms of nature we call culture and civilization. By using Ong's ideas to explore some of what we know of the history of rhetoric, we can, I think, come to a fruitful new understanding of why rhetoric assumed the forms it did and how it has changed and is changing today.

The discipline of rhetoric, as it had evolved from the classical period through the eighteenth century, was an absolutely male—and thus a quintessentially agonistic—discipline. Along with logic, its counterpart, it reified in technical disciplinary form the sometimes inchoate agonistic longings of a patriarchal society. Classical rhetoric is, plain and simple, about fighting, ritual fighting with words; this agonistic tone carried over into all rhetorical study up until the nineteenth century. Feminist scholarship has clearly shown how women had to fight their way into many intellectual disciplines during the last two millennia of Western culture; but no discipline was as closed to them as rhetorical study. Through most of Western history, women were not encouraged to learn to read or write, though those skills—even the "higher" skills of Latin and Greek—were grudgingly allowed to women of high social or economic status. Rhetoric, however, was simply and clearly forbidden to women. Like battle skills, rhetorical skills were assumed by men to be both beyond women's capabilities and beneath their natures.

This exclusion of women from rhetoric was absolute, and it deeply affected the discipline. Feminist scholarship in rhetorical history has scoured all existing records; there are, of course, many women who used rhetoric, who were known as admirable stylists or influential figures (Glenn). But we have found not a single woman prior to 1800 who defined herself, or was defined by those around her, as a rhetorician. This central discipline, one of the three legs of the trivium of Western knowledge, was denied women completely. Through the classical era, the idea of women rhetoricians was either

frightening or humorous to male orators. In the patristic period, Pauline misogyny denied women the right to speak in the churches, the central rhetorical forums of the time. Throughout the medieval period, the influence of the Church kept women from rhetorical training or public speaking before mixed audiences.

During the Renaissance, when education for women first came to be a real issue, we might expect to see a new attitude toward women's abilities to conduct public affairs, but even such liberal scholars as Leonardo Bruni and Juan Luis Vives worked to close down the emerging possibilities that women might be taught rhetoric. And through the seventeenth and eighteenth centuries, though colleges developed and became more specialized, women continued to be completely excluded from the capstone discipline of traditional education. Finally, in America during the nineteenth century, women demanded and received access to higher education, and rhetoric changed forever in the face of their determination to have access to it.

Until the nineteenth century, American women shared no higher schooling of any sort with men. There were no colleges for women; education of young women was reserved for the wealthier classes and was carried on, if at all, by private tutors and masters in the parents' home—which was, of course, a young woman's only proper sphere. The strict classical curriculum long taken for granted in all-male colleges was for most of Western history completely unavailable to women, who were shut out even of reading about educational questions and issues because they were seldom taught Latin, the language in which most learned discourse was conducted. Both on the Continent and in the British Isles, women were educationally disenfranchised, and colonial America, where for many years the majority of people of both genders were only minimally educated, merely followed suit in its attitudes.

Even with the establishment after the American Revolution of common grammar schools, higher education for women over twelve years of age was rare. A few female seminaries grew up in the late eighteenth century, but they taught mainly ornamental and domestic skills—sewing, penmanship, music. As American culture matured, however, and the essentially agrarian nature of the society began to give way to manufacturing, a newer urban bourgeoisie evolved, and the status of women in America changed. As Ann Douglas argues in *The Feminization of American Culture*, women in America shifted from producers to consumers during the nineteenth century, from the center of a household-based production economy to the main demand element in a consumption economy based on specialization, industrialization, and nonagrarian extrahousehold workplaces for men (48–68). Women in the American Northeast after 1800 were becoming a more leisured class, and in the egalitarian world of Jacksonian democracy, it was inevitable that institutions would spring up to serve and educate this new class.

The first female academy offering rigorous classical courses was established at Troy, New York, in 1821. The Hartford Female Seminary was established by Catherine Beecher in 1828, Mount Holyoke Female Seminary, in South Hadley, Massachusetts (later Mount Holyoke College), in 1837.

Women were demanding their right to an education, and over the next fifty years, the first all-women's colleges were established: Georgia Female College in 1836, Elmira Female College in the mid-1850s, Vassar College in 1860, Smith and Wellesley in 1875, Bryn Mawr and Mount Holyoke in 1888 (Rudolph, 314–19). Separate education for women—including the entire classical course—was a reality by a decade after the Civil War.

More apposite to this study than the general movement for women's colleges, however, is the change wrought on previously all-male colleges by the admission of women. It is in coeducational institutions that we first see truly extraordinary changes in the discipline of rhetoric. The movement toward allowing men and women to go to college together began around the same time the first all-women's colleges were established—the 1830s and 1840s. Oberlin was the first college to allow women to take courses with men, in 1837, but coeducation was a movement slow to be accepted; many educators feared that coeducation would produce "unmanly" men and "unwomanly" women, and fewer than six colleges were coeducational before the Civil War. With the passage of the Morrill Land-Grant Colleges Act in 1862, however, each state was empowered to found an Agricultural and Mechanical College. These schools, especially in the booming Midwest and West, were to become the major state universities. Unshackled by the all-male traditions of many eastern schools, these western universities were nearly all coed from the beginning. By 1872, there were ninety-seven coed schools (sixty-seven of which were in the West). By 1880, 30 percent of all American colleges admitted women, and by the turn of the century this figure had risen to 71 percent (Rudolph, 322).

From no women in colleges in 1830 to three-quarters of all American colleges admitting women by 1900 was a change in educational culture unprecedented in modern history. What we see, within seventy years, is an absolute revision of the all-male enclaves that colleges had been for over a millennium. There were, of course, schools that remained all-male—some even to the present day—but the college experience was ineluctably changed by the gradual influx of young women. This is not the place to detail the horrified objections, the often frantic attempts to safeguard the portals, the manifold arguments advanced against coeducation (Woody, vol. 2). Women were on the move and would not be denied. And where women and men went to college together, the atmosphere and curriculum changed as a result: the atmosphere and tone of life, with startling rapidity; and the curriculum, more slowly but just as certainly. No discipline was as much affected as rhetoric.

Rhetoric entered the nineteenth century as a central argumentative discipline—respected training that was desired by students, was primarily oral, and had a civic nexus. Rhetoric exited the nineteenth century as "composition," a marginalized, multimodal discipline—compulsory training that was despised by most students, was primarily literary, and had a personal, privatized nexus. Coeducation and the decline of agonistic education strongly affected these changes in rhetoric and can be seen to tie together many elements of shifting American discourse education, in particular: (1) the change

of student-teacher relationships in rhetoric courses, from challenging and judgmental to nurturing and personalized, a change still in process today; (2) the shift from oral rhetoric to writing as the central classroom focus; (3) the shift from argument as the primary rhetorical genre to a multimodal approach that privileged explanation; and (4) the decline of abstract, distanced subjects for writing and the rise of more personal assignments.

METHOD: FROM AGON TO IRENE

The most general change wrought in the teaching of rhetoric by the influence of women involved the tone and methods of the classroom. From cold, distanced, demanding lecture-recitation teaching and agonistic competition, rhetoric has become, at its most typical, a personalized editorial coalition and, at its most progressive, an irenic, nurturing partnership between teacher and student.

It is difficult for us today to understand what all-male rhetorical education really was like before 1860, because our own experiences are so different. But in an all-male atmosphere, whether the methods were practical or theoretical, rhetorical instruction meant contest—and kinds of contest that had not changed importantly for millennia. In the practical instruction, the methods used were debates and carefully staged persuasive orations—all opportunities for personal display of talent, for contest, for the thrill of victory and the humiliation of defeat. The theoretical instruction, too, was intensely agonistic, using memorization and defense of theses or lecture-and-recitation methods that asked students to take detailed notes of the master's theoretical lecture one day and spit back his own words to him the next in a detailed catechetical recitation. Anyone in a class could be chosen to recite, and woe betide the unprepared reciter, who would be subjected to the severest humiliation and scorn from the master at any hint of error in reciting. "Habitual duel for those in the ranks provided the indispensable sense of security for the men in command," as Laurence Veysey puts it (299).

This constant testing defined the school and college curriculum. It was a tense, rigorous, and demanding curriculum, one that required good students to be perpetually ready to pick up a challenge, answer a point, refute a position, come up with a turn of phrase, and in general protect their vitals from one another and from the master. It is in this kind of agonistic school situation that the long-standing hostility that existed between college faculties and college students grew up.

Education in all-male institutions was set up as a struggle for dominance; one had to wrest authority from the teacher by proving one could "master" the subject—and the proof was by ordeal. The closest comparable phenomena we have today to the older forms of education are probably military boot camps and certain sports rituals; but even these are short-lived reflections of the continuous conduct of all-male education in the past. There was no sense in which student and teacher were assumed to be friends; that is a modern concept. For students of most colleges before 1850, the faculty

was the enemy. This may seem a strong statement, but to anyone who has looked into college histories, the dark side of student-faculty relations is very clear.[1] There was no camaraderie and little personal interaction. As W. L. Phelps has testified, the classroom atmosphere was often poisoned by distance, humiliation, and constant testing: "In the classroom, [the faculty's] manners had an icy formality; humour was usually absent, except for occasional irony at the expense of a dull student" (qtd. in Veysey, 295).

The dislike that students often felt for faculty members is not hard to understand, in light of the power of the old-time faculty and the ways they could use it. Before the growth of an administrative bureaucracy in the nineteenth century, all conditions of colleges were set by faculty vote. As Burton Bledstein puts it in *The Culture of Professionalism*, "the tutor played the role of a judge rather than a teacher, and his relationship to the students was normally imperious and unfriendly. The feelings of antagonism were mutual" (229). Of course, this antagonism usually played itself out verbally, and thus rhetorically, in the continuing ritualized test, attack, and defense of the agonistic oral educational tradition. Up until the midnineteenth century, most final exams were oral and public. They were ordeals, and anyone might press the candidate with questions: "College graduates in the audience, like the masters of arts in the medieval universities, were privileged to inject questions of their own or to criticize the answers of the candidates" (Schmidt, 100). This system, which can be traced back to the classical period, often led to lasting distrust and bad feeling between students and teachers. Although students often hated this contestive milieu, faculty members felt that such testing was their only certain method of inculcating knowledge. In the words of Lawrence Veysey, "Only one tactic remained at the disposal of their superiors: the compulsory examination, given at rapid intervals. The continuity of the frequent classroom test in the American system of higher education, from the days of the small colleges down into the period of the new university, revealed a similar continuity of student alienation from the system of which he was supposedly the most essential part" (298). Today, of course, such testing is minimized, and we tend to see professors who engage deeply in it as pathologues; for us, the "defense" of the doctoral dissertation or master's thesis is a curious relic, an atrophied survival of a harder time no one remembers. Few doctoral candidates really have to stand and fight for their theses against determined professorial foes, and it is hard for us to imagine what a student-teacher bond of distrust and hostility might mean.

Among other things, such a relationship meant that the fixed lines of ritual agonism sometimes slipped, and the contest became physical rather than merely verbal. Between 1800 and 1875, there were violent rebellions of students against faculty at Princeton, Miami, Amherst, Brown, the University of South Carolina, the University of North Carolina, Williams, Georgetown, Harvard, Yale, Dartmouth, Lafayette, Bowdoin, City College of New York, Dickinson, and DePauw. Princeton alone saw six violent riots against the faculty between 1800 and 1830. At Virginia, professors were publicly whipped by mobs, and one was shot to death. The president of Oakland College in

Mississippi was stabbed to death. At Yale, one tutor was fatally wounded and another maimed by students. Stonings of faculty houses and other minor acts of violence were too common to catalogue. One paradigmatic episode occurred in 1855 at Davidson College, where the students rioted because their mathematics problems were too difficult. They barricaded themselves inside a dormitory and threw rocks at the faculty members who came to investigate. "One of the latter," reports George P. Schmidt, "a West Pointer, drew a sword, and, following his lead, the professors advanced on the dormitory, battered down the door with an ax, and suppressed the rebellion" (82–83).

It is not surprising, in such an atmosphere of persistent anxiety, insecurity, hostility, and contest, that rhetoric and debate would be important subjects. Prior to 1875, almost all students studied rhetoric, and many joined the extracurricular debating societies that were ornaments of almost every college. Such courses and clubs did prepare students for professional life at the bar or in the pulpit, of course, but they were also popular for the same reason that martial arts schools and street gangs now proliferate in tough neighborhoods: if you are liable to attack, self-defense skills are important. Being able to handle yourself verbally was a prime requisite of success in all-male colleges. Life there before 1875 was in many senses a contest (if not a battle), and rhetoric was the primary weapon.

When women entered colleges, this agonistic rhetorical culture was swept away, and rhetoric itself was changed forever. The primary effect of co-education was the quick decline of public contest as a staple of college life. As Ong argues, the agonistic impulse is a purely male-against-male phenomenon. Males perceive it as honorable to struggle ritually—either physically or verbally—with other males. Even to be bested in such contests preserves honor, if one has obeyed the rules of the contest. The winner and the loser have established a hierarchy they agree on and can shake hands. But to struggle in ritual contest with a *woman?* It was unthinkable. There was no precedent for it, and no psychological rationale (Ong, 51–96). Fighting with a woman, to the agonistically charged male, is ignoble on the face of it. To be victorious in such a contest would confer only slightly less shame and loss of face than to be defeated. Real men don't fight women. Thus, when women entered the educational equation in colleges, the whole edifice built on ritual contest between teacher and student and between student and student came crashing down.

We see evidence of this great change everywhere in reports of college experiences between 1860 and 1900. Living arrangements changed, of course, but of more interest to us are the differences in academic life. The tone of classroom interchange underwent a rapid shift in coed colleges. From having been arenas of contest, the lecture halls and recitation rooms became forums of irenic discussion. The atmosphere changed from one of boredom punctuated by anxiety and hostility to one more decorous. During this period, the lecture-recitation and thesis-defense methods of earlier days gave way to discussion-centered classes, laboratory methods, and seminars—all of

which, it will be noted, minimize the agonism inherent in the constant testing of recitation methods. Participation in classes became elective rather than compulsory, and professors' judgments on student work shifted from oral to written.

Thus, the entire contestive edge of criticism was blunted by distance and undermined by teachers' unwillingness to press women with questions in any "ungentlemanly" way. Professors did not wish to humiliate women by forcing them to match wits or publicly prove their knowledge; male students did not want to look churlish or stupid in front of "the girls." Andrew Dickson White notes that life at the University of Michigan, his alma mater, had changed since coeducation: "Formerly a professor's lecture- or recitation-room had been decidedly a roughish place. . . . Now all was quiet and orderly, the dress of the students much neater." When White asked an old janitor, " 'Do the students still make life a burden to you?' he answered, 'Oh, no, that is all gone by. They can't rush each other up and down the staircases or have boxing-matches in the lobbies any longer, for the girls are there' " (400–01). The tone of classrooms changed completely, and this change was most marked in rhetoric classrooms.

Form: From Public Speaking to Private Composition

The most obvious change in rhetorical instruction itself resulting from these changes was the decline of oral rhetoric and the ascent of writing: the shift from rhetoric as public speaking to rhetoric as composition. To understand this shift, we must first look at oral rhetoric as it related to women prior to the changes that coeducation brought. Women, as early as Anne Hutchinson, had demanded the right to be public speakers, but the culture, still held in check by Pauline stricture, consistently placed blocks in their ways. Public speaking was for men, not for women; most women would not imagine their world being any different. The U.S. Supreme Court, denying Myra Bradwell the right to be an attorney, opined that "the natural and proper timidity and delicacy which belongs to the female sex evidently unfits it for many of the occupations of civil life. . . . The paramount destiny and mission of woman are to fulfill the noble and benign offices of wife and mother. This is the law of the Creator" (Bradwell v. Illinois, 16 Lawrence 130 [1873]). Even educated women knew they had no chance of practicing civic oratory, as Molly Wallace's valedictory oration of 1792 at the Young Ladies Academy of Philadelphia shows: "But yet it may be asked, what has a female character to do with declamation? That she should harangue at the head of an Army, in the Senate, or before a popular Assembly, is not pretended, neither is it requested that she ought to be an adept in the stormy and contentious eloquence of the bar, or in the abstract and subtle reasoning of the Senate—we look not for a female Pitt, Cicero, or Demosthenes" (*Rise and Progress*, 74).

We hear over and over again in the nineteenth century the same refrain: the proper province of women is the home, not the public assembly. In 1837, the Congregational ministers of Massachusetts responded with a harsh

pastoral letter to abolitionist Angelina Grimke's daring to speak to public mixed audiences. The letter condemned "the mistaken conduct of those who encourage females to bear an obtrusive and ostentatious part in measures of reform, and countenance any of that sex who so far forget themselves as to itinerate in the character of public lecturers or teachers" (Hosford, 82).

The situation of rhetorical instruction for women mirrored these attitudes. The early women's seminaries did teach rhetoric to their charges, but it was a curiously old-fashioned analytical rhetoric, not the praxis-based active rhetoric taught to men. Catherine Beecher's Hartford Female Seminary taught rhetoric in the 1830s using Pestalozzian methods that did not include actual speaking: "In rhetoric and logic, the classes are required to analyze the ideas, arguments, and arrangement of certain pieces pointed out by the teacher. They are also required to compose examples of the various figures of rhetoric, and of the various modes of argument, syllogisms, etc., pointed out in logic" (Woody, I, 433). Rhetoric in the Jacksonian era was still essentially argumentative (and even brawling) and could be fed to women only in harmless bits and pieces, stripped of its popular uses. Though women's academies and colleges were founded in increasing numbers through the 1820s and 1830s, the public arts of oratory and debate were forbidden at many women's colleges; the prospectus of Vassar in 1865 announced that methods of education would be womanly and that "no encouragement would be given to oratory and debate." Debating societies, so popular at men's colleges, were pronounced "utterly incongruous and out of taste" for women (Hosford, 83).

This phenomenon is illustrated by the experience of the women at Oberlin College, the first American college to permit coeducation. In the early years, the women of Oberlin, though trained using Whately's argument-based *Elements of Rhetoric,* were given only written composition to do and were denied oratorical training. As Frances Hosford says in her history of co-education at Oberlin, "The women of our earlier decades found every approach to public speaking closed to them, because nobody supposed that any woman in her senses would try to become either a minister or a lawyer. . . . Accordingly, the undergraduate men were trained in debate and oratory, the undergraduate women in essay writing" (71–72).

The women formed a Ladies' Literary Society, after being refused permission to join the men's debating society, and read essays and poems to each other at meetings. They were forbidden, however, to conduct debates, either in class or at meetings, and so in the 1840s Lucy Stone and Antoinette Brown formed a clandestine women's debating society. This society met first in the woods, then in the parlor of a local woman's house, and was forced to post sentinels whenever it met. "We shall leave this college with the reputation of a thorough collegiate course," Stone said at the first meeting, "yet not one of us has received any rhetorical or elocutionary training. Not one of us could state a question or argue it in a successful debate. For this reason I have proposed the formation of this association" (94–95).

The gradual admission of women to the mysteries of rhetoric could not, however, be long gainsaid. They were too insistent, and the reasons for denying them were too weak. Women would be given access to rhetoric or they would take it. We see the crumbling barriers clearly reflected in the changing Oberlin commencement ceremonies. Traditionally, each graduate gave a short, carefully prepared oration at commencement, speaking from memory. In 1841, when the first women were graduated, the college faced the question of what to do with them. Clearly, they must get some recognition, yet they could not be allowed to speak or to sit on the stage. The solution, as reported by the college: "To avoid the impropriety of having the young ladies read from a platform arranged for the speaking of young men, and filled with trustees and professors and distinguished gentleman visitors, the essays of the lady college graduates were read by the professor of rhetoric, the young women coming upon the platform with their class at the close to receive their diplomas" (67–68). Here the private, interior, "feminine" world of writing is clearly juxtaposed with the world of rough display allowed the men. The women agitated against this structure, so demeaning to them as scholars, but it was not until 1859 that they were allowed even to read their own essays upon the stage at commencement. This reading of essays by graduating women persisted for a decade; the graduating men continued to declaim their memorized orations, while the women were expected to read their essays in a monotone, hands at sides, eyes on text. Then came Harriet Keeler of the class of 1870, a known suffragette and radical. She did not plead for the right to join the men in oratory at commencement, to the relief of her professors. As Hosford tells it,

> She did not raise any issue before the crucial moment—and then she stormed and took the last line of defense. Demurely she tripped upon the stage, holding the conventional pages like the other sweet girl graduates. Demurely she read the first sentence, eyes modestly fixed upon her manuscript—and then the paper was discarded, the brave eyes swept the rows of startled faces, and the sweet girl graduate addressed the audience! (102)

The docents of Oberlin held out for four more years and then, in 1874, gave in and allowed full female participation in graduation oratory. The days of such oratory were numbered, though, and by 1885 the custom was done away with completely except for the valedictory address.

As women's colleges became more common and coeducation spread from Oberlin to other schools, teachers of rhetoric, concerned with protecting and developing their discipline, found themselves in an uncomfortable position. Rhetorical theory, which had since 1783 been led in the direction of belles lettres and writing by Hugh Blair's *Lectures*, was beginning by 1830 to turn back toward more traditional oral and argumentative elements under the influence of Richard Whately's *Elements of Rhetoric* of 1828. Just as it seemed Aristotelian argumentative rhetoric was picking up steam, however,

teachers began to find themselves facing classes of women. As discussed earlier, argument and debate could not be major parts of a women's course, and oral thesis defense or thrust-and-parry was out of the question. A new sort of rhetorical instruction was needed, one that minimized the agonistic. Women's colleges and coeducational schools turned increasingly, as had Oberlin, to a form of discourse that no one found threatening from women: written composition. Composition had been a subject in both grammar schools and academies since the early part of the century, of course, but with the beginning of women's education it was given strong impetus in colleges as well.[2] Rhetoric needed to be purged of its public and oratorical elements in order for it to become a safe subject for both men and women. And, between 1840 and 1890, that is what happened, as rhetoric became composition.

Composition was a safer subject than rhetoric to teach to women or to mixed classes for several reasons. Unlike the hurly-burly of oral rhetorical praxis, the composition class was quiet. Writing is an essentially private and interiorized discourse function, and even reading essays aloud creates a distance between reader and audience that oral rhetorical speech is deliberately designed to do away with. The intimacy of rhetorical engagement is thus minimized, as is the opportunity for self-display. Composition is contestive only in the most abstract fashion, because it demands from the teacher no public judgments, no invidious comparisons. The judgment of writing was often given in private conferences or in the form of a written comment. The criteria of good performance in writing were easier to objectify; this attempt at objectification characterizes the composition textbooks of the nineteenth century. Composition, usually taught using a plethora of belletristic models, was more culturally oriented, more literary, more in tune with traditional educational goals for women.

This is not to suggest that composition displaced rhetoric only because women threatened male dominance within traditional oral rhetorical training. There were other important reasons for the rise of written-discourse education: the needs of an increasingly far-flung industrial society for cross-continental communication, the rise of an indigenous literary-intellectual culture centered in the Northeast, the egalitarian system of common schooling that guaranteed an increasing percentage of the population basic literacy skills, and the incentive to refine these skills. The culture needed and came more and more to respect writing. However, these reasons for the growth of written rhetoric, real though they are, do not explain the sharp and unprecedented decay of oral rhetoric and of education in oratory, debate, and argument. Why did oral rhetoric, central to education since ancient Athens, the heart of the trivium, one of the first chairs at any university, decline so ruinously in forty years? That falloff can best be explained by the draining away of public agonism in colleges and the consequent collapse of the educational tradition that had grown up to support it. Written composition—private, multimodal, interiorizing—could be the province of both men and women; public oratory, since it could no longer be the province of men only, ceased to satisfy male psychological needs and was allowed to fall into desuetude.

As women were storming and winning the gates of rhetoric, rhetoric could only mutate. More and more textbooks appeared each year with writing, not speaking, as their primary agenda and, eventually, as their only agenda. In Hugh Blair's *Lectures*, and Richard Whately's *Elements of Rhetoric*, the most popular textbooks in the first half of the nineteenth century, we see the increasingly theoretical nature of rhetoric; from this theoretical base, rhetoric became increasingly differentiated from elocutionary training, which was overtly oral in nature. Textbooks in composition and rhetoric like Samuel Newman's *Practical System*, James Boyd's *Elements*, and George Quackenbos's *Advanced Course* were very popular in women's and coeducational colleges. By 1850, rhetoric had bifurcated into two lines: elocution, which declined, and composition, which prospered and strengthened.

Oberlin's division between men's rhetoric classes and women's essay-writing classes is not singular; throughout coeducational colleges, women were encouraged to study rhetoric as writing or as analysis. In 1867, Sophia Jex-Blake, an Englishwoman, visited various American colleges as an observer of this noble experiment. Oberlin was first on her list, but she also traveled to Hillsdale College in Ohio and to the Mary Institute of Washington University in St. Louis, then on to Antioch College. At both Hillsdale and the Mary Institute, the Oberlin procedure of allowing women "exercises in Composition" weekly, while the men were doing "Composition, Declamation, and Extempore Speaking," was followed. The only rhetoric texts in use at the Mary Institute were Newman's and Boyd's composition-oriented rhetorics and Schlegel's *Dramatic Art and Literature*. At Hillsdale, the women got Quackenbos as freshmen and Whately as juniors but no exercise in oral rhetoric. At radical Antioch, she found the situation somewhat more equal. There was no "Ladies' Course," and "Rhetorical Exercises and English Composition" were expected of everyone.

Oral public discourse was no longer a male enclave, and, its secret agonistic agenda attenuating, it slowly withered. This is not, however, the place for a complete discussion of the decline of oral discourse teaching in America during the latter part of the nineteenth century. Marie Hochmuth and Richard Murphy, writing from a speech-communications point of view, clearly demonstrate how obvious was the decline in elocution. Up until 1825, rhetoric had encompassed writing and its oral delivery, but after 1830 or so the oral aspect of rhetoric, elocution, was increasingly treated as a separate subject. Elocution, which was launched in American colleges around 1825 by the texts of Ebenezer Porter, Jonathan Barbour, and James Rush, hit a tremendous peak of popularity around 1850 and declined thereafter—in almost exact correlation with the entry of women into colleges. Rhetoric was gradually dissociated from the oral agonistic skills of elocution, however, and as Warren Guthrie states, professional connections were shifting as college departments formed: "By 1850 the grouping was not so frequently 'Rhetoric and Oratory' as 'Rhetoric and Belles Lettres' or 'Rhetoric and Composition,' with delivery now relegated to the tremendously popular 'Elocution'" (69).

After the Civil War, however, elocution—especially the old agonistic sort—fell on hard times, for reasons discussed above. It was demoted from a requirement to an elective at most colleges and lost prestige rather sharply, except in the traditionalist (and all-male) colleges of the East, where elocution held on longest. During this time, oral rhetoric and elocution were also changing character, as the old persuasive orations gave way to multimodal and literary effusions in oral, as well as written, discourse. Especially influential in this movement were the theories of the French actor and music teacher François Delsarte (1811–1871), under whose influence "public speaking" began to have a more aesthetic and literary character. From the old, stern Ciceronian tradition of civic oration, public speaking gradually became histrionics, dramatic readings, "interpretations" of poetry, and a host of other completely nonagonistic performances (Shaver, 210). In these, of course, women could share much more easily, and they did.

Earlham College, a coeducational Quaker school, established in 1888 the first speech department in America. Speech contests Earlham was involved in included both orations and dramatic readings and interpretations, but after 1883 there were more dramatic interpretations, as the Quaker ban on dramatics broke down. Such readings as "The Guardian Angel" and a pantomime called "The Romance of Mary Jane" were common, and eventually readings from Shakespeare became most popular. Debating began in 1897, but, in spite of women being allowed in oratorical contests, all debate team members mentioned in Earlham records are men (Thornburg, 216–17).

The last hurrah of oral agonistic rhetoric was, in fact, intercollegiate debate. George Pierce Baker of Harvard was instrumental in setting up these debates in the late 1880s, but the vogue for them was brief. We might view intercollegiate debating as a hothouse flower, a forced blossom of agonism made to grow artificially in a place where it no longer took natural root. As at Earlham, college debating in general was overwhelmingly male-dominated. It never made much headway, however. Bliss Perry describes his own attempts to popularize debate at Princeton during the fin de siècle: "Oratory was beginning in the eighteen-nineties to lose vogue in all the eastern colleges, and the best I could do at Princeton in that field was to prop up for a while a building that was doomed to fall" (135). By the turn of the century even the brief revival of oral agonistic discourse provided by the intercollegiate debate movement was expiring.

Meanwhile, the composition strand of rhetorical studies was rapidly gaining strength at all institutions. Written composition had absolute predominance in actual teaching time after 1870, and college composition courses became an almost universal requirement at exactly the same point when elocution courses were being remanded to elective status. Between 1870 and 1900, rhetoric became, for all intents and purposes, composition. As Albert Kitzhaber shows, after around 1850 most rhetoric texts concentrated on composition, with oratory mentioned, if at all, only as one of the various types of composition (138). By 1885, the term *rhetoric* had begun to give way

to the term *composition* at most schools, and we seldom see it in textbook titles after 1895. The Harvard Reports and the uproar over "illiteracy" sealed the fate of the older oral rhetoric, already on the decline. Composition, that quiet, multimodal, private, non-threatening discourse that could be the province of both men and women, ruled the day.

MODE: FROM ARGUMENT TO MULTIMODALITY

In addition to the change from oral to written discourse, the latter part of the nineteenth century saw a startling decline in the importance of argument and a corresponding rise in interest in other sorts of expression. This transition began long before women entered higher education, of course; multimodal perspectives on rhetoric can be seen as far back as Augustine's *De Doctrina*, and serious modern discussion of nonargumentative modes of discourse began with Adam Smith's rhetoric lectures in 1749 (Connors 1984). The idea that discourse could have ends more valuable than mere persuasion gained credibility from George Campbell's *Philosophy of Rhetoric* of 1776 and was popularized—at least tacitly—by Blair's *Lectures* of 1783, which concentrated on written genres as much as on the traditional oration.

Under Blair's influence, multimodal rhetoric became theoretically very influential in the first three decades of the nineteenth century. Richard Whately's *Elements of Rhetoric* of 1828, however, denied that rhetoric should be "the Art of Composition, universally," and proposed "to treat of Argumentative Composition, generally and exclusively" (6). Whately's book was, next to Blair's immensely popular lectures, the most widely used rhetoric text in American colleges between 1835 and 1865, going through at least fifty-one American printings, and between 1840 and 1850 it began to displace Blair's as the most popular rhetoric text. Under Whately's aegis, it seemed that argument as the primary genre of rhetoric might reappear. We see from the National Union Catalogue records, however, that the popularity of *Elements* diminished substantially after the Civil War, and though it was in print until 1893, only a few colleges used it as a text after 1870.

The reason for the rejection of Whately's text was the increasing popularity of rhetoric textbooks proposing several different modes of discourse. Beginning with Newman's *Practical System* of 1827, American rhetoric textbooks—increasingly and obviously composition textbooks—were supplementing Whatelian argumentative rhetoric with other modes. Teachers were coming to prefer books that offered concrete treatments of the different sorts of communication aims writing obviously served. As writing displaced oral rhetoric, the older insistence on a single argumentative purpose did not serve, and in 1866 the desire for a multimodal rhetorical system was met by Alexander Bain, whose *English Composition and Rhetoric* provided the multimodal system that remains definitive to this day (the "forms" or "modes" of discourse): narration, description, exposition, and argument. Bain's modes by no means constituted the only multimodal system—between 1850 and 1880 more than a dozen modal systems were advanced—but his was the

most popular. It advanced unstoppably into almost absolute acceptance. Within three decades, argument had been displaced; from being the heart of rhetoric, argument became merely one of its forms (Connors 1981). After 1885, the modes of discourse and their related subset, the "methods of exposition," held complete sway. Rhetoric would never again be taught solely as argument, and in fact, expository discourse would gradually come to be the prime desideratum of composition courses.

Like the reasons for the displacement of oral rhetoric by writing, the reasons for the demotion of argument are not singular. Rhetorics that took nonargumentative forms as important had been around for years, and their acceptance and growth merely confirms the validity of nonargumentative aims and their growing importance to a pragmatic and education-minded culture. Even so, however, acceptance of the Bainian modes—of modal rhetoric in general—is so startling and sudden in the years after 1870 that it gives us pause. At least one important reason for the decline of unimodal rhetoric is the decline of public agonism in colleges and the resultant lack of interest in agonism's central genre, argument.

This decline worked itself out quite pragmatically. As women entered colleges, the older rhetoric courses organized around argument and public contest made men (and some women) uncomfortable. Agonistic behavior directed against women during these Victorian times was really disquieting to many. Part of the reason that oral rhetoric declined at coeducational schools was that many *women* did not want it. President Mahan of Oberlin, whose rhetoric course used Whately's *Elements*, sincerely believed in coeducation but found that many women in his first coeducational class, even with his encouragement, refused to face the men in public contest (Bledstein, 133). Elsewhere, the argument-based courses caused similar discomfort, as college men were asked by professors to do the ungentlemanly, unthinkable act of verbally attacking young women. Argumentative battle that had been psychologically meaningful in all-male courses was now, to many men, dishonorable. The overt agonism of rhetorical argument was more than could be borne, and the only solution was to demote argument and allow for other aims within rhetoric.

ASSIGNMENT: FROM ABSTRACT TO CONCRETE

Related to the decline of argument was the slightly later change in the kinds of writing and speaking assignments teachers gave to students. Between 1820 and 1900 the sorts of knowledge that a student in a rhetoric class was expected to command changed radically, in ways that reflected declining agonism (Connors 1987). Students in the older oral rhetoric classes were given abstract, impersonal subjects on which to write and orate. Before 1860, such subjects as "The Baneful Effects of Indulgence" and "The Happiness of Innocence" were commonly assigned—subjects that assumed considerable previous cultural knowledge and had tacit but clear bases in argument. After 1860, however, such abstract topics were increasingly supplanted by subjects based

in personal observation—"A Pleasant Evening" or "Of What Use are Flowers?" These descriptive essays were finally joined in the late 1880s and 1890s by assignments that were concrete and overtly personal in nature—"When My Ship Comes In" and "An Incident From School Life." The rhetorical tasks assigned students during the nineteenth century are indeed one long retreat from abstraction and from subjects based outside of immediate cultural and personal experience.

In part, of course, the rise of personal subjects is explicable as further evidence of romanticism as it entered and came to dominate the psychic climate of the century. Personal writing reflected the literary writing and personally based essays that became popular during the first third of the nineteenth century—exemplified in the work of Lamb, Hazlitt, and Carlyle. It can also be understood as a result of the change from oral- to written-discourse education. It is only natural that as oral-discourse education—public by nature— gave way to writing, the subjects of rhetoric would become smaller scale, more private, more personal. But this change can also be seen as evidence of the decline of agonistic discourse that resulted from women's entrance into the colleges. Personal writing, for whatever reason, had not been a part of rhetoric for twenty-four hundred years, and its admission to rhetoric corresponds exactly to the admission of women to rhetoric courses.

Why might this be? Abstract subjects of the older sort are inherently related to agonistic contest. A large part of dealing with nonpersonal subjects involves the obvious deployment of hard-won extrapersonal knowledge; even if the discourse aim is purportedly explanatory, the most effective rhetor is the one who seems to know the most about the world. That is one important method of establishing ethos, the reputation for good character, knowledge, and perspicacity central to any effective appeal. Indeed, this question of ethos and how much a speaker had to know (or seem to know) was a central issue for both Cicero and Quintilian. They were aware that careful use of abstract knowledge—from maxims to precedents to witness to myth—was the very cornerstone of ethos, which was the heart of rhetoric.

Public display of extrapersonal knowledge is agonistic, as every political debate shows and as every serious player of the board game Trivial Pursuit knows well. Even if such fact-based discourse is not explicitly argumentative, it has as a part of its agenda serious display of self. Dazzling listeners with wit, command of facts, and impressive analysis has been a traditional part of ritual male attitudes toward other males. All of the contemporary male verbal agonistic rituals—flyting, the dozens, trading sports statistics, rapping— are displays of skill with facts and knowledge, not merely displays of argument. While they may sometimes seem to be personal, these rituals actually put fictive personae in play in fictive contests. What is at stake here is the ability to manipulate the stuff of language and of the world. Personal interests and personal confession have to do with these contests only tangentially.

In rhetoric, personal observation writing assignments grew out of teachers' frustrations with the paucity of traditional abstract knowledge noted in college students after 1870, as an ever growing percentage of Americans

attempted college. In place of the truly abysmal writing that increasingly resulted from assignments like "Filial Affection," teachers came to ask for and accept writing based on personal observation. But as opposed to neutral observation, personal narrations and personal feeling assignments were something new in rhetoric, and such a concession cannot be completely explained without looking at the rise of coeducation. There were elements of confession, of intimate personalism, and of antiagonistic admission of weakness in the new topics that could not have existed prior to women's entrance into higher education. "The Loneliness of Freshmen," a suggested topic of 1912, would have been unthinkable half a century earlier; even admitting such a feeling as loneliness would have been hooted at as unmanly in the all-male college of 1860.

Personal writing has been traditionally, though not exclusively, associated with women more than with men. Carol Gilligan, Belenky and her colleagues, and many other feminist critics and scholars have remarked on the commitment to personal feelings and individual emotional reality found in women's writing, and although that case is not accepted by all feminist scholars, it is taken very seriously. Less investigated by scholarship has been the degree to which males are uncomfortable with personal effusions, but evidence does exist in the journal analyses of Cinthia Gannett, who found a clear dichotomy between the full, rich, personal lives recorded in the women's journals in her freshman class and the narrow, uncomfortable, agonistic mentality found in most male journals. The rise of personal subjects in composition is related strongly to women's colleges and to coeducation. Although coeducation was only one influence among many on the changing of rhetorical assignments between 1870 and 1900, if women had not entered the world of higher education, we would today inhabit a very different rhetorical world.

EPILOGUE: THE CREATION OF THE PRESENT

The entry of women into higher education had a profound effect on college rhetoric. In 1870, 1 percent of college faculty were women; by 1890, that figure had risen to 19 percent. By 1920, 33 percent of all bachelors' degrees were awarded to women. Although the early 1920s were a high point for the percentage of women undergraduate and graduate students—after that time, their numbers lagged and at times declined until the 1970s—the great changes in American education had been wrought by 1900. No more was it, or would it be, an all-male world. And composition, more than any other one of the humanities, was influenced by women at all levels. By 1900, over 90 percent of high-school English teachers were female, and when the *English Journal* was begun in 1911 by the fledgling NCTE, women were substantial contributors to it. (By 1920, more than 50 percent of *English Journal* essays were written by women.) During this century, the influence on composition teaching style and methods of these ever larger groups of women teachers and students has been immeasurable.

I do not mean to suggest that the teaching of composition has ever been completely feminized, or that agonistic elements have been purged from writing instruction, or that the feminization of rhetoric has created a perfect world. No one could claim that composition since 1900 has been an irenic love feast or that many of its conditions have been satisfying for teachers or students. However, composition as it has developed is vastly less agonistic than the rhetorical instruction that preceded it; composition has been and remains one of the most feminized college-level disciplines.

It is also, unfortunately, true that composition has been marginalized by the academy, in part at least because it has been so heavily staffed by non-Ph.D.s, especially women. During the first three decades of the twentieth century, between 7 and 16 percent of men in graduate school achieved Ph.D.s within a decade, but that figure never rose from between 3 and 5 percent for women (John 1935, 13–19). Despite the rise in absolute numbers of women in graduate school and the absolute number of female Ph.D.s, there were vastly larger percentages of uncompleted female than male Ph.D.s. Since the Ph.D. was a virtual prerequisite for promotion from instructor rank, most of these women, if they chose to remain in college teaching, were forced to settle into the rank of permanent instructor. And, indeed, Warner Taylor's study in 1929 shows that, of all composition instruction nationwide, 38 percent was being conducted by female instructors (22). This is certainly the highest percentage of female instruction found anywhere in colleges, with the exception of the home economics and nursing departments, and it has surely risen since 1929 (Connors 1990).

The relation between composition theory and women teachers and students during the twentieth century is a fascinating subject, but it cannot be taken up here. Suffice it to say that the current whole-language, writing-process, and social-construction models of teaching seem to be continuing the retreat from agonistic rhetoric that began with coeducation over a century ago. The teaching of composition has been in the hands of women for a long time, but in the last three decades it has evolved into a truly feminized and academically equal discipline—probably the most feminized discipline outside of women's studies. Until the 1970s, the majority of composition theorists were male, but since then a clear preponderance of the most interesting young voices in the field have been women's. No one looking at Ph.D.s in composition since 1980 can doubt that the future of the field—already highly feminized—will be increasingly in the hands of women. So, too, the actual teaching of writing and the direction of that teaching on both secondary and college levels are coming increasingly into the hands of women.

As feminist scholars have pointed out, agonism is not gone from the teaching of writing, and in a pedagogically pluralistic world, it can never—and should never—be gone. Argument and debate, teacher criticism, hierarchies, and personal contest of all subtle sorts will always be with us. But they are no longer at the heart of our discipline, because we have ceased excluding the other half that each man and woman possesses—the nurturing, supportive, interiorized, personal elements in human character that were so long

ignored or sneered at while rhetoric was exclusively male ritual. The task remains ahead of us to develop rhetorical pedagogies that give students access to both sides of themselves, that shortchange neither the outer world of demand, action, struggle, and change nor the inner world of feeling, introspection, and the myriad meanings of the self. Only by nurturing the abilities to deal in both worlds will we be able to say we have been teachers of the whole person.

NOTES

1. I do not, of course, want to claim that all teachers were hated, that all students disliked teachers. There were always, as there are today, extraordinary teachers who were beloved and remembered fondly by their students. Indeed, the fond and nostalgic reminiscences such teachers often provoked from their students years later have grown into a sizable subgenre of literature—a subgenre, I would claim, that has perhaps blinded our eyes to the majority of teacher-student relations that were not eulogized by loving disciples. But these teachers have been the exceptions, not the rule.

2. It is interesting to note that Writing and Composition were at first separate subjects in the women's colleges, the former an adult literacy course involving penmanship and word forms, the latter a course in written rhetoric. Woody shows a steep decline in writing courses after 1830 in female seminaries and a strong increase in rhetoric courses, as the women's schools gave less attention to "practical" educational goals like penmanship and turned to courses patterned on those of the male colleges (418).

BIBLIOGRAPHY

Adams, Charles Francis, E. L. Godkin, and Josiah Quincy. "Report[s] of the Committee on Composition and Rhetoric." Reports no. XXVIII, XLIX, and LXXI. In *Reports of the Visiting Committees of the Board of Overseers of Harvard College*, 117–57, 275–87, 401–24. Cambridge, Mass.: Harvard University Press, 1902.

Bain, Alexander. *English Composition and Rhetoric*. London: Longmans, Green, 1866.

Belenky, Mary Field, Blythe McVicker Clinchy, Nancy Rule Goldberger, and Jill Mattuck Tarule. *Women's Ways of Knowing: The Development of Self, Voice, and Mind*. New York: Basic Books, 1986.

Blair, Hugh. *Lectures on Rhetoric and Belles Lettres*. London: W. Strahan, 1783.

Bledstein, Burton J. *The Culture of Professionalism*. New York: W. W. Norton, 1976.

Boyd, James. *Elements of Rhetoric and Literary Criticism*. New York: Harper and Brothers, 1844.

Campbell, George. *The Philosophy of Rhetoric*. London: W. Strahan and T. Cadell, 1776.

Connors, Robert J. "The Rise and Fall of the Modes of Discourse." *College Composition and Communication* 32 (1981): 444–55.

———. "The Rhetoric of Explanation from Aristotle to 1850." *Written Communication* 1 (1984): 189–210.

———. "Personal Writing Assignments." *College Composition and Communication* 38 (1987): 166–83.

———. "Overwork/Underpay: The Labor and Status of Composition Teachers Since 1880." *Rhetoric Review* 9 (1990): 108–26.

Douglas, Ann. *The Feminization of American Culture*. New York: Knopf, 1977.

Gannett, Cinthia. *Gender and the Journal: Diaries and Academic Discourse*. Albany: State Univ. of New York Press, 1992.

Gilligan, Carol. *In a Different Voice: Psychological Theory and Women's Development*. Cambridge: Harvard Univ. Press, 1982.

Glenn, Cheryl. *Muted Voices from Antiquity through the Renaissance: Locating Women in the Rhetorical Tradition.* Ph.D. diss., Ohio State University, 1989.

Gordon, Ann D. "The Young Ladies Academy of Philadelphia." In *Women of America: A History,* edited by Carol Ruth Birkin and Mary Beth Norton, 68–91. Boston: Houghton Mifflin, 1979.

Guthrie, Warren. "Development of Rhetorical Theory in America, 1635–1850." *Speech Monographs* 15 (1948): 61–71.

Hochmuth, Marie, and Richard Murphy. "Rhetorical and Elocutionary Training in Nineteenth-Century Colleges." In *History of Speech Education in America,* edited by Wallace, 153–77. 1954.

Hosford, Frances Juliette. *Father Shipherd's Magna Charta: A Century of Coeducation at Oberlin College.* Boston: Marshall Jones, 1937.

Jex-Blake, Sophia. *A Visit to Some American Schools and Colleges.* London: Macmillan, 1867.

John, Walton C. *Graduate Study in Universities and Colleges in the United States.* Washington, D.C.: U.S. Government Printing Office, 1935.

Kitzhaber, Albert R. *Rhetoric in American Colleges, 1850–1900.* Ph.D. diss., University of Washington, 1953.

Newman, Samuel. *Practical System of Rhetoric.* New York: Mark H. Newman, 1846.

Ong, Walter. *Fighting for Life: Contest, Sexuality, and Consciousness.* Ithaca: Cornell Univ. Press, 1981.

Perry, Bliss. *And Gladly Teach.* Boston: Houghton Mifflin, 1935.

Quackenbos, George. *Advanced Course of Composition and Rhetoric.* New York: D. Appleton, 1854.

The Rise and Progress of the Young-Ladies' Academy of Philadelphia. Philadelphia: Stewart and Cochrane, 1794.

Rudolph, Frederick. *The American College and University: A History.* New York: Knopf, 1962.

Schmidt, George P. *The Liberal Arts College.* New Brunswick: Rutgers Univ. Press, 1957.

Shaver, Claude L. "Steele MacKaye and the Delsartian Tradition." In *History of Speech Education in America,* edited by Wallace, 202–18.

Taylor, Warner. *A National Survey of Conditions in Freshman English.* Research Bulletin 11. Madison: University of Wisconsin, 1929.

Thornburg, Opal. *Earlham: The Story of the College 1847–1862.* Richmond, Ind.: Earlham College Press, 1963.

Veysey, Lawrence R. *The Emergence of the American University.* Chicago: Univ. of Chicago Press, 1965.

Wallace, Karl R., ed. *History of Speech Education in America: Background Studies.* New York: Appleton-Century-Crofts, 1954.

Whately, Richard. *Elements of Rhetoric.* London: John W. Parker, 1846.

White, Andrew Dickson. *Autobiography.* New York: Century, 1905.

Woody, Thomas. *A History of Women's Education in the U.S.* 2 vols. New York: Science Press, 1929.

The Abolition Debate
in Composition: A Short History

At a 1993 conference on "Composition in the Twenty-First Century: Crisis and Change," sponsored by the Council of Writing Program Administrators and supported by Miami University (Ohio) and the University of Connecticut, Bob weighed in on what has become an increasingly acrimonious debate over whether or not first-year writing courses should be required. Published in the proceedings of that conference three years later as "The Abolition Debate in Composition: A Short History," this essay traces the current controversy back to the inception of required writing courses at Harvard in 1885 and then surveys what Bob identifies as "reformist periods" and "abolitionist periods" across the last hundred years. Along the way, Bob notes a shift in attitude and purpose of those favoring abolition, from self-interest ("getting rid of the composition underclass, or allowing professors to teach courses they liked") to student interest (saying that "students are not as well served by the required freshman course as they could be by other kinds of writing instruction") (292). In the end, Bob tips his hand in favor of the New Abolitionism, joining—with not a little irony— scholars such as Sharon Crowley, with whom he had a long-standing agreement to disagree over historical methodology and questions of ideology. As Bob notes in his concluding paragraph, this debate is by no means settled, and like so many of the other contested issues Bob chose to address, this one is marked by his efforts to inform it.

Since the required course in freshman composition was implemented at Harvard in 1885 and quickly adopted by most American colleges and universities, it has been at the heart of a continuing series of arguments about its worth and standing. Arthur N. Applebee has characterized the history of English teaching in America as being marked by periods of tradition and reform, and in this essay I want to borrow one of his terms and, changing its meaning rather seriously, claim that the history of American

From *Composition in the Twenty-First Century: Crisis and Change*, ed. Lynn Z. Bloom, Donald A. Daiker, and Edward M. White (Carbondale: Southern Illinois UP, 1997), 47–63.

higher education in composition over the last century has been marked by alternating periods of what I will call *reformism* and *abolitionism*. During reformist periods, freshman comp, though problematical, is seen as the thin red line protecting the very life of literacy. Abolitionist periods are times during which at least some English teachers call for the end of freshman composition, declaring the large sums expended on this all-but-ubiquitous course a gross waste.

We see reformist periods—some of which are called literacy crises—of deep interest in improving composition, and abolitionist periods, when some teachers declare it too hopeless to reform, repeat themselves several times across the last 10 decades. Each reformist or abolitionist period is to some degree unique, of course, but they do have certain elements in common, and they ebb and flow according to patterns from which we may learn. We are now involved, if I read the signs aright, in the end of a reformist period and in a new period of abolitionist sentiment, and it may well be worthwhile to ask how or whether these New Abolitionists are like the older ones and whether their movement will go the way of the older ones. To understand the New Abolitionists in context, we need to look back.

The required freshman composition course itself is the product of a reformist period. It was created in direct response to the literacy crisis of the period 1875–1885. This is a story that has been told many times by historians, and we need only outline it here. Harvard College, roused by popular debates on literacy and linguistic correctness, had by 1870 become uncomfortably aware that students entering from the academies that served as its feeders were having problems with its demanding classical courses. In response, Harvard instituted its first entrance examinations in written English in 1874. To the horror of professors, parents, and the American intellectual culture as a whole, more than half the students taking the exam failed it. What had been a vague disquiet crystallized into a sharp alarm. Large numbers of American boys from the best schools were incapable of correct writing, and something had to be done. I call this first crisis the "Illiteracy of American Boys" crisis, after E. L. Godkin's inflammatory article written about it in 1897.

The Harvard exam and the continuing problems students had with it (and with the host of similar writing examinations quickly set up by the many colleges that took Harvard for a model) created the first American college literacy crisis and the first experiments in basic writing instruction on the college level. The Harvard examiners began quickly to agitate for better training on the secondary level and for more effective writing instruction on the college level. Adams S. Hill, Boylston Professor of Rhetoric, had argued strongly as early as 1879 that the sophomore rhetoric course be more oriented toward correctness and composition and be made a required course for freshmen: "The next best step [after improving secondary schools] would be to give to English two hours or more a week during the Freshman year"(12). At first, no room could be found for such a requirement during freshman year, but the exam results kept the pressure on, and in 1885 a basic freshman course, "English A," was

offered at Harvard. Its structure solidified quickly. By 1894, the only required courses for freshmen were English A and a modern language (Rudolph 294). By 1897, the only required course at Harvard for any student was English A. Many other colleges took Harvard's lead on all educational issues, and by 1890 the majority of American colleges and universities had established required freshman composition courses. The formation of these courses nation-wide was a great paroxysm of reformist work, a large-scale curricular endeavor that has no parallel I know of in American college history.

And yet it was very soon after 1890 that the first widespread movement to disestablish these new course requirements arose. This first group of abolitionists consisted primarily of literature teachers in what were then newly established English departments. Their dislike of required composition courses was based in their affiliation with Arnoldian idealism, but their essential rationale for abolishing freshman requirements was based on two more practical claims about college composition: first, the required freshman course was never meant as a permanent English offering but was instead a temporary stopgap until the secondary schools could improve; and second, the teaching of required composition was tiresome, labor-intensive, and a bad use of trained literary scholars.

We see both of these attitudes in William Morton Payne's interesting 1895 collection, *English in American Universities*, which contains 20 reports that had originally appeared in *The Dial* in 1894 on the teaching of college English at different institutions. Though most of the reports detail both literature and composition courses being offered, several are fervid in their triumph at having dispensed with required freshman writing altogether. Payne himself, the editor of *The Dial*, was entirely sympathetic to this movement, and his introduction makes clear why: he was a classic exponent of literature teaching who was in favor of the most stringent entrance requirements possible. He was very doubtful about the Eastern colleges' reliance on the freshman course. "As we go West, we do better and better," he says, noting that Indiana, Nebraska, and Stanford had all abolished freshman composition in favor of strong entrance requirements.

As one examines the reports from those schools, however, it is clear that liberal culture was not the only reason for the abolition. Martin Sampson of Indiana writes that "there are no recitations in 'rhetoric.' The bugbear known generally in our colleges as Freshman English is now a part of our entrance requirements" (93). Melville B. Anderson's report on English at Stanford gives us a genuine feel for the earliest abolitionist sentiments; Stanford, he says, has abolished Freshman English: "Had this salutary innovation not been accomplished, all the literary courses would have been swept away by the rapidly growing inundation of Freshman themes, and all our strength and courage would have been dissipated in preparing our students to do respectable work at more happily equipped Universities" (52). We see here the expected liberal-culture attitudes, of course, but more strongly we see pure self-protection on the part of the tenured faculty. They did not want to teach theme writing, and killing the requirement was the easiest way out of it.

This first wave of abolitionism ebbed after 1900, and Anderson's attitude gives us a key to the reasons why: the growing willingness of universities and colleges to draw on lecturers, instructors, and graduate students to teach their required freshman courses. As I have discussed in more detail in "Rhetoric in the Modern University," the rise of academic specialization and the modern hierarchy of ranks in English departments meant that between 1880 and 1900, most tenured professors were gradually relieved of composition duties by younger and less powerful colleagues or by graduate students. Thus the earliest wave of abolitionism, which had been caused by overwork panic among faculty members, receded because the Andersons and Sampsons no longer had to worry themselves about having to teach freshman composition.

The years between 1885 and 1915 saw a tremendous number of critiques of the freshman course launched, but most of them were oriented toward reforming the course. Not until the end of that period do we see a resurgence of the abolitionist sentiment in the famous article "Compulsory Composition in Colleges," which Thomas Lounsbury of Yale published in *Harper's* in 1911. David Russell, in his essay "Romantics on Writing," has done groundbreaking work on Lounsbury and some of the attitudes that have underlain the early forms of abolitionist argument. Russell describes Lounsbury's abolitionist sentiment as a product of a specific kind of educational idealism that sounds today like liberal-culture literary elitism, tinged throughout by Lounsbury's thinly concealed opinion that undergraduate students were ignorant barbarians. To Lounsbury, the idea that expression could be taught was idiotic, the conception that college students could know anything worth writing about silly, and the position that writing teachers could respond usefully to student writing unlikely. Despite his romantic elitism, Lounsbury makes some telling points against compulsory composition. But Lounsbury was an outsider, a literary scholar. Lounsbury presents an early but completely recognizable version of E. D. Hirsch's cultural literacy argument: writing could not be taught as pure practice-based skill without content. His real and obvious sympathy was with those who had a "cultivated taste begotten of familiarity with the great masterpieces of our literature" (876), and until students' minds were thus furnished, they need not apply, to him at least.

This article caused a small sensation in the English-teaching world, and especially in the still-active circle of composition enthusiasts. Lounsbury had repeated several times in his essay that his was an unpopular minority position, but it was taken very seriously. His article was not followed up in *Harper's*, but it created a long discussion in the *Educational Review* in 1913, and we see here the whole modern reformist/abolitionist debate for the first time. Though some of the *ER* correspondents agreed with Lounsbury, the majority did not. Some commentators saw no problem in the freshman course at all, and they actively praised the course as they had experienced it. Others represented the first wave of what might be called status-quo or modern reformism. These correspondents took the position, as all reformists later

would, that the course was imperfect but necessary and that it would be much improved by their suggestions. N. A. Stedman of the University of Texas admitted that freshman English was useful and yielded some good results, but he saw that its "technical" nature created in students "a distaste for English" and proposed that the course be reformed to create more interest in English (53). Lucile Shepherd of the University of Missouri believed that "the course on the whole is admirable" and that with more humanism and a few tinkerings it would be better still (189).

Lounsbury had some clear allies. Carl Zigrosser of Columbia wrote, "In my estimation prescribed work in English is unnecessary" (188), and George Strong of North Carolina huffed, "My own experience with these courses was profitless. It was, in fact, enough to discourage me from continuing the study of English. I failed to derive any benefit whatever from them" (189). In these responses to Lounsbury, we begin to see proposals for that brand of abolitionism later called Writing Across the Curriculum come hard and fast. Preston William Slosson proposed in 1913 that "the real way to make sure that every Columbia graduate, whatever his other failings, can write whatever it may be necessary for him to write as briefly, logically, and effectively as possible, is not to compel him as a freshman to write stated themes on nothing-in-particular but to insist on constant training in expression in every college course" (408).

But finally, the Lounsbury-based discussion petered out sometime around 1915, after having never attained a solid enough base of agreement from the abolitionists. Reformism began to dominate the professional discussion. At least part of the reason for the failure of abolitionism and the segue we see during the mid-1910s into a clearly reformist period has to do with the growing influence of the ideas of John Dewey. Some of the more widely read teachers of composition were beginning to realize that freshman composition could be more than a mere enforcement of mechanical rules. Helen Ogden Mahin, one of the products of Fred Newton Scott's progressive Michigan graduate program, wrote that she was moved to action by Lounsbury. When she asked her freshman students if they would take the course without the requirement, their answers made her see that "nearly two-thirds of these Freshmen, many of whom had entered the course unwillingly, realized before the end of the first semester that their lives had grown in some way broader and fuller then they had been before" (446). This result, Mahin said, controverted Lounsbury's claims. Required composition could be taught, and should be taught, in such a way that students realize that "writing means simply living and expressing life": "From the testimony of the Freshmen themselves and from the actual results shown in their work the conclusion is very well justified that the student of writing who does not in the course of his study, if that study is rightly guided, become a happier, bigger, and more socially efficient being is the student who, unless he is subnormal in intellect, deliberately sets himself against progress" (450). This concept of "English for life skills" and the "more socially efficient being" is instantly recognizable as based in Dewey's ideas. The theory that writing skills *were*

humane learning and inherently broadening was to become a staple claim of reformism for decades.

The reformist period that began after World War I lasted throughout the 1920s. In examining the professional articles of that period, we see any number of proposals for improving the required course but none that make any version of the abolitionist case. This is not to say that reform periods contain no grumbling or that no teachers exist during them who wish to see freshman composition eliminated. But abolitionism is submerged during reform periods because the mission of the course comes to seem so important that more of value would be lost than gained by cutting the requirement altogether.

By the end of the 1920s, college demographics were shifting strongly. Enrollments had almost doubled between 1920 and 1930, from 598,000 students to more than 1.1 million, and they were beginning to place heavy staffing demands on the single course that had to serve all students (United States, *Digest* 84). As so often occurs, demographic changes in the student body seem to create strains leading to powerful proposals—either radical reformism or some kind or abolitionism. When abolitionism appeared again after the 1920s, however, it came from a place that Fred Newton Scott would not have suspected: the educational research community, which by 1930 was finding a serious voice within English studies. The debate erupted at the NCTE meeting of 1931, in which Alvin C. Eurich of the University of Minnesota reported findings of a study done there in the late 1920s. In one of the earliest controlled experiments conducted of freshman composition, pretest and posttest compositions were required of 54 freshmen passing through the Minnesota course. The results showed that "no measurable improvement in composition was apparent after three months of practice" (211). Eurich's essay is a research report, written with a complete footnoted literature survey, and his findings indicate that the problem with freshman composition rests on "the inadequacy of the administrative arrangement which is based upon the assumption that the lifelong habits of expression can be modified in a relatively short time" (213). To solve this problem, Eurich proposed a sophisticated system in which English teachers would work with teachers in other fields on writing-based assignments—one of the most serious early Writing Across the Curriculum programs.

Eurich's paper at NCTE was answered by one written by Warner Taylor. Taylor's essay is an archetype of reformist objection to abolitionism. Should the course be abolished? he asks. It is problematical, he says, but "as for me, I do not consider the course futile. I do consider it, in general, open to several changes for the better" (301–2). Taylor goes on to discuss a survey he had done that shows freshman courses relying overwhelmingly on handbooks and rhetorics and making a claim that such methods were themselves to blame for the poor showing the course made in Eurich's research. He proposes instead a course that gets rid of rhetorics and handbooks and mixes composition with literature.

This willingness to admit problems and propose reforms rather than agree to abolitionist ideas is a continuing entropic strand in composition discourse from the 1930s forward. It represents a sort of argumentative jujitsu, using the strength and cogency of any abolitionist argument against abolitionism as a position. "The freshman course is problematical, is hated, is boring, does not work? Absolutely true," reformists typically say, "and proof positive that it needs reform—needs, in specific, the reform I am about to propose."

We see here, of course, a certain amount of vested interest on the part of composition reformers. Even as early as 1930, there were teachers and scholars whose careers were primarily concerned with writing pedagogy, and these people associated freshman composition as a course very clearly with "their discipline." It would be almost unnatural for them to admit that the course that was their primary responsibility and interest was so hopelessly compromised and ineffective that abolishing it was the best solution. There is no doubt that reform rather than abolition served the professional needs of most composition specialists best.

The decade of the 1930s saw more lively discussion of reform and abolition than had ever before occurred. The decade of *English Journal* from the 1930s is filled with debates that sound almost incredibly contemporary—proposals for English as training for social experience, for Marxist critique in the classroom, for Writing Across the Curriculum, for research-based reforms of various kinds, for more or less literary influence on composition, for better conditions for teachers. In 1939, the strong liberal-culture side of the abolitionist argument popped up again in Oscar James Campbell's now well known article, "The Failure of Freshman English." Russell has dealt very effectively with the major part of Campbell's position in his "Romantics on Writing," and here we might merely note that literary elitism was not the *entirety* of Campbell's position. He, too, put forward a Writing Across the Curriculum agenda, at least tacitly. As Russell describes, Campbell also makes the familiar claim that composition cannot be taught apart from content, that it is intellectually dishonest as well as futile. He blames freshman composition for teacher disaffection and for reducing the usefulness of literary education.

Campbell's position, though probably sympathetic to most literature teachers, received far less support than Lounsbury's had 25 years before. Unlike Lounsbury, Campbell was facing a composition establishment that was already entrenched and was even building the beginnings of a scholarship and a discipline. Though Campbell was respected, he was not agreed with, and all the responses to his essay were essentially reformist. In 1941, Andrew J. Green's "Reform of Freshman English" took Campbell's arguments on directly, stating squarely that "Freshman English is ubiquitous, inevitable, and eternal" (593).

Campbell also found himself in the unfortunate position of opening a battle immediately before the nation's attention became caught up in an

all-consuming world war. Instead of the debate that Campbell had no doubt hoped to produce, the entire issue of the worth of freshman composition slipped away, as did what had been other engrossing issues of the 1930s—experience curriculum, social conditions, Marxism—in the intellectual conflagration that was the war effort. After 1941, his complaints seem to have been forgotten, and reformism itself was almost blunted for the duration of the war as the needs of the military came to the fore and stressing any American problems seemed somewhat defeatist. Throughout the war years, overt criticism of the course almost disappeared as scholars betook themselves to serve the war effort by keeping up morale.

The postwar world was a different place, one in which the debate that had been damped down during the war emerged in many forms. Particularly hotly debated was the question of the mission and purpose of liberal arts colleges, a question that was always tied in powerfully to the issue of required freshman composition. Ironically, it was not the abolition sentiment of the Campbells but a kind of accelerated reformism that had the greatest abolitionist effect after World War II. The general education movement, which proposed that college curricula since the introduction of the elective system had become too specialized, was first widely enunciated in the Harvard Report of 1945, and, gaining power rapidly after 1948, it produced widespread withdrawal from the traditional freshman composition course.

The general educationists wished to meld the "heritage" model of traditional education with the more recent pragmatic insights of the followers of Dewey and William James (Harvard Committee 46–7), and to do so they proposed that the specialized introductory courses of the freshman and sophomore years be supplanted by much broader general courses, one each in the humanities, the social sciences, and the sciences. The Harvard Committee specifically proposed that the traditional course in freshman composition be replaced by more emphasis on writing in these new general education courses. The static acceptance of required freshman composition courses that had for so long been tacit educational policy was suddenly shaken as "communication" courses replaced the older composition model.

The communication movement, which was the working out of general education ideas in an English context, proposed to unify what had been separate fields of English and speech by rolling together all four of the "communication skills"—speaking, listening, reading, and writing—and creating a new course around them, the communication course. This movement began to take hold in earnest in the late 1940s and prospered through the mid-1950s, when it lost momentum. During that time, however, many traditional freshman writing courses were converted into communication courses, often team-taught by English and speech professors.

It is important to note several things about these communication courses. First, they were not part of anyone's abolitionist agenda. The general education movement itself was not at all against required courses; it was essentially about widening and adding requirements, especially during the first two years of college. Second, the changes that came down during these years

came down from on high as part of a sweeping mandate reaching all the way from Harvard to the federal government. Traditional freshman courses were not transformed by liberal-culture romantics of the old literary sort or even by the kind of Writing Across the Curriculum–oriented attitude we see in Eurich but rather by a temporary enthusiasm for a new sort of reform. This was a specifically successful brand of reformism, perceiving the freshman course in need of change, rather than abolitionism, which perceives the course as hopeless or its change as impossible. It was a reform that changed the name and some of the methods of the traditional freshman composition class in many places but that removed not a jot of requirement anywhere.

Despite the critiques, freshman composition and communication courses flourished throughout the early and middle 1950s. Only at the end of the decade did abolitionism resurge, with the famous statement made in 1959 by Warner G. Rice, chair of the Michigan Department of English, at the NCTE convention of that year and published in *College English* in 1960. Rice's essay, "A Proposal for the Abolition of Freshman English, As It Is Now Commonly Taught, from the College Curriculum," is a classic product of its period; the late 1950s were for colleges a low-stress time during which fewer but much better prepared students were seeking admission. We might think of the period as the antithesis of a literacy crisis: there was no press of new student populations, test scores were rising every year, and there were fewer bachelor's degrees conferred in 1960 than in 1950 (United States, *Digest* 84). The postwar GI boom had not quite been succeeded by the baby boom in colleges, and thus at that moment the need for a required course to remedy freshman literacy problems seemed to many less pressing.

Rice's stance is by now familiar. He made the same claims that abolitionists had always made: basic literacy should be a prerequisite for college; freshman composition in a semester or a year tries to accomplish the impossible and does not really "take"; students are ill-motivated; the course is a financial drain on colleges; English teachers would be happier teaching other courses (361–2). And as Alvin C. Eurich had been answered by reformist Warner Taylor at the NCTE convention 28 years earlier, Rice was answered by reformist Albert R. Kitzhaber in 1959. Kitzhaber's essay, "Death—or Transfiguration?" admits immediately that "no one would want to make an unqualified defense of the present Freshman English course" and goes on to catalog its shortcomings: overambitious aims, lack of agreement about course content, poor textbooks and methods, and impossibility of proving success (367). But Kitzhaber then proceeds to state positive aspects of the course: it subsidizes graduate study, lets young teachers gain experience, and often gets clearly positive results. He also believes that a writing-based course is worthwhile in and of itself (368). Kitzhaber contests Rice's main points, arguing that abolishing freshman composition would not be cheaper to colleges, that faculty in other disciplines would not take up any great part of literacy responsibilities, that the high schools were not equipped yet to handle the responsibilities themselves, and that a more rhetorically oriented freshman English course would help solve the problem (372).

With the eruption of the New Rhetoric in the early 1960s and the gradual growth of composition studies as a scholarly discipline with its own books and journals, its own disseminative and reproductive mechanisms, we entered a new era. It is an era in which reformism was immensely strengthened, becoming, indeed, the backbone of an ever-larger professional literature. Improving the freshman course (through the New Rhetoric, or invention, or classical rhetoric, or Christensen paragraphing, or sentence combining) became the essential purpose of the books and essays that appeared in always-greater numbers.

Abolition sentiment, however, does not die easily, and there was a short period during the late 1960s when the iconoclasm of that time caused the usual reformist consensus to be disrupted again by arguments against the required freshman course. The most interesting abolitionist attack was made in 1969 by Leonard Greenbaum in his article "The Tradition of Complaint." Greenbaum's essay is a piece of historical research on abolitionism written by an author who takes pains to situate himself outside the field of English. (Thus, his stance as an abolitionist himself is easier to understand because he had no professional stake in reform.) In spite of the slapdash nature of Greenbaum's historical research and his tone of classic late-1960s snottiness, his essay is still worth reading, and his essential point goes beyond the liberal-culture self-interest of many other abolitionists: "Freshman English is a luxury that consumes time, money, and the intelligence of an army of young teachers and of younger teaching fellows. . . . It would be better to stop what we are doing, to sit still, to rest in the sun, and then to search for the populations whose problems can be solved by our professional skills" (187). Greenbaum's position as an outsider to composition kept him from having any of the kind of background that could lead to more detailed ideas about what sort of writing instruction he *could* support.

Greenbaum seemed to expect no followers. As his historical survey had shown him, "Freshman English flourishes; its opponents die, retire, languish in exile" (187). But a number of people agreed with him, and for a few years after his essay, as the general cultural upheaval of the late 1960s and early 1970s produced more obvious dissatisfaction with the status quo in American education than had been seen, one of the institutions interrogated most strongly was freshman composition. Ron Smith conducted a survey in 1973 that found that the number of colleges and universities requiring some form of freshman English had dropped from 93.2 percent in 1967 to 76 percent in 1973 (139). Regina M. Hoover published "Taps for Freshman English?" in 1974, making the point that "among the many confusing and often conflicting currents sweeping through considerations of the status of Freshman English these days is one that may make all the rest irrelevant: that the discipline is dying" (149). And Smith, who admired Greenbaum's positions, saw so many continuing changes in the world of academia—"uniform equivalency testing, *true* three-year degree programs, the general elimination or streamlining of lower-division requirements, systems approaches, performance- or competency-based instruction, open-admissions policies, adjustments to

booming and then declining enrollments, and even 'accountability' " — that he was certain that the trend toward deregulation of freshman composition would certainly continue (139). "The change that has occurred these past several years is not going to end very soon," he wrote in 1974. "All signs point to more schools dropping the composition requirement" (148).

Look on my works, ye mighty, and despair. In direct contradiction to Smith's forecast, we see no more of abolitionism after the early 1970s. In the research for this essay, I could not find anything written between 1975 and 1990 in the field of composition that called for general abolition of the course. Now and then a teacher may write about why he or she does not want to teach it anymore, but the requirement itself seems little questioned in the professional literature, and it gradually grew back in the colleges. There can be found every flavor of reformism — the theorizing, the experimental pedagogies, the complaining, the throwing up of hands, the proffering of every sort of solution to the problems that always recur. But abolitionism peters out after 1974, much as it had done after both world wars.

Reasons for the change are complex. Some are culturally bound. The general military draft ended, and the Vietnam War wound down. The last great antiwar protests were rigorously quashed by the Nixon administration in 1971. The antiwar movement imploded into quarreling factions, and the sudden deflation of campus radicalism after 1972 left schools extremely quiet. There was a gas crisis and an economic recession. It was not a propitious time for any proposal for change.

Professionally, the most obvious reason for the decay of abolitionist sentiment was, of course, the rise of open admissions, the movement of a whole new demographic sector into college classrooms, and the resulting "literacy crisis" of the middle 1970s. There is nothing like a new population or a perceived problem of lack of student preparation to put energy back into a composition requirement, and by 1976 we had both in plenty. The "Johnny Can't Write" furor of 1976 was at least as potent as the "Illiteracy of American Boys" furor had been 90 years before, and any chance that abolitionist ideas might have had in the early 1970s was swamped by mid-decade. The "back to the basics" movement, the rise of basic writing as a subdiscipline, even the writing process movement all presumed a required freshman course.

Just as important to the decline of abolitionism, I believe, was the maturation of the discipline of composition studies and its increasing ability to turn out doctoral specialists who could direct and defend programs. The natural tendency early on was for such specialists to talk reform and defend the course, but their very existence tempered the conditions that had made some literary specialists argue for abolition. With the growing availability of a class of tenure-track composition specialists to handle oversight of the course, literary members of English departments could rest increasingly secure from ever having to do *anything* associated with composition unless they chose to do so. Those overseeing required courses had a rising professional stake in them, and thus reform ideas came hard and fast — but not proposals for abolition. So things went, through the later 1970s and most of the 1980s.

This dearth of abolitionist sentiment, by now lasting almost 20 years, makes the historian with even a slight tinge of Toynbeeism begin to expect that the wheel must turn again, and turn again toward abolitionism. And, true to form, we are now seeing a New Abolitionism. The founding statement of the New Abolitionism was made in 1991 by Sharon Crowley in "A Personal Essay on Freshman English," which details her gradual realization that required freshman composition courses implicated her and all composition specialists with any program oversight in structures that could *not* be significantly reformed. The course is simply too tied up with institutional and professional baggage to be amenable to serious reform. "In short," she writes, "I doubt whether it is possible to radicalize instruction in a course that is so thoroughly implicated in the maintenance of cultural and academic hierarchy" (165). Crowley's solution is abolition, not of the course but of the requirement. "Please note," she writes, "that I am NOT proposing the abolition of Freshman English. I am not so naive as to think that the course can be abolished. But it can be made elective" (170). Crowley goes on to argue that eliminating the requirement would get rid of admissions exams, prevent any sort of indoctrination of first-year students, offer administrative control over enrollments in freshman courses, and control teaching assistantships more effectively. She then takes on what she considers good arguments, that is, student needs–based, and bad arguments, that is, institutionally or ideologically based, that can be made against her position.

Crowley's deliberately provocative essay led to the proposal of a round-table session at the 1993 Conference on College Composition and Communication in San Diego titled "(Dis)missing the Universal Requirement." From the quick sketch I have given here of traditional responses to abolitionist arguments over the last century, we might have expected the standard response: reformism. Reformism of a very high standard, no doubt, but, still, reformism: protests that the freshman requirement does more good than harm, or that its methods must be changed to fill-in-the-blank so that it can reach its potential, or that fill-in-the-blank will certainly arrive soon and make it all worthwhile.

But no. No Helen Ogden Mahin or Warner Taylor or Albert R. Kitzhaber stood forth to disagree with Sharon Crowley. Instead, three of the most respected composition scholars and theorists rose, and each one, in his or her own way, agreed with Crowley that the universal requirement should be rethought. Lil Brannon of SUNY at Albany reported that her university had abolished the standard freshman course in 1986 because "a group of faculty from across the curriculum successfully made the case that a 'skills' concept of writing—the very idea of writing that caused the faculty to require Freshman Composition—had no professional currency" (1). David Jolliffe, making an argument based on his historical study, asked whether such a "skills"-based course was a reflection of late-19th-century perceptions. "I wonder if freshman composition isn't a metaphor for a time long passed. I wonder if we shouldn't rethink the position of requiring all incoming students to be 'skilled' in this anachronistic fashion" (1). Calling regular freshman courses

"literacy calisthenics," Jolliffe goes on to argue that they should be replaced with a writing-based sophomore-level elective course that would concentrate on writing about content of their choice. And Charles I. Schuster spoke from the point of view of a practicing composition administrator, saying that freshman composition is the Third World of English studies, "a bleak territory within which students have little power to choose" and in which faculty are underpaid and overworked. Teaching writing is foundational, says Schuster, but "either Freshman Composition has to matter to our departments, or we have to get rid of it—or get rid of our colleagues" (6).

The discussion that followed these three presentations was spirited, and though there was by no means unanimity of opinion, many session attenders agreed with the central points made by the presenters. Within a few weeks, the grapevine of hallway conversations, telephone calls, workshop and presentation discussions, and electronic mail was buzzing with word of the session, and the issue even had its name: the New Abolitionism. This "Dismissing" panel was answered in 1994 by a panel called "Dissing Freshman English: At What Risk?" I am sure the conversation will go on.

We have come a long way from 1893 to 1993, from the oldest to the newest abolitionism movements. Are there any conclusions we can draw from what we have learned? Can our understanding of the past inform our sense of the present—or even the future? Is the New Abolitionism any different from previous similar arguments?

The observer of abolition arguments cannot help noting some salient similarities. The New Abolitionism is like previous versions in its condemnation of the required course as often futile, as a disliked hinterland of English studies, as expensive to run, exhausting to teach, and alienating to administer. Many New Abolitionists are present and former course administrators, as were a large number of abolitionists throughout history. The alternatives proposed by the New Abolitionism are not too dissimilar to alternatives proposed by Slosson in 1913 and Eurich in 1932 and Campbell in 1939: make composition the responsibility of the whole faculty.

The differences between the New Abolitionism and the older movements are, however, even more striking than the similarities. Most obviously different is the professional forum in which the argument is playing itself out. The New Abolitionism is a product of a newly scholarly and professionalized discipline of composition studies, one with many national journals and a constant and ongoing conversation. "Composition people" today are not just course administrators or pedagogy enthusiasts but are increasingly visible in English departments as scholars and researchers with their own claims to respect. The New Abolitionism is the work of insiders—people trained as compositionists from an early point in their careers—and it is based on exactly the opposite conclusion: that writing can be taught, and that experts are needed to teach it, but that the required freshman course is not the most effective forum for attaining the ends we seek.

The intellectual and pedagogical backgrounds for the argument have shifted dramatically as a result of these changes in institutional and

disciplinary cultures, and this background shift will be another important element in any success the New Abolitionism may have. From a very early point, abolitionists have been claiming that freshman composition should be replaced with one or another system that would take responsibility for literacy off English teachers and place it on all faculty members. These were voices crying in the wilderness through much of this century, however. There were no institutional structures that would have helped faculty members in other disciplines make writing more central to their courses, and there was no extant part of English studies with enough credible expertise to do such outreach work. All that has now changed radically with the advent of the Writing Across the Curriculum movement. For the last decade and longer, writing professionals have, with the blessing and help of administrators, been forging professional links that never existed before with extradisciplinary colleagues, bringing contemporary knowledge of writing issues to content-area courses. This is a strong and broadly respected movement, one that is unlikely to go away, and it provides a practical base for the ideas of the New Abolitionism that no previous such movement had.

The arguments we hear from proponents of the New Abolitionism are qualitatively different from those heard in previous avatars of the movement. New Abolitionists typically appeal first to student interests and only secondarily to the interests of teachers, departments, and colleges. Even when previous abolitionists transcended liberal-culture arguments, their calls for the end of the required course were often based in issues of self-interest—getting rid of the composition underclass, or allowing professors to teach courses they liked, or avoiding the criticism of colleagues who thought the course was ineffective. Today's abolitionists are arguing from their scholarly as well as their practical knowledge of writing issues that students are not as well served by the required freshman course as they could be by other kinds of writing instruction. They are ideologically informed in ways that even 1960s radicals such as Greenbaum were not, and they are certainly sympathetic to both students and teachers in ways that few abolitionists have ever been. Most significant, this change in the institutional base of the argument means that we may see fewer reformist claims based in the need to safeguard jobs, turf, and respectability.

Finally, and perhaps most important, the New Abolitionists are in positions to make their critique stick. Since most of them are administrators or advisors to administrators, they know the institutional situation surrounding composition programs, Writing Across the Curriculum, and literary studies. They know what is possible, and they know how to get things done—not just whether they should be done. Because they are respected scholars and teachers, they can and do counter the expectable response from traditionalists and reformists by taking a position of informed sympathy mixed with telling argumentation. And because they are composition insiders, they can make their case from within the discourse of the field rather than complaining scornfully from without, as most abolitionists have done in the past.

It may just be, then, that the New Abolitionism will come to have a real effect. It may be that after a century we will begin to see some actual abolition of the required freshman course in favor of other methods of writing instruction.

Unless. Unless any of the familiar nemeses of abolition, most of which are now quiescent, makes an appearance.

Unless we see another literacy crisis widely cried up in the media. As the literacy crises of the 1870s spawned the freshman course and the literacy crisis of the 1970s saved it from the radical critics of the 1960s, another literacy crisis could send abolitionism scurrying. There is no lack of evidence of literacy problems that can be dug up at any given time; the report in 1992 that 20 percent of American workers could not read well enough to do their jobs most effectively or the more recent news that more than 50 percent of American adults were less than functionally literate are just the two latest lightning strikes ("Workplace"; "Study"). But not every foundation report on literacy can start the sort of large-scale crisis that gets the whole country listening, and we cannot tell which of these scattered grass fires might blow up to be the Class A crown fire that the "American Boys" or "Johnny" crises were. If such a major crisis impends, count on an end to any sort of requirement change in the freshman curriculum and get ready to batten down the "back to the basics" hatches.

Unless the United States gets involved in a serious or lasting war. Twice this century, world wars have created cultural conditions that have meant the end of credible abolition movements, and even the smaller Korean War damped down the pedagogical change of the period 1945–1952. The only exception to the general rule that war is good for the required freshman course was the war in Vietnam, which created a radical backlash on campuses previously unknown in the United States. Wars seem to create a desire for tradition and stasis where they can be achieved on the home front. War does not, thankfully, look likely as of this writing, and the ending of the Cold War may indeed bode well for such curricular changes as abolitionism. But if any major war does involve the United States, kiss curricular change goodbye— if you're able.

Unless there is a serious backlash against abolition of freshman courses on the part of those who teach them. Every abolition proposal during this century has been criticized most strongly by reformists, people who believe that the freshman course is the right answer to the question, albeit one that needs more tinkering. It is difficult to know what the growing split between the scholarly members of the tenure-track composition studies community and the instructor-level teachers in the composition trenches will mean for this issue. As Crowley says, "[T]enured academics have always dictated the terms of Freshman English teaching to its staff, and it is tenured academics who fight over its curriculum" (168), but composition studies is listening to the voices of the teachers who work on the course. If the New Abolitionism comes to look like a clash between tenured academics who want to remove

and ship to some unknown place employment that composition teachers have come to depend on, and those teachers who need or want that employment, we can count on many a painful tale and many a bitter fight on levels ranging from department to CCCC. The New Abolitionism may be our own small version of the jobs/trade debate over the North American Free Trade Agreement, and if it becomes such, reform rather than abolition of the required freshman course will come to seem the only possible compromise. Working people have vested interests even in jobs from which they are alienated.

None of our historical knowledge can really predict the outcome of the New Abolitionism movement. What we can learn, however, is what may promote or block such changes in entrenched curricular practices. My own position, if I have not already tipped my hand, is one of sympathy for the New Abolitionism. I still believe that we have more of a chance today than ever before to rethink in a serious and thoroughgoing way the best methods for working on student literacy issues and that we can do so without harming the best interests of either our students or our colleagues. I look forward to a continuation of the debate and even—could it be?—to real changes in our world of teaching and thinking about writing.

Teaching and Learning as a Man

The opening of "Teaching and Learning as a Man" (*College English*, 1996) is one of the most memorable among Bob's many essays. "He was one of the guys. Burly, thick-necked, he sat in the back of the room in a line with several other guys, [. . .] watching me through lowered eyelids" (295). Every teacher knows this student, and we can imagine readers being drawn, as we were, into this compelling narrative. In it, Bob traces his own process of "finally focusing on my relations, and the relations of male teachers in general, with male students" (297). This focus led him to review once more the history of rhetoric as dominated by males and the changes he saw taking place in the nineteenth century, brought about by the acceptance of women into colleges. Bob's review leads him to contemporary feminism and to what he has gleaned from that movement, as well as to the fairly new field of men's studies, from which he hopes to learn much "about the ways in which gender affects both women and men as we try to teach and learn about writing" (307). The second half of this essay addresses several key questions, including, "Why are our male students often stereotyped as insensitive, or passive, or defensive?" and "Does teaching young men call for pedagogical techniques different from those effective with young women?" and concludes the essay by calling on all teachers of writing to "confront gender issues wholly" (314). We think it's safe to say that the following essay is Bob's most controversial; it elicited dozens of responses on composition listservs as well as critical commentary later published in *College English*.

H e was one of the guys. Burly, thick-necked, he sat in the back of the room in a line with several other guys, wearing the school sweatshirts or the purloined green surgical shirts that were the mandatory badges of individuality in that era. He slumped in his seat, watching me through lowered eyelids. Though he did not volunteer much in class, he was not sullen or challenging, as some of them were. He came to conferences and

---

From *College English* 58.2 (1996): 137–57.

was pleasant and docile, though he never quite met my eyes. His question was always the same: "What do you want me to do?" He would agree eagerly to any suggestion I made on a draft, and the more specific the better. When he had gotten as thorough a set of marching orders as he could draw from me—and I, young prof, was happy to dispense my gems of wisdom in good detail to those astute enough to ask for them—he departed quickly and with relief.

In those days, I required journals from my freshman students. Twice a semester I called them in, and, as the current wisdom of those days went, I did not grade them or even write responses, but merely noted length and wrote a long terminal comment. Twice a semester I spent a good deal of time reading the journals and writing those comments. His journal was like many others, filled with venting about the unfairness of his world, quickly written descriptions of places he would plunk himself in (the dining commons, the Parade Ground, the campus barber shop—always good for a journal entry), and adventure stories about dorm water fights, dangerous drunken outings, incredible rock concerts. I read it all carefully, noted whether it met the requirements for length and number of entries, and wrote my long comment at the end, telling him my opinions of his journal and wishing him a good summer.

Last day of classes. The grades are all done, the papers handed back. They take a few minutes to do their fill-in-the-blanks evaluation forms while I leave the room, then I return, wish them well, tell them to come and see me if they have any future writing problems. I have lugged the large bundle of their journals to the room. "Everybody got journal credit," I announce, "good show! I'll give them back to you and let you go early." I call the names, give back the notebooks as students file past and leave. I call his name, and he comes up, takes the black-and-white marbled book, heads for the door. At the door he pauses, then, studiedly, slowly, his left arm with the notebook comes up to a forty-five degree angle. He dangles the unopened journal for half a second, then releases it. *Bang* into the hollow metal wastebasket by the door. For the first time, his eyes meet mine for a moment. Then he turns and leaves the room.

As I dazedly passed out the rest of the journals, my head swam and emotions eddied about me in waves of hot and cold. The bastard. The bootlicking brown-noser. The disrespectful little twit. Acting interested and submissive to get his grade, and then when he knew he had gotten it, letting me know just how much of his work was an act, and how little he cared for my opinions about his "improvement as a writer."

I wanted to show him. I wanted to make him toe the line. I wanted—for his sake, of course!—to teach him that fleering the teacher is bad policy, son. Maybe I could finagle his grade, find some problem there not seen before, yes, surely that classroom participation was not worth a full B . . .

But my weapon was gone. The temporary artificial dominance that the institution had given me over him had dissipated. The grade was figured, and if I were to refigure it sheerly out of pique, I could not respect the vision I

needed of myself as Fair Arbiter. As I sat in the now-empty classroom, the swirl of final departures dying away down the hall, I knew only that I felt empty, felt rejected, felt useless—and responded to those emotions by allowing myself to feel primarily angry.

That day, I have now come to think, was the beginning of a long process of noticing, paying attention to, and finally focusing on my relations, and the relations of male teachers in general, with male students. It was not comfortable. I had to notice the ways in which male students submit, grudgingly or willingly, to the artificial dominance of a male teacher. I had to notice what sorts of writing young men did, wanted to do, felt they should do. I had to notice how my male students were in the middle of constructing themselves as men—and how difficult and lonely a job it often was. I had to notice how, tacitly or openly, they resisted me and the authority I represented. I had to notice how they sometimes wanted to reach out to a teacher as a mentor or figure of mature wisdom and how seldom they could allow themselves to.

And I had to notice my own attitudes toward the complex relation of power and knowledge my teacherly position forced all of us into—my own desire to initiate, to mentor, to provide a role model, to formalize and hand on rules—and to assert my own hierarchical place, construct my own manhood, find my own spot in the world.

There is not much in the way I was trained as a teacher about how to deal with these issues. My practicum course mentioned discipline issues, but they were general. Erika Lindemann and David Foster and Beth Neman discussed general teaching strategies in their books, but none of them spoke to the subtle and constant questions I would face as a man teaching men. From classical rhetoric and its picture of balanced arguments through the student-centered dialectic of process-oriented teaching, questions of masculinity and the teaching issues that surround it were omnipresent but hardly mentioned.

That was the seventies and early eighties, when gender issues were hardly considered in composition studies. More recently, of course, gender has received intensive attention from the developing feminist theoretic of the past two decades. We are beginning to get detailed accounts of female students and the pressures exerted on them, of women teachers and the problems they face with male students, or of the interaction of male and female students. Feminism has begun to provide a rich discourse about women, but the place of men in this discourse has been marginal. I have seen little that speaks of the underlying sets of questions and challenges that are brought home to me every time I face a group of young men in my classes. Who am I supposed to be? Master? Father? Camp counselor? Buddy?

These sorts of questions—what kind of teacher, what kind of mentor, what kind of man was I supposed to be?—were not being answered for me either in the discourse of education or in the discourse of feminism. A natural reflex for me as a scholar is to try to understand situations historically, so I went to the library to try to find out what I could about men teaching men. I found that there are definite historical reasons for some of the confusions that male teachers and male students are feeling today, reasons grounded in the

nature of composition itself and the ways it defined itself as it succeeded rhetoric as a college discipline.

Throughout most of Western history, the field of rhetoric was the property of men. The historical discipline of rhetoric was shaped by male rituals, male contests, male ideals, and masculine agendas, and women were definitively excluded from all that rhetoric implied. From its inception in the probate courts of early Syracuse, the techniques of rhetoric were evolved for a single purpose: to create persuasive arguments, to develop and win cases, to put forward opinions in legislative fora, to stake out turf and verbally hold it against opponents in public contest. To use a term popularized by Walter Ong, rhetoric was a quintessentially *agonistic* discipline—one concerned with contest. It was ritualized contest, yes, but contest nonetheless. Argument and debate are verbal agonistic displays, and as Ong has shown, ritual contests of all sorts have been central to Western culture for as long as we have recorded history.

In his book *Fighting for Life*, Ong traces the strands of agonistic ritual contest between males that exist in nature and in the convoluted, codified forms of nature we call culture and civilization. He begins by discussing the radical insecurity of male consciousness, which is always subconsciously aware that males are individually far less important to species survival than are females and that they thus represent surplus reproductive value (57–64). Ong has made a powerful case that important elements of human behavior have been unconsciously informed by the radical insecurity and status needs of males, and that agonistic self-display has been the resulting tendency. Put most simply, masculine consciousness tacitly perceives most of life in terms of contest. From day to day, the agonist wins or loses in the constant struggle for power, physical comfort, ego-satisfaction, territory. Staking out "turf," physical, intellectual, social, or emotional, and defending it against all comers seems to be connected to male consciousness in some deep way that females seldom have shared. In *Fighting for Life*, Ong traces a number of the forms through which this agonistic male consciousness has expressed itself, the various ritual contests each culture has evolved to allow males to "prove" superior masculinity. These contests may be overtly physical tests of bravery and ability to withstand pain (the land-diving of the Pentecost Islanders and the self-mutilating Sun Dances of the Plains Indians) or ritualized physical contests (all forms of sports, from the Olympic games to fraternity beer-drinking contests)—or the agonistic verbal contests that have been a part of so many cultures and continue to be an important part of our own (103–15).

Here, on the level of verbal display and contest, is where Ong's argument for agonistic male consciousness begins to intersect with the teaching issues we face. *Fighting for Life* makes a persuasive case for the continuing existence of agonistic verbal display between males in most contemporary cultures. An important portion of Ong's argument concerns the ways in which this agonistic stance has informed education. Academic agonism was historically not just a matter of grades, which are a relatively recent phenomenon, but arises, as Ong puts it, "from a disposition to organize the subject matter

itself as a field of combat, to purvey, not just to test, knowledge in a combative style" (121). From the medieval period forward, college and university courses were conducted as ceremonial ritual contest, in which the teacher and student—both, of course, male—were adversaries. Older students were expected to announce and defend theses against attacks by their professors, and from this practice we get the now-vestigial practice of oral defense of PhD exams and dissertations—a last agonistic remnant of that older oral culture.

Older rhetorical education for all-male groups took several forms, some theoretical, in the form of lectures and memorization, and some practical, in the form of debate and oration. Whether the methods were practical or theoretical, rhetorical instruction meant contest. In both the lecture hall and the classroom, students were set against the master and against each other. Teaching and testing were much more public under this all-male system than they are now. Up until the mid-nineteenth century, most final exams were oral and public. Any man with the credentials might press the candidate with questions, as George Schmidt recounts: "College graduates in the audience, like the masters of arts in the medieval universities, were privileged to inject questions of their own or to criticize the answers of the candidates" (100). Today, of course, such testing is minimized, and we tend to see professors who engage deeply in it as pathologues; for us, the "defense" of the PhD dissertation or Master's thesis is a curious relic, an atrophied survival of a harder time no one remembers. Few doctoral candidates really have to stand and fight for their theses against determined professorial foes, and it is hard for us to imagine what a student-teacher bond of distance and hostility might mean for college life. (For more detail on this agonistic college culture and its downfall in the nineteenth century, see my essay "Women's Reclamation of Rhetoric in the Nineteenth Century.")

College and university culture, from medieval times until after the Civil War, was a culture that pitted man against man in a constant series of ritual tests of worthiness—in the classroom, on the platform, in the debate hall, in the dormitory. In Latin or in English, the agonism was always present. It existed in the argumentative rhetorical theory stretching from Cicero to Whately, in the truncated pragmatism of the elocutionary movement, in the abstract persuasion-based assignments that professors gave, in the forms of thesis and defense, lecture and recitation, in the purring slash of the professor's oral rebuke, in the barking give and take of the debate club's hall, in the silky logical entrapment of the perspiring bachelor's candidate, and in the roaring denunciation of backsliding that issued from the pulpit. College was a man's world, and if it was "red in tooth and claw," it was also a world in which men knew the rules and could use them to define their places in the hierarchy of educational worth.

And what happened to this agonistic educational culture? The older methods of academic defense and attack died out with startling rapidity, says Ong, because of the entrance of women into higher education. After over two thousand years as the central element in schooling, contestive education died

out in the nineteenth and early twentieth centuries, retreating in almost exact proportion to the advances of coeducation in high schools and colleges. Colleges began to mix women and men in the 1840s, and classrooms would never be the same. Contestive, combative educational methods that had worked satisfactorily for all-male schooling now seemed violent, vulgar, silly with women looking on. A man could attack another man verbally, and was expected to, but to attack a *woman*, either physically or intellectually, was thought ignoble.

By 1900 most colleges were coeducational, and this world was a far cry from the old all-male world of higher education. Primarily, it was much more complex. Male psychological agonism did not simply disappear, but it had to be canalized into less overt channels. The most obvious of these—the places where the old male mind still showed most clearly—were intercollegiate athletics, which boomed after 1870, and the "secret Greek letter fraternities" that sprang up to exclude women from at least *some* sanctuaries on each campus. As more and more women entered colleges, the public agonistic tradition was abandoned and less contestive educational methods were pioneered. Instead of the oral, argument-based, male-dominated education of the pre-1850 period, education post-1850 was much more irenic, negotiative, explanatory. Thus the educational structure we inherit is an amalgam of newer irenic values and half-understood survivals from a more agonistic time in education.

Composition, whose forebear was rhetoric, was particularly affected—even in some sense created—by these changes. When women entered colleges, they demanded the full range of courses that men had been used to taking—including rhetoric, which had theretofore excluded women almost entirely. The older oral rhetorical tradition of debates, declamations, hierarchies of expertise, agonistic testing, public contest, would not do. What burgeoned instead at American colleges after 1870 was a newer sort of rhetoric, one suitable for women and mixed classes—the rhetoric of written composition. From 1880 to the present, we have seen the development of composition-rhetoric and the corresponding diminution of purely oral agonistic rhetoric in nearly all American college curricula. Composition-rhetoric, which is interiorized rather than public, multimodal rather than purely argumentative, taught on a one-to-one editorial basis rather than on a public and critical basis, is a much more irenic discourse than the older oral rhetoric.

The gender issues that accompanied this shift have been recognized and discussed recently by a variety of feminist scholars. Historians now have realized that composition-rhetoric evolved during the period 1860–1900 largely around coeducational sites and that the actual teaching of composition has been the most feminized area of college instruction outside home economics for almost a century. The first PhD granted in the field of composition-rhetoric was to a woman: Gertrude Buck in 1898. By 1920, more than half of the articles in the *English Journal* were authored by women. Warner Taylor in 1929 found that 38 percent of all composition instruction in colleges was being done by female instructors, and that percentage has risen

to over 60 percent today (Miller 123). Directors of writing projects testify that over 80 percent of the people who attend them are women.

More importantly, over the last twenty years feminism has come to inform many of the deep structures of the field, and today the teaching of writing is not only feminized but increasingly feminist. What Susan Miller calls "the sad women in the basement" are no longer the only female compositionists; women in the 1990s have both the numbers they always have had in the teaching ranks and increasingly real scholarly and institutional power. The licensing power of doctorates in composition has helped create the current field of composition studies (see Nystrand et al.) as a subfield of English that is rapidly taking its place as a coequal of literary studies, and most PhD programs in composition studies are producing as many female graduates as male—or more. At the same time, the growth of feminist discourse, both theoretical and practical, though it came later to composition studies than to literature, has been extremely rapid—perhaps the most striking movement in the field over the past decade.

This is wonderful, of course. But the shift from a male-dominated rhetoric to a feminized and feminist composition studies has illuminated women's issues in writing while leaving many male teachers uncertain of how or whether they fit in. Few men I know are certain about whether they *can* be feminists, and the decline of older agonistic teaching methods has not produced any model that defines male roles as clearly as those old contestive pedagogies did. Gender does provide a powerful speculative instrument, but I know few men in academia who are sure of their right to wield it or confident in their stance when they do.

Let me speak personally—one of the great gifts that feminism has given to all of us. To be truthful, I must admit that feminism only takes me, as a male teacher, part way toward a satisfying self-definition. I first became aware of what was then called "women's liberation" in college during the late 1960s, and I immediately recognized the importance of the critique that was being mounted. I have been reading feminist work for almost twenty-five years now and have long considered myself a strong advocate of women's issues. But I seldom felt that much of what I read was "about" me in any personal way. Feminism, as I experienced it, was a politics and a system of stances and perspectives not much different from Marxism or poststructuralism. From *The Second Sex* to *In a Different Voice*, I could read and appreciate the analysis or the argument without feeling personally very involved. I could, and did, argue for feminism because I believed in much of what feminist writers were saying about gender equality, but my assent came from my head, not my heart. I knew that as an audience for feminist writers I was a pretty tertiary concern.

When, in the late 1980s, I ran into some writings by people now identified with men's studies or the men's movement—Herb Goldberg, Robert Bly, Sam Keen—I was surprised to find myself much more personally affected by what they were saying. I found an emotional connection in the ways that men's movement writers explored gender issues that had seldom

been there for me as I read women writers discussing women's issues. Questions of constraining roles, of subtle social expectations and tacit fears, of quiet desperation, of blighted relationships and deadly, silent family dramas are there for both men and women. The women's movement gave support for bringing these issues out of the darkness, but the actual discussions that went on in feminism were nearly always about how these issues impinged on women's lives. Men might be in the picture as oppressors, or as support staff, or (very occasionally) as fully drawn figures with problems of their own. But feminist analyses have overwhelmingly dealt with women's roles, issues, and problems. As they should have.

The men's movement writings were trying to give men the same access to discussion about their meaning as gendered beings and about the myths and constraints that have made them and damaged them. That's why they spoke to me in a more emotionally powerful way—because I, as a man, was their primary audience. From men's movement writings I went on to men's studies, of which I had known almost nothing. Intellectually, men's studies engages in cultural criticism by foregrounding gender in historical and cultural settings. Both men's studies and the men's movement thus far have largely concerned themselves with the construction of manhood in modern culture, and many of their concerns have been in the areas of men's interactions, mentoring and bonding issues, fatherhood issues, and issues of power and aggression as they play themselves out among men and between men and women. All of these areas have suggestive applications for me as a male teacher in my relations with all students, but I have found men's studies particularly useful in understanding the work I try to do with male students.

I have come to believe that we—and I specifically indict myself and many male writing teachers—have not been serving male students well. In large part this is because we are reactive. Male intellectuals have been listening to the feminist critique of patriarchy for a long time now, and the result is that we distrust ourselves and our own worth as men; we distrust our own abilities to mentor younger men. We have been told by many sources that the problems of the world arise from machismo and from male sexism, and the natural consequence of hearing this line so consistently is that we shrink from considerations of ourselves as men—as older men, as men of knowledge, as men representative of manhood. Such self-definitions often seem dangerous in the light of what feminism has taught us, but by backing away from engagement with them we have also backed away from powerful heart-reasons for doing what we do.

We should also note that the task with which we are confronted as teachers of young men is demanding today in a way it has not been in the past. In our contemporary academic culture, teaching men can be a confusing task and one filled with cognitive dissonance. As every teacher knows, a class full of young men is not always the Peaceable Kingdom. Often the classroom fills with resistance, self-display, testing, and tacit aggression. As Roy Raphael says in *The Men from the Boys: Rites of Passage in Male America*, "many young males today still feel an urge, a yearning, a mysterious drive to prove them-

selves as men in more primitive terms" (xii). The guys in the baseball caps whispering in the back of the room are not just talkative; they are engaging in what Robert Brooke calls "underlife behavior." Says Brooke,

> By so doing they assert something about their identity. Underlife allows individuals to take stances toward the roles they are expected to play, and to show others the stances they take. . . .
>
> The point is not to disrupt the functioning of the classroom, but to provide the other participants in the classroom with a sense that one has other things to do, other interests, that one is a much richer personality than can be shown in this context. (144, 148)

Brooke does not differentiate underlife activities by gender, but I have certainly noticed more willingness on the part of male students than female to walk the brink, chance the transgressive gesture, or push the disruptive element. Our culture trains young men to do that.

For this reason, really *engaging* with younger men in a writing course (as opposed to merely being "nurturing" or to blandly impersonating a grading-criteria computer) takes a kind of self-confidence that many male teachers of writing find hard to achieve. Being the teacher *does* give us what I call TAD—temporary artificial dominance—over male students, but the dominance, though real, is short-lived and based on sterile institutional power rather than on earned respect or personal choice. Many students resent the artificial dominance of the teacher, and male students are often more explicit in their behavioral interrogation of it. Additionally, many male teachers are uncomfortable with their institutional power and constantly work to give it away.

One solution to the problem of student-teacher relations in a course is to formalize the course structure as thoroughly as possible, with very specific rules and guidelines that control the entire relation of teacher with student. I don't want to suggest that this kind of teaching is injurious. Formulating, testing, and passing on the rules and conventions of a discipline—that is, naming the parts of the world for oncoming generations—is a respectable and necessary part of teaching. But it is also easy to hide behind the rules and conventions, or behind our circumscribed institutional roles. From one point of view, the academic discourse branch of the social constructionism movement in composition studies is exactly about this sort of retreat. These "ordered" roles allow us to bypass issues of our *own* self-definition; defined as "Herr Professor Doktor" or as "Good Buddy Bob," academic initiators, Namers of the Rules, we can put off consideration of whether we are comfortable in our roles as older men, can put off the question of how difficult it is to define ourselves in the eyes of younger men (and I hesitate here even as I write this) as men of wisdom.

(Female reader, are you a woman of wisdom? I hope you are, and I hope you can call yourself that without the need for a self-deprecating smile or a self-critical jibe. If you are capable of thinking of yourself as a woman of wisdom, then the greater part of the feminist objective has been accomplished. I can only

say from my side that it is nearly impossible for me to call myself a man of wisdom in any serious way. I have been to school for twenty-one years; I have read from Plato up to Foucault; I have set up to profess to the young; but if you ask whether I am a man of wisdom I will smile and mutter something rueful and act as if that question has nothing to do with my life as a man or as a teacher. I think most male teachers would respond the same way.)

If male teachers are having problems constructing ourselves as men of wisdom, our male students are having problems simply constructing themselves as men. It is widely acknowledged, I think, that the college years present young people with their most complex challenges of self-definition. Such self-definition is difficult for both women and men, of course, but because of the ways boys and men are acculturated, the construction of manhood in this culture is immensely lonelier than the construction of womanhood. Throughout history, women's worlds have been considered the personal and interpersonal, emotion and relationship, sociality and self-development, and though feminism has allowed women to transcend these personal worlds it has never encouraged leaving them or ignoring their importance.

Young men, on the other hand, are seldom encouraged to consider the personal worlds of feeling and relationship in any except the most narrowly focused ways. Few of them have been encouraged by their culture to go beyond an immature stage of their development. As Robert Moore and Douglas Gillette put it,

> The devastating fact is that most men are fixated at an immature stage of development. These early developmental levels are governed by the inner blueprints appropriate to boyhood. When they are allowed to rule what should be adulthood, when the archetypes of boyhood are not built upon and transcended by the Ego's appropriate accessing of the archetype of mature masculinity, they cause us to act out of our hidden (to us, but seldom to others) boyishness. (13)

Many of the cultural forms that used to ease the passage to manhood in our society—hunting groups, men's clubs and lodges, religious societies, even daily working contact with a father who teaches the son agriculture or trade skills—have pretty well broken down. Outside of a few surviving rites of initiation such as Jewish bar mitzvah and Catholic confirmation, which are usually poorly understood and often rote, young men have no respected and sanctioned social rituals to let them and their societies know they have transcended boyhood and become men.

Traditionally, only men have had the power to bestow manhood on other men, but these young men must do it for themselves, because for them trustworthy elders are hard to come by. The worship of youth and beauty and physical achievement so prevalent in our culture, coupled with the distrust of age and tradition introduced by my own generation, has made the idea of older men as role models exceedingly problematical. As a result, young

men's natural desire to find older men to admire and pattern themselves after has been frustrated, or has fastened on unreal giant-figures such as film stars or sports "heroes"—Rambo or Van Damme or Shaq—or on peer group figures who exemplify whatever qualities of daring or carelessness or brutality are currently admired.

I have talked with few young men of college age who think their fathers are good role models or who want to be like them. In fact, the majority of young men have no adult figures in their lives after whom they wish to pattern themselves, and no way that seems satisfying to fit themselves into the adult world. Lacking such an invitation into adulthood, our young men try to construct their own manhood on the basis of peer wisdom—nearly always a bad source. They try to invent their own initiation and ordeal structures, to achieve in the eyes of their peers what the culture at large denies them, striving "after a catch-as-catch-can image of manhood through a patchwork of ad-hoc initiations" (Raphael 23). They do it by risk-taking, by contest, by sport, by revolt, by artsy alienation. Many seek out reassurance from their peers in the form of groups, gangs, self-created organizations of all sorts. As Anthony Rotundo explains in *American Manhood*, many youth-culture organizations in the past included some social controls—men's lodges, religious organizations, literary societies, YMCA-type clubs all included some older members (67–74). Today, however, our college men have only one extremely limited choice in terms of male organizations: fraternities. We have all seen the results of fraternity membership. As one of my students said about his hazing experience, "They could initiate me into brotherhood, but not into manhood."

One of the results of failed initiation is an emotional constriction. Of the shades of the emotional spectrum, the only hues that most young men feel they may express openly are anger and humor. With little permission to talk about their feelings beyond these "controlled" responses, many college-age men are completely out of touch with the issues that are creating them—and too often creating them as driven, confused, misogynistic, xenophobic obeyers of orders. As a result, much male-to-male contact among students consists of different forms of posing, image creation, and agonistic contest. Despite the confidence they feel they must always display, however, few young men are sure that they are doing well in such contests to demonstrate their manhood.

I saw this clearly in a course I taught last semester that emphasized male gender construction. After the class read a book by Sam Keen, I asked all male students to sit on one side of the room and all female students on the other. "How many people on this side of the room," I asked, gesturing toward the left, "feel comfortable thinking of themselves and calling themselves women?" The sixteen women blinked, shrugged a bit, looked at each other in slight puzzlement, then all raised their hands. "All right. How many people on this side of the room feel comfortable thinking of themselves and calling themselves men?" The fourteen men stirred uncomfortably in their seats. Throats were cleared. They looked sidelong at one another. And finally, three of the fourteen raised their hands.

Most of these students were senior English majors, but in the discussion that followed it came out that even at twenty or twenty-one these men were still uncomfortable thinking of themselves except as "guys"—an age-neutral and even mostly gender-neutral term. Unlike the women, who simply felt that women was what they *were* now that they were not little girls, the "guys" weren't quite sure. "It's sort of like being a man, calling myself a man, is something I have to earn," one of them put it, "but I'm not quite sure what I have to do to earn it."

What *do* they have to do to earn it? And who should we be, then, as male teachers of male students? It is this question to which we all keep turning, and it is this continuing question about the making of masculinities that men's studies and the men's movement are trying to take on. The task is not easy, because the academic mind is still uncertain about the appropriateness of masculine studies. I have heard men's studies attacked as "the macho analysis of machismo," and as a back-formation like the National Association for the Advancement of White People. "Hasn't all scholarship in the West been men's studies?" asks a colleague, "and aren't you just taking energy away from feminist issues?" "Why not just call it gender studies?" asks another. I have gone into bookstores and asked for the men's studies section only to be eyed narrowly by the clerk as if I'd asked for snuff porn before being told that they might have some of "that stuff" down in Sociology. The Women's Studies section takes up three whole double racks, but men's studies is still fortunate to get three bottom shelves.

And all of us, of course, have been invited to join in the more or less constant laugh-fest ongoing about the men's movement and men's weekends. I've collected an office door full of cartoons satirizing such things over the past two years. Of course there *are* elements of the men's movement that are easy to make fun of; the drumming, wildman stuff, spearchucking, and so on, can often seem like Rousseauistic throwbacks. And there are elements out there in the culture only too happy to make fun of them, aren't there? But after thinking about it, which side do you feel more empathy with? The side of *Esquire*, which would like you to laugh at men who feel distorted by the *Esquire/Playboy* culture? Or those who are seeking (yes, sometimes silly-seeming) ways to escape it?

Yes, men's studies and the men's movement are in their early days; yes, we are still casting around for how we should do things, think things through. It's easy to portray us as self-pitying oppressors, balding wimps, failed hippies, whining jerks. But think back to the early days of the women's movement and to the completely unsympathetic presentations the media gave it. In the 1960s, feminists were often presented as crazy or evil—bra-burners, Warhol-shooters, ugly girls with grudges, man-haters. There are powerful vested interests threatened by the men's movement, and they are the same interests that the feminist movement threatens. Next time you see someone sneering at the silliness of the men's movement, ask yourself, *cui bono*? Who gains from this representation?

Again speaking personally, I have come to believe that there is much I can learn, as a man teaching men, from these movements. Men's studies and the men's movement have helped me bring some of my own uncertainties and questions into the open, and I hope to see more discussion about the ways in which gender affects both women and men as we try to teach and learn about writing. To begin the conversation, some of the most immediate questions we face are these:

Why are our male students often stereotyped as insensitive, or passive, or defensive? There is a great danger in stereotyping students, as we all know, but it is easier to casually assume stereotypes about young men than about almost any other group. The one "group identity" joke that is still politically safe is the one with men as its butt. Certainly it was easy for me to angrily place my journal-dumping student into the large category of "dumb yahoos" and think no more about him beyond that identification. We are not often invited to go deeper—especially not by the young men themselves. But as Bruce Ballenger puts it so well, there is nearly always "another face sweating under the mask" of public masculinity, and it is a face we need to try harder to see (11).

Striving to see that face is often not easy for many academic men. As Joseph Harris wrote to me in a critical but helpful letter, English department academics tend to react to male students of a traditional kind as "versions or embodiments of the working-class male, the rough father of the intellectual son and feminized professional." If, like many of us, you were a nerdy kid picked on by the tough guys, dealing from a position of (provisional) power with their contemporary incarnations is a relationship filled with unspeakable issues.

But we must speak of them. We must strive to get beyond our own reactiveness. Our male students are at a very complicated transition point in their lives, questioning their parents' and peers' moral norms and struggling to construct their own. They are changing in response to college culture, in response to the assumption of adult responsibility. They are struggling with what is for some their first exposure to discourse about gender issues and the feminist analysis. They are, to point out the obvious, very much in process, and the public personae they create try to mask this transitional uncertainty. But as writing teachers, we can and should see the uses of this process for them as both writers and readers. Certainly our roles as academic initiators are real and valid ones—but perhaps we should not so soon dismiss other possibilities for more personal mentoring. This may sometimes be uncomfortable, if we are successful at getting "beneath the mask" in male students' writing. But the payoff can be real. As Michael Kaufman, speaking of preventing male violence, puts it,

> Emotional discharge, in a situation of support and encouragement, helps unglue the ego-structures that require us to operate in patterned, phobic, oppressive, and surplus-aggressive forms. . . . Only in situations that

contradict these feelings—that is, with the support, affection, encouragement, and backing of other men who experience similar feelings—does the basis for change exist. (47)

If writing teachers, who have more opportunity to see into students' minds than most other teachers, do not take the responsibility to attempt mentoring, then who will? If we do not work to knock down the stereotypes, who will?

Are there specifically "male" genres of writing? Since I have often had a hard time reading what my young male students want from me, I often feel conflicted as I try to evaluate the venting papers, the macho-thrill, self-display, and adventure papers that they write when asked for personal essays. Personal experience assignments bring out a few tropes over and over again from male students: the wise elder story, the big challenge story, the I-learned-a-lesson story, the best friend story, and the different quest and journey narratives—most told as if they provided their own contexts and meanings—that teachers see again and again. For me, intervening in the process of these narratives has been difficult, because neither the writer nor I is really sure what the narrative is supposed to *do*. *Why* is this story being told? How do I, as teacher and elder, validate its meaning? Is that what I'm supposed to do at all? What gives me the right?

We—and our students, who seldom know any more than we do what real male teacher-to-student engagement on life issues might look like—often seek escape from the uncertain world of mentoring relationships by avoiding personalism completely. As men in this culture, in fact, we are trained from an early age to do precisely this: to focus on task, to put aside personal feelings (consciously, at least), to learn the rules, to do the required job of work, to "take care of business." Liam Hudson and Bernadine Jacot, in their book *The Way Men Think*, call this way of being in the world a result of "the male wound." The male wound, say Hudson and Jacot, exists in most men as a result of male children having to counteridentify with their primary infant caregivers, their mothers. Little girls can model themselves after their mothers, but little boys must tear themselves from that model to become men (44–52). The results of the male wound are both good and bad for men: in negative terms the wound creates physical and psychological hardness, personal insensitivity, and misogyny, while on the positive side the wound results in enhanced ideas of agency, a constant flow of psychic energy, and an attraction for abstract passions and mechanism—all of which we can see in the non-personal writing of our male students.

In light of Hudson and Jacot's idea, it is easier to see why many men turn with relief from the chthonian messiness of personal writing to the structures of rhetoric, the methods of exposition, the classical or Toulmin model of argument. Men love algorithms. Can I put the refutation section up front? How many times does the comparison have to alternate? Does Process Analysis always use the passive? How many grade levels does three comma splices drop me? Does every warrant need backing? Tell Me How To Build It, our male students say, so I can give it to you, you can judge it, and we can both

be on our way. Thus we tend to seek escape from the uncomfortable personalism of real mentoring by turning to distanced, rule- and convention-governed writing—exposition and argument.

It is a commonplace that young men in our classes *want* to write adventure or achievement narratives, quest stories of different sorts, or arguments that allow them to remain emotionally distant or to vent strongly-held opinions. But how much have we constructed these as the male genres we expect? How much do we know about what influences gender conditioning has had on male writing? We need to look more closely at the history of writing instruction and reexamine our ideas of what is "naturally" male. More importantly, we need to try more imaginatively to consider *why* we assume male genres to exist and analyze what such kinds of writing mean or are trying to express. Rather than scornfully dismissing the sorts of attitudes toward work and striving that undergird those sports-apotheosis papers, why not ask *why* our young men seek closeness with others through sports, form their identities through these competitions?

What are the stances available to teachers of male students, and which are the most useful? All teachers are aware that they can move between different roles as they teach, but not all men who teach are consciously aware of the roles they are given permission to slide into in relating to students. I can be the Nurturing Understander, the Institutional Representative, the Formalist Hanging Judge, the Buddy-Buddy, the Distant Scholar, the Daddy Surrogate. There are movements and trends in the sorts of permissions we are given, as well; a century ago I could have chosen the Impersonal Examiner, the Brilliant Lecturer, or the Demanding Humiliator, but very few younger teachers are now given permission to use these roles or to see them as desirable.

Very little has been said about the ethical demands or purposes of such roles. We have moved away from the agonism that informed male teaching and learning up until 150 years ago, but for many male teachers and students, the vortex of conflicting roles left behind has been confusing. What does it mean to mentor a student? What gives us permission or power to do it? How much challenge should exist between teacher and student? How much should teacher and student seem equals? What are the psychological effects of the temporary relationship of dominance that institutional power creates between teacher and student? And, most centrally for me, do male teachers have enough confidence in themselves as men really to accept the responsibility of teaching younger men, and the burden of being models of manhood for their students?

This issue becomes most pressing and practical when we conference or evaluate student papers. Each of our male students is trying to earn the right to call himself a man, but the rules of how manhood is earned are desperately unclear. The result, when we see it in the writing men do in our courses, can sometimes be silly, or disgusting, or horrifying. How are we to deal with the essay defending Rambo films as realistic history, or the argument paper that proposes that Marvel Comics are better than DC Comics, or the paper that pretends to be horrified by fraternity hazing but devotes three lovingly

crafted pages to detailed descriptions of it and ends by saying that "the short-term effects of pledging can be beneficial"? Or the following paper, by which I still feel amazed:

Horsing Around

It was a cold winter day and my two friends, Bill and Jim, decided to skip school with me. I got out of bed and acted as if I were going to school, but instead I went to Bill's house. We sat in his living room drinking alcoholic beverages at 8:00 in the morning, Jim came over at 8:30 to join us.

As we drank beer like fish, we decided we were bored. The three of us had a total of about three dollars, so we could not go anywhere, even out to eat. To help make the time pass, Bill got out his twelve-gauge shotgun and started to clean it. Then a bright idea came to me, so I said, "We have enough guns and ammunition, and we have plenty of wooded area to go shooting in, so let's go!"

We got in Bill's jeep and drove down Party Road to get to the woods. Bill and I both had twelve-gauge shotguns, and Jim had a twenty-two rifle. We were out walking in the woods and Jim saw a crow, black as night, land in a tree. He aimed, shot, and killed the crow. I walked over, picked up the blood-soaked bird, and sat it with its wings spread wide in a small twig tree. I loaded my gun, walked back fifteen to twenty feet, turned, and fired. The bird was blown into about twelve pieces, just like a jigsaw puzzle. The ground was covered with powdery snow, so when the bird was shot a blood spray pattern covered that area.

After this adventure, we walked farther into the woods where we spotted a horse in an open field. Jim dared me to shoot it, but I told him that the horse was too far away to hit. As soon as I said that, though, the huge black and brown horse slowly trotted toward us. Bill was approximately one-hundred feet away from me, and did not know what I was about to attempt. It was a good thing that he did not know, because he is one of those "follow-the-rules" kind of guys. Then Jim said, "Go ahead Adam, I dare you."

Without thinking of the seriousness involved, I raised the gun to my shoulder, took a careful aim, and KABOOM! I nailed him in the left hind quarter and he let out a yelp like a dog getting its tail sliced off. At first I thought I might have killed the animal, but I was too afraid to stick around to find out. All I remember hearing after I shot the gun was the horse yelping and Bill shouting; going into hysterics about what I had done.

At this time we hurried back to the jeep and drove quickly to Bill's house without being caught. Needless to say, Bill doesn't want me to go shooting with him anymore. While in the jeep, Jim was laughing so hard that he wet his jeans. We finished up our unusual and impromptu hunting excursion by cleaning the guns and drinking more beer.

Looking back now, the whole thing seems pretty funny, but I also regret it. I feel bad about hurting the horse and I think the incident probably wouldn't have happened if it hadn't been for the combination of boredom, beer, boyhood.

Horrifying? Yes, of course. This paper, which came to my attention as one of the 21,000 papers Andrea Lunsford and I collected for error research in 1986, presents the teacher with immense questions that go quite beyond the obvious issues of political ideology that have been argued over lately. How this writer came to be who he is, and what we as teachers can or should do about it, is the question. What is the teacher to say about the casual male brutality evident here, brutality of a kind unimaginable from a female student? What is a teacher's duty regarding the moral contents of essays written by young men? How do we reconcile the intelligence and sophistication of some of the writing with this garrulous and self-satisfied tale of puerile cruelty? What are we to *say* to this student?

The easiest tack would be exactly what the teacher in this case seems to have done with an earlier draft: tell the student to provide a "theme," in this case some sort of adult regret, that would transform the purity of the narrative into the teacher-favorite narrative genre of "I did bad and learned a lesson." This is what Adam did, especially in his last paragraph. The teacher's comment: "Adam—Your theme is better-expressed in this draft than in the earlier one. The problem is that besides adding a theme, you have also added some errors—some serious." The rest of the comment deals with paragraph unity and comma splice errors. All of the marginal comments are handbook numbers.

How tempting it is merely to stick handbook numbers on a paper like this, to call for a clearer theme! How simple such a task is in contrast to a fully engaged response from an older man to a younger man. How problematic such an engaged response would be; dare we ask questions of our students like, "Why do you shame yourself so?" or "How have you acted to right this wrong?" How many teachers have any of us ever had who dared to engage us on this level? How much do young men wish to be engaged on such a serious level? (As I remember my own young days, I recall pining for such engagement and discussion—not pontification or lecturing, but serious engagement on the life issues I faced. I also recall getting almost nothing of the sort from older men.)

But these are, and please notice the expression, academic questions. For most college teachers of writing, that engagement with the young, that willingness to name the world for them, is hard to imagine. It is in some ways what academic men are least used to and may even have been trained to distrust programmatically. It is easy today to attack any claim to foundational certainty as megalomaniacal or hegemonic or theoretically indefensible, and it is particularly easy to attack such attitudes in men as more evidence of patriarchal valorization of the subject.

Does teaching young men effectively call for pedagogical techniques different from those effective with young women? Teaching interventions in a writing course must finally, of course, be individualized if they are to be useful. Typing all male students as barbarians, or aggressive strivers, or brown-nosers is not useful; like female students, each one is different. But I have not been able to keep from noticing that men and women often react differently to different sorts of pedagogies.

This difference is very clear in the ways that men and women relate to pedagogies based on collaboration. In distinguishing between "hierarchical" and "dialogic" methods of collaboration on writing tasks, Lisa Ede and Andrea Lunsford in *Singular Texts, Plural Authors* avoid gender stereotypes as much as they can (132–35). Even so, it is impossible for the reader not to associate dialogic collaboration, in which "the group effort is seen as an essential part of the production" (133), with feminism and women's ways of knowing, and hierarchical collaboration, with its product-based goals and clearly defined subordinate and superordinate roles, with the ways men do things. Ede and Lunsford's discussion of these two collaborative methods is sensitive and subtle; they do not demonize hierarchical collaboration in spite of their admiration for (and use of) dialogic collaboration. But because it *is* dialogic, feminist, and "subversive," dialogic work clearly seems more valuable to them, as it does to many teachers of writing. The problem for male students is that many do not come to dialogic collaboration easily, or come to it at all, and if egalitarian, communitarian, consensus-based collaboration is part of a teacher's expectations of group work, male students will consistently disappoint. It is not how men have been trained to do business, and expecting that we can blunt the aggressive individualism that *is* their cultural training in a few weeks is unrealistic.

Young men are simply more drawn to individual work and to hierarchies. Indeed, any writing teacher can illustrate this gender differential by setting up workshop groups segregated by gender. My experience is that the all-women's groups may or may not collaborate dialogically, but that the all-men's groups will certainly proceed hierarchically. A leader will emerge, roles in the project will be assigned, methods will be set up—the whole mechanism of rationalistic Western problem-solving will appear before your eyes. Even the careless or absent member who just "mails it in" in terms of group work is performing a role, and all of us have seen the phenomenon of the "male star" student, one who consistently goes out of his way to create an image, to impress us with his charisma and abilities.

I have also noticed that young men usually want clearly defined individualized credit for the work they do and the roles they play in groups. "Group credit" often seems to them unfair. This cultural training in individualism appears in many forms—and many of them serve young men badly in school settings. The "star" role does not work for everyone. Like the young man who dropped his journal with such telling force into my wastebasket, some of our male students have evolved a serf mentality: to act inexpressive, to take orders for as long as they have to, to give as little as they can, and to rebel in the ways available to them. Newly minted as "adults," they are naturally conflicted by school roles, since the tacit code of male honor they are taught in this culture demands pride, individuality, and resistance, but most find themselves in situations of dependence, powerlessness, and servitude to goals they may not understand or accept.

One of the results of this conflict is that men lag far behind women in educational achievement. Though we hear more in the popular press about the

self-esteem problems of young girls in school settings, in fact girls consistently do better in most school subjects than boys. Women's mean high school class rank has been higher than men's (by a minimum of ten percentage points) at least since the early seventies (Adelman 3). In the 1992 NAEP, twelfth-grade girls outperformed boys by 10.2 points in reading and 21 points in writing on a 500-point scale (National Center for Education Statistics *Report* 462, 486). Since 1978, more women than men have completed bachelor's degrees each year, and today men are a minority—around 46 percent—of both bachelor's and master's degrees awarded (National Center for Education Statistics, *Digest* 245). Honors Programs are even more clearly split, with the one at my own school over 65 percent women (and as much as 80 percent in humanities disciplines). Women's GPAs at my university average 2.90, while men's average 2.65. Men are simply falling behind in college education.

Why is this happening? As Willard Gaylin puts it in *The Male Ego*, the cultural signals that young girls are given to be cooperative rather than physically aggressive often result in more flexible social and interpersonal abilities:

> In many ways this better prepares women for modern life than male biology does. We do not live in a world in which power is measured by grip, height, or size of biceps, but by position, accomplishment, intellectual achievement, and the like. The early lessons the little boys learn about becoming men may tragically become the spears on which their self-respect will be impaled in modern adult life. But the lesson of those early days persists, and men will be trapped testing themselves on an obsolete power basis throughout their lives, if only in symbolic language and metaphorical actions. (35)

The power of these conflicts to harm young men can be seen in the tacit attitudes that many teachers have about their male students. Many have no idea who to *be* in their relations with their students. Most of us have stories about our most disgusting brown-nosers (or were they really just wonderful enthusiasts?), but many are also familiar with what Mary Hiatt calls "the student at bay," usually male, who feverishly agrees with everything a teacher says and takes directions gratefully, does as little as he can, never volunteers, and who leaves the course having given as little of his real self as possible.

How do we get through this serf mentality, break through into the underlife of students? It will probably not be possible until we admit that our young men have different attitudinal responses to teaching and learning than our young women students. Since men's studies and the men's movement are both concerned with the structures that culture uses to construct manhood, it seems natural that we might look to these movements for help in understanding the struggles our students undergo as they submit themselves to the complex institutional structure of higher education.

We must thus ask ourselves: what are male learning styles? As Carol Gilligan and Belenky et al. have suggested, women seem to learn more

happily and naturally in related, collaborative, and nurturing environments. Academic feminism has tended to extrapolate that data into a pedagogy that assumes that female learning styles should be normative, but an honest inquiry into the success of this project reveals serious problems, at least for young men. Inexpressivity, for instance, is a learned behavior in men that serves several functions, but we often tend to read it as simple coldness and write off the student as insensitive (Sattel 355). Our readings of male students are often too simple; males simply do not respond in situations involving motivation, self-disclosure, or collaboration the way that female students do, and to assume that they must learn to in a single semester is unrealistic. Whatever our critique may be of the cultural assignments our young men have received, punishing them as individuals because they don't meet our new standards is unfair. Our job must include understanding them.

These are only a few of the issues we face that men's studies can help us shed light on. If we are to grapple effectively with the attitudes of young men, we cannot continue to view them merely as order-takers, or sulky vandals, or cultural naïfs who can be easily reformed with a dose of cultural studies. The fact is that we are still struggling today with the meaning of the shift away from all-male education that took place 150 years ago, and at this point we have not foregrounded gender issues equally for men and women. The feminism within and the feminization of composition pedagogy that have become such powerful parts of composition studies today have not yet made much room for male students—or male teachers. Although it is understandable why male attitudes, fears, and psychological structures have been either ignored or subjected to offhand dismissal in the discourse of contemporary composition, the result has not been more effective understanding of our students. As writing teachers, we have a unique opportunity to assist or thwart our students' searches. It will require, however, more than our current assumptions that we want to turn out seemingly genderless "writers," or that pedagogies that make collaboration and subordination of the individual normative will work equally well for all. Like it or not, we will produce writers who are young women and young men. We need to confront directly what this means to us as older women and older men. We need, for the first time, to confront gender issues wholly.

WORKS CITED

Adelman, Clifford. *Women at Thirtysomething: Paradoxes of Attainment.* Washington, D.C.: U.S. Dept. of Education, 1991.

Ballenger, Bruce. "The Tuft of Flowers in a Leveled Field." Forthcoming in *Pre/Text.*

Belenky, Mary Field, Blythe McVicker Clinchy, Nancy Rule Goldberger, and Jill Mattuck Tarule. *Women's Ways of Knowing.* New York: Basic Books, 1986.

Bledstein, Burton J. *The Culture of Professionalism.* New York: W. W. Norton, 1976.

Brooke, Robert. "Underlife and Writing Instruction." *CCC* 38 (May 1987): 141–53.

Connors, Robert J. "Women's Reclamation of Rhetoric in the Nineteenth Century." *Feminine Principles and Women's Experience in American Composition and Rhetoric.* Ed. Louise Wetherbee Phelps and Janet Emig. Pittsburgh: U of Pittsburgh P, 1995. 67–90.

Ede, Lisa, and Andrea Lunsford. *Singular Texts, Plural Authors: Perspectives on Collaborative Writing.* Carbondale: Southern Illinois UP, 1990.

Gaylin, Willard. *The Male Ego.* New York: Penguin, 1992.

Gilligan, Carol. *In a Different Voice: Psychological Theory and Women's Development.* Cambridge: Harvard UP, 1982.

Harris, Joseph. Letter to author, 2 March 1995.

Hiatt, Mary P. "Students at Bay: The Myth of the Student Conference." *CCC* 26 (Feb. 1975): 38–41.

Hudson, Liam, and Bernadine Jacot. *The Way Men Think: Intellect, Intimacy, and the Erotic Imagination.* New Haven: Yale UP, 1991.

Kaufman, Michael. "The Triad of Men's Violence." Kimmel and Messner 28–49.

Kimmel, Michael S., and Michael A. Messner, eds. *Men's Lives.* 2d ed. New York: Macmillan, 1992.

Miller, Susan. *Textual Carnivals: The Politics of Composition.* Carbondale: Southern Illinois UP, 1991.

Moore, Robert, and Douglas Gillette. *King, Warrior, Magician, Lover: Rediscovering the Archetypes of the Mature Masculine.* New York: HarperCollins, 1990.

National Center for Education Statistics. *Digest of Education Statistics 1994.* Washington, D.C.: U.S. Dept. of Education, 1994.

———. *The NAEP 1992 Technical Report.* Washington, D.C.: U.S. Dept. of Education, 1994.

Nystrand, Martin, Stuart Greene, and Jeffrey Wiemelt. "Where Did Composition Studies Come From? An Intellectual History." *Written Communication* 10 (July 1993): 267–333.

Ong, Walter J. *Fighting for Life: Contest, Sexuality, and Consciousness.* Ithaca: Cornell UP, 1981.

Raphael, Roy. *The Men from the Boys: Rites of Passage in Male America.* Lincoln: U of Nebraska P, 1988.

Rotundo, E. Anthony. *American Manhood: Transformations in Masculinity from the Revolution to the Modern Era.* New York: Basic Books, 1993.

Sattel, Jack W. "The Inexpressive Male: Tragedy or Sexual Politics?" Kimmel and Messner 350–57.

Schmidt, George P. *The Liberal Arts College.* New Brunswick, NJ: Rutgers UP, 1957.

Taylor, Warner. *A National Survey of Conditions in Freshman English.* Madison: U of Wisconsin Research Bulletin No. 11, 1929.

Introduction to Composition-Rhetoric: Backgrounds, Theory, and Pedagogy

The "Introduction" to Bob's 1997 book *Composition-Rhetoric: Backgrounds, Theory, and Pedagogy* recounts how he came to notice that there was "something wrong" with the picture of rhetorical history he had studied for so long. In brief, he found that what "was missing" was the nineteenth century—for according to traditional rhetorical history, after the publication of Whately's *Elements of Rhetoric* in 1828, "there *was* no rhetorical activity (outside of the jigging of a few stray elocutionists, the only habitants of this waste ground) until Burke's *Counter-Statement* of 1931 or I. A. Richards's *Philosophy of Rhetoric* in 1936" (317). The loosely connected essays in Bob's book challenge that received wisdom, rejecting the description of "current-traditional rhetoric" provided by Richard Young in 1978 and decried by many (including Bob in some earlier essays) as a fairly grim, rule-bound view of writing and writing instruction. In place of "current-traditional rhetoric," with its negative connotations, Bob proposes "composition-rhetoric," a "genuine rhetoric, with its own *theoria* and *praxis*" whose history can be traced from early American, through postwar, to what Bob calls "consolidation composition-rhetoric." This historical account Bob identifies as an attempt to "construct coherent explanations for historical facts and causality, taking archival research as a starting place and consistent control" (332). With now-familiar self-deprecation, Bob says that this is "not 'radical' or 'subversive' history, and I suppose that means I am (sigh) an epistemologically conservative historian" (332).

T his is a book about the rhetoric of written composition that arose in American colleges after 1780 and about its development as a culture, a theoretical apparatus, and a teaching practice down to relatively recent times. Although this story began to be told in detail during the last decade, let me tell you how I happen to be recounting my piece of it. When I began to study rhetoric, back in the mid-1970s, graduate students were all

---

From *Composition-Rhetoric: Backgrounds, Theory, and Pedagogy* (Pittsburgh: U of Pittsburgh P, 1997), 1–22.

quickly made aware of the distinguished work that had been done in rhetorical history during the previous century. Starting from the original nineteenth-century German scholarship and English commentary up through the admirable contemporary work of George Kennedy, Wilbur Samuel Howell, James J. Murphy, James Golden, Edward P. J. Corbett, and Brian Vickers, I traced the history of Greek and Roman rhetoric, patristic and medieval rhetoric, Renaissance and Restoration rhetoric, eighteenth-century and modern rhetoric.

What's wrong with this picture? Something, I slowly became aware, was missing from rhetorical history. It was, of course, the nineteenth century. As those who were trained before 1980 know, that entire century was almost completely excluded from traditional rhetorical history. After Whately's *Elements of Rhetoric* in 1828, if one were to have believed standard histories, there *was* no rhetorical activity (outside of the jigging of a few stray elocutionists, the only habitants of this waste ground) until Burke's *Counter-Statement* of 1931 or I. A. Richards's *Philosophy of Rhetoric* in 1936. At that point, these histories suggest, the whole enterprise miraculously comes back to life and thrives into our own day. As Daniel Fogarty put it in 1959, "with few exceptions of any moment in rhetorical theory, Whately was the last rhetorician until the nineteen-twenties" (*Roots for a New Rhetoric*, 20).

This position is, of course, outmoded and is increasingly being shown as such. It is the result of the first modern rhetorical histories having been written by scholars in speech departments, which were formed in reaction to the poor treatment speech teachers had received in the developing departments of English. As a result, speech-based histories tended to valorize oral discourse—and to downplay written rhetoric, which is the great contribution of the nineteenth century. It came to seem to those of us trained in the 1970s that there *was* no nineteenth-century rhetoric, primarily because there were so few important developments in oral rhetorical theory.

Speech departments, however, no longer control rhetorical scholarship as they once did. Rhetoric at many schools today is in the process of moving from speech to English departments, and scholars of rhetorical history are gradually being made aware of the complexity and importance of this period and this strand of composition-based rhetorical history. Old attitudes die hard, however, and the argument for early rhetorics of written discourse must still be made. During the late 1980s when Patricia Bizzell and Bruce Herzberg were putting together their fine anthology, *The Rhetorical Tradition*, I was one of the historians asked to act as a reader, and I wearied Pat and Bruce with my welkin-rending cries for more nineteenth-century material. At one point when they were for giving the nineteenth century especially short shrift, I wrote to them:

> Your claim seems to be this: after heady new developments from 1590 through 1828, the field of rhetoric just *shut down* for a century, that *nothing* of real interest or importance happened between 1828 and 1928. For rhetoric, there *was* no nineteenth century. There were, of course,

incredibly important nineteenth centuries for chemistry, history, biology, philosophy, psychology, literature, sociology, mathematics, philology— in fact, every other modern discipline was *formed* by the nineteenth century. But not rhetoric. Despite the considerable theoretical arguments it produced, it will seem in this anthology to have generated no important thinkers for a hundred years. Despite the ubiquity of rhetoric and the fact that it had attracted some of the best minds of the period, it will appear that you saw no ideas of importance propounded. The discipline was apparently not affected by its changing culture, nor did it affect the culture in any important sense. It just vegetated, meriting only ten pages of quick, shallow gloss as transition from 1828 to 1928—and most of that gloss will be taken up with discussion of fields only tangentially related to rhetoric—fields with more cachet, more status.

Poor rhetoric. A field without a history for a whole century when every other field was being created. If you were outside observers of this field, knowing nothing about it, can you easily imagine that it could exist as claimed? That there could be *any* field for which the nineteenth century did not exist?

I went on in this vein for months, and Pat and Bruce eventually relented, to the point of including forty pages (including fifteen pages of Nietzsche) of post-Whately, pre-Bakhtin material out of the 1,282 pages of *The Rhetorical Tradition*.

Clearly the argument that indeed there was rhetorical history between 1828 and 1928 needs continually to be made. Several books have made that argument during the past decade, and made it well. James Berlin's *Writing Instruction in Nineteenth-Century American Colleges* and *Rhetoric and Reality* have provided readers with thoughtful introductions to nineteenth- and twentieth-century composition-rhetoric. Sharon Crowley's *The Methodical Memory: Invention in Current-Traditional Rhetoric* and Nan Johnson's *Nineteenth-Century Rhetoric in North America* have delved deeper into specific questions of theory and influence, tying nineteenth-century work inextricably into the older rhetorical tradition. David Russell's *Writing in the Academic Disciplines, 1870–1990* is a splendid example of the tracing of rhetorical influences outside English or speech department walls, and Winifred Bryan Horner's *Nineteenth-Century Scottish Rhetoric: The American Connection* shows how painstaking textual scholarship of a traditional sort can elucidate connections between European and American rhetorics of the period. Albert R. Kitzhaber's groundbreaking 1953 dissertation. *Rhetoric in American Colleges, 1850–1900*, was finally published in book form and made available to general readers. John Brereton's documentary history *Origins of Composition Studies* has given us easy access to many original sources. In addition, scores of articles, chapters, and more recent dissertations have illustrated the importance and complexity of this period and these materials that had been long scanted by traditional rhetorical history.

I place this book in that argumentative tradition. I do not mean it to be only about the nineteenth century or only about composition, though those

areas do bulk large in these pages. I mean here to write a story of people who have studied and taught writing in American schools since the early nineteenth century, to illuminate some elements of that tradition of written rhetoric. I try to show how this composition-rhetoric grew out of and interacted with concurrent cultural trends, as American college and university teaching were shaped by pressures that were economic, political, and theoretical. I mean also to look more closely at specific elements within American composition-rhetoric, trying to determine why some survived and others did not, trying to explore what our theories and techniques of teaching have said about our attitudes toward students, language, and life.

My claim throughout this book is that there *is* a new rhetorical tradition that arose in the United States during the nineteenth century to try to inform an ever increasing demand for literacy skills for the professional and managerial classes. This is a tradition customarily referred to as "current-traditional rhetoric," and indeed, the original title of this book was to have been *Current-Traditional Rhetoric*. I found, however, that as I worked through the chapters one by one I was becoming less satisfied with that widely accepted term for the subject accumulating under my pen. Finally, I simply could not underwrite the term any longer, and in this book I have ventured to suggest a new term, "composition-rhetoric." Let me speak briefly to the reasons for this seemingly wilful refusal.

"Current-traditional rhetoric," as it has been popularly used over the past fifteen years, is a term based on one first proposed by Richard Young in his 1978 essay, "Paradigms and Problems: Needed Research in Rhetorical Invention." Young in that article referred to the older forms of composition teaching and theory as based in a "current-traditional paradigm," a term he derived by adding a hyphen to a term first invented by Daniel Fogarty in *Roots for a New Rhetoric* in 1959. Fogarty was no friend of the composition strand of rhetoric and was anxious to see it supplanted by a new philosophical rhetoric; he called the entire teaching tradition up to that point "current traditional rhetoric" (117). This was not an important term for Fogarty, and little had been made of it before Young's formalization of the phrase reified the concept at a propitious time for new nomenclature. Popularized by the students in Young's 1979 NEH Summer Seminar, many of whom were to become luminaries in their own rights, "current-traditional rhetoric" became the default term for the tradition of rhetoric that appeared specifically to inform the composition courses of the latter nineteenth century and the twentieth century up through the 1960s. Historical studies of composition pedagogy since the eighteenth century were beginning to appear, and historians often collapsed Young's "paradigm" with Fogarty's "rhetoric" in order to have a name for what they were writing about. "Current-traditional rhetoric" as a term seemed to indicate both the outmoded nature and the continuing power of older textbook-based writing pedagogies.

The term was almost unquestioned for many years, although C. H. Knoblauch delivered a thoughtful critique of it at the 1984 Modern Language Association Conference, in a paper called "The Current-Traditional

Paradigm: Neither Current, nor Traditional, nor a Paradigm." Young, said Knoblauch, had stripped Fogarty's term of its intellectual seriousness in order to criticize a classroom tradition he disliked. The "current-traditional paradigm," he charged, was not really a rhetoric at all:

> No major rhetoricians, ancient or modern, have been named as its origi-nators or perpetuators; no works, aside from textbooks, have been iden-tified as constituting it; its concepts have never been formally analyzed or proven systematic. . . . What Fogarty attempts in his book is a linking of school rhetoric to the larger cross-currents of Western thought which are his primary focus, advocating some purposeful changes in the first to accord with his sense of progress of the second. What Young attempts, by contrast, is a portrait of rhetoric from the restricted vantage-point of the classroom. (2)

Knoblauch's critique fell on stony ground, however, since at that time, historians knew little about the nineteenth century except what *was* in classroom textbooks. "Current-traditional rhetoric" became a convenient whipping boy, the term of choice after 1985 for describing whatever in nine-teenth- and twentieth-century rhetorical or pedagogical history any given au-thor found wanting. Got a contemporary problem? Blame it on that darn old current-traditional rhetoric. (No, I do not exempt my earlier work from this charge.)

I have more recently come to believe, however, that the almost unques-tioned acceptance of Young's term has left the field with a stock phrase that was never completely accurate and has become even more problematical since Young's essay appeared fifteen years ago. What we have reified as a unified "current-traditional rhetoric" is, in reality, not a unified or an un-changing phenomenon. It developed over time; the written rhetoric of 1830 is not that of 1870, which is not that of 1910, which is not that of 1960, which is certainly not that of 1995. It evolved differently in different settings: schools, colleges, universities, Lyceums, literary societies, Chautauquas. The develop-ing tradition of written rhetoric was not monadic, was *never* the rhetorical tradition as a whole; it was always a strand unto itself, reliant upon some ele-ments of the earlier oral rhetoric but also filled with materials that would have been meaningless to oral rhetoricians.

"Current-traditional rhetoric," as usually used to describe the reac-tionary and derivative nature of the textbook tradition, is not "current" in any ongoing sense of development. Since 1960, the older forms of written rhetoric have been "current" only in the sense that they still existed and were passed along and taught. To the degree that "current-traditional rhetoric" has been defined and commented upon by those in composition studies, it has been universally condemned as no longer current *enough*. Many "current-traditional" ideas are, after all, no more current than the design of the *Titanic*.

Neither is it "traditional" in the sense of adhering to or developing or-ganically from the older, orally based rhetorical tradition. Nan Johnson and

Sharon Crowley have shown how nineteenth-century rhetoric grew from eighteenth-century epistemology, but the composition-and-textbook "tradition" usually associated with current-traditional rhetoric owes less to Campbell and Blair than it does to pedagogical lore, sheer invention, and sui generis theoretical pronouncements made between twenty and two hundred years ago. Unlike the older rhetorical tradition, it did not exist in any coherent form before 1800. As a body of information, written rhetoric was brought into being between 1800 and 1910.

Since, therefore, the methods and theories associated with teaching writing in America after 1800 are neither changeless, nor unified, nor seriously "current" in today's scholarly field, nor strongly related to traditional rhetoric, I propose in this book to eschew the term "current-traditional rhetoric" and to refer instead to older and newer forms of *composition-rhetoric*. History enthusiasts will recognize that I have appropriated this term from the title of a forward-looking but not very successful secondary school textbook produced in 1897 by Fred Newton Scott and Joseph V. Denney. Like Scott and Denney, I use the term to identify specifically that form of rhetorical theory and practice devoted to written discourse. Writing, of course, had always been a small but necessary part of the older rhetorical tradition, but composition-rhetoric after 1800 was the first rhetoric to place writing centrally in rhetorical work. Although composition-rhetoric was by no means the only strand of rhetoric evolving between 1800 and 1900 (it was related to though increasingly separate from the oral rhetorical ideas that coexisted with it throughout its history, as Johnson has shown in her *Nineteenth-Century Rhetoric*), it was the strand that would burgeon. While oral rhetoric sank into desuetude after 1860, composition-rhetoric waxed, producing the most widely taught course in American colleges after 1900, Freshman Composition.

As opposed to the popular perception of "current-traditional rhetoric," I do not wish to paint composition-rhetoric as essentially degraded or utilitarian. Composition-rhetoric as it existed in ever evolving forms in America does, I believe, represent a coherent tradition of conceptualizing the elements of correct and successful writing, trying to teach students how to find them in extant prose, and encouraging students to create them in their own prose. Contra Fogarty, who thought "current traditional rhetoric" had no philosophy, I see composition-rhetoric as a genuine rhetoric, with its own *theoria* and praxis. Contemporary scholars have strongly criticized earlier forms of it as being pedagogically destructive, but we should also remember that many things we still find useful in writing pedagogy were evolved before 1960.

Composition-rhetoric is a modern rhetoric, quickly changing and adapting, driven by potent social and pedagogical needs, and running on the rails of an ever cheaper, ever quicker, and ever more competitive printing technology. Thus we can never speak of "composition-rhetoric" without stipulation, for it has existed in a variety of forms and constantly evolved. The composition-rhetoric of the schools was different from that of the colleges, which was not that of the universities. The rhetoric of men's colleges was

different from that of women's or coeducational colleges. That of each decade was subtly changed from that of the decade before. So in this book I will be referring to older and newer forms of composition-rhetoric, of school and university rhetorics, of women's rhetoric and men's. To do otherwise would be to reduce the formidable complexity of the situation.

Let me make a quick sketch here of the eras of composition-rhetoric this book means to cover. I am aware that characterization by period represents a sort of taxonomic lowest common denominator, and that it gives less of an impression of analysis than do conceptual taxonomies. Several conceptual taxonomies of this period already exist, however, and I want here to point out how periodization can show us something new about the development of rhetorical ideas. Although I don't want to suggest that composition-rhetoric was absolutely different in any of these periods from its state in previous or succeeding ones, I think an argument can be made that composition-rhetoric developed both as theory and practice through these periods and that each one presents a useful differentiation. Neither do I want to try to make any sort of disingenuous claim that composition-rhetoric is "just like" any of the more familiar disciplines that emerged in modern form out of the nineteenth century. It is not, primarily because the development of composition-rhetoric between 1885 and 1910 was externally imposed. It was a field decreed necessary and continued by social fiat. No other college discipline I know of has had anything like this history. College courses of study have traditionally emerged from the accumulation of a body of knowledge, which is gradually formalized and finally developed to the point where it produces experts who can teach it. Philosophy, history, mathematics, all of the sciences from the oldest to the newest, have evolved using this model. But composition-rhetoric did not, and thus these constructed eras do not mirror the development of any other discipline very closely. Here are the eras I think can be usefully differentiated.

EARLY AMERICAN COMPOSITION-RHETORIC

Although composition of speeches to be memorized and orally delivered has always been a part of the rhetorical tradition, the oldest forms of composition-rhetoric to be discussed here originated in the mixed rhetoric classes of the period 1800–1865, which were organized to teach students both oral and written discourse. These courses, which professed what I will call Early American composition-rhetoric, did not develop in a direct way from earlier purely oral rhetoric courses, although there was some overlap. In spite of Hugh Blair's influential belletrism, there did not exist before the Early American period any serious body of knowledge about how good writing could be successfully taught. The older discipline of rhetoric did contribute some of the ideas and definitions that were in general suspension, but no one was certain how to grid older orally attuned rhetorical concepts to the problems of writing. There was nothing but a teeming marketplace of disparate ideas, which began to appear permanently in competition, since there were no ways to prove their competing claims true or false.

Early American composition-rhetoric courses were usually taught using a combination of the belletristic-stylistic rhetorical theories of Blair's 1783 *Lectures on Rhetoric and Belles Lettres* and of the newer writing-oriented teaching methods pioneered by John Walker in his 1801 public school book *The Teacher's Assistant in English Composition*. These early composition classes were asked to write fortnightly rhetoricals—themes and regular subjects—on relatively abstract assignments like "Fame" and "Trust Not Appearances." They read and analyzed essays by Steele and Johnson, and later Hazlitt and Lamb. As the theoretical side of composition-rhetoric blossomed later in the period, students were often asked to memorize complex discourse taxonomies and lists of stylistic values and formal conditions. They were made to learn lists of figures and tropes and use them programmatically in their essays. Many such courses contained large sections of grammar, usually based on Lindley Murray's very popular *English Grammar* of 1795.

Early American composition-rhetoric was increasingly in transition as the period went on, and by 1860 it was unitary only in a limited sense. Though based in Blair's ideas, the rhetorical theories found in the different texts used by different colleges came to vary more and more widely after 1840; composition-rhetoric thus shows a sort of centrifugal movement throughout the period leading up to the Civil War. In part this fragmentation occurred because the institutional bases of Early American composition-rhetoric were so varied, and were becoming more so. Though the American college scene was small and relatively narrow, devoted to producing doctors, lawyers, and ministers, there were many kinds of colleges, from burgeoning proto-universities like Harvard and Yale to tiny frontier seminaries hardly distinguishable from high schools. Rhetorical theories were fighting for pre-eminence during this time, and training could be very different from college to college.

One element that does run through college experience during this period is the personal attention students got from faculty. Though not all this attention was kindly, and faculty-student relations were sometimes unfriendly, rhetorical training was usually an occasion for intense interaction between students and teachers. Classes were small, and so essays were often checked and commented on in short office conferences by professors. Recitations were held before the entire class, and, in what was usually an all-male college world, students were also usually members of a literary or debating society that continued the rhetorical training taken up in courses. The college world during this period was an intensely rhetorical world. Before the Civil War, composition teaching proceeded in this intense, culturally supported, small-scale, and often tutorial fashion.

POSTWAR COMPOSITION-RHETORIC

After 1865 American college culture changed radically, and composition-rhetoric shifted with it. The Morrill Act of 1862, which established the Agricultural and Mechanical Colleges, brought a large new population of

students to American colleges and helped found the major state universities, which would become important sites for composition teaching over the next five decades. From the province of a small group of elite students, college education became, during this time, much more available to the masses. The colleges were flooded with students who needed to be taught to write, who needed to be taught correctness in writing, who needed to know forms, and who could be run through the system in great numbers. Composition-rhetoric after the Civil War evolved to meet these needs, and in order to do so large portions of it were developed relatively quickly between 1865 and 1885. This is the Postwar period of composition-rhetoric, when scores of competing new ideas were put forward to try to solve the problems of teaching writing.

It was during these two decades that the first great waves of PhDs returned from German universities to establish here the structures of the modern American university. From Germany they brought with them the research ideal, methodologies of detailed analysis, and a scorn for older rhetorical ideas. This Postwar period saw the growth of the modern concept of universities as graduate and professional schools piggybacked on older undergraduate colleges, setting the stage for faculty hierarchies, scholarly specialization, the graduate-student industry, and departmentalization. As a result, between 1865 and 1900 the sites of American post-secondary education changed as they never had before and have not since. During the Postwar period we also see the foundation of a number of all-women's colleges and the rise of coeducation in some established schools, changes that fostered the rise of pure composition classes and helped to diminish the importance of the oral rhetorical tradition.

The size and site of composition courses changed at most colleges during this period as well. Up through the Civil War, most colleges had only a few hundred students, and it was common for college classes to really *be* composed of a whole class—the Class of 1852 or 1836. As colleges grew after the war, courses grew as well, and rhetoric and writing courses grew along with them. Instead of facing a class of thirty-five men, a teacher might find himself striving to grade essays by a class of close to one hundred students. With the rise of the elective system toward the end of the period, some courses could be split, but rhetoric generally tended to remain with the old whole-class system—"sophomore rhetoric" or "senior declamation"—and thus the scene was set for the beginnings of a whole-class freshman course.

During this period of composition-rhetoric, the inventiveness of composition teachers and theorists in America bloomed as it had never done before. Rhetorical and pedagogical theories were spun out by scores of competing writers and were launched into the educational system via an ever more sophisticated industry of school textbook publishers utilizing modern printing methods. This is the heyday of such inventive (and yet finally forgotten) rhetorical theorists as David J. Hill, Henry N. Day, Erastus Haven, Charles Bardeen, and John S. Hart, all of whom produced rhetorics proposing wildly variant ideas about discourse education, all of whom saw their ideas rifled and mostly discarded by the more successful authors of the later 1880s and

1890s. This, too, was the period of the first few very popular and successful text authors, including the Scotsman Alexander Bain and the American Adams S. Hill. The Postwar period saw the first differentiated composition textbooks, the first books identifiable as composition readers and handbooks.

CONSOLIDATION COMPOSITION-RHETORIC

Between 1885 and 1910 occurred the Consolidation period of composition-rhetoric in America, during which the theories and methods of composition teaching were consolidated in colleges and the plethora of ideas produced by the Postwar period were tested, challenged, expanded, discarded, and subjected to the harrowing interrogation of the first waves of compulsory writing courses at most schools. The consolidation of the field came with startling rapidity after 1885, with the advent of written entrance exams at Harvard in 1874 and the general adoption of such exams at most established colleges. The consolidation of composition-rhetoric did not take place because true theory or practice drove out false, but because pressing social problems demanded solutions. When more than half of the candidates—the products of America's best preparatory schools—failed the Harvard exams, a great outcry went up. Trumpeted throughout the nation in newspapers and magazines, "the illiteracy of American boys" became an obsession. College freshmen could not write. This situation could not be allowed. Secondary curricula must change. Teachers must be proselytized. Principals must be warned. Schools must be put on notice.

But though the change in secondary curricula did eventually come, it was not quick enough for Harvard. Adams Sherman Hill, who administered the entrance exam at Harvard, was not satisfied that freshmen were improving quickly enough. He proposed, in the middle 1880s, that Harvard institute a temporary course in remedial writing instruction—just until the crisis had passed—and require it of all incoming freshmen. This was done. The course, not to be dignified with a title, was merely called English A. It was the prototype for the required freshman course in composition that within fifteen years would be standard at almost every college in America. English departments settled into place a two-tiered hierarchy of literature and composition, and freshman "programs" arrived toward the end of the period, standardizing the course and placing it into the hands of those who would teach it henceforward: graduate students, low-level instructors, and beginning professors.

At the same time that institutional structures were consolidating to support composition teaching, the structures of intellectual transmission were falling into place to consolidate rhetorical theory. After the whirling centrifugal generation of competing ideas and theories during the Postwar period, the Consolidation period was centripetal, winnowing down the scores of genres, stylistic qualities, taxonomies, forms, modes, levels, and types into a tested and usable set of teaching tools. Teachability by untrained teachers became an important criterion of whether a theory or pedagogy survived, and

many interesting ideas disappeared while others became hegemonic. The textbook industry in a recognizably modern form was born, belching forth popular texts in huge steam-driven batches of tens of thousands, and these textbooks assumed ever larger roles in disseminating information and training new teachers.

With the advent of Freshman Composition, the melee of competing theory that had been "written rhetoric" was radically simplified. A criterion of choice had been found: teachability. The complex taxonomies and systems of the Early American and Postwar periods melted away, and in their place a few skeletal concepts remained, embroidered differently by different writers but essentially the same. Between 1885 and 1910 what would become Modern composition-rhetoric was shaped and made smooth by the mechanisms of a modernized, centralized textbook marketplace. These ideas were various, but they had in common an attraction for taxonomy and simplicity. They included the four modes of discourse (narration, description, exposition, and argument), the methods of exposition (process analysis, definition, comparison/contrast, classification, and so on), the three levels of discourse (diction, sentence, and paragraph), the "narrow-select-develop-outline" invention structure, the conception of the organic paragraph, the rhetorical and grammatical sentence types, and the static abstractions of Unity, Coherence, and Emphasis. None of these ideas, the very heart-ideas of the composition course after 1910, had existed except sketchily before 1865.

Meanwhile, literacy issues were widely discussed in the new popular magazines and in a growing professional literature of education. Professional organizations like the MLA were formed, and paradigmatic writing programs like Harvard's and Michigan's provided models for all other colleges. The first composition-based celebrities came into being, and the theories and pedagogies they espoused became the nationally accepted methods. The very influential theorists of the 1890s—John Genung, Barrett Wendell, and Fred Newton Scott—introduced pedagogies and rhetorical ideas that still have currency in the teaching of writing a century later. But the consolidation of the field by external forces was to have a heavy price.

MODERN COMPOSITION-RHETORIC

Most issues in composition methodology were decided, one way or another, by 1910, and after 1910 we emerge into what I call the Modern period of composition-rhetoric, a period of relative stasis that is usually associated with the pejorative uses of the term "current-traditional rhetoric." The Modern period of composition-rhetoric is defined by the almost absolute reign of a freshman composition requirement and the habits and industries that grow up around such a dominant institution. During this time, freshman composition programs take on their current forms, under the general direction of but somewhat autonomous from English departments. The huge courses are taught in multiple sections by "section hands" who are either graduate assistants or instructors, many of whom are frustrated literary specialists who teach writing

only because compelled. During the Modern period, it becomes a truism that student dislike for Freshman Composition is exceeded only by the dislike of its teachers.

Theoretically, the Modern period features a heavy reliance on the relatively few rhetorical ideas that lasted through the heavy winnowing of the Consolidation period. These rhetorical ideas are often subsumed into pedagogies that valorize formal and mechanical correctness—what will come to be called the "product" approach to teaching writing—and are given little credence or validity by scholars outside the field of freshman composition. These familiar concepts—the modes of discourse, the methods of exposition, Unity, Coherence, and Emphasis, the levels of style, the select-narrow-expand invention system, and subset outlining—are put forward in a series of textbooks remarkable for their unanimity of view on and their similar treatments of these canonized concepts.

One of the results of this narrowing of theory was to make the teaching of writing an intellectual backwater after 1910. On the level of form and methods, composition-rhetoric was forced by cultural pressures to insist more and more strongly on formal and mechanical correctness after 1900, and this formal obsession became the hallmark of the course. Classes were much larger, and personal conferences were usually impossible, so the typical pedagogy became assigned daily and fortnightly themes, which were turned in, marked up in red ink for the perceived problems each one evinced, and returned to the students, who were either expected to repair all the marked errors or merely to move on to the next assignment and do better. Subjects were nearly always assigned by the teacher, and they were usually devised in a strict adherence to some taxonomic scheme like the modes or methods. Students were nearly always asked for only one draft, which was the one turned in. During the Modern period, mechanical correction methods like correction charts—and eventually handbooks—began to appear to help teachers "correct" student papers more efficiently. Logistical problems of overload that rhetoric teachers had never faced before the 1890s led to new pedagogical methods, and formally, Modern composition-rhetoric tended toward mechanistic solutions to these problems.

This is not the place to rehearse all of the results of Freshman Composition as a phenomenon within the developing socioculture of American academia. For our purposes, we need only note that Freshman Composition, being a really new college subject, presented its teachers with organizational and pedagogical problems that were not well solved in its early days. Literature became the future for promising scholars in the new departments of English. Composition became known as a low-level grind, as a grueling apprenticeship, as a kind of teaching to pass through as quickly as possible.

By 1910, Modern composition-rhetoric was firmly in place, carried forward almost exclusively in textbooks, which represented the only organ of tradition in the field of composition teaching. There, though it was criticized by the journals that began to spring up in the early part of the century, this static form of composition-rhetoric flourished and spread to generation after

generation of new composition teachers—usually graduate students—who knew no other rhetorical or pedagogical way. As Young put it, describing his "current-traditional paradigm," this was a rhetoric consisting of

> emphasis on the composed product rather than the composing process; the analysis of discourse into words, sentences, and paragraphs; the classification of discourse into description, narration, exposition, and argument; the strong concern with usage (syntax, spelling, punctuation) and with style (economy, clarity, emphasis); the preoccupation with the informal essay and the research paper, and so on. ("Paradigms and Problems," 31)

In addition, Gary Tate has identified as other key elements in this form of rhetoric "a focus on expository writing, a belief that reality is located in the external world, a denial of the personal voice of the student writer, a simple-minded prescriptiveness, an emphasis on reason to the exclusion of the other human faculties, a devotion to a simple, linear view of the composing process, and a belief that the primary job of a writer is to transfer to the page ideas that exist already in the mind" ("Current-Traditional Rhetoric," 1).

And so things remained for almost half a century. While literary studies proliferated and evolved research methods, journals, bibliographies, and respected scholars, composition-rhetoric remained a scholarly backwater and a professional avocation, a drudgery, and a painful initiation ritual. The Modern era of composition-rhetoric was informed by practice being divorced from viable roots, left without any means for exploring its field knowledge, condemned to endlessly reinvent the wheel. Writing was the most often taught of college subjects and by a great measure the least examined. Composition was the only college-level course in which the teachers generally gained all their knowledge of the field from the same textbooks they assigned to students. Textbooks themselves emerge during this time as the absolute arbiters of classroom content and practice. Ever more sophisticated in their intent to aid the teacher, they finally reach a point of teachability that can relegate teachers to mere grading assistants to the all-potent text. Textbooks appear in new specialty forms, ranging from the old-style "rhetorics" that contain both theory and exercises, to handbooks to help teachers explain formal errors, to workbooks to give students practice exercises that need no human guide, to anthologies and readers that provide models and grist for discussion.

The Modern period lasts through 1960 or so, after which its tenets are challenged by a variety of rising theoretical and pedagogical movements that had begun in the 1940s. The critique mounted by these disparate movements results in a rather rapid shift after 1960 into the Contemporary world of composition-rhetoric, which is defined by being informed by scholarly work in a new discipline, composition studies. Part of the definition of the Modern period is that it is marked by the slow development of a group of discontented writing specialists, a Loyal Opposition that waxes and wanes,

but always powerfully questions the status quo of current practice. Although true scholarly interest in composition-rhetoric had almost completely died out after 1900, leaving the field in the hands of a few stalwarts based around Fred Scott's Michigan program, a small but continuing scholarly discourse was established in 1911 with the founding of the National Council of Teachers of English (NCTE) and its journal, *English Journal*. Throughout the Modern period, this loyal opposition to the composition establishment continued to publish essays that interrogated the status quo, and after 1945 their numbers and power increased greatly, leading to the dissolution of the Modern unity. Though it was not until after World War II that many tenets of Modern composition-rhetoric were challenged institutionally, at that time the questioning of its received wisdom became vociferous and newly powerful.

There have been several strands to this contemporary interrogation, which has today been institutionalized as the new discipline of composition studies. One of them, the product of a traditional group of academically based scholars, proposed that composition-rhetoric had taken a wrong turn in the nineteenth century in terms of its content. The needed reforms, this group proposed, would involve rediscovering the wisdom of the nearly lost older tradition of classical rhetoric, or paying new attention to the canon of invention, which had been downgraded by composition-rhetoric, or of using new linguistic methods to teach sentence construction. This group of reformers in their earlier incarnations were called the New Rhetoricians. In a later avatar they are associated with a resurrection of Deweyan ideas and today are often called social constructionists. They forced the evolution of Contemporary composition-rhetoric in the direction of new theory.

A slightly later group of scholars identified themselves with the scientific bent in modern research, and they proposed that composition-rhetoric needed to be placed on a firmer research footing. Better-designed experiments and studies would discern what writing really was, what readers really expected, what teaching techniques actually worked. Usually referred to as empiricists or cognitivists, these scholars moved Contemporary composition-rhetoric toward epistemological questions, definitions of problems, data-gathering.

The final strand of post–World War II reform in composition was concerned not so much with what students were taught as how they were taught. In the minds of these teachers, the problem with composition-rhetoric went deeper than mere issues of content, and the received methods of teaching writing were not merely inefficient or unworkable. The way in which composition was taught, to these theorists, was at best a bad method. At worst it was actively destructive, leading to desiccation of the student's creativity, to useless fear about meaningless (and probably fictional) entities such as Emphasis and The Paragraph of Comparison and Contrast, to writer's block paranoia about mechanical issues, and to dead, imitative, ponderous student prose that attempted to mimic the dead, imitative, ponderous prose of academia. These reformers, often referred to by the shorthand notation of "writing-process theorists" (or, by their critics, "expressivists") have

probably been more genuinely subversive of the methodology of Modern composition rhetoric—and the creation of its Contemporary pedagogical form—than either of the other groups.

Under the triple censure of these reformers, composition-rhetoric has changed in the last three decades more quickly and in more ways than at any time since the period 1870–1900. It is not, however, my central purpose here to examine in any depth the more recent history of the discipline of composition studies and its effects on Contemporary composition-rhetoric. There is plenty enough complexity in the story of composition-rhetoric as it developed between 1760 and 1960, which is roughly the period covered by this book. I will not tread very far into the Contemporary (or should it be called the Postmodern?) period of composition-rhetoric here, since we are still much involved in it and have little basis for historical conclusions.

Those looking for a straight chronological history here will, I fear, be disappointed. It does not start with Adam Smith in 1749 and proceed confidently through the years to *Research in Written Composition* in 1963. Such a book might be imaginable, but I am not intelligent enough or knowledgeable enough to write it. Composition-rhetoric exists at the intersection of what a society reads and what it feels it should be able to express, and there is simply too much happening, too many complex connections to be made between composition-rhetoric and the ongoing culture and society that formed it, for me to believe I can provide a coherent "whole picture" that is not unconsciously reductive. Instead I will give you thematic pictures of specific issues in culture and theory that were important in shaping the field as it has come down to us. There is much in this story that has been well told by other authors, and I will try in this book to relate parts of the tale that have not yet been explored.

Composition-rhetoric is neither a stagnant survival nor any of a hundred proposed revolutions. It exists, as it always has, as an ever shifting balance between the old and comforting and the new and exciting, the ways of lore and the ways of theory, the push of societal pressure and the inertia of academic traditions. In the first section of this book we shall look at some of the cultural grounds against which composition-rhetoric was created, partly from the older rhetorical tradition and partly from novel secondary pedagogies. In the second part of the book we shall focus more on specific pieces of the field as it evolved. Though it is a commonplace to say that composition history is written from a critical viewpoint, in this discussion my intention will not be to deride or condemn, but to understand. If history teaches us anything, it is that our own understanding of our historical moment is always necessarily limited. "As I am now, so you shall be," suggests the old New England gravestone, and it is a lesson in humility that we do well as historians to learn.

Examining the history of composition-rhetoric allows us to see our discipline, which seems sometimes to be spinning centrifugally to pieces, as what it truly is: the current avatar of a tradition of studying and using discourse that is as old as literacy and probably older. The ways in which we think of

ourselves and our work, the respect we give each other, the degree to which we think of other researchers and practitioners in composition studies as kin, as "our folks"—these are for me central issues in practicing history. When I sat down to try to write these chapters, one of my central (if tacit) purposes was to provide a shared past, a story of ancestors. I am trying here to build a fire around which we can sit and discover that we do know the same stories, and dance the same dances. Historians may not be the shamans of the field, but we are the storytellers, spinning the fabric that will, we hope, knit together the separate, private stories of the researchers, the theorists, the teachers in classrooms.

We need shared stories because our self-definition is tenuous at best. Although on the one hand composition-rhetoric can trace its lineage back through rhetoric for 2,500 years, on another more pragmatic level we are barely a century old, one of the newest of college subjects. After a quick survey of the field, it is certainly easier to see composition-rhetoric as an arriviste—with all the opprobrium that term implies—on the scene of higher learning today than it is to connect it more carefully to the great tradition of rhetoric. As sociologists of the field as well as historians, we must deal with perceptions as well as with reality; and the general perception of composition is that it is a recent and questionable discipline with a shallow and inauspicious past.

Knowing our history as rhetoricians is particularly useful today, I think, for reasons illustrated by Stephen North in his *Making of Knowledge in Composition*. Only thirty years into the history of the "modern" field of composition (I am here dating the foundation of composition studies as a serious research discipline back to 1963—an arguable point, I realize), we are already pursuing research paths so disparate that many thoughtful people have feared the discipline may fly apart like a dollar watch. Social constructionists criticize cognitivists. Marxists deride expressivists. Social science–based researchers refuse to cater to "uninformed" readers. Theorists cannot easily speak to each other. Philosophers feel ignored by empiricists, experimenters resent the criticisms of rhetoricians, and teachers feel despised by everyone. It is for this reason, I submit, that part of the intellectual task of composition studies today is to understand the story of composition-rhetoric and use that knowledge to attain unity as a discipline.

In order to effect this unity, we must share our stories. If some of them, even recently, are sad or ridiculous stories, we need to know that, too. Indeed, the successes and heroes of composition-rhetoric may be less instructive than its failures and excesses. Helen Thomas's bizarre theories about the paragraph being as formal and algorithmic as a geometry theorem are just as important to learn about as Porter Perrin's progressive condemnation of drill books. The attempted flirtation of wallflower composition with sexy linguistics in the 1950s may not be something we enjoy considering the meaning of, but it is an instructive tale. Like it or not, these have been the ideas that have driven composition-rhetoric. We cannot begin to know ourselves or our current situation without them.

But why is such unity necessary? Why bother? Why not let the centrifuge spin, whipping theorists and empiricists and teachers into separate little boxes? Because we need each other to provide a larger meaning for all our work. We need the communality provided by historical knowledge because of both the peculiarly troubled nature and the unequaled moral power of composition studies as a college discipline. We use our knowledge in unique ways in studying and teaching composition, and we have always thought that our mission was nothing less than to save the world. Composition-rhetoric, for better or worse, is *our* rhetoric, and to know its story is to know our own.

A word about the kind of work I have tried to do here. Though I hope I am not overtly "coughing in ink," as Yeats characterizes dryasdust scholarship, readers of contemporary historiographies will quickly see that the history in this book is (to use currently popular terms) "antiquarian" rather than "critical." It means to construct coherent explanations for historical facts and causality, taking archival research as a starting place and consistent control. In that sense it is not "radical" or "subversive" history, and I suppose that means I am (sigh) an epistemologically conservative historian. Yet as I look back on the series of impulses and enthusiasms over the fifteen-year period that went into the making of this work, I see in myself a more complex movement through historiographic theory, one that the current work of revision has perhaps elided.

I began writing about the history of composition teaching in America (with "The Rise and Fall of the Modes of Discourse" in 1980) with a not very well hidden agenda of reforming current practice through reviewing the genesis of its pedagogy. My training had been New Rhetorical; the foundation of composition studies as a discipline was in full swing; and criticizing the older methods of teaching writing that had been handed down to us was an almost automatic task for one beginning historical study. The theme of my early work was taken almost completely from my admiration for Albert Kitzhaber's historical writing—as filtered through the emotions of a twenty-nine-year-old who had a decade earlier been marching at the Student Strike of 1970. It was a simple theme: our composition predecessors were fools, and we now see through their mediocre work and can transcend it, thus ushering in the millennium. Gathering my data almost completely from textbooks, it was easy to keep up the mood of impatient dismissal I now see in much of that early work. It was certainly critical history in the popular sense of that term.

But, unfortunately for the purity of my Manichaean vision, I kept reading. I began to read the old journal articles and professional books; I began to know the voices, and I began to see the outlines of what our disciplinary ancestors were trying to understand and were up against. By the middle 1980s I knew more about the cultures, and the societal pressures, and the conditions under which people often worked, and the struggle that teaching writing has always been. And, to tell the truth, my earlier mode of critical dismissal, which was based on a shallow reading of one kind of source, became something I could no longer maintain. The more deeply I looked, the more I could

see myself and my colleagues and friends in the words and works of people in 1930 or 1905 or 1870—people for whom, just as for us, times were always clangingly modern and pressures were always great, paper grades were always due, and tomorrow was always mysterious. Who was it who said that to understand all is to forgive all?

Then came a point in the later 1980s when I deliberately turned my gaze outward, away from the development of theory and pedagogy in vacuo and toward the cultural matrix that supported the teaching of writing. It was in this later work that I once again began to move more toward a sort of critical history—investigations of class, social structure, economics, and gender that make up most of the first section of this book. I have not, even in these chapters, gone as far toward ideologically based critical historiography as many people feel contemporary historians should. Such history begins with certain critical assumptions (Marxism, say, or American feminism, or Lacanian psychology) and uses them as an instrument with which to approach archival material. I have not done that here.

I am certainly aware of the arguments of revisionist historiographers, and I must admit I worried over whether or not to turn my book into subversive history. But even if I were starting the book over from scratch, I am not sure how I could address myself to the critical sort of history some readers would apparently like to see. Should it be a poststructuralist bash at the benighted rationalist attitudes or the oppressive patriarchal values that have underlain comp courses? Susan Miller has already done a pass at that in *Textual Carnivals*. Should it be a Marxo-constructivist exposé of the fact that writing instruction has always been in the service of hierarchy, elitism, and a vision of capitalist individualism? The late Wallace Douglas and the late Jim Berlin did a great deal of that sort of work. Should I try for a purely feminist analysis of composition history like Sue Carter Simmons, or an everything-must-go postdeconstructive line like Victor Vitanza? Underlying my interior dialogue about these questions was my fear that unless I foregrounded my ideology and theoretic, the sophisticated critical discourse that more and more makes CCCC sound like MLA would dismiss my book as, in fact, undertheorized. In an academic world that valorizes theory the way ours does today, this is a pretty awful charge, one that carries much unspoken baggage: undertheorized work is naive, politically immature, ill-read, unenlightened, culturally backward.

In defense of my decision to write this book as history instead of historiography, I can only say that *reading* history has taught me one overwhelming lesson, and that is the transitory nature of the current wisdom. Choosing and promoting a theoretical perspective as your own personal Master Trope—the terministic screen through which you propose to look at everything—pins you in time, wriggling like a bug on a board. It will sooner or later relegate your work to the realm of the Historically Interesting. Where are the Archetype Critics of today? The Chicago Formalists? The Socialist Realists? In our field, for that matter, where are the Pure Cognitivists? The Macrorieite Third Way People? The Sentence-Combining Mafia? The Composition Empiricists? (I know—they're at their old stands, *RTE* and *AERA*, but they sure

don't run the show the way they did in 1984, say.) People aren't still reading Herodotus or Gibbon today because of the way they foregrounded their historiographic theories.

If I were to have written this book to conform to one or another of the currently popular theoretical/critical stances (many of whose points, I should say, I agree with, since I live here in this cultural and historical moment, too), I would be afraid that the simple-minded story I hope to tell would get lost in the ideology, would end up serving the theory. I simply have not wit enough to foreground an ideology and also tell the story of what I found and all the complexity I perceive in it. Anyway, the ideologies and theories have plenty of servants already. They don't need my story, too.

This is not to say, of course, that this narrative has no theory behind it. Of course it does. It is based on an essentially rationalist and even empirical kind of traditional textual historical research, assumes Aristotelian causality, and accepts a Deweyan pragmatic epistemology. It drifts toward Marxist class analysis now and then, but finally backs away from any overarching theory of history, either progressive or cyclical. The narrative reflects a politics traditionally called liberal (which now, I suppose, is usually characterized as conservative). Though culture and society—both macro and disciplinary micro—are charged and criticized in several ways throughout, the critique is conducted from the stance of what Richard Rorty calls "banal politics," a deliberate refusal to adhere to any totalizing theoretical or ideological vision of the desirable. (Perhaps this is just another way of saying that the book is, ineluctably, in spite of my hopeless romance with Platonism, a work of postmodernist thought.)

This book seems, then, to be a narrative based on found and on sought archival materials, ordered chronologically on the basis of discrete themes, and interrogated—where they are interrogated—from a limited set of consistent questions based in personal observation of things as they are in the present. I want mostly to tell a story, to identify and pin down as much basic textual evidence as possible, so that further discussion from a theoretical base can then proceed from shareable data. This commitment to narrative and to archival fact means I have had to make constant decisions about what does constitute believable evidence; and in that very basic sense, this book is a critical work.

I make no pretension, however, to have produced a work of criticism. I hope that many different kinds of analysis will be brought to the stories I try to limn here by different critics, and that the carnivals, aporias, dialogues, false consciousness, tropes, gender inequalities, ideological mystification, power relations, and postrational integration that I only sketch or suggest here (or, even more interestingly, fail to sketch or suggest) will be taken up more completely by my partner in crime, the reader. In other words, to use a dichotomy I learned as a first-year master's candidate (and which has probably been discredited while I wasn't looking), this book means to be a work of scholarship rather than of criticism. Whether it succeeds at that goal or not remains to be seen.

Memorial Tribute to
Edward P. J. Corbett, 1919–1998

We could scarcely have imagined that Bob's eloquent "Memorial Tribute to Edward P. J. Corbett, 1919–1998" (*College English*, 1998) would be published just two years before many colleagues turned to writing their own memorial tributes to Bob. In hindsight, this generous and loving portrait of one of Bob's most important mentors seems particularly compelling. Indeed, some of the lines Bob penned in memory of Ed serve us well in remembering Bob: "We shall not see his like again, and the world seems a smaller and less colorful place without him" (336).

Edward P. J. Corbett died June 24 at his home in Columbus. He was seventy-eight. Ed was one of the few remaining members of that astonishing group of teachers and scholars who created the discipline of composition studies in the 1960s, a leader in style studies, a preeminent scholar and brilliant expositor of classical rhetoric whose works made it available to many of us. He was a cornerstone of the pioneering Ohio State University graduate program in rhetoric and composition, helped found the Rhetoric Society of America in 1968, and chaired the CCCC in 1971. As editor of *CCC* during those formative years from 1974 to 1979, he helped many of us get started in publishing. Those who knew Ed also knew that he was a lovely, unpretentious man who taught more by the example of his generosity and humanity than by his writing and scholarship. He was my graduate director and mentor, and I was proud to say he was my co-author and my friend. My own feeling of loss is mitigated somewhat by an awareness of how rich and full a life Ed Corbett lived. Those who knew Ed are sad at his passing, but we are sad for our own sakes, because despite his portion of trouble and suffering—and he had known poverty, and illness, and he knew premature death and loss—Ed's life was a wonderful one.

The names of the students and authors whose lives Ed touched would be an extraordinary list. His annotations of graduate essays were legendary at OSU. He was the first teacher I had who helped me *investigate* my writing, holding up rhetorical analysis as a mirror that allowed his students to see our own work anew. As his assistant on the journal, I filed all of the letters he

From *College English* 61.2 (1998): 141–42.

wrote to the many people submitting essays and saw how wonderfully he advised and supported writers. (This was back in the old days, when the editor of *CCC* read the three or four daily submissions himself and responded to each one with a typed letter of acceptance, revision advice, or rejection.) He had the ability to let authors know, even when their essays were unpublishable, how much he cared about helping them succeed with their work. Then, as later, he gave me a daily illustration of how to work with others, how to be considerate of people while showing them how to improve, how to be delighted with humanity and with life. I wish I could say I had learned those lessons as well as he taught them, but his teaching of them was constant, unconscious, part of who he was. In his every word and gesture, he showed what it could mean to be human.

Everyone who knew Ed has Ed Corbett stories, because he made himself into a kind of dramatic character he sent rambling like Humphrey Clinker or Parson Adams through the adventures of his life and world. Though a truly gifted writer, Ed Corbett was not readily eloquent and knew it; his mind was so well stocked that rummaging through it took more than a beat. In response, he created a public art of the verbal gesture—what his friends called Ed's rhetoric of cliché. There were the archetypal slogan, the elliptical courtliness, the oft-used phrase, the Augustan apothegm, all gradually becoming a sort of spoken stock-in-trade for him and a secret language for his students and friends—"wealthy beyond the dreams of avarice," "What a crushing blow," "carry on in the finest tradition," "utterly humiliated," "Do you think I might possibly be allowed to . . . ?" Some of us will be saying those things to our own students, carrying on the language. But Ed was the fount of it, and like the Gaeltacht, the borders of that land of language will gradually shrink. Our world of discourse is more solemn today. The field that Ed was so important in building will last, and the work he did will continue to serve it well, but the American cultural world that made him and the frontier field of composition that he made are gone now. We shall not see his like again, and the world seems a smaller and less colorful place without him.

It was not hard to love Ed Corbett. His modest, humorous, and generous nature made people who came to him out of scholarly admiration want to meet him again out of pleasure. People responded to him because they sensed how he brought out the best in them. And so, though his professional achievements were numerous and real, few people in any field have lived to see themselves as honored and vividly appreciated while still living as Ed did. He lived to see his family thrive, and to see the children of his mind lead the field that so many credited him with helping build. He saw a *Festschrift* in his honor, publication of his *Selected Essays*, multiple editions of his many successful books, his OSU Distinguished Scholar Award, his CCCC Exemplar award. And he was still vital and committed to his family, friends, and work when he died, not after no suffering, but without prolonged agony or loss of self to pain or medication. We who loved Ed shed tears, as we should. But truly, this was a life to celebrate, and our sadness comes only from not being able to share it any longer.

The Rhetoric of Citation Systems

Part I: The Development of Annotation Structures from the Renaissance to 1900*

In the early 1980s, as the two of us were beginning our research on collaboration and collaborative writing, we became increasingly attuned to the ideology of citation practices. Particularly disturbing to us was the ubiquitous "et al." in footnotes and lists of works cited, and we came to think of this character "et al." as a veritable cheat and thief, the one who made disappear all authors but the first. We remember as well a number of conversations with Bob about such paratextual issues—conversations that touched on some of the work that led to his long two-part essay "The Rhetoric of Citation Systems," published in *Rhetoric Review* in 1998 and 1999. Part I of this essay, "The Development of Annotation Structures from the Renaissance to 1900" (1998), traces in fascinating detail changes that took place in glossing and citations from the earliest days of print texts to the turn of the twentieth century. The title

---

*Readers will notice that this essay violates *Rhetoric Review*'s own citation style, which follows New MLA in asking for endnotes rather than footnotes. I specifically requested this change of the editor, and she has graciously assented. As I will detail in the second part of the article, endnotes were a system that MLA went to in 1977 as the field of English became more populist and the main concern in manuscripts began to be ease of typing and cheapness of typesetting; no one argued, then or since, for any rhetorical superiority of endnotes over footnotes. Indeed, most people agree that from a reader's point of view, endnotes are a pain, whether they are citational or discursive. They force you to search and flip pages when a footnote would allow you to glance at the bottom of the column. The only virtue of endnotes is that they are easier to type on a typewriter.

    This move to endnotes was a situational decision by the MLA. The great word-processing revolution, which would within ten years create a technology that automatically measures and sets footnotes, came just a few years too late; now, of course, all WP programs and graphic programs used by printers can set footnotes automatically and without extra cost. So we're still living in the backwash of a pragmatic decision about note placement that predates our current typographic abilities. Of course, some authors, like Gibbon, may prefer to have their manuscripts run clean-page, without footnotes, as if they were not scholarship. That should be the call of each individual author. The reason I asked specifically that footnotes be used here is the same reason most literary journals have refused to switch to New MLA: I want to make my decisions about how my page will look to readers on a "rhetorical" basis. I have simply found footnotes a more precise system, allowing for a text/note dialogism that endnotes kill completely. And given the fact that the only footnotes still allowed by New MLA are discursive, that dialogism is even more important.

From *Rhetoric Review* 17.1 (1998): 6–48.

to Part I ends with an asterisk, which directs readers' attention to a lengthy footnote at the bottom of the page. Here Bob sets out in brief what becomes the core of his discussion in Part II, beginning with his decision to violate *Rhetoric Review*'s own citation style, which follows "new" MLA style in requiring endnotes rather than footnotes. Why quibble over the placement of these notes? Bob's research led him to conclude that the move to endnotes rested on nothing more momentous than ease and economy of printing, ignoring readers' needs and abjuring any responsibility to demonstrate rhetorical superiority for the endnote. In Part II, "Competing Epistemic Values in Citation" (1999), Bob returns to this rhetorical issue. After surveying the limitations of footnotes, he traces divergences in footnote form in various fields, primarily the sciences and the humanities. Bob does not conclude by arguing for one citation system or another, though his sympathies with "old" MLA are clear. Rather, he urges that our decisions about citation styles "be informed by rhetorical awareness and by a knowledge of the forces that have worked throughout history to affect the ways in which our texts have related to us and to each other" (397).

Communication structures are inescapably social, and humanity throughout recorded history has striven to evolve conventions signaling the fair and proper use of the discourses of other people. Speakers and writers have always known that their "own" words are constantly co-evolving from and with the words of others, and from the earliest written records we see authors' attempts to quote and credit the works of those they used or admired. The field of rhetoric, especially in its written forms, where citations had to be visible and reproducible, inevitably evolved the most formalized conventions for signaling ethical use of others' work. The gradual formalization of written citation systems should not, however, blind us to their essentially rhetorical nature. Every formal structure implies a universe of meanings. Every formal structure declares allegiances and counterallegiances. Every formal structure suggests the ethical and pathetic as well as the logical nature of a discourse. The seemingly "transparent" structures used in formal citation systems have always been as much products and reflections of social and rhetorical realities as all other elements of discourse. In this essay I want to trace the development of the rhetoric of citation systems in Western culture, especially as it has come to exist in the humanities and the social sciences.

Today, of course, the whole issue of ownership, use, and citation of others' works is more vexed than ever before. Scholars have begun to look very seriously into the genesis of the concept of authorship, the ideas behind copyright and limits of intellectual property rights, ownership, and proprietorship of text. There is a small but growing literature on glosses and anno-

tations of texts, and scholars begin to debate the meanings and property values of the margins of text and the foot of the page. I need to delimit the task I hope to accomplish here, since these questions ramify out in so many fruitful and dizzying directions. I want here to concentrate not on legal issues or even broad epistemological issues, but on the specific rhetorical, social, and stylistic questions that have been tied up in formal citation systems. I want to speak to the reasons why these systems evolved and proliferated, what they suggest about authors' feelings of debt and ownership, how they affect the ways we read and process text and the intentions behind it, and, finally, the effects on reading and writing of social decisions to promote and valorize new citation systems and subsystems.

GLOSSING AND CITATION DURING THE RENAISSANCE

How far back should we go? Glossing and annotation are as old as literature; the Hebrew Midrash glossing tradition has *comprised* a literature for twenty-four hundred years. Before the development of printing technology, every manuscript was copied by hand, usually for specific purchasers or for specific purposes. Those who have studied these older manuscripts have described how each one carried the imprint of a scribe; every text is commented on tacitly by the scribe or editor, even if it is copied faithfully. Each palimpsest is a sort of citation system; every annotated manuscript is an example of glossing and of the struggle for proprietorship (Lipking). To begin with individually scribed manuscripts and incunabula simply opens up the field too widely, which is why I propose to begin this inquiry with the advent of the newer forms of public communication made possible by movable type.[1]

The structure of the type-printed page is the ground on which all glosses, annotations, and citations exist; it is like the sculptor's marble or the artist's canvas and pigments, allowing some possibilities and constraining others. Johannes Gutenberg printed his Forty-Two Line Bible in Mainz in 1455, after developing his typefaces, casting methods, presses, type alloys, and inks in secret for at least ten years before. It took time, however, for printers to learn more complex uses of the printing frame structure that Gutenberg developed to lock his sticks of type into. The first marginal annotations used in printed texts do not appear until 1481 (Tribble 59); before that time, commentaries from editors were printed separately, or at least on separate pages. But once printers caught on to the possible uses of the locking forms, they quickly adapted manuscript styles of annotation to typography.

The classic annotation form developed by scribal technology consisted of the widely spaced original text written in large, ornate letters, surrounded by opportunistic remoras of glossing text in much smaller letters. These were

---

[1] For discussion of some of the earlier forms of glossing and notation, see the essays in Barney as well as Grafton, *The Footnote*, 27–31.

the scribal texts coming down into the printing technology of the High Renaissance, the cultural point at which a growing *secular* culture of learning was forced to come to grips with its relationships both to ancient texts and to contemporary commentators. The classical texts being rediscovered in monasteries and old villas spoke to the people of the Renaissance about a developed society, its thought and culture, its arts and philosophies, in an intoxicating manner. After a millennium of heavenly preoccupation, Europeans began seeking again the kingdom of earth, and the old texts were a way in. But the texts disagreed and were often incomplete, so careful comparative editing was needed to establish good texts. Arising from such editing came a need for informed historical and linguistic commentary, and from these industries came the first great wave of Western secular scholarship.

Much has been written about the process through which classical learning began to become secular authority during the Renaissance.[2] From Latin being the language of the Church and its doctors and clerks came the secular culture based around learned Latin that Walter Ong has described, a secular culture that lasted until the nineteenth century.[3] Knowledge of the Latin and Greek classics in great detail (and with great and unforgiving rigor) became intellectual coin of the realm for European scholars from 1400 through 1900. And it was during the Renaissance that citation formats began to coalesce, to proliferate, and to disagree. Evelyn Tribble's *Margins and Marginality* provides thoughtful coverage of some of the elements of these beginnings.

The first editions of the classical authors to be printed did not use margins or page bottoms, but included notes and annotations in separate printed signatures or appended after the works themselves. In 1481 a Venetian edition of Horace appeared with marginal commentaries by Acro and Porphyry, and after that point printers used the margins for glosses and notes in order to save the cost of paper—then, as now, the most costly of their materials. The early scholarly editors were often also the printers, and as soon as printers discovered the uses of margins, they immediately began to compete to see who could gather the most glossing commentary into margins. Editions of Horace appeared with two complete commentaries, then four, and in 1546 an edition appeared with five complete commentaries in the margins and notes by ten more humanists! These texts *cum notis variorum* (with the remarks of different commentators) were set up adjacent to each other in a complementary, additive way rather than as competitors, but by their sheer bulk, they came to overwhelm the original text, as Figure 1, a page from Sebastian Brant's 1502 edition of Virgil indicates.[4]

---

[2] See, for considerable detail on the specifics of this process, Grafton, *Commerce with the Classics.*

[3] See Ong, *Rhetoric Romance, and Technology,* 113–41, and *The Presence of the Word,* 241–55.

[4] Tribble reproduces a page of Ascensius's 1519 Horace on which only two lines of an Horatian ode fit, the rest of the page being taken up with commentary.

FIGURE 1 Sebastian Brant's 1502 edition of Virgil

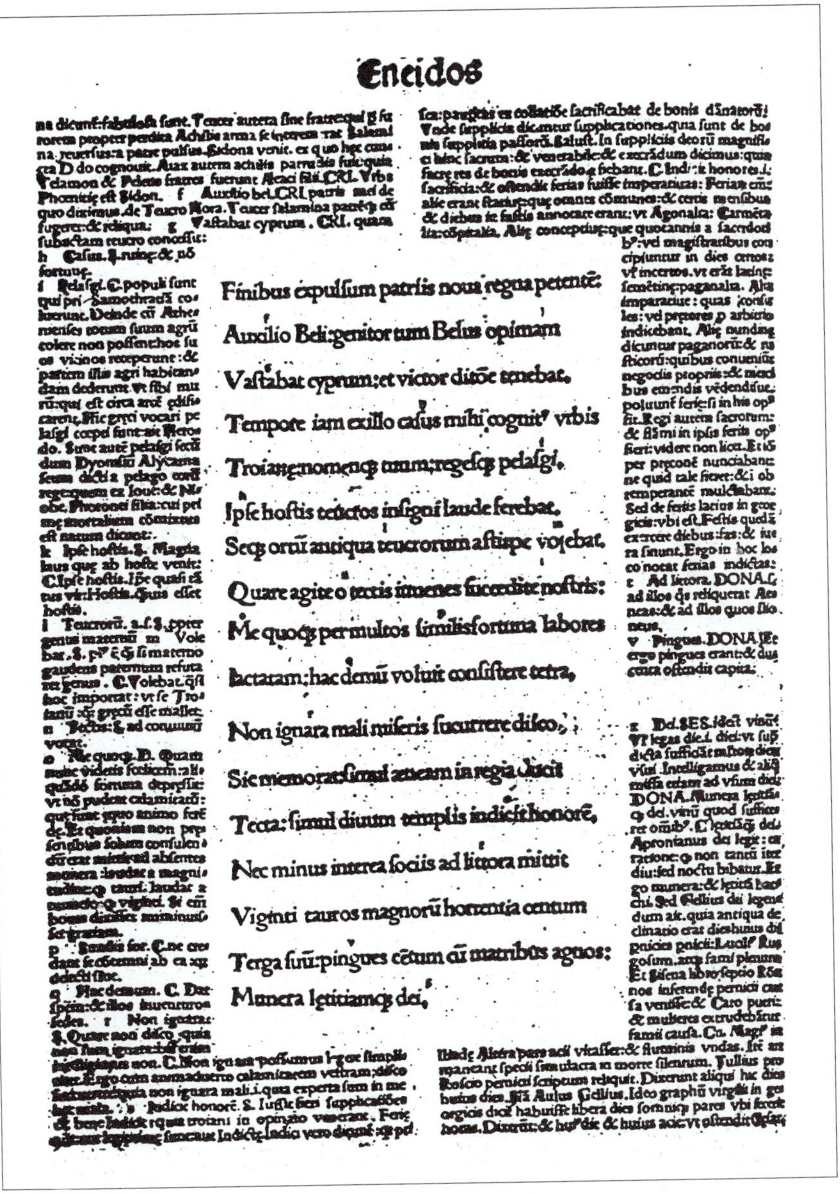

Eneidos

Finibus expulsum patriis noua regna petentē:
Auxilio Beli: genitor tum Belus opimam
Vastabat cyprum: et victor ditiōe tenebat.
Tempore iam ex illo casus mihi cognit⁹ vrbis
Troianę nomenq; tuum: regesq; pelasgi.
Ipse hostis teucros insigni laude ferebat.
Seq; ortū antiqua teucrorum a stirpe volebat.
Quare agite o tectis iuuenes succedite nostris:
Me quoq; per multos similis fortuna labores
Iactatam: hac demū voluit consistere terra.
Non ignara mali miseris succurrere disco.
Sic memorat: simul aeneam in regia ducit
Tecta: simul diuum templis indicit honorē.
Nec minus interea sociis ad littora mittit
Viginti tauros magnorū horrentia centum
Terga suū: pingues cētum cū matribus agnos:
Munera letitiamq; dei.

But humanist scholarship was learning quickly that the simple ability to produce heaps of commentary in the margins might not mean that such additive comments were the most useful form. Aldus Manutius, the Venetian printer and editor who invented italic type, published in 1501 an edition of Horace that simply printed Horace's odes alone on the page. Aldus had done

the necessary comparative scholarly editing, and he did include a few notes at the back of the book, but his edition was meant to showcase the edited text rather than merely to accrete the commentaries. It was Aldus's example that gradually prevailed, and by the 1570s, printers were printing classical works that showcased the original text while using the resources of typography to allow readers easy access to notes and comments, usually at the end of each original work.

By this latter part of the sixteenth century, the humanist use of glosses, commentaries, and notes had become a whole discourse world unto itself. Constant reference to classical sources became a staple of all learned talk and writing, and the scholarly uses and correct citation of these sources had become demanded passwords into the discourse community of educated people. Tribble specifically cites the example of Ben Jonson, the printed versions of whose masques and plays were filled with a constant marginal roar of classical citation. More than any other English writer of the High Renaissance, Jonson seemed to feel that he needed to back his work up with endless references to his learning, and thus to insulate himself from the rejection of the *hoi polloi* by appealing to "the Learned." His *Sejanus His Fall* of 1605, for instance, carefully cites the classical authors from which Jonson drew his material in long marginal notes in Latin (Figure 2). Jonson takes advantage of the complete marginal glossing structure that scholars had been assembling for the previous century, citing with lower-case letters, mentioning specific editions, tomes, and pages, and in general battering any potential critics into silence with the weight of his research and learning. Such citation is, as David Bartholomae has said of writing itself, an act of aggression disguised as an act of charity. Jonson is not only signaling his own accomplishment here but is also indicating the nature of a "fit"—that is, an educated—audience. It is no accident of history that he was never as popular a playwrite as the less overtly learned Shakespeare.

Jonson considered himself both an author and a scholar, but the issue of the proprietorship of the margins of a page was a natural site for conflicts and disagreements between authors and scholars. Writers were beginning to realize that they had rhetorical choices to make about their uses of notes and annotations, and that the typographic structures they chose would mark them as members of one or another kind of discourse community. In general, authors and writers chose to use fewer marginal notes and to use informal sets of citation symbols while scholars identified themselves through use of the complex full-cite, letter-and-number systems that used Latin terms. By the turn of the seventeenth century, these appurtenances of scholarship—and the ethos they projected—had become so well established in writing and publishing that they could be fit subjects for satire and criticism.

One extraordinary example of the authorial attack on scholarly citations came in Thomas Nashe's hilarious *Have With You to Saffron-Walden* of 1596, an attack on the Cambridge scholar Gabriel Harvey. The basis of their quarrel is not apposite to this inquiry, but Nashe uses a huge armamentarium of sar-

FIGURE 2   Ben Jonson, *Sejanus His Fall*, edition of 1605

SEIANVS.

Now, for fhe hath a Fury in her breft
More, then Hell euer knew; and would be fent
Thither in time. Then is there one ᵃ *Cremutius*
Cordus, a writing fellow, they haue got
To gather Notes of the præcedent times,
And make them into *Annal's*; a moft tart
And bitter fpirit (I heare) who, vnder coulor
Of prayfing thofe, doth taxe the prefent ftate,
Cenfures the men, the actions, leaues no trick,
No practife vn-examind, paralells
The times, the gouernments; a profeft Champion
For the old liberty : T⟨ɪ⟩ʙ. A perifhing wretch.
As if there were that *Chaos* bred in things,
That Lawes, and Liberty would not rather choofe
To be quite broken, and tâne hence by vs,
Then haue the ftaine to be preferu'd by fuch.
Haue we the meanes to make thefe guilty, firft ?
Seɪ. Truft that to me; let *Cæfar*, by his power,
But caufe a formall meeting of the *Senate*,
I will haue matter, and Accufers ready.
T⟨ɪ⟩ʙ. But how ? let vs confult.   Seɪ. We fhall mifpend
The time of action. "Councells are vnfit
"In bufineffe, where all reft is more pernicious
"Then rafhneffe can be. Acts of this clofe kinde
"Thriue more by execution, then aduife :
"There is no lingring in that worke begonne,
"Which cannot praifed be, vntill through donne.
T⟨ɪ⟩ʙ. ᵇ Our *Edict* fhall forthwith, commaund a Court.
While I can liue, I will præuent Earths fury ;
ᶜ E'μοῦ Sανόντ⟨Θ⟩ γαῖα μιχSάτω πυρί.

POSTVMVS. SEIANVS.

Pos. My Lord *Seianus* ? Sғɪ. ᶜ *Iulius Poftumus*,
Come with my wifh ! what newes from *Agrippina's*,
Pos. Faith none. They all lock vp themfelues, a'late;
Or talke in character : I haue not feene
A company fo chang'd. Except they had
Intelligence by Augury' of our practife.
E

Side notes (right margin):

ᵃ *Vid. Tac.*
Ann. lib. 4.
pag. 83.
Dio. Hift.
Rom lib. 57.
pag. 710.
et Sen.conf.
ad Mar.
cap. 1. et
fufius. cap.
22.

ᵇ *Edicto vt*
plurimum
Senatores
in curiam
vocatos có-
ftat. Tacit.
Ann. lib. 1.
pag. 3.
ᶜ *Vulgaris*
quidā ver-
fus, quem
fæpe Tiber.
recitaffe
memoratur.
Dio. Hift.
Rom lib. 58.
729.
ᵈ *De Iulio*
Poftumo.
vid. Tacit.
Ann. lib. 4.
Seɪ. *pag. 77.*

casm, parody, and outright insult against Harvey and the scholarly tradition he represented. In an earlier work, *Pierce Pennilesse*, Nashe had used scholarly Latin footnotes, but Harvey attacked him for searching "every corner of his Grammar-schoole witte, (for his margine is as deeplie learned, as *Fauste precor gelida*)" (1:195) in order to do so.[5] *Have With You*, which is a response to Harvey's *Pierce's Supererogation*, is structured as a dialogue, and it is clear that Nashe has disdainfully left the field of scholarly annotation to Harvey. One of the questioners asks Nashe why he does not use marginal notes, and his response is classic:

> *Import*: . . . I wonder thou setst not downe in figures in the margent, in what line, page, & folio a man might find everie one of these fragments, which would have much satisfied thy Readers
>
> *Respon*: What, make an *Errata* in the midst of my Booke, and have my margent bescratcht (like a Merchants booke) with these roguish Arsemetrique gibbets or flesh-hookes, and cyphers or round oos, lyke pismeeres egges? Content your selfe, I will never do it: or if I were ever minded to doo it, I could not, since, (as I told you some leaves before,) in more than a quarter of that his tumbrell of Confutation, he hath left the Pages unfigured; foreseeing by devination (belike) that I should come to disfigure them. (44)

Here Nashe is engaging in his trademark flyting language, but he is also making a serious point about the slavish overreliance Harvey himself displays on classical sources, with only a quarter of his pages free of marginal notes. Nashe analogizes such notes to an Errata, or list of printing or research errors, often bound into books after they had been printed. In the few marginal notes he does use, he is never citational or scholarly. His notes are in English, are marked by Greek letters ("Arsemetrique gibbets or flesh-hookes") in a jibe at the scholarly apparatus of his opponents, and exist as parodic asides in a dialogue with the main text. Nashe is creating a new form here, using conventional marginal forms in order to make fun of scholarship and propriety (Figure 3).

The satire of scholarly overkill that we see in Nashe is one of the earlier evidences of the author/scholar duality that was to present serious writers of the next two centuries with such complex rhetorical choices. On the one hand, serious writers during the period 1600–1800 knew that they could be rendered respectable only by showing their membership in the community of classical learning that defined education as control of the Greek and Latin writers. On the other hand, the gradually developing conception of "original

---

[5] Harvey seems to be attacking Nashe here for his use of some poetic citations in marginal notes in Nashe's previous blast, *Pierce Pennilesse*. Harvey may also be asserting that Nashe's learning is not truly classical, going no farther back than the neo-Latin poet Mantuan, whose eclogue "Faustus: On Happy Love" is quoted here.

FIGURE 3   Thomas Nashe, *Have With You to Saffron-Walden*, 1596

The Epiſtle Dedicatorie.

noble Science of ♉ deciſion and contraction is im- *ʋ For diuiſiõ &*
mortally beholding to him, for twice double his *contrac-*
Patrimonie hath he ſpent in carefull cheriſhing & *tion.*
preſeruing his pickerdeuant : and beſides a deuine
vicarly brother of his, called *Aſtrologicall Richard*, ſome few yeares ſince (for the benefit of his
countrey) moſt ſtudiouſly compyled *a profound
Abridgement ʋpon beards*, & therein copiouſly
dilated of the true diſcipline of peakes, & no leſſe
fruteleſſely determined, betwixt the Swallowes
taile-cut, & the round beard like a rubbing bruſh.
It was my chaunce (O thrice bleſſed chaunce) to
the great comfort of my Muſe to peruſe it, although it came but priuately in Print : and for a
more rateſied paſport (in thy opinion)that I haue
read it and digeſted it,this title it beareth,*a ſ De-* *ſ Ther-*
fence of ſhort haire againſt Syneſius and Pieri- *fore be-*
us : or rather in more familiar Engliſh to expreſſe *like bee gaue it*
it, a Daſh ouer the head againſt baldnes, verie ne- *that ti-*
ceſſary to be obſerued of al the *looſer* ſort,or *looſe* *tle, becauſe it*
haird ſort of yong Gentlemen & Courtiers, and
no leſſe pleaſant and profitable to be remembred *was*
of the whole Common-wealth of the Barbars. *moſt of it ſhort*
The Poſie theretoo annexed, *Prolixior eſt breui-* *haire his*
tate ſua, as much to ſay, as Burne Bees and haue *father*
Bees, & hair the more it is cut the more it comes: *made*
lately deuiſed and ſet forth by *Richard Haruey,* *ropes of.*
          the

composition" and a fear of scholarly affectation meant that one's classical learning must be worn lightly, must be in the service of precision rather than pedantry. This could be a difficult line to which to hew, and during this period we see authors attempting a variety of different solutions to the problem of how to indicate one's deep classical learning without the braggadocio of Harvey-style marginal notes. From the available models—biblical glosses, humanist classical annotations, even the railing satires of the Marprelate controversy and Nashe, Renaissance writers began to construct a rhetorical world of citation styles.

THE AGON OF BIBLICAL GLOSSES

If secular writers were evolving a part of citational rhetoric, the religious controversies of the same time were central to the development of another part. The Reformation battle over glosses of the Bible also provides important background to the ways in which textual annotation works in Western culture. The beginnings of the religious glossing tradition were not agonistic, though they were complex. Figure 4 is a page from the *Glossa Ordinaria*, a thirteenth-century manuscript of a standard textbook-style work used in training priests and theologians in scriptural commentary. The biblical text was surrounded and penetrated by a variety of marginal and interlinear glosses and notes from different theologians and teachers, the more important of whom included Walafrid Strabo, Anselm of Laon, and Peter Lombard (Smalley 197–207). In this version the scribes have used medium-sized glossing letters for large blocks of rhetorical commentary and very small interlinear lettering for comments on specific words. (This is a system still used today by teachers of composition.) Printers adapted this structure by placing all the original text in the middle of the page, and creating a whole world of commentary from editor or theologians in large surrounding margins.

By 1528 printing technology had advanced to the point where Nicholas of Lyra's printed *Glossa Ordinaria* could allow full marginal glosses, interlinear word-level glosses, and even extramarginal biblical citations (Figure 5). This *Glossa* was printed at Lyon; France was even then becoming famous for the precision and sophistication of its printers. Printed versions of the *Glossa* quickly found themselves at the center of the tremendous religious controversies swirling through the sixteenth century. It's not hard to see why. If we read the essential impulse behind the Reformation as a desire to free the word of God from layer upon layer of dogmatic institutional corruption, then the complex scriptural glosses of the *Glossa Ordinaria* could easily be read as that corruption made into text. The *Glossa*, with its layers of *commentaria, commentariola, expositiones, glossae, glossulae, lectiones, lecturae,* and *postillae*, represented the "official word" of canonical interpretation of all scriptural text, and thus Protestant writers condemned it as at best obscuring a direct relation with the scriptures and at worst providing

FIGURE 4   Manuscript *Glossa Ordinaria*, thirteenth century

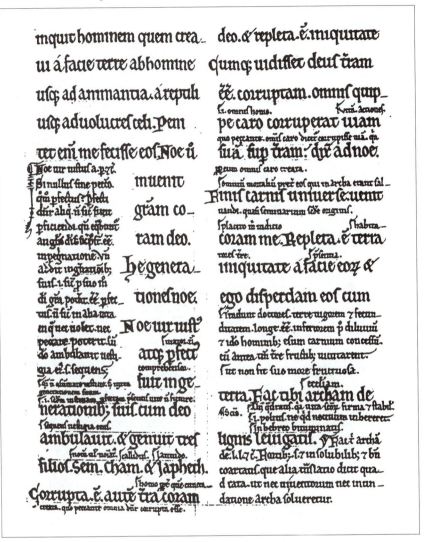

incorrect or misleading ideas about them. As Philip Melanchthon wrote in 1518, "Now let's get rid of all these frigid little glosses, concordances, discordances and other such obstructions to our natural abilities. When our hearts have reflected upon the sources, we shall begin to discern Christ."[6]

---

[6] This was Melanchthon's inaugural address at Wittenberg, from the Latin *Melanchthonis Opera* in the collection of Reformation documents *Corpus Reformatorum*, 23. My amateurish translation.

FIGURE 5 Nicholas of Lyra's printed *Glossa Ordinaria*, Lyon, 1528

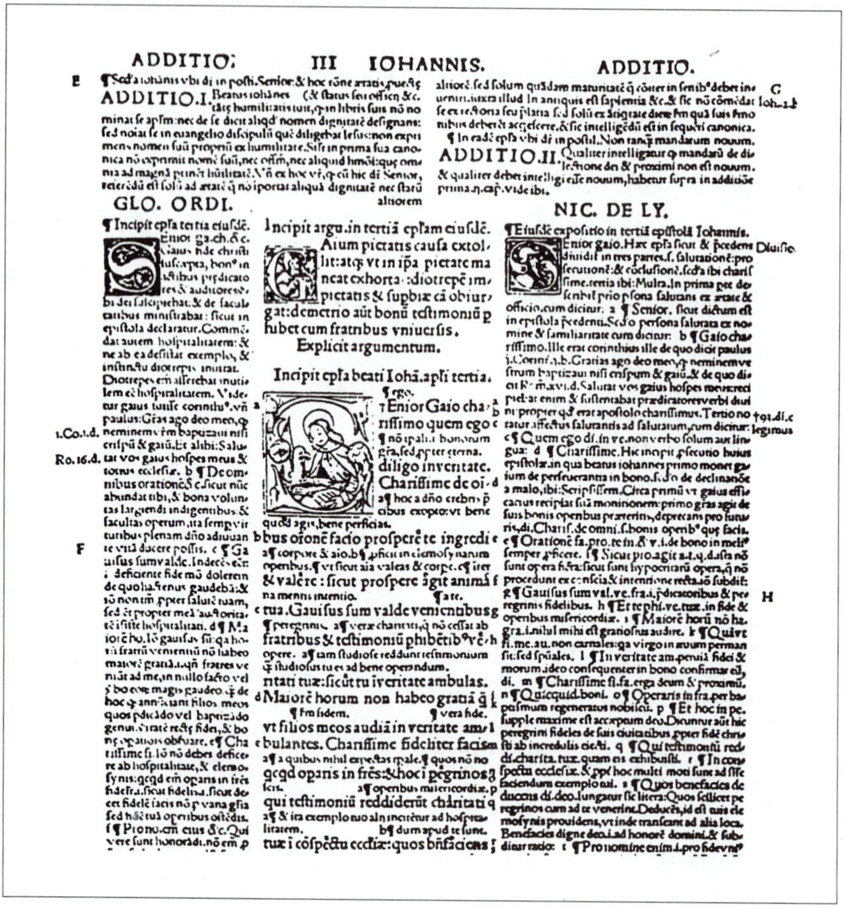
ADDITIO. III IOHANNIS. ADDITIO.

GLO. ORDI.

NIC. DE LY.

Incipit argu.in tertiã eplam eiusdē. Aium pietatis causa extol- lit: atq; vt in ipa pietate ma neat exhorta-: diotrepē im- pietatis & supbiæ cã obiur- gat: demetrio aũt bonũ testimoniũ p hibet cum fratribus vniuersis. Explicit argumentum.

Incipit epla beati Iohã.apli tertia.

The best treatment of this war of glosses is found in Tribble's first chapter, which details the wars of biblical glossing that went on in England during the period 1500–1630. The European Protestant intellectuals from Luther on attacked the whole tradition of marginal and interlinear glossing of biblical text that had gone on since the beginning of scholasticism in favor of exposing readers to the unmediated truth of scripture. They especially objected to the *Glossa Ordinaria*, in which even the large type of the scriptural passage does not prevent its being "swallowed up," as Tribble says, "in a sea of commentary both marginal and interlinear" (12). As William Tyndale put it, Catholics had "blinded the scripture . . . with glosses and traditions," and Tribble reads the Reformation as in part a struggle for control of textual margins and their proprietorship over the text they purport to serve.

As might be guessed, Catholics generally supported the canonical readings found in the centuries-old *Glossa*, making the claim that they had the im-

primatur of the holy councils and doctors of the church. The scripture itself was not, however, given centrality.[7] For the Catholic Church, the traditions and doctrines found in canon law, in breviaries, and in missals were enough textual universe for average (literate) communicant, and there was little need for a direct, nonmediated source of scriptural text. Protestants, however, claimed complete primacy for scripture and for the individual's understanding of its meaning. At first, they simply condemned glossing, but since doctrinal divergences with Catholic traditions soon became evident and even standardized, and since Protestantism was so essentially text-based anyway, there soon arose a contesting set of Protestant glosses of scripture to rival orthodox Catholic ones.

As the Reformation got under way, more than doctrine began to be at stake in the selection of one's biblical glosses. In England the uncertainty about what glosses might be acceptable under the new dispensation of Henry VIII's Church of England led to the printing in 1539 of the *Great Bible*, sponsored by Henry. The editors had originally meant to include annotations, but the entire question of which were doctrinally acceptable, and to whom, was so vexing that Miles Coverdale, the main editor, finally settled on a series of small pointing hands throughout the text, indicating passages that *would* have been glossed (with endnotes) had the glosses been allowed.[8] Coverdale warned that those specific passages were pointed out so readers would know that no "private interpretation" of them would be countenanced; these passages were the property of the Church of England. The margins were mostly white space (Figure 6).

Such doctrinal delicacy would not last long in the controversial world of the sixteenth century, however. The Protestants had too many actual doctrinal

---

[7] We might make the epistemic case, indeed, that citation itself, with the whole universe of socially sanctioned and institutionally underwritten knowledge it represents, is an essentially Catholic impulse. Uncited prose is out to find truth by itself, antinomian, animated by an inner light, and thus quintessentially Protestant. We might make that case. But we won't.

[8] Our popular citation systems might have been very different if Coverdale had been allowed by Henry to use the original system of citations he proposed. In a letter to Cromwell, Henry's Lord Privy Seal, in August of 1538, Coverdale proposed a much more complete system of annotations for the Great Bible. In addition to the pointing hand, indicating "some notable annotacion," Coverdale wanted to use a three-leaf clover, indicating that "vpon the same texte there is diuersite of redynge amonge the hebrues, Caldees and Grekes and latenystes," the feather, showing "that the sentence written in small letters is not in the hebrue or Caldee, but in the latyn," and finally the dagger, indicating that "the same texte which followeth it, is also alledged of christ or of some apostle in the newe testament" (Pollard 237–38). Cromwell refused permission for any marks except the pointing hands, and then refused permission for Coverdale's proposed table explicating them. Had he not, we might today be using tiny clovers and feathers rather than asterisks and crosses.

                          †

FIGURE 6   The *Great Bible*, 1539

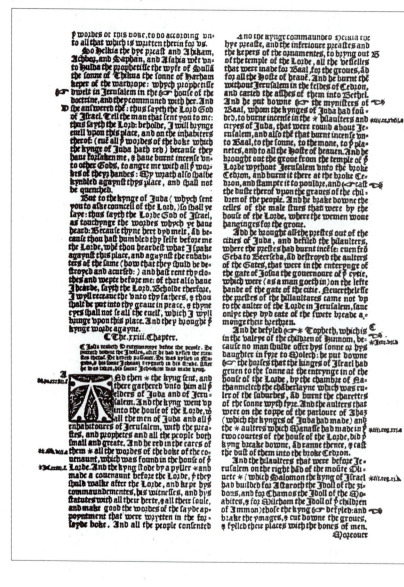

quarrels with Catholic dogma to long refrain from using the inviting margins of their bibles as battlefields. Edmund Becke's version of Matthew's Bible of 1547, the English-made Geneva Bible of 1560, and the Bishops' Bible of 1568 all plunged heavily into marginal glossing and complex, polemical citation systems. The Geneva Bible, free from the fears about state approval of controversial annotation because printed outside of England, was the most openly elaborate and particular in its marginal glossing, filling the margins of its pages with commentary. The Geneva Bible and Bishops' Bible show how typograph-

ical sophistication had grown by the 1560s; they both use textual letter citations—a, b, c, d—to refer to glosses printed in small type in the margins and at the foot of the page. The Bishops' Bible also uses a system of reference symbols ranging from the pointing hands of the Great Bible to asterisks and brackets. The discursive notes in these bibles are not signed and they do not reference specific theorists, but they do create a coherent Protestant reading using "expositions" or commentaries, "annotations" or specific translation/explanation notes, and references to typological precedents and cross-meanings in other biblical books.

As might be expected, the Catholics fired back in this battle of annotation, bringing out in 1582 the Rheims New Testament. As opposed to the "heretical corruptions and false deductions" found in the Protestant bibles, the Rheims version proposed to show "the Apostolike traditions, the expositions of the holy fathers, the decrees of the Catholike Church and the most auncient Councels." Whoever ignored these solid sources in favor of "his private judgement or the arrogant spirit of these Sectaries," says the Preface, "shall worthily through his own wilfulness be deceived." The Rheims New Testament used a system of endnote glosses following each chapter of each book of the New Testament. This is one of the first usages of endnotes I have found, and they are used here to solve a Catholic rhetorical problem: how do you *appear* to foreground the scriptural text when you actually have such a massive glossing apparatus to purvey? The older marginal method of the *Glossa* was not meant to be put into agonistic play in this way, and it was under attack itself. The Rhemish scholars therefore determined on endnotes—a method we will see authors turn to again and again to minimize the rhetorical effect of extensive notational apparatus. The source of each gloss is marked in the text with a double quotation mark ("), referring the reader to the notes at the end of the chapter (Figure 7). The notes, which sometimes take up considerably more space than the passages they gloss, are written in a mixture of English and specialized citational Latin; they assume an audience already educated in the Vulgate and in biblical notation. The interpretations in these notes, unlike the anonymous Protestant notes in the Geneva Bible, were often attributed to orthodox Catholic theologians from Ambrose to Cyprian to Augustine to Gregory. They are overtly polemical, often referring to Protestants as "the adversaries" or "the hereticks." The work assumes familiarity with a body of commenting literature; it uses specialized Latinate "insider" terminology to direct readers around within its field of interlocking claims and support; it uses these citations to support specific textual positions recognizable within a discourse community; and it backs its positions by careful reference to accredited masters working previously within that community. The Rheims New Testament is, in other words, a scholarly work of a completely recognizable sort.

The Rheims New Testament also introduces in a very clear fashion the two elements of citation style that would ever after exist: the dialogic (or substantive or discursive) note and the citation (or reference) note. The dialogic note, which carries on a running subcommentary in relation to elements of the main text, is still used today in all systems of citation; it simply represents

FIGURE 7   The Rheims *New Testaments,* 1582

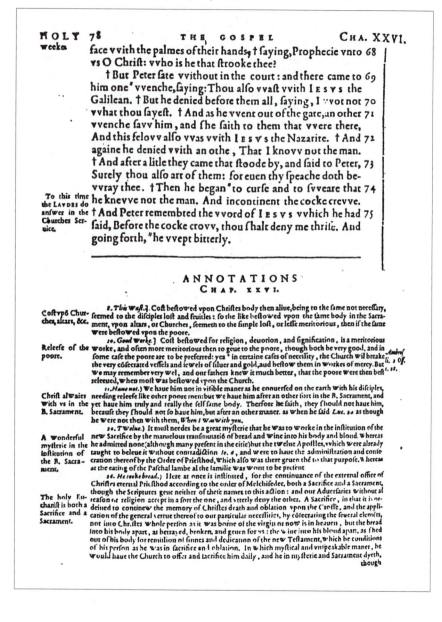

rhetorical possibilities that can't be achieved through any other typographical convention. The citation note is meant to provide a very specific kind of
access to the sources used or quoted by the author. Instead of vaguely declaring, "As St. Augustine says . . . ," the citation note states that "This quote is
found in St. Augustine, *De Doctrina Christiana,* Book 4, Augsberg edition of
1501, page 31." The *full* citation is the key here, for it assumes that the reader

is immersed enough in the universe of the discourse to want to follow it back to specific points in the source works. It invites the reader to doublecheck the point and accuracy of the quotation or idea cited. Citation notes thus assume a dialogic seriousness themselves, treating the reader as a respected co-owner of textual knowledge who is owed a full exposition of the workings and backing of the argument.[9]

The predictable outcome of the battle of biblical glosses that took up the last part of the sixteenth century was a version in which the scriptural text itself represented only a minor percentage of the work, with the majority of text being devoted to glossing controversy and agonistic refutation. This book, a New Testament published by William Fulke in 1589, was a direct refutation of the Rheims New Testament. For every note created by the Rheims commentators, Fulke created a counternote, publishing the entirety of the Catholic gloss and then his refutation of it side by side (Figure 8). Determined to undermine the authority of the Rheims text by using what Bruce Lincoln calls "corrosive discourse" (*Authority* 78), Fulke was as adept at using patristic sources as the Rhemish scholars, and his New Testament reads less like scripture than like extended warfare. As Tribble says, "The plain text, which Tyndale so boldly foregrounded some fifty years before, itself almost disappears in this battle for control. The central impression of Fulke's volume is that of competition and contestation: competing typefaces, competing notes, competing interpretations. In this manifestation the printed page becomes a locus for a bitter struggle over possession of the text" (50).

Finally, this battle of glosses was brought to an end in England by James I's determination that his approved biblical translation would contain no glosses. James was concerned by the increasing vituperation in glossing and by the antimonarchical tone in some of the glosses of the Geneva Bible. In 1603 he called his counselors together and gave orders for a new translation. "Marry, withal, hee gave this caveat . . . that no marginall notes should be added, having found in those which are annexed to the *Geneva* translation . . . some notes very partiall, untrue, seditious, and savouring too much of daungerous and trayterous conceites" (*Summe and Substance*, in Pollard 46). James's instructions to his bishops and translators was to use no marginal glosses except small cross-marked comparative notes referencing parallel passages in other biblical books or variant readings of words. (This usage marks the first time crosses as well as asterisks were used in citation systems.)

Thus the English-speaking world was presented with the stripped-margin Authorized Version of 1611, which we know as the King James Bible. It became the standard English Bible, bringing to a sudden halt the contention of agonistic glosses that threatened to make the Holy Scripture a perpetual battleground. But despite the forced conclusion to this war of

---

[9] For the Rheims scholars, sending readers back to Augustine was also use of the topic of authority. But direct reference to specific sources is a double-edged sword for authors whose readers are antagonistic and may disagree about interpretations—as Fulke's Bible was to show.

FIGURE 8   William Fulke, *The Text of the New Testament of Iesvs Christ, translated ovt of vulgar Latine by the Papists of the traiterous Seminarie at Rhemes . . . Whereunto is added the translation out of the original Greeke, commonly vsed in the Church of England. With a confvtation of all svch argvments, glosses, and annotations,* 1589

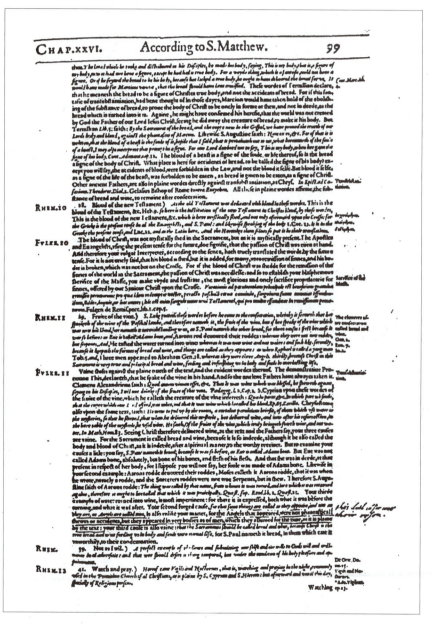

glosses—in England, at least—it left in the hands of Renaissance editors, scholars, and printers an entire heritage and technology of annotation methods, page and form setups, citation structures, and the necessary symbol and italic fonts. We might think of the sixteenth century, with its quickly developing printing technology, its linguistic inventiveness, its political and religious disagreements, as having created a sort of hothouse within which our entire system of scholarly authorization and citation grew rapidly. Its evolution of classical scholarship with all of the hierarchical and competitive elements of comparative work, its battles of competing bible glosses, driven by passionate emotional commitments to truth and the creation of reality through textuality, and its ever-increasing access to texts of all kinds were the cradle of modern Western literacy practices. Although, as Tribble says, at the beginning of the seventeenth century "the legal and cultural mechanisms that will result in a fully proprietary conception of authorship have yet to be formed," the physical and textual structures through which they *will* be formed have been invented (57).

ENLIGHTENMENT EXPERIMENTATION AND FORMALIZATION

The technae of citations and annotations would move forward through experimentation. Several formats were tried and abandoned by the gentleman-authors of the seventeenth century. Robert Burton, in his 1621 *Anatomy of Melancholy*, used a system of text-based translations into English of his classical sources, with the original Greek and Latin (and citation information) in numbered marginal notes (Figure 9). Burton was one of the few early users of citations to present actual quotations from his sources rather than summaries or paraphrases. Though his quotation structure has some problems of readability because it interrupts the reading of the main text for citation information, using the margins for Latin and Greek original versions, at least Burton is using quotes.[10] Thomas Browne, in his *Urn-Burial* of 1658, eschewed the specific citation structures of Burton, and provided no source information except author's name and title, but his margins were still active with overt display of classical learning (Figure 10). Without wanting to appear antiquarian, or "scholarly" in a pedantic way, Burton and Browne still need to appear learned and "authorial," and they cannot do so without some classical structure.

By the end of the seventeenth century, the scholar-author division had become fairly rigid, largely as a result of the rise of empirical science and of

---

[10] Burton's rhetorical choices here probably reflect the linguistic transition of his times. More and more English people were being taught reading and writing in their native language, and Burton used the system he did to provide readers who had no classical languages with translations they could read while allowing classical language speakers to check and rate his translations. Burton may also be continuing in his citation forms the elaborate knowledge game he is playing with the reader. But it is an inescapably transitional system and provides a bumpy read.

Figure 9   Robert Burton, *Anatomy of Melancholy*, 1621

Part. 1. Sec. 2.   *Causes of melancholy.*   Memb. 5. Subf. 3.

226   onely. I am of *Capivaccius* mind for my part. Now this humor according to *Salvianus*, is fometime in the fubftance of the Braine, fometimes contained in the Membranes and tunicles that couer the Braine, fometimes in the paffages of the Ventricles of the Braine, or veines of thofe Ventricles. It followes many times [a] *Phrenfie, long difeafes, agues, long abode in hote places, or vnder the Sun, a blow on the head,* as *Rhefis* informeth vs: *Pifo* addes folitarineffe, waking, inflammations of the head, proceeding moft part [b] from much vfe of fpices, hote wines, hote meats; all which *Montanus* reckons vp *concapite, cap. 23. fil. 22.* for a Melancholy Iew; and *Hernius* repeates *cap. 1.2. de cMania,* hote bathes, garlick, onions, faith *Guianerius,* bad aire, corrupt, much [c] waking &c. retention of feed, or abundance, ftopping of *hæmorrogia,* the Midriffe mifaffected; and according to *Trallianus l. 1. 16.* immoderate cares, troubles, griefes, difcontent, ftudy, meditation, and in a word, the abufe of all thofe 6. non-naturall things. *Hercules de Saxonia cap. 16. lib. 1.* will haue it caufed from a [d] cautery, or boyle dryed vp, or any iffue. *Amatus Lufitanus cent. 2. curâ 67.* giues inftance in a fellow that had a boyle in his arme, *and* [e] *after that was cured, ran mad, and when the wound was open, he was cured againe. Trincavelius confil. 13. lib. 1.* hath an example of a melancholy man fo caufed by overmuch continuance in the fun, frequent vfe of Venery, and immoderate exercife. And in his *confil. 49. lib. 3.* from an [f] headpeece overheated, which caufed head melancholy. *Profper Calenius* brings in Cardinal *Cefius* for a patterne of fuch as are fo melancholy. by long ftudy: but examples are infinite.

[a] Melancholia capitis accedit poft phrenefim aut longam moram fub fole, aut percuffionem in capite, cap. 23. lib. 1.
[b] Qui bibit vina potentia, & fæpe fiunt fub fole.
[c] Cura valide largioris vini & aromatum vfus.
[d] A Canterio & vkere exficcato.
[e] Ab vlcere curato incidit in infaniam, aperto vulnere curatur.
[f] A galea nimis calefacta.

Svbsect. 4.

Caufes of Hypocondriacall or windy Melancholy.

IN repeating of thefe caufes, I muft *crambè bis coctam apponere,* fay that againe which I haue formerly faid, in applying them to their proper Species: of *Hypocondriacall* or flatuous

the first great generation of serious textual scholars at English universities. It is difficult for those trained up in standard English literary history to see these men in any original light, for they have come down to us in literary tradition as comic figures, pedants and buffoons. They had the bad fortune to be the enemies and butts of Alexander Pope and Jonathan Swift in one of the

FIGURE 10   Thomas Browne, *Urn-Burial and Cyrus-Garden*, 1658

---

116   *Cyrus-Garden,* Or

square. For though they might be fix-
teen in Rank and file, yet when they
fhut clofe, fo that the fixt pike advanced
before the firft, though the number
might be fquare, the figure was oblong,
anfwerable unto the Quincunciall qua-
drate of *Curtius.* According to this fquare
Thucydides delivers, the *Athenians* dif-
pofed their battle againft the *Lacedemoni-*
f ᾳ πλαι-   *ans* f brickwife, and by the fame word
δῳ.   the Learned *Guellius* expoundeth the qua-
g *Secto via*   drate of g *Virgil,* after the form of a brick
limite qua-
dret. Com-   or tile.
ment. *in*   And as the firft ftation and pofition of
Virgil.   trees, fo was the firft habitation of men,
not in round Cities, as of later foundati-
on ; For the form of *Babylon* the firft City was fquare, and fo fhall alfo be the
laft, according to the defcription of the
holy City in the Apocalyps. The famous
pillars of *Seth* before the flood, had alfo
the like foundation, if they were but
antidiluvian Obelisks, and fuch as *Cham*
and his *Ægyptian* race, imitated after the
Floud.
But *Nineveh* which Authours acknowledge to have exceeded *Babylon,* was of
h *Diod. Sic.* a h longilaterall figure, ninety five Fur-
longs

---

best-documented—and one of the most partially reported—intellectual
controversies of the late seventeenth and early eighteenth centuries: the
"Ancients and Moderns" battle. Though the scholars may have won this intellectual battle against the authors, they lost the historical war and are
known today, if at all, as hapless targets. The three greatest of this first generation of textual scholars were William Wotton, Richard Bentley, and
Lewis Theobald. Their defense of Enlightenment learning was the first serious indication that English culture had reached a point at which it could
begin to transcend rather than to merely appropriate the classical sources
and writers.

Wotton, Bentley, and Theobald, though they may not have been entertaining or popular figures as Pope and Swift, were the first Englishmen to apply the tenets of critical thought and the relatively new discipline of textual editing and analysis to modern as well as ancient sources. Respect for the findings of the new science, careful comparative scholarship ranging easily from the classics through Milton, and willingness to stand their ground against powerful and sometimes aristocratic intellectual foes mark the work of these writers. The first gun was fired in 1692, when Sir William Temple's "Essay on Ancient and Modern Learning" made the case that the ancients surpassed the moderns in all branches of human endeavor. Contemporary scholars fought back in print. Wotton's 1694 work *Reflections upon Ancient and Modern Learning* was less a condemnation of Temple or of classical works than it was an impressive demonstration of the scope and power of modern discoveries. The book looks familiar to us today because the scholarly apparatus in it is essentially modern—a simple and easily read form of the humanist marginal citation notes that had been evolving for the previous century, defined by repeating alphabetical notes that give complete bibliographical information (Figure 11). Wotton's page is clean, his marginal citations clear and apposite.

A few years later, the battle became specifically textual. Bentley's 1697 *Dissertation upon Phalaris*, a critical examination of Charles Boyle's careless edition of the spurious *Epistles of Phalaris*, drew down upon him the satire of Jonathan Swift, friend of Boyle and Temple, in *The Battle of the Books* and *The Tale of a Tub*. And Theobald angered Pope when in 1723 he took the poet to task for his careless editing of Shakespeare in *Shakespeare Restored*, leading to Pope's attack on him—and on Bentley—in the *Dunciad* and then in the *Dunciad Variorum*, Pope's satire on pedantic scholarship. These works show that citation systems were shifting. Printers were finding that their older methods—based in their imitation of the scribal techniques of leaving large margins for learned annotations—were harder to set in type, requiring two sticks per line per form. Paper, too, was dearer than ever, and extending the text closer to the edge was a natural move. But what, then, could be done with the marginal notes as the margins contracted? They could be placed at the bottom of the page and marked, as marginal notes had been marked, by letters, numbers, or symbols. Thus, around the turn of the eighteenth century, we finally come to the use of footnotes.

They probably began on the Continent. The evolution of scholarly apparatus had been ongoing, especially in continental Europe, for more than two hundred years, and by the later seventeenth century, it had attained considerable sophistication and analytical methodology. One key text is Louis-Sebastien le Nain de Tillemont's massive *Ecclesiastical Memoirs* of 1693, which is a history of the first six centuries of Christianity. Tillemont exhibits clearly how sophisticated authors and printers on the Continent had become since the 1650s (Figure 12). In this English translation from 1731, we see that Tillemont was using no fewer than three forms of citation structure: a num-

FIGURE 11   William Wotton, *Reflections upon Ancient and Modern Learning*, 1694

174   *Reflections upon*

learn who firſt found out the Properties
of Convex and Concave Glaſſes in the
Refraction of Light. Dr. *Plot* has collected a great deal concerning F. *Bacon*,
in his *Natural Hiſtory of Oxfordſhire*;
which ſeems to put it out of doubt that
he knew that great Objects might appear
little, and ſmall Objects appear great;
that diſtant Objects would ſeem near,
and near Objects ſeem afar off, by different Applications of Convex and Concave Glaſſes; upon the Credit of which
(n) Diop-   Authorities, Mr. *Molineux (n)* attributes
tric. Pag.
256, 257, the Invention of Spectacles to this lear-
258.   ned Friar, the Time to which their ear-
lieſt Uſe may be traced, agreeing very
well with the Time in which he lived;
but how far F. *Bacon* went, we know
not: So that we muſt go into *Holland* for
the firſt Inventors of theſe excellent In-
ſtruments, and there they were firſt found
(o) Borel- out by one *Zacharias Joannides (o)*, a
lus *de vero* Spectacle-maker *(p)* of *Middleburgh* in
Inventore
Teleſcopii, *Zeland*; in 1590 *(q)* he preſented a Tel-
pag. 30.   leſcope of Two Glaſſes to Prince *Maurice*,
(p) Ibid.   and another to Arch-Duke *Albert*, the
Pag. 35.
(q) Ibid.   former of whom apprehending that they
Pag. 30.   might be of great Uſe in War, deſired
him to conceal his Secret. For this Rea-
(r) Diop-   ſon, his Name was ſo little known, that
tric.   neither *Des Cartes (r)* nor *Gerhard Voſ-*
ſius (ſ)

bered marginal system cross-referencing other parts of the book, a Greek-
letter footnote system referencing the scriptures and the church fathers, and a
symbol footnote system underneath it for dialogic notes and commentary.
Here, indeed, is God's plenty.

But Tillemont's church history was a specialized book. Anthony
Grafton's *The Footnote: A Curious History*, which deals with the epistemic evolution of footnote content in historical scholarship, places the birth of modern
footnoting methodology with Pierre Bayle's *Dictionaire Critique et Historique*
in 1697 (192–99). Beginning with the credulous and sometimes fictionalizing
antiquaries and compilers of the earlier Renaissance and with the ecclesiastical historians from Eusebius on, careful comparative and analytical historical

FIGURE 12   Louis-Sebastien Le Nain de Tillemont, *Ecclesiastical Memoirs of the Six First Centuries: Made Good by Citations from Original Authors*, 1694, translation of 1731

Saint P A U L.   165

his particular friend, but as a General of the chriftian army, as a lion, as a   A. D. 43.
burning and fhining lamp, as a voice capable of founding through the whole
earth.   + Having found him, he brought him to ' Antioch, where they ' Note 12.
lived a whole year, ' going to the affembly of the church, and inftructing a * ἀυταχθῖται
great number of infidels. ⁕ No one difturbed the progrefs of the faith by ἐστῆ ἐκκλησίᾳ
any perfecution, [which proceeded fo far as to oblige S. Paul to remove;
though there might be one of lefs violence:] ⁑ For in the fourth century
they fhewed fome caverns at the foot of the mountain near Antioch, whither
they held that this apoftle retired, and concealed himfelf.

  β It was no fmall happinefs to Antioch to have been the ⁕ firft city, fays
S. Chryfoftom, that had S. Paul for it's preacher, and to have enjoyed him fo
long: [For we fhall fee, that he returned thither feveral times.]   But the
preaching of S. Paul procured to it another honour, which renders it illuftrious
throughout the whole church.   γ For it was at Antioch, that the difciples
began at that time to be called by the name of *Chriftians*; δ which title communicating to us the adorable name of J E S U S C H R I S T our Saviour, renders
us alfo partakers of all the others that belong to him, and obliges us to fhew
forth the vertues and perfections thereof in our life.   ε S. Gregory Nyffen fays,
that it was ζ by the order of the apoftles, that we were called by this title. ⁸ κατὰ τὸ
ζ Another Father is of opinion, that the Holy Spirit was pleafed in this ἐγγύα.
manner to fulfil what the prophets had promifed, that God would give a
new name to his fervants. η And fince there was no name upon earth to
be found that was common to us, becaufe we are not one people, but a
collection of different nations, it was neceffary that we fhould receive one
from heaven. θ Hitherto they who had embraced the faith, were called *Thofe
of the way*, [which fignifies nothing in particular,] or Difciples, or Believers.
But the title of Chriftians prevailed in a little time above all the others.
[It was immediately carried from Antioch to Rome, if it be true, that
S. Peter, who ufes the word in his firft epiftle, wrote that epiftle this year,
⁕ as fome are of opinion.   The Pagans had hardly any other name for our ⁴See S.Peter,
religion :] ι but not knowing the myftery of the divine unction, from whence §. 28, 31.
the word Chriftian is derived in the Greek, they took it from + another
word of the fame language, which fignifies good and ufeful.

  ⁕ While S. Paul was at Antioch, feveral prophets came thither from Jerufalem, one of whom named Agabus foretold, that there would be a great
famine throughout the whole earth; ς which accordingly happened in the ⁵See the De-
days of Claudius who reigned [at that time,] λ and in the fourth year of ſtruction of
his ⁸ reign.   ⁕ This famine, by which God punifhed the fins of the Pagans ⁶A. D. 44.
and the malice of the Jews againft them, was an advantage to the
Chriftians. For it gave them an opportunity of practifing divers vertues;
ρ and contributed to unite the Gentiles, [who were the principal part of the
church of Antioch,] to the Jews who had embraced the faith in Judæa.
[The latter ρ had quitted their eftates, or been pillaged of all that they had.] ⁷See S.Peter,
ξ For which reafon the Faithful of Antioch refolved to fend them relief, §. 7, 11.
every one according to his ability. S. Paul and S. Barnabas carried their alms
to Jerufalem, where they delivered them into the hands of the priefts.

---

‡ Acts 11. v. 25, 26.   ⁕ Chry. h. 25. p. 235. d, e.   ι Thdrt. v. P. c. 2.
p. 782. c.   β Chry. p. 233. a.   γ Acts 11. v. 26.   ʃ Nyf. chri. t. 3.
p. 270. | perf. p. 295. d.   ε p. 295. d.   ζ Cyr. cat. 17. p. 205. b.   ⁕ Amb.
pf. 36. p. 685. m.   θ Chry. in Act. h. 25. p. 233. b.   ⁕ C. à Lap. ib. p. 205. |
Bar. 43. §. 13.   κ Acts 11. v. 27, 28.   λ Euf. chr.   μ Chry. in Act. h.25.
p. 233. d, e.   ρ p. 235. b.   ξ Acts 11. v. 29, 30.

  * [S. Paul had already preached the faith at   preached at Antioch in the capacity of a doctor.
Damafcus, and perhaps likewife in Arabia and   *Acts* 13. *v.* 1.
other places. But it may be faid, that he was   + Inftead of *Chriftiani* they faid *Chreftiani*,
not, as far as appears, looked on then as any   from the greek word χρηςὸς. *Juſt. ap.* 2. *p.* 55.
more than as an ordinary difciple,] whereas he   *a.*| *Tert. ap. c.* 3. *p.* 5. *a.*| *Lact. l.* 4. *c.* 7. *p.* 367.

methodologies gradually emerged during the sixteenth century and were tested and refined during the seventeenth. Jacques-Auguste de Thou, Joseph Scaliger, Cesare Baronio, Athanasius Kircher, Mosheim, Tillemont, and many other Renaissance historians and scholars helped to create the early Enlightenment intellectual culture within which claims must be supported by marginal or footnoted evidence, and Bayle's *Dictionaire* took full advantage of their work.

Bayle was an extraordinarily learned polymath, and his typographical choices were to have a powerful effect on subsequent writers and printers. The *Historical and Critical Dictionary* was printed in large folio volumes with tall columns of small print. Each page is set up with a relatively small amount of entry text at the top of the folio columns, followed by the larger bulk of Bayle's dialogic "Remarks" (indicated by capital letters) underneath, and finally, with citation notes in the margins (Figure 13). Like Tillemont, Bayle colonized the foot of his page, and the dialogic possibilities it offered him were definitive of his work. The *Dictionary* was seen as a vital, if polemical, work of learning and reference throughout learned Europe. The book was translated, widely read, heatedly argued over, and almost every educated European came to know its typographic formula. After Bayle, the foot of the page becomes a much more important site for notes (though his own citation notes were in the margins), and marginal notes gradually give way to footnotes.[11]

Though it may have been Tillemont or Bayle, no one knows for sure what book was first printed with footnotes rather than marginal notes. The two systems continued side by side for some time. The first English book I have found with true footnotes is the 1710 fifth edition of Swift's *Tale of a Tub*. The first edition of 1704 had used only marginal notes in the old style, but by 1710 Swift had changed the typography to use *both* marginal notes and footnotes marked by symbols.[12] Swift meant this promiscuous use of notational

---

[11] Even in the atmosphere of proliferating scholarly seriousness of 1703, however, we still see some serious divisions on the question of notes and their contents. Grafton quotes Jean-Baptiste Thiers' criticism of Boileau's *L'Histoire des Flagellans* of 1700, which Thiers considered full of officious and unnecessary citation information. "Often," huffed Thiers, "he cites the year and place of publication of books, the names of the printers or publishers, the pages and leaves of the books. . . . What purpose do all of these meticulous and affected citations serve, except to enlarge his history?" (qtd. in Grafton, *The Footnote*, 219–20). Such criticism may seem strange to us, but to Thiers, used to the older gentleman-amateur-antiquarian tradition, Boileau's "booksellers' learning" was pedantic and superfluous. Boileau was operating within a newer scholarly tradition that would, during the next hundred years, coalesce into something very like modern historical methodology; naturally, we tend to understand him better.

[12] The genesis of these various symbols presents an interesting problem. They seem to have been cast as type by early printers and to have been added to as needs arose. In order of their generality of use, they came to include the asterisk, the cross or dagger, the double asterisk, the double cross, the double dagger, the two vertical lines, the three vertical lines, and the doubled parentheses (section mark or whirlwind).

FIGURE 13 Pierre Bayle, *Dictionaire Historique et Critique,* 1697

ARISTOTE 359

une belle mort (*Q*), & il jouït de la (*R*) fecilité éternelle. Il composa un très-grand nombre de livres, dont une assez bonne partie est parvenuë jusques à nous. Il est vrai que certains Critiques forment mille doutes sur cela. Nous parlons des avantures de ces livres dans les remarques * sur l'article *Tyrannion.* Il fut extremement honoré dans sa (*S*) patrie, & il y a eu des heretiques (*T*) qui veneroient son image conjointement avec celle de JESUS-CHRIST. Je n'ai point trouvé que les Antinomiens *portassent plus de respect à ce sage Payen qu'à la sagesse increée,* * ni que les *Aëtiens ayent été excommuniez, parce qu'ils donnoient*

* Voyez ci-dessus les remarques de l'article Andronicus, pag. 271. 272.

† Rapin, compar. de Platon & d'Aristote p.m. 392.

donnée beaucoup de Docteurs Catholiques „ sont „ toutes chimeres, qui ont pris leur origine & „ fondement sur ce qu'il dit en son premier li- „ vre du ciel parlant du nombre ternaire ; Διὸ „ παρὰ τῆς φύσεως εἰληφότες ὥσπερ νόμους ἐκείνης „ καὶ πρὸς τὰς ἁγιστείας τῶν θεῶν χρώμεθα τῷ ἀριθμῷ „ τούτῳ, c'est-à-dire, *Quapropter hoc à natura numero sumpto perinde atque quadam illius „ lege, & in Deorum sacrificiis celebrandis uti so- „ lemus.* Duquel passage on ne sauroit conclure „ autre chose, sinon qu'Aristote dit que l'on se „ servoit en son tems du nombre de trois aux sa- „ crifices, ce qui nous est aussi temoigné par „ Theocrite. „ Après cela Naudé remarque que le Cardinal Bessarion (*a*) *se moque de Trapezonce, de ce qu'il avoit tant pris de peine pour prouver par ce texte qu'Aristote avoit eu une entiere conoissance de la Trinité.*

(*Q*) *Il fit une belle mort.*] Se sentant (*b*) proche de sa fin il versa un torrent de larmes, & tout penetré de douleur & d'esperance il implora la misericorde du souverain Etre. Il aprouvoit extremement une sentence d'Homere, qui porte qu'il ne sied pas mal aux Dieux de se revêtir de la nature de l'homme, afin d'éclairer le genre humain. C'étoient des pressentimens de l'Incarnation du fils de Dieu. Voilà ce que nous lisons dans Cœlius Rhodiginus. Son autorité dans un fait de cette nature ne vaut gueres mieux que rien. D'autres parlent bien autrement des dernieres heures d'Aristote. (*c*) Ils „ disent qu'il mourut de deplaisir de n'a- „ voir pu comprendre la cause du flus & du „ reflus de l'Euripe. Sur quoi quelques Mo- „ dernes ont inventé cette fable qui depuis a eu „ cours, que ce Philosophe se precipita dans „ l'Euripe en disant ces paroles, *Que l'Euripe „ m'engloutisse puis que je ne le puis comprendre.* „ Diogene Laërce (*d*) cite un Auteur nommé Eumelus, qui avoit dit qu'Aristote s'étant refugié à Chalcis s'empoisonna à l'âge de 70. ans. Apollodore (*e*) me paroît plus digne de foi : il a dit que ce grand homme mourut de maladie à l'âge de 63. ans.

(*R*) *Il jouït de la felicité éternelle.*] Sepulveda (*f*) l'un des plus savans hommes du XVI. siecle, n'a point hesité à le placer parmi les bienheureux : il a soutenu publiquement son opinion, & par écrit. Le Jesuite Gretserus (*g*) le reprend d'avoir été trop hardi ; mais neanmoins il avouë qu'il incline en faveur d'Aristote aussi bien que Sepulveda, dont *il n'improuve en cela que la façon de parler affirmative.* Joignez à ceci ce que j'ai cité de Cœlius Rhodiginus, & ce que des gens de poids ont remarqué touchant la raison qui obligea Aristote à sortir d'Athenes. Albert le Grand a soutenu qu'on le chassa à cause de ses bonnes mœurs; *Propter morum rectitudinem pulsus* (*h*) *Athenis.* Gretserus (*i*) dans sa dispute contre Sepulveda touchant le salut d'Aristote, *ne doute point qu'il n'ait voulu éviter par ce bannissement volontaire la necessité où on vouloit le reduire, de rendre à des idoles un culte qu'il croyoit n'être dû qu'à Dieu seul.* Nous avons donc en sa personne un illustre Refugié pour la vraye Religion. Origene (*k*) a favorablement interpreté cette fuite d'Aristote, car lors qu'il explique le precepte que nôtre Seigneur (*l*) donne à ses Apôtres, *de fuir d'une ville où ils seroient persecutez dans une autre,* il dit à Celsus qui se mocquoit de cela *avec ses profanations ordinaires, que l'éloignement d'Aristote dont nous parlons a été conforme à la Morale de l'Evangile, & qu'il fit la même chose étant poursuivi calomnieusement, que* JESUS-CHRIST *conseille à ses disciples.*

(*S*) *Extremement honoré dans sa patrie.*] Elle avoit été ruïnée par le Roi Philippe, mais Alexandre la fit rebâtir à la priere d'Aristote. Les habitans pour reconoître ce bienfait (*m*) consacrerent un jour de fête à ce Philosophe, & lors qu'il fut mort à Chalcis dans l'Ile d'Euboée, ils transporterent ses os chez eux, ils dresserent un autel sur son monument, ils donnerent à ce lieu le nom d'Aristote, & y tinrent dans la suite leurs assemblées. Mandeville (*n*) dans la fabuleuse relation de ses voyages dit que tout cela subsistoit encore de son tems, c'est-à-dire dans le XIV. siecle.

(*T*) *Il y a eu des heretiques qui veneroient son image . . . . que les Antinomiens portassent plus de respect.*] Voici un passage du P. Rapin. „ (*o*) Les Carpocratiens (*p*) furent condamnez „ pour avoir mis l'image de ce Philosophe avec „ celle de JESUS-CHRIST, & pour l'avoir „ adorée par une extravagance de zêle pour sa „ doctrine. Les Aëtiens (*q*) furent excommu- „ niez par l'Eglise, & par les Ariens même dont „ ils étoient sortis, parce qu'ils donnoient à leurs „ disciples les Categories d'Aristote pour Cate- „ chismes. Les Antinomiens (*r*) allerent jus- „ ques à cet excés d'impieté, que de porter plus „ de respect à ce sage Payen qu'à la sagesse in- „ créée. „ Je n'avois jamais si bien connu qu'en cet endroit-ci, que cet agreable Ecrivain ne se donnoit pas la peine de consulter les originaux. J'avouë que Baronius sous l'année que le P. Rapin cite dit que les Carpocratiens avoient des images, & entre autres celle de JESUS-CHRIST qu'ils disoient avoir été faite par Pilate, celle de Pythagoras, celle de Platon, celle d'Aristote, & qu'ils leur rendoient la veneration que les Payens rendoient aux idoles; mais cela ne meritoit pas d'être allegué : car outre que Baronius ne dit point que c'ait été la raison pourquoi on condamna ces heretiques, il ne paroît pas qu'ils ayent eu plus de zêle

(*a*) Cap. 15 lib. 3. adversus calumniat. Plat.

(*b*) Proditum & illas monumentis est quam philosophus hic extremis ubi ingrueret praesentisset dolore ac ipse in lacrymas amplius profusum primae causae misericordiam intentius implorasse. Quia & Homeri sententiam ex Odyssea vehementer approbasse, qua non esse immortalibus diis indecorum pronunciatur hominis induere naturam, quo ab erroribus revocentur mortales. Qua in re CHRISTI praesensisse adventum auguratur nonnulli ejus viri gloriae in primis addicti. Cael. Rhodigin. L. 17. c. 34.

(*c*) Le P. Rapin. p. 310. qui cite Justin. in adm. ad Gentes. Greg. Naz. contra Jul. Voyez aussi Rhodiginus l. 29. c. 8. Quant aux citations du P. Rapin voyez la remarque Z.

(*d*) In Arist. n. 6. (*e*) Apud Laërt. ibid. n. 10.

(*f*) Lib. de anim. p. apud la Mothe le Vayer tom. 5. pag. 114.

(*h*) Lib. 5. Ethic. c. 1. apud Rapin. p. 310.

(*i*) De variis coel. Luth. cap. 13. apud la Mothe le Vayer ib. p. 109.

(*k*) Lib. 2. contra Celsum apud eumdem.

(*l*) Matth. chap. 10. v. 23. ibid.

(*m*) Ammonius in vita Arist.

(*n*) Itinerar. c. 2. apud Hornium, hist. philos. l. 3. c. 15. pag. 197.

(*o*) Compar. pag. 392.

(*p*) Baronius Ann. Eccl. ad ann. 120.

(*q*) Ibid. ad ann. 208.

(*r*) Eusob. Hist. c. 27.

FIGURE 14   Jonathan Swift, *A Tale of a Tub*, fifth edition, 1710

SECTION XI   195

Curiosity attracted Strangers to Laugh, or to Listen; he would of a sudden, with one Hand out with his *Gear*, and piss full in their Eyes, and with the other, all to-bespatter[1] them with Mud.

*IN Winter he went always loose and unbuttoned, and clad as thin as possible, to let *in* the ambient Heat; and in Summer, lapt himself close and thick to keep it *out*.[2]

†IN all Revolutions of Government, he would make his Court for the Office of *Hangman* General; and in the Exercise of that Dignity, wherein he was very dextrous, would make use of ‖no other *Vizard* than a *long Prayer*.[3]

HE had a Tongue so Musculous and Subtil, that he could twist it up into his Nose, and deliver a strange Kind of Speech from thence. He was also the first in these Kingdoms, who began to improve the *Spanish* Accomplishment of *Braying*;[4] and having large Ears, perpetually exposed and arrect,[5] he carried his Art to such a Perfection, that it was a Point of great Difficulty to distinguish either by the View or the Sound, between the *Original* and the *Copy*.

HE was troubled with a Disease, reverse to that

* *They affect Differences in Habit and Behaviour.*
† *They are severe Persecutors, and all in a Form of Cant and Devotion.*
‖ Cromwell *and his Confederates went, as they called it,* to seek God, *when they resolved to murther the King.*

---

structure as part of his satire of the new learning, but he did not invent it (Figure 14). By 1720 footnotes were a standard system, and marginal notes became rarer and rarer. The last purely marginal notes I have found in a serious scholarly book are in Theobald's 1723 edition of *Shakespeare Restored*, and Theobald was using a specific taxonomic system of Pope's editing errors that would have made footnotes less effective for his purposes.

Footnotes, like marginal notes, could take different forms. They declared their cultural allegiances by the forms they took; those writers who wished to appear learned but not scholarly used footnotes marked by symbols and a freer range of citation forms. Scholars, whose work was accountable to other scholars in a way that could be very polemical, marked their trail through the forest with more formal letter- and number-marked systems. We see an example of the first of these systems in Bernard Mandeville's *Free Thoughts on Religion* of 1720 (Figure 15), which is almost nonchalant in the informality of its cited information. The second is satirized by Pope in his *Dunciad Variations* of 1729. As we see in this page (Figure 16), Pope is completely familiar with what by then were the conventions of the scholarly, as opposed to the

FIGURE 15   Bernard Mandeville, *Free Thoughts on Religion*, 1720

2 1 0   *Of Tolleration*

befides *Servetus*, who every Body knows
was burnt for Herefy, * *Alciatus*, † *Blandrata*, ‡ *Gribaldus*, and fome others, would
have met with the fame Fate, if they had
not faved themfelves by Flight, and even
after the Life of that great Reformer,‖ *John
Valentinus Gentilis*, who, like the reſt,
was fled, and got into *Moravia*, ventur'd,
upon the Death of his moſt dreadful Ad-
verfary, to return into *Switzerland*, but
was laid hold of, profecuted by the Cal-
viniſts, and had his Head ** ſtruck off
for oppugning the Myſtery of the Trinity
in the Territories of *Bern*; glorying that
he fuffer'd for the Honour of G o d the
Father.

††*C A S T A L I O*, who likewife has been
forc'd to quit *Geneva* on the Score of Hete-
rodoxy, publiſhed a Book a little after the
Execution of *Servetus*, in which he blam'd
that Action, and fpoke up for Tolleration,
‖‖ difguifing himfelf under the Name of
                                      Martinus

* John Paul Alciatus, *a Gentleman of* Milan.
† George Blandrata, *an* Italian *Phyfician, born in* Picd-
mont.
‡ Mathew Gribaldus, *a learned Civilian of* Padua.
‖ *He was a Native of* Cofenza *in the Kingdom of* Naples.
** Aretius. Hiſtor. Reform. Polon.
†† *A learned* Savoyard, *who was many Years Profeſſor of
the* Greek *Tongue at* Bafil, *where he dy'd,*
‖‖ Ant. Faytus. in vita Beze.

gentlemanly, footnote: the numbers, the Latin references—*ibid, op cit, loc cit, pag. ult.,* etc.—the nitpicking edition and page numbers.[13]

If footnotes were largely standard by 1740, they were brought to a state almost completely modern by the later part of the century. David Hume's *History of England* from 1767 gives an idea of how standard historical works were footnoted around midcentury (Figure 17). Hume tells us here what he has read, but, like Tillemont's, his citations make no judgments about the

---

[13] Probably the greatest satire on pedantic scholarship ever written, the *Dunciad Variorum* was a true variorum, to which Pope invited Swift and other friends to submit parodic "notes" (which were signed "Bentley" and "Theobald" among other names). The language's most scathing satire on scholarly forms thus evolved hardly three decades after the forms themselves coalesced.

FIGURE 16   Alexander Pope, *The Dunciad Variorum*, 1729

---

2   TESTIMONIES of AUTHORS.

tors are wont to infift upon fuch, and how material they feem to
themfelves if to none other.   Forgive me therefore gentle reader, if
(following learned example) I ever and anon become tedious; allow
me to take the fame pain to find whether my author were good or
bad, well or ill-natured, modeft or arrogant; as another, whether his
were fair or brown, fhort or tall, or whether he wore a coat or a caffock?

WE purpofed to begin with his Life, Parentage and Education : but
as to thefe, even his Cotemporaries do exceedingly differ.   One faith,
he was educated at home 1; another that he was bred abroad at St.
Omer's by Jefuits 2; a third, not at St. *Omer*'s, but at *Oxford* 3; a
fourth, that he had no Univerfity education at all 4.   Thofe who allow
him to be bred at home, differ as much concerning his Tutor: One
faith, he was kept by his father on purpofe 5; a fecond, that he was
an itinerant prieft 6; a third, that he was a parfon 7; one calleth
him a fecular clergyman of the church of *Rome* 8; another, a Monk 9.
As little agree they about his Father; whom one fuppofeth, like the
father of *Hefiod*, a tradefman or merchant 10; another a hufband-
man, *&c.* 11   Nor hath an author been wanting to give our Poet fuch
a Father, as *Apuleius* hath to *Plato*, *Iamblicus* to *Pythagoras*, and divers
to *Homer*; namely a *Dæmon:* For thus Mr. *Gildon.* 12   " Certain it
" is, that his Original is not from *Adam* but the devil, and that he
" wanteth nothing but horns and tail to be the exact refemblance of
" his infernal father."   Finding therefore fuch contrariety of opinions,
and (whatever be ours of this fort of generation) not being fond to
enter into controverfy, we fhall defer writing the life of our Poet, till
authors can determine among themfelves what parents or education
he had, or whether he had any education or parents at all?

---

1 *Giles Jacob*'s Lives of Poets, vol. 2. in his life.   2 *Dennis*'s reflect. on the Effay on Crit.
3 Dunciad diffected, p. 4.   4 Guardian, Nº. 40.   5 *Jacob, ib.*   6 Dunc.
diff. *ibid.*   7 Farmer P. and his fon, *ibid.* verfe 32.   8 Dunc. diff.   9 Characters of the Times, p. 45.   10. Female Dunciad, pag. ult.   11 Dunc. diffect.
12. Whom Mr. *Curl* (Key to the Dunc. 1ft. edit.) declares to be author of the *Character of*
Mr. *Pope* and his writings, in a letter to a friend, printed for S. *Popping.* 1716. where this paffage
is to be found, pag. 10.

Proceed

---

trustworthiness or acuity of his sources. Hume's footnotes are flat, passive,
purely citational—albeit with little publication information. The footnote
was awaiting its definitive artist, and in Edward Gibbon he arrived. The
bottom note as a literary form probably reached no higher point than it did
in the hands of Gibbon, whose 1776 *Decline and Fall of the Roman Empire*

FIGURE 17 David Hume, *History of England*, edition of 1767

R I C H A R D I. · · · 333

the rabble fet fire to the houfes, and made way thro' the flames to exercife their pillage and violence * ; the ufual licentioufnefs of London, which the fovereign power with difficulty reftrained, broke out with fury, and continued thefe outrages ; the houfes of the rich citizens, tho' Chriftians, were next attacked and plundered † ; and wearinefs and fatiety at laft put an end to the diforder : Yet when the King impowered Glanville, the jufticiary, to inquire into the authors of thefe crimes, the guilt was found to involve fo many of the moft confiderable inhabitants, that it was deemed more prudent to drop the profecution ; and very few fuffered the punifhment due to this enormity ‡. But the diforder ftopped not at London. The inhabitants of the other cities of England, hearing of this execution of the Jews, imitated the barbarous example ‖ ; and in York, five hundred of that nation, who had retired into the caftle for fafety, and found themfelves unable to defend the place, murdered their own wives and children, threw the dead bodies over the walls upon the populace, and then fetting fire to the houfes, perifhed in the flames §. The gentry of the neighbourhood, who were all indebted to the Jews, ran to the cathedral, where their bonds were kept, and made a folemn bonfire of the papers before the altar ╪.

THE antient fituation of England, when the people poffeffed little riches and the public no credit, made it impoffible for the fovereigns to bear the expences of a fteady or durable war, even on their frontiers ; much lefs could they find regular means for the fupport of fuch diftant expeditions as thofe into Paleftine, which were more the refult of popular frenzy than of fober reafon or deliberate policy. Richard, therefore, knew, that he muft carry with him all the treafure requifite for his enterprize, and that both the remotenefs of his own country and its poverty made it unable to furnifh him with thofe continued fupplies, which the exigencies of fo perilous a war muft neceffarily require. His father had left him a treafure of above an hundred thoufand marks * ; and the King, negligent of every intereft, but that of prefent glory, endeavoured to augment this fum by all expedients, however pernicious to the public, or dangerous to royal authority † : He put to fale the revenues and manors of the crown ; the offices of greateft truft and power, even thofe of forefter and fheriff, which antiently were fo important ‡, became venal ; the dignity of chief jufticiary, in whofe hands

* Ann. Waverl. p. 163. Knyghton, p. 2401.   † Hoveden, p. 657. Bened. Abb. p. 560. M. Paris, p. 108. W. Heming. p. 514.   ‡ Diceto, p. 647. Knyghton, p. 2401.   ‖ Chron. de Dunft. p. 43. Wykes, p. 34. W. Heming. p. 516. Diceto, p. 651.   § Hoveden, p. 665. Bened. Abb. p. 586. M. Paris, p. 111.   † W. Heming. p. 518.   * Hoveden, p. 656.   † Bened. Abb. p. 568.   ‡ The fheriff had antiently both the adminiftration of juftice and the management of the King's revenue committed to him in the county. *See Hale of Sheriff's Accounts.*

w23 ;

(1776–1787) remains today both a research wonder and a stylistic masterpiece. Gibbon excelled at both citation and discursive notes, melding them into a consistent learned descant that weaves through his text.[14] His citation

---

[14] We are so used to reading Gibbon as a dialogue, with one eye on the notes, that it comes as something of a shock to learn in Gibbon's *Memoirs* that his preference was

notes are very complete, including author, title, volume, place of publication, and section or page; and his discursive notes are impressive and wide-ranging in their learning, blending immense comparative reading with Gibbon's own cool wit and subtlety. Gibbon's footnotes act as a textual antistrophe, juxtaposing his decline narrative of the millennia-long decay of Rome with a progression narrative about the rise and development of defensible analytical historical methods culminating in him, Gibbon, and his book, a phoenix out of the ashes of Rome (Figure 18).[15]

PROFESSIONALIZATION AND FORMALIZATION

During the nineteenth century, the footnote techniques of Gibbon's time were formalized but not radically changed. The term *footnote* itself does not enter the language, according to the *Oxford English Dictionary*, until 1841. The great formalizers of scholarly writings were, of course, the German scholars and scientists of the early and middle nineteenth century. Leopold von Ranke, Hermann von Helmholtz, Alexander von Humboldt, Wilhelm Wundt, and other famous German scholars set a tone and created methodologies that no scholar anywhere in the Western world could afford to ignore. But in terms

---

for his notes to be at the end of each volume, or, better yet, bound into separate volumes at the end of the series. (The Basel octavo edition of 14 volumes, Gibbon's favorite, was without footnotes; all notes were packed into the last two volumes.) Indeed, his first volume of the first edition of *Decline and Fall*, printed in February 1776, contains no footnotes; all notes are at the end of the quarto volume. Not until the second and third volumes were published in 1781 do we see the familiar complex footnotes. Gibbon states regretfully in the *Memoirs* that "public importunity" had forced him to move his notes from end of volume to foot of page, though it was probably pressure from his printer, William Strahan, who had received a letter from David Hume praising the book but complaining about the note structure of the first edition.

Gibbon's preference for endnotes over footnotes is almost inexplicable except in terms of his own internal conflicts over issues of readability. Looking at the rare copies of his first volume without footnotes, one can see that the page *is* less busy and more inviting than the more familiar be-noted pages of later volumes. Gibbon also had no ready models of genuinely well-written and completely sourced writing; within the immense world of antiquarian learning he had explored for twenty years before beginning his project, there were beautifully written books and there were completely cited books, but almost no books that coupled scholarly apparatus with modern stylistic appeal. Bayle came closest, but his dialogic textual relations were arbitrary and scattered (though often delightful and witty). Most footnoted texts were turgid and pedantic. Gibbon himself had no Gibbon as his model for successful dialogic and citational integration. Thus, despite his book's success, he distrusted to the end of his life the stylistic possibilities of notational strategies that he (and Strahan) had invented in the *Decline and Fall*, complaining in 1791 that "I have often repented my complyance" with the public importunity for footnotes (194).

[15] And when one picks up one of the synoptic nineteenth-century editions of Gibbon, like H. H. Milman's, which evaluate his use of sources with their own footnotes, one gets the vertiginous dialogic prospect of hearing a conversation in which, for instance, Milman comments on Guizot's comments on Ste. Croix's comments on Gibbon's comments on Quintus Curtius.

FIGURE 18   Edward Gibbon, *History of the Decline and Fall of the Roman Empire*, Volume 2, 1781 (with footnotes rather than endnotes)

180   THE DECLINE AND FALL

C H A P.   who, in the firſt moments of his reign, acknowledged and adored
XX.   the majeſty of the true and only God ². The learned Eufebius has
           aſcribed the faith of Conſtantine to the miraculous ſign which was
           diſplayed in the heavens whilſt he meditated and prepared the Italian

A. D. 312. expedition ³. The hiſtorian Zoſimus maliciouſly aſſerts, that the em-
           peror had imbrued his hands in the blood of his eldeſt ſon, before he

A. D. 326. publicly renounced the gods of Rome and of his anceſtors ⁴. The
           perplexity produced by theſe diſcordant authorities, is derived from
           the behaviour of Conſtantine himſelf. According to the ſtrictneſs of
           eccleſiaſtical language, the firſt of the *Chriſtian* emperors was un-
           worthy of that name, till the moment of his death; ſince it was only

A. D. 337. during his laſt illneſs that he received, as a catechumen, the impo-
           ſition of hands ⁵, and was afterwards admitted, by the initiatory
           rites of baptiſm, into the number of the faithful ⁶. The Chriſtianity
           of Conſtantine muſt be allowed in a much more vague and qualified

---

² Lactant. Divin. Inſtitut. i. 1. vii. 27. The firſt and moſt important of theſe paſſages is indeed wanting in twenty-eight manuſcripts; but it is found in nineteen. If we weigh the comparative value of thoſe manuſcripts, one of 900 years old, in the king of France's library, may be alleged in its favour; but the paſſage is omitted in the correct manuſcript of Bologna, which the P. de Montfaucon aſcribes to the ſixth or ſeventh century (Diarium Italic. p. 409.). The taſte of moſt of the editors (except Iſæus, ſee Lactant. edit. Dufreſnoy, tom. i. p. 595.) has felt the genuine ſtyle of Lactantius.

³ Eufeb. in Vit. Conſtant. l. i. c. 27—32.

⁴ Zoſimus, [illegible].

⁵ That rite was *always* uſed in making a catechumen (ſee Bingham's Antiquities, l. x. c. 1. p. 419. Dom. Chardon, Hiſt. des Sacremens, tom. i. p. 62.), and Conſtantine received it for the *firſt* time (Eufeb. in Vit.

Conſtant. l. iv. c. 61.) immediately before his baptiſm and death. From the connection of theſe two facts, Valeſius (ad loc. Eufeb.) has drawn the concluſion which is reluctantly admitted by Tillemont (Hiſt. des Empereurs, tom. iv. p. 628.), and oppoſed with feeble arguments by Moſheim (p. 968.).

⁶ Eufeb. in Vit. Conſtant. l. iv. c. 61, 62, 63. The legend of Conſtantine's baptiſm at Rome, thirteen years before his death, was invented in the eighth century, as a proper motive for his *donation*. Such has been the gradual progreſs of knowledge, that a ſtory, of which Cardinal Baronius declared himſelf the unbluſhing advocate, is now feebly ſupported, even within the verge of the Vatican. See the Antiquitates Chriſtianæ, tom. ii. p. 232; a work publiſhed with ſix approbations at Rome, in the year 1751, by Father Mamachi, a learned Dominican.

2   ſenſe;

---

of citation structures, they added little to the synthesis that Gibbon had already achieved. In Figure 19 we can see a page from the 1844 English translation of Ranke's magisterial *History of the Reformation in Germany* of 1839. Ranke, like Gibbon, masterfully mixes citation and discursive notes (though his discursive notes are nowhere near as witty or dialogic-with-text as Gibbon's). His extraordinary command of his sources, from ancient church documents through contemporary nineteenth-century scholarship, is clear. But Ranke's footnotes assume a bifurcated readership more clearly than

FIGURE 19 Leopold von Ranke, *History of the Reformation in Germany*, 1839, translation of 1844

days, others to which one for 7000 or 8000 years are attached: one morning benediction of peculiar efficacy was sent by a pope to a king of Cyprus; whosoever repeats the prayer of the venerable Bede the requisite number of times, the Virgin Mary will be at hand to help him for thirty days before his death, and will not suffer him to depart unabsolved. The most extravagant expressions were uttered in praise of the Virgin: " The eternal Daughter of the eternal Father, the heart of the indivisible Trinity:" it was said, " Glory be to the Virgin, to the Father, and to the Son."[1] Thus, too, were the saints invoked as meritorious servants of God, who, by their merits, could win our salvation, and could extend peculiar protection to those who believed in them; as, for example, St. Sebaldus, "the most venerable and holy captain, helper and defender of the imperial city of Nürnberg."

Relics were collected with great zeal. Elector Frederick of Saxony gathered together in the church he endowed at Wittenberg, 5005 particles, all preserved in entire standing figures, or in exquisitely wrought reliquaries, which were shown to the devout people every year on the Monday after Misericordia.[2] In the presence of the princes assembled at the diet, the high altar of the cathedral of Treves was opened, and " the seamless coat of our dear Lord Jesus Christ," found in it; the little pamphlets in which this miracle was represented in wood-cuts, and announced to all the world, are to be found in the midst of the acts of the diet.[3] Miraculous images of Our Lady were discovered;—one, for example, in Eischel in the diocese of Constance; at the Iphof boundary, by the road-side, a sitting figure of the Virgin, whose miracles gave great offence to the monks of Birklingen, who possessed a similar one; and in Regensburg, the beautiful image, for which a magnificent church was built by the contributions of the faithful, out of the ruins of a synagogue belonging to the expelled Jews. Miracles were worked without ceasing at the tomb of Bishop Benno in Meissen; madmen were restored to reason, the deformed became straight, those infected with the plague were healed; nay, a fire at Merseburg was extinguished by Bishop Bose merely uttering the name of Benno; while those who doubted his power and sanctity were assailed by misfortunes.[4] When Trithemius recommended this miracle-worker to the pope for canonization, he did not forget to remark that he had been a rigid and energetic supporter of the church party, and had resisted the tyrant Henry IV.[5] So intimately were all these ideas connected. A confraternity formed for the purpose of the frequent repetition of the rosary (which is, in fact, nothing more than the devout and affectionate recollection of the joys of the Holy Virgin), was founded by Jacob Sprenger, the

[1] Extracts from the prayer-books: Hortulus Anime, Salus Animæ, Gilgengart, and others in Riederer, Nachrichten zur Büchergeschichte, ii. 157-411.

[2] The second Sunday after Easter, so called from the Introit for that Sunday in the Roman Missal, which begins, "Misericordia Domini plena est terra," and gives the key to the variable parts of the Mass. Zaygung des Hochlobwürdigsten Heiligthums, 1509. (The Showing of the most venerable Relics, 1509.) Extract in Heller's Lucas Kranach, i., p. 350.

[3] Chronicle of Limpurg in Hontheim, p. 1122. Browerus is again very solemn on this occasion.

[4] Miracula S. Bennonis ex impresso, Romæ 1521, in Mencken, Scriptores Rer. Germ. ii. p. 1887.

[5] His letter in Rainaldus, 1506, nr. 42.

Gibbon's, in part because "historian" is already becoming a professional self-definition for Ranke that it never completely became for Edward Gibbon, Esquire.

Gibbon's audience in 1776 had consisted of general intellectual readers—most of them men who had been educated, as he had, in the classics. When he was attacked for his cool and agnostic assessment of early Christianity, it was on doctrinal rather than on methodological grounds. Gibbon's notes reflect enough bibliographical information to allow such an audience to find the texts he was using and to check him if they so desired, but the audience for his notes was assumed to be gentleman-scholars like him—men who had not read as deeply or widely as he had, perhaps, but not historical specialists.[16] Ranke is not in quite the same position, though his notes look much the same. By 1839, within a German scholarly tradition then over fifty years old, Ranke's audience was divided. He did have lay readers, who could read his detailed narrative of the sixteenth century for the important cultural history it was without consulting or judging his use of sources, but he was also writing for other specialist historians—some of them his enemies—who could and would scan his footnotes closely for evidence of what he had found and what he had missed. For the former audience, detailed publication information about nonarchival materials in citation notes was not needed; for the latter audience, it was redundant. Ranke does not have to give a complete reference citation to Milman's *History of Latin Christianity* because there was only one edition of it; his audience either would not seek it out or probably already owned it.

But Ranke had to consider such issues, as do we.[17] It is this gradual professionalization of German scholarship, with its competitive and even agonistic edge, that would drive the forms and methods of citation systems henceforward, especially in the developing American academic world. When American scholars returned from German universities in the nineteenth century to establish the American university system of graduate research institutions superadded to undergraduate colleges, they brought with them the German attitude toward citation rather than the English. This loyalty to scholarly precision met the more indigenous English-based attitude of gentleman-amateurism in writing from sources, and the resulting mixture of attitudes took more than a century to sort out. Should sourced writing con-

---

[16] Says Gibbon in his *Memoirs,* "Twenty happy years have been animated by the labour of my history; and it's [sic] success has given me a name, a rank, a character in the world to which I should not otherwise have been entitled . . . [An author] should not be indifferent to the fair testimonies of private and public esteem. Even his social sympathy may be gratified by the idea, that, now in the present hour, he is imparting some degree of amusement or knowledge to his friends in a distant land: that, one day his mind will be familiar to the grandchildren of those who are yet unborn" (187–88). Twenty happy years! Amusement *or* knowledge! This is a voice antithetical to professionalism. For Gibbon, it was his mind that would live in his history, not his professional methodology.

[17] See Grafton's excellent chapter on Ranke and his professional methodological detractors and enemies in *The Footnote.*

ceive of a popular or a specialist audience? Were footnotes a necessity or mere "booksellers' learning"? From 1865 onward the movement in citation systems in America—which increasingly provided the world a model—was toward more professional formalization. More and more, in all fields, scholarly work was seen as written for a delimited discourse community that wanted specific sorts of information about, attitudes toward, and access to the works that undergird the text at hand. But what forms were to be used, standardized upon? Early disciplinary journals—even *PMLA*—show a riot of different notational systems at work, ranging from rudimentary symbol-based notes to completely modern-looking numbered notes a la Gibbon. There were no formal rules.

Here is the historical point at which the genre of printers' manuals, which had existed in cruder forms at least since the seventeenth century, begin to segue over into formal manuals for authors and editors—into style manuals. The US Geological Survey published its *Suggestions for the Preparation of Manuscript* in 1892, beginning the regularization of formats within the government. The booklet, authored by William Croffut, proposed footnote format consisting of author, full title, place of publication, date, and page (13).[18] In 1894 the US Government Printing Office issued its first *Manual of Style*, which relied on Croffut and on the earlier English *Hart's Rules for Compositors and Readers* from the Oxford University Press. These were still primarily printers' manuals, however, that detailed the conventions of word-splitting, spellings of names of countries, and of punctuation usage for professional compositors (Howell x–xi). The first style manual really to be used primarily by authors and editors was the University of Chicago Press *Manual of Style*, whose first edition was published in 1906. Though this book was still largely for use within the publishing house, it does contain four pages of "Hints to Authors and Editors" and three pages on "Footnotes" (Figure 20).

It was not until this first *Manual of Style* appeared that some real standardization appeared in footnoting. The Chicago *Manual* formalized the elements of footnoting that scholars had recognized de facto for centuries as necessary for useful source searching: It provided for consecutive numbered footnotes, for a limited amount of latinate reference to prevent repetition, and for standardized publication information. For book references, it suggested author, title, place of publication, date, and pages; for periodical references, it required journal title, volume number, date, and pages. Both of these *Manual of Style* formats assumed that readers might want to search out and use all the sources mentioned by an author, and the information required was meant to do that, and nothing more.

---

[18] Croffut's pithy little book is still worth reading today. "The primary function of a foot-note," he says, "is the publication of matter which is unimportant to most readers but important to a few. It is also legitimately used for parenthetic and partially irrelevant matter of such extent that its insertion in the main text would interrupt the logical sequence. These considerations should determine doubts as to whether given matter should be included in the text or in foot-notes" (7).

FIGURE 20   University of Chicago Press, *Manual of Style*, 1906

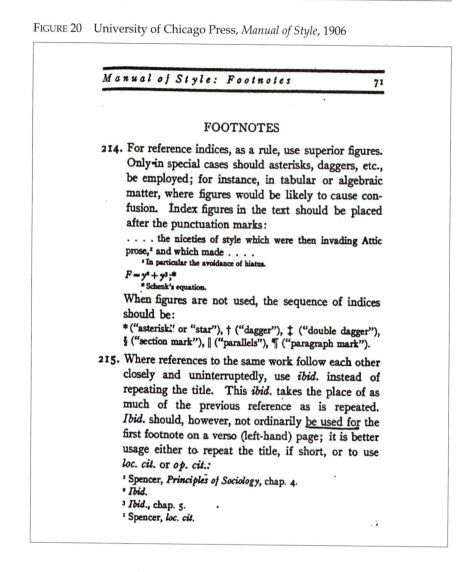

Manual of Style: Footnotes   71

FOOTNOTES

214. For reference indices, as a rule, use superior figures. Only in special cases should asterisks, daggers, etc., be employed; for instance, in tabular or algebraic matter, where figures would be likely to cause confusion. Index figures in the text should be placed after the punctuation marks:

. . . . the niceties of style which were then invading Attic prose,¹ and which made . . . .

¹ In particular the avoidance of hiatus.

$F = y^2 + y^3;$*

* Schenk's equation.

When figures are not used, the sequence of indices should be:

* ("asterisk," or "star"), † ("dagger"), ‡ ("double dagger"), § ("section mark"), ‖ ("parallels"), ¶ ("paragraph mark").

215. Where references to the same work follow each other closely and uninterruptedly, use *ibid.* instead of repeating the title. This *ibid.* takes the place of as much of the previous reference as is repeated. *Ibid.* should, however, not ordinarily <u>be used for</u> the first footnote on a verso (left-hand) page; it is better usage either to repeat the title, if short, or to use *loc. cit.* or *op. cit.:*

¹ Spencer, *Principles of Sociology*, chap. 4.
² *Ibid.*
³ *Ibid.*, chap. 5.
¹ Spencer, *loc. cit.*

The Chicago format was gradually adopted, either formally or informally, by many presses and most humanities disciplines. It was used with elasticity, however, and a flexible adaptation to the "house style" of different journals. The Modern Language Association, which had been founded in 1884 to promote the study of the vernacular languages, had from the beginning provided de facto models of citation style for the humanities in its journal, *PMLA*, but for many years its requirements were informal. Authors for early numbers of *PMLA* could, for instance, still choose to use the "gentlemanly" English system of footnote symbols rather than numbers. After 1906, however, many *PMLA* articles began to move toward Chicago style (Figure 21). Through the first half of this century, few changes were rung on Chicago

FIGURE 21   *PMLA*, 1909

372   WM, A. NITZE.

Now the least Christian feature in the legend is the Fisher King and his cult.   The parallelism with Christ apparently stops with the name Fisher.   If we disregard for the moment the version of Robert, the ritual in which he appears is certainly not founded on the synoptic accounts of the Last Supper, and the striking features of it have no immediate counterpart in Christian or Biblical lore.[1]   The true explanation I believe is to be sought elsewhere.   Before proceeding further, however, it will be well to grasp clearly his salient traits as they present themselves in the various versions of the legend.

The following abbreviations will be used :

  C. Crestien, before 1180.[2]
  W. Wolfram, about 1217.[3]
  Wa. Wauchier de Denain.[4]
  G. Gerbert de Montreuil.[5]
  M. Manessier.[6]
  R. Robert de Boron.[7]

[1] I do not wish to imply that the Eucharist and the Grail ceremony may not go back to similar primitive rites ; see Eisler, *Origins of the Eucharist*, cited below.

[2] Wechssler, *Sage*, 148 ff.   The *Conte del Graal* is dedicated to Philip of Flanders.   Inasmuch as Philip was a patron of letters (cf. Brakelmann, *Les plus anciens chansonniers français*, 1891, p. 13), Crestien's praise of him requires no special explanation.   Thus we can agree with Gaston Paris (*Journal des Savants*, 1902, p. 305), that the poem was written about 1175.

[3] Martin, *Parzival*, p. xiii.

[4] Paul Meyer, *Rom.*, XXXII, 583.   For the best synopsis see Jessie L. Weston, *Legend of Sir Perceval*, London, 1906, ch. II.   Wauchier also translated a series of Saints Lives for Philip, Marquis de Namur.   I do not here distinguish between Wauchier and Pseudo-Wauchier (see Heinzel, *op. cit.*), as I am not yet prepared to take sides on the question ; see Jeanroy, *Revue des lang. rom.* (1907), L, 541–544.

[5] Also author of the *Conte de la Violette*; see Kraus, *Ueber Gerb. de Montreuil*, 1897 ; Wilmotte, *Gerb. de M. et les écrits qui lui sont attribués*, Brussels, 1900, and Gröber's *Grundriss*, II, 509.

[6] Martin, *op. cit.*, p. li.

[7] Cf. above ; the abbreviation (R.) will be used only for the Metrical *Joseph.*

footnote style within the humanities, and hundreds of thousands of students were put through their paces on footnote conventions for research papers. By 1927 the *Chicago Manual* had grown considerably, to a ninth edition of four hundred pages, and it had become a rather forbidding and specialized tome. The University of Chicago Press asked Kate Turabian, who was Dissertation Secretary at the Harper Library, to write a simpler and more directive version of the *Style Manual*'s guidelines for dissertation and thesis writers, and in

1937 the first edition of Turabian's *Manual for Writers of Dissertations* appeared. Turabian's book became the popular version of the *Style Manual*, and "Turabian style" came over the next six decades to be a standard for the humanities.

By the middle of the twentieth century, most citation formats had been brought to a recognizable state of modernity. In the second part of this essay (*Rhetoric Review 17.2, Spring 1999*), we will see how those formats demanded different epistemic values and how different fields made self-defining choices by their use of them.

WORKS CITED

Achtert, Walter S., and Joseph Gibaldi. *The MLA Style Manual*. New York: MLA, 1985.

Agger, Ben. *Soci(onto)logy: A Disciplinary Reading*. Urbana: U of Illinois P, 1989.

Barney, Stephen A., ed. *Annotation and Its Texts*. New York: Oxford UP, 1991.

Browne, Thomas. *Urn-Burial*. London: Henry Brome, 1658.

Burton, Robert. *Anatomy of Melancholy*. Oxford: John Litchfield, 1621.

The Chicago Manual of Style, Thirteenth Edition. Chicago: U of Chicago P, 1982.

Cochrane, J. A. *Dr. Johnson's Printer: The Life of William Strahan*. Cambridge: Harvard UP, 1964.

Conarroe, Joel. "Editor's Column." *PMLA* 97 (May 1982): 307–08.

Conference of Biological Editors. *Style Manual for Biological Journals*. Washington, DC: CBE, 1960.

———. *Scientific Style and Format: The CBE Manual for Authors. Editors, and Publishers, 6th Edition*. Cambridge: Cambridge UP, 1994.

Croffut, W. A. *Preparation of Manuscript and Illustrations for Publication by the U.S. Geological Survey*. Washington, DC: USGS, 1892.

Gibaldi, Joseph, and Walter S. Achtert. *The MLA Handbook for Writers of Research Papers, Theses, and Dissertations,* 2nd ed. New York: MLA, 1984.

Gibbon, Edward. *Memoirs of My Life*. Ed. Georges A. Bonnard. New York: Funk and Wagnalls, 1969.

Grafton, Anthony. *Commerce with the Classics: Ancient Texts and Renaissance Readers*. Ann Arbor: U of Michigan P, 1997.

———. *The Footnote: A Curious History*. Cambridge: Harvard UP, 1997.

Harvey, Gabriel. *Four Letters and Certain Sonnets. The Works of Gabriel Harvey*. Ed. Alexander B. Grosart. 3 vols. London: Privately printed, 1884–85.

Heilbrun, Carolyn G., et al. "Report of the Advisory Committee on Documentation Style." *PMLA* 97 (May 1982): 318–24.

Howell, John Bruce. *Style Manuals of the English-Speaking World: A Guide*. Phoenix: Oryx, 1983.

Hume, David. *Letters of David Hume*. Ed. J. Y. T. Greig. Oxford: Oxford UP, 1932.

"Instructions in Regard to Preparation of Manuscripts." *Psychological Bulletin* 26 (Feb. 1929): 57–63.

Lincoln, Bruce. *Authority: Construction and Corrosion*. Chicago: U of Chicago P, 1994.

Lipking, Lawrence. "The Marginal Gloss." *Critical Inquiry* 3 (Summer 1977): 609–55.

Loewenstein, Joseph F. "*Idem*: Italics and the Genetics of Authorship." *Journal of Medieval and Renaissance Studies* 20 (Fall 1990): 205–24.

Louttit, Chauncey M. "The Use of Bibliographies in Psychology." *Psychological Review* 36 (July 1929): 341–47.

Manual of Style: Being a Compilation of the Typographical Rules in Force at the University of Chicago Press, To Which are Appended Specimens of Types in Use. Chicago: U of Chicago P, 1906.

McFarland, Thomas. "Who Was Benjamin Whichcote? or, The Myth of Annotation." In Barney, 152–77.

Melanchthon, Philip. "Inaugural Lecture." *Melanchthonis Opera, Corpus Reformatorum.* Ed. Carolus Bretschneider. Vol. xi. Halis Saxonum: C. A. Schwetschke, 1834, 21–30.

Modern Language Association. *The MLA Handbook for Writers of Research Papers, Theses, and Dissertations.* New York: MLA, 1977.

———. "The MLA Style Sheet." *PMLA* 66 (April 1951): 3–31.

———. *The MLA Style Sheet, Second Edition.* New York: MLA, 1970.

Nashe, Thomas. *Have with you to Saffron-Walden. The Works of Thomas Nashe.* Ed. Ronald B. McKerrow, III. Oxford: Basil Blackwell, 1958. 1–139.

Ong, Walter J. *The Presence of the Word.* Minneapolis: U of Minnesota P, 1967.

———. *Rhetoric, Romance, and Technology.* Ithaca: Cornell UP, 1971.

Pollard, Alfred W., ed. *Records of the English Bible.* London: Oxford UP, 1911.

"Preparation of Articles for Publication in the Journals of the American Psychological Association." *Psychological Bulletin* 41 (June 1944): 345–76.

"Publication Manual of the American Psychological Association." *Psychological Bulletin* 49 (July 1952): 389–449.

Rose, Mark. "The Author as Proprietor: *Donaldson vs. Becket* and the Genealogy of Modern Authorship." *Representations* 23 (Summer 1988): 51–85.

Smalley, Beryl. "The Bible in the Medieval Schools." *The Cambridge History of the Bible.* Vol. 2. Cambridge: Cambridge UP, 1969: 197–219.

Sprat, Thomas. *The History of the Royal Society of London.* London: J. Martyn, 1667.

Timperley, C. H. *The Printer's Manual.* London: H. Johnson, 1838.

Tribble, Evelyn B. *Margins and Marginality: The Printed Page in Early Modern England.* Charlottesville: U of Virginia P, 1993.

Turabian, Kate L. *A Manual for Writers of Dissertations.* Chicago: U of Chicago P, 1937.

Turabian, Kate L. *A Manual for Writers of Term Papers, Theses, and Dissertations,* 2nd ed. Chicago: U of Chicago P, 1955.

The Rhetoric of Citation Systems

Part II: Competing Epistemic Values in Citation

I n the first section of this essay, we followed the development of the mainstream citation form within Western intellectual culture, the
footnote reference. In this section we will examine the epistemological under-
pinnings of the footnote and resulting challenges to its form.

THE RHETORIC OF FOOTNOTES

With the professionalization of scholarship that was well advanced by 1910
came some competing epistemic demands, and the story of citational rhetoric
in the twentieth century is a mixed and complex one. In order to examine the
changes in the rhetoric of citation structures that have taken place in this century, we must first step back for a moment and look again at something we
have been taking for granted: the note itself. What do notes, marginal or footnote, actually do? From the first use of marginal glosses through the sophisticated citation and discursive forms of the nineteenth century, we have seen
notes work in a dialectical exchange with the body text in question. The notes
may gloss a basic text *cum notis variorum* like parasitic plants; they may support body text with citations of other works that the author embraces or re-
jects; they may enlarge on issues that would blunt the flow of the text's argument if included in it; they may create a parallel discourse on a related set of
questions, as Gibbon's footnotes do with issues of historical judgment; they
may show off the author's wide reading or membership in a discourse community; they may appropriate and manage the reading of a text.

Traditional notes can accomplish these ends because they inhabit the
same space as the body text. Whether they are marginal or footnotes,
whether they overwhelm the text in numbers of lines or specificity like the
Glossa Ordinaria or exist as a single small-type footnote, whether they use
symbols or superscript numbers or letters—traditional notes represent a typographical system that grew organically, over decades and centuries, out of
the needs of authors to relate to their material and to their readers in specific
ways. It is not hyperbolic to say that the note form as it grew up after
Gutenberg shaped—we might say, allowed—some forms of Western prose
style. They were nonpareil for constructing a prose style that, like Gibbon's
or Ranke's, needed to display vast research—but also to control the display
stylistically for enjoyable reading. By separating text and notation, notes
granted readers elective access to the citation or to the parallel discourse. By

From *Rhetoric Review* 17.2 (1999): 219–45.

allowing easy reference, they gave writers permission to elide specificity in text that could be provided in margins or on page foot. By providing, in their later forms, full bibliographic information, notes kept the reading process centered on the page at hand.

Dialogic notes, though their use may be more or less welcome in differing discourse communities, are irreplaceable.[1] But as a typographic convention linking sources with textual reference, citation footnotes—for we may as well speak of the more modern forms—had some serious limitations, which were apparent fairly early. The most obvious limitation has to do with the amount of space that footnotes take up on a page. We saw early on how glosses could proliferate until they had a tendency to overwhelm the text from which they depended, and since footnotes inevitably steal page space from body text, a scholarly text demanding large numbers of notes or significant discursive space in notes creates a war of notes with body. The more complex and judicious the apparatus, the greater the danger that the note structure will need to slide over onto the next page or pages, producing a Bayle-like page with a tiny crest of text balanced over a crashing wave of notes and reference.

Such humanities scholars as Gibbon occasionally ran into this problem in large books of comparative scholarship like *Decline and Fall*, leading to Gibbon's chagrin at Strahan's insistence on the use of footnotes. Not until the nineteenth century, however, did notational needs regularly become so large that scholars began to formalize alternates to the footnote. The problem was most acute in the sciences. When Alexander von Humboldt was writing his *Physical Description of the Earth* in the 1850s, he found that his notes were so thick and rich that he would have needed more than a page of notes for every two pages of text, thus overwhelming his text (and his reader) with citation and discussion of it. Humboldt's typographical world offered him few solutions, and he chose to use one of the earliest forms of endnotes (Figure 22). These endnotes were signaled by parenthesized superscript numbers, leading to the need for the reader interested in Humboldt's sources or comments to read with a finger held later in the book, since almost half of the 1866 English translation of Humboldt is taken up with these extensive endnotes.[2]

Part of the problem Humboldt and others faced is inherent in notes themselves; they can lead to certain stylistic habits dangerous to pursue.

---

[1] We might think of hyperlinks in electronic text as a sort of natural extension of marginal notes, providing extensive—though not infinite, if the work is a finite creation of a mind or minds—dialogic possibilities for rearrangement of reading and understanding processes within the work. Who would doubt that Thomas Nashe, if he lived today, would be writing flyting hyperlinks?

[2] This was Hume's problem with Gibbon's first volume. As he wrote to Strahan. "One is also plagued with his Notes, according to the present Method of printing the Book; When a note is announced, you turn to the End of the Volume, and there you often find nothing but the Reference to an Authority" (letter of April 8, 1776, in *Letters*, II, 313).

FIGURE 22 Alexander von Humboldt, *A Physical Description of the Earth*, 1855, translation of 1866 (text page and endnotes page)

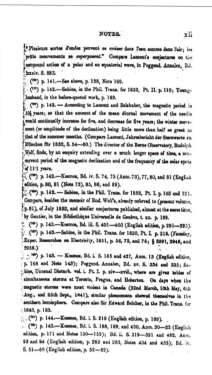

Footnotes tend to invite writers to bifurcate their intentions into separated streams: the high street of the text, which is not supposed to be soiled with specific reference, and the alleys, closes, and mews of the notes, which carry on the necessary but less genteel business of citation and analysis. The tacit understanding during the nineteenth century came to be that textual reference was supposed to be minimal and could often be dispensed with altogether, replaced by the small superscript number that readers knew carried the keys to the sources. The result of this bifurcation was text that was often barren even of general or introductory references and footnotes given permission to be technical, stylistically graceless, marked by ugly abbreviational parsimony. They often sounded and looked like what they were: the secret handshake known only to members of the secret society, filled with the latinate citation jargon that had grown up since the Renaissance—*e.g., et seq., ibid., loc cit., op cit., et passim., viz., s.v.,* etc. Notation forms almost demanded repetition, which this quiver of latinisms was meant to help manage, but no number of *ibids* or *op cits* could make a page bottom citing the same work five times look any less silly and superfluous.

Footnotes also presented formal problems with the reference itself, especially with dating and use of dates. The initial note gave the place and date of

the cited work's publication, of course, but the primary reason for the date's appearance was to allow a reader to find the cited edition, not to establish precedence of publication. Scholarship in the humanities was tacitly perceived to exist in a world where precedence of publication was vastly less important than quality of statement. New "discoveries" in this sphere did not automatically displace older ones, and for an eighteenth-century scholar, Cicero was a writer with vastly more ethical appeal than the much later Priscian. Thus dates in notes were important, but not for reasons of historical precedence or even easy reference; they were simply there to identify editions. The dating structure of footnotes grew up around these attitudes, and it left a legacy of increasing problems for readers and scholars, especially those that proceeded by cumulating empirical knowledge.

The problem for readers exists because footnotes only present publication dates one time, at first citation. Whether subsequent references are by author or by *ibid.*, they include no dates. In a long work with many references, a reader who forgets a date or does not seek it at first reading may have to scan back through many, many pages of notes to find the reference data she needs, and there is no easier way to seek such information. As a result, footnote date information makes it difficult for a reader to remember who said what when, to determine precedence of publication—who wrote first, who was responding to or correcting whom. In other words, footnote dating obscures chronological relationships, making assessments about authorial relations and cumulating knowledge more difficult. For the sciences, this lack of easy chronological access was keenly felt, because new scientific discoveries *do* displace older ones, and footnotes by 1900 were becoming a very troubling and cumbersome way to report that reality.

One attempted solution to the problem was the creation of a new scholarly form, the alphabetical "Bibliography" appended to the end of a footnoted work. The Bibliography, which came to be a feature of some (but by no means a majority of) scholarly books after 1900, accomplished its task of easier reference at the cost of tremendous repetition. Every footnoted item had to be re-cited in a different form in the Bibliography, so it was not a structure that most journals ever allowed due to space limitations. The Bibliography eventually came to be more an academic exercise than anything else; students writing research papers and doctoral candidates writing dissertations became the main users of the algorithmic rules for Bibliography citation.

Finally—and this is not to be discounted as a minor problem—footnotes were difficult to type and expensive to typeset. As typewriters came into wide use in the period after 1900, expectations of a "finished" appearance to manuscripts grew. The typewriter, after all, made each user a miniature Gutenberg. Authors and typists were expected to present work that looked neat and well spaced, and footnotes represented a real challenge, since the typist had to estimate each page separately, calculate the number of notes and the size of each note, and then figure how many notes and how many lines of body text the page could hold. It was a pain. Many a luckless dissertation writer spent sleepless nights in the production of a neatly footnoted

typescript that could pass successfully under the gimlet eye of the library depository dragon. Printers, too, hated footnotes, since they required the same calculations about a page that typing did as well as the use of smaller superscript type, and two different sizes of body type in both standard and italic fonts. Printers in the first half of the eighteenth century had charged an extra shilling per sheet for composition of text with "bottom notes," and even after hot type came in, Linotype operators setting footnoted pages worked much more slowly than those casting regular pages. It remained standard for printers to charge extra for each footnote they had to set.[3]

DIVERGENCES FROM NOTE FORMS

Some of these reference problems were amenable, as we have seen, to solution by use of endnotes rather than footnotes, but the note citation form itself was inescapably part of the problem. As a result of decades-long frustrations, some fields in the sciences and social sciences decided after 1900 that they must break with the note-citation format altogether. Journals in geology, biochemistry, and psychology dropped footnotes and began to experiment with new citation forms, most based around parenthetical rather than note citation forms. Different journals and different disciplines often enforced formally different versions of the parenthetical format, but all of them shared the idea of a parenthetical text citation followed at the end of the work by the key element of an alphabetical list of the references used.

The sciences, as might be expected, began the movement toward citation structures that would allow cumulation and easy reference. Though nineteenth-century science journals used footnotes almost exclusively, the first decade of the new century saw a gradual movement toward other formats. The *Annals of the Entomological Society of America* began using List of References form in 1908, *Phytopathology* in 1912, *Journal of Heredity* in 1924, *Botanical Gazette* in 1926. Many journals allowed varied citation forms for years. The *American Journal of Science*, for instance, published its first list of references at the end of an article in 1918, but it continued to publish footnoted articles without reference lists until 1948. Many journals moved as slowly. The *Journal of Paleontology* moved gradually away from footnotes around 1936; the *Geological Society of America Bulletin* switched in 1938, the *Philosophical Transactions of the Royal Society* in 1939, the *Journal of Geology* in 1948, the *Archives of Physiological Medicine* in 1953. By the late 1950s, most hard-sciences fields had abandoned footnotes.

---

[3] J. A. Cochrane reports that in the first half of the eighteenth century, compositors were paid 12 shillings for a folio sheet and 13 s 8 d a sheet for folio with marginal notes (17). And around a century later, Charles Timperley reports that compositing costs have not changed much, with a sheet with "bottom notes" subject to an extra charge of 1 shilling and with "side notes" an extra charge of 1 s 6 d (*Printer's Manual* 76). As late as 1978, when I was editorial assistant on *CCC*, Edward P. J. Corbett, the editor, would discourage authors from using footnotes because they cost so much to typeset.

We must be aware, however, that the same rhetorical forces at work in the humanities and social sciences hold sway in the sciences, and tradition is an important element. The field that defined science in the nineteenth century as physics defined it in the twentieth was chemistry, and chemistry imported a very specific citation structure from its beginnings in Germany, a superscript structure based in footnotes that it has been loath to give up. The *Zeitschrift fur Physiologische Chemie* was using this structure from 1877 onward (Figure 23), and British and American chemical journals picked it up and used it (without the parentheses) for decades. This structure is almost the worst imaginable, since it provides no list of references and begins footnote numbering anew on each page, but it was used by the majority of chemical journals in all languages for decades and, with small changes, is still in wide use today.[4] (The *Zeitschrift* itself went to an endnotes system in 1973, but the endnotes are still not alphabetical.) The sciences, not having any need to prove anything about their status, are hard to predict, and each field and journal tends to be individualistic. A surprising number of science journals kept and adapted the German system, which most resembles footnotes. *Reviews of Modern Physics* did not move to a parenthetical format until 1969, the *Annals of the Assn. of American Geographers* did not switch over until 1982, *Math Teacher* waited until 1986, the magisterial *Physical Review* only moved away from footnotes to a Number system in 1991, and the *American Journal of Archeology* is still using a pure footnote system. The refusal of scientific fields to be dictated to by format purveyors makes the humanities look submissive.

In general, scientific journals have been much less directive and much less formally demanding about citation forms than might be guessed. The Conference of Biological Editors, publishers of today's all-sciences manual *Scientific Style and Format*, did not become active as formalizers even of biology style until 1960, when their first edition, *Style Manual for Biological Journals*, appeared. The CBE delineates two main families of scientific citations, each of which has a number of variations: the earlier Number system, which uses parenthetical numbers keyed to numbers in the Works Cited lists (Figure 24), and the Name-Year system (which resembles the current APA system).[5] The Number system, which grew out of the older German superscript-number system, was probably more popular in the sciences until recently, in

---

[4] The *Journal of the American Chemical Society*, for instance, finally moved in 1922 from starting superscript numbers anew on each page, but though it now sequences its numbers, it *still* does not provide a list of references. The *Journal of the Chemical Society of London* moved from a super-APA-like parenthetical system to the German superscript number system in 1956. *Mathematische Annalen* used footnote symbols for its references until 1920. And the *Journal of Biological Chemistry* only began to use a Bibliography in 1922.

[5] The current edition of the *Style Manual*, today's *Scientific Style and Format: The CBE Manual, Sixth Edition*, now calls these two systems Citation-Sequence and Name-Year, and they also seem to have gained the informal rubrics of "Vancouver" and "Harvard," whose etymologies remain mysterious. The "Harvard" system is also sometimes called the "British system."

FIGURE 23   The early German system in *Zeitschrift fur Physiologische Chemie*, 1877

Ueber die Synthese von Aetherschwefelsäuren und das Verhalten einiger aromatischer Substanzen im Thierkörper

von **E. Baumann** und **E. Herter.**

(Aus dem physiologisch-chemischen Institute zu Strassburg i. E.)

(Der Redaction zugegangen am 10. Oktober 1877.)

Durch die Entdeckung Wöhler's, ([1]) dass aus Benzoë-säure und Glycocoll im Thierkörper Hippursäure gebildet wird, war zum erstenmale der direkte und sichere Nachweis einer Synthese im Organismus geliefert. Seitdem haben wir kennen gelernt, dass die synthetischen Processe im Thier-körper überhaupt eine grosse Rolle spielen. Analogieen der Vereinigung von Benzoësäure und Glycocoll zu Hippursäure wurden festgestellt für Nitrobenzoësäure([2]), Chlorbenzoë-säure([3]), Salicylsäure([4]), Anissäure([5]), Toluylsäure([6]), Mesitylen-säure([7]), ebenso paaren sich die Gallensäuren mit Glycocoll und mit Taurin, andererseits vereinigt sich das Taurin im Thierkörper auch mit dem Reste der Carbaminsäure und bildet damit einen substituirten Harnstoff, die Taurocarbamin-säure([8]). Ausserdem sind die Synthesen von Harnstoff aus

([1]) Tiedemann's Untersuchungen über die Natur des Menschen. Bd. I., pag. 142. 1824. Berzelius, Lehrb. d. Chemie, 1831, Bd. IV., pag. 376.

([2]) Bertagnini, Annal. d. Chem. u. Pharm. Bd. 78, pag. 100, 1851. Jaffé, Ber. d. d. chem. Ges.. Bd. VII., pag. 1673, 1874.

([3]) O. Schultzen u. C. Graebe, Reichert's u. Du Bois Reymond's Arch. 1867, pag. 167.

([4]) Bertagnini, Annal. d. Chem. u. Pharm. Bd. 97, pag. 248, 1856.

([5]) Schultzen u. Graebe, loc. cit. pag. 168.

([6]) Kraut, Neubauer u. Vogel, Analyse des Harns. 6. Auflage. pag. 136.

([7]) L. v. Nencki, Arch. exper. Pathol. u. Pharm. Bd. I. 1873, pàg. 420.

([8]) E. Salkowski, Ber. d. d. chem. Ges., Bd. VI., pag. 744, 1312.

part because it is a less overt break with footnoting practice than the Name-Year system. Indeed, the earlier forms of the Number system simply replaced the German superscript footnotes with bracketed numbers without changing anything else: their Lists of References were organized by sequence rather than alphabetically. Only in the last few years have Name-Year systems, which provide more meaning in exchange for the parenthetical interruption, come to have more currency in the scientific literature.[6] But scientific journals still use a number of variants on these two systems, and the *CBE Manual* has always acted as a handmaiden rather than an arbiter to science editors.

The interesting fields to examine in terms of citation rhetoric, of course, are the social science and humanities fields, and it is in the history of these

---

[6] Though it was certainly specified by some journals, the first mention of the Name-Year style I can find in any style manual is in the 1955 second edition of Turabian, which quickly covers scientific styles, mentioning first the older Number system and then the Name-Year system (53). It was not until after the APA's adoption of Name-Year in 1957 that it established an identity.

FIGURE 24   Conference of Biological Editors, *Style Manual for Biological Journals*, first edition, 1960

LITERATURE CITED

Basic considerations in making bibliographic references are accuracy, readers' convenience, and librarians' time.

In the text, citations should be made consistent (according to the practice of the journal) by use of one of the following systems:

1) *Name-and-year system*. Depending upon the construction of the sentence, the citation will appear as: Smith and Jones (1960), (Smith and Jones, 1960*a, b, c*). With not more than three authors, name all in the first reference, e.g., Doe, Miller, and Wilson (1960), but subsequently use Doe et al. (1960); four or more authors should be cited Doe et al. (1960) in the first instance.

2) *Number system*. Depending upon the construction of the sentence, the citation will appear as: Smith and Jones (1), or (Smith and Jones, 1), or merely (1). If citations are to be numbered number them after all additions and deletions have been made.

List citations at the end of the paper in alphabetical order. Inclu only those cited in the text. Do not cite unpublished work unless paper has been accepted for publication. Citations should contain all data necessary to locate the source easily in a library. Check all part: each citation against the original. An inaccurate or incomplete refere: wastes time of readers and librarians.

fields' choices that we see social and disciplinary affiliation dreams acted out most obviously. The field of psychology represents perhaps most clearly what Stanley Fish calls "theory hope," a desire for the cachet of mature disciplinary status going all the way back to the medical training of Charcot, Freud, Jung, and the early psychoanalytic movement. In the early days of the field, however, many psychologists were conversant with good models of writing, and they resisted the scientizing of their texts if it came at the expense of their prose style. Thus we see the APA's *Psychological Bulletin*, which published short report-style clinical articles, switching (by editorial fiat) completely to Number style, the early parenthetical style based in footnotes, in 1911. The *Psychological Review*, which published longer, more essayistic pieces, allowed its authors to use footnote citations until the late 1930s. (The *Review* found that some of its authors, well-known figures in the field, simply refused to use a parenthetical form for stylistic reasons.) The *Journal of Educational Psychology* took many years to determine what it would ask of its authors; its first List of References appeared in 1918, but it continued to allow footnote citations until 1953. And the *American Journal of Psychology* did not leave footnote citations until 1970! The road to science styles in psychology has always been mediated by subsets of the psychology community.

Official APA citation style has long been central to this constructed situation, and its history is an interesting one in itself. It was clear by the 1920s that psychological literature was proliferating at a tremendous rate; between 1910 and 1915, the number of bibliographies in APA journals tripled (Louttit 344). In its earliest versions, APA style was not the strong break with

footnoting it would later become. The first version of the *APA Style Manual* was published in the *Psychological Bulletin* in 1929 as "Instructions in Regard to Preparation of Manuscripts." The committee writing the article was modest: "The committee realizes that it neither has, nor wishes to assume, any authority in dictating to authors; but it suggests the following recommendations for use as a standard of procedure . . ." (57). The citation form recommended was either footnotes or bibliographical references placed in alphabetical order at the end of the article.[7] This latter suggestion was a formalization of a structure that had grown up in APA literature since 1911. In practice, it consisted of a boldface number in parentheses keyed to numbers in the alphabetized list of references found at the end of the article (Figure 25). This system was formalized further in 1938, when the APA adopted the scientific bibliography style of using only lower-case letters in titles except for initial capitals and proper nouns.[8] The revised "Preparation of Articles for Publication in the Journals of the American Psychological Association" appeared in the *Bulletin* in 1944. This version marginalized footnotes, suggesting that footnotes only be used when an article had five or fewer references. Otherwise, the numbered cumulative list of references was to be used.

This first APA Number System was a sort of halfway measure, since its numbering system did not severely interrupt the text, but it gave no real citation information in the parenthesis; a reader still had to turn to the reference list for dates or even authors' names. This system held sway in APA journals through 1957, when it was finally swept away in the first separately printed *APA Publication Manual* of that year. This "New APA" style, with a few changes, is the name/year system used today in APA and many social-science publications (Figure 26). This is probably the least prose-friendly citation form extant, but by 1957, APA authors who had been trained in a tradition of professional writing that emphasized readability or rhetorical success per se were nearly all retired or dead.[9] Since 1957, the *Style Manual of the APA* has been revised and enlarged in 1967, 1974, 1983, and 1994, and, despite its

---

[7] This nondirective humility is curious, given the fact that the *Bulletin* had been *de facto* enforcing APA Number Style on its authors since 1911!

[8] In the German chemical literature and the English work that followed it may be a clue to the beginning of the movement to decapitalize all nonproper nouns in titles. German usage capitalized all substantive nouns but no other words in titles. In moving to English, early citation stylists in the sciences followed the German form in many things but not in capitalization, removing all capitals except names and initial capitals. We first see this in the 1890s, and all scientific forms since then have eschewed capital letters in titles.

[9] This 1957 APA *Manual* is a fascinating little piece of work for the epistemological power struggle it seems to reveal. During the course of its preparation, the project coordinator, Chauncey Louttit, died and was replaced. The booklet was apparently already in press and, indeed, set in type, showing the older APA citation style (parenthetical boldface numbers in text and numbered list of references at end). But after Louttit's death, the Council of Editors, acting at the last moment, overrode his revision and printed his original pages *struck through* with black lines. Their contents have been replaced by tipped-in errata pages, numbered 28a, etc., that detail the "new" APA

Figure 25   "Old APA" style in *Psychological Bulletin,* 1915

JAMES BURT MINER

attention, perception, memory, association and motor control. It raises the question whether the low correlations found may not be due to using the teachers' grades without conversion. Hart and Spearman (24), with their numerous tests, conclude that their comparatively low correlations of tests with estimates of ability is due to inaccuracies in the latter. Vickers and Wyatt (47) also present an extended study of the intercorrelations of tests. Arithmetical and reasoning tests are studied by Winch (50, 51), Dockerill and Fennings (15), and Davies (13). The inter-relations between the fundamental arithmetical operations as given by the Courtis tests are shown by Bell (5). Arithmetic stands apart in its lack of correlation with school subjects (7). Frailey and Crain (19) study the relations of school standings intensively, but fail to simplify their statements by giving correlations. Baldwin (3) provides the most valuable data available for consecutive measurements on the same children and states some of the observable relations, but without coefficients. General intelligence correlates .32 with ability in group games with allowance for constant age. The importance of estimating the influence of age is shown by Smith's study (41). He demonstrates empirically that brothers and sisters correlate in pitch discrimination no closer than younger and older children from different families. Unless partial coefficients for age constant are calculated, therefore, the size of correlations with heterogenous age groups lacks meaning. Sylvester (46) finds a minus relation, — .384, between age and motor control in the form board test.

References

1. ADLER, H., WILLIAMS., M., & WASHBURN, M. F. The Correlation Between Accuracy of the Visual Memory After-Image and Control of Visual Imagery. *Amer. J. of Psychol.,* 1914, 25, 293–295.
2. ANDERSON, VON O. Nochmals über "The Elimination of Spurious Correlation Due to Position in Time or Space." *Biometrika,* 1914, 10, 269–279.
3. BALDWIN, B. T. Physical Growth and School Progress: A Study in Experimental Education. *U. S. Bur. of Educ. Bull.,* 1914, No. 19.
4. BARRETT, M. A Comparison of the Order of Merit Method and the Method of Paired Comparisons. *Psychol. Rev.,* 1914, 21, 278–294.
5. BELL, J. C. A Class Experiment in Arithmetic. *J. of Educ. Psychol.,* 1914, 5, 467–470.
6. BOYD, W. The Value of the Combination Method for Examination Purposes. *J. of Exper. Ped., &c.,* 1914, 2, 449–456.
7. BRADFORD, E. J. G. A Psychological Analysis of School Grading. *J. of Exper. Ped., &c.,* 1914, 2, 431–440.
8. BRIDGES, J. W. An Experimental Study of Decision Types and their Mental Correlates. *Psychol. Monog.,* 1914, 17, No. 72. Pp. 72.

complexity (there are separate books completely devoted to *explaining* the *Style Manual*), APA style has flourished. Sociology, originating in an older humanistic tradition, clung to footnotes through the 1960s, but most of its journals switched to APA-type formats by 1970.[10] APA style now bids fair to become the de facto standard for all fields over the next five decades.

---

style (name/date in parentheses). The APA journals began to enforce the new style absolutely a year later. Why and how this occurred is lost in the mists of time, but it certainly *looks* like some kind of *coup de style* against the deceased editor.

[10] For instance, the *American Sociological Review* left footnotes in 1968, and *Sociology Quarterly* switched to APA style in 1969.

FIGURE 26   "New APA" style in *Written Communication*, 1993

486   WRITTEN COMMUNICATION / OCTOBER 1993

tices of disciplinary communities is "picked up" in the local milieu of the culture rather than being explicitly taught. As Brown et al. (1989) suggested

> Given the chance to observe and practice *in situ* the behavior of members of a culture, people pick up the relevant jargon, imitate behavior, and gradually start to act in accordance with its norms. These cultural practices are often recondite and extremely complex. Nevertheless, given the opportunity to observe and practice them, people adopt them with great success. Students, for instance, can quickly get an implicit sense of what is suitable diction, what makes a relevant question, what is legitimate or illegitimate behavior in a particular activity. (p. 34)

Brown et al.'s argument here is based on their own as well as other studies of situated or "everyday" cognition (Engestrom, 1987; Lave, 1977, 1988a, 1988b; Lave & Wegner, 1991; Rogoff, 1990; Rogoff & Lave, 1984; Scribner, 1984). These studies owe a debt to the work of Russian activity theorists such as Vygotsky, Leontiev, and others, which has also influenced recent educational research (see Cazden, 1989; Clay & Cazden, 1990; Cole, 1985, 1990; Daiute, 1989, 1990; Dyson, 1987, 1988, 1990; Galimore & Tharp, 1990; Wertsch, 1991). We believe that these latter studies are also relevant to our inquiries concerning the nature of genre knowledge.

Wertsch (1991) observed that Bakhtin and Vygotsky held a number of ideas in common:

> First [they shared] the assertion that to understand human mental action one must understand the semiotic devices [such as language] used to mediate such action. . . . Second [they held] the assumption that certain aspects of human mental functioning are fundamentally tied to communicative processes. . . . that human communicative practices give rise to mental functioning in the individual. (pp. 12-13)

These views undergird much of what has recently been written about the situated nature of individual concept development. For example, Brown et al. (1989) argue that acquiring conceptual knowledge, like learning the use of tools, is

> both situated and progressively developed through activity. . . . People who use tools actively rather than just acquire them . . . build an increasingly rich, implicit understanding of the world in which they use the tools and of the tools themselves. The understanding, both of the world

THE TERGIVERSATION OF THE MLA

Meanwhile, back at the footnote style, the other major player in the formalization of citation style, the Modern Language Association, finally decided to stake out its position around mid century. The MLA asked William Riley Parker in 1951 to convene a committee to formalize MLA style, and the first

MLA Style Sheet was published in that year in *PMLA*. It was a relaxed reflection in most ways of Turabian forms, dictating consecutively numbered citation footnotes providing author, title, place of publication, and date. The MLA style was little more than a codification of the scholarly practice that had existed since Gibbon, but it largely mirrored the *Chicago Manual,* and most literary journals adopted it. The little booklet printed under the title *The MLA Style Sheet* sold over a million copies in the next two decades.

The *Style Sheet*'s section on documentation tries to deal with problems of footnote repetition by suggesting that references, if brief, could be inserted in parentheses. Abuses of footnote structures were clearly on Parker's mind. "Let the test be whether or not it interferes seriously with ease in reading, remembering that the footnote number, which teases the reader to look at the bottom of the page,[11] may be more of an interruption than such a simple reference in your text as (II, 241) or (page 72)" (14). This first MLA structure did not require a bibliography; indeed, Parker refers to the term "bibliography" in quotes, as if it were some annoying newfangled invention. But the history of MLA Style is a history of populist expansion, and of the waning of notes and the waxing of bibliography. The second edition of the *Style Sheet* in 1970 finally followed the 12th edition of the *Chicago Manual* of 1969 in creating the footnote form most familiar to those trained up in the 1970s: author, title, place of publication, publisher, and date. (By that time, scholarship had become such an industry and scholarly works so specialized that the name of the publisher was needed to make certain that the correct text was, indeed, specified.)

But by 1970, discontented rumblings can also be heard offstage. Between 1951 and 1970, the older elite traditions of literary scholarship had been broken up by the two great waves of demographic change in the American academy: the GI Bill generation, which by 1960 had stocked faculties with new faces, many of whom would never have gone to college but for the war, and, a little later, their children, the wave of baby-boomer students. College enrollments quadrupled during those two decades, from two million to eight million, and teaching scholarly writing forms was no longer a vocation, but a mass industry. Footnotes, which are so easy to misuse or to use poorly, began to give teachers pause as they faced the boomer masses. The committee's preface states a version of the problem:

> *Readability* is a prime consideration of scholarly writing. American scholarship over the past quarter century has moved away from fact gathering for its own sake and a system of annotation virtually independent of the text. Prose is more pleasant to read if it does not require one to jump constantly to the foot of the page or to the back of the book. Every effort should be made to make the text self-sufficient, to make the annotation

---

[11] Like this. And suppose you had found only "*Ibid.*" [This footnote is a direct quote from footnote 4 in the *Style Sheet*. Clearly there was dissatisfaction on editors' parts with some authors' uses of footnotes, cleverly reflected here by Parker. —RJC]

unobtrusive, and to consolidate footnote references. Yet scholarship will continue to differ from the personal essay in that its facts and inferences are fully documented. Successful scholarly writing achieves that most difficult feat of blending maximum interest and readability with maximum accuracy and evidence. (3)

The MLA was clearly aware of the problems with the footnote system, particularly its repetitiveness and its tendency in less-experienced hands to throw explanatory and context-creating weight on reference footnotes that they cannot bear. But its only recourse was recommending expertise.

The problems with reference were also tacitly addressed in 1970 by addition of a citation form for following bibliographies (the quotes were gone). Dissertations, theses, and term papers were allowed to have bibliographies, though they are not mentioned for scholarly articles. This second MLA edition also mentions endnotes more seriously, demanding that article authors type their footnotes double-spaced on separate sheets at the end of the article. Dissertation authors cannot take advantage of this easy way out of complex typing tasks, since their work will be photographed by University Microfilms and must provide citations that stand by themselves on their own pages, but undergraduate term papers are allowed to use endnotes because they're "easier for the student to type"—though they must then be secured by paper clips and not staples for easy reference (31–32).

The *Style Sheet*'s "little green book" lasted for only seven years before it was replaced by a larger perfect-bound version called something new: the *MLA Handbook for Writers of Research Papers, Theses, and Dissertations*. This perfect-bound 163-page book was meant as an aid to students, but it quickly outsold the old *Style Sheet*, which went out of print. Graduate and undergraduate schools were humming along, and in this 1977 version, student usages have taken over. We hear the last hurrah for MLA notes, which are now all endnotes. Footnotes, unforgivably tedious to type and expensive to typeset, have descended to the status of an unfortunate survival in dissertations. Bibliographies by 1977 are de rigueur for all papers except dissertations, and for the first time the MLA discusses parenthetical styles as a valid alternative to note-based styles for "papers requiring very few citations or in bibliographical studies" (94).[12] From its splashy rainbow cover to its concern with typing convenience, the *Handbook* is a populist document for populist scholarship. It has passed from William Riley Parker's orientation toward prose style and the convenience of the reader in 1951 to a system designed to make the tasks of the writer less onerous.

The 1977 *Handbook* suggested that the traditional humanities citation structures were in a crisis, and the MLA finally brought the ax down on them in the 1984 second edition of the *Handbook*. This book reflected the watershed decision finally to do away with the reference note altogether in favor of a

---

[12] The method recommended is, however, impossibly clunky, placing *all* information normally in a footnote directly into the text.

modified version of the APA parenthetical style. The MLA had been looking into such a change since 1978, when it constituted an Advisory Committee on Documentation Style, chaired by Carolyn Heilbrun. This committee worked for four years on changes to MLA style, introducing its resulting system in the May 1982 issue of *PMLA*. The committee's "Report," published in that issue (which also featured articles that had all been rewritten to model the new style) explained the problems with footnote systems—dating, repetition—most complained about. The professionalization of literary scholarship and the resulting proliferation of materials needing citation were mentioned, as were rising printing costs, the defection to APA-type styles of linguists and interdisciplinary scholars, and the rise of single-journal styles.

The committee attempted with its style recommendations to hew to a middle course, they reported, between "mindlessly endorsing the past and wildly embracing what may prove faddish" ("Report" 319). They wished to further humanistic scholarship, be compatible with current publishing practices, conform to other recognized authorities (particularly the *Chicago Manual* and Turabian, which were including coverage of parenthetical styles by this time), and "help bridge the gulf that exists in practices of documentation between the humanities and other disciplines, while remaining faithful to the spirit of humanistic scholarship" (319). The stalking ghost throughout the "Report" is, of course, the *APA Style Manual*, which was gathering more and more adherents in the scientistic and professionalized world of early 1980s humanities (inter)disciplines. The APA is actually mentioned only once, however, in a list of professional organizations using parenthetical formats (323).[13]

PMLA editor Joel Conarroe reported in May 1982 that 200 scholars and editors had been consulted about the new style and that most of them had been "remarkably positive" ("Editor's Column" 307). Some of the dissenters, however, "expressed themselves with considerable force," though Conarroe suggests that these objections were either personalistic, vague, or based on misunderstandings (307).[14] He invited the *PMLA* readership to comment, but though he said that opinions on the new style would "be received with special interest," no letters printed in the *PMLA* "Forum" column over the next four years ever mentioned the new style system.[15] Though *PMLA* adopted the new style in 1982, it remained a set of "recommendations" until 1984,

---

[13] This list, which consists almost entirely of social-sciences and hard-sciences organizations like the Linguistic Society of America, the American Mathematical Society, the Association of American Geographers, and the American Physiological Society, is interesting for the traditional humanities fields it does *not* mention.

[14] Conarroe's column is especially interesting in that it suggests—as the official "Report" does not—that the committee's initial proposal involved a name-date-page system like APA's, and that powerful resistance to that idea led to the dropping of the parenthetical dating.

[15] Doubtless this silence indicates the perfect satisfaction MLA members felt with the new system.

when the *Handbook* appeared. Given the fact that this decision probably affected the real lives and activities of more MLA members than any other decision the organization has made in decades, one might have expected some extended discussion and a rationale for it in the 1984 *Handbook*. The *Handbook*, however, presented the results apodictically and without comment on the purposes, rationale, or import of the change. The style itself of the 1984 *Handbook* needs little description; it is the citation style being used in this essay. It was restated in more detail in the 1985 *MLA Style Manual* and remains little changed today except for necessary updating to reflect the need to cite electronic sources. "New MLA," as it was at first called, tries to avoid both the readerly inefficiencies of the footnote system and the astylistic provision of date-centered information that marks the APA form. The typical parenthesis contains only an author's name and a page number, and the MLA guides contain sections on readability that recommend keeping parenthetical references as brief as possible and placed as naturally as possible at pause points in a sentence (*Style Manual* 164–65).

Though the MLA guides still gave information on how to cite information in reference notes (and still today glumly recommend that dissertations to be microfilmed should use footnotes), it was clear after 1985 that the world had been announced changed; the note reference for scholars in the modern languages was pronounced dead.[16] But the multidisciplinary tale of affiliations and complexities of choice that followed the decision of the MLA is still ongoing. Journals in the humanities had nearly all specified that their authors use MLA style before 1984, and we in English studies might have tended to assume that all humanities journals would have made the switch to parenthetical citations as automatically as we did. In my own field, composition studies, every journal not using APA had made the change to New MLA by 1987. Despite a certain amount of complaining by authors and editors, the feeling seemed to be that the change was inevitable, that you couldn't fight City Hall (or Astor Place).

I was thus somewhat surprised to learn while researching this essay that the new MLA style had provoked a considerable amount of revolt within the humanities. The wholesale acceptance of the new MLA style that I had assumed was by no means universal, with many journals continuing to specify the style of the 1977 MLA *Handbook* as their preferred style even into the 1990s. (Despite pleas for its continuation, the MLA took the 1977 book out of print in 1986, when the last copies [of over 860,000] were sold.) Many journals in traditional humanities areas have defected from MLA style back to the *Chicago Manual* footnote style, which includes reference notes *and* a bibliography.

---

[16] It is ironic that the MLA should give the quietus first to the footnote and then to the endnote just at the point when technology, in the form of easily available word-processing programs, was making the typing and formatting of such notes simple and automatic. If WordPerfect had been available in 1975, the pressure to move away from hard-to-type note systems might have been considerably less.

The Modern Language Association has always been thought of as a primarily literary organization, but the majority of traditional literary journals have rejected current MLA style in favor of more traditional footnote styles. A survey of some of the leading literary journals indicates a considerably less flexible constituency within MLA than the Committee on Documentation Style expected. Between 1984 and 1990, each literature journal was forced to make a decision about its relation to MLA style, and most chose to part company with the MLA.[17] Though there are a few English-language literary journals that have made the move to new MLA style, they are a distinct minority.[18] And most journals in the foreign languages and literatures have remained with footnotes as well.

The new MLA style was, of course, never adopted by history, classics, political science, or the other traditional humanities, and in placing its weight behind a parenthetical system, the MLA seems to have underestimated the traditionalism of its core constituency, literary scholars. Although linguists were instrumental in the development of new MLA, nearly all linguistics journals use either APA style or one of the more scientific styles. Though it is widely adopted in composition journals and widely taught at the undergraduate level, new MLA style remains a sort of citation-style version of the metric system in America: a well-meaning and heavily promoted rationalistic system that people reject for reasons essentially human and emotional.

---

[17] For instance:

American Literary History still specifies the *MLA Style Sheet* of 1970.

American Literature specified the 1977 *MLA Handbook* until 1990, when it went to its own Chicago-based house footnote style.

English Literary Renaissance specifies the *MLA Handbook*, second edition, but actually uses footnote form.

English Language Notes specifies the endnote form (which does receive coverage, albeit as the repudiated system) in the current *MLA Style Manual*.

English Literature in Transition moved from the *MLA Handbook* to Chicago footnote style in 1986.

English Studies still specifies a footnote style most like the first edition of the *MLA Style Sheet*.

Eighteenth Century Studies moved from MLA to Chicago style in autumn 1984, as soon as the *Handbook* second edition appeared.

From specifying no specific style. *ELH* moved to Chicago footnote style in 1985.

The *Journal of American Studies* moved from the 1977 *MLA Handbook* to Chicago style in 1986.

Nineteenth Century Literature asks for citations to be done according to Section 5.8 of the current *MLA Style Manual*—the footnotes/endnotes section.

Victorian Poetry moved from the *MLA Handbook* to Chicago style in 1988.

Though this is by no means an exhaustive list of literary journals, it does give a reasonably accurate picture of the variety of journals that have solidly rejected the recommendations of their major professional organization.

[18] Four that my quick survey found were *American Literary History, Victorian Studies, Milton Quarterly*, and *Modern Fiction Studies*—a group with few commonalities other than relative recency of founding.

CITATION FORMS AND RHETORICAL CHOICES

The movement toward parenthetical citation forms suggests powerful episte-mological shifts in the ways that readers are expected to perceive and use the literature. Citation systems comprised of notes, whatever their form and wherever they were placed, all share the central idea that the citations and annotations should *interrupt* the text as little as possible. Whether marked by symbols or by a letter or number system, notes were an *elective* reading expe-rience; readers could choose or not choose to follow up the back trails or side tracks they represented. Note systems, even those that surrounded a block of text with glosses and annotations, assumed the reading experience of the reader with the main text to be sacrosanct. Parenthetical citation systems called this assumption into serious question. We need to look at the rhetorical values suggested by parenthetical systems.

Parenthetical reference systems were formulated to allow authors to dis-play complete control over previous work in their special field. In disciplines that advance by cumulating knowledge and building it in small increments upon previously accumulated data, a natural opening for a work is such a display of the author's command of previous works. Without this literature survey, with which the author builds ethos by her display of the necessary background knowledge, the current incremental addition to the cumulation of knowledge would seem to float in space. However uninteresting the litera-ture survey may be as a reading experience, it presents field specialists with the author's *bona fides*, and parenthetical systems allow this presentation with no meaningless gestures toward prose style.

These new systems had as their clearest purpose the easing of a reader's task of finding and accessing cited sources. The one thing all early parenthet-ical systems had in common was the use of an alphabetical list of references at the end of the essay or book. In comparison to the repetitious (and seldom used) Bibliography of note systems, the List of Works Cited structure of par-enthetical systems is at its very center, and the date is the keystone. Paren-thetical citations gave new importance to the date of published works as they diminished the importance of the author.[19] Rather than being "Samuel John-son," the author becomes "(Johnson 1755)" in the text and "Johnson, S. (1755)" in the List of Works Cited. Rhetorically, authors lose agency here, as their surnames become nametags for works. As parenthetical systems evolved during the twentieth century, dates of publication within the text ci-tation became more important, as is only natural when investigation is ongo-ing in rapidly moving fields and "getting there first" with research results is of prime importance.

---

[19] Humanities readers often feel that in some obscure way works lose agency, too, when they lose their title capitals, as in APA and the scientific forms. Though tradition is the only real rationale for capitalizing all substantive words in a title, it can't be de-nied that such references as *The mill on the Floss* or *The taming of the shrew* seem to lose some largeness of being with their capitals. We might think of it as aesthetic formal nostalgia, or, as rationalists would say, love of kitsch.

The need actually to quote sources is another way in which the two systems diverge. Footnote systems evolved organically in humanities discourses with specific page-level identifications of their sources. The exact formulation of a quoted author's words was important in the humanities in ways it was not often so important in the sciences. A science citation is much more apt to mention the work in passing, to summarize it or paraphrase it, than to quote it directly. Prose formulations are not primarily what sciences are about. They are, however, what the humanities have always been about, and footnotes always incorporated the ability to specify section, page, even paragraph and line, as necessary. The early German chemical system allowed this specificity as well, but as science progressed, citations came more and more to be of a whole article rather than of specific pages. Name-year and name-title forms like APA and New MLA cannot carry page numbers off without bulking up the parenthetical citation, which is almost certainly why many humanities authors still view them with suspicion.

Rhetorically, parenthetical citations, by their foregrounding of citation structure and placement of it within the body of the text, relegate issues of readability and prose style to tertiary importance. They represent a resolution to make scholarly prose a vehicle of purest instruction rather than of instruction *and* delight. No matter how hard an author using parenthetical style may work to include authorial references within her text, she will always be forced to pepper her writing with, at a minimum, parenthetical page number references. More commonly, authors must use fuller references that can be as lengthy as "(Gibbon, *Decline and Fall*, iv, 342–3)."[20] The elective reading of footnotes is here replaced by the inescapable reading of parentheses, some of which may be long enough to seriously interrupt the stylistic flow of the prose and all of which force the reading process from content to reference issues willy-nilly. Obviously, this movement is not so severe or disruptive that it keeps the reader from making sense of the main text, but there is no question that it changes the reading experience.

Many authors in the sciences and social sciences felt at first that parenthetical citations disrupted and even degraded their prose style and the experience of their readers. Others disliked the use of lists of references at the ends of essay, for the reason that they make essays *look* scientific rather than traditionally scholarly. These are among the reasons that adoption of parenthetical citation systems has been a debated issue in many fields during this

---

[20] Or "(Gibbon, 1781, iii, 342–3)." The alternate, of course, is to place Gibbon's name in the text, or perhaps Gibbon's name and the title or date of the work, so as to minimize the length of the parenthetical reference. But we must notice what a stylistic balancing act this really is. Does the author want to clog up the text or the citation with the reference specifics? The one option she does *not* have is simply to stick the whole schmeer into a footnote.*

---

* Unless she cheats and writes a citation footnote in the guise of a dialogic footnote—"For more on this issue, see Gibbon, *Decline and Fall*, iii, 342–3." Who among us can cast the first stone?

century and why such adoption is such an inescapably social and rhetorical act. What seems to undergird the decision of fields (or of individual journals, since there are fields in which different journals use radically different citation systems) to change over from note to parenthetical systems is an attitude toward cumulation of knowledge and supersession of outdated knowledge in a field.

Decisions about which citation style will be specified seem to be made on the basis of each journal's perception of its readership. Some of the more obvious continua along which the decision is made are level of traditionalism, affinity to science, and concern with readability. Many of the journals and fields that have moved to new MLA style are either themselves new or wish to reflect a concern with modern ideas and a rejection of traditionalism. Composition studies was being pulled strongly in the direction of APA style in the early 1980s, a movement toward social-sciences affiliation that was stopped by the social-construction coup of 1987, with its antiscientistic and literary-theory orientations. Into this seething vacuum, sans affiliation with *any* easily identifiable scholarly tradition, came the New MLA form, meant to please everyone. In the case, it pleased only composition studies and the vast numbers of composition teachers purveying the research paper each term. Conversely, literary scholarship had enough of a self-concept to give New MLA the back of its hand; most of the older literary journals have been doing citation business similarly since before there *was* an MLA style, and their historical commitment to footnote structures will not be quickly shaken by any committee.

The issue of affinity to science we have already discussed in terms of APA style and its effect on new MLA, but it underlies this affiliation question powerfully. The key term here is *efficiency*. We might think of disciplinary affinity as existing on a continuum bounded on one end by the demonstrative sciences and the other end by history. The closer a social sciences/humanities journal perceives its readership and tacit affiliations to be to the demonstrative sciences, the more likely it is to choose to use the pragmatic efficiency of APA style or—a little farther to the right—new MLA style. Conversely, the more a journal associates itself with history and the epistemological traditions and prose decorums associated with that culture-old discipline, the more likely it will be to continue with a footnote style.

The final continuum journal editors consider is readability, and this is a vexed and complex area. The journals that have remained with footnote style are taking a contemporary version of the position taken by the Ancients in that eighteenth-century feud. The authors of footnoted articles, whatever the depth of their display of learning, tacitly perceive themselves as in the tradition of amateurs, in the original sense of that word. Their articles are essays, not research reports. Each essay is a discrete, personal piece of writing, concluding not with a quantitative list of other people's writings but with an institutional affiliation telling where the author is. These essays are not mere collections of facts or literature surveys, but prose works in their own right

meant to appeal as pieces of writing. Readers are assumed to want commerce with them for pleasure as well as for learning.

Footnotes grew out of this tradition and allow this stylistic line. Rhetorically, they are about precise stylistic control of information. A sentence from Parker's original *Style Sheet* of 1951 that lasted through the 1977 *Handbook* reflects this concern: "The test (for footnotes) should be whether or not the reference interferes with ease in reading." That test, ease in reading, still remains the primary concern in any footnote style. Despite Parker's concern that poor use of footnotes would force readers to go down to multiple "*ibids*" at page bottom, the most obvious point of superscript footnoting is that the journey to page foot is *elective*. Readers can choose to follow up the note number or not. Even the best-executed parenthetical style creates either an unavoidable lump in the text—(Jespersen, *Philosophy of Grammar* 311)—or foregrounds author and title of all cited works to avoid doing so—"As Otto Jespersen puts it so well in his *Philosophy of Grammar* . . ." Footnote systems allow an author to choose exactly how much will go into or be elided in the text; in this sense, they are the most precise and delicate of citation systems.[21] This control of information delivery allows other sorts of control, over prose rhythm, lengths of clauses and sentences, structuring of ethical and pathetic appeals.

Practitioners of the sciences and social sciences have not for decades found this sort of control meaningful or useful. Like the Moderns in the old debate, they are interested in expressing "so many things, almost in an equal number of words . . . bringing all things as near the Mathematical plainness, as they can" (Sprat 113). Systems like APA and new MLA are simply more rational in terms of providing immediate access to citation information. Parenthetical systems are simpler to use and easier to teach the use of because they are designed to be more efficient in terms of information transfer. Driven by their closing lists of references, they suggest an epistemological world in which new data are always accruing and cumulating, where mastery of previous work is the primary ethical duty of an author and needs to be constantly proven. The fields out of which these systems rose were not style-proud; in fact, from the beginning, sciences has considered prose style an enemy and argued for complete flatness in discourse. So if parenthetical citations interrupt the reading process, it is not considered an important problem. If authors' first names are reduced to initials, they should get over it. If "the research" is made to have more reality than the persons who conducted it, so much the better (See above Figure 26). What is important is that the march of science not be impeded by any issues that would cloud the referential efficiency of what is, after all, a professional literature.

---

[21] Of course, since they allow so much more delicate control, footnote systems were always liable to ill-use in the hands of beginners. Older teachers can recall a variety of footnote use errors in student papers, ranging from multiplication of "*ibids*" to serious problems of contextualization of information. These problems with the system in the hands of tyros were, I suspect, one strong unstated reason for its rejection by MLA.

The rhetoric of citation systems is fascinating because it has so silently undergirded the enterprise of Western intellectual activity. Though these systems constrain many of the ways we deal with each other and each other's work, they have largely gone unremarked. We are fond of saying that every formal choice is rhetorical, but our citation choices have always seemed *so* formalized that they have remained submerged, little discussed. Having been left in the hands of committees, functionaries, and to the choices of individual editors of journals, citation rhetorics only occasionally seem like anything individual authors can control. We have complete academic freedom—unless we try to control the citation structures we use. Then we are enmeshed in a control arrangement that makes the Star Chamber look liberal.[22]

The historical tendency of citation structures has been toward formalization, and for the past two decades it also seems to be toward convergence. Like various dialectal structures under the pressure of a unifying written grapholect in the seventeenth and eighteenth centuries, citation systems seem to be moving toward a slow unification. Since the sciences broke from footnote structure early in this century, the convergence seems to be gradually working toward the hegemony of some form of the APA name-date citation system. The APA itself made its move in 1957. New MLA is already a long step in that direction. The 13th edition of the *Chicago Manual of Style* of 1982 began to recommend the Name-Year system for all sciences and social sciences because it was "most economical in space, in time (for author, editor, and typesetter), and in cost (to publisher and public)—in short, the most practical" (400). In the 14th edition of 1995, the book has broken out a whole long chapter on APA-like Name-Year citation style in its recommendations for the first time, as has the sixth edition of Turabian. The University of Chicago Press is now encouraging all authors who can use this system to do so. In the sciences, the 1994 edition of the CBE style manual, *Scientific Style and Format*, clearly wishes to promote this convergence in style throughout all of the sciences, not just biology. For the first time, this sixth edition itself adopts the Name-Year system rather than the older Citation-Sequence system used in the five previous editions. The editors hasten to say that this choice is "not an endorsement" of the Harvard over the Vancouver system (6), but clearly a convergence is taking place.

---

[22] The business of gathering and publishing style manuals has also become large and lucrative. Examining the publication history of the four major style manuals is like watching the inflation of a colorful hot-air balloon. The 1906 first edition of the *Chicago Manual of Style* was only 201 pages, and many of those were examples of typefaces; today's 14th edition of 1995 takes up 921 pages. The first *MLA Style Sheet* of 1951 was 32 pages long, and today's 1995 *MLA Handbook* is 293 pages. APA's first separate *Publication Manual* in 1957 was 70 pages, and today's complex version takes up 368 pages. The Conference of Biology Editors wins the giantism award, though; its first *CBE Style Manual* was 92 pages, while today's 1994 version, *Scientific Style and Format*, weighs in at 825 pages. Style manuals are big business for the organizations that produce them—a fact we do well to remember.

Such epistemic and formal shifts do not take place quickly. In psychology over forty years had to elapse before the last footnoters died off and the field could be shifted to parenthetical forms. Scholars in history and in English, it seems to me, must make an informed and considered choice of what sets of conventions we wish to use, and then must make our wishes known, or be willing to drift along with this tide of tacitly approved convergence around a scientifically based style. We can consciously approve this movement toward an APA-like style, declaring that we see our fields as rational, efficient, and cumulative, and that in the service of that accumulating knowledge, we are willing to give up some elements of prose style. Or we can consciously move back toward investment in a humanities-wide footnote system, a sort of Turabian rationalized by parentheses to mark oft-cited sources, rendered technologically simple to use by word-processing and computer typesetting, and buttressed by a list of references at the end for easy source information. There will be arguments made on both sides. But whichever choice we make about our citation structures, it should be informed by rhetorical awareness and by a knowledge of the forces that have worked throughout history to affect the ways in which our texts have related to us and to each other.

WORKS CITED

Achtert, Walter S., and Joseph Gibaldi. *The MLA Style Manual*. New York: MLA, 1985.

Agger, Ben. *Soci(onto)logy: A Disciplinary Reading*. Urbana: U of Illinois P, 1989.

Barney, Stephen A., ed. *Annotation and Its Texts*. New York: Oxford UP, 1991.

Browne, Thomas. *Urn-Burial*. London: Henry Brome, 1658.

Burton, Robert. *Anatomy of Melancholy*. Oxford: John Litchfield, 1621.

The Chicago Manual of Style, Thirteenth Edition. Chicago: U of Chicago P, 1982.

Cochrane, J. A. *Dr. Johnson's Printer: The Life of William Strahan*. Cambridge: Harvard UP, 1964.

Conarroe, Joel. "Editor's Column." *PMLA* 97 (1982): 307–08.

Conference of Biological Editors. *Style Manual for Biological Journals*. Washington, DC: CBE, 1960.

Conference of Biology Editors. *Scientific Style and Format: The CBE Manual for Authors, Editors and Publishers, 6th Edition*. Cambridge: Cambridge UP, 1994.

Croffut, W. A. *Preparation of Manuscript and Illustrations for Publication by the U.S. Geological Survey*. Washington, DC: USGS, 1892.

Gibaldi, Joseph, and Walter S. Achtert. *The MLA Handbook for Writers of Research Papers, Theses, and Dissertations*. 2nd ed. New York: MLA, 1984.

Gibbon, Edward. *Memoirs of My Life*. Ed. Georges A. Bonnard. New York: Funk and Wagnalls, 1969.

Grafton, Anthony. *Commerce with the Classics: Ancient Texts and Renaissance Readers*. Ann Arbor: U of Michigan P, 1997.

Grafton, Anthony. *The Footnote: A Curious History*. Cambridge: Harvard UP, 1997.

Harvey, Gabriel. *Four Letters and Certain Sonnets. The Works of Gabriel Harvey*. Ed. Alexander B. Grosart. 3 vols. London: Privately printed, 1884–85.

Heilbrun, Carolyn G., et al. "Report of the Advisory Committee on Documentation Style." *PMLA* 97 (1982): 318–24.

Howell, John Bruce. *Style Manuals of the English-Speaking World: A Guide*. Phoenix: Oryx, 1983.

Hume, David. *Letters of David Hume*. Ed. J. Y. T. Greig. Oxford: Oxford UP, 1932.

"Instructions in Regard to Preparation of Manuscripts." *Psychological Bulletin* 26 (1929): 57–63.

Lincoln, Bruce. *Authority: Construction and Corrosion*. Chicago: U of Chicago P, 1994.

Lipking, Lawrence. "The Marginal Gloss." *Critical Inquiry* 3 (1977): 609–55.

Loewenstein, Joseph F. "*Idem*: Italics and the Genetics of Authorship." *Journal of Medieval and Renaissance Studies* 20 (Fall 1990): 205–24.

Louttit, Chauncey M. "The Use of Bibliographies in Psychology." *Psychological Review* 36 (1929): 341–47.

Manual of Style: Being a Compilation of the Typographical Rules in Force at the University of Chicago Press. To Which are Appended Specimens of Types in Use. Chicago: U of Chicago P, 1906.

McFarland, Thomas. "Who Was Benjamin Whichcote? or, The Myth of Annotation." In Barney, 152–77.

Melanchthon, Philip. "Inaugural Lecture." *Melanchthonis Opera, Corpus Reformatorum*. Ed. Carolus Bretschneider. vol. xi. Halis Saxonum: C. A. Schwetschke, 1834: 21–30.

Modern Language Association. *The MLA Handbook for Writers of Research Papers, Theses, and Dissertations*. New York: MLA, 1977.

Modern Language Association. "The MLA Style Sheet." *PMLA* 66 (1951): 3–31.

Modern Language Association. *The MLA Style Sheet, Second Edition*. New York: MLA, 1970.

Nashe, Thomas. *Have with you to Saffron-Walden. The Works of Thomas Nashe*. Ed. Ronald B. McKerrow. III. Oxford: Basil Blackwell, 1958: 1–139.

Ong, Walter J. *The Presence of the Word*. Minneapolis: U of Minnesota P, 1967.

———. *Rhetoric, Romance, and Technology*. Ithaca: Cornell UP, 1971.

Pollard, Alfred W., ed. *Records of the English Bible*. London: Oxford UP, 1911.

"Preparation of Articles for Publication in the Journals of the American Psychological Association." *Psychological Bulletin* 41 (1944): 345–76.

"Publication Manual of the American Psychological Association." *Psychological Bulletin* 49 (1952): 389–449.

Rose, Mark. "The Author as Proprietor: *Donaldson vs. Becket* and the Genealogy of Modern Authorship." *Representations* 23 (Summer 1988): 51–85.

Smalley, Beryl. "The Bible in the Medieval Schools." *The Cambridge History of the Bible*, vol. 2. Cambridge: Cambridge UP, 1969: 197–219.

Sprat, Thomas. *The History of the Royal Society of London*. London: J. Martyn, 1667.

Timperley, C. H. *The Printer's Manual*. London: H. Johnson, 1838.

Tribble, Evelyn B. *Margins and Marginality: The Printed Page in Early Modern England*. Charlottesville: UP of Virginia, 1993.

Turabian, Kate L. *A Manual for Writers of Dissertations*. Chicago: U of Chicago P, 1937.

———. *A Manual for Writers of Term Papers, Theses, and Dissertations*, 2nd edition. Chicago: U of Chicago P, 1955.

Adversus Haereses:
Robert J. Connors Responds to Roxanne Mountford

In *"Adversus Haereses,"* Bob responds to reviews of *Composition-Rhetoric*—reviews that were particularly critical of his treatment of gender issues. In defending his position, Bob traces his interest in and work on gender and rhetoric back to 1986, noting that he had persistently explored the relationship between two sets of facts: "(1) Between 1820 and 1910, women entered American post-secondary education in both all-women's colleges and coeducational settings. (2) Between 1820 and 1910, rhetorical education in American colleges shifted powerfully from its [. . .] concern with oral, argumentative, non-personal discourse to a new concern with written, multi-modal, and more personalized discourse. 'Rhetoric' became 'composition,' and the remnants of the oral rhetorical tradition were marginalized [. . .]" (400). Far from assuming a direct causal connection between these two sets of facts, as he says he is accustomed to doing, Bob argues that he has been careful to identify women's entry into higher education and into rhetorical practice as only one factor in the change he identifies. This response, which appeared in *JAC*'s online "Reviews Reviewed" in 1999, constitutes the last published commentary on his own work of which we are aware and is thus of particular interest for what Bob has to say about his writing life.

Perhaps it's because of the personal plea at the end of the review, or perhaps because Roxanne Mountford's own scholarship has been around religious rhetoric. But I must admit at this point to feeling the vague spiritual guilt of the recalcitrant heretic rejecting the kindly counsels of orthodox doctors of the church. As Roxanne points out, I have been given many opportunities to recant with only minimal discipline—opportunities I have spurned, through blameworthy antinomian pride, no doubt. My interrogators have offered their corrections of my fallacious opinions time and again, yet I will not learn from them. I have not yet been shown the instruments, but I fear that will be the next step. Heresy is an ugly business, but with revealed truth available, it must be exposed.

From *JAC Online* 19.3 (1999): http://jac.gsu.edu/jac/Reviewsreviewed/connors.htm.

If we assume a *secular* intellectual world, though, we have here a curious situation. Two reviewers of my book, Sharon Crowley and Roxanne Mountford, have chosen to devote four-fifths of each of their lengthy reviews to melancholy critiques of a gender thesis that informs one of the book's eight chapters. For each of these reviewers, the other seven-eighths of the book are decidedly minor. We might think that the gender issue is the pivot on which everything turns; we might think that the book was not about the history of composition in American colleges. That is why it seems to me that what we have in these reviews is not so much the need to review a book as to expose an error, confute a heresy. What's at issue seems more than merely intellectual; as the tone of Roxanne's last page indicates clearly, we have gone here into questions of ideology, attitude, and community that have some deep emotional roots. It's not just this one chapter of the book for Roxanne, but my *CE* article and responses to it, my arguing back against powerful criticism— my whole refusal to accept all of the tacit ideological positions of some monolithic version of feminist rhetorical history that she seems to feel she and Sharon represent.

I don't believe that such a unified condemning circle of feminist historians exists; the feminist rhetorical-history community is more thoughtful and individual than that. On my side, I feel like I've been straw-manned by both Sharon and Roxanne, who seem determined to draw invidious conclusions from my work that I do not see there. What is this infamous "feminization theory" which I so notoriously refuse to abandon? It is the idea that during the nineteenth century, women in America began to stake a claim to rhetorical education that was one of the reasons for powerful changes in American rhetoric. Not the only reason, not even, perhaps, the most important reason. But a reason.

I have been working on this idea since 1986, and I evolved it to try to deal with two groups of facts that will, I think, not be argued:

1. Between 1820 and 1910, women entered American post-secondary education in both all-women's colleges and in coeducational settings.

2. Between 1820 and 1910, rhetorical education in American colleges shifted powerfully from its 2500-year-old traditional concern with oral, argumentative, non-personal discourse to a new concern with written, multi-modal, and more personalized discourse. "Rhetoric" became "composition," and the remnants of the oral rhetorical tradition were marginalized as elocution and dramatic recitation.

There are three possible relations between these two generally accepted sets of facts:

a. There is an absolute causal correlation.

b. There is some causal correlation.

c. There is no causal correlation.

The "feminization theory" is a working out of some of the implications of position (b.). I do not—as Roxanne admits in one of the very few quotes

the book is allowed in her review—claim any absolute causality. I am aware of *post hoc ergo propter hoc*. On p. 54, I go out of my way to list other reasons for the displacement of oral rhetoric by composition. But I do argue that women's entry into American colleges after 1820 is one factor in that change. I do supply evidence from a variety of sources to the effect that coeducation wrought powerful changes to the atmospheres and workings of American colleges, and that it had rhetorical consequences. Both position (a.) and position (c.) are extreme, and anyone proposing one of them would have as difficult a time arguing for no causal correlation as would the person arguing for an absolute causal correlation. Yet both Roxanne and Sharon seem to believe that there can be no causal correlation.

Just to try to halt the manufacture of straw-man versions of my argument, let me state here explicitly what I am *not* claiming, in the book or anywhere else. I do not argue that:

1. Women before the nineteenth century never used rhetoric or engaged in public speaking.

2. Women cannot engage in agonism or contestive behavior.

3. Women do not argue as well as men.

4. Women shrink from oral discourse.

5. Rhetoric is male and composition is female.

6. Rhetoric is good and composition is bad.

I challenge anyone to find evidence in my work that I support any of these ideas. I do and will argue that:

1. Men and women do and always have engaged in gender-differentiated behaviors.

2. For cultural and perhaps biological reasons, men have traditionally engaged and have been expected to engage in public agonistic and contestive activities more than women have.

3. Rhetoric is the discipline that formalized and reified one important set of public contestive activities.

4. In western culture, women were excluded from formalized training in rhetoric and from forums within which oral civic discourse could be practiced almost absolutely before the seventeenth century and in most situations before the nineteenth.

5. Beginning in the late eighteenth century, women began successfully to demand access to coequal education with men and specifically to rhetorical education.

6. As women entered colleges and won access to education, faculty-student relations shifted, the older all-male oral teaching methods changed, and agonistic activities lost their power and centrality in both the curriculum and the extracurriculum.

7. Changes in rhetorical education were part of this larger change in American college life.

These claims are general and institutional, and they are *not* about the rhetoric of writing, but of public oral discourse. With a very few exceptions—which we must see in context, as exceptions—oral rhetoric was a male-dominated activity until after 1820. If I had been able to find more than a persecuted handful of women who attempted to engage in oral civic rhetoric before the nineteenth century, I would not have made such claims. If rhetorical education had been widely available to women before 1820, they would be rendered trivial or false.

As I have said, my claims are not absolute. They are about general trends and tendencies. I have no arguments with Roxanne's statement that hundreds of Methodist women preached during the eighteenth and nineteenth centuries. I detail myself (pp. 37–40) the rise of the female Quaker preaching tradition after George Fox and Margaret Fell in the mid-seventeenth century. We have, as Roxanne says, knowledge of a few women preaching and prophesying from Paul on down. The point I make about these female preachers was not that they did not exist, but that they were very few—because they were marginalized, persecuted, tortured, and even killed by a patriarchal western culture determined to keep women out of the public sphere. Our laudable desire to find rhetorical foremothers cannot blind us to the power of the forces arrayed against them, forces that were hegemonic and overwhelmingly successful. It is no accident that Cheryl Glenn, in revising her dissertation into a book, moved from the title *Muted Voices* to *Rhetoric Retold*. The old field of rhetoric did mute women's voices all too successfully, and we are forced to retell the story of rhetoric, to move it out from the traditional oral, civic, argumentative and pedagogical tradition if we are to find more than a very few women in rhetoric before 1820.

Human history will show almost no absolutely successful prohibitions, but some powerful constraints are relatively complete, and this is one of them. The hundreds of Methodist and Quaker women preaching after 1660 cannot blind us to the millions of women of all other Christian faiths forbidden to speak in the churches or to the obloquy those women preachers received from the mainstream cultures they inhabited. Samuel Johnson's gibe against women preaching in the 1770s ("Sir, a woman's preaching is like a dog's walking on his hinder legs. It is not done well; but you are surprised to find it done at all.") is a truer reflection of his time than our admiration today for Ann Lee. And women who proposed to preach and prophesy had an easier time of it than women who proposed to engage in secular public speaking; if they existed historically, their stories have been transmitted, like those of Aspasia, in controversial or equivocal forms, or they stand out strongly, like the story of Hortensia, as exceptional. We simply have no good historical evidence that women were permitted to engage in oral civic rhetoric before the nineteenth century, and the desperate and horrified struggle waged after 1800 *against* the very women who pioneered oral public rhetoric should tell us how powerful the disciplining forces had been for over two millennia preceding.

I must confess to being a little surprised at the animus directed here against my chapter. Yes, the exclusion of women from a field we think of as our own is discouraging. Yes, it is tempting to focus on the few women who broke the taboo and to paint them as representative. Yes, it may be necessary to broaden the definition of rhetoric to include convent homiletics and written discourse, in which women always engaged much more freely. But we cannot turn our backs on the cumulation of so much inductive evidence about the nature of the field that has *called* itself rhetoric. It was a male field for most of its history. This very fact, though, makes the changes of the nineteenth century all the more notable. As I did the research, I found myself thrilled by the courage and resourcefulness of the college women who demanded and won access to rhetorical training at that time. My title for a book chapter about that movement is "Women's Reclamation of Rhetoric in the Nineteenth Century," and I thought of it as in most ways a story of triumph. That it has been read as insulting to women—that some readers seem to *need* to find positions in the chapter that I do not take—mystifies me a bit.

As I look back on the last thirteen years, I can also see that this research has, for me, been less about women than it has been about men, and that fact may finally be more important than anything else. When I heard Walter Ong present his theories about male agonistic behavior in 1982, what he said explained much that I had experienced in my training as a male in this culture, and from his theories of agonism it was a natural step to the history of rhetoric. Finally, my "feminization theory" (and I should say here that I have never used that term in any of my own titles) is really about how traditional patriarchal culture was challenged and was changed forever during the nineteenth century, and how American manhood would not be the same after that. Finally, the theory is not really about women and was not meant to be.

Now I'm no less in love with my own ideas than anyone else and am loathe to give them up, but I'm not, I hope, a solipsist or a monomaniac. Show me evidence, and I'll recant. But I'd need more and better arguments than I've seen so far to do so in this case. What would such evidence look like? It would have to have certain facts on display. It would have to show that:

1. Traditional rhetoric and rhetorical education were not agonistic.

   OR

2. Women have always been part of the tradition that called itself rhetoric. Women before the nineteenth century were widely invited to engage in oral rhetorical training and given access to oral rhetorical forums.

   OR

3. Rhetorical training in the nineteenth century did not change substantially.

   OR

4. All the changes in American rhetorical education during the nineteenth century are explicable with no reference to gender issues or to the single most striking change in colleges, the entrance of women.

I do not see such evidence forthcoming. And although I cannot quite follow Roxanne in calling the sort of history I have tried to write "empirical" (I think we'd need Mr. Peabody's Wayback Machine for historical empiricism), my own examination of the textual evidence available makes me suspect it will not be forthcoming.

And despite Roxanne's suggestion that book reviewing is agonistic, our little written give-and-take here is really fairly mild compared to rhetorical agonism of the old sort. Roxanne, let's imagine that you and I were upon a stage in front of hundreds of our CCCC colleagues. Our intentions would be simple: you would seek to attack me and my ideas with every tactic and piece of evidence and skill you possess, and I would seek to defend my ideas and to show that your motives were ideological. No reading of prepared papers, no hiding behind citations or French theory or literature surveys. You attack; I parry. The audience responds immediately and loudly to every point made, every hit scored. Back and forth it goes, mounting to the heights of eloquence, dipping into the muck of personal invective, thrust and counter-thrust, until we are both exhausted. And then the audience votes on a winner and one of us is chaired out of the hall to huzzahs while the other bitterly collects notes and goes out silently, escorted by a few sullen seconds.

Now *that's* agonism. And we don't see it much in college anymore. The irenic discourse that replaced it—this stuff we're doing—does not have to be about sweetness and light. We may indeed disagree. All that I would ask, of both you and of Sharon, is that when you are asked to do a book review, you do the author the simple courtesy of reviewing—that is, describing and evaluating—his or her book, not taking the five pages of journal space you are given as a unilateral forum for attacking one idea in the book while more or less ignoring everything else the book is proposing to be about. We don't actually disagree about that much, after all, and there are issues about which people of good will may disagree.

Unless my opening idea about heresy holds water. Because for true believers, religious or ideological, the difference between *homoousion* and *homoiousion* is, literally, the difference between heaven and hell.

Composition History
and Disciplinarity

The first Thomas R. Watson Conference on Rhetoric and Composition was held at the University of Louisville in the fall of 1996. Bob's "Composition History and Disciplinarity" provided the keynote address, and his essay appears first in the volume that bears the name of that first conference theme: *History, Reflection, and Narrative: The Professionalization of Composition, 1963–1983* (1999). The period Bob focuses on in his essay, a period he calls the "Era of Disciplinarity" in composition-rhetoric, begins in the late 1960s and early 1970s with the burgeoning of doctoral programs, journals, book series, and conferences devoted to this subject. After describing the second and third generation of modern composition-rhetoric scholars (Bob places himself in the third-generation group), Bob goes on to explain what he sees as the advantages and the disadvantages of disciplinarity, focusing particularly on composition studies' move away from practice and toward theory. He concludes with a stark description of composition-rhetoric's possible futures: "we can continue to follow the example of literary studies, making theoretical sophistication, specialized expertise, and sheer scholarly output the prime criteria of success in the field" (420) *or* we can "embrace teaching and service as indispensable parts of the world of [our] research, and [put] scholarly research in the service of action in colleges and universities" (420). Bob's own sympathies lie with the second choice, and he closes by urging that we serve our students and society rather than "concentrating on narrow career goals or sterile intellectual puzzles" (421). Readers may think, as indeed we do, that this binary between service and scholarship need not hold, but with his characteristic determination, Bob insists that we confront the hard choices that creating the future of composition-rhetoric will entail.

G rowing older within any intellectual field has both its pleasures and terrors: The excitement and stress of entry into the Burkean parlor, the whitewater canoe ride of achieving tenure and disciplinary

From *History, Reflection, and Narrative: The Professionalization of Composition, 1963–1983*, ed. Mary Rosner, Beth Boehm, and Debra Journet (Stamford, CT: Ablex, 2000), 3–21.

maturity, the (always unexpected) revelation of the extra work that comes with seniority, and, finally, the gradual letting go into younger hands of the work to which one has devoted one's life. This pattern holds for every intellectual discipline, but I suspect that the pleasures and terrors are a bit sharper for those of us who have been working in composition studies since the 1960s. We are so new; most of our Ph.D. programs are less than two decades old. One of our most noted award winners was barely 50 years old when she was named an Exemplar to the field. The very name of our discipline has only been around for 15 years. Those of us who have been active over the past 30 years are aware that we were present at the making of something.

The 1996 Watson Conference at Louisville was in some ways the outward and visible sign of who we have become. The reality of what we have been making is all around us at every Conference on College Composition and Communication, but the Watson Conference was the first meeting I know of that was specifically meant to look at the meanings of our making. What *does* it mean, what *will* it mean, for us to be a recognizable discipline, as opposed to the group of marginalized enthusiasts coming together for support and sympathy that we were 35 years ago?

I'm a historian, so this question presents itself to me—as do most questions—against the background of our past. What it means for us to have become a discipline can only be understood in reference to what we were before. Without an understanding of history, a field of action has no memory, and without memory it cannot measure movement outside the realm of a narrow, incremental present. That is why the developed sciences still retain, as important field information, the archaeologies of their theoretical explorations. Chemists today do not need knowledge of the phlogiston theory nor linguists knowledge of early transformation-based theory except to understand where their fields have been and are not anymore—and why this is. Development of a field is always understood comparatively, which is why I'm bemused by people in the field today who say they don't need to know about rhetorical history or past developments in composition teaching.

HISTORICAL AWARENESS AND DISCIPLINARY ROOTS

Part of the way in which historians have always made meaning, and a method I'd like to adopt here to help make sense of the part of the disciplinary story we are currently traversing, is to look at events as occurring in related "periods." Reductive and simplifying as such periodization can be, it seems an inevitable result of the way our hearts, if not our too-active minds, conceive the past. The "Age of Chivalry," the "Plague Years," the "Ante-Bellum Period," the "Era of Good Feeling"—these terms may not be completely descriptive of everything that was going on during those times, but we respond to them as accurate enough descriptions of what we want to call out for attention. As a historian, I want to call this time in our historical development the "Era of Disciplinarity" in the field of composition studies.

What is it that allows us to use this term? I don't ask the question lightly, because the history of people who teach writing in American colleges is peppered with a number of previous unrequited romances with disciplinarity. What do we have now that we didn't have then?

I hope those who were there, or who have heard these stories, will forgive me for quickly rehearsing them. I do so because our modern relationship with history is implicated in and contemporaneous with our disciplinarity, and it illustrates how gaining a historical sense means gaining a self. American composition-rhetoric before 1850 was still strongly attached to the traditional discipline of rhetoric, and such early American teachers of writing as Edward T. Channing and Henry Day, in addition to their biweekly writing conferences, worked from a deep knowledge of sources ranging from Aristotle to Whately. But then the Germanic scholarly approach to learning, with its overt scientistic disdain for rhetoric, was imported to America after the Civil War. Tradition-based rhetoric came gradually to be despised by the new scholars, who preferred social science, philology, and literary scholarship, and who built the new academic departments around them.

Without a historical component, American composition-rhetoric before 1950 lacked connections to any tradition and was rendered weak and vulnerable. Our first great chance at disciplinarity was lost in the 1890s, when Fred Newton Scott determined to found his pioneering University of Michigan doctoral program on psychological and linguistic bases, while downplaying rhetorical and historical elements. Scott's Ph.D. students, oriented toward modern educational and psychological theory but unwilling or unable to dialogue successfully with literary or classical colleagues, found themselves excluded from academia or trapped in English or speech departments, where they were aliens. Scott's intellectual line of psychological and philosophical composition died out after his retirement in 1927.

Rhetorical history never died, but the bulk of the work done there from the 1920s through the 1940s was the effort of scholars in the relatively new field of speech communication. Unlike compositionists, speech rhetoricians had never severed their ties to the history of rhetoric, and they were thus able to grid historical methodologies onto their work in ways immediately recognizable as scholarly. As a result, speech departments had established the legitimacy of their discipline and were granting their own doctorates a scant decade after declaring the secession of speech teachers from the National Council of Teachers of English in 1914. They were speaking a language the rest of the academy could understand and accredit.

But in English departments there was no reception, and it was some time after the demise of Scott's experiment that the first historians of the rhetoric of teaching writing arose. It's not accidental that these torches in the darkness were also preeminent among the intellectual figures striving to create, out of the oppressed and unmemoried activity of teaching required composition, some sense of what it meant to do so. Porter Perrin's 1936 dissertation, entitled *The Teaching of Rhetoric in the American Colleges Before 1750*, was a history of rhetoric in America during the 18th century, and Perrin went on to

become an important voice, demanding self-awareness and seriousness in composition teaching during the late 1930s, 1940s, and 1950s. Perrin is little-recognized today, because he was active during a time in American educational history not friendly to the possibilities for composition as a developed intellectual field. Only toward the end of his life did he see the stirrings of what would become composition studies—a field that should honor him as a progenitor.

A sense of our own place in history and tradition was a surprisingly late entry on our professional scene, one that began with a realization of lost roots. The Conference on College Composition and Communication was founded in 1949 on principles considered very modern, as part of a nation-wide movement to break down what were seen as rigid disciplinary boundaries. As the Harvard Committee on the Objectives of a General Education in a Free Society put it, "Specialization enhances the centrifugal forces in our society. . . . Our conclusion, then, is that the aim of education should be to prepare an individual to become an expert both in some particular vocation or art and in the general art of the free man and the citizen" (1945, pp. 53–54). The General Education movement and its subset, the Communication movement, wanted to bring together fields that had grown too specialized, and thus courses in writing or in speech were brought together into communication courses, which incorporated the four communication skills of reading, writing, speaking, and listening. But these modern, reformist ideas led, as they often do, to a new realization about history and its centrality. Staffing these courses was a group of teachers who had been raised in English and speech departments, and the result of their meeting was a new dialogue between writing teachers and their speech counterparts—public-speaking teachers, who had kept alive the history and theories of Western rhetoric far more completely than had English. Though the Communication movement did not outlast the mid-1950s except in a few places, its supporters from both speech and English had come into touch with each other around the issue of rhetoric, and an organization had been formed that would allow important disciplinary developments in the future.

The CCCC was a necessary, though not a sufficient, cause for composition's becoming a discipline. The people around whom composition studies would coalesce were becoming active in the early 1950s, but the content of their work was still scattered and noncumulative. Few had much sense of the source their work and ideas had derived from because English department compositionists tended to concentrate on immediate pragmatic issues. But forces were at work, and it was Albert R. Kitzhaber, a graduate student of Porter Perrin's, who wrote the first definitive history of American composition. Our modern history really begins with his 1953 dissertation *Rhetoric in American Colleges, 1850–1900*, a work in which Kitzhaber concentrated on material about the teaching of writing in America that had been almost completely elided in the rhetorical histories done in the field of speech communication. Though Kitzhaber's work was a secret classic, destined to have an im-

mense impact on a group of later historians, it was hardly known to most composition specialists until two decades after its creation.

We had a journal and a conference, but still not much of a sense of our own history, and our second failed attempt at disciplinarity played out during the 1950s around that lack of a center. During that time, many composition teachers were tending to seek disciplinary validity by reaching out and subordinating themselves to more developed or seemingly impressive fields of learning. There was an early 1950s fling with general semantics, then popular. In particular, that time saw an unhappy rekindling of composition's old affair with grammar in the form of structural linguistics, a smooth-talking Lothario that swept us off our feet through the late 1950s and early 1960s. Structural linguists were so confident, so scientific, so sure that their hard-edged analyses would allow composition to become respectable—how could we resist? When Harry Warfel told us that structural linguistics was analogous to atomic physics and that "a widespread familiarity with the principles of structural linguistics will work a similar revolution in the teaching of verbal composition" (1959, p. 212), his claims were forceful. Many writing teachers came to believe that linguistics would give composition a leg-up to disciplinarity, but when the Chomskian revolution swept structural linguistics away after 1963, those who had invested heavily in structural analysis were left wondering and discouraged. It began to appear that affiliation with a language science most people could not at all understand offered no obvious road to any new status for composition.

The New Rhetoric of the 1960s, to which it is easy to trace our primary lines of disciplinarity, was both a blossoming of the promise of the earlier Communication movement and a new social movement coming from within English departments. Elsewhere, I have made comparisons between the New Criticism and the New Rhetoric, not in terms of their theoretical origins, but in terms of their both representing populist movements growing out of the new GI Bill-socioculture of English departments (Connors, 1989). Though a part of the New Rhetoric movement was genuinely interdisciplinary, especially in relation to new connections made with philosophy (and to lesser degrees with linguistics and psychology), its most important effects were felt within English departments and within composition programs. It influenced English courses, its proponents were English teachers, and its literature was read by English department scholars. It was resolutely traditional in its historical and analytical backgrounds, presenting English scholars for the first time with a vision of composition that was based on a classical past, with even deeper roots in Western culture than their own Anglo-Saxon roots.

New Rhetorical scholarship for the first time could hold its own as a literature that argued positions by relying consistently on previous scholarship in a dialectic. It went beyond the narrow presentism that had previously cursed composition journals. Examine an issue of *College Composition and Communication* from 1960 and contrast it to an issue from 1970 and the difference will immediately become apparent to you. I think we can trace the

possibility of the field of composition studies from this point; what had been scattered and mostly rootless conversations was evolving into a dialogical and cumulating scholarly literature. The rebirth of classical rhetoric, the development of tagmemic rhetoric, the prewriting movement, sentence combining, the writing-process movement, Christensen rhetoric, and the entire new seriousness of the research strand in composition—with its new journal, *Research in the Teaching of English*—all date to the middle and late 1960s. Disparate as these ideas and movements look to us in retrospect, collectively they were the New Rhetoric, and they represent a huge leap forward for the discourse of the field. We were not yet a discipline, but the conditions were coming together.

TRADITION AND REPRODUCTION

The 1970s, rather than the 1960s, were the founding decade of the disciplinarity of composition studies because two elements coalesced then that had not existed before. The first we have already seen in the beginning of the 1960s (and some would place it even earlier): methods of intellectual tradition in a great burgeoning of journals and books. The 1970s was the first decade since the 1890s to see large numbers of serious-minded scholarly and practical books appearing concerning themselves with the problems and issues of rhetoric and composition. It was also a decade of astounding journal foundings. In addition to new vitality in the NCTE journals *College English, College Composition and Communication,* and *Research in the Teaching of English,* we saw the foundings of *Freshman English News, Teaching English in the Two-Year College, Journal of Basic Writing, Rhetoric Society Quarterly, Writing Lab Newsletter,* and *Writing Program Administration.* The 1960s and 1970s were times of hero-editors who made a literature: Richard Ohmann, Ken Macrorie, Don Gray, Bill Irmscher, Ed Corbett, Gary Tate, Mina Shaughnessy, Muriel Harris, and Richard Braddock.

In addition to a method of tradition, however, a discipline needs a method of scholarly reproduction, and this we had never had before the 1970s. The failure to endure of the first American composition boom—lasting from 1885 to 1905—provides an example of how methods of tradition alone cannot keep a discipline alive without some system that can continue to provide a community of accredited disciplinary authors and informed readers. In practical institutional terms, that means a doctorate.

I have elsewhere discussed reasons why written rhetoric did not evolve a doctoral capacity until almost a century after it began to be institutionally taught (Connors, 1991). Though there existed a strong interest in and dialogue about teaching writing between 1885 and 1905, the great generation of experts from the 1890s—John Genung, Barrett Wendell, and Adams Hill, to name a few—either did not or could not train replacements for themselves. As I've mentioned, the only person who had the will and the resources to try was Fred Newton Scott at Michigan. He fought almost alone for a composition-based Ph.D., but he could not succeed as the only such program in the

United States. When he retired in 1927, his doctoral program in rhetoric was folded back into the Michigan English department, and the 23 doctorates in rhetoric he produced between 1898 and 1930, finding no jobs and no support system for their training in the departments that proposed to hire them, gradually drifted into other professions or other parts of English studies. And with the exceptions of those speech-trained rhetoricians like Warren Guthrie, whose interests included the 19th century, and very few English- and education-based students like Porter Perrin and Al Kitzhaber, there were no more composition-oriented doctoral students in American colleges until the late 1960s.

The "first generation" of modern composition specialists, such GI Bill- generation scholars as Kitzhaber, Jix Lloyd-Jones, Priscilla Tyler, Donald Murray, and Ed Corbett, began work in the field between the late 1940s and the early 1960s. They were mainly literary in background and were forced to be rhetorical autodidacts, often in their spare time. Their writings and ex- ample helped create the "second generation," which includes such people as Dave Bartholomae, Susan Miller, and Erika Lindemann. Trained in the late 1960s, when there was a literature and a lot of excitement but no possibility of official doctoral recognition, this second generation, too, had to retool as writing specialists after literary doctorates. It was only after 1970 that a groundbreaking change occurred, with the appearance of the first rhetoric doctorates in English departments. I don't know who the "first Ph.D." was, and it's probably not a useful question, but sometime between 1970 and 1975, such universities as Texas, Michigan, Ohio State, USC, and UCSD began to allow their faculty composition specialists to develop and teach graduate courses in rhetoric and composition, and then the freedom to examine stu- dents and direct dissertations in these fields.

This new group of students, the "third generation" of modern composi- tion people, was the first generation of fully composition-trained Ph.D.'s in America since the 1920s and Fred Scott. This generation—and I am a mem- ber of it—saw its mission clearly: it was to go forth and multiply, establish- ing doctoral programs almost everywhere it went. As a result of our success, the third generation quickly became leaders within the field as it grew rapidly, and relatively young people, such as Lee Odell, Andrea Lunsford, and Nancy Sommers, have now assumed almost elder statesperson roles within the field.

With both methods of tradition and methods of reproduction burgeon- ing for composition studies, the decade of the 1980s saw full-blown growth of disciplinarity. We discovered our own history as Kitzhaber's 1953 disserta- tion began to circulate in microfilm and photocopied *samizdat* form in the 1970s. A copy of it was a *sine qua non* for the new generation of young profes- sors who wanted to know about the past times of composition. This genera- tion of historians—Kate Adams, Jim Berlin, Sharon Crowley, Nan Johnson, Tom Miller, David Russell, and Bill Woods—at first wrote history simply be- cause they were fascinated by it and wanted to explore the trails that Perrin and Kitzhaber as well as other early historians such as Warren Guthrie,

Glenn Hess, and Wallace Douglas had blazed. But, half-realized, we were also writing history in order to create ourselves as members of a discipline, and then in order to inform that discipline and try to unify it. We even, rather quickly, had a name: composition studies.[1] The Educational Resources Information Center (ERIC) shows 46 examples of its use between 1983 and 1991, and 46 more between 1992 and 1994. The journal *Freshman English News* became *Composition Studies* in 1992. We began to assume a definable position as a field coequal with other fields within English studies.

THE SOCIOCULTURE OF DISCIPLINE

It is easy to see the positive results of our growing disciplinarity. We now have what we did not have before. We write and publish serious scholarship in journals that are professional and respectable. We have diverse interests, and there are a plethora of positions and theoretical stances with which we can affiliate ourselves. We have our places in the hierarchy of discourse circles—both our own and those outside. Composition scholars are capable of performing conscientious critical analyses of a sort that allows us to hold up our ends in conversations at both MLA and AERA. We are part of a field whose intellectual vitality is still growing, as opposed to some fields that seem exhausted. Locally, we get better salaries and enjoy more respect in the English departments that are still home for most of us. We have in those departments graduate students to mentor, often among the most intelligent and capable of the crop, and the pleasures of reproduction are real ones.

The negative results of our disciplinarity have been less explored in public, if not less considered privately. "An intellectual hatred is the worst," says Yeats, and it seems that one of the inevitable concomitants of disciplinarity is intellectual hatred. If we are more real as a discipline, we are also more hierarchical and exclusive. If the credulous wheel-reinventing of our earlier journal articles was replaced with more rigorous means of testing and discussing writing and its teaching, the supportive good fellowship of earlier composition dialogue was also replaced with something more pointed—and more divided.

Disciplinarity has not been, in this sense, an unmixed blessing. Our understanding of writing has undoubtedly deepened, as doctoral research of many sorts was bent to the psychological and then the social understanding of it, but with the Ph.D. research orientation have come unexpected side effects. Between 1970 and 1990, as we were building composition studies, 4C's ceased being the love-feast of a marginalized minority and came to be marked more and more by a theoretical-camps mentality of inclusion and exclusion. "Special interests" came more and more to the fore, and identity politics of every kind popped up in the program. We have seen the growth of sharp disagreements, simmering dislikes, and warring factions, sometimes within the same city. The skirmish of egotisms that was always one of the least admirable aspects of literary studies has come home to composition over the last 15 years as people have built reputations, staked out turf, and

gotten famous. Like every other discipline, we have evolved our own jargon and code terms, which are sometimes part of standard dialogic lore, but use of which (or failure to use of which) can also represent ideological purity tests. The Passchendaele sense of entrenched and warring intellectual cliques, with their creation of friend and enemy lists, that so troubled me when I began to go to MLA in the 1970s has become a too-familiar phenomenon even at CCCC. Nearly all of us are familiar, at least tacitly, with the growth of hierarchy in the field—hierarchies of graduate programs, journal placements, and awards.

Within a discipline, the power to critique is also the power to destroy. Since 1970, the power of cumulating criticism within the field has been getting more marked. In the 1970s, critiques of tagmemic rhetoric were enough to cause it to lose momentum, and in the early 1980s we saw the dominating juggernaut of sentence combining brought to a shivering halt by a combined attack from linguistic and expressivist criticism. A little later, expressivism itself was rendered disreputable, at least theoretically, by cultural and ideological critiques. And in the most recent and potent example of a line of research being overthrown, we saw the psychology-based research approach that had marked the early 1980s essentially terminated by criticism from the more theoretical social and cultural-studies approach that has been ascendent since 1987. In the wake of that event, theory wars gradually made their way from literary and cultural studies into composition studies. Our graduate students are now expected to know their Gramsci, Bakhtin, and Foucault as thoroughly as they know their Quintilian and Elbow.

Curiously, as some aspects of the field have been moving closer to those in literary and cultural studies, others are coming to resemble the practices of the "hard" sciences. The critique of individualism underlying much of the current theoretical construction of the field has had both explicit and tacit elements. Explicitly, we see the rise of constructivism, intellectual-property theory, collaborative methodologies, and collaboration-based pedagogies. Tacitly, the concept of author-blind peer review has come to have almost absolute control over our publications and conferences. Peer review has always been dominant in scientific publication, of course, and scientific fields still provide a tacit model for disciplinary maturity. Thus, with social construction of scholarly acceptability as prime desideratum, we have seen the rise of the idea that no individual can or should control the gates of public dialogue. The "hero-editors" who constructed our journals in the heady 1970s and early 1980s have thus disappeared in favor of "facilitator-editors," who solicit blind readings for acceptance of journal articles and even conference papers. The replacement of the more traditional footnoting citation systems in favor either of "new MLA" or APA parenthetical systems in composition journals is another reflection of the social orientation of the field. Parenthetical citation systems, designed for easy reference to previous work in literature survey form, won out over the more individualistic (albeit natural and reader-friendly) footnote and endnote in the social sciences, and their quick acceptance by composition studies (as opposed to literary studies, which is

still convulsed by disagreements about "new MLA") indicates where some of our affinities lie. These more communitarian ideas of scholarship have led to more defensible and more replicable research at the same time that they have filtered a certain amount of unpredictability and polemical energy out of many of our journals.

It cannot be a surprise that scholarly communities tend to enforce scholarly norms. If I may speak personally, the most disturbing corollary of our movement into disciplinary status has been a change in our attitude toward our service identity. The growth of our disciplinary literature has, let us admit, been marked by a retreat from pragmatic pedagogical issues more than by any other single phenomenon. The origin of most doctoral programs in English departments left us open to a sort of "theory-pride," and to a resulting reflexive movement away from teaching issues and writing pedagogy as too "ed-school." The Ph.D. licensure in English has for several decades usually meant safety from the danger of having to teach freshman composition on a standard rotation, and it has increasingly come to mean the same thing even in composition studies. New composition doctorates may be asked to teach first-year composition or even basic writing once or twice a year, but usually they are hired primarily to coordinate programs, teach graduate courses, run writing centers, and assist in writing-across-the-curriculum (WAC) programs. It's a rare college that hires a composition doctoral specialist simply to teach undergraduate writing; the tacit feeling on all sides is that such duties would be a waste of valuable training.

As a result, composition studies as a discipline has moved farther and farther from our original teaching duties and the awarenesses that went with them. We have all seen the eclipse of the "Staffroom Interchange" section of CCC, and the journal is simply reflecting the reality that most of its readers don't go into the staffroom anymore, except perhaps to post notices or lead meetings. Let me again speak personally; it's 10 years since I taught more than one writing course in a semester, and today I can choose how often I teach composition and what courses I teach. When I go into the staffroom, the lecturers and instructors there see me essentially as no more one of them than is the Shakespeare scholar down the hall from me.

THE EROSION OF A SERVICE IDENTITY

The conformity that intellectual communities unavoidably enforce operates in ways that are powerful while remaining hidden, and composition studies is no more free of such conformity than any other field. To the degree that we have bound ourselves to scientific methods of knowledge construction, more and more of what we do is, in Kuhnian terms, "normal science"—even if it critiques scientism. A field constructs itself, in part, by excluding the alien, and the range of variation of ideas that will be allowed before a person is effectively read out of the community is smaller than it has been. We do not mean to enforce conformity; it's just what communities do. And increasingly, what our community does is marginalize practitioners. In a talk at the 1991

Boston CCCC, Alice Calderonello made the claim—a strong one, and supported strongly—that composition disciplinarity is in part defined by devaluing practitioner knowledge. Donald Murray, who represents practitioner knowledge better than almost anyone, has told me that for over five years he has been unable to get his essays accepted by the major journals. Blind reviewed, his articles come back to him with readers saying they cannot recommend publication because the essay is "too quaint" or, in one case, "too Murrayesque." He has effectively given up on publishing in journals he helped make reputable. We cannot really blame journal editors for this situation, since they must listen to their reviewers. It is the socioculture of composition studies that has changed, out from under Murray and people like him.

The book publishers, too, have lined up on one side or the other, and there has been some movement toward marginalizing those presses that show an overt orientation toward serving teachers rather than scholars. Bob Boynton once told me that during the six years of Richard Larson's editorship of *CCC*, not a single Boynton/Cook book was reviewed in the journal. (That changed, of course, in the last Larson-edited issue, which carried three separate reviews of Knoblauch and Brannon's *Rhetorical Traditions and the Teaching of Writing* [1984].) Even the NCTE Press, which had for years been one of only two serious presses to publish composition material (SIUP being the other), entered a long decline in its reputation during the early 1980s, during which it was thought to be not quite serious enough, not quite scholarly enough—too "teacherly," in other words.

On the other side of the street, we've also seen a strong movement into composition of the specialty presses that had long served the social sciences: Ablex, Sage, Greenwood, Guilford, Erlbaum. These presses are happy to sign a narrow-focus scholarly book that will sell only 600 copies, mostly to libraries. Their economies of scale are much different from those of even university presses, since they typically price their books so high that they can make a profit on a small press run. The only people who lose are graduate students and those other scholars who cannot afford these expensive books. All of us have probably had the experience recently of planning a graduate course and being shocked to find that the five books we've asked students to buy total hundreds of dollars. Specialization and its attendant movement away from large markets for our writings is an inescapable result of disciplinarity.

Of course, the growth of our disciplinary identity is only part of this movement away from a primary identity as teachers of writing. In part, we seem not to believe quite so strongly that our practical work can make a difference. The world has changed around us, and we are far from the heady days of the 1970s when the doors of colleges were thrown wide to anyone who wanted to try and writing teachers plunged into trying to serve this new population. Mina Shaughnessy once told us that the process of coming to teach basic writers began, usually, with the attitude of wanting to "convert the natives." Elitist or wrongheaded though that attitude might have been, it was still determinedly optimistic. Today, however, with Shaughnessy's own

City University of New York open-admissions program shut down and with fewer and fewer colleges seeming to care about basic writers, how many new doctorates emerge from their programs with that sort of wrongheaded but idealistic missionary attitude? How many in our newly meritocratic world pine to tackle the problems of seriously underprepared students?

As the teaching and service elements of composition studies attenuate, the theoretical side of our field is, then, coming more and more to the fore. And for many of us, the question is beginning to arise: *Whom* does the theory serve? This is not simply querulous idealism, but a very practical question, because we have historically gained intellectual vitality from teaching and service. If we look at the geneses of the two most recent important theoretical developments in the field, we note that cognitivism grew out of questions that arose while teaching professional writing, and social constructionism originated in questions raised by basic writing. The development of theoretical approaches means that they can come to exist far from their pragmatic roots, as both those approaches often have. But both had deep roots in teaching, and the question still nags: out of service to whom will grow today's theories and tomorrow's? What connections are we forging to our world—to students and their needs—with the work we are doing in our journals and our conferences? From what practical or service question will the new theoretical ideas of tomorrow emerge?

I ask these questions of myself first, because I have seen so much change so quickly in this field, which I had never even heard of before 1975. After I entered it, I pushed as hard as I knew how for the respect that disciplinary status would bring to composition studies—and now I find myself thinking about the problems of answered prayers.

We wanted to escape the endless reinvention of the wheel that had long marked composition, that "what-to-do-Monday-morning" practical pedagogy that got our journals dismissed by literary scholars. We wanted to be a new kind of composition professional, and we are that. But what have we left behind in that staffroom? We sought seriousness in our literature, and we got it, in spades. We watched *CCC* covers turn from multicolored to brown to gray, and many writing teachers thought the contents of the journal followed the cover colors. And although the membership of CCCC has continued to grow, we have no way of knowing how many people who used to be members and who used to read *CCC* have fallen away. I was once shown a rejection letter from a journal stating that acceptable articles should "advance knowledge, not merely use it," and that dictum automatically cuts out a whole segment of the kind of people who formerly *were* the CCCC. In talking to instructors in my own program, I certainly hear that most of what's in the journals is no longer accessible to them, even if they used to read the literature. When Steve North, in his 1987 book *The Making of Knowledge in Composition*, put forward the concept of "practitioners" as differentiated from other people in the field, he was simply being truthful about a hiatus between teachers and scholars in composition that had been growing for more than a decade.

What I'm worried about is that our movement toward disciplinarity may be a movement away from the human meaning of what we do. In many of our specialized scholarly and theoretical books today, you are much more likely to find discussion of "writing" or of "discourse" than you are of "students." In fact, whether the favored theory is poststructuralism or cultural criticism, the tendency in today's professional dialectic is to problematize the student to the point where he or she becomes a theoretical counter on a conceptual board rather than the living, breathing person we formerly saw ourselves—naively, no doubt—as trying to help out. Some of us, indeed, have become so oriented toward doing our "real" work—research, publication, administration, public service—that we are in danger of becoming the sort of intellectual mandarins we once disliked when we met them in literary studies.

Mandarinism seems to me the worst danger attending our move into disciplinary status, because it nearly always means devaluation of service and teaching in favor of scholarship and reputation. We saw it in literary studies nearly a century ago, when literary scholars were determined to do away with the MLA's Pedagogical Section because the MLA was *not*, in the words of its president, James Bright, "a Gild of Barbers . . . a Teachers' Agency," or a group friendly to the "known class of advocates of 'methods of teachings,'" who were treated by the MLA to a "gentle but unflinching suppression" (1902, pp. xlvii–xlviii). We see the results in today's MLA. Though it is hard to imagine composition studies ever divorcing itself from teaching as thoroughly as the MLA has, our successes are increasingly defining us, and our growing identity as a discipline is endangering our traditional commitment to personally serving students. The American Council of Learned Societies has just admitted the NCTE, dropping its previous objection that our organization was too pedagogical, too little oriented toward research and too much oriented toward teaching students to write. So now we are officially learned. But with all our learning, there may be some simple truths we are in danger of forgetting.

POSSIBLE DISCIPLINARY FUTURES

Every developed discipline has its tacit or explicit ideological dictates, and every disciplinary dictate works in part by effacing some defined Other. The New Rhetoric marginalized what we used to call Current-Traditional Rhetoric. The Writing Process movement worked to erase the old formal correctness-based composition teaching. Cognitivism had an antipathy for "soft" theories and for politics. Constructivism ravaged empiricism and positivism and ended up all but obliterating cognitivism. Today, poststructuralism and feminism marginalize essentialism and foundationalism. Such intellectual enmities are all too familiar to anyone who has followed the history of literary studies over the past five decades. But composition teaching and the study of it have in the past served other needs and other primary ends. Issues of teaching students to write were once more than a background for the

movement of theoretical concepts, more than the profane and quantitative raw material of tenure cases and scholarly fame. Our successes have marked us, and they have changed our world. Will we return to that earlier and more service-based world again, and, can we?

I can only offer a few provisional thoughts. I am a historian, and social history teaches us to watch the demographics, because they undergird many other things. Our disciplinary demographics are shifting, and it may be that those changes will have a more profound impact on where we go from here than any theoretical shifts.

In 1977, there were eight doctoral programs in composition, the pioneering programs that produced most of the members of what I have called the third generation of composition scholars. Based mainly around rhetorical ideas, these programs were the only ones in a position to try to meet the need for composition specialists that resulted from the much-cried-up literacy crises of the late 1970s. New doctoral programs founded by the second and third generations of composition scholars burgeoned between 1977 and 1987, when Gary Tate and David Chapman found that there were 38 Ph.D. programs. But if the rate at which programs were founded went down after 1987, the sheer numbers of programs did not, and when Brown, Meyer, and Enos redid the Chapman and Tate survey in 1993, they found that there were 72 doctoral programs. By now it seems reasonable to assume that there are over 80 programs currently turning out composition Ph.D.'s.

There is a connection here between the growth of our discipline and the market's need for our students. Indeed, it would be a determined idealist who would argue that some large part of our growth into a discipline over the past three decades has not been built on the success our candidates have enjoyed on the otherwise terrible academic job market. We have all heard or experienced stories of composition students getting 15 or 25 job interviews at MLA, being wooed at campus interviews, and having their choice of good tenure-track jobs. At the same time, we have for two decades been watching talented literature candidates scrambling for any sort of position, knowing that their vitas would fall into that stack of 500 other vitas, knowing they were up against competition from elite schools as well as desperate assistant (and even associate) professors looking to improve their lots with a move. The terrific boom in composition jobs created a hothouse atmosphere that forced composition studies into bloom. Graduate students are not fools, and once the job market signals became clear, they responded. The older graduate student attitude (which some of you may remember from the 1970s) that composition-oriented doctoral students were "dupes" or "feebs" who could not compete in literary studies evaporated very quickly. The movement of many good graduate students into composition studies was what really fueled the foundation of the many programs that Brown, Meyer, and Enos found in 1993, when they estimated there were 1,174 students pursuing doctoral work in composition studies.

My point here is that the job market, which for the past two decades had been radically out of balance in favor of the seller, is returning, as markets do,

to equilibrium. We owe much of our rapid disciplinarity to the degree to which our doctoral candidates moved directly into good jobs that had to compete for them, but the seller's market we have so long counted on is coming to an end. It is not that good composition jobs are disappearing, but there *are* fewer of them than there used to be in the 1980s. In 1989, 158 of the 1,057 jobs in the October *Job Information List* were entry-level composition positions. We owned 15 percent of a large job market. In October of 1998, we owned almost 16 percent of the listed jobs in the *JIL*—but there were only 875 jobs in total, and only 139 were for our applicants. We are having to live in times of a shrunken market, but the real issue is that we are producing so many more people to fill the fewer jobs that are being advertised. In 1980, there were fewer than 50 people with composition Ph.D.'s; today, there are hundreds. If we assume that there are around 80 doctoral programs turning out Ph.D.'s today, and further assume that each program turns out an average of one finished candidate a year, then there is probably a job for every candidate. There are even some candidates—the very best ones, from the very best programs—who get multiple campus interviews, and even more than one job offer.

But are we now, will we be producing only 80 doctorates a year? With 1,200 doctoral students in the pipeline, even assuming some are on the 8-year plan, it is inescapable that we will soon be producing well over 100 doctorates a year, and perhaps closer to 200. Meanwhile, the boom in program foundations that produced the doctoral rush of the past two decades is easing off; most of the universities that want composition doctoral work in their programs have already built up their faculties in the field, and we are not likely to see huge new demands for ground-floor program creation. The need for good administrators will remain steady in both first-year programs and other writing-based programs such as writing centers and WAC programs, but these jobs are better suited for—and are usually filled by—experienced administrators or department veterans.

It may well be, in other words, that the 20 fat years that have forced our hothouse disciplinarity so quickly are coming to an end. The unbalanced seller's market that fueled our program growth, our journal foundings, and our presses and publishers is slowing, and composition studies will be affected—is already being affected—by its coming more into balance. More of our students will not get tenure-track jobs. Journals will have a harder time attracting enough subscribers to break even. University presses will not sign as many books. And our disciplinarity, for so long nurtured by kindly influences, will once again be shaped by other social effects. "Pull down thy vanity," says Pound in the Cantos, and the next 10 years may well work to bring us down closer to the same earth trod by other English department people.

I want to suggest that the end of the boom may not be a bad thing. During the late 1960s, when the left causes he had always fought for were in something of a vogue, the famous organizer Saul Alinsky said to his younger colleagues, "Don't worry, boys, we'll weather this storm of approval and emerge as hated as ever." Most of us entered the field of composition studies

not, God knows, because of careerism or the status the field could bring us, but because we really believed in the work and wanted to be of service to our worlds. The 20 fat years made us, but they also changed some of the ethical dimensions of the work, and not always for the better. I know I am not the only one here who has viewed the growing success and status—what I think of as the "MLA-ization"—of the field with strongly conflicted feelings. We entered composition work out of a deep dissatisfaction with the fatuity of overly specialized and theoretical literary studies—but we brought more baggage from that world than we meant to.

From here, it seems to me, our path of disciplinarity can go in one of two directions. In one model, we can continue to follow the example of literary studies, making theoretical sophistication, specialized expertise, and sheer scholarly output the prime criteria of success in the field. Approval of the approved theorists, mastery of one or two deep, tiny slices of the world of knowledge, and evidence of success in the form of the single-author critical book or the sheaf of articles from respectable journals—these will be our demands of composition scholars, and fulfilling them will be the unwritten law. We will be a modern discipline of the very sort blessed by the ACLS, and it will be natural for us to become more and more interlinked with the interests and professional attitudes of our literary colleagues. Though we'll be asked to run composition programs a little more often than our Americanist or cultural-studies friends, and though such service expectations will be considered one of the tiresome aspects of our choice of field, we won't need to worry about teaching writing ourselves any more than we want to. Under our direction, writing programs will run smoothly, staffed by instructors and graduate students we supervise. We'll teach our graduate courses on theoretical issues that interest us. Composition studies will end up being smaller, and a bit more competitive, but we'll be a completely familiar scholarly subfield of English studies, pursuing our own research in honorable obscurity and bothering no one.

The other possible model for composition studies as a discipline is less clear in outline, more muddled and uncertain. It produces scholars who embrace teaching and service as indispensable parts of the world of their research, and puts scholarly research in the service of action in colleges and universities. It exults in the complex and imperfect bungle of pedagogy and teaching issues as much as in the cool abstractions of research and theory. Doctoral candidates in composition studies are trained in administrative and programming issues as well as in history and theory, spending serious time in writing centers, staffrooms, WAC programs, and cross-curricular outreach as well as in English department classrooms. Publication is still expected for advancement, but it can take many forms—websites, textbooks, software packages, and program guides, as well as the more familiar books and articles. We remain open to many interdisciplinary influences, but with a skeptical enthusiasm rather than the credulous acceptance that marked our past. Most centrally, teaching writing and working with writing teachers are and remain the fundamental functions for specialists in composition studies.

In this model, working rhetorically in the world with writers is the continuing key to defining the field.

I don't know which of these models, or what combination of them, we will see. Analogies from the past take us only so far. We have made ourselves a *new* discipline, and despite our uncertainties, I don't think that most of us who helped build this world would choose to go back to a time when we were less self-aware. But real decisions loom up at us about where we will take this thing we have made. Primarily, we are still deciding whom we will serve—our students and our communities, or some more abstract and ideal world of scholarly discovery that is only tangentially attached to our originary roles as writing teachers. I think I have probably sufficiently betrayed my own biases. I am a composition teacher, defining myself as that before anything else. I'm also a scholar, and I hope to continue studying our history, which shows me over and over that whatever problems we have had in the past, the constant commitment of our best people has been to work with their students and serve their society rather than concentrating on narrow career goals or sterile intellectual puzzles. Teaching writing was the path of Ned Channing in 1850, of Fred Newton Scott and Gertrude Buck in 1900, and of Porter Perrin in 1950. Here, on the doorstep of the millennium, we could do far worse than try to follow in their footsteps.

NOTE

1. I feel curiously implicated in this naming, since I seem to have been the first to use the term in a journal article, "Composition Studies and Science," in January 1983. But the term was in the air, and though it was not completely accepted for several years—some people liked just "composition," some liked "literacy studies," some wanted to stay with "rhetoric"—the name seemed to stick.

REFERENCES

Bright, J. W. (1902). President's address. *Proceedings of the MLA, 18*, xli–lxii.

Brown, S. C., Meyer, P. R., & Enos, T. (1994). Doctoral programs in rhetoric and composition: A catalog of the profession. *Rhetoric Review, 12*, 240–387.

Calderonello, A. (1991, March). *Professionalization of rhetoric/composition: Consequences and commitment.* Paper presented at the Conference on College Composition and Communication, Boston. (ERIC Document Reproduction Service No. ED333 464)

Chapman, D. W., & Tate, G. (1987). A survey of doctoral programs in rhetoric and composition. *Rhetoric Review, 5*, 124–185.

Connors, R. J. (1983). Composition studies and science. *College English, 45*, 1–20.

Connors, R. J. (1989). Introduction. In R. J. Connors (Ed.), *Selected essays of Edward P. J. Corbett* (pp. xi–xxii). Dallas, TX: Southern Methodist University Press.

Connors, R. J. (1991). Rhetoric in the modern university: The creation of an underclass. In. R. Bullock & J. Trimbur (Eds.), *The politics of writing instruction: Postsecondary* (pp. 55–84). Portsmouth, NH: Boynton/Cook.

Harvard Committee on the Objectives of a General Education in a Free Society. (1945). *General education in a free society.* Cambridge, MA: Harvard University Press.

Kitzhaber, A. R. (1953). *Rhetoric in American colleges, 1850–1900.* Unpublished doctoral dissertation, University of Washington, Seattle.

Knoblauch, C. H., & Brannon, L. (1984). *Rhetorical traditions and the teaching of writing.* Upper Montclair, NJ: Boynton/Cook.

North, S. M. (1987). *The making of knowledge in composition: Portrait of an emerging field.* Upper Montclair, NJ: Boynton/Cook.

Perrin, P. G. (1936). *The teaching of rhetoric in the American colleges before 1750.* Unpublished doctoral dissertation, University of Chicago.

Warfel, H. R. (1959). Structural linguistics and composition. *College English, 20,* 205–212.

Frances Wright: First Female Civic Rhetor in America

Having written at length about the feminization of the nineteenth- and early-twentieth-century classroom and of the rhetorical instruction that took place within it, Bob became increasingly interested in particular women of the period, such as Angelina Grimke and Harriet Keeler. But "Frances Wright: First Female Civic Rhetor in America" (*College English*, 1999) is his first, and only, full essay devoted to a woman speaker. Bob tells her story with panache, summoning up the physical presence of Wright and describing the overwhelming response of the huge audiences she was soon able to attract. Bob's claim that Wright was "the first important woman who was a true civic rhetor" may or may not be upheld (425). The claim, however, is unnecessary to the story Bob weaves, based on a wealth of archival data that enriches our understanding of the milieu in which Wright came to national attention. Bob sees her career as, eventually, a failure brought on by pedanticism, an extreme reliance on rationalism and empirical observation, and her stands on child care, abolition, and the Woman question. In fact, Bob concludes that Wright "created conditions that hurt every woman speaker for fifty years after" (445). The orator who emerges in this essay calls out for our attention, and for further analysis, not only of her writings but of the cultural conditions and the ideologies in and that shaped those writings.

Sunday, July 13, 1828, a day of Ohio Valley summer, with oppressive heat and humidity.[1] Outside the brick Federalist-style Court House in Cincinnati, Ohio, a group of amazed citizens swirled, some seeking entrance, some there merely to gawk. Inside, the building was about half full; over two hundred men and a few women waited, murmuring about the extraordinary sight they had been promised. A woman was going to lecture, to a mixed audience of men and women, on a secular subject! She was known to some as a popular travel writer, to others as the founder of a notorious experimental community. Some of the audience members were excited, some

---

From *College English* 62.1 (1999): 30–57.

were merely curious—but a large number were ready to sneer, jeer, and hiss. This woman, famous though she might be, was by her behavior offending some of their most dearly held ideals about the proper conduct of womanhood.

At exactly seven o'clock, the crowd's babbling hushed as a tall figure in white made her way up the aisle to the platform. Frances Wright was thirty-three years old. She was unusually tall for a woman of that time, over five feet ten inches, and was dressed in a white muslin gown simply cut in the neo-Grecian style that was becoming popular. She wore no head covering and her dark hair was simply arranged, falling in natural ringlets. She stood for a moment facing her audience, which could see that she held a small paper book with her lecture in it. She was, then, perhaps merely going to read without looking up. That would not be so bad. She might yet be lady-like. Frances Wright lowered her face for a moment, took a breath, and looked out at the sea of friendly and unfriendly faces.

"Who among us," she began, not glancing at the book she held, "that hath cast even an occasional and slightly observant glance on the face of society, but must have remarked the differing opinions which distract the human mind; the opposing creeds and systems, each asserting its claim to infallibility, and rallying around its standard pertinacious disciples, enthusiastic proselytes, ardent apologists, fiery combatants, obsequious worshippers, conscientious followers, and devoted martyrs?" (*Popular Lectures* 4). She went on in a strong, clear, confident voice, with a slight Scots accent, delivering her first lecture, "On the Nature of Knowledge," which attacked religious enthusiasm and proposed that empirical and sharable evidence of a scientific sort was the only trustworthy knowledge.

The lecture took more than two hours, and as the preceding sample indicates, it was not simple. Yet the audience, which had come out of curiosity and perhaps to jeer, was increasingly quiet and attentive. Wright, though never given official training in rhetoric, was a natural orator. She consulted her notes only rarely, having memorized the great majority of her speech. She used facial expressions and gestures adapted from Gilbert Austin's *Chironomia*. Her diction was elegant, her presentation modest yet forceful, and one by one, she won her hearers. Frances Trollope, the mother of novelist Anthony Trollope, was traveling in America and had met and befriended Wright. She was in the audience that night and reported that "all my expectations fell far short of the splendor, the brilliance, the overwhelming eloquence of this extraordinary orator," and said that Wright's lecture produced "an effect unlike anything I had ever seen before or expect to see" (64). At the end of the lecture, the audience exploded in an uproarious ovation. Men and women cheered Wright enthusiastically. She was swept triumphantly away by friends, returning to finish her course of lectures over the next two Sundays to houses now packed, and then repeating, by popular demand, the entire course in August.

During the remainder of 1828, and then through early 1830, Wright toured the major cities of the Midwest and mid-Atlantic—St. Louis,

Louisville, Baltimore, Boston, and Philadelphia, ending up in New York—giving her lectures to great acclaim. She bought an abandoned church and turned it into a rationalist Hall of Science. She became a force in New York politics. For two years, no woman in America was more talked about. And yet today she is hardly known outside of a small circle of feminist historians, and she has had very little attention paid her by rhetorical history. In this essay, I want to look more closely at Frances Wright's career as a rhetorician and try to determine why she remains less known today than any other major female figure of the nineteenth century—a footnote to other, more understandable nineteenth-century feminists.

As Cheryl Glenn has demonstrated in *Rhetoric Retold*, women have always sought and found ways to utilize rhetoric. Since the medieval period, women's writing has been an important rhetorical performative act. A few women even managed to achieve roles as public speakers, usually in religious contexts. Frances Wright was not the first woman to speak in public. She was not the first woman to speak on nonreligious matters, and she was not even the first woman to speak to mixed audiences of men and women. But I believe that a strong case can be made for her as the first woman who was a true civic rhetor.[2] This is a stipulative definition, but each of the stipulations is historically important. A civic rhetor must be able to achieve ethical appeal, attain public notice, garner a forum for oratory, have access to a freely selected and voluntary mixed public audience, use rhetorical technae, and complete a non-homiletic oration to that audience in that forum. If we take these elements as our criteria for rhetorical practice, then Frances Wright was clearly the first important female practitioner of rhetoric to be found in American culture.

But Frances Wright is very little known in comparison to other, more sympathetic feminist foremothers. She is not found in the list of women orators in Karlyn Campbell's 1993 book *Women Public Speakers in the United States, 1800–1925*. Campbell regrets the omission (xix), but she never explains it. Wright is one of the subjects of Helen Heineman's *Restless Angels* (1983), which traces the letters and friendships of six nineteenth-century women friends, and merits a chapter in Elizabeth Ann Bartlett's *Liberty, Equality, Sorority* (1994), which discusses those three ideas in the feminism of Wright, Sarah Grimke, and Margaret Fuller.[3] But even Susan S. Kissel, who devotes more research to Wright than any nonbiographical book, says in her *In Common Cause* (1993) that Wright and her once-friend Frances Trollope, "remain virtually unknown throughout America today. . . . Few contemporary American women's histories or literary anthologies give more than a brief mention to either figure" (i). Frances Wright was and remains something of a pariah. Atheist, rationalist, anti-abolitionist, relentlessly abstract, she *is* an outsider, a figure genuinely alien to the women's public speaking tradition that developed in the United States in the nineteenth century. She stands outside the Christian-based, reform-minded women's rhetorical tradition that began with Maria Stewart and Angelina Grimke, riding the great emotional moral cause of abolition. She stands apart from the community-building

mutual-aid women's rhetoric of the Seneca Falls Convention and the temperance and suffrage movements. She stands apart, indeed, from her time, seeming to today's reader to have much more to do with the ideas behind the French Revolution than with those behind the American. Frances Wright was born perhaps too late; she was not really a reformer at all, but a visionary and revolutionary who had more in common psychologically with Condorcet than with Lucretia Mott or Sojourner Truth.

But she emerged as a woman of talent, privilege, and education into the ferment of Jacksonian America. The result was that she was the first female civic orator and that she was, finally, a failure as an orator. She took on huge issues in her lectures and orations, but she seemed to have no idea that successful oratory demanded emotional as well as rational appeal. Her style, always dense and periodic, became more and more turgid as she grew older, until her speeches became almost unlistenable. Imbued with the idea that an intellectual vanguard must show the masses the truth, she was almost completely insensitive to the feelings and predispositions of many of her hearers, even the most liberal, and she eventually alienated most of her friends and supporters. Although thousands flocked to hear her for a few years, her audiences then melted away because she had little idea of the practical elements of ethos or pathos. Rather than preparing the way for the slightly later group of abolitionist and feminist speakers, Frances Wright's legacy to them was a poisoned distrust of women speakers that proved an obstacle to female rhetors as late as the Civil War.

Feminist scholarship has shown clearly how women had to fight their way into many intellectual disciplines during the last two millennia of Western culture, but *no* discipline was as closed to them as rhetorical study. The essential stricture placed on women's speaking was to *public mixed* audiences of men and women, not on speaking to private family gatherings or to more public audiences of women only. Mixed gatherings of men and women were called "promiscuous" gatherings, from the Latin *promiscuus*, mixed or indiscriminate. It was only with Quakerism in the seventeenth century that a widely popular and evangelical Christian sect first began programmatically to claim the right of women to preach. During the eighteenth century, real strides were made in the areas of women's education, but the Quaker flouting of age-old proscriptions against women's speaking to public mixed audiences continued to be the exception to the rule. Such midcentury English bluestockings as Hannah More, Elizabeth Montagu, and Hester Chapone also argued that women's educational boundaries needed to be expanded — but each of them stopped short of claiming that women should preach or be trained in rhetoric or oratory. The most far-reaching and powerful work to emerge from the eighteenth century on this question was Mary Wollstonecraft's *Vindication of the Rights of Woman* in 1792. Wollstonecraft argues that education of men and women should be equal, that they should all learn together, and that superior students of both sexes should be taught "the dead and living languages, the elements of science, and continue the study of his-

tory and politics, on a more extensive scale, which would not exclude polite literature" (353).

In America such coeducation after grammar school was particularly slow in coming. Until the nineteenth century, women never shared higher schooling with men. As the authors in Catherine Hobbs's *Nineteenth-Century Women Learn to Write* have demonstrated, women in many spheres had to struggle to even learn to read, and more women read than wrote. The strict classical curriculum long taken for granted in all-male colleges was for most of history completely unavailable to women, who were even shut out of reading about educational questions and issues because they were seldom taught Latin, the language in which most learned discourse was conducted. Even with the establishment after the American Revolution of common grammar schools, higher education for women over age twelve was rare. As American culture matured, however, and the essentially agrarian nature of the society began to give way to manufacturing, a newer urban bourgeois class grew up, and the status of women in America changed (see Hobbs 5–19). Women in the American Northeast after 1800 were becoming a more cultivated class, and in the increasingly egalitarian world of late Federalism, it was inevitable that many of the old strictures that kept women from more public lives would be challenged. This was the world into which Frances Wright emerged when she and her sister Camilla first sailed from Glasgow to New York in 1818.

Born in 1795, Frances Wright was twenty-three when she first landed on the soil of the country to which she had devoted so much study. An orphan since age three, she had been raised in Scotland and Devonshire by a maternal aunt. Finding their aunt's attitudes too conservative, Wright and her sister left her house in 1816 to live with their great-uncle James Mylne, Professor of Natural Philosophy at the University of Glasgow. Mylne, who was called by his students "Old Sensation" for his insistence that knowledge comes only through the senses, held the chair at Glasgow that had been Adam Smith's. Wright became interested in America as a result of her growing awareness of the injustices suffered by the poor of England and Scotland. In her autobiography, she writes (as always, in the third person):

> Her sympathies were powerfully drawn toward the sufferings of humanity, and thus her curiosity was vividly excited to discover their causes.... Upon one occasion, peculiarly distressing to her feelings, her soliloquy was to the effect that some strange secret—some extraordinary vice, lay at the foundation of the whole of human practice. What [sic] should she devote her whole energies to its discovery? At the close, she pronounced to herself a solemn oath, to wear ever in her heart the cause of the poor and the helpless, and to aid all that she could in redressing the grievous wrongs which seemed to prevail in society. (*Biography* 11)

For Wright, the United States represented a way out of the political and cultural stasis she felt in Europe. As a teenager, she had found in her aunt's

trunk an Italian history book about the American Revolution, which fascinated her. As she says in her autobiography,

> From that moment she awoke, as it were, to a new existence. Life was
> full of promise; the world a theater of interesting observation and useful
> exertion. There existed a country consecrated to freedom, and in which
> man might wake to the full knowledge and full exercise of his powers.
> To see that country was now, at the age of sixteen, her fixed but secret
> determination. (11)

Much of Wright's subsequent autodidactic education revolved around
her interest in this nation, which was the closest thing the post-Napoleonic
world offered to a large-scale radical social experiment.

So now, in the late summer of 1818, Wright and her sister walked down
the gangplank of the *Amity* into New York City. During this first visit to
America, which lasted from 1818 through 1820, Wright and Camilla traveled
through many of the states of the Northeast, met and became friends with
several prominent families, and even met President Monroe. They did not go
into the American South, because Wright was so revolted by the sight of slavery in Washington and northern Virginia that she could not go farther into its
stronghold. As she wrote to her friend Robina Millar in Scotland, "the sight
of slavery is revolting everywhere, but to inhale the impure breath of its
pestilence in the free winds of America is odious beyond all that the imagination can conceive" (*Views* 267). Throughout the two-year journey, Wright sent
a steady stream of letters back to Mrs. Millar, and when she and Camilla returned to England in 1820, Wright arranged, rewrote, and added material to
these letters to produce a book manuscript, which was published in 1821 as
Views of Society and Manners in America.

Views became an immediate best-seller in both England and America and
made Wright famous. The book went against the grain of most English travelogues about America, which tended to be very critical; Wright praised most
aspects of the new nation effusively—its beauty, its cities, its people, and especially its liberty. Most Americans loved it, and Whigs in England praised it
as well. Wright became a friend of the influential utilitarian philosopher
Jeremy Bentham on the basis of its success and added his ideas to her expanding philosophy. The book also sold well in France, as a result of which
Wright emboldened herself, on a visit to Paris in 1821, to introduce herself to
the sixty-four-year-old Marquis de Lafayette, hero of the American and
French Revolutions, at his estate, La Grange. This meeting, which she described as being fraught with her tears of emotion at meeting the hero of the
Revolution, began the relationship between her and Lafayette that was to
provoke so much scandalous whispering. She all but joined Lafayette's family circle, wrote him copiously while away from him, and in general seems to
have adopted him as the father she had never known. When Lafayette was
invited in 1824 to tour the United States and receive the thanks of the current
generation, Wright and Camilla joined him on the tour and traveled through-

out America in 1824 and 1825, both in Lafayette's entourage and by themselves.

While traveling through the Midwest, Wright met Robert Owen, who
had been working to set up his communal town of New Harmony, Indiana.
Owen, who had been a wealthy millowner in England, had become one of
the most radical philosophers in the English-speaking world, condemning
private property, marriage, and religion. He wanted New Harmony to prove
that communal living need not be based on religious ideas, and Wright was
much impressed by the town she saw and by Owen's ideas.[4] During this tour
of America, the Wright sisters did venture south into the slave states, and
once again Wright was horrified at the reality as well as the idea of slavery.
She began to meditate on a plan to end slavery without stripping slaveholders of the millions of dollars of capital they had tied up in their human
"stock." Melding the communal ideals of the antireligious Robert Owen and
the mystical George Rapp that she had seen at New Harmony with the intention of freeing slaves, she came up with her own plan to end American slavery: Wilderness land and some slaves would be bought; the slaves would
work the land for cotton during the days and be educated in communal
schools at night; since the slaves knew they were working for themselves,
they would strive hard, and all the produce of the plantation would be sold
in order to allow the slaves to buy their freedom with the proceeds of their
own work. Thus slaves could work for six or eight years to purchase their
own freedom, and white slaveholders would not be robbed of their property.

Wright felt it had to work. Leaving Lafayette, she and her sister traveled
to Tennessee with Robert Owen's son, Robert Dale Owen, to start their own
slave-freeing community, which they called Nashoba. With some of her inheritance, she and Camilla bought 2,000 acres near Memphis and fifteen or so
slaves. Both sisters tried hard to convince their English and Scots friends and
correspondents, including Frances Trollope and Julia and Harriet Garnett, to
move to Nashoba and join the community. From 1826 through 1830, Frances
worked at, lived in, defended, and was deeply involved with the two communal endeavors, Owen's New Harmony and her own Nashoba.

Both communities failed. By 1827 the lack of a powerful central doctrine
or a charismatic enough leader had reduced New Harmony to the beginning
of a gradual privatization. Though Nashoba faced a much more difficult
physical situation—a plantation had literally to be torn from a woodland
and living places built from nothing—it had seemed to go well through 1826
and early 1827. As long as Wright was there, the high ideals of community and education seemed to prevail over the frontier hardships, but when
the climate made her very ill in the spring of 1827, she was forced to leave
Nashoba for Europe or face death. In her absence, the community was run by
Camilla, who did not have her sister's strength of will, and by James
Richardson, a Scotsman who had joined Wright earlier when she was buying
land. In Wright's absence, Richardson ran Nashoba in very authoritarian
ways and published a description of the community's activities in the abolition newspaper *The Genius of Universal Emancipation* in 1827. This description

was unconsciously horrific in its portrait of the life of the slave-workers at Nashoba,[5] but its greatest effect arose from its final section: "June 17 [1827]. James Richardson informed [the slaves] that, last night, Mamselle Josephine [a quadroon, daughter of Mamselle Lolotte] and he began to live together; and he took this occasion of repeating to them our views on color, and on the sexual relation" (*Genius*, 28 July 1827).

This admission that Nashoba stood for open sexual commerce between black and white members without benefit of marriage led to the characterization of Frances Wright in all her later life. Returning from France, Wright wrote a long statement she published in the Memphis newspaper defending racial mixing, condemning marriage as "tyranny," and claiming that the marriage law had no force at Nashoba. It would have been difficult to come up with positions in 1827 that would have defied the proprieties of the era more completely. Many of the Wright sisters' friends shrank from them, especially after both Camilla and Wright defended Richardson in letters and in print. After the attendant publicity, Wright became the "red harlot of infidelity," and Nashoba became known as "Fanny Wright's free love colony." She became a somewhat notorious national figure. Even Professor Mylne, the Wright sisters' rationalist uncle, was appalled, writing a friend that "I rather fear that her excessive passion for Notoriety has led to an incipient disorder of the mind."[6]

By the time she returned to Nashoba in 1828, it was becoming clear to Wright that the commune was a failure. The slaves, who could not see eight years of indentured servitude as a realistic road to freedom, would not work unless forced, the community had lost a great deal of money instead of making it, and the remaining trustees drew up a new charter that dissolved the most radical aspects of the colony. Robert Dale Owen returned to New Harmony, and in May of 1828 he invited Wright and Camilla to join him there. Nashoba as a radical social experiment was over. Wright moved in May to New Harmony, her communal experiment a failure but her desire to serve her time undiminished. In New Harmony, Wright began to edit the *New Harmony Gazette* with Robert Dale Owen. It was here, during this summer, that she was to begin her career as a lecturer and orator. She was asked to give the July Fourth address at New Harmony Hall, and did so, her address marking the practical beginning of her speaking career (though since New Harmony was still at this time made up mostly of friendly Owenites, this address was not completely "public," as were her later ones). She then proceeded to Cincinnati, where she gave the first of her public lectures.

Wright saw her immediate purpose, especially when she began her lectures, as arguing against the growing tide of Protestant revivalism that was sweeping America, a tide we now know as the Second Great Awakening. Southern Ohio was particularly hard hit by this powerful religious movement, and Wright's teeth were set on edge by the growing power of what she could only see as irrational "priestcraft." Women were especially victimized by this "odious experiment on human credulity," and as she says in the Preface to her first book of lectures, "a circumstantial account of the distress and

disturbance on the public mind in the Ohio metropolis led me to visit the afflicted city; and since all were dumb, to take up the cause of insulted reason and outraged humanity" (*Life, Letters, and Lectures* ix). For three weeks in July and again for three weeks in August, Wright delivered her lectures in Cincinnati. She argued for reasoned knowledge based on sharable empirical facts, against the "insatiate priestcraft" that lay behind American Christianity with all its hostility toward social reform, in favor of equality between men and women, against slavery, and in favor of a system of national education that would create equality of knowledge, a prerequisite for equality of condition. Each of her lectures was packed, at least in part because they were free and people were anxious to see something so unusual. And unusual it was.

It is difficult for us today to understand the power of the prejudice that Wright flouted by speaking in Cincinnati. As Mrs. Trollope put it, "[t]hat a lady of fortune, family, and education . . . should present herself to the people in this capacity would naturally excite surprise anywhere . . . but in America, where women are guarded by a seven-fold shield of habitual insignificance, it has caused an effect which can scarcely be described" (63). In part this sensational effect created great popularity for her lectures, and with the Cincinnati series, Wright began what was to be the most successful and notorious two years of her public life. She finished her second course of lectures in late August and returned to New Harmony by way of Hamilton, Ohio, and Louisville, Kentucky, where she also gave the lectures. At each stop, she was lionized, even mobbed, and invited to stay in the homes of leading liberal citizens. In September she was back at New Harmony, making plans with Robert Dale Owen to turn the small *New Harmony Gazette* into a national paper devoted to the cause of reform and liberal thought—a paper to be called *The Free Enquirer*. In October she and Camilla returned to Nashoba to begin winding up things there, since she had by then decided that it was "a poor appropriation of her talents to sit down and devote herself to the emancipation of a few slaves" when she could do so much more good by lecturing and editing the *Gazette* (qtd. in Eckhardt 181). She planned a national lecture tour, without Camilla but with Robert Dale Owen and Robert Jennings, an associate from New Harmony.[7] She would go by steamboat from Nashoba up to St. Louis, then across Illinois and Indiana by stage, back to Louisville, then up the Ohio River back to Cincinnati, to Wheeling, West Virginia, disembarking at Pittsburgh, then by stage across the Alleghenies to Baltimore, to Philadelphia, and finally to New York City, the intellectual and cultural heart of America. She set out from Memphis in early November, and on December 31 found herself off Manhattan, after two months of amazing and exhausting travel and lecture.

Why did Wright embark on this course of lecturing, so unusual, so much opposed to the customs of her time? The answers seem to be multiple. First, with the failure of Nashoba, she needed a public cause. She had gotten used to a certain amount of public notice as an author, as Lafayette's friend, as a reformer and communard, but all that was now in the past. With the restlessness that had been a hallmark of her entire adult life (she seems to have

crossed the Atlantic no fewer than seventeen times between 1818 and 1850, to say nothing of her travels within Europe and America), she sought movement outward, away from the old and the failed. In editing the *NHG* and in her lectures, she found a forum that would allow her to see herself and her friends as a vanguard of progressive thinkers, using the paper and her lectures to prepare the way for the new vision that America had been promised and deserved. She wished to obtain subscriptions to the paper and did indeed sell hundreds in each city in which she lectured. Wright also thought that the country desperately needed to hear what she had to say—and needed to hear her say it. Though Wright's philosophy was primarily synthetic (the ideas behind Nashoba and her first lecture tour were compounded of Owenite antimarriage and antireligion themes, the utilitarianism of Bentham, the rationalist empiricism of Adam Smith, the commonsense philosophy of Thomas Reid, the feminism of Mary Wollstonecraft, and the antislavery feelings of British Whiggery) her synthesis was timely, and her energy and vitality in promoting her radical philosophy, her imposing physical presence, and above all, her gender, made her and her ideas a beacon and a lightning rod for the next few years. Her absolute refusal to honor what she thought of as outdated prejudices freed her to take on roles no other woman had approached; by condemning religion, segregation, racial purity, and marriage law, she opted out of the conventional moralities of her time. She was utterly fearless in saying and doing things no other woman could or would say or do during that period, and she took the shrill scorn of her critics coolly.

Her first lecture tour was a success on its own terms and a *succès de scandale* as well. Everywhere she went, huge crowds turned out to hear her; in the letter after letter she wrote back to Camilla (who was pregnant and had to stay at Nashoba) about her successes, we get an idea of the huge interest people had in hearing a woman speak publicly: "I gave my lecture here [Memphis] last night. I think we shall do good and did so then in preventing the foundation of churches and the introduction of preachers in the place"; "My last discourse at St. Louis produced an effect beyond any I have yet delivered"; "They are very anxious for us to settle in Cincinnati, and were we to do so I have little doubt but that we should gradually unite the great mass of the population in a wider knowledge of true moral principle and practice"; "I gave five lectures in successive nights [in Baltimore] to an audience whose pressure seemed to endanger the building. I can give you no conception of the stir in the public mind which my lectures have occasioned during the past week. . . . [In Philadelphia] there was difficulty in procuring a building large enough and the pressure was so excessive that men and women fainted dead away, notwithstanding which the attention was so highly wrought that order and silence were never interrupted" (qtd. in Perkins and Wolfson 220–24). It seems clear that the lectures themselves were well known and that Wright was becoming famous.

The attacks on Wright during this tour were mild in comparison to those she would see later. Someone tried to disrupt one of her Baltimore lectures by

shouting "Fire!" in the theater, but the audience, noting Wright's stoical refusal to panic, did not trample out. In Louisville the *Focus* attacked her broadly, announcing that she "has with ruthless violence, broken loose from the restraints of decorum, which draw a circle round the life of women; and with a contemptuous disregard for the rule of society, she has leaped over the boundary of female modesty, and laid hold upon the avocations of man, claiming a participation in them for herself and her sex" (qtd. in *Free Enquirer*, 10 Dec. 1828). She seems mostly to have been attacked during this tour from pulpits. Clergymen were completely accurate in thinking of Frances Wright as their worst enemy, and they castigated her as a "priestess of Beelzebub," a "female monster," an "unnatural woman." Still, her two-month tour was successful. She then arrived, at the end of 1828, in New York City, where she determined to settle and work because "all things considered, this is the most central spot, both with respect to Europe and this country" (Wright to Camilla, 5 Jan. 1829, qtd. in Waterman 168).

Wright would stay in New York, lecturing and editing *The Free Enquirer*, until July 1, 1830, when she left for Europe. It was an extraordinary eighteen months. She began lecturing in early January, and all of the New York newspapers sent correspondents to cover her speeches (including the young journalist Walt Whitman, who remained dazzled by Wright until his death). The first reports on Wright's lectures ranged from coldly descriptive to amazedly complimentary. William L. Stone of the *Commercial Advertiser*, who would become Wright's worst critic, was initially charmed by her abilities as a speaker:

> Her enunciation is perfect and she has complete command over it. Her emphasis and pauses and the whole of her delivery are excellent, and her gestures appropriate and graceful. So far as these qualifications constitute an orator, we believe her unrivaled by any of the public speakers of any description in this city.... That there was much eloquence of style added to that of manner and the keeping of the whole performance was so good that the sensation of the ludicrous naturally suggested by its novelty was entirely suppressed. (qtd. in Perkins and Wolfson 228)

Charles King in the *New York American* described the first lecture in a less admiring tone:

> A tall ungainly figure, of masculine proportions, dressed in broadcloth, evidently a woman's riding habit.... In her hand, neither white nor well-turned, her lecture. A gold watch suspended from her girdle.
>
> An English face proclaimed the welcome fact that she was no country woman of ours. Hair parted in the middle, ringlets on either side, complexion reddish and wind-worn. Her eye bold and fearless yet glazed and unsteady as if its energies had been wasted by midnight study or its lustre marred by indulgence and by sorrow.
>
> She stood unmoved, broke silence in a clear strong voice, uttered coldly and with scrupulous enunciation a string of truisms.

> Opinions half-way between later Scotch metaphysicians of the School of Reid and the inductive philosophy of Lawrence and the London Physiologists. (qtd. in Perkins and Wolfson 228)

Other newspapers were, if not complimentary, at least not condemnatory.

These were, we must note, the reactions to Wright's first lecture, which was meant to set the stage for her later ones. It dealt mainly with epistemology and did not go into the radical social prescriptions of her later speeches. When the genuine tenor of her beliefs became known a few weeks later, the welkin of New York rang with ever more-heated denunciations of her. Her criticism of Christianity and the clergy in particular maddened her enemies. While she was still at the Masonic Hall, someone placed a barrel of turpentine in the doorway and set it on fire; only Wright's coolness of mind prevented a panic. At another lecture, someone turned off the gas, leaving the hall in darkness. She rented a theater for a second set of lectures, and the *Evening Post* issued a dark warning to the theater owner:

> Suppose the singular spectacle of a female, publicly and ostentatiously proclaiming doctrines of atheistical fanaticism, and even the most abandoned lewdness, should draw a crowd from prurient curiosity, and riot should ensue, which should end in the demolition of the interior of the building, or even in the burning it down—on whom would the loss fall? (26 Jan. 1829)

And William Stone, after hearing more of Wright's ideas, turned against her viciously, deriding "her pestilent doctrines, and her deluded followers.... She comes among us in the character of a bold blasphemer, and a voluptuous preacher of licentiousness.... No rebuff can palsy her—no insult can agitate her feelings. It is iron equally in her head and heart; impervious to the voice of virtue, and case-hardened against shame!" (qtd. in Eckhardt 186)

Even with the attacks coming from all directions—at this point not a single New York newspaper supported her—Wright's lectures were vastly successful, turning away thousands of people and attracting an increasing number of women. She settled in upper Manhattan, renting a large house, and in April 1829 she used more of her inheritance, paying $7,000 for an old Baptist church and converting it into a Hall of Science, with a seating capacity of 1,200, offices for the *Free Enquirer*, and a bookstore. Camilla moved from Nashoba; Robert Dale Owen came from New Harmony; William Phiquepal D'Arusmont, the New Harmony printer, came with three students to help print the paper; and by June 1829 Wright had established her own small community of like believers. She plunged into politics with her usual energy, acting as a central figure to a group calling themselves the Free Enquirers, writing new lectures to add to her series, speaking out strongly on questions of workingmen's rights, women's rights, and democratic education. The rights of workingmen and the dangers of centralized economic power came to be more and more important to her analyses, and she entered

into a second East Coast tour, giving her growing course of lectures in Wilmington, Delaware, Philadelphia, and Boston.

The summer of 1829 was the height of the Jacksonian era in American politics, and doctrines more radical than had theretofore been seen in America were openly discussed. Though Wright did not share the most radical opinions involving proposals to end private property, her lecture on "Existing Evils and Their Remedy," delivered first in Philadelphia, put forth a proposal even more radical: that children be taken from their parents at the age of two and raised and educated by the state, which was the only institution that could guarantee true equality of opportunity. She continued to rail against the clergy, who could no longer dismiss her as marginal. Lyman Beecher in Boston felt compelled by the work of Wright and her friends to respond to the threat of "political atheism" they represented:

> About this time the female apostle of atheistic liberty visited the city, and her lectures were thronged, not only by men, but even by females of respectable standing. And the effect of these lectures on such listeners was not the mere gratification of curiosity. She made her converts, and that, too, not among the low and vicious alone. Females of education and refinement—females of respectable standing in society—those who had been the friends and associates of my own children—were numbered among her votaries, and advocated her sentiments. (92–93)

Beecher's fears about Wright's effects on women were widely shared. At this time, too, Wright began to speak out against other corruptions, corruptions in the press, in the Second Bank of the United States, in Tammany Hall. She also began to attack the radical abolitionist position of William Lloyd Garrison and his growing group of followers, saying that she found among them "more party violence than enlarged philanthropy. Hatred of the planter seemed oftentimes to be a stronger feeling than interest in the slave" (qtd. in Perkins and Wolfson 256). Once again the issue of the property value of slaves kept Wright from joining the growing antislavery consensus for total abolition, and she continued to recommend gradual emancipation on the cooperative principle, as had been attempted at Nashoba.

And the Nashoba experiment now loomed again, interrupting this most successful public portion of Wright's life. She had promised to conduct the Nashoba slaves to Haiti, the only black-led state in the Americas, and free them there. In October, following one last frantic round of lecturing in the Northeast, she and Phiquepal D'Arusmont, who knew Haiti and spoke the language, left New York. Traveling by land and water through New York state, through Pittsburgh and Cincinnati, to Nashoba, then downriver to New Orleans and by ship to Haiti, Wright used this trip to lecture at every stop. She and Phiquepal took ship for Haiti with their slaves in January 1830. They spent two months in the black republic, during which time she ceremoniously liberated her slaves and later met with Haiti's president. In the spring, she returned to New York, where she began lecturing again

immediately, with her usual great success. She was attacked by the main-stream press as usual, but instead of her usual ability to turn the other cheek, even to unfair and personal slurs, Wright this time seemed to feel she should withdraw. On June 8, she announced that she was returning to Europe, since she had become so much a target that her name was hurting rather than helping causes she believed in. On July 1, she took ship with Camilla for France, where she promptly disappeared from the ken of all her American friends.

The actual reason for Wright's rapid resignation of the ground in New York was personal: She was pregnant by Phiquepal and was due around the end of the year, and she could neither marry him nor bear an illegitimate child in America. She had sworn public opposition to marriage and said she would never marry. In what must have been an intensely painful and con-flicted decision, she fled to Europe and disappeared into France with Camilla, not to return to America until 1835. We know very little of Wright's life during this period, but Celia Eckhardt has pieced together what must have happened: Wright arrived in France in the summer of 1830 and gave birth to her daughter Sylva around December. Wright married Phiquepal in July 1831 under unknown psychological circumstances. She gave birth again in April 1832, but the child died before the age of three months, and Sylva was given this dead child's birth date, a fiction that Wright maintained all her life (as did Sylva). During this time, Wright seems to have had some break in relations with Camilla, who was living separately in Paris at the time of her death in February 1831 (Heineman 86), kept in only the most tenuous touch with her American and English friends, and generally seems to have suffered some sort of breakdown.

By the time Wright returned with Phiquepal to America in 1835, she faced a very different cultural situation, and the country in which she had once found fame as well as notoriety was now prepared to give her only the latter. Jacksonianism, which had been in full tide in 1830, was now embat-tled, and Nat Turner's 1831 rebellion had pushed the slavery question onto a completely different and much more desperately contested level, with both sides forcing all public figures to declare their principles. Wright plunged back into public lecturing, starting in Cincinnati, but to her still powerful abilities to draw a crowd was now added a lurid notoriety. Wright was known for her opinions on religion, marriage, and racial mixture, and she never seemed to realize that people came to see her speak after 1836 because those opinions were so universally rejected that she had become the most in-famous woman in America. "Fanny Wrightism" became the sobriquet for any position that people wished to ridicule as extreme. Though she contin-ued to describe herself as a reasonable rationalist, her popular image was that of a crazed radical.

In addition, she was now taking positions that satisfied neither her old friends nor her new allies. She remained steadfast to Jacksonian ideas, which led her to support Martin Van Buren in 1836 after having earlier condemned party politics completely. More important, she seemed trapped by the Demo-

cratic party's general support of the property rights of slaveholders and continually spoke out against the radical abolitionist wing of the antislavery movement: "I now *fully know* what I formerly surmised, that the question of slavery is . . . a pretext for the fomenting of disorder and the breeding of disunion" (*Popular Lectures II* x). Although abolition was the burning question of the day, she continually tried to minimize its importance when she spoke, claiming that it was just one part of the larger issue of the degradation of labor, and that slavery could be ended by the purchase and repatriation to Africa of all slaves—through mechanisms she did not specify. Increasingly, she spoke abstractly of the evils of the Bank of England and its conspiracies against the working people, abetted by its weaker analogue, the Second Bank of the United States.

Wright's career as a speaker after 1835 was never the progress of liberal triumph she had enjoyed from 1828 to 1830. She was denied use of theaters for many of the lectures in 1836 and once had to lecture in an abandoned factory. The newspaper responses to her lectures were even more vicious and apoplectic than six years earlier, and now that Wright was middle-aged and less attractive, they became personally insulting as well. The New York *Commercial Advertiser* called Wright "a great awkward *bungle* of womanhood, somewhere around six feet in longitude, with a face like a Fury, and her hair cropped like a convict's" (20 Oct. 1836). Catharine Beecher, herself active in the movement for women's education, could not abide Wright's attacks on religion and descended to personal insults:

> Who can look without disgust and abhorrence upon such an one as Fanny Wright, with her great masculine person, her loud voice, her untasteful attire, going about unprotected, and feeling no need of protection, mingling with men in stormy debate, and standing up with barefaced impudence, to lecture to a public assembly. . . . There she stands, with brazen front and brawny arms, attacking the safeguards of all that is venerable and sacred in religion, all that is safe and wise in law, all that is pure and lively in domestic virtue. . . . I cannot conceive any thing in the shape of a woman, more intolerably offensive and disgusting. . . . (22–23)

Beecher speaks here for all women who felt that Christianity was no enemy but a bulwark for their efforts to change their culture. Almost universally they rejected any comparison of their positions with Frances Wright's.

Wright continued to write and lecture, but by 1838 the culture had changed so radically that a woman with her background could not continue as a public speaker. In September 1838, she began a series of five lectures on the Independent Treasury Bill at the Masonic Hall in New York—the place she had lectured to such approbation nine years before. The first lecture was calm. At the second, the audience exploded, both shouting imprecations and applauding enthusiastically. Wright was able to calm that outburst and continue, but a week later her third lecture was broken up by the roars of the mostly male mob, who shouted, "'Put her out! Put the old bitch out!

Down with her!' etc., accompanied with sundry expressions too indecent to mention" (*New York Gazette*, 12 Oct. 1838). The next Sunday was the most extreme. There were five thousand people in the hall and Wright completed her lecture, but meanwhile over ten thousand had surrounded the Masonic Hall. They demolished the platform after her lecture and attacked her carriage as she was leaving (Gilbert 71). This was the closest Wright had come to serious violence against her person, but she was nothing if not fearless. When she finished the series a week later, a wave of revulsion for the violence offered to women had swept the city, and she was not molested.

But her days as a lecturer were almost over. She was unable to rent Tammany Hall after the Whigs won the 1838 elections, so she rented a small hall in a bad part of town for a series of twelve lectures (now lost) given from January through April 1839. It was a sad ending to what had had a mighty beginning. "When I look round this narrow space," said an obviously disappointed Wright in her first lecture, "I feel that both they whom I address and I who speak want that inspiration which the presence of thousands alone can impart" (qtd. in Eckhardt 269). Elizabeth Oakes Smith has left us a report on what Wright's last course of American lectures was like:

> I remember that we went upstairs and turned into a very dirty, dimly lighted hall, filled with straight wooden benches, and only three persons in them. The appointed hour had already arrived, and slowly, men, one after another, sauntered in—several women also, some with babes in their arms, and all bringing an atrocious odor of tobacco, whiskey, and damp clothing. At length there might have been fifty persons, not more, present, and these began to shuffle and call for the speaker. It was all so much more gross and noisy than anything I had ever encountered where a woman was concerned, that I grew quite distressed, and the bad atmosphere nearly made me faint, but I was too eager to hear to admit the idea of going out.
>
> Finally the door in the rear of the desk opened, and a neat foot was placed upon the platform. . . . She was a full-sized woman, handsomely shaped, dressed in black silk with plain linen collar and cuffs. Her head was large but not handsome, forehead low, but broad, indicating force and executive ability. She wore her hair short, but it could hardly be said to curl, waving slightly. Her features were all good, and the smile, sweet, with a touch of feminine sadness, eyes well set under the broad, not high, brow, which was marked by long horizontal lines. She was pale, but not sallow, and there were an earnestness and wholesomeness about Fanny Wright that made their way to the mind and heart.
>
> Her gestures were very few and natural, and in good taste. . . . She was at intervals applauded but did not seem to expect or care for it. I should not call her eloquent. She imparted no glow, but she was argumentative and forceful. She made no religious allusion, and said not one word which any sound-minded man might not have said with approval. (83–85)

Wright finished her series of lectures, but she was deeply disappointed. From thousands of adoring admirers in 1830, she was speaking now to "a mere haphazard audience curious to see the woman whom everybody abuses" (Wolfson's copy of lecture notes, qtd. in Eckhardt 269). The newspapers had decided that the best way to work against her was to ignore her completely. Criticism and even hatred she could stand, but being ignored was almost unbearable. She ceased her last lecture with abuse of her audience: "Since it seems, however, that mere curiosity is the only motive which drew [the audience] in the first place, it is certainly more than time for me to desist not only from the present but from all other labors in the public service" (final lecture, qtd. in Perkins and Wolfson 339). She sailed with Phiquepal and Sylva for the Continent six weeks later and never lectured in America again. She attempted a lecture comeback in 1847 in England, speaking at a radical Unitarian chapel on "The Mission of England Considered with Reference to the Civilizational History of Modern Europe," but she canceled the series after her fourth lecture, claiming a nervous attack but probably discouraged by the small numbers in the audience.

The rest of Wright's story is unhappy and soon told. She worked on and published in 1848 a book called *England, the Civilizer*, which was too hermetically written and filled with radical fantasia to be very popular. She traveled extensively, moving around in England and Scotland and to France and America with a velocity that suggests today's jet travel rather than the sail and steam of the 1840s. She lived apart from her husband and daughter much of the time, and her driven need to be active and activist eventually drove a wedge between her and her family. Sylva chose to live with Phiquepal, and when he chose—monstrously and against all their previous understandings of marriage—to assert his husbandly right over Wright's property, she sued for divorce, which was granted in 1850. She won her property suit, but she was completely alienated from her daughter. In January 1852, she slipped on ice in Cincinnati and broke her thigh. After intense suffering for almost a year, she died of complications of the injury on December 13, 1852.

So what are we to make of Frances Wright as a rhetor? What were the reasons for her success and for her failure? Wright knew rhetorical theory and ideas and had great natural talents. We must ask, then, why her speaking career, which began so well, ended so badly, leaving her without an audience and leaving a popular impression of women orators that would be a burden for female abolition and suffrage speakers in America for decades to come.

We should first consider what *kind* of rhetorical training and experience Wright had. Her uncle, James Mylne, was a respected philosopher in his own right and a conduit through whom his nieces met some of the major figures of the still vital Scottish Common Sense School of philosophy, a rationalistic and empirically based epistemological movement that was to have powerful effects on Wright's own philosophy. Elizabeth Ann Bartlett has carefully traced the intellectual environment within which Wright moved while living with her uncle and has been able to draw lines of influence from the ideas of

Locke, Berkeley, Voltaire, Condillac, Condorcet, Wollstonecraft, Stewart, Reid, Smith, Hume, and Jefferson (30–31). During the three years Wright and Camilla spent living with the Mylnes in Glasgow, they were not allowed to take university courses officially but were given complete access to the university library. Here Wright certainly came into contact with the classical philosophies and particularly the Epicurean ideals that informed her first writings, and here she almost certainly came into contact with the Scots New Rhetorics of the period 1749–1781—the ideas of Smith, Campbell, and Blair. We can, unfortunately, only speculate on the rhetorical reading and conversations to which she may have had access. Her reading included great numbers of classical authors, but we do not know the depth of her reading in the great classical rhetoricians. It is reasonable to assume that Wright had read Campbell and Blair and knew rhetoric in its belletristic and epistemological senses.[8]

She knew, in other words, mostly theoretical rhetoric; her rhetorical skills were all from books. Though Blair does deal some with practical preparations for speaking, neither his book nor Campbell's was meant as a rhetorical handbook of practice. The rhetorical tradition specifies, of course, that the rhetor must be trained in both *ars* and *exercitatio*, but there was little possibility for guided rhetorical praxis for girls in Glasgow in 1815. Even assuming that Wright read Austin's *Chironomia* or Thomas Sheridan's books on elocutionary techniques, she had no cultural or educational milieu in which to practice them or to have her efforts critiqued by a trusted mentor until long after she was a formed intellect with ingrained habits. Thus her rhetorical preparation was nearly all done in isolation. Joel Brown, a carpenter who came to know Wright in 1843 when she had moved back to Cincinnati, wrote a memoir of her (still in manuscript) in which he describes her preparation:

> Her manner of getting up an address was new to me. She would write a few minutes, then get up and walk whispering to herself, repeating what she had written. She learned all of her lectures by heart and delivered them extempore. I have often met her in the street talking to herself in whispers. . . . I have known her to walk three miles to see friends, whispering to herself, looking neither to the right nor to the left. She was never idle, always reading, writing, or repeating what she had read. She had a wonderful memory. (6–7)

Clearly, Wright's rhetorical skills were all self-taught, with the strengths and weaknesses of such isolation.

Just as Elizabeth Ann Bartlett examines Wright's philosophy in terms of its relations to the ideas of liberty, equality, and sorority, a useful way of examining her rhetorical career is in terms of the classical appeals: ethos, pathos, and logos. In terms of ethos, the appeal of the character of the speaker, we need to look beyond the large ethical issue of her femaleness. Wright presented her audience with huge paradoxes, and her public career is a tale of bright beginnings and blighted endings. This ethical failure was not, it seems, a result of any diminution of her powers as a speaker; even at the

ghastly end in the Clinton Theater, Smith's description is of a woman who still offers much traditional ethical appeal. Something else had changed, and it destroyed Wright's abilities to project herself as a person of probity and trustworthiness. We could put the problem down to the world changing around Wright, as it certainly did between 1828 and 1848, but the world is always changing around any rhetor. Although the heady days of Jackson's first term were certainly more propitious times for political ideas of a very radically populist sort than a few years later, changing times cannot be the whole case. Wright *did*, in fact, change some of her ideas in later years, finally rejecting racial mixing as a solution to slavery—but it did not help. People still did not want to listen to her.

The problem with Wright's ethos lies in what we can only refer to as her solipsism—another effect of her rhetorical isolation. She was so sure of herself and her ideas that she simply would not make very strong attempts to forge bonds with any community. Even those people and institutions she admired for a time—such as Lafayette, Robert Owen, and New Harmony— she eventually left behind. Toward the end of her life, she had systematically cut her ties with almost everyone who had been her friend in earlier years. Her marriage lasted so long primarily because she and Phiquepal lived together so little. She brooked no opposition to her will, and when questioned by friends or supporters, she would simply cut the relation, as she did with Fanny Trollope, Julia Garnett, Robert Jennings, Robert Dale Owen, and many other people who had been loyal friends. Even her worshipful sister Camilla realized that Wright excluded her.[9] Wright seems to have developed early on a sort of megalomania, the idea that she was meant to play a central role on the world's stage as a leader and prophet, and she was not sensitive to the overtones of self-aggrandizement this attitude created. The epigraph to her second volume of lectures from 1836—which is today much rarer than the first volume—illustrates this tone deafness:

> To the People of the United States: Receive, Fellow-citizens of my adoption! this second volume of discourses, prepared, as was the first, for your mental instruction—at all times indispensable for, and now, more certainly than ever, preparatory to, an increase of moral contentment and physical ease. Receive it, Fellow-citizens! and study it in the same spirit which has inspired its counsels; namely, a spirit of active, untiring, and all-devoted love to this nation and to humankind.

As Eckhardt, a very sympathetic biographer, says, at some point "the self-confidence she had needed to break from her past—to dare things that women had not dared before—had hardened into a blinding self-importance" (250).

In terms of her public life and persona, Wright's increasing alienation meant that she had and seemed to want no part in the powerful liberal social movements that were forming after 1835. Where in 1828 the cause of what she called "liberalism" (those who supported her on her tours she often

referred to in letters as "the libs") embraced many possibilities and could include people of many social-improvement beliefs, by the late 1830s the movements had begun to sharpen their focus on two main causes: to abolish slavery and to gain women political rights. Although both of these causes were dear to Wright and she spoke of them often, her solutions were her own and she would accept no others. She wanted a Nashoba-style solution to slavery, not Garrisonian unconditional emancipation, and so she rejected the political group that would have been her most natural ally. Women's rights would come, she believed, from an understanding of the need for general state-sponsored education for all, and not from suffrage movements or women's-rights conventions like Seneca Falls. As Bartlett says, "Wright viewed our humanity as fundamental, and she denied the significance of subdivision by sex, race, or any other category" (51). Most important, Wright consistently rejected the religious and specifically Christian bases that gave the abolition, temperance, and suffrage movements so much of their own ethical appeal. By declaring so early in her life a rejection of religion and making secular rationalism the basis of everything she argued for, Wright lost any possibility of using the ethos inherent in sharing a metaphysic with her audience. Thus we see such a fearless writer as Margaret Fuller ignoring Wright in *Woman in the Nineteenth Century*.[10] Thus we see her attacking and being attacked by abolitionists, from whose ranks the next great American female civic rhetor, Angelina Grimke, would come in 1837,[11] and thus we see early feminists such as Lucy Stone and Antoinette Brown striving to distance themselves from her by the 1840s, when "Fanny Wrightist" or "Fanny Wright man" were synonyms for crazed radicalism among women (Lasser and Merrill 35). In 1850 Sarah J. Hale wrote about Wright, "[i]f such women are trained rightly, what noble beings they become!" but lamented that "the misfortune of her early training" had led her into "the heavy servitude of infidelity" (842–43).[12] Only after Wright's death did some American suffragists feel they could praise her contributions to the ideas that undergirded their movement.[13]

For her own part, Wright was never much interested in portraying herself as part of any movement she did not lead. It is ironic that early biographies characterize her as a "reformer," because that is exactly what she refused to be. In her uncompromising dedication to her own radical ideas, in her admiration for the French leaders of 1789, in her thoroughgoing critique of life as it actually was lived and in her demand that it be renovated from the ground up, Wright was always a revolutionary. "Every passing event announces the dawn of a new era," she said in late 1829, "proclaims a new epoch in the history of man, foretels [sic] for all the civilized world, and first for this nation, as first in the ranks of civil liberty—foretels a REVOLUTION" (*Popular Lectures* 174–75). And her revolutionary refusal to join forces with the proponents of mere reform—in the person of abolitionists and early feminists—led to the diminution of her ethical appeal. Ethos is, after all, the appeal that reveals to the audience that the speaker is like them, has their attitudes and interests at heart, is *of* them. Wright was not of them, but set her-

self up increasingly as an uncompromising teacher. She had fewer and fewer pupils as the years went on.

Wright's handling of pathetic appeal, the appeal to audience emotions, seems always to have been her weakest point. As "Oliver Old-School" said in criticizing her Cincinnati lectures, "[i]f chaste diction, and logical deduction from assumed data, delivered with an air of determined purpose . . . be eloquence, she possesses it" (Cincinnati *Saturday Evening Chronicle*, qtd. in *Free Enquirer*, 1 Oct. 1828). She either did not know how to approach moving the emotions of an audience or, more likely, she did not believe in doing so.[14] Though she would sometimes address audiences with fervor—"Oh, my fellow beings! let us leave these inconsistencies to those who teach them!"— Wright was bitterly resentful of what she thought of as spurious uses of pathos by the revivalist preachers of the Second Great Awakening, and it is probable that she deliberately set out to be a speaker antithetical to their tactics and uses. In her "Address to Young Mechanics," she shows that she is aware of pathos as a necessity—"Whosoever in these days, would be listened to, *must* address himself to the reason; but in so doing, he will be most injudicious who neglects the conciliation of the feelings, or even who despises the pleasing of the ear"—but the whole tenor of her discussion of oratory is disparaging of rhetoric as it was practiced in her day (primarily by preachers): "No art has been more abused than that of oratory. . . . It has been pressed, even openly, into the service of injustice, falsehood, hypocrisy, superstition, and corruption" (*Supplement* 203).

From her practice, Wright seems always to have believed that right knowledge itself would move hearers to do what was right—to use Campbell's terms, she assumed that addressing the understanding would move the will. The result of this assumption was a speaking style that is relentlessly high-minded, relentlessly explanatory, and emotional only in the sense of reflecting outraged reason. Wright's style of speaking had hardened as early as 1829; after seeing her speak in November, Frances Trollope wrote to a friend about "that dry, cold, masculine, dictatorial manner that has been growing . . . since [Wright] commenced her public lectures" (letter to Julia Garnett Pertz, 12 March 1830). In all the descriptions we have of her lectures and speeches, there is not a single indication that she ever moved her hearers to any emotion other than rational enthusiasm for or virulent anger against her ideas. There is no suggestion that she *sought* a wider emotional range. Of any attempt to move her auditors to sorrow, pity, mirth, swelling outrage, righteous indignation, fear, or any other primary emotion, we hear nothing. As a rationalist, Wright probably took pride in her cerebral speaking and would have bridled at the suggestion that emotion should be part of the human response to persuasion. (As Smith said, when Wright was applauded she "did not seem to care for it.") We also know how unmoved she was by verbal abuse, which she could take and give back smartly. Fervent support and howling condemnation alike were milieus with which she was comfortable, but no other emotions seem to have entered her rhetorical vocabulary.[15] This dismissal of pathetic appeal partly explains Wright's essential difference

from Stewart, Grimke, Martineau, Stone, and the other early female civic rhetors who followed her. It also may illuminate why her speaking career faded while theirs blossomed. As long as Wright could count on ethos and logos working to bring an audience in, she could discount the element of pathos, but when ethos faded and logos no longer spoke to popular issues or positions, her deliberate rejection of emotional appeal left her largely without an audience.

In terms of logos, Wright had some great strengths but some corresponding weaknesses. If you turn back to the opening of this essay and look again at the first sentence in Wright's first lecture, you will begin to get an idea of the situation. Here, obviously, is the voice of a woman who knows her subject, has thought about and digested it, and who has a clear idea of how she wants to begin treating it. Wright's lectures—especially the early ones, when she had not entered the solipsistic isolation of her later period—are logical, rigorous, philosophical-sounding expositions of her positions on such issues as religious revealed truth. As philosophical disquisitions on rationalism, these lectures are effective. But they are, as we have noted, relentlessly abstract. As one of her correspondents wrote her in 1829, he was surprised that he could understand her at all, "as many of the remarks and positions laid down by you were necessarily of an abstract and metaphysical nature" (qtd. in Eckhardt 210). Even when she was arguing for specific candidates such as Van Buren or specific policies such as the Treasury Act, Wright's natural tendency in treating subjects was to speak from the large, abstract, and metaphysical side of an issue. She was *not* adept at moving from abstract to specific and back again—a movement necessary for successful oral delivery more than for writing. Her lectures smack of the schoolroom.

In terms of her stylistic effect, Wright's writing would not sound strange to any reader of Blair or Hume. She was a classic English prose stylist of the period of her youth—which is to say, of the late eighteenth century.[16] Here is a typical example from her lecture on religion:

> For myself, pretending to no insight into these mysteries, possessing no means of intercourse with the inhabitants of other worlds, confessing my absolute incapacity to see either as far back as a first cause, or as far forward as a last one, I am content to state to you, my fellow creatures, that all my studies, reading, reflection, and observation, have obtained for me no knowledge beyond the sphere of our planet, our earthly interests, and our earthly duties; and that I more than doubt, whether, should you expend all your time and all your treasure in the search, you will be able to acquire any better information respecting unseen worlds, and future events, than myself. ("Religion" 67)

As many testified, her language was pure and her diction admirable, but from our vantage point we can also see that her stylistic choices were better suited to written prose than to oral delivery. She was addicted to periodic sentences, which must be handled with great subtlety in oral discourse, and

she overused them at times. What is simple is thus made more complex for style's sake: "The more I considered the evil of slavery, and approached it in comparison with the other evils that corrode the face of society, the more distinctly I perceived them to have not only the same root, but to be, in fact, only different phases of one and the same thing" (*Popular Lectures II* 78). Even her loose sentences were often very long, strung together with many added clauses, and all too often she approaches turgidity. Unlike her extant letters, which can be informal and can show a keen sense of human-to-human interaction (especially her earlier letters to Camilla), her lectures are didactic, high-sounding, and a little pompous. She was, in other words, more naturally a prose stylist than a speechwriter. In the final analysis, she was impressive as a lecturer but pedantic as an orator: a clear, precise, rather dry, and ultimately rather dull speaker.

Frances Wright's story is one of the most extraordinary and finally one of the saddest in the history of rhetoric. She was a woman of amazing talent and ardor for good, and the vision she shared with others in her Transcendentalist generation of a better life for all through "just knowledge" resonates today. But like the French Deputies of 1789 she so admired, Wright was a failed revolutionary. She wanted to live according to her powerful theories about renovating humanity and was tormented by her own inability to do so. Her culture changed around her rather cruelly, and she seemed unable to change with it. She alienated her friends and family, and her only child, unable to bear her mother's company, became a conservative religious antifeminist. Throughout her life, there seemed to be whole levels of feeling and significance she would not or could not pay attention to. At the end, her name synonymous with craziness, loose morals, and bad judgment, Wright was remembered with derision by her enemies and with regret by those who would have been her friends. As a pioneer woman speaker, she did not blaze a trail that made others' travels easier, but instead created conditions that hurt every woman speaker for fifty years after. And today Wright's beliefs are no more in vogue than they were in 1835. Her extreme reliance on rationalism and science; her absolute trust that empirical observation alone can produce true knowledge; her idea that taking children from their parents at age two for a proper state-run education could solve the world's problems; her extreme respect for property, which prevented her from supporting abolitionism though she hated slavery; her complete lack of interest in the women's movement, which was born during a very active phase of her public life, make her as alien to the ideas and ideals of today as she was to the nineteenth century. She is still too radical in too many eccentric ways for most academics today, and so instead of the commemoration of Wright we might expect from the current generation of historians recovering women's rhetorical history, she is the least well known of that group of extraordinary nineteenth-century women who brought us into the modern era of gender relations. I hope this essay will help to give Frances Wright the rhetorical status she deserves, for as our first female civic rhetor, her seriousness, intelligence,

and success—fleeting though it was—have still not been recognized completely today.[17]

NOTES

1. There is some uncertainty about the date of Frances Wright's first course of lectures, illustrating problems modern scholars have with her story. The primary materials are gone. Both Waterman in 1924 and Perkins and Wolfson in 1939 had access to a trunk of Wright materials belonging to Rev. Norman Guthrie, Wright's grandson, who was very elderly when Perkins and Wolfson took notes from his materials. The trunk included letters, clippings, lecture notes, a scrapbook Camilla Wright kept for her sister, and many other irreplaceable items. The trunk has since disappeared, and when Eckhardt came to write her modern biography in 1984, she was forced to rely on secondary sources—on Waterman, who is precise but stilted and sometimes lacking detail, on Perkins and Wolfson, who are talky and sometimes careless, and on Theresa Wolfson's notes taken on the Guthrie trunk materials. Wolfson's notes are valuable, but they are, like much of Perkins and Wolfson's scholarship, hurried, incomplete, and often lamentably imprecise. Working with Frances Wright materials is textual carnivalization in action.

So, the date of the first Cincinnati lecture. Eckhardt, who is reliant on public primary sources, gives it as August 10, on the basis of a mention in the August 27 *New Harmony Gazette* as "Sunday the tenth of last month," since no Sunday in July fell on that date (316, n. 10). But both Waterman and Perkins and Wolfson, who had access to the now missing trunk of Wright materials, state that Wright delivered her first three lectures twice in Cincinnati that summer, the first time at the Court House on three successive Sundays in July, "and again by special request on three successive Sundays in August at the theater on Main and Sycamore streets" (Perkins and Wolfson 211). Since we know Wright was at New Harmony on Friday, July 4, and that the journey up the river to Cincinnati must have taken at least three days, she could not have given her first Sunday lecture until July 13, with succeeding lectures on the 20th and 27th. Eckhardt's surmise is reasonable, but I tend to trust Waterman and Perkins and Wolfson more than she does, especially where they had access to primary sources that she did not. Thus the date in the *NHG* is probably a typographical error or a misreading by Phiquepal, the printer, of what must have been a longhand story sent back from Cincinnati by Robert Dale Owen. Specific data on the Cincinnati lectures is also found in a letter from Camilla to Harriet and Julia Garnett, dated November 20, 1828:

> The prejudice regarding her opinions was there [Cincinnati] as elsewhere so strong that her first lecture was but thinly crowded & scarcely one female form was to be descried. The second the house was crowded, and at the 3rd upwards of 500 individuals were obliged to return without accommodations. . . . Having delivered four lectures she was publicly requested to repeat them, which she did with renewed success & increased interest. (qtd. in Heineman 73)

2. I use the term "civic rhetoric" in the same sense that Gregory Clark and S. Michael Halloran use it in discussing the civic basis of oratorical culture in their *Oratorical Culture in Nineteenth-Century America*. I am obviously using a slightly different definition of "civic rhetor" here than that proposed by Janet Carey Eldred and Peter Mortensen in their recent *College English* article. Civic rhetoric in their work is "grounded in an oral, neoclassical tradition" but actually found in "texts that represent women's schooling" (174). My stipulative definition of civic rhetoric is more traditionally disciplinary, demanding that the text be orally delivered in a fully public secular rhetorical situation.

3. Bartlett finds Wright to be strong in her support for the feminist ideas of liberty and equality for women but weaker in her support for the feminist ideal of sorority.

Given Heineman's uncovering of the way in which Wright took for granted and then all but abandoned her devoted sister Camilla, who died soon after, it is easy to accept Bartlett's assessment. But Bartlett, like other contemporary scholars, tends to elide those ideas of Wright's that are still anathema to feminist theory today, such as her anti-abolitionist stance, her denigration of the suffrage movement as bourgeois, and her utopian tendency to see the family as the root of most human evil. Bartlett does not deal in any detail with any of the ideas Wright advanced after 1844. As this essay was in galleys, I saw Carol Mattingly's fine essay, "Friendly Dress: A Disciplined Use" in the Spring 1999 issue of *Rhetoric Society Quarterly*, an essay which speaks of Wright at more length than any other I know in the field. Mattingly devotes five pages to Wright, mostly concerned with her physical presentation of self and its public reception. Mattingly made me aware of how this essay, too, opens with a description of how Frances Wright *looked* as she gave her first lecture. Even so keen an observer as Mattingly, however, seems to equate Wright's antislavery feelings with pro-abolitionist positions — which she never accepted.

4. It should here be noted that the physical site of New Harmony had been bought by Owen from George Rapp, who had founded his religious community of Harmonie there nine years earlier. Rapp moved on to Economy, Pennsylvania, with his band of hardy German religious pioneers, leaving to Owen the beautiful small town they had built for a payment of $125,000. The New Harmony communal experiment lasted only from 1824 to 1827, after which the community gradually turned into another small Indiana town.

5. The slaves were not, for instance, permitted to eat except at public meals. Children were taken from mothers and put into the care of a central authority, whose permission had to be gotten before parents could even see their children. A slave woman who was sexually molested in her bedroom by a male slave was refused a lock for her door as a door lock was "inconsistent with . . . a doctrine we are determined to enforce, and which will give to every woman a much greater security than any lock can possibly do" (*Genius*, 28 July 1827). The editor of the *Genius* did not publish several other parts of Richardson's report, in which he describes whipping female slaves with a leather belt and reprimanding parents for speaking to and feeding their children. As Celia Eckhardt puts it, the overseers of Nashoba, however good their intentions, seem to have been "made monsters by theory" (145).

6. James Mylne to Julia Garnett, August 12, 1827. This letter shows clearly how shocking Wright's racial and sexual views were even to "enlightened" European rationalists. Mylne was horrified by Wright's and Camilla's defenses of the Nashoba sexual situation, especially after he had tried to suppress news of it in Glasgow by buying up all available copies of the newspaper in which it appeared, *The Genius of Universal Emancipation*. He was also shocked that Wright had gone to Europe to recover from an illness, leaving Camilla alone at Nashoba in the society of negroes or "whites whose intellects seem to be destroyed & whose moral feelings are I fear ruined by the absurd principles of her senseless system." Mylne was particularly disappointed because he expected so much of Wright's genius and thought she could advance rather than retard the cause of atheism and rationalism. But he despairs of his "poor and infatuated niece," fearing he may in future be forced to conceal their relation. For the ways in which this eventually affected both sisters, but most especially Camilla, see Heineman 35–80.

7. Camilla could not travel because she was pregnant at this time by Richeson Whitby, a Quaker who had joined the Nashoba group. Against Wright's and her own stated views on marriage, Camilla had married Whitby, writing to her friend Julia Garnett that she could only explain why in person. The marriage was not a happy one and did not continue long; the baby died suddenly in 1829. See Heineman 35–45.

8. Though Wright reports only her readings concerning the United States, it is difficult to imagine that she did *not* know the important rhetorical ideas of her day. This

is surmise, of course, because we have few details of her earlier life or reading, but it seems completely reasonable to assume that Wright, while living with Professor Mylne, read and spoke with others about the popular New Rhetorics of Campbell and Blair—perhaps even Adam Smith's rhetorical ideas were mentioned, though they did not then have wide printed currency. We know, for instance, that in addition to Mylne's occupying Adam Smith's chair at Glasgow, he and his nieces were friendly with the Millar family, which had been close to Smith. George Campbell of Aberdeen had died in 1796, but his *Principles of Rhetoric* was recognized as the primary Scottish-School statement on rhetoric, and of course Hugh Blair of nearby Edinburgh, dead for only sixteen years, had published his famous *Lectures on Rhetoric and Belles-Lettres* in 1784. These were intellectual Scots educators, and though the great days of the Hibernian universities were over, Scots contributions to the tradition of rhetoric were part of what they could point to with pride over the previous fifty years.

9. Camilla wrote to Harriet Garnett in February 1830, while Frances was in Haiti with Phiquepal, "Yes, dear Harriet, to your bosom I will confide the painful truth—the sister—the friend with whom I have suffered much & with whom I have sympathised still more is no longer the sharer of my thoughts & feelings & only ceased to be so from my discovery that *I shared not hers*" (qtd. in Heineman 83). The rest of this passage goes on with a wrenching rationale in which Camilla accuses herself of selfishness in expecting that "minor objects of interest" in Frances's life, such as her sister, should have any precedence over Frances's commitment to her public life, the "cause worthy of her talents & which I consider as all important to the welfare of generations yet unborn." Thirteen months later, Camilla was dying alone in Paris, with her sister living across town.

10. This was, of course, the same Margaret Fuller who would conduct her "conversations" on literature and culture at Peabody's bookshop from a seated rather than from a standing position, so that no one would take her for a public lecturer.

11. Grimke herself was aware of how damaging any association with Wright could be to her and her cause, and at first she lectured only to all-women's gatherings to avoid the charge of conducting "Fanny Wright meetings." Only gradually was she able to gain enough ethos and confidence to open her meetings to mixed audiences. See Lumpkin 98–113.

12. Hale's entire short article is worth reprinting here for the insight it gives us into the ways in which women viewed Wright late in her career. Appearing in Hale's compendium *Woman's Record*, this was written, we can guess on the basis of internal evidence, around 1850:

> Darusmont, Frances. Better known as Miss Fanny Wright, was left an orphan at the age of nine years, with a younger sister, the two being heirs to a considerable property. They were placed under the guardianship of a man who was an accomplished adept in the philosophy of the French Encyclopaedists. Her parents had been strict Presbyterians, and, apparently, she was brought up in that faith; yet the poison of the French philosophical ideas was instilled with zeal into her young and eager soul, that should have been moulded by a pious mother's wise care; for, with warm feelings and a mind of strong powers, Fanny Wright had an enthusiasm of nature which *would* have its way. If such women are trained rightly, what noble beings they become!
>
> When Miss Wright came of age, she found that the Old World was a hard field for her philanthropic plans. She had been taught by her infidel friend, and honestly believed, that religion, or the priest, rather, was the greatest obstacle in the way of human happiness and social improvement. She therefore came to the New World to see another phase of society. Her travels and observations at that time extended through three years, from 1818 to 1820; and her work, "Views on Society and Manners in America," evinced a hopeful mind, enlarged and liberal political views, with no expressed hostility to the Christian religion, which she

found here not in state establishments, but in the hearts of the people. Her second work, "A Few Days in Athens," published in 1822, is dedicated to Jeremy Bentham. In this she endeavours to prove the truth and utility of the Epicurean doctrine—that pleasure is the highest aim of human life. It is written with vigour, and the classic beauty of its style won much praise; but its tendency is earthward.

Miss Wright returned to America about 1825, and settled at Nashoba, Tennessee, with the avowed intention of cultivating the minds of some negroes whom she emancipated, and thus proving the equality of races. Her philanthropy was doomed to disappointment. She finally abandoned her plan; came to the eastern cities and began a course of lectures, setting forth her particular views of liberty. She was followed and flattered by many men in New York, particularly, who formed "Fanny Wright Societies," with notions of "reform" similar to those of the present communists of France. Rarely did an American woman join her standard, and so Miss Wright could find no true friend; for between the sexes there can be no real bond of generous sympathy without Christian sentiment hallows the intercourse. Miss Wright left America for France, where she had before resided. Here she married M. Darusmont; a man who professed her own philosophy; the result has not been happy for her. They separated some years ago; she returned with their only child, a daughter, to America, where she owns landed property. Her husband is endeavouring to wrest this from her, and the matter is now undergoing investigation in the law courts of the West. Meantime, Madame Darusmont has recommenced her philanthropic labours on behalf of the coloured race. In justice to her, it must be said that she is not like the fanatics who would destroy the Union to carry out an abstract principle of human rights—she seeks to prove the slave may be made worthy of freedom, and she does this at her own care and cost. There is no doubt that she has sought to do good, and it is a sorrowful thought that such a mind should have been so misdirected in its forming-time. We have been told by a lady who lately conversed with Madame Darusmont, that she ascribes her errors of opinion (there is no substantial charge against her purity of conduct) to the misfortune of her early training; that she has freed herself from many of these errors, and we hope she will yet be redeemed from the heavy servitude of infidelity, and find that true liberty and happiness which the Gospel only can give the human soul. (842–43)

Both the general tone of Christian regret and the factual errors and elisions tell us much about the attitude of liberal but nonradical women like Hale.

13. By 1860 Ernestine Rose was praising Wright at the Tenth National Women's Rights Convention, and in 1881, Elizabeth Cady Stanton, Susan B. Anthony, and Matilda Joslyn Gage used a portrait of Wright as the frontispiece of their massive *History of Woman Suffrage 1848–1861*. But posterity has remembered Stanton and Anthony and left the difficult Wright much less known. For excellent detail about the early suffragists and liberals who most admired Wright, see Kissel 94–114. Kissel's coverage of Rose's and Lucretia Mott's admiration for Wright is particularly useful, as is her discussion of how much Walt Whitman admired Wright throughout his life. Kissel does not speak directly to the evidence found elsewhere of how toxic Wright's reputation remained during her lifetime, even among most suffragists and feminists.

14. In *Views of Society and Manners*, Wright states that successful orators display "[a]nimation, energy, high moral feeling, ardent patriotism, a sublime love of liberty, a rapid flow of ideas and of language, a happy vein of irony, an action at once vehement and dignified, and a voice full, sonorous, distinct, and flexible" (374). Note the qualities, such as a sympathetic heart and an understanding of an audience and its feelings, that Wright does not mention.

15. Wright herself admitted that she did not seek demonstration from her audience; in a letter to Julia Garnett, she said even before 1831 that human coldness "has made me hold cheap both the public censure and the public praise" (frag. 30, n.d.).

16. She was also a poet of some skill in the Byronic vein, but as she aged, she increasingly rejected poetry as she valorized reason. For an example of her poetry, see Owen.

17. This essay is a palimpsest of editorial help, and I want to thank John Trimbur, who originally suggested it and who helped shape the first version, the readers for *College English*, who brought me up to date on current Wright scholarship, and Louise Z. Smith, whose careful editorial suggestions curbed my habit of swamping readers in a welter of data.

WORKS CITED

Bartlett, Elizabeth Ann. *Liberty, Equality, Sorority: The Origins and Interpretation of American Feminist Thought: Frances Wright, Sarah Grimke, and Margaret Fuller.* Brooklyn: Carlson, 1994.

Beecher, Catharine. *Letters on the Difficulties of Religion.* Hartford: Belknap, 1836.

Beecher, Lyman. *Lectures on Political Atheism.* Boston: Jewett, 1852.

Brown, Joel. Unpublished memoir of Frances Wright. Public Library of Cincinnati and Hamilton County: 6.

Campbell, Karlyn Kohrs. *Women Public Speakers in the United States, 1800–1925.* Westport: Greenwood, 1993.

Clark, Gregory, and S. Michael Halloran, eds. *Oratorical Culture in Nineteenth-Century America: Transformations in the Theory and Practice of Rhetoric.* Carbondale: Southern Illinois UP, 1993.

Eckhardt, Celia Morris. *Fanny Wright: Rebel in America.* Cambridge: Harvard UP, 1984.

Eldred, Janet Carey, and Peter Mortensen. "'Persuasion Dwelt on Her Tongue': Female Civic Rhetoric in Early America." *College English* 60 (1998): 173–88.

The (New-Harmony Gazette and) Free Enquirer. New Harmony, Indiana; New York, 1825–1835.

Garnett-Pertz Papers. Houghton Library, Harvard University, Cambridge.

The Genius of Universal Emancipation. Baltimore, Maryland, 1826–1828.

Gilbert, Amos. *Memoir of Frances Wright, the Pioneer Woman in the Cause of Human Rights.* Cincinnati: Longley, 1853.

Glenn, Cheryl. *Rhetoric Retold: Regendering the Tradition from Antiquity through the Renaissance.* Carbondale: Southern Illinois UP, 1997.

Hale, Sarah J. *Woman's Record, or, Sketches of All Distinguished Women.* New York: Harper, 1870.

Heineman, Helen. *Restless Angels: The Friendship of Six Victorian Women.* Athens: Ohio UP, 1983.

Hobbs, Catherine, ed. *Nineteenth-Century Women Learn to Write.* Charlottesville: UP of Virginia. 1995.

Kissel, Susan S. *In Common Cause: The "Conservative" Frances Trollope and the "Liberal" Frances Wright.* Bowling Green: Bowling Green State U Popular P, 1993.

Lasser, Carol, and Marlene Deahl Merrill. *Friends and Sisters: Letters between Lucy Stone and Antoinette Brown Blackwell, 1846–1893.* Urbana: U of Illinois P, 1987.

Lumpkin, Kathryn Du Pre. *The Emancipation of Angelina Grimke.* Chapel Hill: U of North Carolina P, 1974.

Mattingly, Carol. "Friendly Dress: A Disciplined Use." *Rhetoric Society Quarterly* 29 (Summer 1999): 25–45.

Owen, Robert Dale. "An Earnest Sowing of Wild Oats." *Atlantic Monthly,* July 1874: 67–77.

Perkins, A. J. G., and Theresa Wolfson. *Frances Wright, Free Enquirer: The Study of a Temperament.* New York: Harper, 1939.

Smith, Elizabeth Oakes. *Selections from the Autobiography of Elizabeth Oakes Smith*. Ed. Mary Alice Wyman. Lewiston: Lewiston Journal, 1924.

Trollope, Frances. *Domestic Manners of the Americans*. New York: Bell, 1904.

Waterman, William R. *Frances Wright*. New York: Columbia University, 1924.

Wollstonecraft, Mary. *A Vindication of the Rights of Woman*. (1792.) *A Mary Wollstonecraft Reader*. Eds. Barbara H. Solomon and Paula S. Berggren. New York: Mentor, 1983.

Wright, Frances. "Religion." *Course of Popular Lectures*. London: Watson, 1834, 53–68.

———. *Supplement Course of Lectures*. London: Watson, 1834.

———. *Views of Society and Manners in America*. London, 1821; Cambridge: Harvard UP, 1963.

Wright D'Arusmont, Frances. *Biography, Notes, and Political Letters*. New York: Windt, 1844.

———. *Course of Popular Lectures, Volume II*. Philadelphia: n.p., 1836.

———. *England, the Civilizer*. London: Simpkin, 1848.

———. *Life, Letters, and Lectures, 1834–1844*. New York, Arn., 1972.

The Erasure of the Sentence

Bob Connors's last essay was published posthumously, just three
months after his death. "The Erasure of the Sentence" (*College Composition and Communication*, 2000) is replete with methods and topics that had consumed Bob's interest throughout his career: the desire to construct narratives of disciplinary progress and change (the
rise and fall of sentence-based writing instruction); a predilection
and talent for creating taxonomies (the categorization of sentence-
based pedagogies); the attention to historical context (the career of
sentences and sentence-based instruction across the decades); and
an ongoing brief for the uses of formalism and empiricism within
our field. In this essay, as in many others, Bob chooses one strand
of composition-rhetoric and examines its fortunes within the field.
The fall from fashion of sentence pedagogies can be traced, Bob argues, to the "inevitable hardening into disciplinary form of the
field of composition studies as a subfield of English studies" (472),
whose disdain of formalism, behaviorism, and empiricism are
long-standing. And while he acknowledges some of the problems
associated with sentence pedagogies, Bob sees their passing as part
of a general "destruction in the wake of the disciplinary formation
of composition studies" (473), and warns that the wholesale
sweeping away of the past leaves us with "curious vacuums in the
middle of our teaching" and "few proofs or certainties not ideologically based" (473).

I n the 1980s, as composition studies matured, theoretical
and critical interrogation of much of the field's received wisdom began in
earnest. The field of composition studies, increasingly in the hands of the
new generation of trained specialist Ph.D.'s, began to do more and more effectively what intellectual fields have always done: define, subdivide, and
judge the efforts of members. Some elements of the older field of composition
teaching became approved and burgeoned, while others were tacitly declared dead ends: lore-based and therefore uninteresting, scientistic and

---

From *College Composition and Communication* 52.1 (2000): 96–128.

therefore suspect, mechanistic and therefore destructive. Little attention has been paid to these preterite elements in the older field of composition; they have been dropped like vestigial limbs, and most of those who once practiced or promoted those elements have retired or moved to more acceptable venues, maintaining a circumspect silence about their earlier flings with now-unpopular ideas such as paragraph theory, or structural linguistics, or stage-model developmental psychology. Of all of the inhabitants of this limbo of discarded approaches, there is no more dramatic and striking exemplar than what was called the school of syntactic methods. These sentence-based pedagogies rose from older syntax-oriented teaching methods to an extraordinary moment in the sun during the 1970s bidding fair to become methodologically hegemonic. But like the mayfly, their day was brief though intense, and these pedagogies are hardly mentioned now in mainstream composition studies except as of faint historical interest. The sentence itself as an element of composition pedagogy is hardly mentioned today outside of textbooks. But we can learn as much from watching the working out of Darwinian intellectual failures as from participating in the self-congratulatory normal science of the current winners, and so I offer this history of syntactic methods since 1960 in the spirit of the old New England gravestone: "As you are now, so once was I; as I am now, so you shall be."

From the earliest point in American composition-rhetoric, the sentence was a central component of what students were asked to study, practice, and become conversant with. From the 1890s onward, chapters on The Sentence in most textbooks were fairly predictable. Western rhetorical theories about the sentence date back to classical antiquity, with roots in Latin grammar and in the oral rhetorical theories of the classical period, and they came to their nineteenth-century form by a long process of accretion. Traditional sentence pedagogy assumed grammatical knowledge of the sort inculcated by Reed and Kellogg diagrams, but the prime elements in these textbook chapters were taxonomic, all this time focused on their place in sentence construction. Along with the breakdown of sentences by grammatical types—simple, compound, complex, and compound-complex—which was usually taken up in the grammar chapters of textbooks, the traditional classification of sentences is by function: declarative, imperative, interrogative, and exclamatory sentences. The traditional rhetorical classifications of sentences were also covered: long and short, loose and periodic, and balanced. In addition, sentence pedagogy nearly always included coverage of the old abstractions that informed modern composition-rhetoric from 1890 through the present: those of Adams Sherman Hill (clearness, energy, force), Barrett Wendell, (unity, coherence, emphasis), or C. S. Baldwin (clearness and interest).[1]

All of these traditional sentence pedagogies included many exercises and much practice, and we fail to understand them if we think of them only as defined by their abstractions and classifications. Most sentence chapters in textbooks asked students to create many sentences, and indeed, sentence-level pedagogy was an important part of traditional writing courses. It became even more central during the 1950s, a period when composition

teachers were looking to structural linguistics with expectation and sentence-writing was much discussed. But as I have discussed in more detail elsewhere (*Composition-Rhetoric* 162–70), it was just as structural linguistics was gaining a serious foothold in composition pedagogy that its theoretical bases came under sustained and successful attack from Noam Chomsky and the theory of transformational-generative grammar.

Here we enter a more familiar modern territory, the post-1960 era of composition and composition studies. And it is here that we find the beginnings of the three most important of the sentence-based rhetorics that were to seem so promising to writing teachers of the New Rhetoric era: the generative rhetoric of Francis Christensen, imitation exercises, and sentence-combining. I want to take up these three more modern syntactic methods in roughly chronological order, beginning with the ideas of Francis Christensen.

CHRISTENSEN RHETORIC

Francis Christensen, a professor of English at the University of Southern California, began to publish essays in the early 1960s complaining that traditional theories of the sentence widely taught throughout the first sixty years of this century were primarily taxonomic rather than generative or productive. Except in providing examples, they were not of much real help to teachers in showing students how to write good sentences. In 1963, Christensen published what is arguably his most important article, "A Generative Rhetoric of the Sentence." In this article and in other works published up to his death in 1970, Christensen described a new way of viewing sentences and a pedagogical method that could be used to teach students how to write longer, more mature, more varied and interesting sentences.

In the opening sentence of "A Generative Rhetoric of the Sentence," he announced his intentions: "If a new grammar is to be brought to bear on composition, it must be brought to bear on the rhetoric of the sentence" (155). Christensen was certain that the sentence is the most important element in rhetoric because it is "a natural and isolable unit" ("Course" 168). Complaining that the traditional conceptions of the sentence were merely descriptive, Christensen argued that traditional sentence pedagogy simply did not help students learn to write. "We do not really teach our captive charges to write better—we merely expect them to" ("Generative" 155). Christensen indicated that both the grammatical and rhetorical classifications of sentences are equally barren in the amount of real assistance they give to students. "We need a rhetoric of the sentence that will do more than combine the ideas of primer sentences. We need one that will generate ideas" ("Generative" 155).

Christensen rhetoric did not follow the traditional canons of rhetoric, which begin with conceptualization or invention; instead it opted for a view that all other skills in language follow syntactic skills naturally. According to Christensen, you could be a good writer if you could learn to write a good sentence. His pedagogy consisted of short base-level sentences to which students were asked to attach increasingly sophisticated systems of initial and final modifying clauses and phrases—what he called "free modifiers." Effec-

tive use of free modifiers would result in effective "cumulative sentences," and Christensen's most famous observation about teaching the cumulative sentence was that he wanted to push his students "to level after level, not just two or three, but four, five, or six, even more, as far as the students' powers of observation will take them. I want them to become sentence acrobats, to dazzle by their syntactic dexterity" ("Generative" 160).

For some years after 1963, Christensen's syntactic rhetoric was widely discussed, praised, and damned. His few short articles—and all of them were contained in *Notes toward a New Rhetoric*, a book of 110 pages—created an intense interest in syntactic experimentation and innovation. Several experiments confirmed the effectiveness of using generative rhetoric with students. During the early 1970s, two published reports appeared on the use of the *Christensen Rhetoric Program* (an expensive boxed set of overhead transparencies and workbooks that had appeared in 1968). Charles A. Bond, after a rather loosely controlled experiment, reported that there was a "statistically significant difference" between the grades of a group of students taught using Christensen methods and those of a control group taught by conventional methods; he also mentioned that his students were enthusiastic about cumulative sentences. R. D. Walshe, teaching a group of adult night-class students in Australia (it is hard to imagine two groups of native-speaking English students as far removed from one another as Bond's American first-year students and Walshe's Australian working people), found that although some of Christensen's claims for his system were inflated, the *Christensen Rhetoric Program* generally worked well and was liked by his students.

These tests of Christensen's program were unscientific and anecdotal, and it was not until 1978 that a full-scale empirical research test was done on the Christensen system. The experiment's creator, Lester Faigley, began with two hypotheses: First, that the Christensen sentence method would increase syntactic maturity in those who used it (for a fuller discussion of the concept of syntactic maturity, see the next section of this paper), and second, that the Christensen rhetoric program as a whole would produce a measurable qualitative increase in writing skill. Faigley tested four experimental sections and four control sections in his experiment. The experimental sections used Christensen's *A New Rhetoric*, and the control sections used a well-known content-oriented rhetoric textbook, McCrimmon's *Writing with a Purpose*. Faigley proved both of his hypotheses; he found that the writing produced by the Christensen program not only was measurably more mature but also received better average ratings (.63 on a six-point scale; statistically significant) from blind holistic readings ("Generative" 179). Faigley's experiment showed that the Christensen method does produce measurable classroom results.

IMITATION

The argument about Christensen rhetoric was in full swing during the middle 1960s when another syntactic method was first popularized: imitation exercises. Unlike Christensen rhetoric, imitation was part of the rediscovered trove of classical rhetorical theory that was coming to light in English departments.

From the time of Isocrates and Aristotle, exercises in direct imitation and in the copying of structures had been recommended by theorists and teachers of rhetoric, and after Edward P. J. Corbett published his essay "The Uses of Classical Rhetoric" in 1963 and his *Classical Rhetoric for the Modern Student* in 1965, the use of imitation exercises in composition classes enjoyed a renaissance of popularity. There are, of course, different meanings for the term *imitation*, but in rhetoric it has always meant one thing: the emulation of the syntax of good prose models by students wishing to improve their writing or speaking styles. The recurring word used by the ancients concerning imitation, according to Corbett, was *similis*; the objective of imitation exercises was to make the student's writing similar to that of a superior writer ("Theory" 244). This similarity does not imply that the student's writing will be identical to the writing she imitates; the similarity that imitation promotes is not of content, but of form. Corbett recommends several different sorts of exercises, the first and simplest of which involves "copying passages, word for word from admired authors" ("Theory" 247). For students who have spent some time copying passages, Corbett recommends a second kind of imitation exercise: pattern practice. In this exercise, the student chooses or is given single sentences to use as patterns after which he or she is to design sentences of his or her own. "The aim of this exercise," says Corbett, "is not to achieve a word-for-word correspondence with the model but rather to achieve an awareness of the variety of sentence structure of which the English language is capable" ("Theory" 249). The model sentences need not be followed slavishly, but Corbett suggests that the student observe at least the same kind, number, and order of phrases and clauses.

After Corbett's initial arguments for imitation, other scholars took the method up as an important technique. As Winston Weathers and Otis Winchester put it in their 1969 textbook on imitation, *Copy and Compose*, writing "is a civilized art that is rooted in tradition" (2). The assumption that imitation makes about contemporary student writing is that it is often stylistically barren because of lack of familiarity with good models of prose style and that this barrenness can be remedied by an intensive course in good prose models. Weathers and Winchester—whose *Copy and Compose* and *The New Strategy of Style*, as well as Weathers's *An Alternate Style: Options in Composition*, recommended imitation as a primary exercise—became the most notable proponents of imitation. Weathers and Winchester used a slightly more complex model of imitation than did Corbett: They asked their students first to copy a passage, then to read a provided analysis of the model's structure, and finally to compose an imitation. During the 1970s, Frank D'Angelo, William Gruber, Penelope Starkey, S. Michael Halloran, and other writers all supported classically based imitation exercises as effective methods for attaining improved student sentence skills. A second set of imitation exercises proposed during the late 1960s and early 1970s were called "controlled composition exercises," and were actually a hybrid, melding some aspects of imitation and some aspects of sentence-combining. Controlled composition, according to Edmund Miller, is "the technique of having students copy a passage as they introduce some systematic change" (ii).

From the middle 1960s onward, a small but significant number of voices kept reproposing the value of imitation. Frank D'Angelo noted that imitation connoted counterfeiting and stereotyping in most people's minds, when it should connote originality and creativity. A student who practices imitation, he suggests, "may be spared at least some of the fumblings of the novice writer" for forms in which to express his thoughts (283). A "student will become more original as he engages in creative imitation," claimed D'Angelo (283). Weathers and Winchester took the argument further: "Originality and individuality are outgrowths of a familiarity with originality in the work of others, and they emerge from a knowledge of words, patterns, constructions and procedures that all writers use" (*Copy and Compose* 2).

Like Christensen rhetoric, imitation was put to the test, in this case by Rosemary Hake and Joseph Williams, who performed an experiment in 1977 that compared sentence-combining pedagogy with an imitation pedagogy that they evolved under the term "sentence expansion." Hake and Williams found that the students in their imitation group learned to write better expository prose with fewer flaws and errors than students using sentence-combining pedagogies ("Sentence" 143). Since sentence-combining was known by the late seventies to produce better syntactic results than non-sentence methods, this finding was important. Imitation, proponents claimed, provided students with practice in the "ability to design" that is the basis of a mature prose style. The different imitation techniques, whether they consist of direct copying of passages, composition of passages using models, or controlled mutation of sentence structures, all have this in common: They cause students to internalize the structures of the piece being imitated; as Corbett points out, internalization is the key term in imitation. With those structures internalized, a student is free to engage in the informed processes of choice, which are the wellspring of real creativity. William Gruber, writing in 1977, argued that imitation assists in design: "Standing behind imitation as a teaching method is the simple assumption that an inability to write is an inability to design—an inability to shape effectively the thought of a sentence, a paragraph, or an essay" (493–94). Gruber argued that imitation liberates students' personalities by freeing them of enervating design decisions, at least temporarily. Without knowledge of what has been done by others, claimed proponents of imitation exercises, there can be no profound originality.

THE SENTENCE-COMBINING JUGGERNAUT

Sentence-combining in its simplest form is the process of joining two or more short, simple sentences to make one longer sentence, using embedding, deletion, subordination, and coordination. In all probability sentence-combining was taught by the grammaticus of classical Rome, but such exercises have tended to be ephemera, and none has come down to us. Shirley Rose's article of 1983, "One Hundred Years of Sentence-Combining," traced the use of similar techniques back to the nineteenth century and argued that teachers asking students to combine short sentences into long ones was a pedagogy

growing out of schoolbook grammar and structural grammar as well as more modern grammatical ideas (483).

While combining exercises can be found in the 1890s, it was not until 1957, when Noam Chomsky revolutionized grammatical theory with his book *Syntactic Structures*, that the theoretical base was established upon which modern sentence-combining pedagogies would be founded. This base was, of course, Chomskian transformational-generative (TG) grammar, which for a while caused tremendous excitement in the field of composition. TG grammar, which quickly swept both traditional and structural grammar aside in linguistics between 1957 and 1965, seemed at that time to present to composition the possibility of a new writing pedagogy based on the study of linguistic transformations. In 1963, Donald Bateman and Frank J. Zidonis of The Ohio State University conducted an experiment to determine whether teaching high-school students TG grammar would reduce the incidence of errors in their writing. They found that students taught TG grammar both reduced errors and developed the ability to write more complex sentence structures. Despite some questionable features in the Bateman and Zidonis study, it did suggest that learning TG grammar had an effect on student writing.

The Bateman and Zidonis study was published in 1964, and in that same year a study was published that was to have far more importance for sentence-combining: Kellogg Hunt's *Grammatical Structures Written at Three Grade Levels*. Francis Christensen had been using the term "syntactic fluency" since 1963, but Christensen's use of it was essentially qualitative and impressionistic. Hunt's work would become the basis for most measurements of "syntactic maturity," a quantitative term that came to be an important goal of sentence-combining. To recap Hunt's study quickly: He wished to find out what elements of writing changed as people matured and which linguistic structures seemed to be representative of mature writing. To this end he studied the writings of average students in the fourth, eighth, and twelfth grades and expository articles in *Harper's* and *The Atlantic*. At first Hunt studied sentence length, but he quickly became aware that the tendency of younger writers to string together many short clauses with "and" meant that sentence length was not a good indicator of maturity in writing. He studied clause length, and as he says, he "became more and more interested in what I will describe as one main clause plus whatever subordinate clauses happen to be attached to or embedded within it" ("Synopsis" 111). This is Hunt's most famous concept, the "minimal terminable unit" or "T-unit." "Each T-unit," says Hunt, is "minimal in length and each could be terminated grammatically between a capital and a period" (112).

The T-unit, Hunt found, was a much more reliable index of stylistic maturity than sentence length. Eventually he determined the three best indices of stylistic maturity: the average number of words per T-unit, the average number of clauses per T-unit, and the average number of words per clause. When applied to writing at different grade levels, he found that these numbers increased at a steady increment. Below is a chart that Frank O'Hare

adapted from Hunt's work and from similar work by Roy O'Donnell, William Griffin, and Raymond Norris:

TABLE 1   Words per T-unit, Clauses per T-unit, Words per Clause

	Grade Level						Superior Adults
	3	4	5	7	8	12	
Words/T-unit	7.67	8.51	9.34	9.99	11.34	14.4	20.3
Clauses/T-unit	1.18	1.29	1.27	1.30	1.42	1.68	1.74
Words/Clause	6.5	6.6	7.4	7.7	8.1	8.6	11.5

O'Hare (22).

As you can see, the rise in these three indices over time is obvious. Although these preliminary studies of Bateman and Zidonis and of Hunt used no sentence-combining at all, they did represent the bases from which high-modern sentence-combining sprang: the methodological linguistic base of TG grammar and the empirical quantitative base of Hunt's studies of syntactic maturity.

These two bases were brought together in the first important experiment involving sentence-combining exercises, that of John Mellon in 1965. Mellon called the 1969 report of his experiment *Transformational Sentence-Combining: A Method for Enhancing the Development of Syntactic Fluency in English Composition*, and his was the first study actually asking students to practice combining kernel sentences rather than merely to learn grammar. "Research," wrote Mellon, ". . . clearly shows that memorized principles of grammar, whether conventional or modern, clearly play a negligible role in helping students achieve 'correctness' in their written expression" (15). What *could* help students do this, reasoned Mellon, was instruction in TG grammar plus practice exercises in combining short "kernel sentences" into longer, more complex sentences.

With Mellon's initial publication of his work in 1967 and then with the national publication by NCTE in 1969, sentence-combining was established as an important tool in helping students write more mature sentences. But the grammar question still remained open. Since Mellon had to spend so much time teaching the principles of TG grammar in order to allow his students to work on his complex exercises, there was doubt as to which activity—learning the grammar or doing the exercises—had gotten the results. After all, Bateman and Zidonis had gotten error reduction—though admittedly not scientifically measured growth—from mere TG grammar instruction alone. How much importance did the sentence-combining exercises really have?

These questions were put to rest once again and for all in 1973 with the publication of Frank O'Hare's research monograph *Sentence-combining: Improving Student Writing without Formal Grammar Instruction*. This study, which

was the spark that ignited the sentence-combining boom of the late 1970s, showed beyond a doubt that sentence-combining exercises, without any grammar instruction at all, could achieve important gains in syntactic maturity for students who used them. Testing seventh graders, O'Hare used sentence-combining exercises with his experimental group over a period of eight months without ever mentioning any of the formal rules of TG grammar. The control group was not exposed to sentence-combining at all.

O'Hare's test measured six factors of syntactic maturity and found that "highly significant growth had taken place on all six factors" (55). His experimental group of seventh graders, after eight months of sentence-combining, now wrote an average of 15.75 words per T-unit, which was 9 percent higher than the 14.4 words per T-unit Hunt had reported as the average of twelfth graders. The other factors were similarly impressive. Just as important as the maturity factors, though, were the results of a second hypothesis O'Hare was testing: whether the sentence-combining group would write compositions that would be judged better in overall quality than those of the control group. Eight experienced English teachers rated 240 experimental and control essays written after the eight-month test period, and when asked to choose between matched pairs of essays, chose an experimental-group essay 70 percent of the time. The results suggested that sentence-combining exercises not only improved syntactic maturity but also affected perceived quality of writing in general.

The O'Hare study focused interest in sentence-combining, which had been associated with Mellon's complex directions, as a pedagogic tool. A follow-up study by Warren E. Combs found that the gains in writing quality that were produced by O'Hare's methods persisted over time and were still notable as long as two months after the sentence-combining practice had been discontinued. Textbooks began to appear using sentence-combining exercises, notably William Strong's *Sentence-Combining: A Composing Book* in 1973, which used "open" exercises, and O'Hare's own *Sentencecraft* of 1975. There remained now only one important question about sentence-combining: Was it useful for first-year students in college, or were they too old to be helped by the practice it gave? There was no doubt that it worked at the secondary-school level, but an article by James Ney in 1976 describing his attempts to use sentence-combining in a first-year class cast doubt on the technique's usefulness for eighteen year olds. Some teachers who had tried small doses of sentence-combining in first-year classes anecdotally reported no noticeable change in student writing.

Were college students too old for syntactic methods? This last question was answered in 1978 by the publication of the first results of a large and impressively rigorous study conducted under an Exxon grant at Miami University of Ohio by Donald A. Daiker, Andrew Kerek, and Max Morenberg. This college-level study used ninety of William Strong's "open" exercises and others created by the Miami researchers. These "open" exercises, some of which were lengthy and gave considerable stylistic and creative leeway to students, gave no directions on how best to complete them, and thus there was no

"correct" answer or combination. Daiker, Kerek, and Morenberg's experimental and control groups each consisted of six sections of first-year college students, and their experiment was conducted over a fifteen-week semester (245–48). The Miami researchers found that their experimental group, like O'Hare's, evidenced both statistically meaningful gains in syntactic maturity and a gain in overall quality of the writing they produced. Daiker, Kerek, and Morenberg's sentence-combining group moved during the experiment from a high-twelfth-grade-level of syntactic maturity to a level approximating high-sophomore- or junior-level college writing skills. In addition, their experimental group showed statistically significant gains in three qualitative measures of general essay quality: holistic, forced-choice, and analytic (Morenberg, Daiker, and Kerek 250–52).

The late 1970s, just after the Miami experiment, were the high-water mark for sentence-combining. The literature grew so fast it was difficult to keep up with it; Daiker and his colleagues hosted an entire large conference devoted to sentence-combining at Miami in 1978 and another in 1983; scores of normal-science experiments were conducted using it in classrooms across the nation during the early 1980s. The lesson of sentence-combining was simple but compelling; as O'Hare said, "writing behavior can be changed fairly rapidly and with relative ease" (68). The result: Sentence-combining was a land-rush for a time. Between 1976 and 1983, there were no fewer than 49 articles in major journals about sentence-combining and hundreds of papers and conference presentations.[2] The success of the method provoked nasty quarrels about who "owned" it or had a moral right to profit from it. Revisionist narratives about development of the technique were published. Everyone, it seemed, wanted a piece of the pie now that it had been proven so tasty.

With the potency during the early 1980s of the movement toward empirical research—a movement that had been materially strengthened by the popularity of some of the sentence-combining research—we might expect that sentence-combining would have continued as a potent force in the developing field of composition studies. The research was there; the pedagogy was usable by almost any teacher and provided results that could be seen impressionistically as well as measured; the method had powerful champions. It had been long assumed that sentence-combining could be a useful part of a complete rhetoric program, but by the late 1970s, the venerable Kellogg Hunt was suggesting that sentence-combining was so useful that it should take up all class time in a first-year course, that "in every sense, sentence-combining can be [a] comprehensive writing program in and of itself, for at least one semester" ("Anybody" 156).

Look upon my works, ye mighty, and despair.

THE COUNTERFORCES

In an astonishing reversal of fortune for sentence rhetorics, the triumphalism, the quarrels, and the debates of the early 1980s—now mostly forgotten—died away after 1983 or so. The articles on sentence issues fell away radically, and

those that were written were more and more about applications to learning disabilities, or English as a second language, or special education. Erstwhile syntactic rhetoricians turned to other issues. The devaluation of sentence-based rhetorics is a complex phenomenon, and we need to approach it with circumspection. Let me first try to establish the reality of what I'm calling the "erasure of the sentence" in clearly numerical terms. Table 2 lists raw numbers of books and articles appearing in general-composition journals about the three sentence rhetorics discussed in this essay.

While I can't claim that this chart, which I derived from a combination of ERIC searching and my own research, is exhaustive or even directly replicable, the numbers themselves are less important than the trends they show. And these numerical trends strongly match our intuitive sense of what has been going on. We see, starting with Christensen's first articles in the early 1960s, a strong interest in sentence-writing that was mostly taken up with generative rhetoric and imitation during the early period of the New Rhetoric, say, 1963–1975. After 1976, the interest in Christensen begins to peter out as sentence-combining gathers momentum; a truly extraordinary burst of activity occurred in the late 1970s and early 1980s. But after 1984, general articles on sentence-combining died out, and more and more of the essays published had to do with use of sentence-combining in classes in English as a second language or with behaviorally disordered or autistic students; an ERIC search shows only three essays published on general-composition sentence-combining after 1986. The few general articles that were published after 1986 came more and more to be critical, but even the criticisms died away. After the mid-1980s, the sentence rhetorics of the 1960s and 1970s were gone, at least from books and journals.[3] Shirley Rose's 1983 article on the history of sentence-combining, which probably felt when she wrote it like a historical background to a vital part of the field, now looks more like the *ave atque vale* of the field to sentence-combining.

TABLE 2   Books and Composition Journal Articles about Sentence Rhetorics, 1960–1998

	Christensen	Imitation	Sentence-combining
1960–1965	4	1	1
1966–1970	13	2	2
1971–1975	12	5	3
1976–1980	6	4	31
1981–1985	2	3	23
1986–1990	2	5	3
1991–1998	1	2	2

What iceberg did this *Titanic* meet? It was not a sudden ending, certainly; there had been criticisms of sentence rhetorics going back to the 1960s. There

had been some sentence-combining studies reporting equivocal results. There had been arguments over the differences between Christensen's "syntactic fluency" and Hunt's "syntactic maturity." And there had been ongoing questions about the meaning and validity of T-units and the relationship between syntactic maturity and holistically rated writing quality. But all of these had been essentially in-house issues, methodological or pragmatic, mostly waged in the pages of *Research in the Teaching of English.* By the early 1980s, sentence rhetorics had been criticized by some theorists for over fifteen years—but finally the criticisms were coming to bite.

That this devaluation of sentence rhetorics took place slowly meant that it was not noticeable as such by most people in the field. But once noted, it stands out as quite an extraordinary phenomenon. The story of sentence rhetorics is analogous, perhaps, to that of the U.S. space exploration effort of the 1960s. John F. Kennedy determined in 1961 that we would beat the Russians to the moon, and as a result of amazing effort, technological breakthrough, heart-rending sacrifice, and incalculable spondulix, Apollo 11 landed on the Mare Tranquilitatis in 1969. We went back a few more times, put up flags, drove about in dune-buggies, collected dusty gray rocks, and came home. We had seen what it had to offer. And after a while, we did not go back any more.

Similarly, in the early 1960s, a few scholars in composition determined to update the ages-old notion that students needed to be able to write good sentences before they could write good essays. Through new discovery, imaginative application of literary ideas, grammatical theory, and empirical research breakthroughs, methods and measurements were evolved that could determine whether student writers were writing better sentences. Teaching methods relating to the measurements were tested, and they succeeded, repeatedly and incontrovertibly, in producing better sentence writers. In addition, researchers determined that there was indeed a correlation between sentence skill and general perceived writing skill, discovering repeatedly that experimental sentence-writing groups were also holistically rated better writers. The techniques were honed and refined for different levels, and they finally appeared in easily usable textbooks available to all. We had said we wanted newer and better teaching techniques, and the sentence rhetorics of the 1960s and 1970s provided them. And, as a discipline, we then peered quizzically at what we had wrought, frowned, and declared that no, this was not what we had really wanted. We had seen what it had to offer. And after a while, we did not go back any more.

To understand the reasons for the erasure of sentence rhetorics, we need to look at the kinds of criticisms that were leveled at them almost as soon as they demonstrated any success. It will become apparent, doing this, that sentence rhetorics were not dragged under by any sudden radical uprising in the early 1980s, but rather finally succumbed to an entire line of criticism that had been ongoing for at least fifteen years. The reasons for the erasure of the sentence are multiple and complex, but as we look back over the varied critiques of syntactic rhetorics that were leveled beginning with Johnson, I think

we can induce some general themes—themes that I would argue represent an important, if sometimes tacit, set of underlife definitions for composition studies in the past two decades.

The first and most obvious of the lines of criticism that would engulf sentence rhetorics was what we might call anti-formalism—the idea that any pedagogy based in form rather than in content was automatically suspect. Some part of this anti-formalist position is a result of distrust of traditional textbook pedagogies, what we might call the reaction against rhetorical atomism. For much of rhetorical history, and certainly for all of the history of composition, the pedagogical method of taking discourse apart into its constituent components and working on those components separately had been accepted almost absolutely. In American composition-rhetoric, this meant the familiar textbook breakdown of the "levels" of discourse—the word, the sentence, the paragraph, the essay. The great difference between the early New Rhetoric of the 1960s and 1970s and the work that came after it is largely found in the New-Rhetoric acceptance of atomistic formal levels up until the late 1970s and the later rejection of them. The first exposition of this point was by James Moffett in his classic 1968 book *Teaching the Universe of Discourse*, in which Moffett surveyed sentence rhetorics (including Christensen and early [Mellon] sentence-combining) and concluded that teachers must "leave the sentence within its broader discursive context" (186). Teachers can help students relate to syntactic options only in the context of a whole discourse, Moffett believed, and thus a teacher can only help a student "if the units of learning are units larger than the hindsight sentence." He criticized traditional writing pedagogy for moving from "little particle to big particle" toward the whole composition. "For the learner," Moffett wrote, "basics are not the small-focus technical things but broad things like meaning and motivation, purpose and point, which are precisely what are missing from exercises" (205). This was a line of attack that came to be heard more and more often.

We first see it in responses to Francis Christensen's work, which began to draw criticism almost as soon as it was formulated. The ink was hardly dry on the large and ambitious *Christensen Rhetoric Program*, Christensen's expensive boxed set of workbooks and projector overlays, when the first serious critique of his theory was published in 1969. Sabina Thorne Johnson, in an article called "Some Tentative Strictures on Generative Rhetoric," admitted that Christensen offered "a revolution in our assessment of style and in our approach to the teaching of composition" (159), but she also had some important reservations about the *generative* nature of the cumulative sentence. Johnson's critique was essential: "Christensen seems to believe that form can generate content (*Program*, p. vi). I don't believe it can, especially if the content is of an analytical or critical nature" (159). Johnson went on to criticize Christensen's reliance upon narrative and descriptive writing for his examples and as the basis for his theory, complaining that narrative and descriptive skills seldom carry over to exposition. She initiated a line of argument against syntactic methods that later came to seem conclusive: that

students need training in higher-level skills such as invention and organization more than they need to know how to be "sentence acrobats."

Christensen himself died (of natural causes) shortly after Johnson's article appeared, and the attack on his theory led to a colorful exchange between Johnson and Christensen's widow Bonniejean that can be surveyed in back issues of *College English*. This debate was joined by A.M. Tibbetts, who made several telling points. Although Christensen is useful in the classroom, said Tibbetts, the claims he made for his system are simply "not empirically true as stated" (142). It is true that pattern practice with cumulative sentences can help students learn to use free modifiers, Tibbetts continued, but that is only one of the skills writers need. While he admitted that Christensen's method produced clever sentences from students, Tibbetts complained that that was part of the problem. "What we are generally after in expository writing," Tibbetts warned, "is accuracy rather than cleverness" (144). He rearticulated Johnson's reservations about the formal generativity of the Christensen rhetoric program. Christensen's theory, argued Tibbetts, is not designed to teach young people how to do the most valuable things any grammar-rhetoric should be designed to teach—how to think; how to separate and define issues; how to isolate fallacies; how to make generalizations and value judgments—in brief, how to express the truths and realities of our time and how to argue for improvements. He criticizes, as did Johnson, Christensen's "fiction fallacy," as he calls it: the idea that students should learn to write like Welty and Faulkner. Narrative and descriptive writing, Tibbetts claims, require no logical analysis and lead to "arty, false descriptions of adolescent mental states" (143). If you want nothing but "sentence acrobats," Tibbetts warned, "you are likely to get what you deserve—dexterous rhetorical acrobats who dexterously tell untruths" (143).

W. Ross Winterowd, no enemy to linguistic issues in composition, also questioned Christensen's work in 1975, when he pointed out that Christensen rhetoric exercises "take sentences out of the living content of the rhetorical situation and make them into largely meaningless dry runs" (338). Although he was himself trained in linguistics, Winterowd had deep reservations about large claims made for formalist "technologies":

> I can envision no "technology" of composition, no effective programming of students for efficiency in learning to write—nor would most composition teachers want such efficiency. From my point of view, "efficient" exercises in sentence-building, for instance, are downright morbid because they miss the point concerning the creative act of producing meaningful language in a rhetorical situation. (90)

And when James Moffett reacted to the formalist orientation of early sentence-combining, his Parthian shot—"It's about time the sentence was put in its place" (187)—could have been the watchword on syntactic rhetorics for a whole group of theorists whose work was gaining power.

The two *loci classici* of this anti-formalist position were the papers given at the second Miami sentence-combining conference in 1983 by Donald Murray and by Peter Elbow (their invitation by the Miami group seems in retrospect not unlike Brutus's decision to allow Antony to speak at Caesar's funeral).[4] Murray's essay is one of the wildest and most subtle he ever wrote, an almost unreadable melange of brainstorming lists, poem drafts, and endless badly combined sentences that commit formal mayhem on sentence-combining while never mentioning the technique, inviting students to write as badly as he does here in order to learn to write well. Elbow was much more open in his challenges to the formalist assumptions of sentence-combining, and he deserves to be quoted at length:

> I think sentence-combining is vulnerable to attack for being so a-rhetorical—so distant from the essential process of writing. In sentence-combining the student is not engaged in figuring out what she wants to say or saying what is on her mind. And because it provides prepackaged words and ready-made thoughts, sentence-combining reinforces the push-button, fast-food expectations in our culture. As a result the student is not saying anything to anyone: The results of her work are more often "answers" given to a teacher for correction—not "writing" given to readers for reactions. (233)

Though Elbow followed up this frontal barrage with a quick statement that these were his misgivings in their most extreme form, the remainder of his essay is a careful assessment of the dangers of making sentence-based work any very important part of writing instruction. Believing that "every one of our students at every moment is *capable* of generating a perfectly intelligible, lively sentence," Elbow says that the way to bring student skills out most usefully is "by leaving syntax more alone—that is, by learning to do a better job of writing down words in the order in which they come to mind" (241). Indeed, the whole thesis of Elbow's essay is that students do better and are truer to their own language when they leave their syntax alone. Elbow's final word on form-based work is that it is not, cannot be, genuinely generative. "[Sentence-combining] gives the wrong model for generating by implying that when we produce a sentence we are making a package for an already completed mental act" (245).[5]

The second strand of criticism leveled against syntactic rhetorics is related to anti-formalism; we might call it anti-automatism or anti-behaviorism. This set of critiques was based in the idea that pedagogies that meant to tap into non-conscious behavioral structures and to manipulate them for a specific end were inherently demeaning to students. The debate on behaviorism had been raging since the 1950s, of course, but it was given new impetus in composition in 1969 with the notorious publication of Robert Zoellner's "Talk-Write: A Behavioral Pedagogy for Composition" in *College English*. Zoellner's open plea for consideration of behavioral aspects to writing pedagogy struck a powerful nerve; *College English* printed no fewer than eight passionate rejoinders to Zoellner in 1969 and 1970. Behaviorism in psychology was the subject of deep

distrust on the part of most humanists, and any proposal for pedagogical uses of it was bound to be regarded with suspicion. It was here that syntactic pedagogies were problematical, because they all used exercises to build "skills" in a way that was not meant to be completely conscious. These skills would then be on tap for all conscious student-writing purposes. What most syntactic theorists wanted from their pedagogies was a systematic and intense exposure of student writers to models and activities that would not only teach them "correct structure," but would rather, as W. Ross Winterowd suggests, "activate their competence" in language so that it "spills over into the area of performance" (253). Effective generation, imitation, or combination would be praised, and incorrect syntactic manipulation could be corrected and criticized. But for many critics, the behaviorist, exercise-based formats of these pedagogies were deeply troubling. They were perceived as a-rhetorical, uncreative, and in some senses destructive of individuality.

Imitation exercises in particular were perceived as actively insulting to the creativity of student writers. Probably the most controversial of the syntactic methods in the 1970s, imitation exercises seemed to ask their team to play defense from the beginning. Objections to imitation were made on several grounds, and most theorists who discussed imitation even in the 1970s felt compelled to defend their interest in it. Frank D'Angelo claimed in 1973 that popular feeling against imitation existed because it was perceived as drudgery, "dull, heavy, and stultifying" (283), and spent his essay explicating how imitation was actually close to invention. But the complaint about drudgework was only a part of the reason that imitation was a pedagogy besieged from its inception. The main reason for the unpopularity of imitation was that it was perceived as "mere servile copying," destructive of student individuality and contributory to a mechanized, dehumanizing, Skinnerian view of writing. The romanticism of the age, seen clearly in much of the anti-Zoellner criticism, would grow more and more potent as the 1970s segued into the 1980s. Teachers and theorists reacted against any form of practice that seemed to compromise originality and the expression of personal feelings, and imitation exercises were among the most obvious indoctrinations to "tradition" and "the system." As a result of this fear of loss of individuality and originality in student writing, those who recommended imitation were fighting a battle that they were the first to join and, ultimately, the first to lose.

Although imitation's defenders sought to clear it of the charges of automatism leveled against it by the age, arguments against imitation never disappeared, even during its heyday, since it was the most overtly anti-romantic of the sentence-based writing pedagogies. D'Angelo noted in 1973 that imitation connotes counterfeiting and stereotyping in most people's minds, when it should connote originality and creativity. William Gruber, whose essay is titled "'Servile Copying' and the Teaching of English," knew that imitation was distrusted by many teachers when he argued that imitation does not affect creativity. Gruber argued that imitation exercises liberate students' personalities by freeing them of enervating design decisions, at

least temporarily. Without knowledge of what has been done by others, he claimed, there can be no profound originality: "Self-expression is possible only when the self has a defined area to work in" (497). But Gruber admitted that imitation "seems, I suppose, an 'inorganic' way of teaching writing" (495) and that his students initially seemed suspicious of it. "The greater part of students' mistrust of imitation . . . seems to derive more from emotional factors than from intellectual ones: for they grew up during the sixties, and they seem either to balk at any extreme formalization of the process of education, or to want one instant set of rules for all writing" (496). Gruber was indeed up against the powerful psychological backwash of the 1960s, as were, eventually, all proponents of sentence rhetorics.

The problem was in the exercises. Critics pointed out that sentence-combining exercises were quintessentially *exercises*, context-stripped from what students really wanted to say themselves. James Britton and his colleagues called such exercises "dummy runs," a term Britton's group evolved to describe tasks unrelated to the larger issues of creative composing in which a student is "called upon to perform a writing task in order (a) to exercise his capacity to perform that kind of task, and/or (b) to demonstrate to the teacher his proficiency in performing it" (104–05). And, as early as 1968, James Moffett was defining exercises as the central definition of old and discredited pedagogy:

> An exercise, by my definition, is any piece of writing practiced only in schools—that is, an assignment that stipulates arbitrary limits that leave the writer with no real relationships between him and a subject and an audience. I would not ask a student to write anything other than an authentic discourse, because the learning process proceeds from intent and content down to the contemplation of technical points, not the other way. (205)

Moffett was primarily attacking the old workbook "drill and kill" exercises that had stultified students since the 1920s, but he reports here on a keen resentment that had been building against all pedagogies based in the older ideas of exercises as "mental discipline." The wholesale (and heartfelt) assault on the teaching of grammar in composition that had been set off by Richard Braddock, Richard Lloyd-Jones, and Lowell Schoer's *Research in Written Composition* in 1963 was a related phenomenon. Many teachers had simply come to disbelieve in the efficacy of any exercise-based teaching. By 1980, this attack on the "from parts to the whole" tradition associated with exercises and textbooks had become much more general. Despite the flashy research claims to the contrary, many people felt that syntactic rhetorics were really not that much different from the old-time "grammar workbook" exercises whose usefulness had been aggressively challenged.

The final line in the congeries of criticisms that brought down syntactic rhetorics was anti-empiricism. Now we are in complex territory, and I must be careful to limit my claims. The empirical-research strand in English stud-

ies had existed since the 1920s, when educational psychometricians first began to try testing classroom pedagogies against one another. Modern empirical research in composition, however, was much newer, dating back primarily to the potent critiques of Braddock, Lloyd-Jones, and Schoer in *Research in Written Composition*, which had pointed to serious methodological problems in most extant English research and laid the ground for defensible studies. In 1966, Braddock had founded the journal *Research in the Teaching of English* to publish the newer and better work he envisioned, and most compositionists cheered. For the next two decades the empirical strand in composition waxed powerful, with syntactic methods as its first great success and with the cognitive psychology-based research associated mainly with Carnegie-Mellon as its second. In the Big Tent atmosphere of the New Rhetoric era of the 1960s and early 1970s, there was a general air of good feeling produced by the vision, widely shared, that all—rhetoricians, process-based teachers, linguists, stylisticians, experimenters, psychologists—could work together to reform and improve the teaching of writing; workers in different vineyards need not be enemies. Once sentence rhetorics began to get serious ink in the late 1970s, however, a number of teachers looked at them more closely and began to feel some discomfort, especially with their pre- and post-test scientism, their quantifications, their whole atmosphere of horse race experimentalism. This discomfort was not eased by the huge success of sentence-combining, with its Huntian movement toward a possible pedagogical hegemony. So in the late 1970s, we see the first serious signals of an open anti-empiricism movement within the coalescing field of composition studies.

Anti-scientism and anti-empiricism were not completely novel in the field, of course. We saw a sort of prequel to the movement in the point-counterpoint debate about psychology and invention heuristics in 1971 and 1972 between Janice Lauer and Ann Berthoff.[6] In its modern form, however, the movement probably begins with Susan Wells's and Patricia Bizzell's work in the late 1970s. Wells looked carefully at Christensen's work, arguing that it was empiricist in both method and epistemology, with an asocial contemplation of static phenomena at its center. The natural attitude for a student doing Christensen exercises, said Wells, is

> minute and unquestioning attention to his or her own perceptions, passive receptivity to the messages of sensation, and the desire to work in isolation. . . . These characteristics amount to a sort of contemplation. . . . Contemplation is not distinguished by its objects, but by the relation of thinker to thought, and Christensen's rhetoric enforces a contemplative relation. (472)

And, in an important essay in 1979, Pat Bizzell made the point, which she and others would sharpen over the next decade, that cultural and community traditions would be "as important—if not more important—in shaping the outcome of our debate, as any empirical evidence adduced and interpreted by the competing schools of thought" (768).

This humanist- and theory-based criticism found its first voice in the late 1970s and early 1980s in attacks on the most obvious and successful empirical research going: syntactic pedagogical research.[7] We can see echoes of the anti-empirical position in some of the arguments I've mentioned against generative rhetoric and imitation, but the real edge of this criticism was directed at sentence-combining, whose basis in quantitative methods was almost total. One criticism resulting from this reliance on empiricism was that sentence-combining was a practice without a theory, a method without a principle, an *ars* without an *exercitatio*. As Winterowd complained in 1975, "in our self-made ghetto, compositionists have neglected theory, opting to concern ourselves with the pragmatics of everyday teaching" (90–91). James Kinneavy brought this complaint down to specifics in 1978, noting that "... few efforts have been made to place sentence-combining into a larger curricular framework," and that it still awaited a philosophic rationale (60, 76). This lack of a general theory was not seen at first as a particular problem, since the new research strand of sentence-combining was so novel and powerful that it submerged other questions.[8] But by 1983, when Miami held its second sentence-combining conference, the problem of theory had become obvious to many participants. The book that emerged from that conference, *Sentence Combining: A Rhetorical Perspective*, is a fascinating collection, the last major statement made by the discipline about sentence rhetorics, and as a collection it shows clear awareness of the changing weather around sentence rhetorics.

By 1983, it was no longer enough to report that sentence-combining "worked" if no one could specify *why* it worked. Stars of the 1978 Miami conference Rosemary Hake and Joseph Williams were back, this time with more questions than answers. "Sentence-combining is at this moment operating at a very crude level of sophistication," they claimed, "... interesting theoretical speculation about sentence-combining has been very infrequent" ("Some" 100–01). Kenneth Dowst, in his essay "An Epistemic View of Sentence-Combining: Practice and Theories," takes on directly the popular perception that sentence-combining was "a practice devoid of a theory" (333). After examining the relation of sentence-combining to epistemic rhetoric, Dowst comes to the conclusion that sentence-combining *has* a theory, but that it is "a theory that many teachers are finding problematic and many students inadequately relevant. To wit: formalism" (333). The connection with formalism is not the only one possible, says Dowst, but other connections, to rhetoric or epistemic theory, "remain only to be enacted" (333). Despite the hopes expressed at the 1983 conference, they never were. And in the increasingly theoretical world of composition studies post-1985, practice without theory was increasingly associated with the lore-world of earlier composition and condemned.

Another criticism was that sentence-combining represented methodological hegemony of a kind destructive to a truly humanistic epistemology. Michael Holzman, in his "Scientism and Sentence Combining" in 1983, dry-gulches sentence-combining with such energy that he almost appears para-

noid about its possibilities. After slashing and burning all the research findings down to the affirmation that "sentence-combining exercises do appear to help students learn how to combine sentences (although this skill deteriorates rapidly)" (77), Holzman makes his central claim for an end to "scientistic" research. "The humanities are the sciences of man," he writes. ". . . It would be a serious mistake to allow the fascination of methodologies for social scientific research to bring us to doubt that literacy is primarily a humanistic attainment" (78–79). Holzman's fear—that the clear-cut successes of the sentence-combining research might slant the whole evolving discipline of composition studies away from traditional humanistic/rhetorical lines and into the camp of social sciences and psychology—was beginning to be widely shared in the early 1980s and came to its real fruition four years later, with the wholesale reaction against cognitive approaches and empiricism in general that marked the beginning of the Social-Construction Era.[9] The best-known example of this methodological critique was Stephen North's famous chapter on the experimentalists in his *Making of Knowledge in Composition* in 1987, which calls out the Miami researchers in particular for criticism (although not as harshly as it does some other experimentalists).

The result of all of these lines of criticism of syntactic methods was that they were stopped almost dead in their tracks as a research program and ceased being a popular teaching project just a little later. The degree to which the attacks succeeded can be seen in the curious growth of the truly lore-oriented conception that "research has shown that sentence-combining doesn't work." When preparing to write this essay, I asked a number of friends and colleagues in composition studies what had ever happened to sentence-combining. At least half of them replied that it had lost currency because it had been shown not to work, not to help students write better. So far as I can determine, this is simply not true. Outside of a few essays, including Marzano's and Holzman's, that really did take a slash-and-burn attitude toward reporting balanced opinions of the research, I can find no work that genuinely "disproved" the gains created for students through sentence practice. It is true that Lester Faigley showed, in two essays in 1979 and 1980, that Hunt's concept of syntactic maturity did not correlate with generally perceived writing quality ("Problems"; "Names"). But Faigley himself did not question the holistic quality gains of the sentence-combining students, stating that the answer must be that sentence combining and generative rhetoric "affect some part of the writing process more fundamental than the enhancement of syntactic maturity" ("Problems" 99).[10]

Warren Combs and Richard Smith published an essay in 1980 that reported that students would write demonstrably longer sentences if simply told to do so by the teacher ("Overt and Covert Cues"), but their experiment was short-term, and they specifically stated that their "findings in no way call the efficacy of SC [sentence-combining] instruction into question" (35).[11] It is true that the Miami group's last report, which appeared in the non-mainstream *Perceptual and Motor Skills*, found that absent other writing work, the gains made by the sentence-combiners were self-sustaining, but that the

advantage that the experimental group had shown over the control group disappeared after two years. The control group, in other words, caught up to the sentence-combiners after twenty-eight months. This shows, as the Miami researchers comment, that the sentence-combining practice "simply accelerated the positive changes that would have occurred after a longer period of normal maturation and experience" (Kerek, Daiker, and Morenberg 1151). In other words, syntactic gains, if not practiced, only persisted for two years. But by this criterion, if our methods in any given first-year composition course don't measurably put our students ahead of other students *forever*, they don't work and are not worth doing. That's a high hurdle for any pedagogy to clear. There were, finally, a few articles published with "Questions" in their titles: Mary Rosner's "Putting 'This and That Together' to Question Sentence-Combining Research" in 1984 and Aviva Freedman's "Sentence Combining: Some Questions" in 1985, but these essays were concerned with specific queries about technical style and abstracting ability. Neither questioned the general writing success of students using the technique.

It really does seem that the current perception that somehow sentence rhetorics "don't work" exists as a massive piece of wish-fulfillment. Leaving aside the question of syntactic fluency or maturity entirely, the data from holistic and analytic general essay readings are unequivocal. George Hillocks, reviewing the research in 1986, looked closely into all the major sentence-combining research and found many lines of inquiry that needed to be followed up. But after his careful dissection, he still concluded his section on sentence rhetorics with a quote that recognized the value of the technique: "Even with so many questions left unanswered, one is tempted to agree with Charles Cooper (1975c) that 'no other single teaching approach has ever consistently been shown to have a beneficial effect on syntactic maturity and writing quality' (p. 72)" (151). In other words, if people believe that research has shown that sentence rhetorics don't work, their belief exists not because the record bears it out but because it is what people want to believe.

Why we want to believe it is the interesting part.

So what was it that erased the sentence, wiped what had been the "forefront in composition research today . . . at the cutting edge of research design" in 1980[12] off the radar screen of composition studies? What reduced it from a vital, if unfinished, inquiry into why a popular stylistic method worked so well to a half-hidden and seldom-discussed classroom practice on the level of, say, vocabulary quizzes? It was not, as we have seen, that sentence rhetorics were proved useless. Neither was this erasure the simple playing out of a vein of material before the onslaughts of the normal scientists who followed the major researchers of sentence rhetorics. If the last important work in sentence-combining, Daiker, Kerek, and Morenberg's *Rhetorical Perspective*, shows anything, it is that many of the most interesting questions about sentence rhetorics were still being raised and not answered.[13]

I think that we have, to a large extent, already seen what it was. The sentence was erased by the gradual but inevitable hardening into disciplinary form of the field of composition studies as a subfield of English studies. The

anti-formalism, anti-behaviorism, and anti-empiricism that marked the criticism of sentence rhetorics can be found in some earlier writers and thinkers in the older field of composition, but not with the hegemony they gradually achieved as disciplinary structures were formed after 1975. These three attitudinal strands are hallmarks of English studies and not of works in the other fields—speech, psychology, education—from which composition grew after 1950. Departmental structures are lasting and durable, and as it became apparent that composition studies as a field would almost universally find its departmental home in the same place its primary course identity—first-year composition—resided, cross-disciplinary elements in the older composition-rhetoric world were likely to fade. The graduate students after 1975 who would make up the core of composition studies were, for better or worse, English graduate students, and they would go on to become English professors.

On a sheer demographic basis, it is not strange to see many default attitudes based around English departments—textuality, holism, stratification by status, theory-desire, distrust of scientism—gradually come to define composition studies. However complex the feelings composition people had and have about English departments, such departments are usually our native lands. Even if we reject much of the culture, we still speak the language. And one result of the increasing English-identification of composition studies has been a gradual movement away from connections that had helped define an earlier, looser version of composition that arose in the 1950s. We have dropped much of our relationship with non-English elements—with education and with high school teachers, with speech and communications and with oral rhetoric, with psychology and with quantitative research.

This is not the place for a complete discussion of the changing demographics of composition studies as it became a clear subfield of English. In this article I wanted to show, in a very delimited instance, evidence of the movement's power and potency by examining one part of its effects. When a phenomenon is hard to see or define, looking at what it has done may point to important realities about it. In this case, as in a tornado documentary, the effects exist as a trail of destruction. There was indeed much destruction in the wake of the disciplinary formation of composition studies, but since most of it was destruction of things few people after 1980 had ever believed in or fought for, the destruction was not noticed by many. Who remembers a vital NCTE College Section? Who mourns for the Four Communications Skills or the modes of discourse? But we should remember that swept away with the modes and the five types of paragraphs were other, newer, and potentially more valuable things. The loss of all defense of formalism has left some curious vacuums in the middle of our teaching. Rejection of all behaviorist ideas has left us with uncertainties about any methodology not completely rationalistic or any system of pedagogical rewards. Distrust of scientistic empiricism has left us with few proofs or certainties not ideologically based. More has been lost than sentence-combining here, but it seems somehow part of human nature to forget about the preterite. Many people still professionally active today have deep background as generative rhetoricians or imitation

adepts or sentence-combining pioneers, but they have lost most of their interest; they do not do that much anymore. They have cut their losses and gone on. We all must.

NOTES

1. C. S. Baldwin's terms, clearness and interest, were not used in his earlier textbook, *A College Manual of Rhetoric*, in 1902, which adopted Hill's version of Whately's terms. They are found in his later text, *Composition: Oral and Written*, from 1909.

2. These numbers do *not* include conference papers at the two Miami sentence-combining conferences, which became 45 separate essays in the two proceeding books.

3. Notice I'm not claiming that sentence rhetorics were gone from teaching. Anecdotal evidence seems to suggest that some teachers have continued to use sentence-combining and Christensen rhetoric even absent any mention of them in books or journals. They have thus become part of what Stephen North calls teacher lore. But isn't it ironic that such techniques, which made strong moves toward grammatical analyses and empirical proofs, have ended up as lore, which North defines (23) as being driven by pragmatic logic and experiential structure?

4. William Strong attempted to respond to Murray and Elbow in a heart-breaking piece with which the 1983 Miami conference (and collection) closes. Strong has read their papers, and his essay is an attempt to explain to them, and to the world at large, that sentence-combining is both more and less than they think and fear. Called "How Sentence Combining Works," Strong's essay admits that sentence-combining is not, cannot be, "real writing," and that it cannot and should never take the place of naturalistic experience. Still, though, Strong will not admit that sentence-combining is a-rhetorical or non-naturalistic, and he believes that "the language in sentence combining often triggers metalinguistic thinking beyond its own discursive content" and "helps students transfer power from oral language performance to writing" (350). Strong's is an extraordinary rhetorical performance, struggling at the end of the Era of Good Feelings for tolerance from a group that was moving inevitably away from him. But finally, his plea for compromise and understanding fell on stony ground. Composition studies after 1980 did not like or trust exercises. Any kind of exercises.

5. Today, more than fifteen years after the first cannonades were fired at the various movements associated with the term "process," we are used to thinking of our world as "post-process" and of "expressivism" as a devil term and a dead letter. As an intellectual field, we have managed with considerable success to marginalize that movement, at least insofar as it existed as ongoing intellectual or non-pedagogical discourse. Its greatest champions—Moffett, Britton, Garrison, Emig, Murray, Macrorie, Stewart, Rohmann—have died or retired, leaving Peter Elbow nearly alone to carry the banner. Many people see expressivism today—not unlike sentence-combining, ironically—as a hoary pedagogical survival, *exercitatio* with *ars*, old-time staffroom lore and instructor prejudice, the body still moving after the head has been cut off. It is difficult, on first consideration, to imagine the writing-process movement as a potent destructive force, or to think that we, in our shining theoretical plumage, are still living in the backwash of its great primary act of pedagogical creation/destruction: the wreck of formalism in all its versions.

But the powerful revolutionary doctrine of the process movement was, finally, terribly simple. It wished to do away with whatever was not authentic in writing and teaching writing. Its great enemy was modern composition-rhetoric, that huge carpet-bag of textbook nostrums about modes and forms and methods and sentences and rules and paragraphs and vocabulary and punctuation and exercises and unity and

coherence and emphasis. If rhetoric was a fox that knew many small things, process was a hedgehog that knew one great thing: you learn to write by writing and rewriting things important to you with the help of a sympathetic reader/teacher. Everything else is, finally, flummery. Formalism and atomism were huge and inescapable parts of modern composition-rhetoric, and the writing process movement laid down a constant challenge to them from 1960 onward. If, as was the case, formalism or atomism were charges that could be applied even to New Rhetoric ideas such as syntactic rhetorics, then applied they must be. Sadly, regretfully applied, yes, since many sentence-combiners had been friends. But when you build a set of positions based completely on authenticity and anti-formalism, you cannot easily choose some formalism you will be friends with.

Max Morenberg of the Miami sentence-combining group certainly had no doubt who had burnt his topless tower. In two conference presentations, in 1990 and 1992, he surveyed the wreckage and protested against the attitudes that had wrought it. His somewhat bitter titles tell the story: In 1990 he delivered "Process/Schmocess: Why Not Combine a Sentence or Two?" and in 1992 he delivered " 'Come Back to the Text Ag'in, Huck Honey!' " Both blamed dichotomizing process/product thinking for the demise of sentence rhetorics. Unfortunately, Morenberg never published either talk outside of ERIC.

6. This whole argument can be seen most easily in Winterowd's *Contemporary Rhetoric* (99–103), along with Winterowd's thoughtful commentary on it.

7. Only a few people saw then that this movement would a few years later in 1987 enlarge the criticism to include the equally powerful cognitive-psychology strand of research; in retrospect it seems clear that the real relation between sentence research and cognitive research lay in their common nemesis. The enlarging reaction against quantitative research would eventually come to include all but the most narrative and humanistic qualitative research as well, and the results would, in the end, be the same: the effective ending of whole lines of research within mainstream composition studies. Of course, much research is still carried on, but it tends to be reported at NCTE and American Educational Research Association, rather than at CCCC. See Charney for the reaction of many researchers to this movement within composition studies.

8. As late as 1981, even such a noted practitioner of theory as the late James Berlin was co-authoring purely practical essays on sentence-combining containing such statements as, "In sum, the 'sentence skills' unit should not be relegated to a few hours devoted to 'style,' but should be seen as central to some of a writer's major concerns" (Broadhead and Berlin 306).

9. In my "Composition Studies and Science," published just a month before Holzman's essay, I made almost the exact plea for the primacy of humanities-based (which I called rhetorical) inquiry over social-science inquiry. Although I made my own howlers in that piece (lumping Pat Bizzell in with all other Kuhn-quoters as an advocate of empirical science!), I was not, I hope, slanting evidence as obviously as Holzman seems to do in his condemnation of sentence-combining, whose whole train of successes he dismisses with a sneer.

10. Faigley's and Holzman's work led to Forrest Houlette's 1984 article on reliability and validity in external criteria and holistic scoring, a piece that seems to suggest that neither criterion can be considered empirically dependable under all conditions without the context of the other. This was the level of epistemological humility syntactic research had reached by 1984: There was no longer any dependable way to determine what writing was actually good.

11. Richard Haswell and his co-authors recently mentioned the study of Combs and Smith as a rare example of replication of research in composition studies (5), and in terms of careful numerical enumeration of syntactic growth, this is true. But Combs

and Smith studied their students over a much shorter period (six days) than did O'Hare or the Miami researchers and made no attempt to cover holistic writing-quality issues. (There is also some evidence that the overtly cued students [those told that their teacher would grade long sentences more favorably] simply began to string long sentences together in a few simple ways, since their T-unit numbers went up but their clause numbers did not [see pp. 33–35].)

12. This rather embarrassing quote is from my dissertation, written in 1979 and 1980. It's humbling to watch your own doxa turn into historical grist.

13. Janice Neuleib suggested, after hearing an earlier version of this paper, that another possible reason for the decline of sentence-combining was not that *all* of the research had been done, but that all of the impressive and groundbreaking research had been done. No one is much interested in the quotidian mopping-up work of normal science, especially in social science–based fields. The specialized and smaller scale studies that were called for (but not done) after 1983 were not career-makers. Although I thought at first that this idea might be too cynical, I have been gradually forced to admit its possibility.

WORKS CITED

Bateman, Donald R., and Frank J. Zidonis. *The Effect of a Study of Transformational Grammar on the Writing of Ninth and Tenth Graders.* Urbana: NCTE, 1966.

Bizzell, Patricia. "Thomas Kuhn, Scientism, and English Studies." *College English* 40 (1979): 764–71.

Bond, Charles A. "A New Approach to Freshman Composition: A Trial of the Christensen Method." *College English* 33 (1972): 623–27.

Braddock, Richard, Richard Lloyd-Jones, and Lowell Schoer. *Research in Written Composition.* Urbana: NCTE, 1963.

Britton, James, Tony Burgess, Nancy Martin, Alex McLeod, and Harold Rosen. *The Development of Writing Abilities (11–18).* Basingstoke: Macmillan, 1975.

Broadhead, Glenn J., and James A. Berlin. "Twelve Steps to Using Generative Sentences and Sentence Combining in the Composition Classroom." *College Composition and Communication* 32 (1981): 295–307.

Charney, Davida. "Empiricism Is Not a Four-Letter Word." *College Composition and Communication* 47 (1996): 567–93.

Christensen, Francis. "A Generative Rhetoric of the Sentence." *College Composition and Communication* 14 (1963): 155–61.

———. *Notes Toward a New Rhetoric: Six Essays for Teachers.* New York: Harper, 1967.

———. "The Course in Advanced Composition for Teachers." *College Composition and Communication* 24 (1973): 163–70.

Christensen, Francis, and Bonniejean Christensen. *A New Rhetoric.* New York: Harper, 1975.

Combs, Warren E. "Sentence-Combining Practice: Do Gains in Judgments of Writing 'Quality' Persist?" *Journal of Educational Research* 70 (1977): 318–21.

Combs, Warren E., and William L. Smith. "The Effects of Overt and Covert Cues on Written Syntax." *Research in the Teaching of English* 14 (1980): 19–38.

Connors, Robert J. "Composition Studies and Science." *College English* 45 (1983): 1–20.

———. *Composition-Rhetoric: Backgrounds, Theory, and Pedagogy.* Pittsburgh: U of Pittsburgh P, 1997.

Cooper, Charles R. "Research Roundup: Oral and Written Composition." *English Journal* 64 (1975): 72–74.

Corbett, Edward P. J. *Classical Rhetoric for the Modern Student.* New York: Oxford UP, 1965.

———. "The Theory and Practice of Imitation in Classical Rhetoric." *College Composition and Communication* 22 (1971): 243–50.

Daiker, Donald A., Andrew Kerek, and Max Morenberg. "Sentence-Combining and Syntactic Maturity in Freshman English." *College Composition and Communication* 29 (1978): 36–41.

———, eds. *Sentence-Combining: A Rhetorical Perspective*. Carbondale: Southern Illinois UP, 1985.

———, eds. *Sentence-Combining and the Teaching of Writing*. Conway, AR: L&S Books, 1979.

———. *The Writer's Options: College Sentence-Combining*. New York: Harper and Row, 1979.

D'Angelo, Frank. "Imitation and Style." *College Composition and Communication* 24 (1973): 283–90.

Dowst, Kenneth. "An Epistemic View of Sentence-Combining: Practice and Theories." Daiker et al. *Sentence-Combining: A Rhetorical Perspective*. 321–33.

Elbow, Peter. "The Challenge for Sentence Combining." Daiker et al. *Sentence-Combining: A Rhetorical Perspective*. 232–45.

Faigley, Lester L. "Generative Rhetoric as a Way of Increasing Syntactic Fluency." *College Composition and Communication* 30 (1979): 176–81.

———. "Problems in Analyzing Maturity in College and Adult Writing." Daiker et al. *Sentence-Combining and the Teaching of Writing*. 94–100.

———. "Names in Search of a Concept: Maturity, Fluency, Complexity, and Growth in Written Syntax." *College Composition and Communication* 31 (1980): 291–300.

Freedman, Aviva. "Sentence Combining: Some Questions." *Carleton Papers in Applied Language Studies* 2 (1985): 17–32.

Graves, Richard L., ed. *Rhetoric and Composition: A Sourcebook for Teachers*. Rochelle Park, NJ: Hayden, 1976.

Gruber, William E. " 'Servile Copying' and the Teaching of English Composition." *College English* 39 (1977): 491–97.

Hake, Rosemary, and Joseph M. Williams. "Sentence Expanding: Not Can, or How, but When." Daiker et al. *Sentence-Combining and the Teaching of Writing*. 134–46.

———. "Some Cognitive Issues in Sentence Combining: On the Theory That Smaller Is Better." Daiker et al. *Sentence-Combining: A Rhetorical Perspective*. 86–106.

Halloran, S. Michael. "Cicero and English Composition." Conference on College Composition and Communication. Mineapolis. 1978.

Haswell, Richard H., Terri L. Briggs, Jennifer A. Fay, Norman K. Gillen, Rob Harrill, Andrew M. Shupala, and Sylvia S. Trevino. "Context and Rhetorical Reading Strategies." *Written Communication* 16 (1999): 3–27.

Hillocks, George Jr. *Research on Written Composition: New Directions for Teaching*. Urbana: NCTE, 1986.

Holzman, Michael. "Scientism and Sentence Combining." *College Composition and Communication* 34 (1983): 73–79.

Houlette, Forrest. "Linguistics, Empirical Research, and Evaluating Composition." *Journal of Advanced Composition* 5 (1984): 107–14.

Hunt, Kellogg W. *Grammatical Structures Written at Three Grade Levels*. Urbana: NCTE, 1965.

———. "A Synopsis of Clause-to-Sentence Length Factors." Graves 110–17.

———. "Anybody Can Teach English." Daiker et al. *Sentence-Combining and the Teaching of Writing*. 149–56.

Johnson, Sabina Thorne. "Some Tentative Strictures on Generative Rhetoric." *College English* 31 (1969): 155–65.

Kerek, Andrew, Donald A. Daiker, and Max Morenberg. "Sentence Combining and College Composition." *Perceptual and Motor Skills* 51 (1980): 1059–1157.

Kinneavy, James L. "Sentence Combining in a Comprehensive Language Framework." Daiker et al. *Sentence-Combining and the Teaching of Writing.* 60–76.

Marzano, Robert J. "The Sentence-Combining Myth." *English Journal* 65 (1976): 57–59.

Mellon, John. *Transformational Sentence-Combining: A Method for Enhancing the Development of Syntactic Fluency in English Composition.* Urbana: NCTE, 1969.

———. "Issues in the Theory and Practice of Sentence-Combining: A Twenty-Year Perspective." Daiker et al. *Sentence-Combining and the Teaching of Writing.* 1–38.

Miller, Edmund. *Exercises in Style.* Normal, IL: Illinois SUP, 1980.

Moffett, James. *Teaching the Universe of Discourse.* Boston: Houghton Mifflin, 1968.

Morenberg, Max. "Process/Schmocess: Why Not Combine a Few Sentences?" Conference on College Composition and Communication. Chicago. March 1990. ERIC ED 319040.

———. " 'Come Back to the Text Ag'in, Huck Honey!' " NCTE Convention. Louisville. November 1992. ERIC ED 355557.

Morenberg, Max, Donald Daiker, and Andrew Kerek. "Sentence-Combining at the College Level: An Experimental Study." *Research in the Teaching of English* 12 (1978): 245–56.

Murray, Donald. "Writing Badly to Write Well: Searching for the Instructive Line." Daiker et al. *Sentence Combining: A Rhetorical Perspective.* 187–201.

Ney, James. "The Hazards of the Course: Sentence-Combining in Freshman English." *The English Record* 27 (1976): 70–77.

North, Stephen M. *The Making of Knowledge in Composition.* Upper Montclair, NJ: Heinneman-Boynton/Cook, 1987.

O'Donnell, Roy C., William J. Griffin, and Raymond C. Norris. *Syntax of Kindergarten and Elementary School Children: A Transformational Analysis.* Urbana: NCTE, 1967.

O'Hare, Frank. *Sentence Combining: Improving Student Writing without Formal Grammar Instruction.* Urbana: NCTE, 1973.

———. *Sentencecraft.* Lexington: Ginn, 1975.

Rose, Shirley K. "Down From the Haymow: One Hundred Years of Sentence Combining." *College English* 45 (1983): 483–91.

Rosner, Mary. "Putting 'This and That Together' to Question Sentence-Combining Research." *Technical Writing Teacher* 11 (1984): 221–28.

Starkey, Penelope. "Imitatio Redux." *College Composition and Communication* 25 (1974): 435–37.

Strong, William. "How Sentence Combining Works." *Sentence-Combining: A Rhetorical Perspective.* Ed. Daiker et al. 334–50.

———. *Sentence-Combining: A Composing Book.* New York: Random House, 1973.

Tibbetts, A. M. "On the Practical Uses of a Grammatical System: A Note on Christensen and Johnson." *Rhetoric and Composition: A Sourcebook for Teachers.* E. Richard Graves. Rochelle Park, NJ: Hayden Books, 1976. 139–49.

Walshe, R. C. "Report on a Pilot Course on the Christensen Rhetoric Program." *College English* 32 (1971): 783–89.

Weathers, Winston. *An Alternate Style: Options in Composition.* Rochelle Park, NJ: Hayden Books, 1980.

Weathers, Winston, and Otis Winchester. *Copy and Compose.* Englewood Cliffs, NJ: Prentice-Hall, 1968.

———. *The New Strategy of Style.* New York: McGraw-Hill, 1978.

Wells, Susan. "Classroom Heuristics and Empiricism." *College English* 39 (1977): 467–76.

Winterowd, W. Ross. *Contemporary Rhetoric: A Conceptual Background with Readings.* New York: Harcourt Brace, 1975.

Zoellner, Robert. "Talk-Write: A Behavioral Pedagogy for Composition." *College English* 30 (1969): 267–320.

IN MEMORY OF
ROBERT J. CONNORS

The memorial reflections with which this volume concludes appeared in 2000 in *JAC* and *CCC*. We believe that they speak, albeit in an inevitably partial way, to the richness and complexity of Bob Connors's life and work.

In Memoriam: Robert J. Connors, 1951–2000

PATRICIA A. SULLIVAN

Bob Connors died early Thursday evening, June 22. He was driving home from the University of New Hampshire on his motorcycle when a late afternoon thunderstorm darkened the sky and then unleashed a fury of rain. Bob was struck by a young driver in a pickup truck only a mile from his house and died from his injuries en route to the hospital. Still conscious at the accident scene, he spoke to his wife Colleen on a cell phone. The last words she said to him were: "I love you. I'll see you at the hospital in a few minutes." As Colleen clutched me Friday morning, sobs wracking her body, she said, "Pat, I never imagined for one second that Bob would die!"

Who among us could have imagined that Bob Connors would die at forty-eight, with so much of life still ahead of him? Even as I write these words, two weeks after the funeral I attended with several hundred other mourners, I am struggling to accept the fact that he is gone.

Bob would say that I'm struggling with the wrong entity: facts are famously remiss—drearily empty—when it is meaning we need and seek. Bob knew this in his marrow. As a historical scholar, Bob Connors had a respect for fact, to be sure: he often labored for days in a university archive to uncover the precise data upon which a scholarly essay—some small mystery or wonder he was tracking—turned. But for Bob, it was what he and we

From *Journal of Advanced Composition* 20.3 (2000): 483–504.

might make of facts that mattered, and making them matter was the province of rhetoric—and Bob's remarkable gift.

Bob's affinity for the nineteenth century is legendary. Indeed, he attributed to "pure dumb luck" and to "karma, cruel bastard!" the great misfortune of his birth date: he was born a hundred years later than the schoolmasters, rhetoricians, public orators, and skilled artisans who were his kindred spirits. He knew that for most of us the nineteenth century was little more than a crypt whose bones he was excavating on the chance that he might find something to instruct us or give us pause or even charm our jaded souls. But Bob himself *dwelled* in the nineteenth century—its moral sensibilities, its codes of discursive decorum, its latinate locutions, its aesthetic (especially its aesthetic), its prescriptions and proscriptions for a life of letters. I would venture to say that it was Bob's felt sense of existential dislocation—his inhabiting of two disparate eras—that gave rise to his singular and celebrated career as a historical scholar. He possessed not only a researcher's curiosity but an inborn need to connect the present with the past. His quest to discover how things were—from the social and civic milieus of oratory and written rhetoric to particular classroom practices and pedagogies—invariably began in the present. The vital question, he said, was, "How did things come to be this way?"

What Bob Connors made of the facts he gleaned so assiduously from archives often vexed colleagues who insisted on more contemporized, more consciously politicized accounts. He was far more comfortable than many of us were with the conclusions he rendered because he had a deep and abiding faith in historical reality: this happened, then this, for this reason. Even his appreciation of contingency and exigence, the narrative twists and turns of historiography, was infused with a desire to tell us something certain, something we could take away from his scholarship and say we know. His approach to history and its underlying epistemology placed him at odds with ideological theorists and historians like James Berlin, Sharon Crowley, Susan Miller, and Pat Bizzell. A walking anachronism (and self-professed antiquarian), he could never fully countenance ideologically inflected histories of rhetoric and composition. He eschewed postmodernism, social constructionism, anti-foundationalism, and to an appreciable extent, feminism. He was an unabashed, unrepentant essentialist. "How things came to be this way" applied to a complex web of social interactions, political circumstances, technological inventions, and pedagogical interventions, but not to our essential, inescapable selves.

On these points, he and I argued—respectfully, affably, always with a good measure of humor—but, to my mind, too infrequently. Bob preferred to work and write in solitude and I respected that, though I wish we engaged more often in face-to-face conversations when he and I were contemplating similar issues from notably divergent viewpoints (for example, gender, the place of personal writing in first-year composition, the first-year writing requirement, the working conditions of writing teachers). As a teacher he practiced and modeled agonistic modes of argument—holding classroom de-

bates and embracing a literal definition of the thesis defense—but in his personal life and demeanor he harbored a deep distaste for confrontation.

Like nearly everyone I've talked to in the days since Bob's death, I found Bob complicated—all the more so, perhaps, because he and I worked together and because so much of work life is play. The Robert J. Connors who could wax so imperiously on a listserv about the deplorable state into which composition has fallen was the same man who would meet his classes wearing a day-glo tie and "Hello Kitty" socks. The Bob who flirted with joining the National Association of Scholars and found much to admire in the Promise Keepers was also an ex-hippie, a shroomie, a Deadhead, a lifelong Democrat, a collector of underground comics, an apologist for the schmaltz-fest of professional wrestling, a Simpsons and Dilbert fan, an ardent biker. Bob could fix a truck engine and craft a Tiffany lamp from stained-glass pieces he made. He planted orchards, loved animals, relished vast rural spaces. He once drove to three McDonald's restaurants in a single day—and consumed three Happy Meals—to get his daughter the Beanie Baby she coveted. He was far and away the funniest man at any English department meeting I attended. It may well be Bob's sense of humor and his own hearty gust of a laugh—a sound I was always thrilled to provoke—I will miss most.

In the conclusion to his essay on historical method, "Dreams and Play," Bob said that "we write histories to define ourselves on the stage of time." In his own brief hour on the stage, Bob Connors undertook the demanding role of defining us to ourselves, and he performed this role, over and over again, with conviction, perspicacity, and quiet eloquence. We have lost a wise soul and a devoted friend. Our loss is truly profound.

University of New Hampshire
Durham, New Hampshire

Remembering Dr. Bob

DAVID EDWARDS

When I first heard the news of Bob Connors' passing, a darkness swept over me and blocked my view of the future. I hated myself for being so selfish in that moment. My loss certainly could not compare to that of his wife Colleen and daughter Aillinn, for whom this was the greatest tragedy of all. Still, in the moments just after my friend Bronwyn told me the news, my numb mind turned instinctively to thoughts of the future, to a life after Bob. This was the man who was going to chair my exam committee next spring, oversee my dissertation, guide and direct the final

stages of my PhD odyssey. We were supposed to grow old together: he at the University of New Hampshire, continuing his work and supporting mine; I at a smaller, local institution, hoping to make a difference. The stories he told me about his teacher, Ed Corbett, matched my own private fantasies of a lifelong relationship with a model teacher and scholar. I was neither ready nor prepared for the sudden and inexplicable loss of the most important person in my professional career. Bob Connors was my coach, my philosopher, my friend.

I met Bob before I even knew who he was. In 1996 I had just applied to, and had been rejected from, graduate study at the University of New Hampshire. I stubbornly moved to Newmarket, New Hampshire, got an apartment, and took summer classes to improve my chances during the reapplication process. And because I wanted to work with the writing center—having been a peer consultant at my undergraduate school—I was told to meet with some guy named . . . oh, it's written down somewhere . . . here it is, a Professor Robert Connors.

I found my way to his office one August afternoon. I was greeted by stacks of books piled below overflowing bookshelves, two desks masquerading as paper shrines, and little room remaining for human habitation—your typical faculty office. Then a large man—wearing a plaid shirt and jeans, with a scraggly beard and tight, shiny eyes—greeted me and invited me to sit beside him in one of two armchairs set side by side. I remember being struck by this arrangement: he never conferenced with students while seated behind a desk; rather, he preferred to greet them as if they were guests in his living room.

As we talked about writing center policies and training, I remember thinking how his appearance and personality seemed at odds with one another. It was as if the powers that be had placed the gentle spirit and wit of an English professor in the body of a woodsman. An axe wanted to be in those hands, not a pen. When I learned later that he rode a motorcycle and was once a trucker, I nodded silently. Yet, over the years, as I understood more about him and his love of literature, writing, rhetoric, and history, I came to see this bulky, bearded man as the gentle giant of the English Department at UNH, a teddy bear with a soul. And only after I had read a dozen or more articles authored and coauthored by Robert J. Connors, articles that helped to shape and define the discipline I now study, did I understand that the quiet, humorous, unassuming man sitting next to me that day was one of the central figures in the field.

Without my realizing or seeking it, Bob became my mentor. Slowly I discovered, through three courses and our contact at the writing center, that I wanted to emulate him. Bob impressed and inspired me. He knew everything, it seemed, about rhetorical history, writing center administration, composition theory, and literature; he also knew a great deal about plants, carpentry, old books, old furniture, meteorology, the politics of universities, cigars, and Louisiana cuisine. Yet, he maintained the attitude of a lifelong

student, constantly researching, writing, and learning. He was the model of the scholar and teacher I feared I could never be but wanted so desperately to become.

Bob gave me style, which is not to say that he taught me fashion sense. Only Bob could successfully manage to wear a tweed jacket, aquamarine shirt, and multi-hued tie to class without looking clownish. Rather, Bob introduced me to what we both suspected was a diminished canon of classical rhetoric: style. His own mentor, Ed Corbett, had explored the subject extensively, and Bob continued to "carry the torch," as he put it, hoping to pass that torch along to someone worthy of the task. Bob invited me to hold that torch at the 1999 CCCC convention in Atlanta. In my first appearance at a professional conference, I sat, terrified—the nameless graduate student between Dr. Robert Connors and Dr. Ross Winterowd—clutching a paper about the history of style in composition and feeling terribly out of my league. After Bob impressed and amused a standing-room audience of a hundred peers, speaking on the decline of sentence-combining theory, he turned to me and, noting the panic in my eyes, said, "You'll be fine." And, remarkably, I was.

That is how Bob invited me into the field and under his wing. He gave me confidence when I had none, encouraged me in the comments he wrote on a dozen of my papers written for his classes, and smiled at me when I was choking on the words I spoke in front of a hundred people who surely knew more than I. These things I remember, and I remember the "extracurricular" help as well. He was the first to invite me to the Oak Room, the faculty dining hall at UNH, where we would discuss the nineteenth-century German university system, our children, master's theses, or nothing but the movement of air masses over New England. Complaining one day, unexpectedly, about my very young and turbulent marriage and my continued inability to provide financial support to that union, I watched Bob laugh as he told me that, for some time, I would be the "net income sucker" in that relationship. He always did have a way with words.

Strangely, what I think I will remember best, and miss the most, are the chance encounters in the basement of Hamilton-Smith Hall. Bob had two offices at opposite ends of the basement—an office in the writing center and his faculty office with the comfortable chairs—so he was constantly patrolling the hallways. My own office was also in the basement, so at least once a week, and often once a day, I would see Bob approaching me, slightly stooped to reduce his height and bouncing gently as if he were hearing a tune in his ear. I would call out, "Hey, Dr. Bob," which was my way of paying respect and having fun with him at the same time. And he would always reply, "Hey, Dr. Dave," which was his way of telling me that he believed in me and expected great things in the years to come. I will miss that confidence, and I hope I can still live up to those expectations without my beloved, bearded rhetorician there to convince me that I belong.

University of New Hampshire
Durham, New Hampshire

Remembering Bob Connors

ANDREA ABERNETHY LUNSFORD
AND LISA EDE

T his is the second time in two years that we find ourselves writing a memorial tribute for someone close to us. Two years ago we
commemorated the death of Edward P. J. Corbett, our friend and mentor.
When Ed died on June 24th, 1998 at the age of 79, we mourned his passing,
but we also celebrated his long life and many contributions to the field. We
could not have imagined that almost precisely two years later we would be
mourning the untimely death of Bob Connors, who died in a motorcycle accident on June 22.

There is much to celebrate about Bob's life and work, including his long
and productive association with Ed Corbett. But since Bob died at forty-
eight, not seventy-nine, our epideictic task feels harder to carry out. Bob
should have had thirty more years—years of productive work and joyful living with his wife Colleen and daughter Aillinn. While we grieve for those
missing thirty years, we know that Bob lived his forty-eight years solidly in
the present, and that he did so on multiple levels.

Our readers are aware, we are sure, of Bob's many contributions to the
field of composition studies. A graceful and prolific writer, Bob produced
countless articles and books, some of which we worked on collaboratively.
Bob's research has been particularly important for the history of rhetoric and
composition: from his "The Rise and Fall of the Modes of Discourse" to his
most recent book, *Composition-Rhetoric: Backgrounds, Theory, and Pedagogy*,
Bob identified critical issues and developed powerful arguments that matter
today—and will continue to matter in the future. But Bob's interests ranged
much more broadly than this. Over the last twenty-five years, he wrote about
many topics, ranging from the theoretical (historiography, the nature and future of composition studies as a discipline) to the pedagogical (error in student writing, the relevance of the classical tradition for contemporary students). In a recent e-mail exchange, Bob wrote about his interest in what he
saw as an important lack of attention to the sentence in recent research. He
asked, "Why was research on this topic so important in the 1970s, and so absent in the 1990s?" These are important and difficult questions. When we
think back to Bob's many and varied studies, we realize that this ability to
ask hard questions was a hallmark of his work.

When you know and work with someone as long as we did with Bob,
disagreements are inevitable. Indeed, in recent years we have not always
agreed with Bob's responses to some of the questions he formulated. We

have doubted Bob's "take" on current historiographic debates, on the feminization of rhetoric, and on the role that men's studies should play in theory and practice in composition—and we had plenty of friendly debates on these issues. What we never doubted, however, was the seriousness with which Bob engaged these issues and the intelligence, wit, and insight he brought to his scholarly and pedagogical work.

Bob was, we now realize, always willing to take unpopular stands. When Maxine Hairston published "The Winds of Change: Thomas Kuhn and the Revolution in the Teaching of Writing," we (like many in the field) were eager to hail the revolution. Bob was more cautious. In "Composition Studies and Science," Bob reminded readers of the specific material and rhetorical context of Thomas Kuhn's work, and he raised important questions about the extent to which the field was—and was not—experiencing a paradigm shift. Similarly, in his most recent book, *Composition-Rhetoric*, Bob challenges readers to look harder at conventional disciplinary narratives that portray current-traditional rhetoric as essentially degraded or utilitarian. Whether scholars agree or disagree with Bob, the field's understanding of this period is significantly enriched because of his willingness to tell another story about it.

As a historian, Bob recognized the importance—and power—of telling stories. In the introduction to *Composition-Rhetoric*, he calls for scholars and teachers to "share our stories." We would like to close this tribute with stories, stories that speak to us, and that we hope will also speak to you.

The first story is one of family. The last time that we saw Bob with his immediate family, Colleen and Aillinn, was at the 1999 International Society of the History of Rhetoric in Amsterdam. Aillinn had somehow grown from a toddler into a girl of seven. Scholarly conferences are not of great interest to seven-year-olds, but Aillinn bore with us as we eagerly exchanged news. We learned of Colleen's continued artistic efforts (which range from poetry to illustration to clothes design), of the new home that meant so much to both Bob and Colleen. We talked of times in the past, and of the future—of the toy sailboat they had just purchased for their lake, of Aillinn's schooling and Bob's woodworking and stained-glass projects.

Those who know Bob primarily through his scholarly work may be surprised by our second story, which tells of his love of cars, motorcycles, and all things mechanical. Bob worked as a truck driver in a stint between his undergraduate and graduate studies, and there was a part of Bob that would always love both the open road and the care and tending of various engines that made time on the open road possible. Of course, this love had to be expressed in some writerly way—hence his articles published in *Car and Driver*. Bob used to say that he valued this recognition as much as any scholarly award, and he meant it.

Like many his (and our) age, Bob grew up loving music and defining himself in important ways through it. Bob loved New England, which was his home and source of much pleasure during the last two decades. And he loved crafts—stained glass, for instance. In recent years, he lovingly oversaw the building of an authentic replica of a Victorian home. He himself did

much of the interior finish work for this home, finding and restoring old mantelpieces, building new ones, locating antiques. Bob planted an orchard, cultivated a garden.

Had he lived to be seventy-nine, Bob would have been able to see that orchard mature and Aillinn grow up. Undoubtedly, he would have seen countless new scholarly projects through to maturity as well. But had he lived longer, Bob's life would not have been richer or more productive than it already was. Bob lived every day fully, with a deep awareness of the importance of living in the present. We were reminded of this awareness when, in preparing to write this memorial, we read the words Bob wrote and published in *JAC* upon Ed Corbett's death. In concluding his tribute, Bob wrote about Ed's respect for others, his "abstention from warring cliques and dirty political hatreds, the social acceptance of difference, [and his] fullhearted appreciation of all good work." This, Bob said, was Ed Corbett's legacy to scholars and teachers of composition. "And to be worthy of that legacy is simple, really," Bob added. "All we have to do is love life and love one another" (401).

And so we do. Though we, like many others, will miss Bob, we want to honor who and what he was—even as we mourn his loss.

Stanford University, Stanford, California
Oregon State University, Corvallis, Oregon

Remembering Bob

CHERYL GLENN

Bob would let me fiddle with just about any other part of our *St. Martin's Guide to Teaching Writing*, but not the opening:

> There it is in black and white. You've been assigned to teach a college writing course: first-year composition. Sentences, paragraphs, essays. "Me—teach writing? I never took a writing course in my life, except freshman English, which I barely remember. What am I going to do?"

I never liked that opening—not when we used it in 1988 for our first edition, not when we used it in the fifth edition. But Bob did. He wouldn't budge on it. He thought it was a "grand invitation" to the teaching of writing. Every time we'd begin the revisions for our next edition, and every time I'd bring up that opening, he'd tell me, "New TAs like that opening."

Now that he's gone, I wouldn't dream of changing that opening. Besides, Bob was right.

Bob and I go far enough back that I, like so many *JAC* readers, feel that Bob was an old and trusted friend. When I was a graduate student at Ohio State University, we were studying Robert Connors' 1982 Richard Braddock Award winner, "The Rise and Fall of the Modes of Discourse." Until then, I had thought that rhetoric (that is, history) and composition (that is, practice) were separate fields. Bob showed us how very much rhetoric and composition need and interanimate each other. When "Robert" Connors came to campus that spring, he behaved in his inimitable self-deprecating way, bashfully brushing off the praise for "Modes" and moving ahead to important matters: shouldn't we try to get a seat at his favorite gyro place just north of campus. Gyros—not praise—were what he was after that day, and the days that followed were much the same: he'd change the subject from himself to something he thought more entertaining—food, for instance, or fireworks, or clothes.

Last summer, Bob came to the Penn State Conference on Rhetoric and Composition—his first visit to our campus and to the conference. He was genuinely delighted—and honored, he told me—to be invited as a "featured speaker." He wanted to attend a conference on "Rhetorical Education in America"; he wanted to hear practical, theoretical, and historical papers; he wanted to eat, talk, and walk with the other conferees. He was in his element. After Kathleen Hall Jamieson gave her Fourth of July keynote address, many conferees looked for a cold drink or returned to their rooms. Not Bob (even though he'd driven his Jaguar from New Hampshire that day). He wanted to see State College and the fireworks. He wanted to talk with folks. So Bob and Marie Secor invited him along to see the fireworks display.

The next morning, Bob rushed up to tell me how much he liked breakfast, the conference, and especially the fireworks! He was having a good time in Happy Valley.

As the conference wore on, I'd see Bob surrounded by scholars of all ages, talking about papers, ideas, articles. Bob was a natural magnet for conversation, with his kindly ways, his good humor and wit, and his strong opinions. But during one early confab, he broke away to ask me a sartorial question. He'd noticed that another conferee had been wearing a "cool Hawaiian shirt," and Bob wanted to find one. I gave him directions to the three men's clothing shops in town and sent him on his way. When he returned, after lunch, he was proudly sporting his new Tommy Bahama shirt.

Bob and I didn't always agree—how could any collaborators who had worked on five editions of a book? We didn't always agree about how our *Guide* should sound or look or change, how women could be—had been, in fact—written into the history of rhetoric, how graduate students might best be professionally prepared. There were times when I wanted to bean him— and I'm sure there were plenty of times he wanted to bean me, too. But our disagreements, agreements, and loyalty truly mark our enduring friendship, just as his commitment to Colleen and Ailleen, his generosity to his friends, and his intellectual investment in the field of rhetoric and composition mark Bob as the fine man he truly was. We'll all miss him.

When Bob accepted his Braddock Award, he thanked the folks who'd helped him, quoting Yeats, "Say my glory was I had such friends." Indeed, Bob had many such friends. Our glory was having him as one. I'd give anything to catch a glimpse of our friend at the Denver CCCC convention heading out to find a cool western shirt.

Pennsylvania State University
University Park, Pennsylvania

Canonical Bob

LYNN Z. BLOOM

Canonical scholars are exciting. That their work is immediately recognized by the cognoscenti as cutting edge goes without saying. That their work is the product of passionate concern, deep understanding, and incalculable effort is not surprising. But it is remarkable that their ways of knowing and explaining their subjects, however arcane or esoteric— such as Balinese cockfights, the Panopticon, or the contact zone—kindle reciprocal passion in the otherwise cool-headed or indifferent, whether they be sophisticated scholars or newcomers to the field. The work of canonical scholars is transformative; it moves the marginal to the mainstream; it changes the flow of the course of knowledge. We take it to our minds, our hearts—even while the occasional radical who dares to disturb the universe (Galileo comes to mind) is being carted off to prison. Yet, because canonical work is foundational—with or without struggle—it becomes embedded in the newly-configured field. Its definitions, concepts, methodology—once dazzlingly new—are taken for granted, as if we had always known and understood them.

That Bob Connors was a canonical scholar is beyond question. That his work immediately became canonical is not surprising. The status accorded the early work of many of his contemporaries—Peter Elbow, David Bartholomae, Nancy Sommers, Mike Rose, Andrea Lunsford, and Lisa Ede— attests to the newly burgeoning field's immediate recognition of groundbreaking work. Indeed, when Connors earned his PhD from Ohio State University in 1980 with a dissertation directed by Ed Corbett—"A Study of Rhetorical Theories for College Writing Teachers"—the ancient discipline of rhetoric was in the process of rebirth ("composition studies" had not yet been labeled). Connors contributed to its renascence. His second published article, "The Rise and Fall of the Modes of Discourse," won the CCCC's 1982 Richard Braddock Award. His first book, *Essays on Classical Rhetoric and Modern Dis-*

course, coedited with Lisa Ede and Andrea Lunsford, received the MLA's 1985 Mina P. Shaughnessy Award. That these still remain among Connors' most widely cited works is further evidence of his canonicity. Around fifty percent of academic publications in all fields are never cited anywhere; another twenty-five to thirty percent are cited a few times (often by their own authors); the remaining heavy hitters are usually cited frequently during the first decade after publication and then hardly at all. But the work of canonical figures remains vital and central, often throughout the lifetime of the author—and long beyond.

The rest, as they say, is history—to be specific, the history of rhetoric and composition studies, particularly in American colleges in the nineteenth and early twentieth centuries. Much of what we know about this broad area we have learned from Bob Connors, who continued to fulfill his early promise, year in and year out. His illuminating work has appeared without fail since 1980, despite minimal research support, most of it produced at the University of New Hampshire, where he taught from 1984 until his death in June. There, after physically transporting a vanload of Richard Beal's papers to campus, he established the Beal Collection, a composition archive (Connors, the purist, preferred the singular) of historical correspondence, out-of-print journals, and composition textbooks that evolved into the National Archives of Composition and Rhetoric.

Connors contributed to all the major journals. His most recent article, "Frances Wright: First Female Civic Rhetor in America," which focuses on a woman I never knew I wanted to know about until I read it, characterizes his scholarly methodology: sophisticated and eclectic. Drawing on a wealth of primary and secondary sources—no matter how obscure, fugitive, and controversial—Connors combines biography and nineteenth-century American cultural, intellectual, social, and political history with rhetorical analysis to assess Wright's life and work as a principled, initially engaging, and ultimately quixotic and self-defeating orator. He observes, "As a pioneer woman speaker, she did not blaze a trail that made others' travels easier, but instead created conditions that hurt every woman speaker for fifty years after." As is always the case with canonical research, the subject emerges, as thoroughly compelling in interest and significance. How could we have overlooked Frances Wright before? How can we forget her now? The articles that are my personal favorites, however—the ones I expect my graduate students to understand, address, and even argue with—are not historical but contemporary: "Frequency of Formal Errors in Current College Writing, or Ma and Pa Kettle Do Research" (with Andrea Lunsford) and "Teaching and Learning as a Man." The latter is much more moderate and reasonable than might have emerged in less gracious hands. For instance, he concludes:

> If we are to grapple effectively with the attitudes of young men, we cannot continue to view them merely as order-takers, or sulky vandals, or cultural naïfs who can easily be reformed with a dose of cultural studies. The fact is that we are still struggling today with the meaning of the shift

> away from all-male education that took place 150 years ago, and at this point we have not foregrounded gender issues equally for men and women. The feminism within and the feminization of composition pedagogy that have become such powerful parts of composition studies today have not yet made much room for male students—or male teachers. (*College English* 58 [1996]: 156)

Connors wrote chapters for many books, such as the theoretically sophisticated and subtle "Dreams and Play: Historical Method and Methodology," which appears in Pat Sullivan and Gesa Kirsch's *Methods and Methodology in Composition Research*. He was an invited speaker at the numerous conferences that began to flourish in the 1990s, among them *Composition in the Twenty-First Century: Crisis and Change*. At this WPA conference featuring the field's movers and shapers, Connors delivered a prescient plenary speech, "The Abolition Debate: A Short History," establishing that "Today's abolitionists are arguing from their scholarly as well as their practical knowledge of writing issues that students are not as well served by the required freshman course as they could be by other kinds of writing instruction." With Andrea Lunsford, Connors wrote a major textbook, *The St. Martin's Handbook*, which represents his continuing legacy to the composition classroom.

The centerpiece of Connors' legacy to the profession is his major book, *Composition-Rhetoric: Backgrounds, Theory, and Pedagogy*, a volume dedicated to restoring the nineteenth century to rhetorical history—a period hitherto slighted when not ignored altogether. Connors concentrates on "the rhetoric of written composition that arose in American colleges after 1780 and . . . its development as a culture, a theoretical apparatus, and a teaching practice down to relatively recent times." His methodology is Gibraltar-solid. He draws on an ingenious and eclectic mix of primary documents (letters, histories, treatises, textbooks), and an "economic, political, and theoretical" knowledge of the history of rhetoric from classical times to the present. Connors takes nothing for granted, exploding such pervasive concepts as "current-traditional rhetoric": "What we have reified as a unified 'current-traditional rhetoric' is, in reality, not a unified or an unchanging phenomenon." Its default label, invented by Daniel Fogarty in 1959 and promulgated by Richard Young in 1978, is inaccurate as well. In this book, as elsewhere, Connors shores up his claims with evidence presented with such offhand grace that the wealth of scholarly underpinning is unobtrusive. Like many of the best writers in composition studies (or anywhere), Connors has the ability to express complex ideas with simple clarity; what readers see is the elegant superstructure that in some ways overshadows the complicated and massive support that is solidly in place.

Connors learned from the best of mentors, Ed Corbett, and continued to learn from and teach with a wealth of colleagues and students not only at the University of New Hampshire but throughout the country. Portions of his "Memorial Tribute" to Corbett published in *College English* could, with a few revisions, be applied to Connors himself. But, punctilious as Connors was about keeping most deadlines, there is one he kept too early, too soon. I wish

we could say some thirty years from now that, like Corbett, Bob Connors "lived to see his family thrive, and to see the children of his mind lead the field that so many credited him with helping build." Cut down in his prime, Bob did not live to see his young family thrive. That the children of his mind lead the field, as they have done for twenty years, is a claim we can make, in certainty and in sorrow. The canon is eclectic and expansive. Bob Connors' larger-than-life presence helped that canon—and all of us—to grow.

University of Connecticut
Storrs, Connecticut

Masculinity, Feminism, and Motorcycles: Memorial Reflections

ELIZABETH A. FLYNN

The cycle swings into each curve effortlessly, banking so that our weight is always down through the machine no matter what its angle is with the ground. The way is full of flowers and surprise views, tight turns one after another so that the whole world rolls and pirouettes and rises and falls away.

–ROBERT PIRSIG

Most of the sight lines along the mile-long strength of Route 5 that I walk are good, but there is one place, a short steep hill, where a pedestrian heading north can see very little of what might be coming his way. I was three-quarters of the way up this hill when the van came over the crest. It wasn't on the road; it was on the shoulder. My shoulder. I had perhaps three-quarters of a second to register this. It was time enough to think, My God, I'm going to be hit by a school bus, and to start to turn to my left. Then there is a break in my memory. On the other side of it, I'm on the ground, looking at the back of the van, which is now pulled off the road and tilted to one side. This image is clear and sharp, more like a snapshot than like a memory. There is dust around the van's taillights. The license plate and the back window are dirty. I register these things with no thought of myself or of my condition. I'm simply not thinking.

–STEPHEN KING

B ob Connors and I were graduate students together at Ohio State University in the 1970s. I finished coursework before he started his and then spent two years in Europe, so we didn't meet up until the mid-1970s. But we were both involved in the composition program when I returned, so our paths crossed from time to time. My most distinct memory of an association with him during this period was our being paired up in a workshop focusing on pedagogical issues in which we wrote an on-the-spot collaborative piece. I realized then that he was both an assertive and a skilled writer. I also had a sense when we were at Ohio State that he had clear priorities: he was a scholar first.

I was not surprised, then, that as soon as he obtained a tenure-track position he started publishing immediately and within a few years had established himself within rhetoric and composition as a historian of classical rhetoric, composition studies, and technical communication. I took note of his being the person who coined the term "composition studies," of his providing one of the first maps of the field of technical communication, of his winning the Richard Braddock Award (1982). His was definitely a rising star. We chatted from time to time at the annual CCCC convention, met again at one of the New Hampshire conferences in the 1990s, had overlapping terms on the CCCC Executive Committee in the early 1990s, and served on the same Executive Committee subcommittee. It was after one of these subcommittee meetings that we shared stories about our daughters. Mine was a toddler and his was a baby. I distinctly recall his mentioning that he had given himself permission to take time off from his scholarship to help with Aillinn. I remember thinking that he certainly could afford it and deserved it. He nevertheless was able to publish *Composition-Rhetoric: Backgrounds, Theory, and Pedagogy* in 1997. I also remember seeing him in his black leather motorcycle jacket after the 1996 CCCC session, "Beyond Zen: The Rhetoric of Writers Who Ride" — a session he shared with David Schwalm and Toby Fulwiler.

Bob was no one to contend with in writing so I am fortunate not to have gotten into a wrangle with him in print. I guess I learned that lesson in graduate school. My personal contacts with him were entirely pleasant, so I am probably better situated than some to reflect on his gendered writing and life. Many of us who got PhDs at Ohio State in the late 1970s and obtained academic jobs were women who were then feminists or became feminists when the field of rhetoric and composition turned its attention to feminist concerns in the late 1980s. The English department at the University of New Hampshire where Bob obtained his second academic position (his first job was at Louisiana State University) hired a number of strong feminist women in the wake of controversy over Annette Kolodny's discrimination charges in the mid-1970s. These women (from what I understand) represent a strong force within the department. It is perhaps not surprising, then, that Bob began to turn his attention to gender issues earlier than most others in rhetoric and composition and that he demonstrated sympathy for feminism. But his relationship to feminism was no doubt more complicated than that—hence his

turn to men's studies. His considerable achievements and his tragic death re-mind us of the limitations of dichotomous conceptions of gender and of monolithic rejections of men and male modes of behavior. While obviously an expression of male freedom and independence, motorcycle riding, after all, has its pleasures and its aesthetic dimension, as Robert Pirsig's description makes clear. It also has its vulnerabilities. A motorcycle is smaller than other vehicles on the road, and the motorcyclist does not have the protection provided by other vehicles; in this sense, motorcycle riding more closely resembles bike riding or walking than driving. Stephen King's description of his near-fatal accident while walking on a highway in Maine makes clear the vulnerabilities of walkers in the face of powerful machines such as vans. Although motorcycle riders are frequently the victims in accidents—hence the controversy over the need for helmet laws—they are rarely the perpetrators in accidents. They are more like English teachers in an academy dominated by hard scientists than like patriarchs that dominate others. Bob Connors' death reminds us that in the midst of our work on women's special needs and problems, we need to attend to those of men as well.

Michigan Technological University
Houghton, Michigan

Struggling with Manhood: Remembering Robert Connors

PATRICK McGANN

Bob, Jim Catano, and I are standing together at the 1998 CCCC convention in Chicago, a little uncertain about how to continue discussing the politics of masculinity, men's studies, and composition. I notice each of us has a beard. Bob and I have just participated in a roundtable with Gesa Kirsch and Eileen Schell focusing on the relationship between women's and men's studies in composition studies; Jim was in the audience. Although Bob is disappointed that only about seventy people were present, I am ecstatic, never before having presented to a group that size. I am the newcomer, the only person on the roundtable without substantial publications and therefore perhaps a bit giddy. Bob and Jim seem frustrated by the profession's disinclination to embrace the issue of masculinity. When I suggest the need for an edited anthology, they both say, "Who's going to do all that work? Not me," and they laugh.

Jim leaves and Bob turns to me. He seems bear-like—both lovable and intimidating. I saw him present at the CCCC convention ten years earlier,

slimmer, and talking about agonistic rhetoric. He would like, he says, to sit down with me sometime to talk more about men's studies and masculinity. He says that maybe the next CCCC convention we could get together over a meal.

"Sure, I'd like that," I say. We shake hands.

I never knew Bob Connors well. After his "Teaching and Learning as a Man" appeared in *College English,* I wrote a response that appeared in the December 1996 "Comment and Response" section. That eventually led to some e-mail exchanges and to an invitation from Bob to participate in the round-table mentioned above. My reply to his essay was more rebuttal couched as questions than appreciative inquiry, my approach to men's studies and masculinity differing significantly from Connors'. In many ways I viewed "Teaching and Learning as a Man" as fodder for my own platform; for two years after its publication, almost all of my scholarly writing, in one way or another, challenged the assumptions and ideas in "Teaching." Bob represented my antithesis—or I transformed him into one—in ways that at present seem overly simplistic to me. This essay is an attempt to set things right, to honor our points of contact and the work Bob Connors did for the profession in the area of masculinity studies.

Bob's collected works in men's studies and composition is not large—especially compared to other areas of his scholarship. There are primarily two: "Teaching and Learning as a Man" and a special issue of *Pre/Text* that he edited entitled *Constructing Masculinities.* Although small in number, there is indication that his masculinity work has made an impact on the profession—especially "Teaching and Learning as a Man." That essay is a call to begin to "confront gender issues wholly" in composition by using men's studies to help us deal with the complexities of teaching writing to young men. Connors raises issues he considers important to male teachers, scholars, and students that he believes feminisms fail to address: what positive role models are available to men who teach writing; how might male teachers mentor male students; and are feminist theories and models of writing appropriate for male students? He invokes both the men's movement and men's studies as means of answering these questions.

I can't help but believe that when Bob published "Teaching," he must have known the controversy it would create—especially among feminists. *College English* devoted two sets of responses to the essay, one in the December 1996 issue and one in the April 1997 issue. The first article to appear in response to Connors' piece was Laura Micciche's "Male Plight and Feminist Threat in Composition Studies: A Response to 'Teaching and Learning as a Man,'" published in the spring 1997 issue of *Composition Studies.* Both Micciche and Cathleen Breidenbach, whose response is in the April 1997 *College English,* are critical of Connors' oversights and representations of feminism, as is Gesa Kirsch's piece in the December 1996 responses.

My own response, written from a profeminist perspective, takes a similar stance. Profeminists who study masculinity acknowledge a debt to feminism; without its theories and insights, the study of gender in its fullest sense

would not be possible. And they tend, generally, to focus on critiques of male privilege and sexism. But profeminism is one perspective among many that interpret and explain masculinity. Books such as Kenneth Clatterbaugh's *Contemporary Perspectives on Masculinity* and Michael Messner's *Politics of Masculinities* identify and evaluate the threads of men's responses, positive and negative, to the second and third waves of the women's movement, and to heterosexual, hegemonic masculinity. Clatterbaugh names six perspectives: conservative, profeminist, men's rights, spiritual, socialist, and group-specific. Messner identifies some of the same and a few more: mythopoetics, Promise Keepers, men's liberation, men's rights, profeminists, socialists, racialized identity politics, and gay liberation. My intent here is not to explain each of these perspectives and movements, but to suggest that a number of complex ideologies are tied to manhood. To invoke the men's movement and men's studies, as Bob does, then, leads to the question: which movement and which men's studies? It seems to me that Bob's work was more or less free-floating, wandering from one masculinist ideology to another without any acknowledgment that differing ideologies exist. Some are anti-feminist, some are profeminist, and some are a mixture of the two. I tried to pin him down at various times and he refused to be pinned.

I intentionally use the wrestling image—being pinned. At the time, I was frustrated that he avoided positioning himself and his work. But now, looking back, I think he simply rejected playing the very typical masculine game I was trying to engage him in: the battle of ideologies. I admit I wanted to be right, and in another sense, the good male. I don't think Bob was invested in winning. I was, and so I was a bad listener.

Now, when I listen to his work on men's studies and composition, I hear it say something more complex, something along the lines of what Timothy Beneke, a well-known profeminist, claims: "I start from the recognition that men have enormous work to do to end sexism and that men's writing about sexism should serve that end. But I also recognize that men are not likely to venture forth as moral soldiers striving to end sexism unless they perceive it to be in their simple self-interest" (*Proving Manhood*, U of California P, 1977, xii). And men's self-interest is tied to the pain and difficulties that compulsive masculinity sometimes causes them. Certainly, Bob's scholarship focused on the harms of manhood rather than its privilege. In his introduction to the issue of *Pre/Text* he edited, he cites a litany of wounds tied to masculinity: men attending college in fewer numbers than women; men experiencing more school disciplinary problems than women; men committing more crimes than women, and killing other men in large numbers, and so on. The danger in focusing on how men are harmed by masculinity is, of course, that it is easy to lose sight of men's entitlement. Bob tried to walk that tightrope. He was not always successful in my view, but I admire his attempt to strike a balance. He is one of the people who have helped me realize that working on masculinity issues is not an either/or proposition, that we somehow have to pay attention to men's privileged positions at the same time that we consider the ways masculinity damages them.

I do not think that Bob would have ever dared to claim that he had everything figured out about manhood, that he had the answers. More typically questions permeate his work on men's studies and composition. Conversation defined his interests more than finality, as is clear in his reply to comments made about "Teaching and Learning as a Man." He writes in his response to Cathleen Breidenbach that he wants the essay "to begin a conversation about the construction of masculinities in the college writing class, not to finish one." The roundtable I participated in with Bob took place because he and Gesa Kirsch had a lengthy discussion about their responses to one another in which they both realized that their differences were not so extreme.

Bob and I never met at the next year's CCCC convention and had our conversation, and now I feel that loss more than ever. For one reason or another, we drifted our separate ways. But I am comforted by the conversation he began about men's studies in composition, and by his willingness to make a space for me in the discussion.

George Washington University
Washington, DC

Saying Farewell to Bob: A Twisted Turn of Fate

SHERRIE GRADIN

When Robert J. Connors died suddenly and tragically on June 22, the discipline lost an extraordinary scholar, a man of letters, a man who believed in the life of the mind. Many of us lost a friend, a teacher, a mentor. Professor Connors became my teacher at the University of New Hampshire in 1986, and my professional and personal lives have since been the richer. As I write this, I cannot forget Bob's recent memorial tribute to his own teacher and mentor, Edward P. J. Corbett. I am incredulous, angry, railing at the gods for this twisted turn of fate that now has me doing the same for my teacher. And yet, I am honored and hope that by writing I will begin an act of healing, both for myself and for others who knew him professionally and personally.

Bob was a complicated guy in some ways. He was "Robert J.," the quintessential academician, a tad stuffy at first glance, a bit traditional. And he was "Bob," the truck driver and biker, his hair blowing in the wind—anything but the quintessential academician. I first knew Robert J. through his publications. His writing awed me. I could only imagine the man behind

such eloquent prose. "Textbooks and the Evolution of the Discipline," "Mechanical Correctness as a Focus in Composition Instruction," "Historical Inquiry in Composition Studies," "Composition Studies and Science"—none of these are topics I would choose to write about, but all are beautifully crafted arguments in stellar prose. I was lulled, mesmerized, hypnotized into believing his arguments by his seamless, smooth, and polished academic style. Here was an academic writer to emulate.

It was Robert J. I had expected to meet when I first arrived at his office on a hot August day. But it was Bob, the man who wrote not for *Rhetoric Review* but for *Yankee Magazine* about the humor of, and his compassion and fear for, a little skunk who, in dire straits, wandered around the yard with a jar stuck on its head. "We are so glad you decided to come to UNH," he said. "We need people like you." Foolishly, I thought he was going to say something about my potential as a member of the profession, perhaps a word about a paper I had submitted with my application. But no, for that would have been Robert J. Connors and this was definitely Bob Connors: "What got you in were all those A's in trapshooting. But Sherrie, why did you take the easy way out and withdraw from the rodeo classes?"

Later, we walked out of the building together, Bob heading for the library and I for my car parked in front of it. He was like an eighteen-year-old when he saw my maroon, 1971, Boss 302 Mach Mustang. (Months later he drove it and thanked me for never having put stabilizers on the rear.) In this moment I knew I had a mentor, but I also knew I had a friend. And while I am at the moment bereft at the loss of this friend, I will keep him alive in my heart and mind not only by remembering these more personal moments, but also by continuing to teach his work to my students. I want my students to know the joy of his prose, to grapple with the historical tales he has spun, to see historical method in action.

Like all of you, I will miss cracking open the newest volumes of our premier journals to read what Connors has set before us. We will miss his thorough scholarship, his attention to detail, his treasure hunts for obscure primary sources. We will miss his contributions to our discussions on teaching and our understanding of our history. We will miss his intellect. We will miss his wit. Until we meet him again, I like holding a vision of him sitting around a Burkean parlor of sorts with James Britton, Don Stewart, James Kinneavy, Jim Berlin, Ed Corbett, and Jim Corder, gleefully engaging in a bit of male agonistic rhetoric. Until then, Bob, *adieu*. And yes, I still have some things to say to you about this agonistic rhetoric stuff. . . .

Ohio University
Athens, Ohio

In Memoriam: Robert J. Connors

THOMAS NEWKIRK

Bob Connors was killed in a motorcycle accident on June 22, 2000. It occurred in the late afternoon when he was returning home from the last class of a summer school course and was caught in a violent and sudden thunderstorm, which may have caused a truck to enter his lane. Although grievously injured, Bob was able to call his wife before being taken to the hospital. But severe bleeding caused him to lose his pulse on the way, and he was dead upon arrival.

Bob was part of a talented and productive group of scholars (including James Berlin, Sharon Crowley, John Brereton, Nan Johnson, and others) who helped to map out the history of composition teaching in this country. Bob's specialty, and great love, was the nineteenth century. He had an encyclopedic knowledge of the teaching materials. He could trace in intricate detail the evolution of correction symbols, the common topics offered to students, or, moving into the twentieth century, the history of the handbook. When he and Andrea Lunsford developed the *St. Martin's Handbook*, they followed the historical precedent of John Hodges, the original author of the *Harbrace Handbook*, in examining a huge body of corrected student writing in order to have an empirical base for their work. And in the role of Ma and Pa Kettle, they reported the results of this research.

Bob established himself as a major figure in the field immediately after graduate school when his essay, "The Rise and Fall of the Modes of Discourse," won the Braddock Award in 1982. The title itself suggests something of his temperament as a historian. Although this early essay was anchored to a careful study of archival material, the title evokes Gibbon and a sense of grand historical sweep that would be his trademark. Bob disarmingly labeled himself an "antiquarian" historian, driven to find a story in the mass of detail he uncovered. His histories were invariably dramatic, filled with movements, contests, key turning points, rises and falls, heroes and villains. He was openly critical of attempts to use the historical record to bolster ideological points, and on this issue he clashed with James Berlin. Yet Bob's own histories were not without an ideological intent, particularly his controversial assertions about the feminization of composition. He saw coeducation and a personalistic approach to writing as driving out the older ideal of an outward looking, public, agonistic—and male—form of rhetorical instruction. And I believe he felt this loss on a personal level.

From *College Composition and Communication* 52.1 (2000): 9–11.

In many ways Bob resembled another historian, Henry Adams, who, throughout his celebrated biography, bemoans the fact that he is an eighteenth-century man stranded in the nineteenth century. Bob was a nineteenth-century man often ill at ease in the twentieth century. He built a Victorian home with such exacting authenticity that workmen had to relearn old techniques for steaming and molding wood in order to make the turrets. He loved the ornate, even anachronistic turn of phrase. More significantly for his work in composition, he abhorred the often glib postmodern constructionism that seemed to reduce value, morality, and religious belief to transitory social conventions. In one of his favorite Zippy cartoons a young man questions the oracular Mr. Toad:

"Mr. Toad, are there any universal truths?"

"We make everything up."

"Right? Wrong? Good? Evil? Pain? Pleasure?"

"All constructs."

"Do you really believe that?"

"Yes and no."

"Are you toying with me, Mr. Toad?"

"Eskimo questions, Italian no lies."

He felt this lack of a solid foundation most acutely on issues of masculinity and in the last years of his life began to raise uncomfortable questions about the alienation and poor performance of men in educational institutions. He introduced a popular but controversial course in "men's literature," and he regularly reminded leaders at the University of New Hampshire that only 40 percent of the student body was male, an underrepresentation that would normally be a cause for alarm. In his powerful and revealing essay, "Teaching and Learning as a Man," he discusses his concern for the uncertain place of male students in schools. Like Henry Adams, Bob was able to utilize his own longings and discomfort to prompt investigation and, in the end, to produce scholarship that sometimes approached the level of art.

Although Bob would present himself as the sober nineteenth-century scholar, his irrepressible sense of humor would undercut the image. His pants, coat, and sweater vest might be shades of brown, but his socks would be bright pastel stripes. The cuckoo clock in his office would momentarily deflate any serious conversation that ran past the hour. He could talk about one of his recent passions, professional wrestling, with the same kind of interest he brought to stylistics. He loved metaphors, the more extravagant the better. Once I asked him how he managed get a Ph.D. in *composition* in 1980 (before there really *were* any programs). He answered, "I had the great good fortune to watch Andrea Lunsford scale the sheer rock face that was the Ohio State English Department." His laugh was high and light and generous— and often directed at himself.

On his door at the time of his death, Bob had posted the first amazon.com review of his book, *Composition-Rhetoric*. The reviewer gave the book one star and wrote

> The book examines the development of a compositional trend nobody but this obscure and self-important author recognizes or really cares about. It might contain some valuable information for those willing to wade through Connors' bombastic, pseudo-Victorian prose. The cover is lovely, though.

Bob had circled this quotation and had written beside it "My Public."

He was wrong, though, and I suspect he knew it. He was a shrewd judge of scholarly achievement and knew how high he had set the bar for himself—and that there was a public for such work. The outpouring of grief from colleagues across the country, many who had never met him in person (and many who disagreed with him), is evidence of his true public. And as we ponder his death, we may find that it was his unconventionality and originality—his willingness to be "the dog in the manger" (one of his favorite self-descriptions)—that we treasure the most.

University of New Hampshire
Durham, New Hampshire

BIBLIOGRAPHY FOR ROBERT J. CONNORS

BOOKS

Essays on Classical Rhetoric and Modern Discourse (co-edited with Lisa S. Ede and Andrea A. Lunsford). Carbondale: Southern Illinois UP, 1984.

The St. Martin's Guide to Teaching Writing (with Cheryl Glenn). New York: St. Martin's, 1989. (2nd ed. 1992; 3rd ed. 1995).

The St. Martin's Handbook (with Andrea A. Lunsford). New York: St. Martin's, 1989. (2nd ed. 1992; 3rd ed. 1995).

Selected Essays of Edward P. J. Corbett. Dallas: Southern Methodist UP, 1989.

The Everyday Writer (with Andrea A. Lunsford). New York: St. Martin's, 1996.

The St. Martin's Pocket Guide to Research and Documentation (with Andrea A. Lunsford and Marcia Muth). New York: St. Martin's, 1996.

Composition-Rhetoric: Backgrounds, Theory, and Pedagogy. Pittsburgh: U of Pittsburgh P, 1997.

Easy Writer: A Pocket Guide (with Andrea A. Lunsford and a section for multilingual writers by Franklin E. Horowitz). New York: St. Martin's, 1997.

Classical Rhetoric for the Modern Student (with Edward P. J. Corbett). 4th ed. New York: Oxford UP, 1998.

Style and Statement (with Edward P. J. Corbett). New York: Oxford UP, 1998.

The New St. Martin's Handbook (with Andrea A. Lunsford). Boston: Bedford, 1999.

The New St. Martin's Pocket Guide to Research and Documentation (with Andrea A. Lunsford and Marcia Muth). Boston: Bedford, 1999.

The New St. Martin's Guide to Teaching Writing (with Cheryl Glenn). 4th ed. Boston: Bedford, 1999.

ARTICLES AND BOOK CHAPTERS

"Deregulating English." *Moreover* 9 (1979): 3–6.

"The Differences between Speech and Writing: Ethos, Pathos, and Logos." *College Composition and Communication* 30 (1979): 285–290.

"Current-Traditional Rhetoric: Thirty Years of *Writing with a Purpose*." *Rhetoric Society Quarterly* 11 (1981): 208–221.

"The Rise and Fall of the Modes of Discourse." *College Composition and Communication* 32 (1981): 444–455. Rpt. in Gary Tate and Edward P. J. Corbett, eds. *The Writing Teacher's Sourcebook*. 2nd ed. New York: Oxford UP, 1988.

"The Rise of Technical Writing Instruction in America." *Journal of Technical Writing and Communication* 12 (1982): 329–352. Rpt. in Teresa C. Kynell and Michael G. Moran, eds. *Three Keys to the Past: The History of Technical Communication*. Stamford: Ablex, 1999.

"*Actio:* A Rhetoric of Manuscripts." *Rhetoric Review* 2 (1983): 64–73.

"Composition Studies and Science." *College English* 45 (1983): 1–20.

"Handbook Bibliography." *Rhetoric Society Quarterly* 13.2 (1983): 171–176.

"Handbooks: History of a Genre." *Rhetoric Society Quarterly* 13.2 (1983): 87–98.

"Static Abstractions and Composition." *Freshman English News* 12.1 (1983): 1–12. Rpt. in Gary Tate, Edward P. J. Corbett, and Nancy Myers, eds. *The Writing Teacher's Sourcebook.* 3rd ed. New York: Oxford UP, 1994; and in Edward P. J. Corbett, Nancy Myers, and Gary Tate, eds. *The Writing Teacher's Sourcebook.* 4th ed. New York: Oxford UP, 2000.

"Computer Analysis of Reviewing and Revision: The RECOMP Project" (with Mark P. Haselkorn). *Collected Essays on the Written Word and the Word Processor.* Ed. Thomas Martinez. Villanova: Villanova UP, 1984. 267–279.

"Historical Inquiry in Composition Studies." *The Writing Instructor* 3 (1984): 157–167.

"Journals in Composition Studies." *College English* 46 (1984): 348–365.

"The Revival of Rhetoric in America" (with Lisa S. Ede and Andrea A. Lunsford). *Essays on Classical Rhetoric and Modern Discourse.* Ed. Robert J. Connors, Lisa S. Ede, and Andrea A. Lunsford. Carbondale: Southern Illinois UP, 1984. 1–15.

"The Rhetoric of Explanation: Explanatory Rhetoric from Aristotle to 1850." *Written Communication* 1 (1984): 189–210.

"Computer Analysis of the Composing Process" (with Mark P. Haselkorn). *Computers and Composition: Selected Papers from the Conference on Computers and Writing.* Ed. Lillian Bridwell and Donald Ross. Houghton: Michigan Technological UP, 1985. 139–158.

"Mechanical Correctness as a Focus in Composition Instruction." *College Composition and Communication* 36 (1985): 61–72.

"RECOMP: Gathering Data on the Composing Process" (with Mark P. Haselkorn). *Collegiate Microcomputer* 3 (1985): 263–273.

"The Rhetoric of Explanation: Explanatory Rhetoric from 1850 to the Present." *Written Communication* 2 (1985): 49–72.

"Genre Theory in Literature." *Form, Genre, and the Study of Political Discourse.* Ed. Herbert W. Simons and Aram A. Aghazarian. Columbia: U of South Carolina P, 1986. 25–44.

"Grammar in American College Composition: An Historical Overview." *The Territory of Language: Linguistics, Stylistics, and the Teaching of Composition.* Ed. Donald McQuade. Carbondale: Southern Illinois UP, 1986. 3–22.

"Greek Rhetoric and the Transition from Orality." *Philosophy and Rhetoric* 19 (1986): 38–65. Rpt. in Edward P. J. Corbett, James L. Golden, and Goodwin F. Berquist, eds. *Essays on the Rhetoric of the Western World.* Dubuque: Kendall/Hunt, 1990.

"The Rhetoric of Mechanical Correctness." *Only Connect: Uniting Reading and Writing.* Ed. Thomas Newkirk. Upper Montclair: Boynton/Cook, 1986. 27–58.

"Textbooks and the Evolution of the Discipline." *College Composition and Communication* 37 (1986): 178–194.

"Basic Writing Textbooks: History and Current Avatars." *A Sourcebook for Basic Writing Teachers.* Ed. Theresa Enos. New York: Random House, 1987. 259–274.

"Personal Writing Assignments." *College Composition and Communication* 38 (1987): 166–183.

"Frequency of Formal Errors in Current College Writing, or Ma and Pa Kettle Do Research" (with Andrea A. Lunsford). *College Composition and Communication* 39 (1988): 395–409.

"The Politics of Historiography" (octalog with other historians). *Rhetoric Review* 7 (1988): 5–49.

"Rhetorical History as a Component of Composition Studies." *Rhetoric Review* 7 (1989): 230–240.

"Overwork/Underpay: Labor and Status of Composition Teachers since 1880." *Rhetoric Review* 9 (1990): 108–126.

"Rhetoric in the Modern University: The Creation of an Underclass." *The Politics of Writing Instruction: Postsecondary.* Ed. Richard Bullock, Charles I. Schuster, and John Trimbur. Portsmouth: Boynton/Cook, 1991. 55–84.

"Writing the History of Our Discipline." *An Introduction to Composition Studies.* Ed. Erika Lindemann and Gary Tate. New York: Oxford UP, 1991. 49–71.

"Dreams and Play: Historical Method and Methodology." *Methods and Methodology in Composition Research.* Ed. Gesa Kirsch and Patricia A. Sullivan. Carbondale: Southern Illinois UP, 1992. 15–36.

"Exorcising Demonolatry: Spelling Patterns and Pedagogies in College Writing" (with Andrea A. Lunsford). *Written Communication* 9 (1992): 404–428.

"The Exclusion of Women from Classical Rhetoric." *A Rhetoric of Doing: Essays on Written Discourse in Honor of James L. Kinneavy.* Ed. Stephen P. Witte, Neil Nakadate, and Roger D. Cherry. Carbondale: Southern Illinois UP, 1992. 65–78.

"*Actio:* A Rhetoric of Written Delivery (Iteration Two*)." *Rhetorical Memory and Delivery: Classical Concepts for Contemporary Composition and Communication.* Ed. John Frederick Reynolds. Hillside: Lawrence Erlbaum Associates, 1993. 65–77.

"Teachers' Rhetorical Comments on Student Papers" (with Andrea A. Lunsford). *College Composition and Communication* 44 (1993): 200–223.

"Crisis and Panacea in Composition Studies: A History." *Composition in Context: Essays in Honor of Donald C. Stewart.* Ed. W. Ross Winterowd and Vincent Gillespie. Carbondale: Southern Illinois UP, 1994. 86–105.

"The Abolition Debate in Composition: A Short History." *Composition in the Twenty-First Century: Crisis and Change.* Ed. Lynn Z. Bloom, Donald A. Daiker, and Edward M. White. Carbondale: Southern Illinois UP, 1996. 47–63.

Guest editor and "Foreword." *Pre/Text* 16.3–4 (1995): 183–187.

"The Modes of Discourse." *Encyclopedia of English Studies and Language Arts.* Ed. Allen C. Purves, Sarah Jordan, and Linda Papa. Vol. 2. New York: Scholastic, 1994. 2 vols. 816–818.

"The Morning and the Afternoon (Counterpoint)." *Journal of Advanced Composition* 15 (1995): 314–316.

"The New Abolitionism: Toward a Historical Background." *Reconceiving Writing, Rethinking Writing Instruction.* Ed. Joseph Petraglia. Mahwah: Laurence Erlbaum Associates, 1995. 3–26.

"Women's Reclamation of Rhetoric in the Nineteenth Century." *Feminine Principles and Women's Experience in American Composition and Rhetoric.* Ed. Louise Wetherbee Phelps and Janet Emig. Pittsburgh: U of Pittsburgh P, 1995. 67–90.

"Edward P. J. Corbett." *The Encyclopedia of Rhetoric and Composition.* Ed. Theresa Enos. New York: Garland, 1996. 150–151.

"Henry Noble Day." *The Encyclopedia of Rhetoric and Composition.* Ed. Theresa Enos. New York: Garland, 1996. 161–163.

"Teaching and Learning as a Man." *College English* 58 (1996): 137-157. Rpt. in Nancy V. Wood, ed. *Perspectives on Argument.* 2nd ed. Englewood Cliffs: Prentice Hall, 1997.

"The Rhetoric of Citation Systems—Part I: The Development of Annotation Structures from the Renaissance to 1900." *Rhetoric Review* 17 (1998): 6–48.

"Frances Wright: First Female Civic Rhetor in America." *College English* 62 (1999): 30–57.

"The Rhetoric of Citation Systems—Part II: Competing Epistemic Values in Citation." *Rhetoric Review* 17 (1999): 219–245.

"Afterword." *Coming of Age: The Advanced Writing Curriculum.* Ed. Rebecca Moore Howard, Linda K. Shammon, and Sandra Jamieson. Portsmouth: Boynton/Cook, 2000. 143–149.

"Composition History and Disciplinarity." *History, Reflection, and Narrative: The Professionalization of Composition, 1963–1983.* Ed. Mary Rosner, Beth Boehm, and Debra Journet. Stamford: Ablex, 1999. 3–22.

"The Erasure of the Sentence." *College Composition and Communication* 52 (2000): 96–128.

REVIEWS

Rev. of *A Vulnerable Teacher,* by Ken Macrorie. *College Composition and Communication* 29 (1978): 108–109.

Rev. of *How a Writer Works,* by Roger Garrison. *Rhetoric Review* 2 (1984): 185–188.

Rev. of *Rhetoric: Theory and Practice for Composition,* by Walter Minot. *College Composition and Communication* 36 (1985): 110–112.

Rev. of *Student Writers at Work: The Bedford Prizes,* eds. Nancy Sommers and Donald McQuade. *Rhetoric Review* 3 (1985): 228–232.

Rev. of *The St. Martin's Guide to Writing,* by Rise B. Axelrod and Charles R. Cooper. *Rhetoric Review* 5 (1986): 106–110.

Rev. of *Writing Instruction in Nineteenth-Century American Colleges,* by James A. Berlin. *College Composition and Communication* 37 (1986): 247–249.

Rev. of *Analyzing Prose,* by Richard Lanham. *Journal of Advanced Composition* 5 (1988): 191–196.

Rev. of *The Muse Learns to Write: Reflections on Orality and Literacy from Antiquity to the Present,* by Eric A. Havelock. *Quarterly Journal of Speech* 74 (1988): 379–381.

Rev. of *A Short History of Writing Instruction from Ancient Greece to Twentieth-Century America,* ed. James J. Murphy. *Rhetoric Society Quarterly* 21.2 (1991): 47–49.

Rev. of *Nineteenth-Century Rhetoric in North America,* by Nan Johnson. *Rhetoric Society Quarterly* 21.4 (1991): 37–39.

Rev. of *The Methodical Memory: Invention in Current-Traditional Rhetoric,* by Sharon Crowley. *Journal of Advanced Composition* 12 (1992): 217–221.

Rev. of *The Origin of Composition Studies in the American College, 1875–1925: A Documentary History,* by J. C. Brereton. *Rhetoric Review* 15 (1997): 422–425.

Rev. of *Assuming the Positions: Cultural Pedagogy and the Politics of Commonplace Writing,* by Susan Miller. *College Composition and Communication* 51 (1999): 272–283.

MISCELLANEA

"The Last Ride." *Cavalier* July 1976: 45–49. (short story)

"Ode to the Age of the Beetle." *Yankee* Feb. 1981: 78–81, 174–179. (nonfiction essay)

"The Reluctant Vampire." *Yankee* Oct. 1981: 98–103. (short story)

Response to Don K. Pierstorff's comments on "Journals in Composition Studies." *College English* 46 (1984): 723–724.

Response to Patricia Bizzell's comments on "Composition Studies and Science." *College English* 46 (1984): 181–182.

"The Genius." *Road & Track* Aug. 1985: 58–60, 64. (short story)

Response to Tim D. P. Lalley's comments on "Journals in Composition Studies." *College English* 47 (1985): 79–80.

"How in the World Do You Get a Skunk out of a Bottle?" *Yankee* June 1991: 68–71. (nonfiction essay)

Response to Patrick McGann and Gesa Kirsch's comments on "Teaching and Learning as a Man." *College English* 58 (1996): 968–974.

Response to Catherine Breidenback and Kristie S. Fleckenstein's comments on "Teaching and Learning as a Man." *College English* 59 (1997): 475–478.

"In Memory of Edward P. J. Corbett." *College Composition and Communication* 50 (1998): 8–9.

"Memorial of Edward P. J. Corbett." *Journal of Advanced Composition* 18 (1998): 399–401.

"Memorial Tribute to Edward P. J. Corbett, 1919–1998." *College English* 61 (1998): 141–142.

Acknowledgments (continued from page iv)

"Handbooks: History of a Genre" by Robert J. Connors. From the *Rhetoric Society Quarterly* 13, Spring 1983, pp. 87–98. Reprinted with permission.

"The Rhetoric of Explanation: Explanatory Rhetoric from Aristotle to 1850" by Robert J. Connors. From *Written Communication* 1, April 1984, pp. 189–210. Copyright © 1984, Sage Publications. Reprinted with permission.

"The Rhetoric of Explanation: Explanatory Rhetoric from 1850 to the Present" by Robert J. Connors. From *Written Communication* 2, January 1985, pp. 49–72. Copyright © 1985. Reprinted with permission.

"The Genius" by Robert J. Connors. From *Road & Track* (1985). Reprinted with permission.

"The Rhetoric of Mechanical Correctness" by Robert J. Connors. From *Only Connect: Uniting Reading and Writing* by Thomas Newkirk, ed. Copyright © 1986. Used with permission of Boynton/Cook Publishers, Inc.

"Textbooks and the Evolution of the Discipline" by Robert J. Connors. From *CCC* 37, May 1986, pp. 178–194. Copyright © 1981 by the National Council of Teachers of English. Reprinted with the permission of NCTE.

"Grammar in American College Composition: An Historical Overview" by Robert J. Connors. From *The Territory of Language: Linguistics, Stylistics, and the Teaching of Composition*, edited by Donald McQuade. Copyright © 1986 by Southern Illinois University Press. Reprinted with the permission of the publisher.

"Personal Writing Assignments" by Robert J. Connors." From *CCC* 38, May 1987, pp. 166–183. Copyright © 1987 by the National Council of Teachers of English. Reprinted with the permission of NCTE.

"Frequency of Formal Errors in Current College Writing, or Ma and Pa Kettle Do Research" by Robert J. Connors. From *CCC* 39, December 1988, pp. 395–409. Copyright © 1988 by the National Council of Teachers of English. Reprinted with the permission of NCTE.

"Introduction" by Robert J. Connors. From *Selected Essays of Edward P.J. Corbett*, edited by Robert J. Connors. Copyright © 1989. Courtesy of Southern Methodist University Press.

"Overwork/Underpay: Labor and Status of Composition Teachers since 1880" by Robert J. Connors. From *Rhetoric Review* 9, Fall 1990, pp. 108–125. Reprinted with permission.

"How in the World Do You Get a Skunk out of a Bottle?" by Robert J. Connors. From *Yankee*, June 1991, pp. 68–71. Reprinted with permission.

"Writing the History of Our Discipline" by Robert J. Connors. From *An Introduction to Composition Studies*, edited by Gary Tate and Erika Lindemann. Copyright © 1991 by Oxford University Press, Inc. Used by permission of Oxford University Press, Inc.

"Dreams and Play: Historical Method and Methodology" by Robert J. Connors. From *Methods and Methodology in Composition Research* edited by Patricia Sullivan and Gesa Kirsch. Copyright © 1992 by the Board of Trustees at Southern Illinois University. Reprinted by permission.

"Teachers' Rhetorical Comments on Student Papers" by Robert J. Connors. From *CCC* 44, May 1993, pp. Copyright © 1983 by the National Council of Teachers of English. Reprinted with the permission of NCTE.

"Women's Reclamation of Rhetoric in the Nineteenth Century" by Robert J. Connors. From *Feminine Principles and Women's Experience in American*

INDEX